Pro SQL Server 2005
Database Design: Building
Quality OLTP Databases

Louis Davidson

Apress™

Pro SQL Server 2000 Database Design: Building Quality OLTP Databases
Copyright © 2004 by Louis Davidson

ISBN (pbk): 1-59059-302-2

Printed and bound in the United States of America 12345678910

Trademarked names may appear in this book. Rather than use a trademark symbol with every occurrence of a trademarked name, we use the names only in an editorial fashion and to the benefit of the trademark owner, with no intention of infringement of the trademark.

Technical Reviewer: Craig Weldon

Editorial Board: Dan Appleman, Craig Berry, Gary Cornell, Tony Davis, Steven Rycroft, Julian Skinner, Martin Streicher, Jim Sumser, Karen Watterson, Gavin Wray, John Zukowski

Assistant Publisher: Grace Wong

Project Manager: Kylie Johnston

Copy Editor: Mark Nigara

Production Manager: Kari Brooks

Production Editor: Kelly Winquist

Proofreader: Patrick Vincent

Compositor: Katy Freer

Artist: April Milne

Cover Designer: Kurt Krames

Manufacturing Manager: Tom Debolski

Distributed to the book trade in the United States by Springer-Verlag New York, Inc., 175 Fifth Avenue, New York, NY 10010 and outside the United States by Springer-Verlag GmbH & Co. KG, Tiergartenstr. 17, 69112 Heidelberg, Germany.

In the United States: phone 1-800-SPRINGER, email orders@springer-ny.com, or visit http://www.springer-ny.com. Outside the United States: fax +49 6221 345229, email orders@springer.de, or visit http://www.springer.de.

For information on translations, please contact Apress directly at 2560 Ninth Street, Suite 219, Berkeley, CA 94710. Phone 510-549-5930, fax 510-549-5939, email info@apress.com, or visit http://www.apress.com.

The information in this book is distributed on an "as is" basis, without warranty. Although every precaution has been taken in the preparation of this work, neither the author(s) nor Apress shall have any liability to any person or entity with respect to any loss or damage caused or alleged to be caused directly or indirectly by the information contained in this work.

The source code for this book is available to readers at http://www.apress.com in the Downloads section. You will need to answer questions pertaining to this book in order to successfully download the code.

This book is dedicated to Dr. Paul Durham. He didn't know a dang thing about data-bases, but he was a great man, a minister with a huge heart, and an interesting teacher. I count the members of his family among my best friends....

Acknowledgments

God, the Creator for giving me the ability to design and program computer software.

My wife Valerie and daughter Chrissy, who have to put up with looking more at my laptop than my face for the past few years....

My Mom and Dad, without whom I would never have had the tenacity to pull off such an amazing amount of work....I still miss you Dad....

Chuck Hawkins for writing the chapter that I never could have....

Chip Broecker, Donald Plaster, Mike Farmer, and the best friend I ever had, all of whom have been important personal influences (in reverse chronological order!).

All of the professors, academics, authors (of books and various web pages), presenters, and so on who have influenced me, not the least of which is E. F. Codd, who passed away between the first two editions of the book.

In no particular order, the following persons who have worked with me on getting this book to you: Tony Davis, Kylie Johnston, Craig Weldon, Mark Nigara, Kelly Winquist, Sarah Neidhardt, Jessica Dolcourt, Beckie Stones, Beth Christmas, and of course Gary Cornell for trusting my work enough to publish it. I hope I haven't forgotten to mention anyone!

The editors, who made this book (both editions) better than it might have been.

Contents at a Glance

Introduction   xix

Chapter 1: Introduction to Database Concepts   1

Chapter 2: Gathering Information for a Database Project   13

Chapter 3: Fundamental Database Concepts   27

Chapter 4: Entities, Attributes, Relationships, and Business Rules   55

Chapter 5: Data Modeling   91

Chapter 6: Normalization Techniques   129

Chapter 7: Advanced Normalization Topics   165

Chapter 8: Ending the Logical Design Phase   191

Chapter 9: Planning the Physical Architecture   219

Chapter 10: Building the Basic Table Structures   245

Chapter 11: Declarative Data Protection   315

Chapter 12: Programmatic Data Protection   341

Chapter 13: Advanced Data Access and Modification   367

Chapter 14: Determining Hardware Requirements   459

Chapter 15: Completing the Project   511

Index   543

Contents

Introduction   **xix**

Chapter 1: Introduction to Database Concepts   1

Introduction 1

History of Relational Database Structures 1

    The Four Modules of the Modern Database System 3

    Online Transactional Processing 4

    Operational Data Store 5

    Data Warehouse 6

    Data Marts 7

    Architecture 9

An Overview of the SQL Server Database Design Process 9

Case Study Introduction 10

Summary...11

Chapter 2: Gathering Information for a Database Project   13

The Database Design Team 14

Documentation and Communication 15

    Client Approval 16

Minimum Information Requirements 16

Database Prototypes 16

Client Interviews 17

    Questions That Need Answers...18

Other Places to Look for Information 21

Outline of the Case Study...22

    Client Interview 23

    Preliminary Documentation 24

Summary...26

Chapter 3: Fundamental Database Concepts   27

Introduction 27
The Relational Model 28
Database 28
Table 28
    Rows and Columns 30
    Row Identifiers 35
    Optional Attribute Values 38
    Rowcount 38
    Additional Considerations for Entities 39
Relational Operators 42
Relationships 48
    Binary Relationships 48
    Nonbinary Relationships 50
Definitions of Essential Concepts 51
    Functional Dependency 51
    Multivalued Dependency 52
Summary 53

Chapter 4: Entities, Attributes, Relationships, and Business Rules   55

Introduction 55
    Divorcing Yourself from the Final Structure 56
Identifying Entities 57
    People 58
    Places 58
    Objects 59
    Ideas 59
    Other Entities 60
    A List of Entities 61
Identifying Attributes 62
    Identifiers 62
    Descriptive Information 64
    Locators 65
    Related Information 66
    A List of Entities, Attributes, and Domains 66
Relationships Between Entities 68
    One-to-n Relationships 68
    Many-to-Many Relationships 70
    Listing Relationships 70
Identifying Business Rules 71
Identifying Fundamental Processes 73
Is This Trip Over Yet? 75
    Identification of Additional Data 75

Review with the Client 76
Repeat Until Gaining Customer Acceptance 77
Case Study 77
Client Interview 77
Documents 79
Bank Account Object Listing 82
Business Rules and Processes...86
Best Practices 88
Summary..88

Chapter 5: Data Modeling   91

Introduction 91
Data Models 92
Data Modeling Format 93
Entities..93
Entity Type...94
Naming 95
Attributes..96
Primary Key 96
Alternate Keys 97
Foreign Keys 98
Domains 98
Naming 100
Relationships 101
One-to-Many 103
Identifying Relationships 103
Nonidentifying Relationships...103
Mandatory 105
Optional 105
Cardinality 106
Role Names 107
Other Types of Relationships 108
Recursive 108
Categorization Relationships 110
Many-to-Many 112
Verb Phrases (Relationship Names) 113
Alternate Methods of Relationship Display 115
Descriptive Information 119
Case Study 120
Best Practices 127
Summary..128

Chapter 6: Normalization Techniques   **129**

Why Normalize? 130
    Reducing NULLs..130
    Eliminating Redundant Data 131
    Avoiding Unnecessary Coding 131
    Maximizing Clustered Indexes 131
    Lowering the Number of Indexes per Table 131
    Keeping Tables Thin...132
The Process of Normalization 132
Attribute Shape 133
    All Attributes Must Be Atomic 133
    All Instances in an Entity Must Contain the Same Number of Values 135
    All Occurrences of a Row Type in an Entity Must Be Different.........................136
    Programming Anomalies Avoided by the First Normal Form 136
    Clues That Existing Data Isn't in First Normal Form 139
Relationships Between Attributes 139
    Second Normal Form 140
    Third Normal Form 145
    Boyce-Codd Normal Form..150
Case Study 155
    First Normal Form..155
    Boyce-Codd Normal Form..157
    Model 162
Best Practices 163
Summary...163

Chapter 7: Advanced Normalization Topics   **165**

Introduction 165
Fourth Normal Form 166
    Ternary Relationships...166
    Lurking Multivalued Attributes 173
    Attribute History 176
Fifth Normal Form..179
Denormalization..180
Case Study 181
    Example 1–Account.BalanceDate...181
    Example 2–Payee.Address Id and Payee.Phone 182
    Example 3–check.UsageType 185
Best Practices 189
Summary...189

Chapter 8: Ending the Logical Design Phase   191

Data Usage 192
    Common Processes 193
    Reporting 194
    Determine Data Usage and Ownership 198
    Interfacing with External Systems 200
Volumetrics 204
Project Plan 204
    Test Plan 205
Final Documentation Review 206
    Future Requirements 207
Case Study 208
    User and Process Identification 208
    Interfacing to External Systems 212
    Volumetrics 213
    Project Plan 215
    Test Plan 215
    Final Documentation Review 216
Best Practices 216
Summary 217

Chapter 9: Planning the Physical Architecture   219

Reporting Issues 221
    Size of Data 221
Performance Concerns 225
    Connection Speed 225
    Amount of Data 228
    Budget 228
    Number of Users 229
SQL Server Facilities 230
    Replication 230
    Linked Servers 231
    Data Transformation Services 232
    Distributed Transaction Controller 232
    SQL Data Management Objects (SQL-DMO) 233
    COM Object Instantiation 233
    SQL Mail 234
    Full Text Search 234
    SQL Server Agent 235
Basic Topology Discussion 235
    Thin Client vs. Thick Client 235
    Client to Data Configurations 238
Case Study 242
Best Practices 242
Summary 243

Contents

Chapter 10: Building the Basic Table Structures   245

Database Generation Tools 246
Physically Designing the Schema...246
Transforming the Logical Design..247
    Subtypes 247
    A Reason Not to Stray from the Logical Design 251
Tables 251
    Naming 252
    Owner 253
    Limits 254
Columns 255
    Naming 255
    Choosing the Datatype 257
User-Defined Datatypes 262
    Error Reporting Using Rules 263
    Inconsistent Handling of Variables...264
    UDT Cannot Be Modified When in Use 265
    Calculated Columns 266
Physical-Only Columns...267
    Concurrency Control 267
    Collation (Sort Order)..271
Keys...273
    Primary Keys 273
    Alternate Keys 276
    Naming 277
    Other Indexes 278
Relationships 278
    Foreign Keys 278
    Naming 279
    Cascading Deletes and Updates 280
    Cross-Database Relationships 282
Sharing the Details of Your Database with Developers 282
    Information Schema and System Stored Procedures 283
    Descriptive Properties...286
Case Study 292
    Cleaning Up the Model 292
    Preparing the Model for Implementation..298
    Physical Model..309
Best Practices 312
Summary..313

Chapter 11: Declarative Data Protection   315

Example Tables 316
  Constraints 317
  Default Constraints 318
  Check Constraints 322
  Handling Errors Caused by Constraints..329
Case Study 331
  Default Constraints 332
  Check Constraints 333
Best Practices 339
Summary...339

Chapter 12: Programmatic Data Protection   341

Triggers 342
  Using AFTER Triggers to Solve Common Problems....................................343
  Cascading Inserts...344
  Range Checks 345
  Cascading Deletes Setting the Values of Child Tables to NULL...........................346
  Uses of INSTEAD OF Triggers..347
Client Code and Stored Procedures 353
  Mutable Rules 355
  Optionally Cascading Deletes 356
  Rules That Are Based Upon How a Person Feels...357
Case Study 358
  Remove the Time from Transaction Dates Trigger 359
  Validate City and Zip Codes Match Trigger 360
  Transaction Allocations Cannot Exceed the Amount Stored Trigger 362
  Optional Rules...364
Best Practices 364
Summary...365

Chapter 13: Advanced Data Access and Modification   367

Query Considerations 368
  Transactions 368
  Major Coding Issues 372
  Views 388
  Batches of SQL Code 395
Stored Procedures 399
  Returning Values from Stored Procedures..400
  Error Handling 403
  Encapsulation...410
  Security 412
  Transaction Count..413

Contents

Common Practices with Stored Procedures 417
Compiled SQL vs. Ad Hoc SQL for Building Apps 431
    Ad Hoc SQL 431
    Compiled SQL..433
    Tips to Consider 436
Security Considerations..436
Cross-Database Considerations 442
    Same Server 443
    Different Server (Distributed Queries) 445
Case Study 446
    Base Stored Procedures..446
    Custom Stored Procedures 452
    Security for the Processes 455
Best Practices 456
Summary...457

Chapter 14: Determining Hardware Requirements   459

Types of Databases 460
    OLTP Databases 460
    OLAP Databases 460
Growth of OLTP Tables..461
    Rapid Growth 461
    Slow Growth 461
    No Growth 462
Growth of OLAP Tables..462
    Batch Growth..462
    Growth Through Company Growth 463
    "We Need More Reports!"...463
    Don't Forget the Indexes 463
Calculating Complete Table Size..463
Data Size Calculation 464
    Reviewing Index B-Tree Structures 467
Index Size Calculation 468
Transaction Log Size 471
Archive Data When It Makes Sense 473
    The Cost of Archiving 473
    Archiving Details..474
    Archiving by Time Period 474
    Archiving by Fact Table Date-Partitioning...................................475
    Archiving by Fact Table Characteristics.......................................475
    Accessing Archived Data 476
Server Performance 477
    Windows Server 2003 Editions 477
    Memory Subsystems 478
Memory Performance Monitoring...481

The Art of Performance Monitoring 482

Memory Tuning: The Operating System and SQL Server 483

SQL Server 2000 Dynamic Memory Tuning...484

Free Memory Target 486

Multiple Instance Memory Tuning 486

SQL Server Process Memory Tuning 488

Adjusting Server Performance 488

CPU Subsystems 490

CPU Performance Monitoring...491

Textile Management 492

Disk Subsystems..492

The Basic Disk Subsystem 493

The RAID Subsystem 494

Multiple Controller/Channel Solutions 497

Disk Tuning and Performance Monitoring 498

User Connections...499

Locking and Blocking 501

Monitoring Blocking 502

Case Study 504

Summary..509

Chapter 15: Completing the Project   511

Performance Tuning 512

Read-Only Support Databases 513

Modeling the Transformation 515

Uses...527

Enterprise Data Models 531

Moving from a Test Environment 533

Development 534

Quality Assurance 535

Production 536

Case Study 537

Best Practices 541

Summary..542

Index   543

Introduction

If you're standing in your favorite bookseller, flipping thorough this book because it's in the technical book section, I know you're probably thinking, "Hey, where is all of the code and settings and such?" Well, this isn't exactly that kind of book. (Not that there is anything wrong with that kind of book; I alone have a gaggle of them around my desk.) This book intends to balance the thin line between the very implementation-oriented SQL Server books–which are concerned solely with DBCC settings, index options, and all of the knobs and handles on SQL Server–and the truly academic tomes that go deep into the theory of databases, but provide little or no practical information.

Database design can be thought of as an interesting blend of art and science. The science of database design is well established, with a number of mature methods for designing database structures, the most common of which is normalization. In fact these methods are almost ancient in computing terms, and it isn't terribly difficult to follow these rules when designing your database structures. As you'll see, it's also relatively straightforward to translate such a design into SQL Server tables.

This book presents straightforward techniques that will help you to design better databases in a way that is clear enough for novices, but at the same time helpful to even the most seasoned professional. One thing should be made clear before you start reading. Working with the design and architecture of a database requires a very different approach than performing database setup and administration. For example, in the role of data architect, I seldom create users, perform backups, or set up replication or clustering. This is the role of the DBA.

Though it isn't uncommon to wear both of these hats (and others such a programmer, tester, and so on), I think you'll find that your designs will generally be far better thought out if you can divorce your mind from the more implementation-bound roles.

In this book you'll look in depth at how to design, architect, and implement the SQL Server database tables and their accompanying access methods; you'll also examine the physical hardware, system software, and other aspects of a database system. You'll start from the point where someone mentions to you that they want to store some data, and begin generating tables and implementing access to these tables.

The real mission isn't so straightforward though. I've reviewed lots of people's code over the years, and no matter how well the object models, supporting code, or even documentation was put together, the database generally ranged from bad to horrible (there were good examples too!). My desire is to provide the information that database architects need to build databases properly. For anyone who has had the pleasure of reading college database textbooks, you know that they can be a bit on the dry side—as dry as the Mojave Desert in a drought. This is actually too bad, because much of the information contained between the covers is useful and relevant.

So my restated mission is to end the communication breakdown between the egghead geniuses and you, the working programmer, in order to provide the necessary knowledge in a way that's applicable to the real world. If you've ever done any programming, you'll undoubtedly disagree with some of the ideas presented in this book. I fully accept that this book is hardly the Gospel of St. Louis of Databases. My ideas and opinions have grown from 12 years of working with, and learning about, databases, and as such I've supplemented them with knowledge from many disparate persons, books, college classes, and seminars. The design methodology presented in this book is a conglomeration of these ideas, with as much credit given to those other folks as I can remember. I hope it proves a useful learning tool, and that by reading other people's works and trying out your own ideas, you'll develop a methodology that will make you a successful database designer.

What's Covered in This Book

This is a book of two halves. The first covers the logical design of databases, and the second looks at the physical design and implementation. The following is a summary of the areas covered chapter by chapter.

❑ **Chapter 1 Introduction to Database Concepts**: As its name implies, a brief introduction to the different database methodologies that are commonly used to implement a fully featured database system, such as OLTP databases, Data Warehouses, Operation Data Stores, and Data Marts.

❑ **Chapter 2 Gathering Information for a Database Project**: In this chapter we give an overview of the process of determining the requirements that the users will have of the database system, by looking at some of the more obscure places where important data hides.

❑ **Chapter 3 Fundamental Database Concepts**: A basic understanding of the concepts of relational theory is fundamental to the process of database design and is considered here. This will provide a basis for the development of our design.

❑ **Chapter 4 Entities, Attributes, Relationships, and Business Rules**: In this chapter we will begin the process of turning the information gathered in Chapter 2 into a logical design of our relational database, in particular by devising the entities we will require.

❑ **Chapter 5 Data Modeling**: Once we have discovered objects, we need to have a way to display and share the information with programmers and users. The data model is the most effective tool for depicting database design information.

❑ **Chapter 6 Normalization Techniques**: Normalization is the process of taking the information we gathered in Chapter 2, and developed in Chapters 4 and Chapter 5, and turning it into a well-structured draft of the data model. In this chapter we consider the normalization rules we must follow in designing a well-structured model for our system.

❑ **Chapter 7 Advanced Normalization Topics**: This chapter builds on the previous one by extending the basic normalization techniques beyond those familiar to most programmers. In this way we are able to fine-tune our logical design so as to avoid, as far as is possible, any data anomalies.

❑ **Chapter 8 Ending The Logical Design Phase**: Once we have designed the "perfect" database, we need to return to the original specifications to ensure that the data we expect to store will serve the data needs of the users. By this point many programmers are ready to code away, but it is important to finish off the logical design phase, by double-checking our model and its documentation to try and minimize the level of changes required when we come to physically implementing it.

❑ **Chapter 9 Planning the Physical Architecture**: In this chapter you'll look at making decisions about how you'll implement the architecture. Here you'll begin to take into consideration the number of users, system size, and how the data will be used.

❑ **Chapter 10 Building the Basic Table Structures**: In this chapter you'll go through the mechanics of choosing datatypes, building tables, and creating indices.

❑ **Chapter 11 Declarative Data Protection**: There are many different issues that govern the data integrity of your system. In this chapter you'll look at how to build data protection into your databases using the base techniques using constraints.

❑ **Chapter 12 Programmatic Data Protection**: In this chapter you go beyond the declarative protections described in Chapter 11 to include methods that are extremely flexible, using triggers and stored procedures.

❑ **Chapter 13 Advanced Data Access and Modification**: In this chapter you'll look at some of the different methods of accessing the data in the databases you've created, in particular through the use of views and stored procedures.

❑ **Chapter 14 Determining Hardware Requirements**: One of the most difficult activities for many data architects is to translate the system requirements into actual hardware requirements. What disk format do I need? How much disk space do I need, and how will these requirements change in the future? How much RAM? How many processors? Too many questions. These are generally questions for the database administrator, but for many architects there may not be an administrator around to help make proper hardware decisions.

❑ **Chapter 15 Completing the Project**: In this chapter you'll look at the endgame. Once you have your data, structures, and queries built, the project is over, isn't it? To wrap up your project you'll consider the fine-tuning you'll need to carry out, including performance issues concerning reporting needs, especially in high usage systems, and the system testing and deployment you must undertake. You'll also look at drawing up disaster plans, in order to protect your data from all those mishaps that Murphy (in his famous law) predicted would occur.

In addition to the material directly in this text of this book, there are several appendices that will be located on the Apress website that supplement the text. These appendices cover material that was not exactly a great fit for a database design book, but useful to explain a concept or a feature of SQL Server or the RDBMS that will extend your experience with the book.

These appendices are:

❑ **Appendix A: Codd's 12 Rules for an RDBMS** A listing of Codd's rules, and a brief discussion of how SQL Server meets these standards that have stood as a measuring stick of relational databases since 1985.

❑ **Appendix B: Indexes** Explains the basic structure of indexes to give you a feel for the best uses of indexes.

❑ **Appendix C: User Defined Functions** An overview of how to code user defined functions.

❑ **Appendix D: Data Type Reference** An introduction to the many different intrinsic datatypes provided by SQL Server. This appendix gives an overview of how they are implemented and how best to use the different datatypes.

❑ **Appendix E: Triggers** An overview of how to code triggers to implement complex business rules.

❑ **Appendix F: Transactions** An overview of how transactions are used in SQL Server code to promote proper concurrency and data integrity.

❑ **Appendix G: Cursors** An overview of the features and settings used in Cursors.

I have moved most of the sections out of the book and onto the website to focus completely on database design, and very little on the mechanics of SQL Server coding. However, these references give you what you need to know to understand and code these objects, if you do not currently possess these skills.

Who Should Read This Book?

Of course it is hard to not say "everyone on earth," but each chapter of this book isn't necessarily relevant for everyone and parts of it will not appeal to every programmer. I wish it did, because there is stuff in each chapter that will enrich every programmer's ability to design and implement databases. However, this is a breakdown of what will be valuable to whom.

Database Architect

If you're already a database architect who is responsible for gathering requirements and designing databases with involvement or responsibility for implementation, then read the entire book. You can skip the third chapter on a first reading.

Database Programmer

If you're only involved in the implementation of database code, you'll be interested in a good part of this book, which will help you understand the reasons why the "insane" data architect wants to implement a database with 50 tables when it seems like it needs only 3.

A first reading might include Chapter 5 on data modeling, and Chapters 6 and 7 on normalization, followed by the entire Part Two of the book. This section describes all of the techniques for implementing database systems.

What You Need to Use This Book

For the first half of the book, you'll be learning about logical data modeling. There are no software requirements for working through this part of the book.

In the latter half that deals with physical design, the only requirement (other than your thinking cap) for working through the examples is an installed copy of SQL Server 2000 and the Query Analyzer tool that comes with it. This can be any edition of SQL Server (Personal Edition upwards), as long as you can connect with Query Analyzer. You'll need a database that you can access with a user who is a member of the db_owner role, because you'll be creating all objects as the database owner.

If you don't have a copy of SQL Server, an Evaluation Edition is available on Microsoft's SQL Server website at http://www.microsoft.com/sql.

Conventions Used

You're going to encounter different styles as you're reading through this book. This has been done to help you easily identify different types of information and make sure that you don't miss any key points. These styles are as follows:

> **Important information, key points, and additional explanations are displayed like this to make them stand out. Be sure to pay attention to these when you find them.**

General notes, background information, and brief asides look like this.

❑ If you see something like, BackupDB, you'll know that it's a file name, object name, or function name.

❑ The first time you encounter an **important word**, it's displayed in bold text.

❑ Words that appear on the screen, such as menu options, are in a similar font to the one used on screen, for example, the File menu.

This is how code samples look the first time they're introduced:

```
Private Sub Command_Click
    MsgBox "Don't touch me"
End Sub
```

Whereas code that you've already seen, or that doesn't relate directly to the point being made, looks like this:

```
Private Sub Command_Click
    MsgBox "Don't touch me"
End Sub
```

Source Code

Full source code for examples used in this book can be downloaded from the Apress website at http://www.apress.com.

Errata

I've made every effort to make sure that there are no errors in the text or the code. However, to err is human, and as such I recognize the need to keep you informed of any mistakes as they're spotted and corrected. Errata sheets are available for all Apress books at http://www.apress.com. If you find an error that hasn't already been reported, please let Apress know.

Introduction to Database Concepts

Introduction

There are some basic database concepts and topics that everyone reading this book should know, and these will be covered in this first chapter. The following topics will be covered:

❑   **History of relational database structures**: Brief overview of why relational databases began

❑   **OLTP and data warehousing**: Compares online transaction processing (OLTP) with data warehousing, plus an introduction to the different modules that make up a complete database system

❑   **Overview of the SQL Server database design process**: Looks at the process followed in developing database applications

❑   **Case study introduction**: Introduces the case study, which you'll build throughout the course of the book

History of Relational Database Structures

The structure of databases has changed significantly in the last few decades. Originally, the only choice was to structure databases in ways optimized for the limited hardware on which they were stored. In the early 1970s E.F. Codd, working for IBM, introduced a new concept that changed forever the way in which data would be stored. His principles for what would become the **relational model** were way ahead of their time. In the relational model, each fact or piece of data is stored once only in the database, related to facts in other tables through key relationships. This leads to far greater consistency of data. Many programmers liked his ideas, but couldn't implement them due to hardware limitations.

Relational database theory continues to evolve but Codd's research, realized in his original three rules of normalization, remain the basis of most of this research. These rules have been expanded on since Codd's original work, and they will be covered later in Chapters 6 and 7 in a real-world manner more relevant to the database designer than Codd's classic, if rather dry, paper entitled "A Relational Model of Data for Large Shared Data Banks." Sadly, Mr. Codd passed away in April 2003 at the age of 79.

As mentioned earlier, it took quite some time after Codd's research was published for relational-style databases such as SQL Server to catch on, mainly because the hardware required for a proper architectural system only became available recently. You'll learn *why* later on, but for now, just take it that normalization requires an increase in the number of database tables, and any refinements to Codd's theory further increases the number of tables needed. Because of the extra hardware requirement this incurs, it hasn't been easy to sell the benefits of greater normalization to typical database programmers. Add to this the fact that a large number of tables with large numbers of joins bogged down the database server hardware and software of the 1980s and 1990s, and it isn't hard to see why database developers failed to properly structure their databases, as much from technological limitations as from lack of understanding.

Fortunately, recent advances in technology mean that things are looking up, and in the three years since SQL Server 2000 was initially released hardware has improved dramatically. Optimizations to database servers for specific uses such as OLTP and online analytical processing (OLAP), plus the fact that Microsoft completely rewrote SQL Server to work optimally with both Windows and the Intel platforms in the past few years has yielded great performance and reliability increases. These factors, along with operating system refinements and concepts such as **data warehousing** (discussed later in this chapter), have produced database servers that can handle structuring data in a proper manner, as defined 30 years ago.

Databases built today are being designed to use better structures, but we still have poorly designed databases from previous years. Even with a good basic design, programming databases can prove challenging to those with a conventional programming background in languages such as C, C++, or Visual Basic. This is because the relational programming language, SQL, requires the programmer to rethink the whole programming paradigm: sets and relations instead of ifs and loops. One SQL statement can expand to hundreds or tens of thousands of lines of procedural code. This isn't to say that Transact-SQL (T-SQL), the language of SQL Server, doesn't have support for loops, and all of the other basic programming language constructs, but even in T-SQL, the more work you offload onto the relational engine, the better. The other problem with SQL that is worth mentioning is that it's relatively easy to learn the basics, and as such it's typically not taken as seriously as other "real" programming languages. However, programming complex SQL isn't easy and should not be taken lightly.

Online Transactional Processing and Data Warehousing

An **OLTP** database is probably what most people are thinking of when they talk of a database, because it deals with the current data needed for the business operations. In contrast, **data warehousing** allows for extremely complex reporting by building repositories for historical data separate from the transactional data. This allows you to investigate long-range trends in business history, while avoiding any performance hits for transactional activities.

There is a tremendous difference between these two paradigms:

- ❑ **OLTP** systems deal with data that is constantly modified. The database is optimized to respond quickly to the insertion of new data, or the modification or deletion of existing data. It's designed to be responsive even when the amount of data is very large, and there are a large number of transactions.

- ❑ **Data warehousing** solves the issues that OLTP systems have in producing reports. OLTP systems have always been sluggish in reporting, because they're optimized to deal with constant modification, rather than collation, of the stored data. When reporting, you may want to query and perform calculations on large amounts of data, and this can seriously reduce the responsiveness of your database. In addition, data updates in the middle of a report may lead to a different outcome. Data warehouses overcome this by storing the data in a manner optimized for complex queries. Data warehouses are a recent history of the data that is stored—you don't query the actual live version of the data, but rather a copy, which is read-only to the user.

This is a little simplistic but highlights the main difference between these two database architectures. Let's now look at them in a little more depth.

The Four Modules of the Modern Database System

Over the past ten years or so there has been a lot of discussion about how corporate data should be structured. One of the most widely agreed-upon approaches is to break down the entire system into functional modules that serve different needs, instead of just forcing a single technology to perform all the tasks. The different modules are as follows:

- ❑ **OLTP**: The OLTP database stores current data—data that the user needs to run its business **now.**

- ❑ **Operational data store (ODS)**: Consolidated data used for day-to-day reporting. Such data is frequently consolidated from several disparate sources, with some degree of pre-aggregation performed, in order to save query time.

- ❑ **Data warehouse**: Grand data store for holding nearly all organizational data and its history.

- ❑ **Data Mart**: Specialized data store optimized for aggregations, used for specific situations, and held as a subset of the data warehouse. Data marts are generally processed using a technology known as **online analytical processing** (OLAP).

3

Referring to these as *modules* may seem incorrect, but the term module is used here to indicate that they're each part of an integrated database system. Each module plays a very different role. For one reason or another, not every database system will require every module. The two biggest factors in choosing which are necessary are the amount of data that needs to be stored, and concurrency (which defines how many users will be accessing the data at any given time). Smaller systems may be able to handle the reporting load without building costly additional modules to handle reporting needs. Chapter 9 deals specifically with deciding which modules to use.

Let's now look a little more closely at the four modules we introduced earlier.

Online Transactional Processing

The OLTP database contains the data used in everyday transactions in the process of conducting business. It has transient qualities that reflect current processing, and serves as the source where data about the enterprise resides. It's characterized by having any number of concurrent users who are creating, modifying, and deleting data. All corporate data should be stored or have been stored (in the case of historical data) in an OLTP database.

The structure of the OLTP data store should be highly normalized, as per the rules laid down in Codd's paper. Normalization reduces the amount of redundant data, thereby helping to prevent modification anomalies such as would occur if you had the customer address stored in two places in the database and only altered it in one. Normalization is covered in detail in Chapters 6 and 7.

A primary goal of the OLTP database is the integrity of current corporate data. This is achieved by following two important principles:

❑ Storing each current piece of data in a single place where it can be edited, so that any change is reflected everywhere else that it's used.

❑ Providing transactional support, so that multiple database alterations all have to take place together. If one of the alterations in the transaction fails, none of the others should be allowed to occur. The rest of the transactions up to that point should be rolled back.

A side effect of this, however, is that querying for useful information can be laborious due to the strictly compartmentalized structure of the data. As the OLTP database is designed with transactional performance and integrity in mind, data is stored in a manner that allows it to be written, but not necessarily read, efficiently. The user will often have to query numerous tables to get a meaningful set of information. This book focuses on the structure and implementation of an OLTP database. For smaller (there is that term again!) systems this may be the only type of database you need to implement.

As an example of the use of OLTP type databases, consider a bank that has customers with various amounts of money stored in their accounts. The bank will typically have a database that contains the names and contact information of all its customers. The bank is also likely to have many distributed databases handling all of the different account types and monetary transactions its customers make.

It might seem like all of this data could be located in the same database, but because a bank has tremendous amounts of data about monetary transactions spanning different branches, different states, and even different countries as well as a large body of contact information about its customers, it's more likely that these details will be held on separate databases. The bank may also have databases (or the same database if it's so inclined) for prospective customer contact information, and so on. Each of these databases would be an OLTP-type database.

Banking systems are among the most complex OLTP databases in today's global economy. While it seems simple enough to use an ATM card anywhere in the world without being able to withdraw more money than you actually have available, the implementation of this system will involve a massive distributed OLTP database system.

> A transaction refers to the mechanism by which you're able to ensure referential integrity (in other words, preserving the defined relationships between tables when records are entered or deleted) and atomicity (the concept that an action should act as a single unit). For a database, this means that you have a known set of outcomes depending upon whether one operation (or a group of operations) fails or succeeds. You'll look at transactions and how to use them in database code in Chapter 13. The most important thing to understand is that one of the main characteristics of OLTP databases is the employment of mechanisms to keep the data contained in them from being corrupted by anything the user does.

Operational Data Store

The idea of the ODS is to have a database in which all of the data you need to run your business on a day-to-day basis is located. A limited amount of historical data may be stored depending upon requirements.

The ODS is designed to address the following problems associated with the OLTP concept:

- ❑ OLTP databases generally have a complicated structure with many tables. The data structures can be quite complex to understand, and querying information may require creative use of the SQL language. Novice query writers commonly lack an understanding of the inner workings of SQL Server and can bring an OLTP system to its knees by executing inefficient queries.

- ❑ Many OLTP databases have a large number of detailed records. Day-to-day operations usually don't require access to every transaction created during the day, but need to be able to obtain summations of the data. If you ran multiple queries on the OLTP system, all of the transactions would need to be recalculated every time a query was made.

- ❑ Not all data is stored in a single source. A typical organization may have data important to the operation of the business stored in many data sources. Much as we would like to see it change, much of the world's data is still housed on mainframes in nonrelational databases written in COBOL.

In the ODS, data is consolidated from all the disparate sources in an organization and summarized as required. It can be refreshed as frequently or infrequently as necessary. The data is characterized by having few, if any, allowable user-modifications, with a moderate amount of history maintained to handle the day-to-day questions and show short-term trends.

In the bank scenario, the ODS would have all of the transactions for the past day, and possibly the past week or month, stored in a manner where a simple query returns any answers you wanted. Some aggregated data may be stored if it's frequently needed. For example, an account list might be stored where a customer's current account balance for the previous day is viewable. The customer could then query this kind of data to see their balance for the previous day as well as any transactions that have been cleared. Hence the entire account need not be summarized every time the customer wants to see their account information. Additionally, notices could be sent based on the data from the summarized rolling account balances.

Storing summarized data isn't a requirement for the ODS. It may just be necessary to make a set of tables that are simpler to query, so that the users can perform ad hoc inquiries. A great example of ODS is a database placed on notebook computers for sales staff who are on the road, or in PDAs for people who walk and work around the office, and don't have a permanent desk. Hence the goal of the ODS can be met by providing users with operational data and keeping them up to date on the short term trends required for making daily decisions.

Data Warehouse

The data warehouse supports decision making by storing as much historical information from the organization as is necessary. **Decision support** is a pretty generic term that refers to being able to answer the difficult questions about how an enterprise is doing. Better decisions can be made when more data specific to the needs of the user is available to be looked through, summarized, and queried. A proper decision support system can form the "intelligence hub" of an organization. For example, if the sales group in your company was able to see sales trends over a ten-year period, correlated with the current advertising models in use at any given time, it would certainly be better than having a single year of the same data. Another goal of the data warehouse, as with the ODS, is to separate the active transactional processing from the reporting aspects of the database system, so that you can perform intensive querying that will not affect your users' ability to create and access the data in your OLTP systems.

An older copy of the data from the OLTP database is stored in the data warehouse. The frequency of updating the information is based on the amount of data, the needs of the users, and the time available to do the copying. This data is stored in a manner efficient for querying—which requires a different structure compared to what's efficient for modifications. No modification should ever be made to the data in the warehouse; any changes should be made to the operational database. The only time that the warehouse changes is when it gets the most up-to-date set of information from the operational database. You should also never use the data to ask questions that require an up-to-date exact answer. The data warehouse is used solely for historical analysis of data, such as looking at trends over a long time.

A comprehensive data warehouse may take several years' worth of data from all heterogeneous sources within an organization—such as legacy mainframe systems, SQL Server, and Oracle databases—and transform it into a single database using common structures. In this manner, the valuable data from legacy databases in an organization can be combined with all of the newer, well-structured databases (as well as third-party databases that are used for various tasks) into one common set of structures that can be used to mine the information needed to make decisions. For instance, human resources data could come from one third-party system, one general ledger from another, and router IP addresses from a third. All of these databases may supply a piece of the puzzle that will provide users with the complete picture they need to make a decision.

One of the most important things you have to consider is the potential range of questions that may be asked. While many questions can be answered directly from the OLTP database ("What is customer X's current account balance?") many will have to be pushed out to a data warehouse ("Over the past year, what is the average amount of money customers have debited or credited to their accounts in ATMs in each region of the country?"). The data warehouse is an ideal place to bring together difficult-to-associate data in a manner that users can deal with.

A data warehouse is a tremendous undertaking, and shouldn't be considered just a quick item to build. You usually want to bring in data from many disparate sources, some of which may change as time passes, especially when the data comes from third-party sources (a new vendor for the Human Resources database, a new version of another system, a systems acquired as a result of a takeover, for example).

While a banking data warehouse will be huge, it will probably be used heavily by the bank's sales and marketing teams. They can use the data to answer questions about which of their programs has worked best when, and what kinds of programs to implement when. The actuarial staff would probably look at the data to see trends in interest rates vs. foreclosures. Having such a vast collection of information in a database makes the new technologies available in SQL Server 2000 so important to data warehousing.

Data Marts

A **data mart** is a distinct subset of a data warehouse and usually pertains to either the specific needs of a division or department, or a specific business purpose within an organization. It's built using special database structures known as star or snowflake schemas. **Star schemas** are actually simple databases, with a single **fact table** (a table containing information that can be summarized to provide details regarding the history of the operation of the organization) connected to a set of **dimension tables** that categorize the facts in the fact tables. It should be noted that the data in the fact table is primarily numeric. **Snowflake schemas** are simply an extension of star schemas in which the fact tables may also be dimension tables.

The other important term from data marts that you must introduce are **cubes**. A cube is another of those fairly strange terms, but it describes how the OLAP tools technology organizes the dimension tables of your star or snowflake schema. The dimensions of the fact table are described by the dimensions of the cube, while each cell of data in the cube represents a fact containing a level of detail for the different dimensions of the cube. Consider the following three questions:

❑   How many viewers in total were there to your website in 2000?

❑   How many viewers in total of your website were there in 2000 and what areas did they visit?

❑   What kinds of viewers of your website in 2000 did you have and what areas did they visit?

Each of these questions will use a different number of dimensions to solve the problem. Your fact table would be concerned with a numeric count of users at a low level, and the dimension tables would be used to group and slice the data according to a user's needs. The cubing mechanisms can be used to pre-aggregate the answers to parts or all of the questions that a user might ask, in order to make answering the question quicker for the users. An in-depth explanation of these data structures is beyond the scope of this book. More details can be found in *Professional SQL Server 2000 Programming* by Wrox Press and *Professional Data Warehousing with SQL Server 7.0 and OLAP Services* by Apress.

Data marts often use SQL Server to store their data, but the data isn't necessarily accessed using classic SQL commands (though it's an option when SQL Server is used to store the dimensional data). Usually they're queried using the SQL-like language **Multidimensional Expressions** (**MDX**), though technically data can also be accessed using a tool with no coding. Suitable tools include Microsoft Excel, Microsoft Access, Cognos Impromptu, and Lotus Approach. The data in data marts is read-only by definition (save for the processes that periodically refreshes it, of course).

The main purpose of the data mart is to show trends on any grouping of data the user wants, by separating the contents of a massive data warehouse into smaller segments that are reasonably easy to access and manage. Each data mart will be architected in such a manner as to solve a very specific set of problems.

Consider the example of an online bookseller. The marketing department wants to have a data mart dealing with products sold. The main fact table contains numeric sales figures, such as quantity of items sold, and their price. Dimensions are then modeled for the following: date of sale; where on the site the user got the information (did they search directly for the item?, did they do a general author search?, or did you entice them to purchase by flashing their information on the screen?); the customer information (where they were from, any other personal information); and finally the products that were purchased. From this information you can see what sales were made over a quarter to persons in Topeka, or any other combination of the dimensions, and thus build vague, or very specific, queries to answer questions. If you were retrieving this directly from your OLTP databases, it would take hundreds of lines of SQL code, as I can verify from painful experience.

In the banking example, you might create specific data marts for different users of the data warehouse. For instance, a marketing user may have a data mart with banking customers segregated by income level, region of the country, payment amounts, interest amounts, and on-time information. From this, queries can be formulated showing the customers from each region, by each income level, who made their payments on time, for which interest level. This could be very powerful information when formulating new deals with special rates in different parts of the country.

Architecture

The overall architecture of the final database solution will vary depending on the size of the problem you're trying to solve. In the following diagram, you take a typical larger system, and break it down so you can see the flow of data through the full database solution.

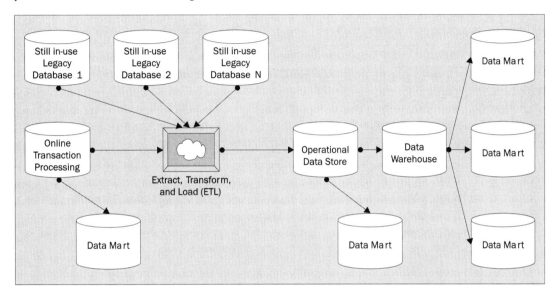

Notice that there are a lot of data marts scattered about the diagram. Data marts are most easily built from the data warehouse, because the data warehouse already has historical information, but data marts can be built at any step along the way.

Note also that you take your source data in the legacy databases and OLTP databases and transform it for use in the ODS first. Generally, once you've transformed the data into an ODS-like format, there aren't too many changes to arrive at the data warehouse format. Actual scenarios may vary from situation to situation.

An Overview of the SQL Server Database Design Process

The process of designing a proper database system has a few things in common with designing efficient computer systems of any kind, as follows:

❏   It's a relatively straightforward task.

❏   It can be very time-consuming.

❏   It's seldom done with the rigor that might be desired.

The database is the central, and therefore most important, cog in most computer systems being created today. The reason for this is simple; the database stores the information that lets you monitor what is going on in a system, and most importantly lets you bill the clients of the system. Take any system, from a phone system, air traffic control, tape library, call center, inventory, and so on, and the backbone is always some sort of data storage. Even in systems that don't seem to have any database involvement, data storage in some form is usually a requirement. This book will concentrate primarily on larger systems that have a database as the focus of the system. Examples of such databases are all around you, on the Internet, in your banks, government, companies, and so on.

The process of designing such databases can be broken down into a few steps:

- **Defining the objective**: Don't laugh this off as being too obvious: Most projects are plagued by the developers having no real idea of what the user base actually wants or needs, yet this is probably the most critical stage of the project. During this phase you define the functional, performance, and reporting requirements for the final system that direct your activities and planning for the rest of the project.

- **Logical design**: Once you have your objectives, you can create a logical path towards achieving them. This is done in an implementation-independent way. The main reason you won't see SQL Server referenced much in the first half of this book is because logical database design is largely independent of physical database design and implementation.

- **Physical design**: Once you have your logical design, you translate it to an implementation-specific design, thereby replacing logical representations with physical ones.

- **Physical implementation**: In this phase you finally build the database by laying out the physical data onto database servers and developing code to it.

- **Review**: This process assesses whether or not the objectives were achieved. Sadly, this remains the most overlooked part of a project because it takes too long and is no fun at all: testing, documenting, and all of the other things you hate to do but know that you should. The review should include user feedback and start a maintenance plan to counter any problems identified now or in the future.

In this book, the first two steps are covered in the "Logical Design" section, and the rest is covered in the "Physical" section.

Case Study Introduction

Throughout the book, you'll walk through a database design case study, incorporating all the aspects covered in the book. The topic of the case study will be a personal checking account register. While the actual amounts of data that will be stored in the resulting databases will be much smaller than might normally require advanced data warehousing, it does make for a manageable example in terms of size.

All the code and data for the case study can be downloaded from http://www.apress.com.

The choice of a checking account register gives just enough leeway to show many of the different types of relationships and structural problems that will be encountered when creating a real database. It allows you to consider the design and implementation of the OLTP ODS database, and the use of SQL Server utilities to perform the extraction, transformation, and loading tasks of the data from the OLTP database into the data mart (generically known as **extract**, **transform**, and **load** or **ETL**) or ODS database.

Summary

In this chapter you learned about the basic foundations of the modern database systems, especially OLTP and data warehousing methodologies. You now know that there are four primary parts to the enterprise database system:

❑   **OLTP** for storing your current data, with only a limited amount of the historical data retained to enable up-to-the-minute decisions.

❑   **ODS** for building a storage mechanism for data needed to make day-to-day business decisions without interrupting the users in the OLTP database.

❑   **Data warehouse**, not to be confused with the general term of data warehousing. The data warehouse is used to store massive amounts of history, thereby enabling you to maintain a consolidated database of as many of your corporate databases as necessary and to help you to see trends over long periods of time.

❑   **Data marts**, which are often confused with OLAP or cubes (which are technologies used in querying the data in the data mart). The data mart is used to take a slice of a data warehouse or in its absence, the OLTP or ODS data, and allow the user to view aggregated data in a flexible manner.

2

Gathering Information for a Database Project

In this chapter, you'll learn about the very first steps that you should take when starting a database design project. Gathering preliminary information for a new database project–such as deciding what is going to be stored in it –is one of the most important tasks, though constraints on time and resources in the real world usually mean that the process isn't carried out as thoroughly as it should be.

Building databases without adequate preliminary analysis is like building a house on sand: Once the first floor is built, the sands shift and you have to start all over again. Situations frequently arise in which a redesign of some overlooked feature is required post-deployment. Proper analysis is the solid foundation for a smooth, successful, and sturdy project.

As you gather the information for your database project, you should avoid the strong temptation to start imposing any kind of structure. Avoid defining too much at first, like tables and fields, however obvious the structure may seem at this point. It's important to approach the process reasonably naively, as if everything the client is telling you is new. Consult all parties involved in the project and listen to their ideas and needs. Too often a structure is imposed and a solution to a problem is begun before enough knowledge of the task is at hand. This chapter precedes the definition of data modeling in order to emphasize this point.

The process of database design involves the collection of a significant amount of information. This information will be useful to other team members now and in the future in order to understand and support the system. A formal documentation policy needs to be considered.

> **Reality Check:** This chapter describes a process for gathering requirements that won't fit every situation. The goal of this chapter isn't to show you a complete project management process, but to point out the basic pieces of information needed to feed the database design process. The actual process employed may be much simpler for small projects, or much more intense for grander projects, such as government contracts.

The Database Design Team

In order to start the information-gathering process, a project team must be organized. While the team may only consist of a single person (in the case of small organizations or projects), there are at least three roles that need to be filled because each serves a very different essential purpose:

- ❑ The **business analyst** fleshes out the business requirements from the users and provides the design team with a functional specification that the team develops into a technical specification. This role also acts as the user's advocate, making sure that the final project solution suits the specified business needs of the client. The role also ensures that any contracts, agreements, and so on are fulfilled.

- ❑ The **data architect** takes the functional specification and develops a technical implementation specification. (The system architect also helps with this task.) The data architect designs all the data storage and access architectures, and also chooses proper storage technologies based on what's needed. *This book focuses only on the responsibilities of this role.* Note that the data architect isn't the same as the database administrator (DBA) who is concerned with implementation and deals with hardware, software, and generally makes things run smoothly. The data architect is concerned with the way the database systems, relational or otherwise, fit together and are structured.

- ❑ The **system architect** designs the entire user interface and middle-tier business objects that the project will require, and is responsible for choosing the front-end and middle-tier technologies. The specific difference between this role and the data architect is that the latter is solely responsible for the database side of the project, while the system architect deals with everything else, though there may be some overlap between the roles.

Each of these roles is present during the design and implementation process. There are other important roles that also contribute as well–for example, the project manager who manages the process; the project sponsor or client representative who provides the finance and will use the finished project; testers; documenters; and so on. However, the three roles listed earlier are the core group that will be involved with the database design. The reason for defining these roles at all is to show that the data architect can focus almost exclusively on how the data is stored as long as different people perform each of the three roles.

Documentation and Communication

If you've ever tried to order take-out food over the phone from a restaurant where the person you're speaking to barely understands your language, you have a good idea of the communications issues involved when management and end users explain to Information Technology professionals what they want in their computer solution. Clients tend to think in the language of their needs, and DBAs tend to think in terms of computer solutions.

During this process of analysis, there is one good habit that you should adopt early on: Document as much of the information that you acquire as is reasonably possible. As a best case, you have reference material to look back on as the project progresses. In the worst case, if one of the project team resigns suddenly after the final design meeting then all of the knowledge in their mind is gone.

So you should document, document, document! It's imperative that information isn't stored only inside the craniums of your design team, lest it's forgotten later in the process. The following are helpful tips as you begin to take notes about your clients' needs:

- ❑ Try to maintain a set of documents that will share system design and specification information. Important documents to consider include the following: design meeting notes, documents describing verbal change requests, and sign-offs on all specifications, such as functional, technical, and testing.

- ❑ Beyond formal documentation, it's important to keep the members of the design team up-to-date and fully informed. Develop and maintain a common repository for all your information.

- ❑ Take minutes of meetings and keep notes of every suggestion, request, or idea that a customer voices.

- ❑ Annotate information that is added as a result of brainstorming, despite the fact that the users haven't actually stated or agreed to it. Even good ideas can become contentious when the user feels that he is being kept in the dark.

- ❑ Set the project's scope early on and keep it in mind at all times. This will prevent the project from getting too big or diverse to be useful.

One of the primary jobs of the design team is to specify the scope (mission statement or mission objectives) of the project. This will be consulted and used for comparison during the design and implementation as well as completion. If, however, the project's objectives and aims are not decided at this early stage and nothing is written down, then there is a strong chance that there will be conflicts between the client's and design team's ideas. Such vagueness or indecision might cause unnecessary discussions, fights, or even lawsuits later on in the process. So, make sure clients understand what is being done for them, and use language that will be clearly understood, yet is specific enough to describe what can be learned in the information-gathering process.

Client Approval

Progressing through the entire database design process, the client will no doubt change her mind on field names, field definitions, business rules, user interface, colors–just about anything that she can–and you have to be prepared for this. Whatever the client wants or needs is what you'll have to endeavor to accomplish, but she must be made aware of the implications on finances or deadlines of design changes once work has begun.

After every meeting, summarize notes in language that all participants can understand, and send them copies. Forward responses to the project manager, and consider keeping folders with communications stored away for later reference.

At any time the client can say, "I never said that," and if there is no documentation to counter their claim, guess what?–for all intents and purposes they never said that. So once again, keep documentation and if decisions have to be made that the client won't like, you should have documentation available as a backup for decisions based on the correspondence.

The best way to avoid conflict (and, as clients change their minds, "scope creep" *will* occur) is to make sure to get client approval at regular stages throughout the design process.

Minimum Information Requirements

Regardless of the size of the design team, there is a set of basic information that must be gathered during the early stages if the team is to continue the design process.

To start with, there is probably a pile of notes, printouts, screen shots, CD-ROMs loaded with spreadsheets, database backups, Word documents, e-mails, handwritten notes, and so on that can help solve the problem. This data will be analyzed to discover the data elements, screens, and reports that you'll need to consider in the design of your applications. Often information is found in the client's artifacts that will be invaluable when putting together the table designs.

Next you'll explore the initial stages of the design process, and the sources of this basic information.

Database Prototypes

Prototypes can be useful tools for communicating how you intend to solve a real-world problem using a computer, or when trying to reengineer the management of a current process. Prototypes are "proofs of concept," an opportunity to flesh out, with the design team and end users, the critical elements of the project on which success or failure will depend.

Sometimes, the data architect will be directed to take a prototype database that has been hastily developed and "make it work" or, worse yet, "polish up the database." Indeed, inheriting an unstructured, unorganized prototype and being tasked with turning it into a production database isn't uncommon.

Bear in mind however that prototypes should only be considered as interactive pictures to get the customer to sign a contract with your company. Time and time again consultants are hired to develop a prototype that looks so good that it's assumed that it must be ready for enterprise deployment. Many people will say, "It works, so why toss it out? Just Band-Aid it and get moving." The problem is, when making a prototype, you piece, slap, and hack together code as you develop ideas in an unorganized way. Proper structure and forethought are generally tossed to the wind. Once the whirlwind prototype development is done, you have a pretty UI and some data; but little or no thought has been put into its architecture.

Many clients think visually in terms of forms, web pages, and simple user interfaces. In many cases clients will have absolutely no understanding or care about how the system is created. The data architect's job is to balance the customer's perceived need with their real need–a properly structured database that sits behind the user interface. Changing a form around to include a new text box, label, or whatever is a relatively simple task and can give the user the false impression that creating a database application is an easy process. For proof, show the user a near-finished prototype application with no database support. The clients may be impressed that something has been put together so quickly, but then run it in the untested sequence and watch it go boom and crash. Rarely will it be understood that what exists under the hood–namely the database and the middle-tier business objects– is where all the main work takes place.

It's better to start from scratch once the customer has signed, thereby developing the final application using structured and supported coding standards. As a data architect, it's very important to work as hard as possible to use prototype code *only* as a working model, that is, as a piece of documentation that enhances the design. Prototype code helps to ensure that you don't miss out on any critical pieces of information that the users need–such as a name field, a search operation, or even a button (which may imply a data element or a process)–but they usually shouldn't tell anything about architectural issues. When it comes to enterprise database design, there can be no sloppy shortcuts.

Client Interviews

The client interview is where the project really gets started, though it's often the case that the data architect will never meet the user, let alone formally interview them. The business analyst and system architect would provide all the information that is required. There may be times, however, when the data architect actually becomes involved in the interview process, depending on the structure of the actual design team. An exhaustive treatment of interview techniques is beyond the scope of this book, but there are a few key points that should be mentioned. Firstly, the word *interview* is used instead of the word *interrogation*. The first suggests a one-on-one exchange of ideas, while the second implies the imposition of ideas upon the paying customer.

Try to set a basic agenda for the interview, so that important areas are covered, but have an open mind. As a starter, one simple question will serve well: "What do you want from this project?" This lets the interviewees tell you what **they** want from the project. Encourage them to explain their initial ideas of how they would achieve it. All of this will give you a clear explanation of what they want and why, thereby preventing preconceived ideas from altering how the problem is addressed. Be prepared to listen, take notes, ask questions, get clarification–and then take more notes.

Make sure to treat every person that is being interviewed for a project as an important individual. Each person will likely have different viewpoints from every other person. Don't assume that the first person spoken to can speak for the rest, even if they're all working on the same project or if this individual is the manager. One-on-one sessions allow clients to speak their mind, without untimely interruptions from colleagues. Be mindful of the fact that the loudest and boldest people might not have the best ideas. The quiet person who sits at the back and says nothing may have the key to the entire project. Make sure everyone who matters is heard. Be careful here to understand what *matter* means. This doesn't mean that you should only talk to the manager. *Matter* refers to people who understand what the problem is and the intricacies surrounding it.

One way to convey to the client that what they're saying is being understood is to repeat the most important points as the meeting progresses. This is also useful for clarification of unclear points and aids in the note-taking process. Never record any conversation without the interviewee's consent. If at all possible, have a person at meetings who has no responsibilities other than note taking.

The more that's written down and filed away, rather than just committed to memory, the more clients can regularly review it. This means that not only the relationships with the clients can be improved, but the chances of identifying the data they need. This also helps to provide the design team with the information required to design the final product.

This book is born out of making mistakes, plenty of mistakes in the database design process, and the client interview is one of the most difficult parts of the process. It might not seem a suitable topic for experienced programmers, but even the best need to be reminded that jumping the gun, bullying the client, telling them what they want, and even failing to manage the user's expectations can ruin even a well-developed system. Good client-interviewing technique is necessary to get a solid foundation for the design process.

Questions That Need Answers

It's very important to make sure that whoever does the interviewing finds out the answers to the following questions.

Who Will Use the Data?

The answer to this question may indicate other personnel that might need to be interviewed, and will be of importance when you come to define the security for the system.

How Will the Data Be Used?

Consider the case of designing a contacts database. You need to know the following:

❑   Will the contact names be used just to make phone calls, like a quick phone book?

❑   Will you be sending mass e-mails or posts to the members of the contact lists? Should the names be subdivided into groups for this purpose?

❑   Will you be using the names to solicit a response from the e-mails, like donations, overdue bills, or new investors?

❑   How important is it to have each contact's correct title (for example, Dr. instead of Mr.)? Do you need any phonetic information? Would you lose a sale if a user mispronounces a customer's name?

Knowing what the client is planning to use the data in the system for is a very important piece of information indeed. Not only will this help in understanding the process, but it also gives a good idea of the type of data that needs to be stored.

What Is Wanted on Reports?

Reports are often one of the most forgotten parts of the design process. Many novice developers leave their implementation to the very last minute. However, users are probably more interested in the reports that are generated by the data than anything else that is done in the program. Reports are used as the basis of vital decision making and can make or break a company.

Looking back at the contact example, what name does the client want to see on the reports?

❑   First name, last name

❑   First name, middle name, last name

❑   Last name, first name

❑   Nickname?

It's very important to try to nail as many of these issues down early, no matter how small or silly they seem at this point. You'll be looking at building a reporting infrastructure later in your project and this kind of information will be necessary.

Where Is the Data Now?

It would be nice once in a while to have a totally new database with absolutely no pre-existing data. This would make life so easy. Unfortunately, this is almost never the case, except when building a product to be sold to end users in a turnkey fashion. Most of the time, the conversion of existing data is important to the end users.

Every organization is different. Some have data in one single location, while others have it scattered in many locations. Rarely, if ever, is the data already in well-structured databases that can be easily accessed. If that were the case, where would the fun be? Indeed, why would the client come to you at all? Clients typically have data in the following sundry locations, just to mention a few:

❑   **Mainframe or legacy data:** Millions of lines of active COBOL mainframes still run many corporations.

❑ **Spreadsheets:** Spreadsheets are wonderful tools to view, slice, and dice data, but are inappropriate places to maintain complex databases. Most users know how to use a spreadsheet as a database, but unfortunately aren't so well experienced in ensuring the integrity of their data.

❑ **Desktop databases such as Access:** Desktop databases are great tools and are easy to deploy and use. However, this often means that these databases are constructed and maintained by nontechnical personnel and are poorly designed, thereby potentially causing large amounts of problems when the databases have to be enlarged or modified.

❑ **Filing cabinets:** Yes, there are still many companies that have no computers at present and maintain vast stockpiles of paper documents. The project might simply be to replace a filing cabinet with a computer-based system, or to supply a simple database that logs the physical locations of the existing paper documents.

Data that needs to be included in the SQL Server database design will come from these and other weird and wonderful sources that will be discovered from the client.

How Much Is the Data Worth?

It's also important to place value judgments on data. Just because data is available, it doesn't necessarily mean that it should be included in the new database. The client needs to be informed of all the data that is available and be provided with a cost estimate of transferring it into the new database. The cost of transferring legacy data can be high. In this way, the client is offered the opportunity to make decisions that may conserve funds for more important purposes.

How Will the Data in the New Database Fit In with the Other Data?

Once you have a good idea of where all of the client's important data is located, you can begin to determine how the data in the new SQL Server solution will interact with the data that will stay in its original format. This may include building intricate gateway connections to mainframes, linking server connections to other SQL Servers or Oracle boxes, or even spreadsheets. You cannot make too many assumptions about this topic at this point in your design. Just knowing the basic architecture you'll need to deal with can be very helpful later in the process.

What Are the Rules Governing the Use of the Data?

Taking the previous example of contacts, you might discover the following:

❑ Every contact must have a valid e-mail address.

❑ Every contact must have a valid street address.

❑ The client checks every e-mail address using a mail routine and the contact isn't a valid contact until this routine has been successfully executed.

❑ Contacts must be subdivided by type.

Be careful not to infer any rules like this. Confirm them with the client. The final product might be unacceptable because you've placed a rule the client doesn't want on the data.

Other Places to Look for Information

Apart from interviews, there are other sources to consult in the search for data rules and other pieces of information relevant to the design project. Often the project manager will obtain these documents.

Request for Quote or Request for Proposal

Two of the primary documents are as follows:

❑   **Request for Quote** (**RFQ**): A document with a fairly mature specification that an organization sends out to firms to determine how much something would cost.

❑   **Request for Proposal** (**RFP**): A document for less mature ideas that an organization wishes to expand on using free consulting services.

A copy of an RFP or an RFQ needs to be added to the information that you need later on in the process. While these documents generally consist of sketchy information about the problem and the desired solution, they can be used to confirm the original reason for wanting the database system and for getting a firmer handle on the types of data to be stored within.

Contracts or Client Work Orders

Getting copies of the contract is a fairly radical approach to gathering design information. Frankly, in a corporate structure, fighting through layers of management to make people understand why it's necessary to see the contract at all can be quite a challenge. Even if you're granted access, contracts can be inherently difficult to read due to the language that they're written in. However, be diligent in filtering out the legalese, and uncover the basic requirements for the database system–requirements that must be fulfilled exactly or you might not get paid.

Note that not only is the contract to build the system important, but you must take into consideration any contracts that the system has to fulfill.

Level of Service Agreement

One important section of contracts that is very important to the design process is the required level of service. This may specify the number of pages per minute, the number of records in the database, and so on.

Don't Forget About Audits

When building a system, you must consider if it's likely to be audited in the future and by whom. Government, ISO 9000 clients, and other clients that are monitored by standards organizations are likely to have strict audit requirements. Other clients will also have financial audit processes. These audit plans may contain valuable information that can be used in the design process.

Old Systems

If you're writing a new version of a currently operating database system, then access to the existing system can be both a blessing and a curse. Obviously, the more information you can gather about where the system was previously is very important. All of the screens, data models, object models, user documents, and so on, are extremely important to the design process.

However, unless you're simply making revisions to the existing system, it's very important to use only the old database system as a reference point. It's very easy to think in terms of tweaking existing code and utilizing all of the features and data of the existing system as the basis of updating the system. In a minority of cases, this might be a correct implementation, but generally speaking, it isn't. On most occasions, the existing system to be replaced will have many problems that will need to be fixed, rather than emulated.

Reports, Forms, Spreadsheets

Quite a large percentage of computer systems are built around the filling out of forms: government forms, company forms, all kinds of forms. Be assured that all this data is going to be scattered around the company, and it's imperative to find it *all*. It's virtually certain that these sources will contain data that you'll need for the project, so make sure that the client gives up all such items.

Outline of the Case Study

The main goal of the case study in this chapter isn't so much to illustrate the information-gathering part of the process–it's unlikely that the data architect will do this in most teams–but rather just to set up a manageable example that you can follow throughout the book. For convenience, try to imagine that you're a one-person design team (with the exception of some input from the business analyst), ignoring any kind of user interface.

You receive an e-mail from the programming manager stating that the accounting department needs a database to handle checking account maintenance. After meeting with the IT manager, you're referred to the accounting manager, Sam Smith. An interview is set up with Sam to get an idea of what his requirements are.

Client Interview

The following notes are created and distributed from this meeting:

Meeting with Sam Smith,
Accounting, Nov 24, 2000, 10 AM,
Large Conference Room

Attendees: *Louis Davidson, Data Architect;*
                        Sam Smith, Accounting Manager;
                        Joe Jones, Business Analyst

Initial Meeting

Additional documentation attached: Bank register, sample check, sample statement, as well as electronic format of statement.

Currently using paper check register, just like a basic home register.

Have looked at the possiblility of using canned product, but we have found none that offer all that they want. And most offer way too many features.

Need to have multi-user capabilities (entry and viewing). Share over intranet.

Process:
Need to have very up to date information about account.
Currently balancing account once a month. Using the statement from bank. Takes an entire day to get balanced at least. Would like to keep the account balanced weekly using internet data.

Only interested in checking, not savings, stocks, bonds, etc. Already have a system for this.

Will be audited yearly by a major auditor. Don't have an audit plan as of yet.

Once Sam was finished, asked him about vendor tracking:
It would be nice to be able to have payee information for most of the checks we write.

Also about categorizing check, Sam said it would be nice, but not completely needed at this point.

Looking back over the notes, there are several items you need to gather from the accounting department: check register, bank statement, audit plan, and a voided check, if available.

Preliminary Documentation

Sample Check Register

Number	Date	Description	Category	Amount	Balance
12390	12/15/00	Thinburger	Employee Appreciation	▬	▬
12391	12/15/00	UnAllied Mortgage	Building payment	▬	▬
12392	12/16/00	TN Electric	Utilities	▬	▬
12393	12/16/00	Deposit	N/A	▬	▬

Account
Running Total

Sample Bank Statement

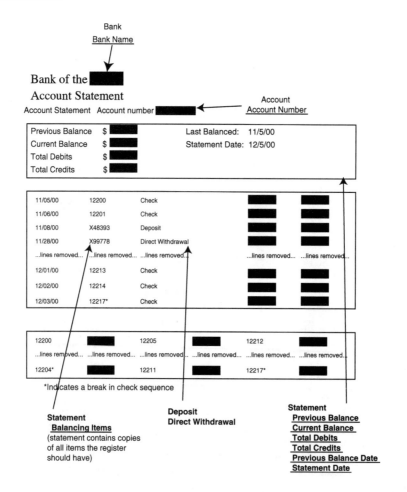

Bank
Bank Name

Bank of the ▬

Account Statement

Account Statement   Account number ▬

Account
Account Number

Previous Balance	$ ▬	Last Balanced:	11/5/00
Current Balance	$ ▬	Statement Date:	12/5/00
Total Debits	$ ▬		
Total Credits	$ ▬		

11/05/00	12200	Check	▬	▬
11/06/00	12201	Check	▬	▬
11/08/00	X48393	Deposit	▬	▬
11/28/00	X99778	Direct Withdrawal	▬	▬
...lines removed...	...lines removed...	...lines removed...	...lines removed...	...lines removed...
12/01/00	12213	Check	▬	▬
12/02/00	12214	Check	▬	▬
12/03/00	12217*	Check		

12200	▬	12205	▬	12212	▬
...lines removed...	...lines removed...	...lines removed...	...lines removed...	...lines removed...	...lines removed...
12204*	▬	12211	▬	12217*	▬

*Indicates a break in check sequence

Statement
Balancing Items
(statement contains copies
of all items the register
should have)

Deposit
Direct Withdrawal

Statement
Previous Balance
Current Balance
Total Debits
Total Credits
Previous Balance Date
Statement Date

Notice that all figures have been blacked out in the previous statements. Unless it's extremely important to have exact figures on documents, block out any sensitive information that might cause problems if it got into the wrong hands.

Sample Bank Register Data Stream Format

Column	Datatype	Required
Transcation Date	Date Only	Yes
Transaction Number	String(20)	Yes
Description	String(100)	Yes
Item Amount	Money	Yes

Transcation
Transcation Date
Transaction Number
Description
Item Amount

Note that this data stream isn't from your analysis. Rather it's a paper document explaining what the bank will be providing to the client to support the electronic balancing of accounts.

Sample Check

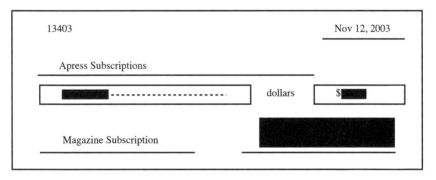

This is as far as you'll go with the case study in this chapter. You have now made a good start–the scope of your project is extremely small and you've gathered as much information as you can at this point–but there will come a time later on when you have to ask for more information. In later chapters, you'll look back at these notes and documentation when you come to assemble the database itself.

Summary

In this chapter you've concentrated on a significant preliminary step in database design: the information-gathering process. The real message behind all that you've seen is to get as much information as possible and document it. Look everywhere that is reasonable–leave no stone unturned while procuring as much information as the client is willing or able to give about the problem. Sometimes it's clear exactly how to solve the problem even after the first e-mail. At other times, it will take months of digging around to get enough information to tackle it. This balance will be based on the scope of the requirements, but the steps are almost always pretty much the same. Designing well-structured systems and databases is hard work that takes a relatively long time to accomplish if done correctly. The first step is to understand the problem before trying to solve it.

Always keep in mind that it takes more time to redo a poorly implemented task than it does to do it right the first time. You'll look at what "right" means during the physical data-modeling phase of database design later in this book.

3

Fundamental Database Concepts

Introduction

The goal of this chapter is to clarify terminology used by database professionals and academics. The question often arises as to whether or not reading about database design theory is at all worthwhile. Of course it is–would you fly in a plane with a pilot who didn't understand the theory of flight, or drive on a bridge designed by an engineer who didn't understand physics? No, so why expect your customers to come to you for database expertise if you don't understand the theory that supports database design?

In this chapter, you'll look at some of the aspects of relational theory, and compare them to the SQL concepts and methods that you in the field should already know. Because there are numerous other books on the subject, this book won't delve too deeply into academic territory; rather you'll learn a basic foundation in useful database concepts.

The relational concepts will be presented largely from a SQL-oriented point of view, which means that you'll be comparing theoretical concepts with SQL terms that are already familiar. However, you won't get bogged down in implementation; you'll just get an overview. For further information, you should delve into the other sources suggested in Chapter 1.

During this chapter you'll be looking at the following:

❑   Relational model: Examines the terminology used for the essential blocks; you'll then build upon this knowledge in later chapters.

❑   Definitions of additional database concepts.

The Relational Model

As mentioned in Chapter 1, E. F. Codd devised the relational model in the early 1970s. In this section, you'll take a look at its more important parts from a SQL Server standpoint.

As you'll see, SQL Server implementation has much in common with this model, but it isn't nearly the same thing. Many relational purists cringe at how all of the variations of SQL (not just SQL Server) are implemented, but this book isn't the place to discuss these objections.

Database

The first item to define is a database.

> **Simply, a database is a collection of data arranged for ease and speed of search and retrieval.**

This could be a card catalog at a library, a SQL Server database, or a text file. Technically, there is no corresponding concept in relational theory, but because you'll make use of this term frequently, it's important that you're introduced to it.

> **In SQL Server, a database is a collection of objects and data that is grouped together logically.**

Table

The most important element you'll deal with is the table itself. A table is the physical representation of some *thing,* either real or imaginary. As you design tables, you'll be looking for people, places, things, or ideas (**nouns**) that need to have information stored about them. Understanding the concept of treating tables as a noun, and nouns as tables is the first step to designing proper tables. Later, you'll examine what you should store in tables in more detail. You'll look at how to identify tables and other objects in the next chapter.

The term **table** is a very implementation-oriented term and has the following meaning:

> **An orderly arrangement of data. Especially one in which the data is arranged in columns and rows in an essentially rectangular form.**

Two common versions of tables are an Excel spreadsheet and the result of a simple SQL Query on the Northwind database. The latter is shown here.

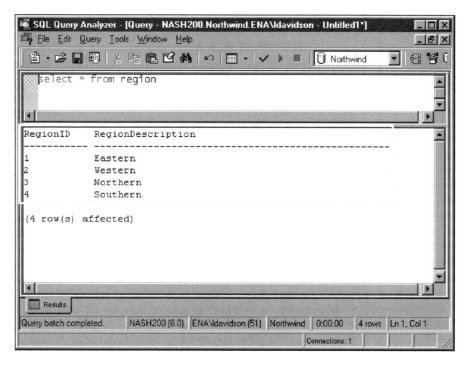

Even before computer spreadsheets, people were working on paper ones containing rows and columns (though they would not have called it a spreadsheet). You'll take a more in-depth look at rows and columns later in this section.

The following table is just a very generic one that represents some basic information about several restaurants, with a few columns defined. Each of the terms in the table will be defined later in this chapter.

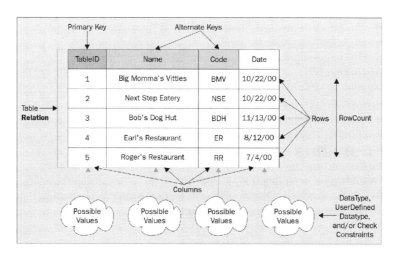

Note the use of the term *relation*. This is a theoretical term that correlates approximately to a table. **Relation** is defined as follows:

> *A structure composed of attributes (individual characteristics, such as name or address, corresponding to the columns in a table) and tuples (sets of attribute values describing particular entities, such as customers, corresponding to the rows in a table). Within a relation, tuples cannot be repeated; each must be unique. Furthermore, tuples are unordered within a relation; interchanging two tuples doesn't change the relation.*

This definition may seem a little confusing at the moment. Don't worry; everything will become clearer as you work your way through this chapter.

A relation is a very strict mathematical concept based on set theory, whereas a table is a physical implementation of a relation with special properties. That is to say, a relation can be used to define all tables, but not all relations can be manifested as a table. However, it's reasonable to suggest that the differences between the two are so subtle as to be nearly meaningless in practice.

> One of the most common misconceptions about the relational model is that the term relational refers to the relationships between tables. In actual fact, it refers to the term relation (the mathematical name for a table), which is considered to be (almost) synonymous with the term table. As you'll see, the relational model applies different names to not only a table, but also the elements contained within it.

There is another term that is used in logical modeling that is approximately equivalent to a table. This is the term **entity**; you'll see this term throughout the logical modeling part of this book, and it means the "conceptual" version of a table. The term emphasizes that a table is in fact a representation of something. Once you start calling it a table, you start to visualize it as a rectangular shape of rows and columns. The other concern is that "table" has a totally different meaning outside of computer science circles, so it tends to be a confusing term to use when discussing database design with a non-techie customer. The first time I told someone I built a table they thought I might have been lying about my profession: "I thought you were in computers?" they asked.

The term *entity* has fewer overheads and is less tied to implementation. In the next chapter, when we start to identify tables, we'll first identify them logically as entities to avoid being forced into the structure that tables inherently have. Whenever you talk in the physical sense, we'll use the term table as normal.

Rows and Columns

In SQL, you deal with tables containing rows and columns. The table definition is much like the class in object-oriented programming (OOP), and each column in the table is like an OOP property. Each row indicates an instance of the entity, but instances in SQL are slightly different from instances in OOP.

The main reason for the distinction is really an implementation issue. Because SQL is heavily built around accessing data, it's very easy to see multiple instances of a SQL "object" at any time; so many programmers fail to notice the parallels between an OOP object and a SQL Server row. As we look further into data and object modeling in later chapters, we'll investigate further some of the parallels between OOP methodologies and relational database programming.

As you can see in the following figure, the relational model has very different names for rows and columns. Rows are **tuples** (pronounced like couples) or instances, and columns are **attributes**. The term *tuple* is one of those funny terms seldom used outside of academia. According to legend, the word "tuple" has no other meaning, and presumably was coined during the formation of Codd's relational model specifically as a word with no preconceived notions attached to it. It does avoid the confusion generated by terms such as table.

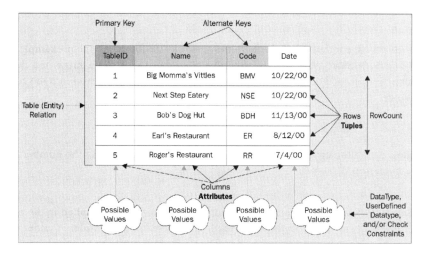

While the term *tuple* is pretty obscure to many programmers, *attribute* is a far better name for what a column represents. Each column should contain a characteristic or attribute of the instance of the row or tuple, or more simply put, each column contains an attribute that describes the row. When thought of in this manner, column usage makes way more sense. The analogy to OOP properties should be reasonably obvious to anyone who has done any OOP. A column is a property of an instance (or row) of a table (or relation or entity).

One of the tenets of relational theory is that attributes have no inherent ordering within an entity. Obviously, this isn't usually the case in practice, as SQL users want a constant set of columns to be returned, not to mention that the columns have to be efficiently stored on some physical media. The most important point here is that it's much better to avoid assigning meaning to the physical ordering of columns. There are a few common column-sorting basics that data architects generally follow when designing tables, such as primary keys at the left of the table, followed by more important columns near the left, and less readable columns near the right, but this is specifically for programmer or user convenience only. You'll look at this further when you actually start to model tables in Chapter 5. The last item you need to learn about is **degree**, which corresponds to the number of attributes in the entity. This term isn't used all that frequently, but I've seen it mentioned in some documents, and it's worth noting here for completeness. Each instance of an entity must contain the exact same set of attributes. Each attribute must have a name that's unique among the attributes in that particular entity. This may seem obvious, but is worth mentioning.

The Attributes of an Attribute

It's important to understand that each attribute in a entity has attributes of its own. The most important of these (besides the attribute's name, which has been discussed) are as follows:

- ❑ The domain of the attribute
- ❑ Whether or not the attribute is used to identify the specific instance (row)
- ❑ Whether or not a value is required for the attribute

The next few sections will deal with these in more detail.

Domain

The domain of an attribute indicates the legal values that may be stored in it. For example, say the goal is to store a person's salary; the **domain** would be a number value, not a string or a Boolean. SQL Server tables have several methods for restricting the values that can be entered into the resulting columns, as follows:

- ❑ Type of data (for example, string, numerical, binary datatypes)
- ❑ Constraints within the chosen type of data (for example, only allowing the numbers 1 to 12 within a numerical datatype)

Each of these serves a distinctly different purpose and should generally be applied in the order listed. In relational terminology, as shown in the following figure, these are all considered under the heading **domains**. A domain is defined as the set of valid values for a given attribute.

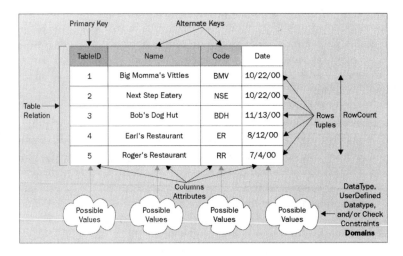

Type of Data

The datatype must be defined as well as the intrinsic range of the input. One additional detail to mention is that every datatype also supports a value of NULL, unless you specify otherwise. For example, consider the following datatypes that are supported by SQL Server:

❑ An integer datatype variable requires whole numeric input and may be between -231 (-2,147,483,648) and +231 (2,147,483,647).

❑ A tinyint datatype also requires whole numeric input, but has a range of nonnegative integers between 0 and 255.

❑ A varchar(20) requires ASCII character data between 0 and 20 characters.

Choosing the precise datatype of a column is one of the most important choices that is made during the physical design process. The datatype is the simplest form of domain enforcement mechanism in SQL Server.

During the logical phase of design, at a minimum, the general type of data that is to be stored will need to be determined. General classes of data might include the following:

binary	Streams of binary data
blob	Large streams of binary data
character	Streams of alphanumeric data
date	Calendar dates
logical	Boolean values of either true or false
numeric	Number values, either integer or real
time	Time of day, or length of time

It's also advisable to define custom domains (known in SQL Server as user-defined datatypes). You'll then define the rules that govern what data can be stored in the attribute. This enables you to create many attributes from the same template, and have it control the values that are entered. This can reduce design time greatly. Once you reach physical implementation, you choose physical datatypes to store the values in, and define how you implement the rules for data storage, and you're done.
In addition to these base datatypes, it will be useful to come up with your own domains during the design process. As a simple example, you might define the following domains:

❑ IntegerFromOneToTen: Defined as an integer, with a rule that restricts values entered to between one and ten inclusive

❑ SocialSecurityNumber: Defined as a nine-character string, or an eleven-character string that is restricted to having dashes in the fourth and seventh places, and all other characters are numeric

It should also be noted that user-defined datatypes need not be simple base datatypes as defined by relational theory. It's legal to have more complex datatypes as long as they don't have repeating groups in them. For example, consider the following datatype:

❑   2DGraphPoint: Defined as X–integer, Y–integer

But you cannot have an array datatype with an unlimited number of attributes. This would only be legal in cases such as the graph point where the two values X and Y actually make up a single attribute, in this case location.

> *Note that SQL Server doesn't currently support the creation of complex datatypes.*

Constraints

Constraints are predicates that you use to define what can be stored in an attribute. A predicate is simply a truth or a rule that the database will assert is true. There are three classes of constraints that you can define this way:

❑   **Optional constraints**: You define optional constraints to confirm whether or not a value must always exist for an instance. These will be translated to NULL constraints. A NULL value in relational theory indicates that an attribute has an unknown value, generally thought of as a maybe. It's important to understand that when two NULL values are compared, they are never equal.

❑   **Check constraints**: You define an allowable range of values for an attribute. For example, you can create a constraint on an attribute that represents the month of the year and only allows a value of 1 through 12.

❑   **Foreign Key**: Used to define that an entity is related to another. This is done by ensuring that a value in one entity matches the key of a different entity. Foreign keys are used both to ensure data integrity and to maintain relationships between entities. Although these won't be covered in any more depth in this chapter, it's important to simply mention their existence in the role of domain constraints for an attribute.

You'll study optional attributes and foreign keys in more detail later in this chapter. It's necessary to mention them here to introduce you to domains, because they're part of domains, but they also merit a deeper discussion.

A Note About Terminology

In this book, we'll generally use the term **domain** during logical design to indicate a datatype description such as number, integer, string, and so on together with a general description of the legal values for the attribute. Try to use the same domain for every attribute that has the same attributes. For example, you might define the following domains in a typical database:

❑   **Amount**: A monetary value, with no domain, that always requires a value

- ❏ **String**: A generic string value that contains alphanumeric values, which always require a value

- ❏ **Description**: A string value that is used to further describe an instance of an entity, which always requires a value

- ❏ **FutureDate**: A date value that must be greater than the current date when entered, which always requires a value

- ❏ **SocialSecurityNumber**: An 11-character string of the format *###-##-####*, which always requires a value

As you identify new attributes, you'll see if the new attribute fits any existing domain, and if so, you assign it appropriately. If not, then you create a new domain. This will give you attributes that allow you to build databases in a quicker, easier, and more consistent manner.

In this book the term **business rules** indicates the **predicate** for the entity or database as a whole. As an example of this, let's consider the `SocialSecurityNumber` domain. This domain came with a predicate that the value stored in an attribute that used it would always be in the format "*###-##-####*". Although I'm not enamored with the term business rules, it's a fairly common term today. Throughout this book the term business rules will require explication, because of its broad usage.

Very often you won't identify your *business rules* as part of the entity definitions; rather, the *business rules* will be located throughout your documentation and implementation.

Row Identifiers

In relational theory, a relation isn't allowed to have duplicate tuples (analogous to duplicate rows in a table). In a physical table, there is no limitation that says that there must not be duplicate rows, but it's always a bad situation when there are duplicate rows, for a number of reasons:

- ❏ It's impossible to determine which row is which, meaning that you have no logical method of changing or deleting a single row.

- ❏ If more than one instance has the exact same attributes, it's likely to be describing the same object, so if you try to change one row, then the other row should change; this means that you have a dependency.

For those who have SQL Server experience, it seems pretty clear that you should define an index to deal with the situation of identical rows. However, in relational theory, there is no concept of an index; instead, you have the concept of a **key**. A key is used to enforce uniqueness over an attribute or set of attributes. An entity may have as many keys as is required to maintain the uniqueness of its columns. A term that is also used is **candidate key**, which has the exact same meaning.

In both relational theory and SQL implementation you also have the concept of **primary keys** and **alternate keys**. A primary key is the candidate key used as the primary identifier for a entity, and alternate keys are the other candidate keys over which uniqueness must be maintained so that you can always identify the row by the alternate column values, as you can see in the following table.

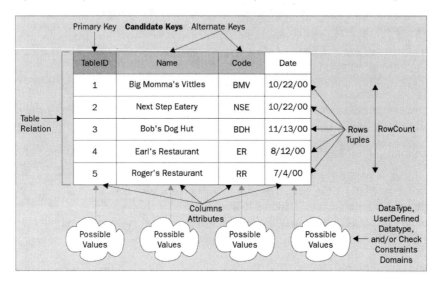

The choice of keys is a very important one. A large percentage of databases errors are the result of failing to define all the possible keys. When you get to the normalization rules in Chapter 6, you'll study the choices of candidate keys in more detail.

Composite Key

Although it's best to use as few attributes or columns as possible when forming keys, it's possible to make them up from any number of attributes; sometimes it's even necessary to use more than one attribute for the key.

For example, imagine the situation in which you have a Book entity with the following attributes: `Publisher_Name`, `Publisher_City`, `ISBN_Number`, and `Book_Name`. For anyone who doesn't know, the ISBN is the unique identification number assigned to a book when it's published.

From these attributes, you can decide to define three keys as follows:

❑ `Publisher_Name`, `Book_Name`: Obviously, a publisher will publish more than one book. Also, it's safe to assume that book names aren't unique across all books. However, it's probably true that the same publisher will not publish two books by the same name (at least we'll assume that it's true).

❑ `ISBN_Number`: It should be clear to you that `ISBN_Number` is unique.

❑ `Publisher_City`, `ISBN_Number`: Because `ISBN_Number` is unique, it follows that `ISBN_Number` plus any other attribute combined is also unique.

Both the first and third keys we've defined are **composite keys**. The third one needs a bit more discussion. Without prior knowledge that ISBNs are unique, anyone looking at the third key might assume that the implication of this key is that in every city, it's possible to reuse the ISBN_Number, a fact that isn't true. This is a very common problem with composite keys when they aren't thought out properly.

> As a brief aside, it's important not to confuse unique indexes with keys. There may be valid performance reasons to implement the Publisher_City, ISBN_Number unique index in your SQL Server database. On the other hand, you wouldn't want to identify this as a key of a table.

Primary Key

The primary key is a candidate key that is chosen to uniquely identify an instance (row) in an entity (table). You'll examine the precise logic surrounding this choice in the section on physical design, but for now it's enough to consider the meaning of the terms.

Artificial Keys

An artificial key is a contrived one, and usually the only reason for its existence is to identify the row. It's usually an automatically generated number (Identity column), or a globally unique identifier (GUID), which is a very large, randomly generated identifier that is unique on all machines in the world. An artificial key's main use is to provide an internal key that an end user never has to view, and never has to interact with. Be aware that the table should have other keys defined as well, or it isn't a proper table.

The concept of an artificial key is a kind of troubling one from the perspective of a purist. Because it doesn't describe the entity at all, can it really be an attribute of the entity? Artificial keys probably shouldn't even have been mentioned in the logical design section, but it's important to know of their existence, because they'll undoubtedly still crop up in some logical designs. In Chapter 6 you'll study the pros and cons of such an approach.

Alternate Keys

Any candidate key that isn't chosen as the primary key is referred to as an **alternate key**. Alternate keys are very important to a successful database. For one reason or another, most entities have more than one way of identifying their instances. This is particularly true when one uses artificial keys as primary keys.

Optional Attribute Values

Optional values are a can of worms that I'd rather not open, but I must. Entities have attributes for which the contents aren't yet known or are unnecessary in a given context. Unfortunately, there is only one mechanism to denote this fact built into SQL. This is the value NULL. NULL is defined as an unknown value, rather than nothing. Because of this, no two values of NULL are considered equivalent, and NULL can be a very confusing concept.

Depending on the way an optional column value (NULL) is actually implemented, a value of NULL may have a couple of possibilities as follows:

- ❑ The value isn't known yet, but maybe there is a value that should be here.
- ❑ There is never going be a value for this attribute.
- ❑ A value in this attribute doesn't make sense in this given situation.

It should be obvious from the list of different meanings of NULL that this isn't the best way of handling such situations. Putting invalid data (such as a date of Dec 31 9999) is even more troubling than NULL, for two reasons. First, you may very well discover that there is stored data with the exact same value that has just been entered–a problem if the attribute being used is a key. Second, invalid values may not stand out in the same way that NULL values do to the user, and therefore they're unlikely to be recognized as invalid.

Some theorists would prefer NULL to be done away with altogether. I would rather see a set of NULL-type values implemented to say **why** the value is NULL. There are set techniques for dealing with optional data without NULLs, but the implementation can require quite a few tables. You'll learn how to deal with NULL values in Chapter 13.

Finally, you cannot use an optional attribute in the primary key. The Integrity Independence Law (Number 10 of Codd's 12 Laws, see Appendix A on the Apress web site) requires that no column in the primary key can be an optional column.

Rowcount

The number of rows in a table has a special name in relational theory. As shown in the following figure, it's called **cardinality**. This term is seldom used to indicate the number of rows in the table; however, the term is used to indicate the number of rows that can meet a certain condition. You'll look at another form of cardinality more during the discussion on relationships later in this chapter.

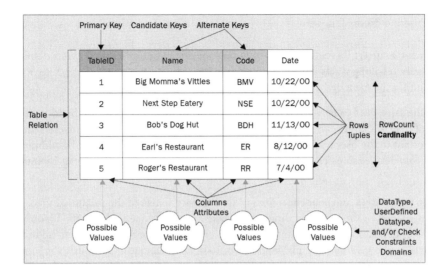

Additional Considerations for Entities

In this section you'll look at some of the additional considerations for entities in relational theory.

Foreign Keys

When is a key not a key? When it's a foreign key. That's not a joke (well, it certainly wasn't funny anyhow). A foreign key is actually an attribute or combination of attributes whose values match the primary key or unique key or another table in the same way. Existence of a foreign key in a table represents the implementation of a relationship between the tables. Relationships will be discussed in more detail later in this chapter. The reason that *foreign key* is a bad use of the term *key* is that a foreign key doesn't have to be a unique value—it can be implemented on columns that allow NULLs, for example.

The Integrity Independence Law (Number 10 of Codd's 12 Laws, see Appendix A on the Apress web site) states that all non-optional foreign key values in the database must have a matching primary key value in the related table.

Views

Views are tables that don't exist as base (actual) tables; in fact, they're virtual tables. A view is the implementation of a named relation as discussed in the "Tables" section of this chapter. In logical design, views should be used very carefully, for example when you need to define one entity from the existence of two or more other entities.

Views appear as tables to the user and should cautiously be considered as tables. Based on Codd's Laws, views are supposed to be updateable, thereby greatly enhancing their ability to appear as tables. In fact, in SQL Server 2000, you can implement any view as being updateable by using several new features. You'll look at this in some detail in the "Physical Design" part of the book when you look at the problems that can and cannot be solved using views.

Views can be used to do the following:

- **Implement security**: By including or excluding specific columns from the view definition, then specifically revoking rights from the base table and giving rights to the view, security can be provided for the excluded columns.

- **Allow the same data to be viewed by different users in different ways**: By building different views of the data, users can be given a view that suits their needs. In this manner, data that is unimportant to the user can be hidden from them to improve readability. In addition to this, foreign key relationships can be resolved and data from the related table can be shown to the user.

- **Provide logical data independence**: One of the primary tenets of the relational theory is that the implementation of the database should not make any difference to the users. If something changes in the database implementation, the user shouldn't notice. Views can be used in much the same way to give the user insulation from base table changes. Obviously the view is dependent on the structure of the underlying table, but if a column is added, the view need not have it added, unless it's needed. If a column is removed or moved to a different table, the view could be modified to return a default value, or to get the value from the new table.

Views are a very important part of any relational database implementation. However, they're considered a physical implementation issue, so this is the last time you'll look at views in this part of the book.

Restricting Entity Values

So far predicates for attributes have been discussed, but now you must look at predicates that govern the use of the entity. As a reminder, the term *predicate* is a fancy word for a rule that governs the range of values in the database. The predicate of every entity should be stated during logical design as fully as possible. By listing the predicates for the entity in prose, they will have meaning to the developer as well as to the user, who needs to ratify the rules. The predicate should contain any rule that governs the input of data. For this you have at your disposal code-based "constraints," generally known in SQL Server as triggers.

Triggers are devices that allow code to be fired whenever data in a table is entered or modified. This gives you the power to make sure that the entire table is in a consistent state before you accept the changes that a user is attempting to make. You should also briefly mention that stored procedures can be used to implement domains, as can any code that is written to insert data into the attribute. In Chapter 11, you'll investigate triggers and stored procedures as data integrity mechanisms in great detail.

Let's briefly discuss situations in which the need to restrict data requires access to different attributes. You can break these down into three typical scenarios:

❑ Inter-attribute dependencies

❑ Inter-row dependencies

❑ Inter-entity dependencies

Each of these poses quite a different type of problem to the implementation as follows:

❑ **Inter-attribute dependencies**: Inter-attribute dependencies deal with the situation in which the value stored in one attribute requires a certain domain of values in another attribute.

For example, say you have the attributes `hasDriversLicense` and `driversLicenseNumber`. If `hasDriversLicense is False`, then you don't want the user entering a value for `driversLicenseNumber`.

Generally, you solve this problem with a simple table `CHECK` constraint.

❑ **Inter-row dependencies**: Inter-row dependencies describe the situation in which one row in the same table dictates the value in a different row.

An example of this might be a banking system. When a user goes to make a withdrawal from their account, all transactions they've previously made need to be summarized to see if they have enough money to make the withdrawal. Actually this might not be implemented in exactly this way, but logically speaking this is what occurs.

Generally, this type of situation must be solved using a trigger, or less desirably, a stored procedure. One of the real problems with the inter-row dependencies in SQL Server is that it's easy enough to prevent overages (too many rows of too high a value) but very difficult to prevent too few values from being entered, because you need a certain number of values before the trigger will fire. For example, say you want to keep the sum of a set of rows as long as the sum is between 10 and 20. This is easy enough to roll back when the sum is over 20, but if it's less than 10 you can add another row later that takes the sum over 10 after the trigger has fired, thereby violating the rule. This topic will be returned to in Chapter 12, when you start to implement this sort of problem.

❑ **Inter-entity dependencies**: Another situation occurs when a value exists in one entity, but you don't want this value to be filled in a related entity.

An example of such a constraint might be personal information for a user. One entity will keep a row with the person's name and age, and another may intend to store that person's address and phone number. If the person is under a certain age, it may actually be illegal to store their address and phone number.

As with the inter-row dependencies, this must also be solved using a trigger, or less desirably, using a stored procedure or middle-tier object. Inter-entity dependencies have the same difficulties as inter-row dependencies.

Relational Operators

Regarding sets of data such as the ones found in the tables in this chapter, it would be wrong to avoid mentioning relational operators. It's interesting to see what sorts of operations will be used to manipulate the data stored in the tables you'll design.

Now you'll look at the relational operators that make up the relational algebra that is the basis for all SQL implementations. All resultsets returned from the SQL SELECT statements can be thought of as tables (even if they're never physically stored as such). A relation must have a unique name for every attribute returned, but this isn't always true for SQL resultsets (even if it should be). The tables that are formed as a result of any relational or SQL operator are referred to as unnamed tables, as opposed to tables and views, which are named.

Originally, Codd formulated eight relational operators. Most of these take the form previously mentioned with one or two relations into the operator, and a single relation out. Only one of these didn't fit this mold, and it isn't implemented in SQL. The following relational operators are the list of operators as first described by Codd in 1972 in *Relational Completeness of Data Base Sublanguages*. They're listed in the order that they're presented in the text, because each logically refers back to the previous one.

❑   Restrict

❑   Project

❑   Join

❑   Product

❑   Union

❑   Intersect

❑   Difference

❑   Divide

These eight operators serve as the basis of most SQL operations, and give a solid, if brief, introduction to the relational operators. It should be noted that most SQL optimizers use the concept of operators to break down SQL Statements into manageable chunks that can be dealt with. Now we'll look briefly at each of the original operators.

> **It's important not to confuse these relational operators with any keyword used in a SQL dialect.**

Restrict

The **restrict** operator is used to limit the rows of a table to those that match a given criteria. This is directly analogous to a simple SELECT statement's WHERE clause. For example:

```
SELECT    columnname, columnname2, … , columnnameN
FROM      tablename
WHERE     columnname > value
```

The WHERE clause is the implementation of the restrict operator, and it should also be noted that the output of this entire operation is an unnamed table that contains the single column columnname and contains all of the rows where columnname is greater than value. In the WHERE clause, you can use any of the common comparison operators (=, >, <, >=, <>, LIKE, etc.).

Project

The **project** operator is used to limit the number of columns in the resulting output table. In the next example, you should expect that more than the single column in the table exists, as follows:

```
SELECT    DISTINCT columnname1, columnname2
FROM      tablename
```

In this manner you can vertically subdivide the resulting table into a single column or combination of columns. In relational theory, any duplicate values would be removed, so you have included the SQL keyword DISTINCT to remove the repeat values.

A common question that arises is "Why is there no DISTINCT operator in relational theory?" Every operator in the discussion here takes in one or two relations and returns a relation. By definition, a relation doesn't have any duplicate rows. Because the output of your query would be a relation, it will have no duplicates, and the DISTINCT operator is effectively redundant. In essence therefore, the DISTINCT operator is built-in.

Again, this is one of the most important differences between the definition of a relation and the implementation of a table.

Join

The **join** operator is used to associate one table with another, based upon the matching of column values, usually the primary key of one table with the foreign key of another.

```
SELECT    columnname
FROM      tablename1
             JOIN tablename2
                ON tablename1.key1 = tablename2.key1
```

Next let's look at the effect of chaining together two JOIN operations, as in the following query:

```
SELECT    columnname
FROM      table1
             JOIN table2
                 ON table1.key1 = table2.key1
             JOIN table3
                 ON table2.key2 = table3.key2
```

The first join operation can be considered as follows:

```
(SELECT *
 FROM    Table1
          JOIN table2
             ON table1.key1 = table2.key1)
                             = derivedTable1
```

So you could rewrite your query as follows:

```
SELECT    columnname
FROM      derivedTable1
             JOIN table3
                 ON derivedTable1.key2 = table3.key2
```

This is as far as we'll delve into joins in this section. The point of this section has been a simple introduction to how the join operator works, and how it relates to current join technology in SQL Server.

Product

One of the least useful and most dangerous of the operations is the **product** operation. The product operator takes two tables and builds a table consisting of all possible combinations of rows, one from each table. In SQL this is denoted by the CROSS JOIN statement.

```
SELECT    columnname
FROM      tablename1
             CROSS JOIN tablename2
```

To better explain this operation, consider the following:

Table1
Fred
Wilbur

Table2
Sam
Bugs
Ed

Table1 product	Table2
Fred	Sam
Fred	Bugs
Fred	Ed
Wilbur	Sam
Wilbur	Bugs
Wilbur	Ed

You can see that the number of rows that will be returned by the product operator is the number of rows in Table1 multiplied by the number of rows in Table2. This number can get quite large, contain duplicate and useless rows, and quickly choke a server, so there aren't too many practical uses of the product operator.

Union

The **union** operator takes as an input two tables of the same structure and builds another table with all of the rows in either of the tables, thereby removing duplicates in the process:

```
SELECT    columnname
FROM      tablename1
UNION
SELECT    columnname
FROM      tablename2
```

To better explain this operation, consider the following:

Table1
Fred
Wilbur

Table2
Fred
Wilbur
Babe

Table1 union Table2
Fred
Wilbur
Babe

This is a good time to remember that the two input tables to the union operator must be of the same type, but this doesn't mean that they have to be base tables. The table may also be a derived table formed from the project operator, as discussed earlier.

Intersect

The **intersect** operator is pretty much the opposite of the union operator. It takes two tables of the same structure, removes the values that don't exist in both inputs, and returns the resulting table.

Table1
Jeb
Silver
Carney

Table2
Jeb
Howie
Bill
Carney
Bob

Table1 intersect Table2
Jeb
Carney

Intersect isn't implemented properly in the SQL syntax. This code snippet shows the primary way to implement an intersect in SQL.

```
SELECT    columnname
FROM      tablename1
            JOIN tablename2
              ON tablename1.columnName = tablename2.columnName
```

Be careful with this code snippet. It may look as if intersect = join. Intersect is like join insofar as it returns rows that match, but it acts more like union, where there tends to be a thin set of data. In this example, there's only a single column, which must be the same column as the column names that are being intersected.

Difference

Difference is an operation that is used quite often when implementing a system. Just like union and intersect, difference again requires tables of the same structure. The gist of the difference operator is that you want every value in one table where there doesn't exist a corresponding value in the other. This is in contrast to the intersect operator, which *removes* a value if it doesn't appear in both tables.

Table1
Jeb
Silver
Carney

Table2
Jeb
Howie
Bill
Carney
Bob

Table1 minus Table2
Silver

What makes this operator interesting is that unlike ordinary arithmetic, the table you're subtracting from the other may contain values that don't matter to the equation. In the example, Howie and Bob weren't involved in the operation, because they didn't exist in Table1.

Difference again doesn't have a specific keyword in SQL. It can be implemented in its most simple form by using the NOT IN operator as shown here:

```
SELECT    columnname
FROM      tablename1
WHERE     columnname NOT IN (SELECT  columnname
                                  FROM    tablename2)
```

Divide

The **divide** operator is one of the stranger operators, and it's seldom used. It takes two relations, one with a single column, one with two columns, and returns a table of values that match (in the column that is specified) all values in the single column relation.

There is no clear way to implement this in a way that will be useful or clear in SQL, so it will be omitted here because it isn't terribly useful for most database architects and SQL programmers.

Other Operators

Additional operators can be separated into two classes, modification types (INSERT, UPDATE, DELETE), and additional retrieval types. The modification type operators won't be discussed in this chapter, because they're very close to how SQL implements them, and also they have very little logical modeling relevance. As far as the retrieval operators go, there have been other relational operators defined in the (nearly) 30 years since the formulation of these eight base operators. In fact all of the data manipulation language (DML) commands in SQL Server are either a result of, or an extension of, these basic operators. You should also note that the **data definition language** (DDL) is basically for defining your objects, and although there would be no relational operator equivalent, any relational language would have to implement some form of DDL to build the objects for the DML.

This book's scope has been stretched to cover these eight original operators, but you should try to understand the relational theory behind SQL operators because it will help you when you're logically designing your databases and writing your code.

Relationships

We have already mentioned the concept of the primary key and the foreign key. Now let's put them together and look at the object that they form: the relationship. Relationships are what make the tables that we have created useful, by linking tables together. However, there is one point that we must make: The relationship types we'll discuss in this section need not take the form of one table's primary key being referenced by another table via a foreign key. While it's true this is how almost all relationships are physically realized, it can take several primary key or foreign key relationships to convey a simple logical relationship. In this section, you'll read about the logical relationship types. The discussion of physical implementation will come later in the book.

Relationships can be divided into the following two basic types:

❑   Binary relationships

❑   Nonbinary relationships

The distinction between the two types lies in the number of tables involved in the relationship. A binary relationship involves two tables, while nonbinary relationships involve more than two tables. This may seem like a small distinction, but it really isn't. SQL and relations are limited to binary relationships, while there is no such restriction in the real world. Here is where it's essential to document each of the possible situations. When you look at data modeling in Chapter 5, you'll learn how to represent each of these in a data model.

Binary Relationships

Binary relationships are relationships between exactly two tables. Most of the relationships you deal with on a regular basis will fit into this category.

The number of child rows that may participate in the different side of the relationship is known as the cardinality. You'll find a discussion on the different cardinalities of binary relationships in this section.

One-to-n Relationships

One-to-n relationships are the class of relationships in which one table migrates its primary key to another table as a foreign key. The table that contains the primary key is known as the **parent** table and the table that receives the primary key, and uses it as the foreign key, is the **child** table. This parent-child terminology only considers itself with the relationship between the two tables. A child may have many parents, and a parent may have many children.

The one-to-n relationship is the most common relationship type. However, there are several distinct possibilities for the cardinality of this relationship, such as the following:

❑ **One-to-one relationships**: A relationship of one-to-one cardinality indicates that for any given parent, there may only exist a single instance of the child. An example of this type of relationship might be house to location, as illustrated in the following figure. A house is obviously in only one location. The discussion of why this would not be in the same table will be left for a later time.

House Id	House Type
1001	1
1002	2
1003	1
1004	3
1005	4

House Id	Location
1001	Database Drive
1002	Administration Avenue
1003	SQL Street
1004	Primary Key Place
1005	Business Rules Boulevard

❑ **One-to-many relationships**: The one-to-many relationship is the most important relation type. For each parent, there may exist unlimited child rows. A sample one-to-many relationship might be state to address, as illustrated by the following figure. Obviously there are many addresses for a single state, though an address can only be in one state.

State Id Number	State
1	Amabala
2	Aksala
3	Sasnakra

State Id No.	Address	No. of bedrooms	No. of bathrooms
1	402 Database Drive	1	1
1	1222 Administrator Avenue	2	1
2	23 Login Lane	2	1
2	246 Cardinality Close	1	1
2	893 Server Street	3	2
3	107 Query Quay	2	1
3	293 Primary Key Place	4	2

❑ **One-to-exactly-n relationships**: Actually the one-to-one relationship is merely a specialized version of this relationship type. This is a rarely used relationship type, but it does actually get used on occasions. For example, a rule might be made that a user may only have two e-mail addresses. The following figure shows how one-to-two relationship cardinality might be used to enforce the user to e-mail relationship.

Employee Reference Number	Name
5001	Bob
5002	Fred
5003	Jean

Employee Reference Number	Email Address
5001	dbo@wrox.com
5001	dbo2@wrox.com
5002	serveradmin@wrox.com
5002	fred@wrox.com
5003	md@wrox.com
5003	jean@wrox.com

❑ **Recursive relationships**: Recursive relationships are where the parent and the child are in the same table. This kind of relationship is used to implement a tree with SQL constructs. The classic example of the recursive relationship is a bill of materials. Take an automobile. In and of itself, it can be considered a part for sale by a manufacturer, and each of its components, which also have part numbers, are a part that makes up the whole. Some of these components are also made up of parts. In this example, the automobile could be regarded as made up recursively of the automobile part and all of its constituent parts.

Many-to-Many Relationships

The other type of binary relationship is the many-to-many relationship. Instead of there being a single parent and one or more children, there would be more than one parent with children. This is impossible to implement using just two tables, but you'll look at the implementation of many-to-many relationships later in the physical modeling part of the book and, specifically, Chapter 10.

An example of a many-to-many relationship is a car dealer. Take nearly any single model of car, and it's sold at many different car dealers. Think in the opposite direction. Take one car dealer; it sells many different car models. So many car dealers are related to many models of car.

Nonbinary Relationships

Nonbinary relationships involve more than two tables in the relationship. This is really quite a common thing. For example, take this common scenario:

Apress provides books for booksellers to sell.

The term for such a relationship is a ternary relationship, because it involves three tables (anything greater than three is referred to as N-ary, where N is the number entities involved in the relationships). You deal with such relationships by breaking them down into multiple entities with binary relationships.

❑   Apress provides books.

❑   Booksellers sell books.

❑   Booksellers are supplied by Apress.

However, now that you have changed the relationship to only use binary relationships, you cannot exactly infer the original ternary relationship. All that can be inferred is the following:

❑   Apress supplies books (presumably to someone, but it cannot be determined who).

❑   Booksellers sell books (which may or may not have been supplied by Apress).

❑   Apress provides something to booksellers (could be books, could be chickens).

For example, from these relationships, you cannot exactly infer the original statement that *Apress provides books for booksellers.* This is a common problem because the original relationship will be identified during the design phase, and then broken down in the design phase, and the meaning of the original relationship is lost, causing data issues once we start implementing the physical design. In Chapter 7, when we discuss advanced normalization rules, we deal with the problems that arise when it's required to store N-ary relationships using only binary relationships.

Definitions of Essential Concepts

Before moving on to Chapter 4, which deals with fundamental database concepts, there are a couple of extremely important concepts that you need to understand. They will become very important later in the process (and possibly clearer as you begin to apply them), and an introduction to them is important to get started with the process.

Functional Dependency

The term **functional dependency** is a very important one. It's also one of those terms that sounds more complex than it really is, but it's actually a rather simple concept. If you apply a function to one value (call it Value1) and the output of this function is *always* the exact same value (call it Value2), then Value2 is functionally dependent on Value1.

Correctly implemented functional dependencies are very useful things, while improper functional dependencies lie at the very heart of many database problems.

A related term is **determinant**. It can be defined as "Any attribute or combination of attributes on which any other attribute or combination of attributes is functionally dependent." So in the previous example, Value1 would be considered the determinant. Two examples of this come to mind:

❑   Consider a mathematical function like 2 * X. For every value of X a particular value will be produced. For 2 you'll get 4, for 4 you get 8. Any time you put the value of 2 in the function you'll always return a 4, so in this case 2 functionally determines 4 for function 2 * X.

❑   In a more database-oriented example, consider the vehicle identification number (VIN) of a vehicle. From the VIN, additional information can be derived, such as the model year, original color, where the vehicle was built, and many other fixed characteristics of the product. In this case, the VIN functionally determines the specific fixed characteristics, because every time the VIN is referenced, the characteristics will be the same.

Functional dependency isn't exclusive: that is, Value1 may not be the only value that returns Value2. For example, take the function X * X. The value 2 will always return 4. However, there are two values that will return 4; -2 and 2.

Relationships were discussed earlier in this chapter, where you learned that there is always a child and a parent in a binary relationship. The child in the relationship will be functionally dependent on the parent in that every child has one parent in the relationship. Every parent on the other hand usually may have many children, unless there are cardinality restrictions.

The key of an entity will functionally determine the other attributes, and when there are two keys, such as the primary key and alternate key of the table, the primary key will functionally determine the alternate key and vice versa. This concept will be central to the discussion of normalization in Chapter 6.

Multivalued Dependency

In the previous section, functional dependency was discussed in a single-valued case. Unlike a single-valued dependency, in which one value determines one value, here, one value determines multiple values.

As an illustration, consider that this book was written by a single author, so if you run the author function on this book, you would have a single value every time. However, if an editor function existed, it would return multiple values, because there are several technical editors of this book; and no matter how many times the function is applied, it will always return the same values. Hence, technical editor is multidependent on book.

You'll come across the concept of the multivalued dependency later in Chapter 6.

Summary

In this chapter you've buzzed through some pretty heavy stuff. You were introduced to many of the database terms you'll make great use of throughout the rest of the book. Next you looked at relational theory, and studied some of the building blocks of the relational programming language SQL.

As a reminder, in the following table you should equate common SQL Server database terms with their synonyms from relational theory and to a lesser degree, logical design terminology.

Common Term	Synonym
Table	Entity (specifically in logical design), Relation (used more in theory discussions)
Column	Attribute
Row	Tuple
The legal values that may be stored in a column, including datatypes, constraints, and so on	Domain
Rowcount	Cardinality
Number of columns	Degree

This chapter has been a technical conference–level overview of some important topics that, at the very least, will give you enough theoretical understanding to help you understand the concept of designing databases. Hopefully, it will make you want to go out and pursue this subject further, because it will make you a far better database architect or programmer.

4

Entities, Attributes, Relationships, and Business Rules

Introduction

Now that we've looked at the basic building blocks of databases, we'll begin to identify these building blocks within the preliminary information you gathered during Chapter 2. During the information gathering phase, you collected a mass of information and notes that are probably pretty much of a mess at this point. In this chapter, you'll add structure to this information as you look for the basic database building blocks, and then gain an overview by summarizing it. You'll go through everything–identifying and assigning initial names to entities, relationships, attributes, and business rules–so make sure that you consult your users for any additional information.

When you finish this process, you'll have your foundation documentation in a format that can be shared with the user without the baggage of technical talk and diagrams (which you'll start to develop later on).

> **Reality Check:** The process you'll outline may be considered overzealous and require more work than what's really necessary. In this book, you'll be looking at best practices. Many accomplished programmers are likely to abbreviate the process that is outlined. That's also true of my personal design process; however, while the steps are less tersely documented, the process is more or less the same. The methods in this chapter could help you avoid the perils of increasing maintenance costs in your project, lessen the frequency with which you'll have to go back later to change your structures and code, and generally decrease the risk of failure.

Divorcing Yourself from the Final Structure

For those readers who are new to database design, or who haven't yet designed any tables, you should follow the principles outlined in this chapter literally to ensure the best result. On the other hand, a more advanced reader may question the simplistic nature of the progress through this chapter. It will probably become clear very rapidly which tables need to be broken down into which constituent parts. However, although doing such operations at an early stage in the design process might seem to save time, you may pay a price later when you have to go back and modify the database, rather than the design document, because you neglected to spend time reviewing your strategy with your client. Don't forget to continue to update your documentation, because the best-looking documentation in the world is useless if it's out of date.

After building a database or two (or two hundred for that matter), you'll find it hard to avoid thinking in terms of the final structure. When you listen to the client explaining what he wants, you'll probably have visions of table-like structures before you've even finished hearing the client out; it will be almost second nature to you. Unfortunately, this isn't always the best situation to be in when in this discovery or organizing phase of the database design process.

Regardless of the tools used to actually consolidate the information (ER diagramming tool, object-oriented programming or OOP diagramming tool, word processor, or even pencil and paper), at this stage you should go through all of the gathered documentation to look for the following items:

- ❏ Entities
- ❏ Attributes
- ❏ Relationships
- ❏ Business Rules

As you proceed through this process, you end up with a much smaller pile of documentation, maybe 10 percent of the size of the original pile, although you should still make sure that you haven't overlooked any important data. With this documentation you can secure acceptance from the user prior to applying a very rigid series of processes, which are outlined in the next three chapters, to the output of this discovery process.

In Chapter 3 you learned that, from that chapter onwards, you should use more implementation-oriented terms to describe an object unless it made sense not to. In this chapter, you'll make use of the terms *entities* and *attributes* because you'll be looking for objects that may never appear as physical structures. You'll begin to use implementation-oriented terms as you start to move towards structures that will begin to resemble what you know as tables and columns.

A Simple Example

This section will illustrate what you've just read using the following example, which could easily be a snippet of notes from a typical design session.

> The company has customers to whom they sell used products, usually office supplies, but it sells furniture as well. Employees identify customers by a number generated by their current system. The company also sells new stuff, but used products represent how it makes its money. Invoices are printed on a weekly basis, but the company makes deliveries as soon as a customer makes an order if they're trusted (no particular credit problems). Any changes to the invoice need to be documented. The company ships all products from the warehouse downtown.

Employees need to store contact information for each customer–phone numbers (fax and voice), addresses, and e-mail addresses. They would like to be able to fax or e-mail product order confirmations. They also want to have free notes for contacts so they can keep a journal of contacts. Through each of the following sections, you'll scan the documentation for pieces of information that need to be stored. Sounds simple enough, eh? It really is much easier than it might seem.

Identifying Entities

Entities are reasonably simple objects to locate while you're scanning through documentation. They're generally used to represent people, places, objects, ideas, or things referred to grammatically as nouns. This isn't to say that entities only store real things. Entities can also be abstract concepts; for example, "new products" is an abstract concept that isn't physical, but rather a convenient way of grouping a range of products. Actually, a more reasonable definition of an entity is as a store for all the descriptive information necessary to fully describe a single person, place, object, or idea, for example:

- ❏ Person: A student, an employee, a driver
- ❏ Place: A city, a building, a road
- ❏ Object: A part, a tool, a piece of electronics
- ❏ Idea: A requirement document, a group (like a security group for an application), a journal of user activity

Note that there is overlap in several of the categories (for example, a building can be a "place" or an "object"). You'll seldom need to discretely identify that an entity is a person, place, object, or idea. However, if you can place it within a given group, it can help to assign some attributes, like a name for a person or an address for a building. This will also help to ensure that you have all the documentation necessary to describe each entity.

How an entity is implemented in an actual database table may be very different from the initial entities that are specified. It's important not to worry about this at this stage in the design process–you should try hard not to get yourself too wrapped up in the eventual database implementation.

People

Nearly every database will need to store information on people entities of some sort. Most databases will have at the very least some notion of a user. While not all users are people, a user is almost always thought of as a person, though a user might be a corporation or even a machine like a networked printer. As far as real people are concerned, a single database may need to store information on many different types of people. For instance, a school's database may have a student table, a teacher table, as well as an administrator table. It may also require only a single table to represent all three. However, during logical design, you want to note the existence of each entity, because they are clearly different things, with some obvious likeness. Later, in the discussion of relationships, you'll determine when entities share commonality and how to deal with them.

In this example, two people entities can be found–contacts and customers.

```
        need to store contact information for each customer ...
```

```
        ... a journal of contacts ...
```

The contact and customer information you'll need to store has yet to be described, so you cannot know whether or not they will be considered as separate entities at this point in the documentation process. You'll look at the specific attributes for the contacts and customers when you get to the attribute section of this chapter.

Places

There are many different types of places about which users will want to store information. There is one obvious place entity in your sample set of notes.

```
        products from the warehouse downtown.
```

Note though that contacts and customers obviously have postal addresses identifying their locations.

Objects

Objects refer primarily to physical items. In your example, you have three different objects.

> ... that they sell used **products** to, usually **office supplies**, but they have **furniture** as well.

Products, office supplies, and furniture are objects, but notice that furniture and office supplies are also products. Obviously, it comes as no shock that the generic products, office supplies, and furniture entities will have *very* different attributes. Whether or not you can roll up the three objects into one abstract entity called Products, or whether you'll need to treat all three as separate entities will totally depend on why you're designing the particular database in the first place.

Ideas

There's nothing that states that entities must be real objects or even physically exist. At this stage of discovery, you'll have to consider information on objects that the user wants to store that don't fit the already established "people," "places," and "objects" categories, and which may or may not be physical objects.

For example, consider documents. For many, the term "documents" refers to tangible pieces of paper containing information that the client wants to keep track of. Technically, this isn't necessarily the case. What if you make a copy of the piece of paper? Does that mean there are two documents, or are they both the same document? For your client, you really are referring to physical pieces of paper, the pieces of paper that are mailed to a customer after the delivery of the client's order.

> ... money. Invoices are printed on a ...

However, you only know that the invoices are printed on physical paper, but when they're mailed or even how they're delivered is unknown at this stage. If the client changed to an e-mail-based invoicing method, would the invoice be a different thing? Sort of, because tracking the invoice may be different, but the purpose of the invoice is the same: to get a customer to pay for something. At this point you simply identify the existence of entities and move along; again, you'll add your guesses as to how the data is used later in this process.

> ... e-mail product order confirmations ...

Here you have a type of document that isn't written on paper—an e-mail message.

Other Entities

At this stage of discovery, you'll have to consider information on entities that the users want to store that don't fit the already established "people," "places," "objects," and "documents" categories.

Audit Trails and Database Logs

A typical entity you'll define is the audit trail or a log of database activity. This isn't a normal entity in that it stores no user data and, as such, should generally be deferred to the physical design stage. The only kinds of entities that you should be concerned with at this point are those that users wish to store data about. As such, statements such as the following probably won't be dealt with at this stage but left until the implementation.

> Any changes to the invoice need to be **documented**.

Events

Event entities generally represent verbs or actions.

> ...they make **deliveries** as soon ...

Whether deliveries are recorded in some physical document isn't clear at this point; the statement merely shows that an event has taken place. These events are important and users will want to schedule events or produce data resulting from an event occurrence. In your example, it may be that you document events after they occur, so it may end up becoming a log of deliveries made.

Another type of event for you to consider might be things like meter readings, weather readings, equipment measurements, and so on.

Records and Journals

The last of the entity types that you'll examine at this stage is a record or journal of activities. **Note that I mean records in a nondatabase sort of way**. This could be any kind of activity that a user might previously have recorded on paper. In this example, the user wants to keep a record of each contact that is made.

> ... so they can keep a **journal** of contacts.

This is another entity type that is similar to an audit log but would potentially contain more information, such as notes about a contact, rather than just a record that a contact had taken place.

A List of Entities

So far you've looked at the following list of preliminary entities:

Entity	Description
Contact	People who are points of contact for customers with whom you need to communicate
Customer	Organization or individuals to whom products, office supplies, and/or furniture are sold
Warehouse	Locations where objects are stored for sale
Deliveries	Events when sold items are delivered to customers
Products	Items that are sold
Office Supplies	A type of product
Furniture	A type of product
Invoice	A physical document that is issued to a customer to request payment for items sold
Product Order Confirmation	An electronic (possibly the only format) document that allows us to alert a customer that an order has been placed
Journal	A listing of all communication with a contact
Journal Entry	The actual record of the contact
Physical Modeling note: Changes to invoices must be logged	

The descriptions are based on facts carefully derived from the preliminary documentation.

Note that in the description for contact, you should avoid making any kind of assumptions about how the data is used while fully describing the basics of what is true, based on what has been previously agreed upon.

Now you have a list of all of the entities that have been specified in your previous documentation. At this point you're still iterating through what the client told you. When you begin to analyze what has been specified you can start to look for details that the client didn't give us. Rather than filling in these holes with assumptions and guesswork, you should (ideally) prepare a list of questions and deliver them to the business analyst, who will revisit the client to extract more information.

❑   Do you have just one warehouse?

❑   Are your customers typically individuals or large conglomerates?

❑   Are there other types of products that you sell? Or are furniture and office supplies so important that you need to store special information about them?

Identifying Attributes

As you look for attributes, you'll be looking for items that identify, make up, and describe the entity you're trying to represent. For example, if the entity is a person, attributes might include a driver's license number, social security number, hair color, eye color, weight, spouse, children, mailing address, and e-mail address. Each of these things serves to represent the entity in part. Note that at this point in the process, an attribute isn't bounded in any way. An attribute might be a simple scalar value, or it might be an array, or an array of arrays. In Chapters 6 and 7 you'll take whatever you gather here and structure it into a better format through the process of normalization.

Identifying which attributes can be associated with an entity requires a different approach from identifying the entities themselves. Attributes will frequently be found by noting adjectives that are used to describe an entity you have previously found.

Because domain information is generally discovered at the same time as the attributes, you'll look for this now as well.

Identifiers

Every entity needs to have at least one identifying attribute or set of attributes. These identifiers are what you defined as keys in Chapter 3. In the previous example, one such identifier is shown as follows:

> They identify customers by a **number** generated by their current system.

Almost every entity that you discover in this phase of design will have some easily found identifier. The reason for this is that, at this point, you're dealing with entities that are easy to pick out because they have natural identifiers.

It's also important to be certain that what you think of as a unique item really is unique. Look at people's names. They're almost unique, but there are actually hundreds of Louis Davidsons in the United States, and that isn't really a common name. There are thousands of John Smiths out there! Some common examples of good identifiers are as follows:

- ❑ For people: Social security numbers (in the US); full names (not always a perfect identifier); or other IDs (like customer numbers, employee numbers, and so on).

- ❑ For transactional documents (invoices, bills, computer-generated notices): These usually have some sort of number assigned when they're sent to other organizations.

- ❑ For books: The ISBN (titles aren't unique).

- ❑ For products for sale: Product numbers (product names aren't unique).

- ❑ For companies that clients deal with: These are commonly assigned a customer or client number for tracking.

- ❑ For buildings: The complete address including zip and postal code.

- ❑ For mail: The addressee's name and address, and the date it was sent.

There are many more examples, but by now you should understand what identifiers are. Thinking back to the relational model discussed in Chapter 3, you know that each instance of a relation (or row if you will) must be unique. Identifying unique natural keys in the data is the very first step in implementing a design. Some of the identifiers listed earlier cannot be guaranteed to be unique; for example, in the case of company numbers and transactional documents, the identifiers could be sequential numbers, which aren't natural keys.

However, in many cases the value may be a **smart** key, which means that there is some other information embedded within it. In most cases, the smart key can be disassembled into its parts. In some cases, however, the data will probably not jump out at you. For example, consider an automotive VIN (vehicle identification number). It's a 17-character code assigned uniquely to every vehicle in the world. In the US, the format is as follows (from http://www.autoinsurancetips.com/vin.htm):

- ❑ First character: Identifies the country in which the vehicle was manufactured, for example: US (1 or 4), Canada (2), Mexico (3), Japan (J), South Korea (K), UK (S), Germany (W), Italy (Z).

- ❑ Second character: Identifies the manufacturer, for example: Audi (A), BMW (B), Buick (4), Cadillac (6), Chevrolet (1), Chrysler (C), Dodge (B), Ford (F), GM Canada (7), General Motors (G), Honda (H), Jaguar (A), Lincoln (L), Mercedes Benz (D), Mercury (M), Nissan (N), Oldsmobile (3), Pontiac (2 or 5), Plymouth (P), Saturn (8), Toyota (T), VW (V), Volvo (V).

- ❑ Third character: Identifies vehicle type or manufacturing division.

- ❑ Fourth to Eighth characters: Identifies vehicle features such as body style, engine type, model, series, and so on.

- ❑ Ninth character: Identifies VIN accuracy as check digit.

- ❑ Tenth character: Identifies the model year. For example: 1988(J), 1989(K), 1990(L), 1991(M), 1992(N), 1993(P), 1994(R), 1995(S), 1996(T), 1997(V), 1998(W), 1999(X), 2000(Y)---2001(1), 2002(2), 2003(3)

- ❑ Eleventh character: Identifies the assembly plant for the vehicle.

- ❑ Twelfth to Seventeenth characters: Identifies the sequence of the vehicle for production as it rolled of the manufacturers assembly line.

Smart keys have their purpose–it's easy to look at the VIN of a car and determine an incredible amount about a car, with only a very small reference sheet–but for logical design you need to discover all of the individual bits of information that make them up. Most of these bits will make up different attributes of the object.

For example, say you have a car entity, and you've identified that the VIN existed as an attribute. From this you can infer that there are several other attributes, such as in the example of a VIN:

- ❏ Country of Manufacture
- ❏ Manufacturer
- ❏ Vehicle Type
- ❏ Vehicle Features
- ❏ Model Year
- ❏ Assembly Plan
- ❏ Sequence of Production

You'll want to identify these as attributes as well.

Descriptive Information

Descriptive information is one of the easiest types to find. Adjectives used to describe things that have already been identified as entities are very common and will usually point directly to an attribute. In your example, you have different types of products: new and used.

> ... they sell **used** products to ... They also sell **new** stuff ...

One great thing here is that you have now identified part of the domain of the attribute. In this case, the attribute is "Type of Product," and the domain seems to be "New" and "Used." Of course, it would be just as valid to identify this as two attributes; an "Is New" attribute, and an "Age of Product" attribute.

In the next example, you'll see that you must have an attribute that identifies the customer's credit worthiness.

> ... as soon as a customer makes an order if they're **trusted (no particular credit problems)**.

How companies find out whether the customer has credit problems is something you'll definitely want to question at some point, because you'll want to know more about how the database can facilitate the process of managing credit worthiness. On the other hand, the following example gives the impression that you have a contact entity which has an attribute of phone number with a domain of fax and voice.

> ... both phone numbers (**fax and voice**), address ...

This is a good place to insert a little reminder that one of the major differences between a column and an attribute is that a column is a physical representation of a single piece of information stored in the same physical entity or table, while an attribute may not be physically stored in the same table.

Locators

Locators are used as a way to locate something, from a physical resource to a categorization, and they can also differentiate and locate a value in a table. An example of a locator is shown here.

> They ship all products from the warehouse **downtown**.

Here you have a warehouse location. The warehouse can only have one physical address, so it's a specific locator. Note that it isn't clear from this sentence fragment whether or not they have more than one warehouse. This will be noted as a question to ask later.

In this next example you have four very typical locators.

> ... *store* contact information *for each customer, both* phone numbers (fax and voice), address, *and* e-mail addresses.

Most entities that are connected with organizations will have many phone numbers, addresses, and e-mail addresses. In this example, you have four attributes for the contact entity. A further review will help you do a better job of determining all the actual needs when it comes to this information. Nevertheless, this is a pretty good list of what's important to the user.

You may be wondering why you should consider an address to be a single attribute, when it's obvious that an "address" consists of apartment number, street, city, state, zip code–clearly there are several values there. The answer to that is that although all these attributes make up the address, individually they aren't important at this point. As discussed in the complex attributes (like a point being made up of X and Y coordinates) section, the address is made up of street information plus locality information.

The important thing to identify at this point is that the address identifies one more piece of information about the customer, namely where they can be contacted. This will make more sense later when you start the structuring process, but for now, it should be enough to realize that when a user sees the word "address" in the context of the example, they think of a generic address used to locate a physical location.

The last attribute comes from the following sentence.

> They would like to be able to **fax or e-mail** product order confirmations ...

The fax or e-mail attribute goes to the delivery mechanism that you use to pass on the product order confirmation. You'll certainly want to keep a record of how and when you sent this to the customer. Hence you'll need an attribute describing the delivery mechanism on the product order confirmation table.

Related Information

In some cases (though not in this example) you'll have related information that you'll need as attributes for your entities. Some examples of this might be:

❑ Additional materials: Anywhere there exists an entity describing a book or some other type of media (think Amazon.com), you'll probably want to list additional resources that the user can also look up.

❑ Contacts: You've already learned about contact entities, but a contact is also technically an attribute of an entity. Whether or not it's decided that the contact is a separate entity at this point or later on, the final database will end up looking exactly the same, because the process of normalization (Chapters 6 and 7) ensures that attributes that need to be implemented as entities are restructured accordingly.

❑ Web sites, FTP sites, or other assorted Web resources: You'll often need to identify the website of an entity, or the URL of a resource that is identified by the entity; such information would be defined as attributes.

A List of Entities, Attributes, and Domains

The following table shows the entities, along with descriptions and probable attribute domains.

Entity	Description	Column Domain
Contact	People who are points of contact for customers with whom you need to communicate	
Fax phone number	Phone number to send facsimile messages to the contact	Any valid phone number
Voice phone number	Phone number to reach contact over voice line	Any valid phone number
Address	Postal address of the contact	Any valid address
E-mail address	Electronic mail address of the contact	Any valid e-mail address
Customer	Organizations or individuals to whom you sell products, office supplies, and furniture	
Customer Number	The key value that's used to identify a customer	Unknown
Credit Trustworthy?	Tells you if you can ship products to customer immediately	True, False
Warehouse	Locations where objects are stored for sale	
Location	Identifies which warehouse–there may only be one at this point, because single domain value identified	"downtown"
Deliveries	Events in which sold items are delivered to customers	
Products	Items that are sold	
Product Type	Identifies different types of products that they sell	"Used," "New"
Office Supplies	A special type of product that is sold	
Furniture	A special type of product that is sold	
Invoice	A physical document that is issued to a customer to request payment for items sold	
Product Order Confirmations	An electronic (possibly the only format) document that allows you to alert a customer that an order has been placed	
Delivery Mechanism Type	Identifies how the product order confirmation is sent to the customer	"Fax," "E-mail"
Journal	A listing of all communication with a contact	
Journal Entry	The actual record of the contact	
Physical Modeling note: *Log any changes to invoices*		

Note the use of the term "Any valid." The scope of these statements will need to be expanded to define what is valid. Many databases that store phone numbers and addresses cannot cope with all of the different formats used in all regions of the world.

Note that you still haven't begun to add anything to the design in this process. It might also be interesting to note that you have a document that is almost a page long from a simple analysis of two small paragraphs of text. When you do this in a real project, the resulting documentation will often be quite large, and there will likely be quite a bit of redundancy in much of the documentation. You'll no doubt do a better job of discovering what data is needed than you've done in the preceding few pages!

Relationships Between Entities

The most important decisions you'll make about the structure of your database will usually revolve around relationships.

One-to-n Relationships

In each of the one-to-n (that is one-to-one or one-to-many) relationships, the table that is the "one" table in the relationship is considered the parent, and the "n" is the child or children.

The one-to-n relationship is frequently used in implementation, but is uncommonly encountered during early database design. The reason for this is that most of the natural relationships that users tell you about will turn out to be many-to-many relationships.

There are two prominent types of one-to-n relationships that you need to discuss. They're really quite simple and an experienced database designer will recognize them immediately.

The "Has-A" Relationship

The main special type of relationship is the "has-a" relationship. It's so named because the parent table in the relationship has one or more of the child entities employed as attributes of the parent. In fact, the "has-a" relationship is the way you implement an attribute that often occurs more than once. Some examples are as follows:

❑ Addresses

❑ Phone Numbers

❑ Children

In the example paragraph, you had the following:

> ... store **contact** information for each **customer** ...

In this case, you have a customer entity that has one or more contacts. Note that the "has-a" relationship is actually the way you define the case where an instance of one entity is an attribute of another. In this case, the contact has an attribute of contact. Because contact is an object, you define a relationship "Customer has-a Contact."

Another example of a "has-a" relationship is found in the following example:

> ... for **contacts** so they can keep a **journal** of contacts.

In this case, a contact has many journal entries. It isn't likely that a journal entry will be associated with multiple contacts.

The "Is-A" Relationship

A special case of the one-to-n relationship is the "is-a" relationship, in which the child entity in the relationship extends the definition of the parent entity. For example—cars, trucks, R/Vs, and so on are all types of vehicle, so a car **is a** vehicle. The cardinality of this relationship is one-to-one, because the child entity simply contains more specific information that qualifies this extended relationship. The reason for having this sort of relationship is conceptual. There would be some information common to each of the child entities (stored as attributes of the parent entity), but there would be other information that is specific to each individual child entity (stored as attributes of the child entity) as well.

In this example, you have the following situation:

> ... they sell used **products** to, usually **office supplies**, but they have **furniture** as well.

In this example you have an entity—products—that is very generic. The product entity is unlikely to have much information about what constitutes office supplies, or what a piece of furniture is made from. This approximates to the concept of inheritance in OOP databases.

> *The "is-a" relationship is loosely analogous to a subclass in OOP. In relational databases there is no such concept as a subclass. You'll read more about this topic when you come to modeling the database.*

Many-to-Many Relationships

Examples of many-to-many relationships are far more common than you might imagine. In fact, as you begin to refine your design, you'll use many-to-many relationships for a large proportion of your relationships. In this example, there is one that is obvious:

> ...**customers** that they sell used **products** to ...

If you incorrectly define this as a one-to-many relationship, you would be stuck with either one customer being able to buy many products, or each product only able to be sold to a single customer. Alternatively, one product could be sold to many customers but each customer could only purchase a single product. Obviously neither of these is realistic. Many customers can purchase many products and many products can be sold to many customers.

Listing Relationships

Let's look at the document you're working on once again, this time after having removed the attributes you added in the previous section to save space and make what you've done clearer.

Entity	Description
Contacts	People who are points of contact for customers with whom you need to communicate
Have journal entries	To identify when they contact people at the customer's address
Customers	Organization or individuals to whom you've sold products, office supplies, and furniture
Purchase Products	Customers purchase products from the client
Have contacts	To store names, addresses, phone numbers, and so on of people at the customer's address
Warehouses	Locations where things are stored for sale
Store products to ship	Products are stored at the warehouse for sale to customers
Deliveries	Events in which sold items are delivered to customer
Products	Items that are sold
Can be sold to customers	Customers can purchase any of the products that are sold
Office Supplies	A type of product
Is a Product	Office supplies are simply extensions of products, presumably so you are able to show more information

Entity	Description
Furniture	A type of product
Is a Product	Furniture is simply the extension of products, presumably so you are able to show more information
Invoice	A physical document that is issued to a customer to request payment for items sold
Product Order Confirmation	An electronic (possibly the only format) document that allows you to alert a customer that an order has been placed
Journal	A listing of all communication with a contact
Journal Entry *Physical Modeling note:* *log any changes to invoices*	The actual record of the contact

Identifying Business Rules

You'll define business rules as statements that govern and shape business behavior. Depending upon an organization's methodology, these rules can be in the form of bulleted lists, simple text documents, or any format that works. They can also be stored in a case tool. For your database design, you'll treat rules the same as the predicates that were discussed in the previous chapter, and use them to cover any criteria that don't fit precisely into your mold of table, column, and domain. The ability to implement the rule isn't implied by the existence of a documented business rule; in fact, at this point in the process you don't really care if the rule can be implemented using any specific technology, only that it must be enforced *somehow*. All you want to do is gather business rules that are concerned with data for later review.

When defining business rules, there is likely to be some duplication of rules and attribute domains, but this isn't a real problem. It's important to get as many of the existing rules as possible documented, because missing business rules will hurt more than missing attributes, relationships, or even entities. Entities and attributes will frequently be found when you're implementing the system, usually out of necessity, but finding new business rules at a late stage can change the entire shape of the design, forcing an expensive rethink or an ill-advised "kludge" to shoehorn them in.

Recognizing business rules isn't generally a difficult process, but it's time-consuming and fairly tedious. Unlike entities, attributes, and relationships, there is no straightforward specific clue for identifying all of them. However, general practice when looking for business rules is to read documents line by line, looking for sentences including language like "once...occurs," "have to," "must," "will," and so on. But documents don't always include every business rule. You might look through a hundred or a thousand invoices and not see a single instance where a client is credited money, but this doesn't mean that it never happens. In many cases business rules have to be mined from two places:

❑ Old code

❑ Clients

Getting business rules from either of these sources can be quite an arduous task. Not every programmer out there writes wonderfully readable code. If you're lucky, business analyst will interview clients for their rules and will be skilled in finding the situations where obscure rules exist.

In the "snippet of notes from the meeting" example, there are a few business rules that you can define. For example, you have already looked at the need for a customer number attribute, but were unable to specify a domain for the customer number, so you take the following sentence.

> They identify customers by a number generated by their current system.

And you derive a business rule like this.

> **Customer numbers are generated from an algorithm in their current system. (Check for meaning in their current numbers.)**

Another sentence in this example suggests a further possible business rule.

> Invoices are printed on a weekly basis ...

From the previous statement you might derive this rule.

> **Invoices may only be printed on a given day each week.**

However, is this an actual business rule? It's unlikely that the client would want to tie the system down so that it only allows invoices to be printed on a certain day in the week. However, you might interpret that this is precisely what the client specified from the original documentation. This is likely to be one of the situations in which common English language isn't technically precise enough to specify important details in such a short form. The previous extract from the example documentation might be implying that the client anticipates that they would only have enough invoices to print weekly, or that it's just convenient to print them weekly. You'll have to find out what was meant by this statement when the document you produce is reviewed with the client.

The last business rule you can identify comes from this part of the document.

> ... but they make deliveries as soon as a customer makes an order if they're trusted (no particular credit problems).

You saw this before when you read about attributes, but therein also lies a highly important business rule.

> **Deliveries should not be made immediately to customers if they're not credit trusted.**

Of course, you need to qualify the following information:

- ❏ What does "immediately" mean here?

- ❏ How do you assess the credit worthiness of the client?

- ❏ When you're finally able to ship products to the customers, how will payments and deliveries be made?

These issues also need to be clarified in further consultation with the client.

This section on business rules is hardly complete. It was easy to give examples of tables, attributes, and relationships, but business rules are far more obscure in nature. To make your example one that could derive a more complete set of business rules, you would have had to greatly increase the amount of information in the example documentation, which would have made the identification of entities and attributes unnecessarily complicated. It's simply very important to locate every conceivable place where you could derive a specific business rule that governs how data is used and that hasn't been specifically handled by column domains. Establishing business rules is a potentially long drawn-out process that should not be sidestepped or cut short in a real project. Missing or incomplete business rules will cause big problems later.

Identifying Fundamental Processes

For your purposes, you'll define a process as "a coherent sequence of steps undertaken by a program that uses the data that you've been identifying to do something." As an example, consider the process of getting a driver's license (at least here in Tennessee):

- ❏ Fill in the learner's permit forms (optional)

- ❏ Obtain learner's permit (optional)

- ❏ Practice (optional)

- ❏ Fill in license forms

- ❏ Pass driving exam

- ❏ Have picture taken

- ❏ Receive license

Each of these steps must be completed before the following steps can proceed. Processes may or may not have each step enumerated during the logical phase, and certainly will have business rules that govern them. In the Tennessee license process, you must be 15 to get a learner's permit, and you must be 16 to get the license, you must pass the exam, practice must be with a licensed driver, and so on. Obtaining the learner's permit is not a requirement before getting a full license to drive, but it's strongly advised. The business analyst helping to design a driver's license project would have to document this process at some point.

Identifying processes is very relevant to the task of data modeling. Many procedures in database systems require manipulation of data, and processes are critical in these tasks. Each process will usually translate into one or more queries or stored procedures, which may require more data than you've specified. Also, each step of a process may require data to be stored, which is only important to the process, and isn't of any use to the user.

In this example, you have a few examples of such processes.

> They have customers that they sell used products to ...

This note tells you that there's a means of creating and dealing with orders for products being bought by the client. On the surface, this may not seem like a groundbreaking revelation, but there will probably be rows in several tables to facilitate the proper creation of an order. You haven't yet specified an order entity or prices of items, though you would undoubtedly need to do so.

> Invoices are printed ...

You've identified invoices and the need to print them, but this "Print invoices" process may require additional attributes to identify that an invoice has been printed or reprinted, such as who the print was for, and whether it can be reprinted. Document control is a very important part of many processes when helping an organization that is trying to modernize a paper system. Note that printing an invoice may seem like a pretty inane event—press a button on a screen and paper pops out of the printer. All you have to do is select some data from a table, so what's the big deal? However, when you print a document that deals with money exchanging hands (not to mention a specific date that the client expects to get paid) you'll probably have to record the fact that the document was printed, who printed it, when it was mailed, and so on. You might also need to indicate that the documents are printed during a process that includes closing out and totaling of the items on an invoice. The most important point here is that you cannot make any assumptions.

Other basic processes that have been listed are as follows:

- **Make delivery**: From "They make deliveries as soon as a customer makes an order if they're trusted."

- **Modify invoice**: From "Any changes to the invoice need to be documented."

- **Ship product**: From "They ship all products from the warehouse downtown."

❑ **Send product order confirmation**: From "Fax or e-mail product order confirmations."

❑ **Contact customer**: From "They also want to have free notes for contacts so they can keep a journal of contacts."

Each of these processes identifies a unit of work that must be dealt with during the implementation phase of the database design procedure.

Is This Trip Over Yet?

It should be very obvious that not all the entities, attributes, relationships, business rules, and processes from even your simple example have been identified at this point. In this section, you'll briefly go over the steps involved in completing the task of establishing a working set of documentation.

Each of the following steps may seem pretty obvious, but they can easily be overlooked or rushed through in a real-life situation. The real problem is that, if you don't go all the way through the discovery process, you'll miss a tremendous amount of information, some of which may be vital to the success of the project. Frequently, when an architect arrives at this particular point, she'll try to move on and get down to the implementation of it. However, there are at least three more steps that you must take before you can start the next stage in the project.

❑ Identify additional data needs

❑ Review the progress of the project with the client

❑ Repeat the process until you're satisfied, *and* (more importantly) the client is happy and agrees with what you've designed (and preferably puts pen to paper in acknowledgment of that fact)

Note that this sort of procedure needs to be going on throughout the whole design process, not just the data-oriented parts.

Identification of Additional Data

The purpose up to this point has been to achieve a baseline to your documentation, so you can stay faithful to the documentation you originally gathered. Mixing in your new thoughts prior to agreeing on what was in the previous documentation can be confusing to the client as well as to yourself. However, at this point in the design, you need to change direction and begin to add the attributes that you know you'll need. Usually there is a fairly large set of obvious attributes and, to a lesser extent, business rules that haven't been specified by any of the users or initial analysis.

For each of the ideas and items identified so far, you need to go through and specify additional attributes that you'll need. For example, take the contact entity defined earlier.

Entity	Description	
Contact	People who are points of contact for customers with whom you need to communicate	
Attributes		
Fax phone number	Phone number to send facsimile messages to the contact	Any valid phone number
Voice phone number	Phone number to reach contact over voice line	Any valid phone number
Address	Postal address of the contact	Any valid address
E-mail address	Electronic mail address of the contact	Any valid e-mail address
Relationships		
Have journal entries	Used to document communications with the contact	

It's likely that you'll want to note that a contact needs the following additional attributes:

❑ **Name**: The contact's full name is probably the most important attribute of all.

❑ **Spouse Name:** The name of the contact's husband or wife. This kind of information is priceless when making contacts if you want to personalize your message to the person or ask about their family.

❑ **Children**

❑ **Birthdate**: If the person's birthday is known, you may send correspondence on that date.

There are certainly more attributes that you could add for the contact entity, but this set should make the point clearly enough. There may also be additional tables, business rules, and so on to recommend to the client so, in this phase of the design, document them and add them to your lists. One of the main things to make sure of is that your new data items stand out from those already agreed upon from previous consultations with the client using the preliminary documentation.

Review with the Client

Once you've finished putting together this first draft document, it's time to meet with the client. It's important to show them everything that has been documented and not to leave anything out. It's absolutely essential to have the client review every bit of this document, so that they come to understand the solution that you're beginning to devise for them.

It's also worthwhile devising some form of sign-off document, which the client signs before you move forward in the process. This could well be a legally binding document.

Repeat Until Gaining Customer Acceptance

Of course, it's unlikely that the client will immediately agree with everything that's said. It usually takes several attempts to get it right, and each iteration should move you closer to acceptance. As you get through more and more iterations of the design, it becomes increasingly important to make sure that you have the client sign off at regular times; you can point to these documents when the client changes his mind later on. (OK, I mentioned reviewing again!)

> *This one hurts, especially when you don't do an adequate job of handling the review and documentation process. I've worked on consulting projects where the project was well designed and agreed upon, but the documentation of what was agreed upon wasn't written too well (a lot of handshaking, not a lot of ink being applied to paper). As time went by, after many thousands of dollars were invoiced, the client reviewed the agreement document and it became obvious that we didn't agree on much at all. Needless to say it was not a success of titanic proportions.*

Case Study

Now you can get back to the real database design example. While looking over the case study that you started in Chapter 2, you'll need to begin the process of entity discovery by following the guidelines already presented in this chapter.

Client Interview

It's always best to start with the client interview notes. First, go through the notes and mark all of the items that you expect to represent entities. In the example, you'll **bold** these items.

Meeting with Sam Smith, Accounting, Nov 24, 2000, 10 am, Large Conference Room
Attendees: Louis Davidson, Data Architect; Sam Smith, Accounting Manager; Joe Jones, Business
Analyst

Initial Meeting
Additional documentation attached: Bank register, sample check, sample statement, and electronic
format of statement.
Currently using paper **check register**, just like a basic home register. Have looked at the possibility
of using canned product, but they've found none that offer all that they want. And most offer way
too many features.
Need to have multiuser capabilities (entry and viewing). Share over intranet.

Process:
Need to have very up-to-date information about **account**.
Currently balancing account once a month. Using the **statement** from **bank**. Takes an entire day to
get balanced at least. Would like to keep the account balanced weekly using Internet data.
Only interested in checking, not savings, stocks, bonds, and so on. Already have a system for this.
Will be audited yearly by a major auditor. Don't have an audit plan as of yet.

Once Sam was finished, asked him about vendor tracking:
It would be nice to be able to have **payee** information for most of the checks they write.
Also about categorizing **check**, Sam said it would be nice, but not completely needed at this point.

You have found the following initial set of entities to deal with:

Entity	Description
Check	A paper document that is used to transfer funds to someone else.
Account	A banking relationship established to provide financial transactions.
Check Register	A place where account usage is recorded.
Bank	The organization that runs the checking account that the checks are written against.
Statement	A document (paper or electronic) that comes from the bank, once per calendar month, that tells you everything that the bank thinks you have spent.
Payee	A person or company to whom you send checks.

The next step is to go through the document and look for attributes (which you'll apply **<u>bold underline</u>**
to) and relationships, which you'll *italicize*.

Meeting with Sam Smith, Accounting, Nov 24, 2000, 10 am, Large Conference Room
Attendees: Louis Davidson, Data Architect; Sam Smith, Accounting Manager; Joe Jones, Business Analyst

Initial Meeting
Additional documentation attached: Bank register, sample check, sample statement, and electronic format of statement.
Currently using **paper check register**, just like a basic home register. Have looked at the possibility of using canned product, but they've found none that offer all that they want. And most offer way too many features.
Need to have multiuser capabilities (entry and viewing). Share over intranet.

Process:
Need to have very up-to-date information about **account**.
Currently balancing account once a month. Using the **statement** *from* **bank**. Takes an entire day to get balanced at least. Would like to keep the account **balanced weekly** using **Internet data**.
Only interested in checking, not savings, stocks, bonds, and so on. Already have a system for this.
Will be audited yearly by a major auditor. Don't have an audit plan as of yet.

Once Sam was finished, asked him about vendor tracking:
It would be nice to be able to have **payee** *information for most of the checks* they write.

Also about **categorizing check**, Sam said it would be nice, but not completely needed at this point.

At the moment, there really isn't a whole lot of information to be gleaned from these notes. Often you find the client interview uncovers very little information, in which case you may want to review why you didn't get the information that you sought. Were you talking to the wrong people in the organization, or were you asking the wrong questions? It's tough answering the question "How did I fail?"—but doing so can make you a much better data architect (as well as a better person) in the future.

Documents

Your case study interview documentation is a bit on the lean side (to keep the example short and sweet) but, fortunately, you have several documents that will shed quite a bit of light on your solution. You'll look at these documents now and mark the attributes (and possibly entities) that you find. The first document you'll look at is the sample check. This sort of document is a fantastic location for finding information. Because you've identified the check entity, each of the fields in this document is likely to be an attribute.

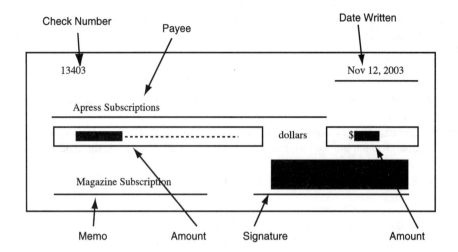

Two things to note from the check:

❏ The amount is specified twice on the check, thereby providing a measure of redundancy and protection from fraud, which probably isn't necessary at this level of design.

❏ Payee has already been specified as a "has-a" type relationship, which is in essence an attribute of the entity, so you won't need to respecify it as an attribute.

The next thing you'll look at is the sample check register. It's simply a record of each check as it's entered.

Number	Date	Description	Category	Amount	Balance
12390	12/15/00	Thinburger	Employee Appreciation	███	███
12391	12/15/00	UnAllied Mortgage	Building payment	███	███
12392	12/16/00	TN Electric	Utilities	███	███
12393	12/16/00	Deposit	N/A	███	███

Account
Running Total

Note that the numbers, dates, descriptions (payee), categories, and amounts are derived from checks themselves, but the balances are new. The balance attribute doesn't fit so well with the check entity, but it does make sense for an account entity. Hence, you'll add a balance attribute to the account entity.

Next, you need to look at the bank statement. You'll mark all of the different attributes just as you did on the check. The bank statement provides attributes for several entities.

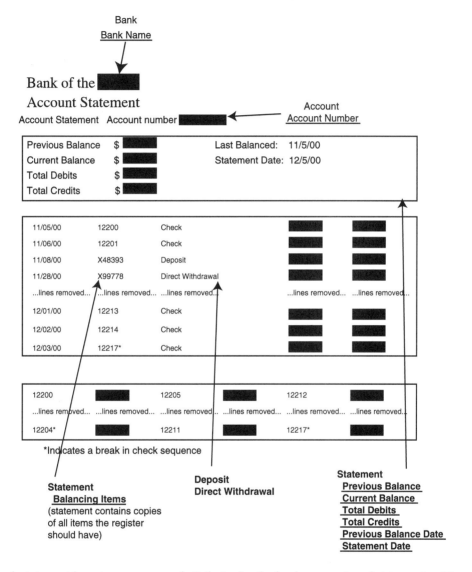

The bank statement has given you several attributes for the bank, account, and statement entities. Here you define two new entities:

❑ **Deposit**: Used to add money to the account

❑ **Direct Withdrawal**: Money is removed from the account without issuing a paper check

Again you see the check date, check number, check amount, and running total (all blacked out for reasons of privacy and security, though it's always a good idea to get sight of some uncensored documents to get an idea of the scale of figures and their format—for example, do check numbers have leading zeros?). Also make note that the deposit and direct withdrawal entities have apparently the same attributes, and they're all in the same table with the running total. So the deposit and direct withdrawal entities will have date, number, and amount attributes. The running total again is the total for the account.

The final piece of documentation you have to look at is the electronic format of the bank register. The electronic version is notably sparser than the paper version. There may be more to the electronic feed, but this is all that you're currently given. This also may be the only thing that you're given because it's truly all you'll need to balance the account.

Column	Data type	Required
Transaction Date	Date Only	Yes
Transaction Number	String(20)	Yes
Description	String(100)	Yes
Item Amount	Money	Yes

Transaction.
  Transaction Date
  Transaction Number
  Description
  Item Account

Although there are no new attributes for existing entities, there is mention of a new entity: the transaction. Interestingly, the bank uses this entity with these attributes to report the values of several other entities. This leads me to believe that there is likely to be a single object that also represents checks, deposits, and direct withdrawals. This indicates that you'll have a transaction entity, with "is-a" relationships to the deposit, direct withdrawal, and the check entities.

Once you've worked your way through these documents, you need to finish your entity document. You'll mark any additional attributes that you add in the far-left column.

Bank Account Object Listing

So this is the draft document that you'll produce from your initial analysis:

Entity	Description	Domain
Transaction	A logical operation that adds or subtracts money from your account	
Attributes		
Transaction Date	The date that the check is presented and money is removed from the account	Valid Dates
Transaction Number	A unique number that is used to identify a transaction	A string
Description	A string description of what the transaction was for	A string
Item Amount	The amount of money to be added to or withdrawn from the account	Real number to two decimal places
Check A paper document that is used to transfer funds to someone else		
Attributes		
Check Usage Type	Used to categorize what check	*Unknown*
Check Type	Used to categorize the check	*Unknown*
Check Number	Number used to uniquely identify the check	Integer
Date Written	The date that the check was written	Valid dates, possibly no future dates
Amount	The amount of money to be withdrawn from the account and remitted to the payee	Real positive number to two decimal places
Memo	Brief description of what the check was used for	Text
Signature	The signature of the person who can sign the check—you likely will simply keep the text version of the name signed	Text
Relationships		
Has Payee	Used to identify the payee that the check was sent to	
Is a transaction	Defines that a deposit is a subclass of the transaction	
Payee A person or company to whom you send checks		
Attributes		
NEW Name	Name of whoever is receiving money	String
NEW Address	Address of the payee	Any valid address
NEW Phone Number	Phone number of payee	Any valid phone number

Table continued on following page

Entity	Description	Domain
Deposit	Used to add money to the account	
Attributes		
Date Written	The date that the check was written	Valid dates, possibly no future dates
Deposit Number	Number used to uniquely identify the check	Integer
Amount	The amount of money to be added to the account	Real positive number to two decimal places
Description	Description from the electronic feed	String
Relationships		
Is a transaction	Defines that a deposit is a subclass of the transaction	
Direct Withdrawal	Used to take money from account without any paper trail	
Attributes		
Date Withdrawn	The date that the check was written	Valid dates, possibly no future dates
Deposit Number	Number used to uniquely identify the check	Integer
Amount	The amount of money to be removed from the account	Real positive number to two decimal places
Description	Description from the electronic feed	String
Relationships		
Is a transaction	Defines that a deposit is a subclass of the transaction	
Account	A banking relationship established to provide financial transactions—you'll probably need to be able to deal with multiple banks	
Attributes		
Account Number	Number that uniquely identifies the account	*Unknown, set by bank, probably a string*
Balance Date	Date and time the checking account was balanced	Valid dates
Running Total	The current amount of money in the account	Real positive number to two decimal places

Entity	Description	Domain
Relationships		
Balanced Using Statement	Identifies where the data came from to balance the account	
Has Transactions	Transactions are made on an account to get money in or out of the account	
Check Register	A place where account usage is recorded	
Attributes		
Register Type	Describes the type of register you're using to hold the account records	"Paper"
Bank	The organization that runs the checking account that the checks are written against—you'll probably need to be able to deal with multiple banks	
Attributes		
Bank Name	The name of the bank you're dealing with	String
Relationships		
Sends Statement	The bank sends a statement so you can balance the account	
Have Accounts	Identifies the bank of an account	
Statement	A document (paper or electronic) that comes from the bank once per calendar month, and tells you everything that the bank thinks the company has spent	
Attributes		
Statement Type	Identifies the type of statement received from the bank	"Internet Data," "Paper"
Previous Balance	Specifies what the balance was supposed to be after the last statement was balanced	Real number to two decimal places
Previous Balance Date	Specifies the date that the account was last balanced	Date
Current Balance	Specifies what the balance of the account is after all of the items in the statement have been reconciled	Real number to two decimal places
Statement Date	Specifies the date that the statement is produced—this will likely be the day that the statement was created by the bank	

Table continued on following page

Entity	Description	Domain
Total Credits	Sum of all items that have added money to the account during the statement period	Real positive number to two decimal places
Total Debits	Sum of all items that have subtracted money from the account during the statement period	Real negative number to two decimal places
Balancing Items	All of the items that the bank has processed and is now reporting back to us	Array of transaction (checks, deposits, direct withdrawals) objects

You can probably see that you're getting to a point where, even for such a small example, this format of documentation is unwieldy. In the next chapter, you'll learn about data modeling, which provides a method of gathering and presenting this data that is much easier to work with. That isn't to say that this manner of specification has no merit. At the very least, you need to be able to produce a document of this sort to share with the clients. This is the reason that you've gone through this exercise, and haven't gone directly into data modeling. The document you've produced does a fair job of describing what you're trying to implement, in a way that can be read by the technical and nontechnical alike.

Business Rules and Processes

For business rules and processes, you should go back and look at your client interview notes. Business rules are *italicized*. Processes are in boxes .

Meeting with Sam Smith, Accounting, Nov 24, 2000, 10 am, Large Conference Room
Attendees: Louis Davidson, Data Architect; Sam Smith, Accounting Manager; Joe Jones, Business Analyst

Initial Meeting
Additional documentation attached: Bank register, sample check, sample statement, and electronic format of statement.
Currently using **paper check register**, just like a basic home register. Have looked at the possibility of using canned product, but you've found none that offer all that they want. And most offer way too many features.
Need to have multiuser capabilities (entry and viewing). Share over intranet.

Process:
Need to have very up-to-date information about **account**.
Currently balancing account once a month. Using the **statement** *from* **bank**. Takes an entire day to get balanced at least.
Would like to keep the account **balanced weekly** using **Internet data**.
Only interested in checking, not savings, stocks, bonds, and so on. Already have a system for this.
Will be audited yearly by a major auditor. Don't have an audit plan as of yet.

Once Sam was finished, asked him about vendor tracking:
It would be nice to be able to have **payee** *information for most of the checks* they write

Also about **categorizing** check, Sam said it would be nice, but not completely needed at this point.

This documentation gives us the following.

Business Rule		Description
	Must have multiuser capabilities	It's likely that more than one person will need to enter transactions at the same time.
	Account must be balanced weekly	You need to be able to balance the account more frequently than monthly, presumably to reduce the time it takes to balance by finding missed transactions more often.
	Will be audited yearly	Some outside firm will check your numbers yearly to make sure that everything is in good shape; you'll probably produce some documentation to facilitate this process.
New	User should get a warning if they attempt to withdraw too much money	Just an idea that the user may want to help avoid an overdrawn account.
New	Should not be able to enter transactions for future dates	Possibly to avoid accidentally post-dating a check.

Process		Description
	Balance Account	Reconcile all transactions that the bank thinks you have to make sure that you have all of them recorded.
	Audit Account	Process to ensure that everything actually works as documented.
New	Enter Transaction	Enter a new deposit, check, or direct withdrawal.

There are probably more business rules and processes to be suggested, but what you have is a solid start. At this point you would take your draft document to your client for approval.

Best Practices

❑ **Be diligent**: Look through everything to make sure that what is being said makes sense. Be certain to understand as many of the business rules that bound the system before moving on to the next step. Mistakes made early in the process can mushroom later in the process.

❑ **Document**: Obviously the point of this chapter has been just that. Document every entity, attribute, relationship, business rule, and process identified. The format of the documentation isn't important. Use a CASE tool, modeling tool, spreadsheet, or pen and paper, but make sure that you have documentation to share.

❑ **Communicate**: Constant communication with clients is essential to keep the design on track. The danger is that if you start to get the wrong idea of what the client needs, every decision past that point may be wrong. Get as much face time with the client as possible.

> *This mantra of "review with client, review with client, review with client" is probably starting to get a bit old at this point. This is one of the last times it will be mentioned, but it's so important that I hope it has sunk in.*

Summary

In this chapter, you've looked at the process of discovering the entities that will eventually make up your database solution. You've weeded through all of the documentation that had been gathered during the information-gathering phase. You did your best not to add your own contributions to the solution until you had processed all of the initial documentation. It should be noted that this is no small task; in the initial example, you had just two paragraphs to work with, yet you ended up with about a page and a half of documentation from it. You also conducted interviews with the client and obtained a sign-off.

It should be noted here that recording all of this information in a simple text document isn't going to be the final ideal version of the data. You've done it this way to keep it simple for the purposes of this book, but normally would use a specialized tool to generate this kind of documentation.

Up until now, you've only been involved with the specification part of the process. This really cannot be helped. Any development process that requires data storage needs to be specified *completely* prior to moving onto the design phase. The implementation design phase will be covered in the second half of this book when you get to physical design. Once the process outlined in this chapter is complete, you have almost everything you need to gather from the client before you build a precise data specification.

5

Data Modeling

Introduction

The document that you started to develop with the tables, columns, and relationships in the previous chapter became unwieldy very quickly, and visualizing the relationships between the different entities was also becoming very difficult. Hence, you need some way to represent the information that you created as tables in a document in a format that's easier to understand.

In this chapter, you'll look at a method of graphically representing a database. This process, known as data modeling, is used to document the structures contained in a database system in a manner that's relatively easy to read. By applying the "picture is worth a thousand words" principle, you'll draw a picture. The only problem is this: What the heck does a database look like? Databases have no actual shape, size, or physical characteristics, other than perhaps one or more machines and hard disks.

What makes data modeling unique is that the picture you end up with has no actual connection to the way the database looks in reality. Because of this, there are several different ways to graphically represent the same thing. You, however, will learn about data models, which are centered around representing the data structures and relationships in a relational database graphically.

Data Models

You'll break down data models into two categories: **logical** and **physical** (with a third type, **conceptual**, simply being a logical model that isn't fully fleshed out). During the process of designing a database system, you first build a logical model and then one or more physical models based on it. If the process goes well, the entire logical model should be functionally equivalent to the physical model(s) once the entire logical model is materialized physically into your SQL Server. In a perfect world, no data that the user needs to see should appear in the physical model without being in the logical model, though it's a reality of life that this isn't always the case.

The logical model represents the basic nature of the information that the client needs to maintain. A logical model can be implemented in a number of different ways, depending upon the needs of the physical implementation. Regardless of whether you use SQL Server 2000, Oracle, Access, or even Excel to implement your data stores, the base logical model can always remain unchanged.

During logical modeling you should be concerned with ensuring that every piece of information is documented so that it can be stored somewhere. Therefore, as you progress through the process of normalization in the next two chapters, your model will grow from the largely disorganized mass of entities that you started to deal with in the previous chapter, into a very organized set of entities. By the end of the process you'll hopefully have identified every single piece of information you may possibly wish to physically store.

The major distinction between the logical and physical models is implementation. Because you use the same modeling language, the logical model will always pretty much resemble the physical model, but during the logical modeling phase of the process it's best to ignore the **HOW** and totally focus on the **WHAT** that will go into the database.

The physical model, which you'll put together in the second half of the book, provides the detailed plan of action for the implementation of the database. This model is where you take the entities you discovered in the previous chapter and turn them into tables. Many different processes are possible, depending on the purpose and usage of the data in the database. Although the logical model should be complete enough to describe the business, the physical data model you'll implement later may make trade-offs for performance, implementation ease, and efficiency versus strict organization.

If the two will differ so much, what is the purpose of logical modeling? This is a valid question. By documenting what should be the optimal storage of data from a consistency standpoint, you increase your ability to produce the best physical databases possible, even if you have to deviate a bit (or a lot) from the logical model. The logical model remains the driving document for later changes to the system and will not be overly perverted by storage details.

Data Modeling Format

There are quite a few different data modeling methodologies, but you'll study one of the deepest, though easiest to read, of them all. This modeling format is, **IDEF1X** (**Integration Definition for Information Modeling**). You'll also look at several other formats, including the other favorite of many database modelers: **Information Engineering**.

While the data modeling methodology may be a personal choice, economics, company standards, or features usually influence tool choice. In this chapter, you'll take a fairly nonpartisan look at some of the tool features that are required or desirable if you want to extend basic graphical modeling. All of the information found in the document you created in the previous chapter needs to be represented and stored in the data model, and you need to be able to get the data out, so it can be shared with the client and programmers.

To cover in any detail a substantial subset of the existing modeling methodologies would be next to impossible. They all serve quite the same purpose, and all have nearly the same objects displayed in slightly different ways. To be fair, there are several modeling methodologies that are pretty much equal for data modeling, such as Information Engineering, and Chen ERD models, and if you're a user of one of these methodologies then you're likely to be quite attached to it, and probably won't wish to change technologies on the basis of this chapter. However, all examples throughout the book will be in the IDEF1X format, which is the one that you'll be learning in detail.

IDEF1X was originally developed by the US Air Force in 1985 to meet the following requirements:

❑   Support the development of data models

❑   Be a language that is robust and easy to learn

❑   Be teachable

❑   Be well tested and proven

❑   Be suitable for automation

For a full copy of the IDEF1X specification, go to http://www.itl.nist.gov/fipspubs/by-num.htm and choose document 184.

IDEF1X does an excellent job of meeting the previous requirements, and is implemented in many of the popular design tools, such as CA ERwin, Embarcadero ERStudio, and Microsoft Visio's Enterprise Edition. It's also supported by other public domain tools, which can be found on the Internet

Entities

In the IDEF1X standard, **entities** (which are synonymous with tables) are modeled as rectangular boxes, which is actually true for most data modeling methodologies. There are two different types of entities that you'll model: **identifier-independent** and **identifier-dependent**, also frequently referred to as **independent** and **dependent,** respectively.

Entity Type

The independent entity is so named because it has no primary key dependencies on any other entity, or to put it in other words, there are no foreign or **migrated** keys in the primary key.

In Chapter 3, you learned about foreign keys, but IDEF1X introduces a related term: **migrated**. This term is common and is included in the specification, but it can be misleading, because to migrate in common English means to move. Rather than actually being moved, the primary key of one entity is "migrated" (copied) as an attribute in a different entity, thus establishing a relationship between the two entities. Hence, it's "independent" of any other entities. All attributes that aren't migrated are owned, because they have their origins in the current entity.

The independent entity is drawn with square edges.

The dependent entity is the converse of the independent entity, because it will have the primary key of another entity migrated into its primary key. In your final physical design, you'll seldom end up using dependent entities in the physical modeling phase of design. This is because the primary key of an entity should usually not be editable in a database, especially when it has dependent entities relying on it. Certainly, the concept of a cascading update does exist, so it's less of a problem, but later in Chapter 10 you'll see the inherent difficulties in building entities in this manner. You'll also look deeper at the idea of independent and dependent entities in the section of this chapter about identifying and nonidentifying relationships.

The dependent entity is drawn with rounded off edges.

What you're beginning to see here is a bit of a chicken-and-egg situation. The dependent entity depends on a certain type of relationship. The later section on attributes has some information that relies on certain types of relationships that you haven't yet covered. If this is your first time ever looking at data models, this chapter may require a reread in order for you to get the full picture, because the concept of independent and dependent objects are directly linked to relationships.

Naming

Though how you name entities isn't a part of the IDEF1X specification, while you're building entities you must mention this subject. One of the most important aspects of designing or implementing any system is how objects and variables are named. Naming database objects clearly is no different, and is possibly a more important task than it is for other programming objects. The names given to your entities (and attributes for that matter) will be translated into names that will eventually be used by end users as well as programmers. The logical model will be considered the primary schematic of how the database was conceived, and will probably evolve as a living document that gets changed before changing any physical structures.

The following are a few basic guidelines for naming entities:

❑ **Entity names should never be plural.** The primary reason for this is that the name refers to an instance of the object being modeled rather than the collection. Besides, it sounds silly to say that you have "an automobiles row." No, you have an automobile row. If there were two, there would be two automobile rows.

❑ **The name given should directly correspond to the essence of the entity.** For instance, if modeling an entity that represents a person, name it *person*. If modeling an automobile, call it *automobile*. Naming isn't always this cut-and-dried, but it's wise to keep names simple and to the point.

Entity names frequently need to be made up of several words. It's totally permissible to have spaces in them when multiple words are necessary in the name, but it isn't required. For example an entity that stores a person's addresses might be named: *Person Address*, *Person_Address*, or using the style I've recently become accustomed to, and the one that you'll use in this book: *personAddress*. A common name for this type of naming is **camel notation**, or mixed case.

> *Note that you're in the logical modeling stage. You generally want to avoid implementing spaces in the names of your physical structures. While it's allowable to have names with spaces, it isn't a good idea for usability. In SQL Server you would have to address these names surrounded by square brackets, [like this] or use quoted identifiers "like this."*

No abbreviations are to be used in the logical naming of entities. Every word should be fully spelled out. Abbreviations tend to confuse, although abbreviations may be necessary or even desirable in the physical model due to naming standards. If abbreviations are used in physical or logical modeling, then it's a very good idea to have a reference to make sure that any word that is abbreviated is always abbreviated the same way every time. This is one of the primary reasons to avoid abbreviations, so you don't end up with attributes named "description," "descry," "desc," "descrip," and "descriptn" all referring to a description attribute.

One word of warning though: It's important not to go overboard with long descriptive sentence names for an entity, such as *leftHandedMittensLostByKittensOnSaturdayAfternoons* (unless the entity stored therein is unique from *leftHandedMittensLostByKittensOnSundayMornings*), because on-screen truncation will make it difficult to read the name. A better name might be *mittens* or even *lostMittens*. Much of what is encoded in that name will likely be entities in their own right: *Mitten, Mitten Status, Mitten Hand, Mitten Used By, Kitten,* and so on. However, this falls more readily under the heading of normalization and will be discussed further in Chapters 6 and 7.

Attributes

All attributes in the entity must be uniquely named within it. They are represented by a list of names inside of the entity rectangle.

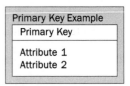

> *Note: This is technically an invalid entity, because there is no primary key defined (as required by IDEF1X). You'll learn about keys in the following section.*

At this point, you simply enter all of the attributes that you've defined in the discovery phase. In practice, you might well have combined the process of discovering entities and attributes with the initial modeling phase. It will all depend on how well the tools are used. Most data modeling tools cater for building models fast and storing a wealth of information to document their entities and attributes.

In the early stages of logical modeling, there can be quite a large difference between an attribute and a column. As you'll see in the next two chapters, the definition of what an attribute can store will change quite a bit. For example, the attributes of a person may start out as simply an address and phone number. However, once you normalize, you'll break these down into many columns (address into number, street name, city, state, zip code, and so on) and likely multiple entities.

Primary Key

As we noted in the previous section, an IDEF1X entity must have a primary key. This is convenient for you, because in Chapter 3 you learned that for a tuple, or an entity, each row must be unique. The primary key may be a single attribute, or it may be multiple columns (a composite key, defined earlier as keys with multiple columns) with a required value for all attributes in the key (physically speaking, nulls are not allowed in the primary key).

The primary key is denoted by placing attributes above a horizontal line through the entity rectangle.

In the early logical modeling phase, I generally don't like to assign any meaningful primary key attributes. The main reason for this is to keep the model clean and make it clear where the origination point of the key is, once the key has migrated around in the model. I tend to use a simple meaningless primary key named after the entity plus the character's ID. This then will migrate to other entities to help you see when there is any ownership. Occasionally an attribute may migrate five or ten tables deep into a model.

Because it's possible that you won't choose the primary key that will eventually be implemented, I generally model all candidate keys (or unique identifiers) as alternate keys (nonprimary key unique keys are defined in the next section). The result is that it's very clear in the logical model what entities are in an ownership role to other entities.

> *This is certainly not a requirement in logical modeling, but is a personal preference that I have found to be a useful documentation method that keeps models clean and corresponds to my method of implementation later. Using a natural key as the primary key in the logical modeling phase isn't only reasonable but, to many architects, preferable. I tend to try to equate even my logical objects to object-oriented classes that are identified not by a primary key, but by a pointer.*

Alternate Keys

As previously defined in Chapter 3, alternate keys are a set of one or more columns whose uniqueness you want to guarantee over the entire entity. Alternate keys don't have special symbols like primary keys and aren't migrated for any relationship. They're identified on the model in a very simple manner.

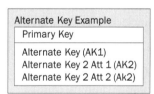

In this example, there are two alternate keys *groups*: Group AK1, which has one attribute as a member, and group AK2, which has two. One extension that CA ERwin (a popular data modeling tool built by Computer Associates; go to http://www3.ca.com/Solutions/Product.asp?ID=260 for more information) uses is shown here.

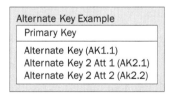

Note that there is an added *<position number>* notation tacked onto the AK1 and AK2 in order to denote the position of the attribute in the key. In the logical model, technically, this information shouldn't be displayed and certainly should be ignored, because ordering isn't important for attributes, nor should it be for the eventual resulting columns. Logically, it doesn't matter which attribute comes first in the key. When a key is physically implemented, it will become interesting for performance reasons only.

Foreign Keys

Foreign keys are also referred to as **migrated attributes**. They are formed by including primary keys from another entity in another entity. These attributes serve as a pointer to an instance in the other entity, thereby forming a connection. They are a result of relationships that you'll look at in the next section. They're indicated much like alternate keys by adding the letters "FK" after the foreign key.

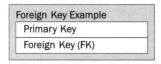

Foreign Key Example
Primary Key
Foreign Key (FK)

The diagram doesn't show what entity the key is migrated from, and confusion can arise, depending on the choice of primary keys. This is a limitation of most modeling methodologies, because it would be unnecessarily confusing to the process if you displayed the name of where the key came from for the following reasons:

❑   There is no limit (nor should there be) on how far a key will migrate from its original owner.

❑   It also isn't unreasonable that the same attribute might migrate from two separate entities, especially early in the logical design process.

This is one of the reasons for the primary key scheme that you'll employ in your logical model where you'll simply build a key named <*entityName*>Id as the key for an entity. The name of the entity is easily identifiable, and is clearer in the examples.

Domains

Domain is a term that you're regrettably going to use in two very similar, but different, contexts. In Chapter 3, you learned that a domain is the set of valid values for an attribute. In IDEF1X, domains have a subtly different definition, which encompasses this definition, but with a useful twist. In this case, domains are mechanisms that not only allow you to define the valid values that can be stored in an attribute, but also provide a form of inheritance in your datatype definitions, as follows:

❑   **String**: A required character string

❑   **SocialSecurityNumber**: An optional character value with a format of ###-##-####

❑   **PositiveInteger**: An optional integer value with an implied domain of 0 to max(integer value)

You can then build subtypes that inherit the settings from the base domain. You'll build domains for any attributes that you use regularly, in addition to domains that are base templates for infrequently used attributes. For example, you might have a basic character-type domain, where you specify that all character data wasn't required. You might also define domains named *name* and *description* for use in many entities, and they'll define that these values are required.

In logical modeling, there are just a few bits of information that you're likely to store, such as the general type of the attribute–character, numeric, logical, or even binary data. You'll also make note of any length or possible values that you know form the boundaries for values stored in the eventual column, plus you'll see whether or not a value is required for the attribute. It's important however to keep these domains as implementation-independent datatype descriptions. For example, you might specify a domain of the following:

❑ **GloballyUniqueIdentifier**: A required value that will be unique no matter where it's generated.

In SQL Server you might use a `uniqueidentifier` (GUID value) to implement this domain. In Oracle, in which the implementation may not be exactly the same, you would implement a `uniqueidentifier` differently; logically it wouldn't matter.

When you start physical modeling, you use the very same domains to inherit physical properties as well. This is the real value in using domains. By creating reusable template attributes that will also be used when you start creating columns, you reduce the amount of effort it takes to build simple entities, which make up the bulk of your work. It also provides a way to enforce companywide standards by reusing the same domains on all of your corporate models.

Later on, physical details such as datatype and constraints will be chosen, just to name a few of the more basic physical properties that may be inherited. Because you should have far fewer domains than implemented attributes, you get the double benefits of speedy and consistent implementation. However, you may not employ the inheritance mechanisms when you're building your tables by hand. Implementation of domains is strictly based on the tools used.

For example, you might define the following hierarchy as shown.

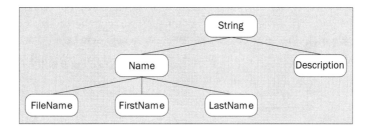

`String` is the base domain from which you then inherit `Name` and `Description`. `FileName`, `FirstName`, and `LastName` are inherited from `Name`. During logical modeling, this might seem like a lot of work for nothing, because most of these domains will share some basic details, such as whether the value is optional (translated to allowing NULLs or not) or blank data. However, it may not always be required to give a `FileName`, whereas you'll always require a `LastName`. It's important to implement domains for as many distinct attribute types as possible, in case rules are discovered that are common to any domains that have been set up.

Domains are one of the cooler features of IDEF1X. They provide an easy method of building standard attributes, thereby reducing both the length of time required for such builds as well as the number of errors that occur in doing so. Specific tools implement domains, with the ability to define and inherit more properties throughout the domain chain to make creating databases easier. Obviously, if you're building databases and models by hand, it's less likely you'll be able to design the model using the inheritance of domains.

The domain may be shown to the right of the attribute name in the entity, as shown here.

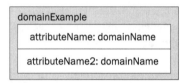

So if you had an entity that held domain values for describing a type of person, you might model in the following way.

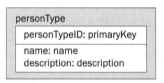

In this case, you have the following three domains:

❑ **PrimaryKey**: A row pointer for a migrating foreign key. In this case, implementation isn't implied by building a domain, so you can implement this value in any manner you decide.

❑ **Name**: A generic domain for holding the name of an instance of an entity. By using this as your standard name domain everywhere you want a name, you maintain consistency. If a given entity name doesn't fit the same mold, you can create a new domain.

❑ **Description**: The same type of domain as the name domain, except it will be used to hold a description of the entity it is a member of.

Naming

Attribute naming is a bit more interesting than entity naming. We stated that the entity name should never be plural. The same is technically true for attributes. However, at this point in the modeling process, you will still have attribute names that are plural. Leaving the name as a plural can be a good reminder that you expect multiple values. For example, you might have a *Person* entity with a *Children* attribute identified. The *Person* entity would identify a single person, and the *Children* attribute would be there to identify sons and daughters of that person.

Standards for naming attributes have always been quite a hot topic with several different naming schemes having been developed over the previous 30 years of databases. You'll look at those in Chapter 10, when you begin to implement your database. The naming standard you'll follow is very simple:

❑ Generally, it isn't necessary (or even desirable) to repeat the entity name in the attribute name, except for the primary key. The entity name is implied by the attribute's inclusion in the entity. Because the primary key will be migrated to other entities, this small concession makes dealing with migration simpler, because you don't have to rename every attribute after migration, not to mention clean up joins in SQL.

❑ The chosen attribute name should reflect precisely what is contained in the attribute and how it relates to the entity being modeled.

❑ As with entities, no abbreviations are to be used in the logical naming of attributes. Every word should be spelled out in its entirety. If any abbreviation is to be used, due to some naming standard currently in place, then a method should be put into place to make sure that it's used consistently, as was discussed earlier in the chapter.

Your basic naming principles will be to keep it simple and readable, thereby avoiding abbreviation. This standard will be followed from logical modeling into the physical phase. Whatever standard is used, establishing a pattern of naming will make models easy to follow, both for the modeler, the programmers, and the users. Any standard is better than no standard.

Relationships

Up to this point, the constructs you've looked at are pretty much constant across all data modeling methodologies. Entities are always signified by rectangles, and attributes are always words within the rectangles.

However, relationships are a very different matter. Every methodology does relationships differently. IDEF1X is quite a bit different from all others, in primarily a good way. You're using IDEF1X because it's a very expressive way of representing relationships. To make this clear, you need to take a look at the terms **parent** and **child**, and an example of a relationship between them.

From the glossary in the IDEF1X specification, you'll find the following definitions:

❑ **Entity, Child**: The entity in a specific connection relationship whose instances can be related to zero or one instance of the other entity (parent entity).

❑ **Entity, Parent**: An entity in a specific connection relationship whose instances can be related to a number of instances of another entity (child entity).

❑ **Relationship**: An association between two entities or between instances of the same entity.

These are remarkably understandable definitions to have been taken straight from a government specification. Every relationship is denoted by a line drawn between two entities, with a solid circle at one end of that line.

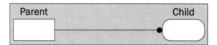

The primary key of the parent is migrated to the child. This is how you denote a foreign key on a model.

You'll attempt to go through all of the different settings in the IDEF1X methodology, followed by a brief look at some of the other methodologies that you should understand, because not everyone will use IDEF1X. There are several different types of relationships that you'll look at, such as the following listed here.

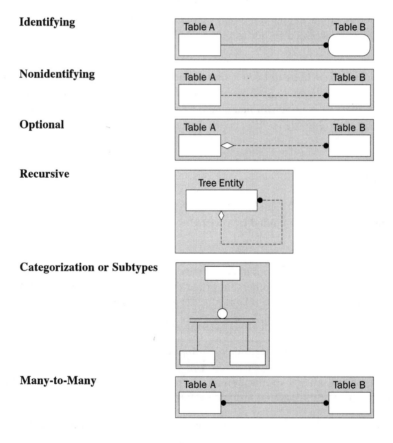

One-to-Many

The **one-to-many** relationship is really kind of a misnomer, and should be considered a one-to-*any* relationship. It encompasses *one-to-zero, one, many,* or perhaps *exactly n* relationships. Technically, you'll see that it's more accurately one-to-(from m to n), as you're able to specify the many in very precise (or very loose) terms as the situation dictates. The more common term is one-to-many.

As mentioned earlier in this chapter, there are two main types of one-to-many relationships: the **identifying** and (unsurprisingly) the **nonidentifying.** The difference, as you'll see, is where the primary key is migrated to. There are quite a few different permutations of one-to-many relationship settings, and you'll look at all of them and how to denote them in this section.

Identifying Relationships

The **identifying relationship** indicates that the migrated primary key attribute is migrated to the primary key of the child as shown here.

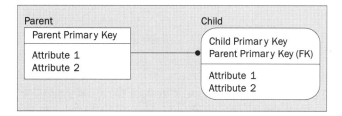

Note that the child entity in the relationship is drawn as a rounded-edged square, which means that it's a dependent entity. The reason this is called the identifying relationship is that you'll have to have a parent instance in order to be able to identify a child instance. The essence (defined as "the intrinsic or indispensable properties that serve to characterize or identify something") of the child instance is at least partially defined by the existence of a parent.

In other words, the identification and definition of the child is based on the existence of the parent. An example is a purchase order and its line items. Without the purchase order, the line items would have no reason to exist. On the other hand, take a teacher and a classroom. Without a teacher defined, there still would be a reason for the class to exist.

Nonidentifying Relationships

The **nonidentifying relationship** indicates that the primary key attribute isn't migrated to the primary key of the child. They are used more frequently than the identifying relationship. Whereas identifying relationships were based on needing the existence of the parent to even have a reason to exist, the nonidentifying relationship is (not surprisingly) just the opposite. Taking the example of the purchase order, you'll now consider the relationship between product vendor and the line item of the purchase order. The vendor doesn't define the existence of a line item. The vendor in this case may be required or not required as the business rules might dictate, but generally business rules will not dictate whether a relationship is identifying or nonidentifying; the data itself will buy its fundamental properties.

Nonidentifying relationships are modeled by a dashed line, as shown here.

Why should you use an identifying instead of a nonidentifying relationship? The reason is actually pretty simple. If the parent entity (as you stated in the previous section) defines the essence of the child, then you'll use the identifying. If on the other hand, the relationship defines one of the child's attributes, then you should use a nonidentifying relationship.

As a contrasting example, consider the following:

❑ **Identifying**: Say you have an entity that stores contacts and an entity that stores the contact's telephone number. The *contact* defines the phone number, and without the contact, there would be no need for the *contactPhoneNumber*.

❑ **Nonidentifying**: Take the entities that you defined for the identifying relationship, along with an additional entity called *contactPhoneNumberType*. This entity is related to the *contactPhoneNumber* entity, but in a nonidentifying way, and it defines a set of possible phone number types ("voice," "fax," and so on) that a *contactPhoneNumber* might be. The type of phone number doesn't identify the phone number; it simply classifies it. If you didn't know the type of phone number, it wouldn't cease being a contact phone number. If you didn't know the contact, logically, you wouldn't have any need for a phone number for that contact.

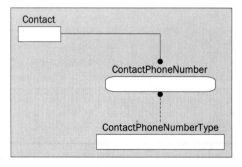

The

contactPhoneNumberType entity is commonly known as a **domain entity** *or* **domain table***. Rather than having a fixed domain for an attribute, you design entities that allow programmatic changes to the domain with no recoding of constraints or client code. As an added bonus you can add columns to define, describe, and extend the domain values to implement business rules. This entity also allows the client user to build lists for users to choose values with very little programming.*

There are two different classes of nonidentifying relationships, mandatory and optional. You'll now take a closer look at these in the next two sections.

Mandatory

Mandatory nonidentifying relationships are so called because the migrated column in the child instance is required. When this relationship is implemented, the migrated key will be implemented as NOT NULL.

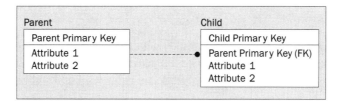

Note that the child entity doesn't have rounded-off corners in this example. This is because both entities are independent, which is because none of the primary key attributes for the child are foreign keys.

Another example of such a relationship might come from a movie rental database.

The relationship might be `Genre <classifies> Movie`, where the `Genre` entity is the one entity, and `Movie` is the many. The mandatory business rule might be that every movie being rented must have a genre so that it can be placed on the shelves.

Optional

You may not always want to force the child to have a value for the migrated key. In this case you'll set the migrated child key to **optional,** which, if implemented in this manner, will dictate allowing null values. Because the nonidentifying relationship denotes that the parent is an attribute of the child, this is the same as having an optional attribute (nullable attribute).

You signify this by an open diamond at the opposite end of the line from the black circle, as shown.

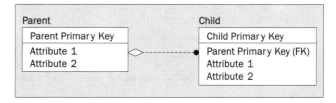

There isn't an optional identifying relationship due to the fact that there may not be any optional attributes in a primary key. This is true for IDEF1X as well as SQL Server 2000.

For a one-to-many optional relationship, consider the following figure.

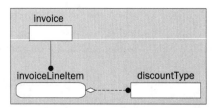

The *invoiceLineItem* entity is where items are placed onto an invoice to receive payment. Then consider that you sometimes will apply a standard discount amount to the line item. The relationship then from the *invoiceLineItem* to the *discountType* entity is an optional one.

Cardinality

The cardinality of the relationship denotes the number of child instances that can be inserted for each parent of that relationship. The following table shows the six cardinality classification types that you can use for relationships.

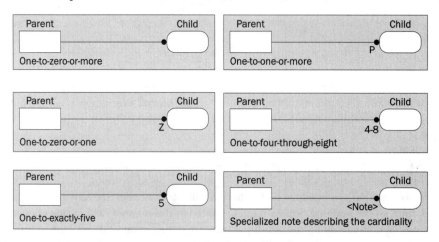

A possible use for the one-to-one-or-more might be to represent the relationship between a guardian and a student in a school database.

This is a good example, because it expresses a relatively complex cardinality situation. It says that for a *guardian* row to exist, a student must exist, but a student row need not have a guardian for you to wish to store their data.

Next, consider the case of a club that has members and certain positions that they should or could fill.

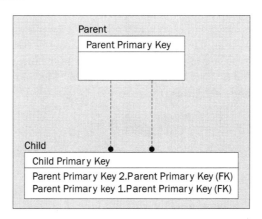

The first example shows that a member can take as many positions as there are possible positions. The second shows that they can only serve in one position, and in the final 0, 1, or 2. They all look about the same, but the Z or 0-2 have far different meanings.

I considered including an example of each of these cardinality types, but in most cases it was too difficult or too silly, so I've merely mentioned a few of the more typical ones. However, it's very nice to have them available in case they do become necessary.

Role Names

A role name is an alternative name you give an attribute when you use it as a foreign key. The purpose of a role name is that you sometimes need to clarify the usage of a migrated key, because either the parent entity is very generic and you want to specify a very specific name, or you have multiple relationships from the same entity. As attribute names must be unique, you have to assign different names for the child row.

You have two relationships from the parent entity to the child entity, and the migrated attributes have been named as [Parent Primary Key 1] and [Parent Primary Key 2]. Note that the name of the column in the migrated attributes for illustrative purposes has been included.

As an example, say you have a *User* entity, and want to store the name or ID of the user who created an *Object* entity. You would end up with a situation like this.

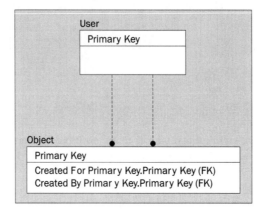

Note that you have two relationships to the *Object* entity from the *User* entity. One is named [Created For Primary Key] and the other is [Created By Primary Key].

Other Types of Relationships

There are a few other, less important relationship types that are less frequently employed. However, knowing about them is extremely important.

Recursive

One of the more difficult relationships to implement, but one of the most important, is the **recursive relationship**, also known as a **self-join**, **hierarchical**, **self-referencing** or **self-relationship**. This is modeled by drawing a nonidentifying relationship not to a different entity, but to the same entity. The migrated key of the relationship is given a role name (I generally add "parent" as a naming convention to the front of the attribute name, but this isn't a necessity).

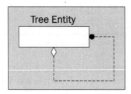

The recursive relationship is useful for creating tree structures, as in the following organization chart.

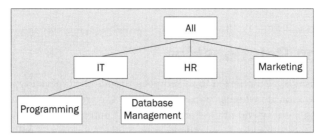

To explain this concept you'll need to look at a set of data that would be used to implement this hierarchy.

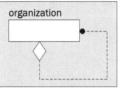

You'll treat the *organizationName* as the primary key and *parentOrganizationName* as the migrated, role-named attribute that indicates the self-reference to the table.

```
organizationName                 parentOrganizationName
-----------------                ----------------------
All                              <null>
IT                               All
HR                               All
Marketing                        All
Programming                      IT
Database Management              IT
```

The org chart can now be rebuilt by starting at "All" and getting its first child, "IT." Then you get the first child of "IT": "Programming." "Programming" has no children, so you go back to "IT" and get its next child, "Database Management," and so on. The recursive relationship is so named because a popular algorithm for implementing such data structures in functional programming languages uses recursion to handle the process simulated in this example.

As one final example, consider the case of a person entity, where you store the name, address, and so on of people that you deal with. If you wish to build this entity with the ability to point to a spouse, you might design the following.

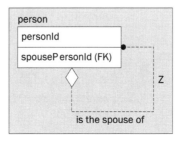

Notice that you also set this as a one-to-zero-or-one relationship, because (in most places) a person may only have a single spouse.

Categorization Relationships

Categorization relationships (also referred to as subtypes) are another special type of one-to-zero-or-one relationship used to indicate whether one entity is a specific type of a generic entity. Note also that there are no black dots on either end of the lines; the specific entities are drawn with rounded-off corners, signifying that they are indeed dependent on the generic entity and will have the primary key of the generic entity migrated to them.

Using this type of relationship you have the following three distinct parts:

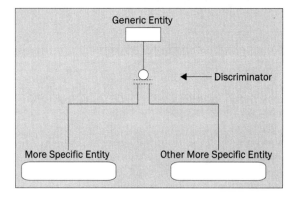

❑   **Generic Entity**: This is an entity that contains all of the attributes that are common to all of the subtyped entities.

❑   **Discriminator**: This is the specification of the attribute that acts as a switch to determine the entity where the additional, more specific information is stored.

❑   **Specific Entity**: This is the place where the specific information is stored, based on the discriminator.

For example, let's look at a video library. If you wanted to store information about each of the videos that you owned, regardless of format, you might build a categorization relationship like the following figure.

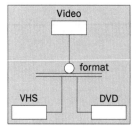

110

These types of relationships are typically known as "is-a" relationships—a VHS is a video, and a DVD is a video.

In this manner, you can store the title, actors, length, and possibly description of the content in the *Video* entity, and then, based on video format (denoted by the discriminator), store the information that is specific to *VHS* tapes or *DVD* in their own separate entities, like special features and menus for DVDs, and long or slow play for VHS tapes.

There are two distinct types of categories: **complete** and **incomplete**. The complete set of categories is modeled with a double line on the discriminator, and the incomplete with a single line.

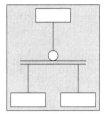
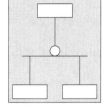

Complete set of categories   *Incomplete set of categories*

The primary difference between the complete and incomplete categories is that in the complete categorization relationship, each generic instance must have one specific instance; in the incomplete case this isn't necessarily true. For example, you might have a complete set of categories as shown here.

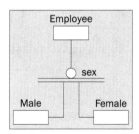

This relationship is read as follows: "An employee *must* be either be male or female." This is certainly a complete category because there are no other recognized sexes. However, look at the following incomplete set of categories.

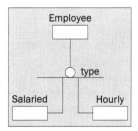

In this case, you have an incomplete subtype, because employees are either salaried or hourly, but there may be other categories, such as contract workers. You may not need to store any additional information about them, so you don't need the specific entity. This relationship is read as: "An employee can be either salaried or hourly or other."

Many-to-Many

The many-to-many relationship is also known as the **nonspecific relationship**, which is actually a better name, but far less well known. It's very common to have many-to-many relationships in your logical models. In fact, the closer you get to a proper database model, the more you find that a large number of relationships will be of the many-to-many type. In the early stages of modeling, it's helpful to define relationships as many-to-many, even if it's obvious that they will likely change during implementation.

Many-to-many relationships are modeled by a line with a solid black dot on either end.

Note that you cannot actually implement this relationship in the physical model, so you sometimes will go directly to a more implementation-specific representation.

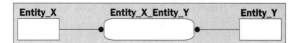

Here the intermediate *Entity_X_Entity_Y* entity is known as a **resolution entity**. In your modeling, you stick with the former representation when you haven't identified any extended attributes to describe the relationship, and the latter representation when you have.

To make that a bit clearer, let's look at the following example.

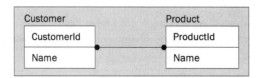

In this situation, you have set up a relationship in which many customers are related to many products. This is a very common situation, because you seldom create specific products for specific customers; rather, any customer can purchase any of the products. At this point of modeling, you would use the many-to-many representation. However, if you discover that the customer can only be related to a product for a certain period of time, you might choose to represent this by the other representation.

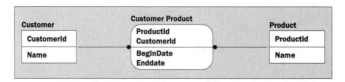

In fact in most cases, you find that the many-to-many relationship requires some additional information to make it complete.

Verb Phrases (Relationship Names)

Relationships are given names called **verb phrases**, which make the relationship between a parent and child entity a readable sentence and incorporate the entity names and the relationship cardinality. The name is usually expressed from parent to child, but can be expressed in the other direction, or even in both directions. The verb phrase is located on the model somewhere close to the line that forms the relationship.

The relationship should be named so that it fits into the following general structure for reading the entire relationship.

> **parent cardinality—parent entity name—relationship name—child cardinality—child entity name**

For example, the following relationship would be read as follows:

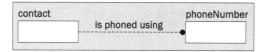

One contact is phoned using zero, one, or more phoneNumber(s).

Of course, the sentence may or may not make perfect logical sense, because this one brings up the question of how a contact is phoned using zero phone numbers. Obviously, if you were trying to present this to a nontechnical person, it would make more sense to read it as follows:

> *One contact is contacted by using a phone using one or more phoneNumber(s) if a phoneNumber exists.*

Obviously the modeling language doesn't take linguistics into consideration when building this specification, but from a technical standpoint, it doesn't matter that the contact is phoned using zero phone numbers; it follows that the contact has no phone number.

Being able to read the relationship helps you to notice obvious problems. For instance, the following relationship looks fine at first glance, as shown in the figure.

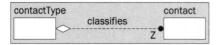

But when it's read like this, it doesn't make logical sense, otherwise why did you even create the contactType?

One contactType classifies zero or one contact

You probably want to correct this situation in your model, as shown in the following figure.

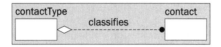

It now reads as follows:

One contactType classifies zero or more contacts.

Note that the type of relationship, whether it's identifying, nonidentifying, optional, or mandatory, makes no difference when reading the relationship.

You can also include a verb phrase that reads from child to parent. For a one-to-many relationship this would be of the following format:

one child row (relationship) *exactly one parent row*

In the case of the first example, you could have added an additional verb phrase (added after the inclusion of a forward slash character "/"):

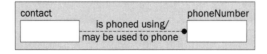

This would be read exactly opposite to the previous examples, as follows:

One phoneNumber may be used to phone exactly one contact

Because you're going from the many to the one, you'll always know that the parent in the relationship will have one related value, and because you're reading in the context of the existence of the child, you can also assume that there is a single child row to consider in the sentence.

Alternate Methods of Relationship Display

In this section, you'll briefly look at two other modeling methodologies that are frequently used when designing databases.

Information Engineering

The IE (Information Engineering) methodology is very well known and widely used. It's really quite popular, and does a very good job of displaying the necessary information. It's also known affectionately as the crow's foot method.

By varying the basic symbols on the end of the line, you can arrive at all of the various possibilities for relationships.

The following table shows the different symbols that you can employ to build relationship representations:

Symbol	Description
	Many: The entity on the end with the crow's foot denotes that there can be greater than one value related to the other entity.
	Optional: Indicates that there doesn't have to be a related instance on this end of the relationship for one to exist on the other. What has been described as zero-or-more as opposed to one-or-more.
	Identifying Relationship: The key of the entity on the other end of the relationship is migrated to this entity.
	Nonrequired Relationship: A set of dashed lines on one end of the relationship line indicates that the migrated key may be null.

The following figure shows the attributes in much the same way that IDEF1X uses them, inside the rectangle.

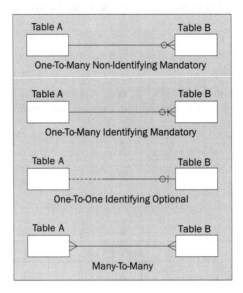

This notation isn't as clean as IDEF1X, but it does a very good job and is likely to be used by some of the documents that you'll come across in your work as a data architect. IE isn't always fully implemented in any tools. However, the circle and the crow's feet are generally implemented properly.

Further details regarding this methodology can be found in the three-volume *Information Engineering* series from Pearson Education.

Chen ERD

The Chen ERD methodology is quite a bit different, but is pretty self-explanatory. In the following figure, you see a very simple diagram with the basics of the Chen diagram.

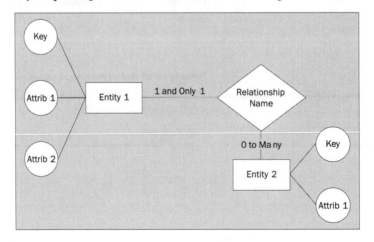

Each entity is again a rectangle; however, the attributes aren't shown in the entity, but are attached to the entity in circles. The primary key is denoted as double underlined. The cardinality for a relationship is denoted in text. In the example, it's *1 and Only 1 Entity1 <relationship name> 0 to Many Entity2.*

The primary reason for including the Chen ERD format is for contrast. At least one other methodology (Bachman) implements attributes in this style, that is, in which the attributes aren't displayed in the rectangle. While I understand the logic behind this (attributes can be thought of as separate objects), I have found that models in this format seemed overly cluttered, even for very small diagrams. It does, however, do an admirable job with the logical model without an overreliance on an arcane symbology to describe cardinality. While I'm not saying it doesn't exist, I personally haven't seen this implemented in a database design tool other than Microsoft Visio, but many of the diagrams found on the Internet will be in this style, so it's worth understanding.

Microsoft SQL Server Diagram Tools

In the Enterprise Manager of SQL Server, a new tool was added to version 7.0 that was pretty neat: a database diagram tool. This also has a fairly interesting manner of displaying entities. The following is an example of a one-to-many relationship.

The primary keys are identified by the little key in an attribute. The relationship is denoted by the line between the entities, with the one end having a key and the many end having an infinity sign.

You can display the entities in several formats, for example by just showing the names of the entities, or by showing all of the attributes, with datatypes.

	Column Name	Data Type	Length	Allow Nulls	
	ParentId	int	4		
	Attribute1	varchar	50		
	Attribute2	varbinary	50	✓	

Parent

In the following graphic, I've made a model of the entire `Northwind` database using the diagramming tool to show that it does in fact do a good job of displaying the model.

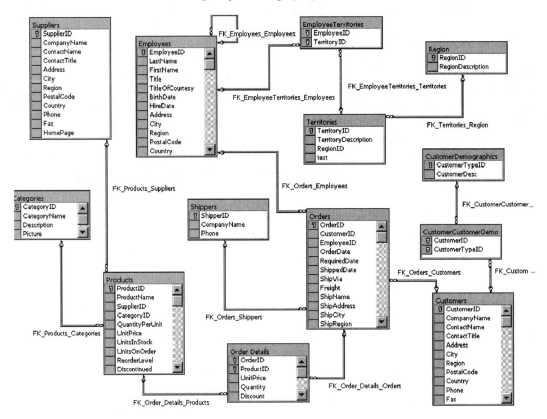

However, while the database diagram tool does have its place, it isn't a full-featured data modeling tool and shouldn't be used as such if possible. You're including the SQL Server modeling methodology because it's included in SQL Server and it's understood that in some situations it's the best tool that you may have access to. It's only a physical modeling tool, but it does give access to all implementation-specific features of SQL Server, including the ability to annotate your tables and columns with descriptive information. It's a great tool for sharing the current structure with database developers. Because it's implementation specific, if you decide to implement a relationship in a trigger it will not know that it exists.

In most cases these tools aren't the optimal way to see actual relationship information that is designed into the database, but it does give a serviceable look at the database structure when needed.

Descriptive Information

By now you've drawn entities, assigned attributes and domains to them, and set up relationships between them, but you aren't quite done. You have learned about naming your entities, attributes, and even your relationships, but even with well-formed names, there may still be confusion as to what exactly an attribute is used for.

You must add comments to the pictures in your model. Comments will let the eventual reader know what was in mind when the model was created. Remember that not everyone who views the models you create will be on the same technical level; some will be nonrelational programmers, or indeed users or (nontechnical) product managers who have no modeling experience.

You've already had a good start on this process in the previous chapter, where you added this information to your Word document. It should be noted that once you find a data modeling tool that you're comfortable with, you'll be able to enter all of the data you entered in the previous chapter and more. This will prove much faster than using a Word document to store all of the information you put into your document, and then transferring it to a data model.

Descriptive information need not be in any special format; it simply needs to be detailed, up-to-date, and capable of answering as many questions as you can anticipate will be asked. Each of these bits of information should be stored in a manner that makes it easy for users to quickly tie it back to the part of the model where it was used, and should be stored either in a document or as metadata in a modeling tool.

You should ask questions such as the following:

❑ What is the object supposed to represent?

❑ How will be it used?

❑ Who might use it?

❑ What are the future plans for the object?

The scope of the descriptions should not extend past the object or entities that are affected. For example, the entity description should refer only to the entity, and not any related entities, relationships, or even attributes unless necessary. Attribute definitions should speak to only the single attribute and where their values might come from.

Maintaining good descriptive information is equivalent to putting decent comments in code. Because the database is often the central part of any computer system, comments at this level can be more important than any others. For example, say you have the following two entities as shown.

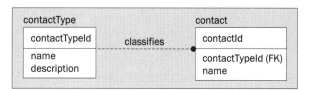

You might have the following very basic set of descriptive information stored to describe the attributes that you've created as shown in the following tables.

The following are entities:

Contact		Persons that can be contacted to do business with
	Attributes	**Description**
	ContactId	Primary key pointer to a contact
	contactTypeId	Primary key pointer to a contactType
	name	The full name of a contact

ContactType		Domain of different contact types
	Attributes	**Description**
	contactTypeId	Primary key pointer to a contactType
	name	The name that the contact type will be uniquely known as
	description	The description of exactly how the contact should be used

The following are relationships:

Parent Entity Name	Phrase	Child EntityName	Definition
ContactType	**Classifies**	Contact	Contact type classification; was required by specifications

Case Study

In the previous chapter, you built a document that has all of the different objects that you need to model. In this case study, you simply want to transfer all of the information that you put in the document and turn it into a set of graphical models where that makes sense.

The first step in data modeling is to model the entities and attributes that you've previously identified.

> *Note: For the rest of the case study, you're usually going to assume that any definitions that you've previously added are contained in the model. You cannot expand all of the columns to show definitions. You will, however, try to give definitions for all new objects that you create.*

So you simply create entities for each of your objects adding all of the attributes, choosing a base type domain as shown in the following figure.

```
Account                    Bank                    Statement
┌─────────────────┐        ┌────────────┐          ┌──────────────────────┐
│                 │        │            │          │                      │
├─────────────────┤        ├────────────┤          ├──────────────────────┤
│ Number          │        │ Name       │          │ Type                 │
│ Balance Date    │        │            │          │ PreviousBalance      │
│ Running Total   │        └────────────┘          │ PreviousBalanceData  │
└─────────────────┘                                │ CurrentBalance       │
                                                   │ StatementDate        │
                                                   │ TotalDebits          │
                                                   │ TotalCredits         │
Transaction                DirectWithdrawal        │ BalancingItems       │
┌─────────────────┐        ┌────────────────┐      └──────────────────────┘
│                 │        │                │
├─────────────────┤        ├────────────────┤
│ Date            │        │ WithdrawalDate │
│ Number          │        │ Number         │      CheckRegister
│ Description     │        │ Amount         │      ┌────────────────┐
│ Amount          │        └────────────────┘      │                │
│ Type            │                                 ├────────────────┤
└─────────────────┘                                 │ RegisterType   │
                                                   └────────────────┘


Check                      Deposit                 Payee
┌─────────────────┐        ┌────────────────┐      ┌────────────────┐
│                 │        │                │      │                │
├─────────────────┤        ├────────────────┤      ├────────────────┤
│ UsageType       │        │ Date           │      │ Name           │
│ Number          │        │ Number         │      │ Address        │
│ DateWritten     │        │ Description    │      │ PhoneNumber    │
│ Amount          │        │ Amount         │      └────────────────┘
│ Memo            │        └────────────────┘
│ Signature       │
└─────────────────┘
```

Now you have all of the entities from the previous chapter's case study in a far more compact and easy-to-follow format.

The next step is to identify any relationships in which the two objects are basically the same thing, and implement them as subtypes. You have one such example in your case study in that the *check*, *deposit*, and *directWithdrawal* entities are all just types of transactions.

Note that you've added the type attribute as your discriminator for the subtypes, and have removed all of the attributes that were duplicates of the ones that were already in the transaction entity.

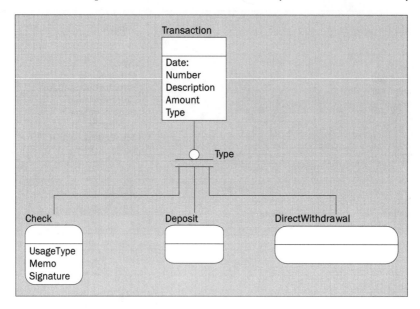

The next step is to add and name all of the relationships on the model. You still haven't added primary keys to the model, so you don't have any migration of keys at this point. It makes the implementation cleaner to start with. You'll actually add them as your last step.

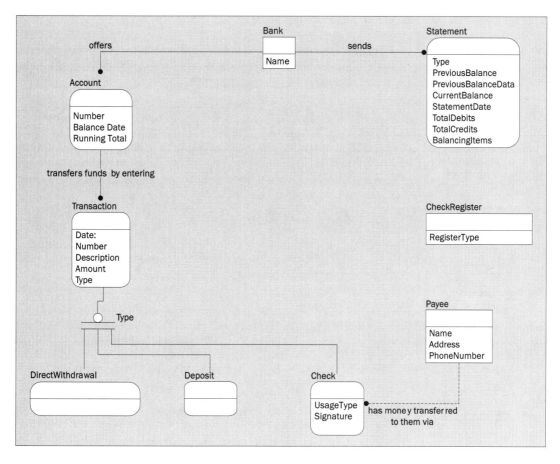

Notice that you see the payee-to-check relationship as a nonidentifying relationship. This is because a check isn't identified by its payee, because the payee is merely an attribute of a check that's nevertheless required.

The final step in building your initial model is to identify any natural unique keys in the data. For instance, in the *account* entity, the number is likely to be a unique value. In the *bank* entity, you have a name of the bank that should be unique. *Transactions* will probably have a unique number to identify them. Your guesses will sometimes be right and sometimes not quite so right, but they are logical guesses. As always, any time a guess is made it must be verified, and the model and supporting documentation should always give an indication of the fact that it was a guess, not a given requirement.

For example, in the *transaction* entity you've set the *number* attribute as unique. This makes logical sense on first pass, but as you progress you'll (hopefully) realize that a transaction's number is only unique for a given account. There are several wrong ways to deal with this situation such as appending the number of the account to the start of every transaction. (This is what is known as a **smart** or **intelligent** key and it may be hard to readily decipher, because it doesn't stand out on the data model.) The right implementation will be to add the *account* entity's primary key to the alternate key you've devised.

123

This will mean that your model now looks like this figure.

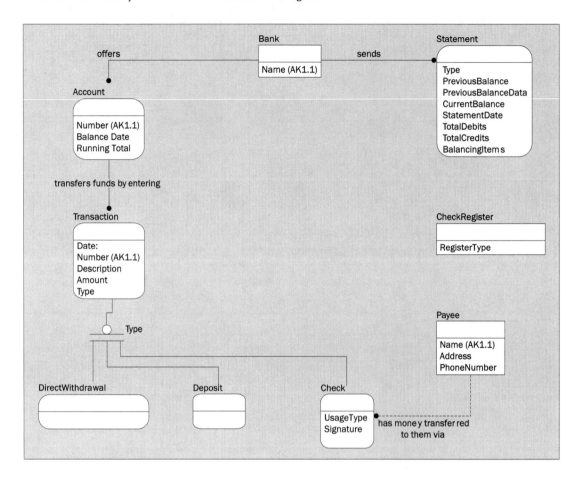

In this model, you'll use meaningless pointers as the primary key to make it clear where the key is migrated from. The choice of primary key, even during logical modeling, is largely a personal choice, but in this book I'm advising that you stick with pointer-oriented primary keys during the logical phase. However, as mentioned earlier, by not choosing a proper primary key at this point, you don't end up with a confusing model developed from keys migrating about until you aren't sure where they initially originated from. Note that every entity gets their own ID column and may also get migrated keys from any entities that they are dependent upon.

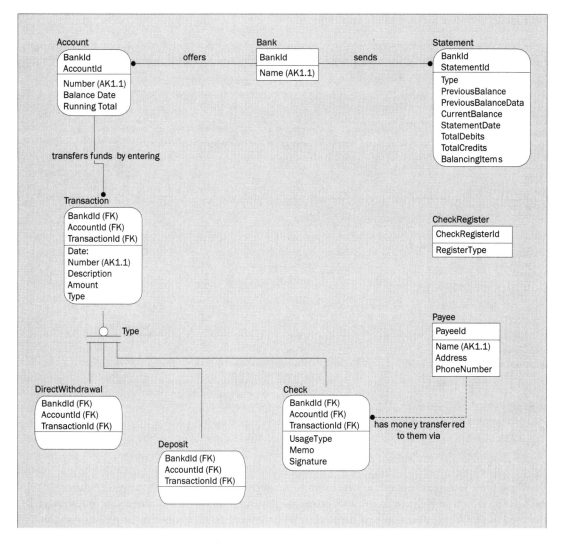

The final step you need to take is to choose logical domains for each of the attributes. The idea at this point is to try to group like attributes in the same domain, as, for example, in the case of the *date* attribute in *transaction,* the *previousBalanceDate* in *statement,* and the *balanceDate* in the **account** entity. For the primary key attributes, you'll give them a domain of primary key, and leave it at that for now.

Your model now looks like the following figure.

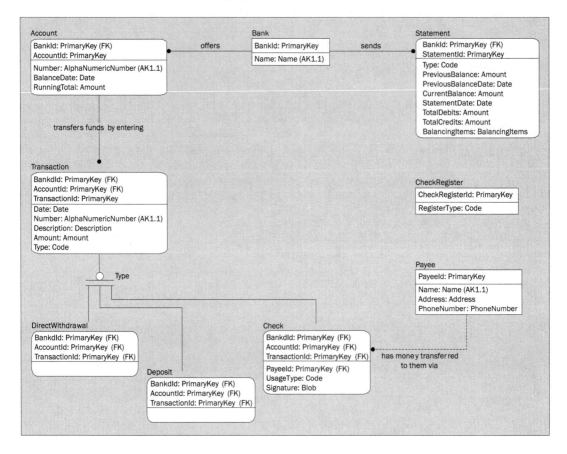

You'll continue to assign domains to every one of the attributes that you create as you continue through the logical modeling phase. At this stage, as shown in the following tables, you've discovered and used the following domains, which you should also make certain to describe as well as you can.

Address	Includes an entire address
AlphaNumericNumber	A value that is generally referred to as a number but actually allows alphanumeric data
Amount	A monetary value
BalancingItems	A group of items you need in order to balance account
Blob	Picture, document store in Binary Large Object format
Code	A value used as a kind of a text pointer
Date	Date value
Name	The readable tag that is assigned to an instance of an entity for easy access
PhoneNumber	Entire phone number
PrimaryKey	Used as a pointer to an instance

You won't be doing much more in terms of assigning predicates to them at this point, because you'll be making quite a few changes throughout the process, and you'll no doubt discover more domains (and remove a few). You will however keep up with the process of adding domains, any time you create a new attribute, because your model becomes more mature.

The model is beginning to get a bit larger and shows signs of an implementable structure. You won't be making a lot of changes to the structure in the upcoming chapters, but the final structure will still vaguely resemble what you have here.

At this point, you'll take the definitions that you gathered previously into your attributes. As an example, let's take the *statement* entity.

Statement	Represents a document (paper or electronic) that comes from the bank once every calendar month that tells you what the bank thinks you have spent
Attributes	**Description**
BankId	Primary key identifier for a bank
StatementId	Primary key identifier for a statement instance
Type	Identifies the type of statement gotten from the bank
PreviousBalance	Specifies what the balance was supposed to be after the last statement was balanced
PreviousBalanceDate	Specifies the date that the account was last balanced
CurrentBalance	Specifies what the balance of the account is after all of the items in the statement have been reconciled
StatementDate	The date that the current statement was issued
TotalCredits	Sum of all items that have added money to the account during the statement period
TotalDebits	Sum of all items that have subtracted money from the account during the statement period
BalancingItems	All of the items that the bank has processed and is now reporting back to you

Best Practices

❑ **Table Names**: Usually shouldn't be plural–the name of the table describes a single instance (or row) of the entity, much like an object-oriented programming object name describes the instance of an object, not a group of them.

❑ **Attribute Names:** Generally, it isn't necessary to repeat the entity name in the attribute name, except for the primary key. The entity name is implied by the attribute's inclusion in the entity.

The chosen attribute name should reflect precisely what is contained in the attribute and how it relates to the entity. As with entities, no abbreviations are to be used in the logical naming of attributes. Every word should be spelled out in its entirety. If any abbreviation is to be used, due to some naming standard currently in place, then a method should be put into place to make sure that it's used consistently, as discussed earlier in the chapter.

❑ **Relationships**: Name relationships with **verb phrases**, which make the relationship between a parent and child entity a readable sentence. The sentence expresses the relationship using the entity names and the relationship cardinality. The relationship sentence is a very powerful tool for communicating with nontechnical members of the project team like customer representatives.

❑ **Define every object created so it's clear what was in mind when the object was created**: This is a tremendously valuable habit to form because it will pay off later when questions are asked about what something is, and it will serve as documentation to give to programmers or users.

Summary

In this chapter, you looked at taking the textual design that you arrived at in the previous chapter, and putting it into a more concise graphic format.

You were introduced to a specific modeling type, namely IDEF1X, and took a detailed look at the symbology you'll need in your design work. The base set of symbols that you outlined will enable you to fully model your logical databases (and later physical databases) in great detail.

The last point to be made is that for every entity, and every attribute you discover during the process you should at the very least identify the following detailed properties:

Property	Purpose
Name	Name that will fully describe the purpose for the entity or attribute.
Description	Full explanation that when read within the context of the attribute and entity will explain what the purpose of the attribute is for the programmer and user alike.
Predicates (Domain)	Generally, predicates indicate ANY rules that govern your data in or out of your database. It's generally acceptable to simply set a domain (single column predicate based on constraints and datatypes during physical modeling) and document other predicates at a table or database level.

You'll use this descriptive information later in the process to build your check constraints, your triggers, and so on, in order to protect and use the data to produce a bulletproof data store. In this way the user can have confidence that what they specified and agreed to will indeed be what is stored in the database.

Having considered the symbology required to model your database, you now need to go on to consider normalizing your design, which you'll do in the following chapters.

6

Normalization Techniques

No matter what database system is being designed, normalization is a vital process. Normalization ensures that the database contained within the system is both accurate and doesn't contain duplicated information. Normalization can be summed up in a single sentence: "Every entity in a database needs to have a single theme" (see http://www.gslis.utexas.edu/~l384k11w/normstep.html). By theme, what is being said is that one entity models one "thing" and is used for just one purpose.

The term "normalized database" is used quite frequently, but it really is a misnomer, because there is no true or false criterion to determine if a database is normal, or otherwise. Normalization is a matter of levels, or steps. The different levels of normalization of a database indicate how well the structure adheres to the recognized standards of database design; although after the third level there is some question as to how useful the further levels are. You'll consider these arguments in the next chapter; this chapter will focus only on the first three levels of normalization, plus one additional level, which is a clearer restatement of numbers two and three.

As you might have guessed, database structure is a polarizing topic for the database architect. Disagreements often arise between database architects and client developers over how to store data. Why? Because no two database designs are the same and there are always several correct ways to structure a database, not to mention that it can take a good deal more time initially to build applications on top of properly structured tables. Logically, if you stored all of your data in one table, you would only need a single interface to modify the data. You can develop this much faster than if you had twenty tables, right? For the most part, there is no easy way to defend this statement. It's clearly true on one level, but completely wrong on many others. This chapter and the next will look at some of the problems with the statement, showing some of the programming anomalies that will be caused by not breaking your entities down into smaller "single-themed" packages.

An OLTP (online transaction processing) database that isn't extremely normalized is generally quicker to build for a client the first time because there are far fewer tables. This benefit soon disappears when minor user changes are required after the system is in production. Expert database designers realize that changes in data structure have large costs associated with them. When there are no rows in a table and no code to access the tables, structure changes may simply take minutes. When you've added a hundred rows to a table, with seven of its related tables having ten rows each, and programmers having written hundreds of lines of code, you can easily burn an hour of prime video game time changing the table structures, domains, and supporting code. Data conversion is also a problem, because if you have to change the table, then you have to fit existing data into the new structures. If there are a million rows in the table, forget about it. Once you've changed the table structure, you then have to change all of the code that accesses the table. Normalization also saves a great deal of storage space, because a major goal is to avoid repeating data. Note also that you do normalization as part of the logical modeling phase. This is because its implementation isn't specific. No matter what RDBMS (relational database management system) you use, you still have the same goals for the normalization process.

The process of normalization also ensures consistent entity structures, which will help you avoid modifying your existing entities in the future. If you've done a decent job on the requirements portion of the project, when you're finished, the normalization process should have weeded out most of the trouble areas in the database. Obviously I'm not saying that it can't be changed once the design has been implemented, because expansions and changes in business practice could create much needed amendments. However, it's easier to add new information and new entities to a fully normalized database.

This chapter and the next will go through the recognized techniques of normalization, and you'll see that the results of normalization minimize the inclusion of duplicated information, and make entities easier to manage and modify as well as more secure—although it will create a lot more entities.

Why Normalize?

There are many reasons to normalize data structures, as you'll see in the following sections.

Reducing NULLs

NULLs can be very detrimental to data integrity and performance, and can make querying the database very confusing. However, NULLs are a tricky subject in their own right; a lot of space can be devoted to how SQL Server 2000 handles them and how to avoid them or minimize their impact. So, rather than digressing here, the rules of NULL handling will be covered in Chapter 14 in more depth. It's enough here to note that the process of normalization can lead to there being fewer NULL values contained in the database, a definite good thing.

Eliminating Redundant Data

Any editable piece of data that isn't a primary key of a table (or part of one) but is a foreign key (or part of one) that occurs more than once in the database, is an error waiting to happen. No doubt you've all seen it before: a person's name stored in two places, then one version gets modified and the other doesn't–and suddenly you have two names where before there was just one.

The problem with storing redundant data will be very obvious to anyone who has moved to a new address. Every government authority requires its loyal citizens to individually change their address information on tax forms, driver's licenses, auto registrations, and so on, rather than one change being made centrally.

Avoiding Unnecessary Coding

Extra programming in triggers, stored procedures, or even in the business logic tier can be required to handle the poorly structured data and this in turn can impair performance significantly. This isn't to mention that extra coding increases the chance of introducing new bugs into a labyrinth of code required to maintain redundant data. Many database projects fail to meet their potential due to the enormous requirement of keeping redundant data in sync.

Maximizing Clustered Indexes

Clustered indexes are used to natively order a table in SQL Server. They are special indexes in which the physical storage of the data matches the order of the indexed columns, which allow for better performance of queries using that index. Typically, the indexes are used to order a table in a convenient manner to enhance performance. Each table may have only a single clustered index. The more clustered indexes in the database the less sorting that will need to be performed, and the more likely it is that queries will be able to use the MERGE JOIN–a special type of very fast join technique that requires sorted data. Sorting is a very costly operation that should be avoided if possible. Clustered indexes and indexes in general will be covered in great detail in Chapters 10 and 11.

Lowering the Number of Indexes per Table

The fewer indexes per table, the fewer the number of **pages** that might be moved around on a modification or insertion into the table. By pages, we're referring to pages of memory. In SQL Server, data and indexes are broken up and stored on 8KB pages. Of course SQL Server doesn't keep the whole database in memory at any one time. What it does do is keep a "snapshot" of what is currently being looked at. To keep the illusion of having the whole database in memory, SQL Server moves the pages in and out of a high-speed fast-access storage space when those pages are required, but this space can only contain a limited number of pages at any one time. The pages are therefore moved in and out of the space on the principle that the most frequently accessed remain in. The operation of moving pages in and out of memory is costly in terms of performance, and especially painful if one or more clients are twiddling their thumbs waiting for an operation to complete. Therefore, to keep performance as high as possible, you should minimize page transfers as much as possible.

When a table has many columns, it may be required to apply quite a few indexes on a table to avoid retrieval performance problems. While these indexes may give great retrieval gains, maintaining indexes can be very costly. Indexes are a very tricky topic because they have both positive and negative effects on performance and require a fine balance for optimal utilization.

Keeping Tables Thin

When we refer to a thinner table, we mean that the table has a relatively small number of columns. Thinner tables mean more data fits on a given page in the database, thus allowing the database server to retrieve more rows for a table in a single read than would be otherwise possible. This all means that there will be more tables in the system when you're finished normalizing. There is, however, a common sense cutoff point (no single column tables!). Bear in mind that in a typical OLTP system, very few columns of data are touched on every data modification, and frequently queries are used to gather the summary of a single value, like an account balance.

The Process of Normalization

If you recall your single sentence description of normalization from the first paragraph of this chapter— "Every table in the database needs to have a single theme"—you can take this to mean that each table should endeavor to represent a single entity. This concept will become more apparent over the next two chapters as you work through the process of normalization.

In 1972, E. F. Codd presented the world with the First Normal Form, based on the shape of the data, and the Second and Third Normal Forms, based on functional dependencies in the data. These were further refined by Codd and Boyce in the Boyce-Codd Normal Form. This chapter will cover these four in some detail.

During the discussion of normalization in this chapter and the next, you'll step through each of the different types, looking to eliminate all of the violations you find by following the rules specified in each type. You might decide to ignore some of the violations for expediency. It's also critical not only to read through each form in the book, but to consider each form while performing logical modeling.

Normalization is a process that can be broken down into three categories:

❑   Attribute shape

❑   Relationships between attributes

❑   Advanced relationship resolution

The discussion of advanced relationship topics will occur in the next chapter.

Attribute Shape

When you investigate the shape of attributes, you're looking at how the data is allowed to look in any single attribute. The **First Normal Form** deals with this topic, and is one of the most important normal forms.

This form is also used in the definition of the relational model of databases, and the definition of the First Normal Form is one of Codd's Twelve Rules, which aren't actually about normalization, but rather a set of rules that define a relational database. These rules are listed and discussed in Appendix A (see the Apress web site).

Entities in First Normal Form will have the following characteristics:

❑ All attributes must be atomic; that is, only one single value represented in a single attribute in a single instance of an entity

❑ All instances in a table must contain the same number of values

❑ All instances in a table must be different

First Normal Form violations manifest themselves in the physical model with messy data handling situations as you'll see shortly.

All Attributes Must Be Atomic

An attribute can only represent one single value; it may not be a group. This means there can be no arrays, no delimited data, and no multivalued attributes. To put it another way, the values stored in an attribute cannot be split into smaller parts. As examples, you'll explore some common violations of this rule of the First Normal Form.

E-mail Addresses

In an e-mail message, the e-mail address is typically stored in a format such as the following:

```
name1@domain1.com;name2@domain2.com;name3@domain3.com.
```

This is a clear violation of the First Normal Form because you're trying to store more than one e-mail address in a single e-mail attribute. Each e-mail address should form one separate attribute.

Names

Consider the name "John Q Public." This is less obviously a problem, but from what you understand about people's names (in English-based cultures at least) it is clear that you have the first name, middle initial, and last name. After breaking down the name into three parts, you get the attributes `first_name`, `middle_initial` (or `middle_name`, which I prefer), and `last_name`. This is usually fine, since a person's name in the US is generally considered to have three parts. In some situations, this may not be enough, and the number of parts may not be known until the user enters the data. Knowing the data requirements is very important in these kinds of situations.

Telephone Numbers

Consider the case of the telephone number. American telephone numbers take the form "1-423-555-1212" plus a possible extension number. From the previous examples, you can see that there are several values embedded in that telephone number, not to mention possible extensions. Additionally, there is frequently the need to store more than just American telephone numbers in a database. The decision on how to handle this situation may be totally based on how often the users store international phone numbers, because it would be a really hard task to build a table or set of entities to handle every situation.

So, for an American-style telephone number, you would need five attributes for each of the following parts in C-AAA-EEE-NNNN-XXXX:

- ❏ (C) Country code: This is the one that you dial for numbers that aren't within the area code, and signals to the phone that you're dialing a nonlocal number.

- ❏ (AAA) Area code: Indicates a calling area that is located within a state.

- ❏ (EEE) Exchange: Indicates a set of numbers within an area code.

- ❏ (NNNN) Number: Number used to make individual phone numbers unique.

- ❏ (XXXX) Extension: A number that must be dialed once after connecting using the previous numbers.

One of the coding examples later in this section will cover the sorts of issues that come up with storing phone numbers.

Addresses

It should be clear by now that all of an address should be broken up into attributes for street address, city, state, and postal code (from here on you'll ignore the internationalization factor, for brevity). However, street address can be broken down, in most cases, into number, street name, suite number, apartment number, and post office box. You'll look at street addresses again shortly.

IP Addresses

IP addresses are a very interesting case because they appear to be four pieces of data, formed like BY1.BY2.BY3.BY4 where BY is short for byte. This appears to be four different attributes, but is actually a representation of a single unsigned integer value based on the mathematical formula $(BY1 * 256^3) + (BY2 * 256^2) + (BY3 * 256^1) + (BY4 * 256^0)$. Therefore, say you have an IP address 24.32.1.128 that could be stored as $404750720 = (24 * 256^3) + (32 * 256^2) + (1 * 256^1) + (128)$. How the value is actually stored will depend in great part to what will be done with the data, for example:

❑ If the IP address is used as four distinct values, you might organize it in four different attributes, possibly named `ipAddressPart1`, `ipAddressPart2`, `ipAddressPart3`, and `ipAddressPart4`. Note that because there will always be exactly four parts, this type of storage doesn't violate the First Normal Form rules: All instances in an entity must contain the same number of values. This is covered in the next section.

❑ One valid reason to store the value as a single value is range checking. To determine when one IP address falls between the two other IP addresses, storing the addresses as integers allows you to simply search for data with a where clause, such as the following: "where `ipAddress` is between `ipAddressLow` and `ipAddressHigh`".

One thing should be clear however, in logical modeling; it's enough to understand that there is an IP address, and that it is in fact one value. While interesting to consider the implications of how you model and store the value, both storage possibilities are equivalent in that in the end you have some representation of the IP address. You may store it as either or both possible values (only one editable value, however) when you actually come to implement your system.

All Instances in an Entity Must Contain the Same Number of Values

This is best illustrated with a quick example. If you're building an entity that stores a person's name, then, if one row has one name, all rows must only have one name. If they might have two, all instances must be able to have two. If they may have a different number, you have to deal with this a different way.

An example of a violation of this rule of the First Normal Form can be found in entities that have several attributes with the same base name suffixed (or prefixed) with a number, such as `address_line_1`, `address_line_2`, and so on. Usually this is an attempt to allow multiple values for a single attribute in an entity. In the rare cases where there is always precisely the same number of values, then there is technically no violation of the First Normal Form. Even in such cases, it still isn't generally a good design decision, because users can change their minds frequently. To overcome all of this, you would create a child entity to hold the values in the malformed entity. This will also allow you to have a virtually unlimited number of values where the previous solution had a finite (and small) number of possible values. One of the issues to deal with is that the child rows created will require sequencing information to get the actual rows properly organized for usage. Note that the actual implementation of addresses will certainly be based on requirements for the system that is being created.

You can use cardinality rules as described in the previous chapter to constrain the number of possible values. If you need to choke things back because your model states that you only need a maximum of two children, and a minimum of one child, cardinality provides the mechanism for this.

All Occurrences of a Row Type in an Entity Must Be Different

This one seems obvious, but needs to be stated. Basically, this indicates that every First Normal Form entity must have a primary (or unique) key. Take care, however, because just adding an artificial key to an entity might technically make the entity comply with the letter of the rule, but certainly not the purpose. The purpose is that no two rows represent the same thing: Because an artificial key has no meaning by definition, it will not fix the problem.

Another issue is keys that use a date and time value to differentiate between rows. If the date and time value is part of the identification of the row, like a calendar entry or a log row, this is acceptable. If the value is simply used like the artificial key to force uniqueness (like indicating when the row was created) then it's a less than desirable solution.

Programming Anomalies Avoided by the First Normal Form

Violations of the First Normal Form are obvious and often very awkward if the columns affected are frequently accessed. The following examples will identify some of the situations that you can avoid by putting your entities in the First Normal Form.

Note that for these programming anomalies you'll switch over into using tables, rather than entities. This is because any issues you overlook now will eventually be manifested in your physical structures. It also gives some detail as to *why* this process is actually useful in your physical tables, and not just academic hoo-haa.

Modifying Lists in a Single Column

The big problem with First Normal Form violations is that relational theory and SQL aren't set up to handle nonatomic columns. Considering the previous example of the e-mail addresses attribute, suppose that you have a table named person with the following schema:

```
CREATE TABLE person
(
    personId int NOT NULL IDENTITY,
    name varchar(100) NOT NULL,
    emailAddress varchar(1000) NOT NULL
)
```

If you let users have more than one e-mail address and store it in a single e-mail address attribute, your emailAddress column might look like the following: "Davidsons@d.com;ldavidson@email.com".

Also consider that many different users in the database might use the `Davidsons@d.com` e-mail address. If you need to change the e-mail address from `Davidsons@d.com` to `Davidsons@domain.com`, you would need to execute code like the following for every person that uses this e-mail address:

```
UPDATE person
SET emailAddress = replace(emailAddress,'Davidsons@d.com',
        'Davidsons@domain.com')
WHERE emailAddress like '%Davidsons@d.com%'
```

This code doesn't seem like trouble, but what about the case where there is also the e-mail address `theDavidsons@d.com`? You would have to take that into account, and it would at the very least be messy. If the e-mail address were split off as its own table apart from the person entity, it would be easier and cleaner to deal with.

Modifying Multipart Values

The programming logic required to change part of the multipart values can be very confusing. Take, for example, the case of telephone area codes. In the United States, you have more phones, pagers, cell phones, and so on than the creators of the area code system ever thought of, and so the communications companies frequently change or introduce new area codes.

If all values are stored in atomic containers, updating the area code would take a single, easy-to-follow, one-line SQL statement like this:

```
UPDATE phoneNumber
SET areaCode = '423'
WHERE areaCode = '615' AND exchange IN ('232','323',…,'989')
```

Instead, if the phone number is stored in unformatted text, you get the following:

```
UPDATE phoneNumber
SET phoneNumber = REPLACE(phoneNumber,'-615-','-423-')
WHERE phoneNumber LIKE '_-615-___-____'
    AND substring(phoneNumber,7,3) IN ('232','323',…,'989') --area codes generally
                                                            --change for certain
                                                            --exchanges
```

This example requires perfect formatting of the phone number data to work, and unless that is forced upon the users, this is unlikely to be the case.

Modifying Rows with Variable Numbers of Facts

One of the main problems with allowing variable numbers of facts in a given row, is dealing with the different situations that occur when one needs to deal with just one of the columns instead of the other. Say you have a very basic structured table such as the following:

```
CREATE TABLE payments
(
    paymentsId int NOT NULL IDENTITY,    accountId int NOT NULL,
    payment1 money NOT NULL,
    payment2 money NULL
)
```

Wherever the user has to make two payments (for some reason), he would be required to enter a payment as the following code snippet shows:

```
UPDATE payments
SET payment1 = case WHEN payment1 IS NULL THEN 1000.00 ELSE payment1 END,
    payment2 = case WHEN payment1 IS NOT NULL AND payment2 IS NULL THEN
        1000.00 ELSE payment2 END
WHERE accountId = 1
```

Of course, you probably will not be using SQL to deal with columns such as this, but even if this logic is done on the client side by giving multiple blocks for payments, or you predetermine which of the payments needs to be made, it should still be clear that it's going to be problematic to deal with.

The alternative would be to have a table that's built like this:

```
CREATE TABLE payment
(
    paymentId int NOT NULL IDENTITY,
    accountId int NOT NULL, --foreign key to account table
    date datetime NOT NULL,
    amount money
)
```

Then, adding a payment would be as simple as adding a new row to the payment table as follows:

```
INSERT payment (accountId, date, amount)
VALUES (1, 'June 12 2000', $300.00)
```

This is certainly a better solution. One thing to note here is that date is seemingly not an atomic datatype (in other words, it is a multivalued column). In fact, SQL Server simply has a datetime datatype that can be thought of as several columns all rolled up into one: day, month, year, hour, minute, seconds, milliseconds, and so on. In all actuality, it technically isn't a problem, because what the column stores is the number of ticks (.003 second per) since a date in the past. The only problem is you quite often deal with the date value and the time value separately.

The `datetime` datatype is used often for convenience reasons, but it gives you quite the same issues as if it were not in the First Normal Form. Because of this, there are a host of functions (`DATEPART`, `DATEDIFF`) in SQL Server designed to make up for the fact that `datetime` and `smalldatetime` aren't proper relational datatypes. There are situations in which it's prudent to implement your own date or time user-defined datatypes and deal with time variables in a reasonable manner.

Clues That Existing Data Isn't in First Normal Form

Next you're going to take a look at how you might go about recognizing whether the data in a given database is already in First Normal Form or not.

Data That Contains Nonalphanumeric Characters

Nonalphabetic characters include commas, brackets, parentheses, pipe characters, and so on. These act as warning signs that you're dealing with a multivalued column. However, be careful not to go too far. For instance, if you were designing a solution to hold a block of text, you have probably normalized too much if you have a word entity, a sentence entity, and a paragraph entity (if you had already been considering it, give yourself three points for thinking ahead). This clue is more applicable to entities that have delimited lists.

Column Names with Numbers at the End

As noted previously, an obvious example of column names with numbers at the end would be finding entities with *child1*, *child2*, and so on, attributes or, my favorite, *UserDefined1*, *UserDefined2*, and others. These are usually pretty messy to deal with and should be candidates for their own table. They don't have to be wrong; for example there always exist two values–this is perfectly proper–but be careful that what is thought of as always, is actually always. Often there will arise "exceptions" that will cause the solution to fail. "A person always has two forms of identification noted in columns ID1 and ID2, except when the manager says they don't have to" In this case always doesn't mean always. `Coordinate_1`, `Coordinate_2` might be acceptable, because it will always require two coordinates to find a point in a two-dimensional space, never any more, or never any less.

These kinds of columns are a very common holdover from the days of flat file databases. Multitable data access was costly, so they put many columns in a single table. This is very detrimental for relational database systems.

Relationships Between Attributes

The next normal forms you'll look at are concerned with the relationships between attributes in an entity and most importantly, the key in that entity. These normal forms deal with minimizing improper functional dependencies. As discussed in Chapter 3, being functionally dependent implies that the output of a function on one value (call it Value1) is *always* the exact same value (call it Value2): Value2 is functionally dependent on Value1.

For example, consider the following situation. You have three values: Owner Name, Product Type, and Serial Number. Serial Numbers imply a particular Product Type, so they are functionally dependent. If you change the Product Type but fail to change the Serial Number, then your Serial Number and Product Type will no longer match and the three values will no longer be of any value. Because the two values are functionally dependent on one another, then they both must be modified.

On this note, let's say that you have two sets of the same values, each alike. If you change the non-key values on one of the sets, and not the others, then there are two sets with the same key, with different values. Now the unique identifier refers to two different values, usually not a desirable condition, and certainly not within a single table. The normal forms you'll look at for the rest of this chapter deal with making sure there are none of these relationships "hiding" in entities.

The following quote will help you understand what the Second Normal Form, Third Normal Form, and Boyce-Codd Normal Form are concerned with:

> *Non-key attributes must provide a detail about the key, the whole key, and nothing but the key.*

This means that non-key attribute have to further describe the key of the entity, and not describe any other attributes. The forms that deal with relationships between attributes are as follows:

- ❑ Second Normal Form
- ❑ Third Normal Form
- ❑ Boyce-Codd Normal Form

Second Normal Form

The first attribute relationship normal form is the **Second Normal Form**. An entity complying with Second Normal Form has to have the following characteristics:

- ❑ The entity must be in the First Normal Form
- ❑ Each attribute must be a fact describing the entire key

> **The Second Normal Form is only relevant when a composite key (a key composed of two or more columns) exists in the entity.**

The Entity Must Be in the First Normal Form

This is very important; it's essential to go through each step of the normalization process to eliminate problems in data. It may be hard to locate the Second Normal Form problems if you still have First Normal Form problems. Otherwise, some of the problems you're trying to fix in this rule may show up in any misshapen attributes not dealt with in the previous rule.

Each Non-key Attribute Must Describe the Entire Key

What is being described here is that each non-key attribute must depict the entity described by **all** attributes in the key, and not simply parts. If this isn't true and any of the non-key attributes are functionally dependent on a subset of the attributes in the key, then the attributes will be data modification anomalies. For example, consider the following structure:

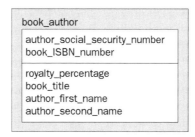

The book_ISBN_number attribute uniquely identifies the book, and author_social_security_number uniquely identifies the author. Hence, these two columns create one key that uniquely identifies an author for a book. The problem is with the other attributes. The royalty_percentage attribute defines the royalty that the author is receiving for the book, so this refers to the entire key. The book_title describes the book, but doesn't describe the author at all. The same goes for the author_first_name and author_last_name attributes. They describe the author, but not the book at all.

This is a prime example of a functional dependency. For every value in the book_ISBN_number column, there must exist the same book title and author (since it's the same book). But for every book_ISBN_number, it isn't true that you'll definitely have the same royalty_percentage–this is actually dependent on *both* the author and the book, and not one or the other, because when books are cowritten, the split might be based on many factors, such as celebrity, how many copies of the book are produced, and so on.

Hence you have problems, so you need to create three separate entities to store this data.

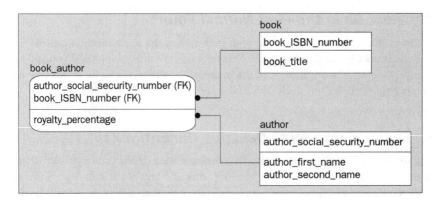

After you split the entities, you'll see that the royalty_percentage attribute is still a fact that describes the author writing the book, the book_title is now an attribute describing the entity defined by the book_ISBN_number, and the author's name attributes are attributes of the author entity, identified by the author_social_security_number.

Note that the book to book_author relationship is an identifying type relationship. Second Normal Form violations are usually logically modeled as identifying relationships where the primary key of the new entity is migrated to the entity where the original problem occurred.

The previous illustration demonstrates this concept quite well. In the corrected example you have isolated the functional dependencies so that attributes that are functionally dependent on another attribute are functionally dependent on the key.

Because there are no columns that aren't functionally dependent on a part of the key, these entities are in the Second Normal Form.

Programming Problems Avoided by the Second Normal Form

All of the programming issues that arise with the Second Normal Form, as well as the Third and Boyce-Codd Normal Forms, deal with functional dependencies. The programming issue is quite simple. Consider the data you're modeling, and how it would be affected if it were physicalized, and if you executed a statement like this, where you're updating an attribute that clearly represents a singular thing (in this case a book's title):

```
UPDATE book_author
SET book_title = 'Database Design'
WHERE book_ISBN_number = '923490328948039'
```

If it were possible to touch more than one row, there are problems with your structures.

The crux of the problems are that many programmers don't have their database design thinking caps on when they are churning out applications, so you get tables created with client screens like this one.

Consider what happens if you use this screen to change the title of a multiauthor book in a database that has book_author tables like the one shown in the first diagram in the previous section, "Each Non-Key Attribute Must Describe the Entire Key." If the book has two authors, there will be two book_author tables for this book. Now a user opens the editing screen and changes the title, as shown here. When he saves the change, it will only alter the book_author table for Fred Smith, not the book_author table for his coauthor. The two book_author tables, originally for the same book, now show different titles.

This problem is rectified by using the Second Normal Form, as shown in the second diagram in that section. In this form, the book table will connect to two book_author tables. Changing the title in this editor screen will change the book_title column in this single book table; the two book_author tables are only linked to the book table by the book_ISBN_number column, so the database will still show both authors as having coauthored the same book. Everything remains in sync.

> **Reality Check: There is nothing sinfully wrong with this screen. If the design calls for this sort of thing to be entered, and this is what the client wants, fine. However, it's clearly best if the underlying structures don't look like this, for the reasons stated. It would also probably be better to give rich functionality to look up the book from the ISBN number and populate the rest of the columns for the book (obviously a table for a book will include more information than its ISBN number and title) but clearly this is a UI design issue, and not a question of database structure.**

Clues That a Table Isn't in the Second Normal Form

The clues for detecting whether entities are in the Second Normal Form aren't quite as straightforward as the clues for the First Normal Form. They take some careful thought, however, and some thorough examination of your structures such as the following:

❏ Repeating Key Column Name Prefixes

❏ Repeating Groups of Data

❏ Composite Keys Without a Foreign Key

Repeating Key Column Name Prefixes

This situation is one of the dead giveaways. Let's revisit the previous example.

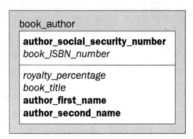

You have author_first_name and author_second_name, which are functionally dependent on author_social_security_number. You also have book_title and book_ISBN_number with the same situation.

Having such obvious prefixes isn't always the case, but it's a good thing to look for because this is a rather common mistake made by novice designers.

Repeating Groups of Data

More difficult to recognize are the repeating groups of data. Imagine executing multiple SELECT statements on a table, each time retrieving all rows (if possible), ordered by each of the important columns. If there is a functionally dependent attribute on one of the attributes, anywhere one of the columns is equal to X, you'll see the dependent column, Y.

Take a look at some example entries from the following table.

author_social_ security_number	book_ISBN_number	royalty_ percentage
DELA-777-888	1-861-000-156-7	2
DELA-777-888	1-861-000-338-1	3
GIBB-423-4421	1-861-000-156-7	3
Book_title	author_first_name	author_second_name
Instant Tiddlywinks	Vervain	Delaware
Beginning Ludo	Vervain	Delaware
Instant Tiddlywinks	Gordon	Gibbon

Book_title is, of course, dependent on book_ISBN_Number, *so any time you see an ISBN number = 1-861-000-156-7, you can be sure that the book title is "Instant Tiddlywinks." If it isn't, then there's something wrong in the database.*

Composite Keys Without a Foreign Key

If there is more than one attribute in the key that isn't a foreign key, any attributes that describe those attributes are likely to be violating the Second Normal Form. This isn't always true of course, considering the previous example of a phone number in which each of the pieces made up the key. However, consider what the composite key values are made up of. In the case of the phone number, the different parts of the phone number come together to form a singular thing, a phone number.

However, the previous example of a key that was made up of the Book ISBN number and Author Identification clearly give you two keys that don't represent the same thing, in this case a Book and an Author.

Coding Around the Problem

Scouring any existing database code is one good way of discovering problems, based on the lifespan of the system you're analyzing. Many times, a programmer will simply write code to make sure the Second Normal Form violation isn't harmful to the data, rather than remodeling it into a proper structure. At one time in the history of the RDBMS (relational database management system), this may have been the only way to handle this situation; however, now that technology has caught up with the relational theory, this isn't the case.

It's important to understand that the case isn't trying to be made that theory has changed a bit due to technology. Actually, relational theory has been very stable throughout the years with few of the basic concepts changing in the past decade. Ten years ago, I had quite a few problems making a normalized system operational in the hardware and operating system constraints I had to deal with, so I cut corners in my models for "performance" reasons.

Using current hardware, there is no need to even begin to cut normalization corners for performance. It's best to resolve these issues with SQL joins instead of spaghetti code to maintain denormalized data. Of course, at this point in the design process, it's best to not even consider the topic of implementation, performance, or any subject in which you aren't simply working towards proper logical storage of data.

Third Normal Form

An entity that's in the **Third Normal Form** will have the following characteristics:

❑   The entity must be in the Second Normal Form

❑   An entity is in violation of the Third Normal Form if a non-key attribute is a fact about another non-key attribute

You can rephrase the second bullet like this:

All attributes must be a fact about the key, and nothing but the key.

The Third Normal Form differs from the Second Normal Form in that it deals with the relationship of non-key data to non-key data. The problems are the same and many of the symptoms are the same, but it can be harder to locate the general kind of violations that this form tends to deal with. Basically, the main difference is that data in one attribute, instead of being dependent on the key, is actually dependent on data in another non-key attribute. The requirements for the Third Normal Form are as follows.

The Entity Must Be in the Second Normal Form

Once again, this is very important. It may be hard to locate the Third Normal Form problems if the Second Normal Form problems still remain.

Non-Key Attributes Cannot Describe Other Non-Key Attributes

If any of the attributes are functionally dependent on an attribute other than the key, then you're again going to have data modification anomalies. Because you're in the Second Normal Form already, you've proven that all of your attributes are reliant on the whole key, but you haven't looked at the relationship of the attributes to one another.

In the following diagram, you take your book entity and extend it to include the publisher and the city where the publisher is located.

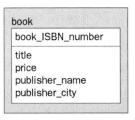

Title defines the title for the book defined by the book_ISBN_number, price indicates the price of the book. The case can clearly be made publisher_name describes the book's publisher, but it's clear that the publisher_city doesn't make sense in this context, because it doesn't directly describe the book.

To correct this situation, you need to create a different entity to identify the publisher information.

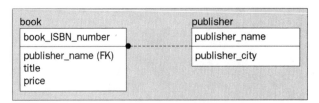

Now the `publisher` entity has only data concerning the publisher, and the `book` entity has book information. What makes this so valuable is that now, if you want to add information to your schema concerning the publisher, for instance contact information or an address, it's very obvious where you add that information. Now you have your `publisher_city` attribute identifying the publisher, not the book. Once we get into physical modeling, we'll discuss the merits of having the `publisher_name` attribute as the primary key, but for now this is a reasonable primary key, and a reasonable set of attributes.

Note that the resolution of this problem was to create a **nonidentifying** relationship: publisher is related to book. Because the malevolent attributes weren't in the key to begin with, they don't go there now.

All Attributes Must Be a Fact Describing the Key, the Whole Key, and Nothing but the Key

If it sounds familiar, it should. This little saying is the backbone for the whole group of normal forms concerned with the relationship between the key and non-key attributes.

Programming Problems Avoided by the Third Normal Form

While the methods of violating the Third Normal Form are very close to the violations of the Second Normal Form, there are a few important differences. Because you aren't dealing with key values, every attribute's relationship to every non-key attribute needs to be considered, and so does every combination of attributes. In the book example, you had the following entity structure:

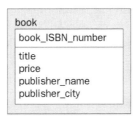

Every attribute should be considered against every other attribute. If entities are of reasonable size (10 to 20 attributes in an entity is probably as many as seems reasonable without violating some normalization rule. Of course, this doesn't always hold, but it's a good rule of thumb.), then the process of weeding out Third Normal Form problems won't be too lengthy a process. In this example, in order to do a "perfect" job of comparing each attribute against each of the other attributes, you need to check each attribute against the other three attributes. Because there are four attributes, you need to consider the N * (N – 1) or (4 * 3) = 12 different permutations of attribute relations to be safe (ignoring the fact that you'll be checking some values more than once). In this example entity you must check the following:

❑   `title` against: `price`, `publisher_name`, and `publisher_city`

❑   `price` against: `title`, `publisher_name`, and `publisher_city`

❑   `publisher_name` against: `price`, `title`, and `publisher_city`

❑   `publisher_city` against: `price`, `title`, and `publisher_name`

From this you'll notice that, when you check `publisher_name` against the other three attributes, it becomes clear that `publisher_city` is functionally dependent on it, hence there's a Third Normal Form violation.

After designing a few thousand entities, some common attributes will jump out as problems, and only a few attributes will have to be considered in routine normalization checks. Note that this example has tailored names to make it seem simple, but in reality, names are often far more cryptic. Consider the following entity.

These names are probably less cryptic than those that might actually exist in some legacy database entities; however, they're already ambiguous enough to cause problems. `City` seems almost fine here, unless you carefully consider that most books don't have a `city`, but publishers probably will. The following example code shows what happens if you want to change the `city` attribute and keep it in sync.

Take, for example, the situation where you have the table as it was built previously:

```
CREATE TABLE book
(
    ISBN varchar(20) NOT NULL,
    pubname varchar(60) NOT NULL,
    city varchar(60) NOT NULL,
    title varchar(60) NOT NULL,
    price money NOT NULL
)
```

This has the Third Normal Form violations that were identified. Consider the situation in which you want to update the city column for ISBN 23232380237 from a value of `Virginia Beach` to a value of `Nashville`. You first would update the single row as follows:

```
UPDATE book
SET city = 'Nashville'
WHERE ISBN = '23232380237'
```

But because you had the functional dependency of the `publisher` to `city` relationship, you now have to update all of the books that have the same publisher name to the new value as well:

```
UPDATE book
SET city = 'Nashville'
WHERE city = 'Virginia Beach'
    AND pubname = 'Phantom Publishing'  --publisher name
```

Although this is the proper way to ensure that the batch code updates the city properly as well as the book, in most cases this code will be buried in the application, not tied together with a transaction, much less one in a batch. It's also easy to forget these types of relationships within the row when writing new processes that are required as the system changes over time.

Any errors in one UPDATE statement, and data can be compromised (clearly something you're trying to avoid by spending all of this time working on your structures). For existing SQL Server applications that are being redesigned, employ the SQL Server Profiler to check what SQL is actually being sent to SQL Server from the application.

Clues That a Table Isn't in the Third Normal Form

The clues for the Third Normal Form are quite similar to those for the Second Normal Form, because they're trying to solve the same sort of problem–making sure that all non-key attributes refer to the key of the entity. These clues are as follows:

❑   Multiple Columns with the Same Prefix

❑   Repeating Groups of Data

❑   Summary Data

Multiple Columns with the Same Prefix

If you revisit the previous example, you'll see that it's obvious that publisher_name and publisher_city are multiple columns with the same prefix.

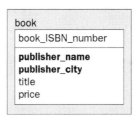

In some cases the prefix used may not be so obvious, such as pub_name, pblish_city, or even location_pub; all good reasons to establish a decent naming standard.

Repeating Groups of Data

You do this the same way that you did for the Second Normal Form, but you'll need to consider more permutations, as discussed.

Summary Data

One of the common violations of the Third Normal Form that may not seem blindingly obvious is **summary data**. This is where columns are added to the parent entity, which refers to the child rows and summarizes them. Summary data has been one of the most frequently necessary evils that we've had to deal with throughout the history of the relational database. There are several new features in SQL Server 2000 that you'll employ to help avoid summary data in your implementation, but in logical modeling there is *absolutely* no place for it. Not only is summary data not functionally dependent on non-key columns, but it's dependent on nonentity columns. This causes all sorts of confusion as I shall demonstrate. Summary data should be reserved either for physical design or the data warehousing systems we introduced in Chapter 1.

Take the following example of an auto dealer. The dealer has an entity listing all of the automobiles it sells, and it has an entity recording of each automobile sale.

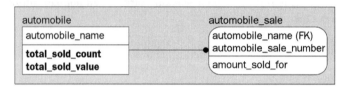

This kind of thing probably has no part in logical modeling, because the sales data is available. Instead of accepting that the total number of vehicles sold and their value is available, the designer has decided to add columns in the parent entity that refer to the child rows and summarizes them.

Is this required during the physical implementation? Possibly, depending on performance, though it's true that the complexity of the implemented system has most likely increased by an order of magnitude, because you'll have to have triggers on the automobile_sale entity that calculate these values for any change in the automobile_sale entity. If this is a highly active database with frequent rows added to the automobile_sale entity, this will tend to slow the database down considerably. On the other hand, if it's an often inactive database, then there will be very few rows in the child entity, and so the performance gains made by being able to quickly find the numbers of vehicles sold and their value will be very small anyway.

The key is that in logical modeling it isn't required, because the data modeled in the total_ columns is actually in existence in the sales table. The information you are identifying in the logical model should be modeled in one and only one spot.

Boyce-Codd Normal Form

During the discussions of the Second and Third Normal Forms, I was purposefully vague with the word **key**. As mentioned before, a key can be *any* candidate key, whether the primary key or an alternate key.

The **Boyce-Codd Normal Form** is actually a better constructed replacement for both the Second and Third Normal Forms; it takes the meaning of the Second and Third Normal Forms and restates it in a stricter way. Note that, to be in Boyce-Codd Normal Form, there is no mention of Second Normal Form or Third Normal Form. The Boyce-Codd Normal Form actually encompasses them both, and is defined as follows:

- ❑ The entity is in First Normal Form

- ❑ All attributes are fully dependent on a key

- ❑ An entity is in Boyce-Codd Normal Form if every determinant is a key

So let's look at each of these rules individually, except for the First Normal Form, which was covered in the Second Normal Form discussion.

All Attributes Are Fully Dependent on a Key

You can rephrase this like so:

> *All attributes must be a fact about **a** key, and nothing but **a** key.*

This is a slight but important deviation from the previous rules for Second Normal Form and Third Normal Form. In this case, you don't specify *the entire* key or just *the* key—now it's *a* key. How does this differ? Well, it does and it doesn't. It basically expands the meaning of Second Normal Form and Third Normal Form to deal with the very typical situation where you have more than one key.

It's noted that the attribute must be fully dependent on a key, and this key is defined as the **unique identifier**. The unique identifier should be thought of as the address or pointer for the entity, regardless of whether you use a natural key or otherwise. The **entity**, as defined, is the logical representation of a single object, either real or imaginary. Think of *every* key as the entity's ID badge, or SSN (social security number), or whole name, and it's easy to begin to understand what each of the attributes should be like.

For example, let's take a person who works for a company and model them. First you choose your key: Let's use the SSN.

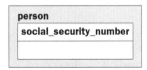

Then you start adding the other attributes you know about your employee—her name, hair color, eye color, the badge number she was given, her driver's license number, and so on. Now you have the following entity:

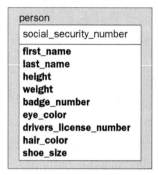

Careful study of the entity shows that it's in the Third Normal Form, because each of the attributes further describes the entity. The `first_name`, `height`, `badge_number`, and others all refer to the entity. The same may be said for the `social_security_number`. It has been chosen as the key, primarily because it was the first thing you saw. In logical modeling, the choice of which attribute(s) are the primary key isn't all that meaningful, and you can change them at any time. (A large discussion of proper primary keys will be dealt with in Chapter 10.) In most cases, even in the logical modeling phase, you'll simply use a pointer as discussed in Chapter 3.

The following sentence basically explains the Second and Third Normal Forms:

> **All attributes must further describe the entity, the whole entity, and nothing but the entity.**

As long this concept is understood, data modeling and normalization become much easier.

An Entity Is in Boyce-Codd Normal Form if Every Determinant Is a Key

The second part of the quest for the Boyce-Codd Normal Form is to make sure that every determinant is a key, or a unique identifier for the entity. The definition of a determinant in Chapter 3 was as follows:

> **Any attribute or combination of attributes on which any other attribute or combination of attributes is functionally dependent.**

Based on your study of the Second and Third Normal Forms, you can see that this is basically the definition of a key. Because all attributes that aren't keys must be functionally dependent on a key, the definition of a determinant is the same as the definition of a key.

The Boyce-Codd Normal Form simply extends the previous normal forms by saying that an entity may have many keys, and all attributes must be dependent on one of these keys. I've simplified this a bit by noting that every key must uniquely identify the entity, and every non-key attribute must describe the entity.

One interesting thing that should be noted is that each key is a determinant for all other keys. This is because, in every place where one key value is seen, you can replace it with the other key value without losing the meaning of the entity. This isn't to say that an alternate key cannot change values– not at all. The driver's license number is a good key, but if the Department of Motor Vehicles issues all new numbers, it's still a key, and it will still identify and describe the entity. If the value of any candidate key changes, this is perfectly acceptable.

With this definition in mind, let's take the example entity you're modeling for this section and look at it again.

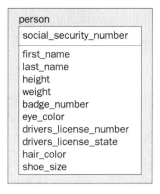

What you'll be looking for now are attributes or groups of attributes that are dependent on the key. The attributes or groups will also be unique to each instance of this entity.

First_name will not be by itself, and it would not be a very good assumption to assume that first_name and last_name are. (It all depends on the size of the target set as to whether or not the user would be willing to accept this. At the very least you would likely need to include the middle initial and title, but this still isn't a very good key.) Height describes the person, but isn't unique. The same is true for weight. Badge_number certainly should be unique, so you'll make it a key. (Note that you don't have badge_issued_date, because that would refer to the badge and doesn't help the Boyce-Codd Normal Form example.) drivers_license_number is probably unique, but consider variations across localities, because two governments may have similar numbering schemes that may cause duplication. Hair_color and shoe_size describe the person, but neither could be considered unique. Even taking the person's height, weight, eye_color, hair_color, and shoe_size together, uniqueness could not be guaranteed between two random people.

So now you model the entity as follows:

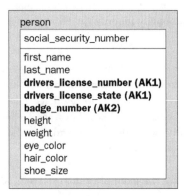

You now have three keys for this object. When you do the physical modeling, you'll choose the proper key from the keys you have defined, or use an artificial key. As discussed in Chapter 3, an artificial key is simply a value that is used as a pointer to an object, much like badge_number is a pointer that a company uses to identify an employee, or the government using SSNs to identify individuals in the US (of course the social security number is actually a smart key, with an artificial key embedded).

It's also worth considering that an SSN isn't always a very good key either. Even if you limit it to only US citizens, you'll find that there are plenty of people who don't have an SSN. And certainly if you want to accommodate people from outside the US, then the SSN will never work. It will certainly depend on the situation, because there are many situations in which the user is required to have an SSN, and some where an SSN or green card is required to identify the user as a valid resident of the US. The situation will always dictate the eventual solution, and it's simply up to the data architect to choose the appropriate path for the situation being modeled.

When choosing a key, you always try to make sure that keys don't completely encompass other keys. For instance, height isn't a unique key, but height and badge_number is! It's important to make certain that individual parts of unique keys cannot be guaranteed unique by themselves; otherwise mistakes can be made by accidentally putting non-unique data in the columns that need to be unique.

Clues and Programming Anomalies

The clues for determining that an entity is in Boyce-Codd Normal Form are the same as for the Second and Third Normal Forms. The programming anomalies solved by the Boyce-Codd Normal Form are the same too.

The main point is that once all of the determinants are modeled during this phase of the design, implementing the determinants as unique keys will be far more likely to occur. This will prevent users from entering non-unique values in the columns that need to have unique values in them.

This completes the overview of the first three normal forms. You'll look at the Fourth and Fifth Normal Forms in the next chapter, but now you'll implement your newly learned concepts into the case study.

Case Study

For this chapter, you'll take your model that you put together in the previous chapter and walk through each of the normal forms, correcting the model according to the rules, and ending with a completed diagram.

First Normal Form

Your model has a few violations of the First Normal Form. You'll break down each of the different violations that may occur.

All Attributes Must Be Atomic

You have one example of this sort of violation. It occurs in the `statement` entity. You should recall that this entity represents the statement that the bank sends each month so that the client can reconcile all of the checks the client has hand-entered as they actually occurred. The `balancingItems` attribute contains all of the transactions that the bank has recorded and needs to be matched up to items in the register. However, this attribute will contain many rows and many columns, hardly a single atomic value, which is required by the First Normal Form.

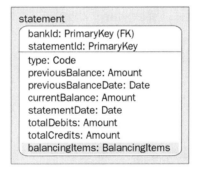

So, you need to add a new entity to contain these items. Because you don't know exactly what will go into this entity, you'll let the attributes migrate from the `statement` entity, then add another pointer to the primary key for uniqueness.

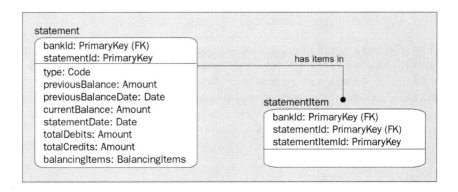

A different type of violation of this same kind must also be looked at. Consider the **payee** entity and the two attributes **address** and **phoneNumber**.

```
payee
payeeId: PrimaryKey
name: Name (AK1.1)
address: Address
phoneNumber: PhoneNumber
```

For your example, yoy'll just look at the **address** attribute. The address is made up of several parts, the street address lines (usually we're happy with two lines to store street information), city, state, and zip code. You'll also expand the **phoneNumber** attribute as we discussed earlier. Once you have finished this process, you're left with the following result:

```
payee
payeeId: PrimaryKey
name: Name (AK1.1)
addressLine1: AddressDescriptiveLine
addressLine2: AddressDescriptiveLine
addressCity: City
addressState: StateCode
addressZipCode: ZipCode
phoneCountryCode: CountryCode
phoneAreaCode: AreaCode
phoneExchange: Exchange
phoneNumber: PhoneNumberPart
phoneExtension: Extension
```

There are no attributes now in this example that overtly violate the First Normal Form and therefore aren't atomic. Actually, you could make the case that the **addressLine1** attribute isn't atomic, since it will contain street number, street name, and other pieces of information. This kind of discussion can be a fun diversion from an afternoon of actual work, but in the final analysis you generally will only model the address down to a level that meets the requirements for your purposes. There are clearly reasons to model the **addressLine1** attribute as **streetNumber**, **streetName**, etc, especially when standardizing addresses in order to save a penny or two per letter on postage fees. Not exciting or valuable unless posting thousands or millions of pieces of correspondence every year. Hence, you stick with the reasonably standard implementation of having unstructured lines for street names and number, apartment numbers, etc.

Notice that you created domains for each new attribute. **addressLine1** and **addressLine2** are the same sort of item. Also of note is the **phoneNumber** attribute. It has the same name as before, but it has a different meaning, because a phone number is made up of country code, area code, exchange, and number. As it has a different meaning, you created a new domain with a new name, since in practice you may still have entities that use the domain.

All Occurrences of a Row Type Must Contain the Same Number of Values

In your new **payee** entity, you have put together a common set of attributes that violate this part of the rule, the `addressLine1` and `addressLine2` attributes. While this is a common solution to the address problem, it's a violation nonetheless. Having a fixed number of address line attributes has bitten me several times when addresses needed more, sometimes even four or five of them. Since not every address will have the same number of items, this is a problem. You solve this by adding another child entity for the address line information:

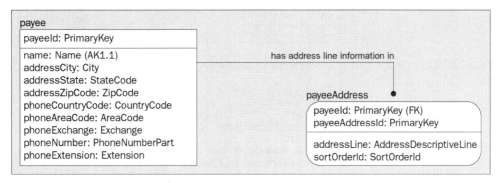

This may seem a bit odd, and it is, considering the way databases have been developed for long periods of time. However, this address design gives you the flexibility to store as many pieces of information as you may need, instead of having to add columns if the situation requires it. This is also a good example of normalization creating more entities.

> **Reality Check: For the most part, it may not be the most user friendly way to store the address, and so the address might be stored using `addressLine1` and `addressLine2`, or considering that what separates `addressLine1` and `addressLine2` is a carriage return and a linefeed, storing it in one large column might also suffice. You'll store it in a different column for discussion purposes.**

All Occurrences of a Row Type in an Entity Must be Different

You have begun to take care of this by adding primary keys and alternate keys to your entities. Note that simply adding an artificial key will not take care of this particular rule. One of your last physical modeling tasks will be to verify that all of your entities have at least one key defined that doesn't contain a non-migrated artificial key.

Boyce-Codd Normal Form

Because Boyce-Codd is actually an extension of the Second and Third Normal Forms, you can consider every one of the violations you have discussed all together.

Summary Data

Summary data attributes are generally the easiest violations to take care of. This is because you can usually just prune the values from your entities. For example, in the `account` entity, you can remove the `[Running Total]` attribute, because it can be obtained by summing values that are stored in the `transaction` entity. This leaves you with:

```
account
bankId: PrimaryKey (FK)
accountId: PrimaryKey

number: AlphaNumericNumber (AK1.1)
balanceDate: Date
```

On the other hand, you have what appear to be summary attributes in the `statement` entity:

```
statement
bankId: PrimaryKey (FK)
statementId: PrimaryKey

type: Code
previousBalance: Amount
previousBalanceDate: Date
currentBalance: Amount
statementDate: Date
totalDebits: Amount
totalCredits: Amount
balancingItems: BalancingItems
```

You have `previousBalance`, `currentBalance`, and so on—in fact, all of the attributes other than `type`—referring to some other entity's values. However, in this case, the `statement` entity is referring to a document, namely the statement from the bank; these attributes represent what the bank *thinks* is on the statement. You'll likely want to keep these attributes and use them to validate the data you'll be storing in the `statementItem` entity.

Multiple Attributes with the Same Prefix

You now have a very good example of this kind of problem in the `payee` entity you've created. `phoneCountryCode`, `phoneAreaCode`, and so on all have the same prefix (note that things won't always be so obvious); likewise for `addressCity`, and so on.

```
payee
payeeId: PrimaryKey

name: Name (AK1.1)
addressCity: City
addressState: StateCode
addressZipCode: ZipCode
phoneCountryCode: CountryCode
phoneAreaCode: AreaCode
phoneExchange: Exchange
phoneNumber: PhoneNumberPart
phoneExtension: Extension
```

You can choose to say that phone numbers and addresses are logically things in and of themselves. Each of the phone attributes doesn't really describe the payee further, but the existence of a phone number does. The same goes for the address attributes. Hence you break them down further like so:

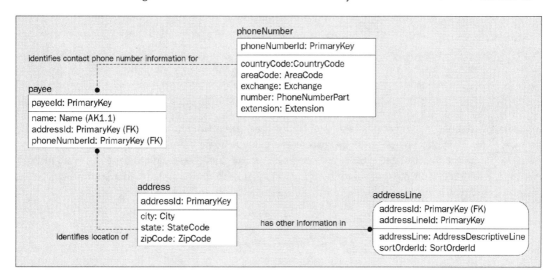

Now that you've satisfied the idea that every attribute refers to a key, because the address and phoneNumber refer to the payee's address and phone number, and the address is defined by its city, state, and zip, plus the street information in the addressLine entity. The phoneNumber is defined by its attributes as well.

Every Determinant Must Be a Key

This is where things can get messy. Consider the payee entity in your previous example. The payeeId–a primary key–and name are the determinants for the entity. You have the following set of dependencies:

❏   For every value of payeeId you must have the same name value.

❏   For every value of name, you must have the same value for addressId and phoneNumberId.

❏   It isn't true that every value in addressId and phoneNumberId has to have the same value for name, because an address or phone number might be used for several payees.

The real issue here is in choosing a proper set of keys. Using a pointer, even in the logical modeling phase, tends to cover up a major issue. Every entity must contain unique values, and this unique value must not include meaningless values, because a pointer is meaningless except to indicate ownership in a relationship.

First you take the phone number entity as follows:

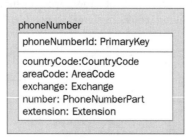

It has no key defined, so you must make one. In this case, the entire entity *without the primary key* will be a key. This illustrates one of the main reasons to maintain single-themed entities. Now that you have the phone number isolated, you're able to make certain that, if two payees have the same phone numbers, you don't duplicate this value. By doing this you keep things clear in your later usage of these values, because if you see duplicate phone numbers, things will get confusing.

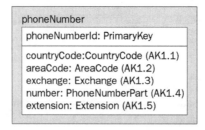

Next you'll look at the address entity:

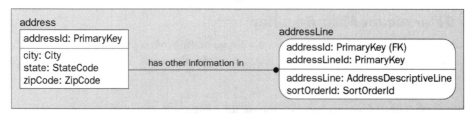

This is a very interesting case to deal with. There is no way that you can make the city, state, and zipCode unique, because you'll almost certainly have more than one address of the same type. In this case, the uniqueness is determined by the city, state, zipCode, plus any addressLine items, which is a valid situation. You may not have any uniqueness in the values in the addressLine entity either, because it's a logical part of the address entity, and address relies on it for uniqueness. You cannot model the situation that only one address may contain the information "101 Main Street" very well. This clearly will not cover every situation, unless you consider only one city, state, and zip. In cases such as this, you would have to simply document that the key of this case is actually city, state, zipCode, plus any number of addressLine values including the sortOrderId. Clearly this cannot be modeled in your data model, but it can be enforced using triggers.

> **Reality Check:** The way you've modeled the address entity in two parts isn't necessarily the way an address would be actually implemented, but the situation in which two tables are required to enforce uniqueness isn't completely uncommon. What you're implementing is an attribute of type array, in which the `addressLine` attribute is actually a repeating value, which in relational language requires additional tables, whereby an array would technically be a better solution.

Finally, consider the `transaction` entity:

```
transaction
bankId: PrimaryKey (FK)
accountId: PrimaryKey (FK)
transactionId: PrimaryKey
date: Date
number: AlphaNumericNumber (AK1.1)
description: Description
amount: Amount
type: Code
```

In this set of attributes, you have a key that is made up completely of migrated keys (`bankId`, `accountId`) and another artificial key. Basically, this means that the migrated account key defines part of the transaction and that it's up to you to look for the proper additional attribute. In this case it will be the `number`, because this is the number that the bank uses to identify a transaction, and you had previously chosen it as a key of its own, as follows:

```
transaction
bankId: PrimaryKey (FK) (AK1.1)
accountId: PrimaryKey (FK) (AK1.2)
transactionId: PrimaryKey
date: Date
number: AlphaNumericNumber (AK1.3)
description: Description
amount: Amount
type: Code
```

You must then go through each of the other entities, making sure a proper key is assigned, and more importantly, checking that there are no attributes that have functional dependencies on another attribute.

Consider also that, now, `bankId`, `accountId`, and `transactionId` functionally determine the attribute `number`, and `bankId`, `accountId`, and `number` functionally determine the `transactionId`. This is a valid situation, which is pretty interesting!

One additional point should be made concerning the following subtyped entities of `transaction`:

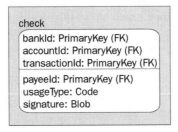

No additional keys are required for this entity because it's in a one-to-one relationship with the transaction entity; hence, its primary key is a valid key.

Model

Here is your model after normalizing up to the Boyce-Codd Normal Form. Note that many of the common modification anomalies should be cleared up. It's far from complete, however. To keep the model simple, you still haven't added any further information to it. You'll be presented a final model with additional columns in the last section of the logical modeling part of the book.

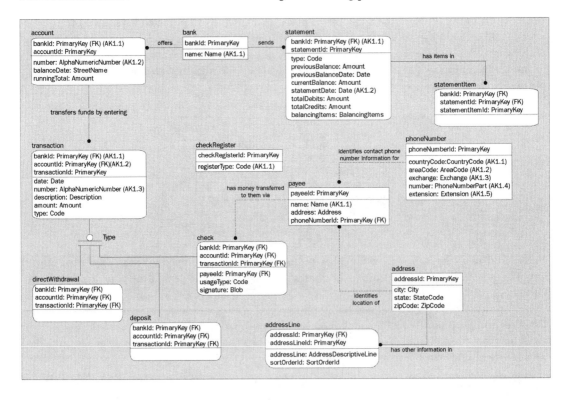

Best Practices

Normalization best practices are deferred until the next chapter.

Summary

In this chapter, you've begun the process of turning your random table structures into structures that will make the storage of data much more reliable. By building these structures in a very specific manner, you'll derive a set of entities that are resilient to change and that have fewer modification anomalies.

This can all seem from the outside like one of the more baffling processes within computer science. This probably explains why a lot of developers don't normalize their databases. However, there's no reason why it should be so. Behind the occasionally esoteric jargon is a set of simple, well-formed rules that lay down how databases should be designed. As for the end result, the case study should demonstrate that the resulting entities you developed are cleaner, tidier, and safer for your data entry, even though the data that is stored will look less and less meaningful to the casual observer.

Now the obvious question: Can you normalize your data any further? Because I've alerted you to the fact that there are seven normal forms of interest, and you've only looked at four, the answer to this question almost certainly is yes.

On the other hand, *should* you normalize further? Most likely! The Third Normal Form has long been identified as the most important plateau of data modeling, and it may be that, when you come to physically implement your solution, you won't need to go beyond this level. However, you're currently in the logical modeling phase and you must not concern yourself yet with performance issues; you should aim for an ideal model. Working through the next normal forms will uncover additional problems with your data that you may not have foreseen.

7

Advanced Normalization Topics

Introduction

If it has been said once, it has been said a million times: "This database is in the Third Normal Form, and that is good enough!" In this chapter, you'll look at one additional very important method for normalization, and you'll be introduced to a few others. The additional methods of normalization aren't commonly used because of perceived drawbacks in terms of both the time taken to implement them, and the cost in performance of the resulting database. In the previous chapter, you looked at some of the different programming anomalies that the Third Normal Form deals with, but as you'll see, there may still be some problems remaining in your logical design, mostly caused by the presence of nonbinary relationships. In essence, while most people think they have completed the normalization process after having reached the Third Normal Form, what they really should be concerned with is *at least* reaching the Third Normal Form in their logical model. A degree of judgment is required in physically implementing a design and determining what level of normalization is appropriate. However, as a general guide, the designer should always attempt to normalize all entities to as high a form as possible.

If, in testing the system, there are found to be performance issues, these can be addressed by denormalizing the system, as will be touched on briefly later in this chapter and also in the physical part of the book.

You'll look in depth at the **Fourth Normal Form** and finally introduce the concepts covered in the **Fifth Normal Form**. One of the interesting points that will be introduced is that the normal forms after the Third require knowledge of not only structures, but also business rules for the entities. Two equal sets of tables might be normalized in one case, and not quite normalized in others. It should become clear that Third Normal Form is a solid baseline, but Fourth Normal Form is actually what is desirable for most systems.

Fourth Normal Form

The rules of normalization so far have resolved redundancies among columns in an entity, but did not resolve problems that arose from entities having composite primary keys while they still possess redundant data between rows. Normalizing entities to **Fourth Normal Form** addresses such problems. In a simple case, moving to the Fourth Normal Form will take care of problems such as the modeling of an attribute that should store a single value but it ends up storing multiple values.

The rules for being in Fourth Normal Form are as follows:

❑ The entity must be in BCNF (**Boyce-Codd Normal Form**). This condition ensures that all keys will be appropriately defined, and all values in an entity will be properly dependent on its key.

❑ There must not be more than one MVD (**multivalued dependency**) represented in the entity. No more than one attribute can store multiple values that relate to a key in any entity, otherwise there will be data duplication. In addition it should be ensured that you don't repeat single valued attributes for every multivalued one.

You shall look at a few examples to help make these ideas clearer. Let's first look at the three main forms that the Fourth Normal Form violations take:

❑ Ternary relationships

❑ Lurking multivalued attributes

❑ Status and other attributes of which you need to know the previous values

Ternary Relationships

You briefly looked at ternary relationships back in Chapter 3. Not all real relationships will manifest themselves in a binary-type relationship, and it's quite common to encounter ternary or even greater relationships in the real world. Any place where you see three (or more) identifying (or nonidentifying relationships all part of a unique key), you're likely to have trouble.

Take, for example, a situation in which you've designed a set of entities to support a conference planner, and you plan to store information concerning the `session`, `presenter`, and `room` where a session is to be given.

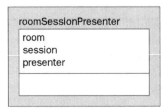

Let's also assume that the following set of very open business rules is being enforced as follows:

❏ More than one presenter may be listed to give a presentation.

❏ A presentation may span more than one room.

The following figure models the relationship: **presenter**-*presents*-**session**-*in*-**room**.

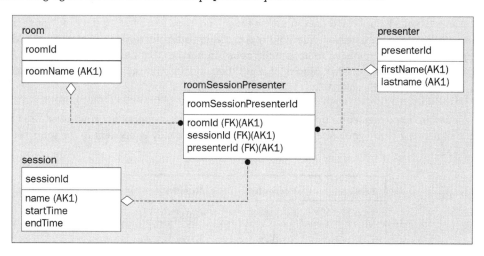

As a reminder, each of these values is nullable, as denoted by the diamond on the opposite end of the line. Remember, too, that unique keys don't require that each attribute should be mandatory.

Each of these entities is a Boyce-Codd Normal Form entity; however, the relationship between the three is troubling. Let's look at a set of sample data.

Session	Presenter	Room
101	Davidson	River Room
202	Davidson	Stream Room
202	Hazel	Stream Room
404	Hawkins	Brook Room
404	Hawkins	Stream Room

In the first row, there is no problem, because you have one row for the `session` *101*, which has one `presenter` *Davidson* and one `room`, the *River Room*. A problem becomes apparent in the next two rows, as one `session` *202* has two different `presenters`, and yet a single `room`. This forces you to repeat data unnecessarily in the `room` attribute, because you have now stored in two places the knowledge that `session` *202* is in the *Stream Room*.

If the `session` moves, you have to change it in two places, and if you forget this property, and update the `room` based on a value that you aren't currently displaying (for example through the use of an artificial key), then you end up with the following:

202	Davidson	Stream Room
202	Hazel	"Changed to Room"

In this example, you've duplicated data in the `session` and `room` attributes, and the *404* `session` duplicates `session` and `presenter` data. The real problem with your scenario comes when adding to or changing your data. If you need to update the `session` number that *Davidson* is giving with *Hazel* in the *Stream Room*, then two rows will require changes. Equally, if a `room` assignment changes, then several rows will have to be changed.

When entities are implemented in this fashion, you may not even see all of the rows filled in as fully as this. In the following entity you see a set of rows that are functionally equivalent to the set in the previous entity.

Session	Presenter	Room
101	Davidson	<null>
101	<null>	River Room
202	Davidson	<null>
202	<null>	Stream Room
202	Hazel	<null>
404	<null>	Brook Room
404	Hawkins	<null>
404	<null>	Stream Room

In this example, you have nulls for some `rooms`, and some `presenters`. You've eliminated the duplicated data, but now all you have is some pretty strange looking data with nulls everywhere. Furthermore, you aren't able to clearly use nulls to stand for the situation where you don't yet know the `presenter` for a `session`. You're in fact storing an equivalent set of data to that in the previous example, but the data in this form is very difficult to work with.

To develop a solution to this problem let's first make the `presenter` the primary entity:

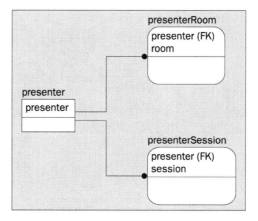

Note that your original implementation was as a nonidentifying relationship. To keep the diagrams as clear as possible, you'll look at the relationships in terms of identifying relationships.

Then you take the data in the `roomSessionPresenter` entity and break it into these entities:

Presenter
Davidson
Hazel
Hawkins

Presenter	Room
Davidson	River Room
Davidson	Stream Room
Hazel	Stream Room
Hawkins	Stream Room
Hawkins	Brook Room

Presenter	Session
Davidson	101
Davidson	202
Hazel	404
Hawkins	404

This is obviously not a proper solution, because you would never be able to determine what room a session is located in, unless a presenter had been assigned. Also, *Davidson* is doing a session in the *River Room* as well as the *Stream Room,* and there is no link back to the session that is being given in the room. When you decompose any relationship and you lose meaning to the data, the decomposition is referred to as a **lossy decomposition**. This is one such case, and so it isn't a reasonable solution to your problem.

Next try centering on the room where the sessions are held.

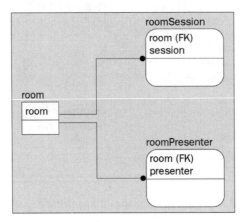

Take the data and fit it into the entities once again.

Room
River Room
Brook Room
Stream Room

Room	Presenter
River Room	Davidson
Stream Room	Davidson
Stream Room	Hazel
Stream Room	Hawkins
Brook Room	Hawkins

Room	Session
River Room	101
Stream Room	202
Brook Room	202
Stream Room	404

Again, this is a lossy decomposition, and as such is an improper solution, because you're unable to determine, for example, exactly who is presenting the *202* presentation. It's in the *Stream Room*, and *Davidson, Hazel,* and *Hawkins* are all presenting in the *Stream Room*, but they aren't all presenting the *202* session. So once again you need to consider another design. This time you center your design on the sessions to be held.

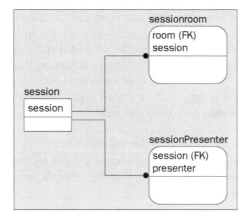

Look at the data again.

Session
101
202
404

Session	Room
101	River Room
202	Stream Room
404	Brook Room
404	Stream Room

Session	Presenter
101	Davidson
202	Davidson
202	Hazel
404	Hawkins

To be certain, you must make sure that the join between the two new tables, sessionRoom and sessionPresenter on their common key returns you back your original set of data.

Session	Presenter	Room
101	Davidson	River Room
202	Davidson	Stream Room
202	Hazel	Stream Room
404	Hawkins	Brook Room
404	Hawkins	Stream Room

In this case, the join agrees with what you have surmised, and this is an adequate solution. This is referred to as a **lossless** decomposition, because you haven't lost any meaning in the process, not to mention that you've made your data more clear. One word of caution: Don't rely on a small set because you have for example to "prove" that the solution is proper. You could have built data that covered any of the situations you tried as you broke down your entities—just as long as they were small. In this particular case, it was fairly obvious from a logical standpoint that the solution was correct, and examination of the data reinforced that point.

Here's a reasonable solution to the problem. From this data you're able to determine precisely who is presenting what and where and you'll have no problem adding or removing presenters, or even changing rooms. Take for example `session` *404*. You have the following data in the `sessionRoom` and `sessionPresenter` entities for this session.

Session	Room
404	Brook Room
404	Stream Room

Session	Presenter
404	Hawkins

To add a `presenter` named Evans to the slate, you simply add another row.

Session	Presenter
404	Hawkins
404	Evans

Now you go back to your model and add in the new tables, leaving you with the following.

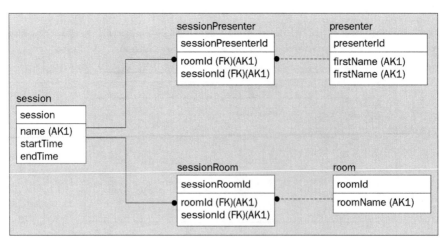

Now that you've set the `session` separate from the `presenter`, the nulls are no longer required in the foreign key values, because if you want to show that a `room` hasn't been chosen, you don't need to create a `sessionRoom` row. The same is true if you haven't yet chosen a `presenter`. More importantly, you can now set multiple rooms for a `session` without confusion.

If you need to have additional data that extends the concept of `sessionPresenter`, for example to denote alternate `presenter` (or indeed primary and secondary `presenter`), you now have a logical place to store this information. Note that if you had tried to store that information in the original entity it would have violated the Boyce-Codd Normal Form because the `alternatePresenter` attribute would only be referring to the `session` and `presenter`, and not the `room`.

Lurking Multivalued Attributes

You should consider some attributes to be **lurking** because they don't always stand out as problems at first glance. This section is one of the reasons why the Fourth Normal Form is far more important than people originally think. Quite often solutions lack the ability to store multiple values for something that was assumed to be only a single value.

In an attempt to illustrate this idea, let's consider the following design model.

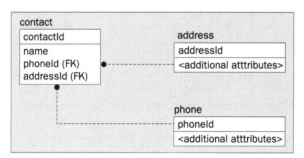

A problem arises here when you consider the `contact` entity, because you have three attributes: the contact's `name` (assume that this name is in the First Normal Form), the `phone` number, and `address`. The `name` is fine, because every contact has a single name that you'll refer to them by, but these days, many people have more than one address and phone number! You therefore have multivalued attributes that require further normalization in order to resolve them. To allow for such multiple address or phone numbers you might modify your design as follows.

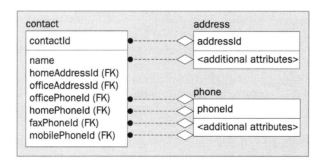

Having multiple phone numbers isn't a violation of the First Normal Form because phone numbers consist of all different types of phone numbers, rather than multiples of the same type. Nevertheless, you do have another problem. Because you've simply added the type attribute to the name of the attribute (for example **homeAddressId**, **fax**PhoneId) you'll have further multivalue attribute problems if, for example, the user has two fax phones, or indeed two mobile phones (who doesn't need at least two?!). Furthermore, you're in the less-than-ideal situation of needing multiple optional values for each of the attributes when values for the reference don't exist (read: nulls needed). This is a messy representation of the relationship. For example, if the client requires a spouse office phone number attribute for a contact, you'll have to change the model, in all probability leading you to rewrite the application code.

Let's further modify the design, so that you can have separate `contact` and `contactInformation` entities.

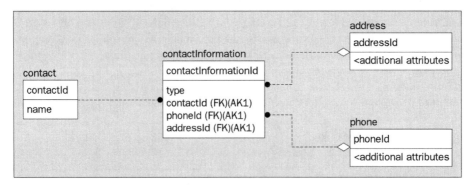

The `type` attribute denotes the type of contact information that you're storing in an instance, so you can now have a `contactInformation` instance with a `type` of Home, and attach an address and phone number to it. This will now allow you to add as many phone numbers and addresses as a user requires. However, because address and phone are held in the same table, you'll end up with null values where a contact has different numbers of home addresses and phone numbers.

At this stage you have to make a decision about how you want to proceed. You may want a phone number to be linked with an address (for example linking home address with home phone number). In your case what you'll do is split the `contactInformation` entity into `contactAddress` and `contactPhone` (though this should not be considered as the only possible solution to the problem).

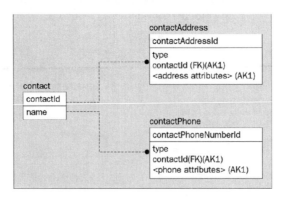

This modification has eliminated the remaining multivalued dependencies, because you can now have many addresses and many phone numbers, independent of one another, and are able to define as many types as desired without the necessity of modifying your entity structures. However, you can take one further step by modeling the phone number and address as different entities in the logical model, and adding domain entities for the type column. In this way, you can prevent users from typing "Home," "Homer," "Hume," and so on when they mean "Home". It will also give you a user-configurable constraint so you can add additional types without having to change the model. You'll add a description attribute to the domain entities allowing you to describe the actual purpose of the type. This allows for situations in which you have an address type of "Away" that is pretty standard for a given organization, but confusing to first-time users. A description such as "Address for contact when traveling on extended sales trips" could then be assigned. Your final model now looks like this.

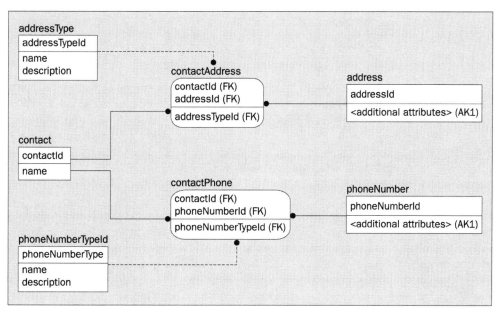

It should be noted that the additional attributes of `address` and `phoneNumber` are alternate keys, so you can avoid duplicating an address every time that it's used in the system. This way, if you have five contacts that have the same address for their office, you only have to change one item. What looks like overkill can therefore actually have benefits, though when you begin to physically model these entities it will be a judgment call about whether or not to implement it to this level, bearing in mind any performance-tuning issues that may arise.

Attribute History

You may also encounter situations in which you need to store status-type information for an instance of some entity. For example, in the following diagram, you've now built two entities that store the header of an order, as well as a domain entity for the order status.

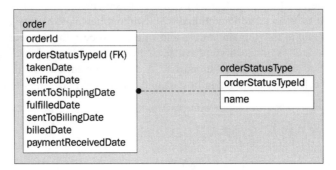

The problem here is that the order status changes (and hence the value of the orderStatusTypeId attribute) based both on the values of the other date attributes, and other external factors. For example, when the order is taken from the customer, the takenDate attribute would be filled in with a date. The order then might be in "Pending" status. After the customer's payment method has been verified, you would then modify the verifiedDate attribute with the date verified, and set the status to "InProcess". "InProcess" could actually mean more than one thing, such as "Sent to shipping" or "Bill sent, awaiting payment."

What you're concerned with here is the orderStatus attribute on the order entity, represented by the relationship to the orderStatusType domain table. It contains the current status for the order instance. When the user wants to answer questions about when an order got sent to the shipping department, or when the order verification department verified the order, how might it be done? The modeler of the data has added several attributes in the order entity to store these bits of information, but what if it failed verification once? Do you care? And is the fulfilledDate the date when the order was either fully shipped or canceled, or strictly when it was fully shipped so you need to add another attribute for canceledDate?

To solve this problem you'll have to change your model to allow the storing of multiple values for each of the attributes you've created.

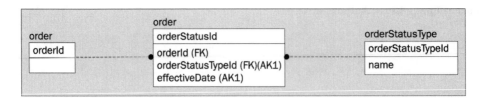

In your physical model, whenever the order status changes, all you'll have to do is add a row to the `orderStatus` table. Whatever row has the latest `effectiveDate` value is the current status; this also allows you to have more than one status value at a time. Of course, in reality, not all statuses are fulfilled in a sequential fashion. The life cycle of an order, for instance, may include sending an invoice to be verified and, on verification, sending it to be processed by shipping, with or without having already received payment, depending on the customers propensity to pay their bills. With the new structure that you've created, when your order fails to be shipped, you can record this. You can also record that the client has paid. Note that, in this case, you only want to model the status of the overall order, and not the status of any items on the order. You should probably also make mention that some statuses may not be represented exactly in this structure, because whether or not a product has been shipped may be recorded in a different entity, and the same can be considered true when discussing the invoiced status.

Solving this type of the Fourth Normal Form situation will sometimes require a state diagram to determine in what order a status is achieved. For example, the following diagram can be used to describe the process of an order being taken, from the time it was ordered to the time it was closed out. (Canceling or modifying an order, or indeed backorders, will not be considered in this example.)

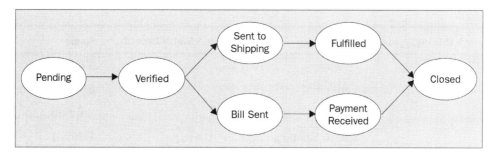

You can model this kind of simple state diagram fairly easily with one additional entity.

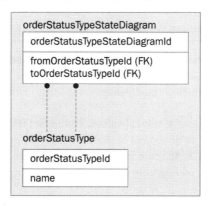

Consider that you have your seven states in the `orderStatusType` entity.

orderStatusTypeId	Name
1	Pending
2	Verified
3	Sent to Shipping
4	Bill Sent
5	Fulfilled
6	Payment Received
7	Closed

To define your state diagram you would need the following instances in the `orderStatusTypeStateDiagram` entity (leaving off the pointer this time, and including `Name` for clarity).

fromOrderStatusTypeId	Name	toOrderStatusTypeId	Name
1	Pending	2	Verified
2	Verified	3	Sent to Shipping
2	Verified	4	Bill Sent
3	Sent to Shipping	5	Fulfilled
4	Bill Sent	6	Payment Received
5	Fulfilled	7	Closed
6	Payment Received	7	Closed

In this manner, you can see whether or not you're in a particular state, what state you were previously in, and what state you can be in next. It also allows you to define the flow of your business rules in data rather than hard-coding a bunch of fixed values.

In this case, your status may go through several values, and in fact may have multiple statuses at any given time. You would then have to document business rules outlining exactly how the process works in a given situation, and as is usually the case, outlining the exception processing will require most of the time, with up to 80 percent of coding time generally spent on the exceptions to the common rules.

Fifth Normal Form

Whereas the First Normal Forms deal with functional dependencies, and the Fourth Normal Form dealt with multivalued dependencies, the Fifth Normal Form deals with join dependence. Unlike the examples for the Fourth Normal Form you considered earlier, not every ternary relationship can be broken down into two entities related to a third. The Fifth Normal Form tries to break tables into the smallest possible pieces while still representing the desired information, in order to eliminate all redundancy within a table. For example, consider the following table of data, noting that this example is different from the previous example in Fourth Normal Form, because here you aren't dealing with a specific session, but only a general day when a session is being given, so multiple things can be going on a given day, not just the single item.

Speaker	Subject	Day
Joe	DB Design	Fri
Joe	XML	Mon
Fred	DB Design	Mon
Joe	DB Design	Mon

The test here is to see if the table can be broken down into two tables without loss. You'll keep it simple and only look at a single permutation of breaking it down, leaving it to you to look at later if you wish. Each of the permutations ends up including one additional row. So now you have two tables.

Speaker	Subject
Joe	DB Design
Joe	XML
Fred	DB Design

Subject	Day
DB Design	Fri
XML	Mon
DB Design	Mon

Note that each table has less data than before, because there were duplicates in each "slice" of the table. Joining the two together on the Subject attribute.

Speaker	Subject	Day
Joe	DB Design	Fri
Joe	XML	Mon
Joe	DB Design	Mon
Fred	DB Design	Mon
Fred	*DB Design*	*Fri*

This join gives you a spurious row (shown in italics).

If you take the third table from the original Entity, produced by taking the `Speaker` and `Day` attributes.

Speaker	Day
Joe	Fri
Joe	Mon
Fred	Mon

You can see that the spurious row will be joined away, because Fred doesn't teach on Fri, which will join out the Fred, DB Design, Friday instance. The original entity was in Fifth Normal Form, and can either be left as a single table, or broken down into three entities.

Generally speaking, an entity is in Fifth Normal Form when it can be broken down into smaller parts (each part having fewer key attributes than the original), and be reconstituted without losing information.

> *The paper "Simple Conditions for Guaranteeing Higher Normal Forms in Relational Databases," by C.J. Date and Ronald Fagin, written in 1972 (available at* http://www.informatik.uni-trier.de/~ley/db/journals/tods/DateF92.html*) notes that one particularly easy way to make certain that a database is in Fifth Normal Form is simply to have only noncomposite keys in an entity. Furthermore, if any key is noncomposite, then it will be in the Fourth Normal Form.*

The Fifth Normal Form is often considered overly esoteric and difficult to deal with, and we won't make any further mention of it. However, it's very important to have some basic understanding of the fact that certain problems that are very difficult to diagnose can occur when ternary (or greater) relationships remain in the implemented data structures because the issues that they cause can be quite hard to notice.

Denormalization

Denormalization is used primarily to improve performance in cases where over-normalized structures are causing overhead to the query processor and in turn other processes in SQL Server, or to tone down some complexity to make things easier to implement. As mentioned earlier in this chapter, although you can argue that denormalizing to the Third Normal Form could simplify queries by reducing the number of joins needed, nevertheless, denormalizing increases the risk of introducing data anomalies. Any additional code written to deal with these anomalies will need to be duplicated in every application that uses the database, thereby increasing the likelihood of human error. The judgment call that needs to be made in this situation is whether a slightly slower (but 100-percent accurate) application is preferable to a faster application of lower accuracy.

I'm contending that during logical modeling you should never step back from your normalized structures to proactively performance-tune your applications. Because this book is centered on OLTP database structures, you should make sure that your design, especially the logical model, represents the entities and attributes that the resulting database will hold. During, and most importantly, *after* the process of *physical* modeling, there may well be valid reasons to denormalize the structures, either to improve performance or reduce implementation complexity, but neither of these pertain to the *logical* model. You'll always have fewer problems if you implement physically what is true logically, and so I would always advocate waiting until the physical modeling phase, or at least until you find a compelling reason to do so (like some part of your system is failing), before you denormalize.

Case Study

Let's now reconsider the logical model that you left at the end of the last chapter. If you apply what you've learned in this chapter to the case study examples, then you discover three examples of Fourth Normal Form violations. These violations are actually more frequent than you might think, and it isn't until you think through each of the attributes and their possible values that the realization hits that you may need to extend the model.

Example 1—Account.BalanceDate

This first example looks at the `balanceDate` attribute in the account entity you originally designed.

The account will be balanced frequently; otherwise any missed transactions or bank mess-ups may cause you to accidentally run out of funds in the account. (If the account isn't balanced, then it will be as bad as my checking account was after I left college!) Because you store data each time the account is balanced, the `balanceDate` attribute represents a multivalued dependency to the account and needs to be relocated. Breaking down this dependency, you introduce the `accountReconcile` entity, along with the `reconcileDate` and `periodEndDate` attributes. These allow for the fact that there may be some latency between the time the statement is received and when it's actually reconciled. The `reconcileDate` is defined as the date when the account was physically balanced. As a final touch, you can add the `statementId` attribute to the `accountReconcile` entity, to record any information that the bank sent the user to balance the account. It will also be better to use the `statementId` as part of the primary key, because it identifies the reconciliation.

With these modifications in place your logical model now looks like this.

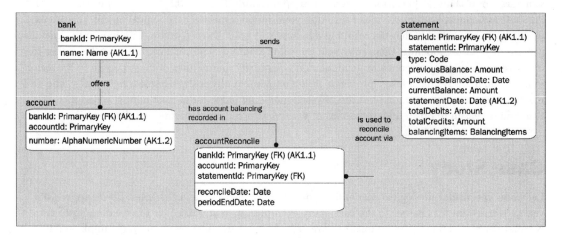

Example 2—Payee.Address Id and Payee.Phone

The second example addresses a particularly common concern—that of needing to have multiple postal addresses and multiple phone numbers. You read about this earlier in the chapter in the Lurking Multivalued Attributes section, and you need to apply the same process to your case study. Your original model contained single entities for both address and phoneNumber, as shown here.

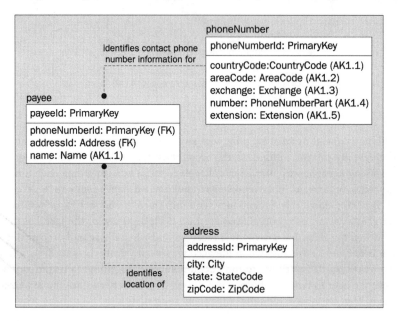

In order to be able to enter multiple phone numbers you create the `payeePhoneNumber` entity, and add a type domain entity to allow the classification of these numbers. In a similar fashion you create the attributes `payeeAddress` and `addressType`. Your new model design now looks like the following figure.

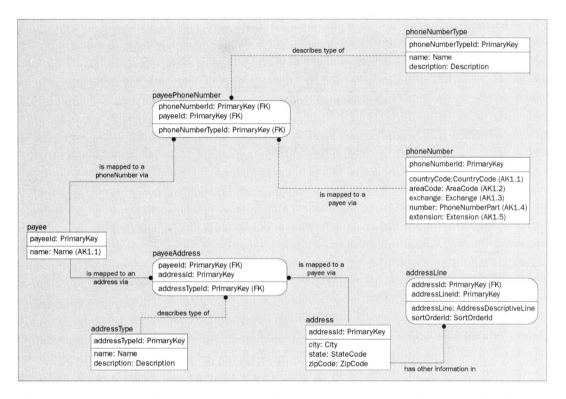

Note that a payee is now allowed to have many phone numbers and many addresses in a flexible manner, thereby allowing you to define new types of address without any additional coding; so the user will never have that same issue when the need arises to store an address.

However if you take a closer look at the address entity you have another small issue, because `city` and `state` are related (non-key) attributes, and therefore violate the Third Normal Form by appearing in the same entity. Both of these are also related to the `zipCode` attribute, because if you know a zip code you can determine the city and state. Splitting the `address` entity leads you to the following modified diagram.

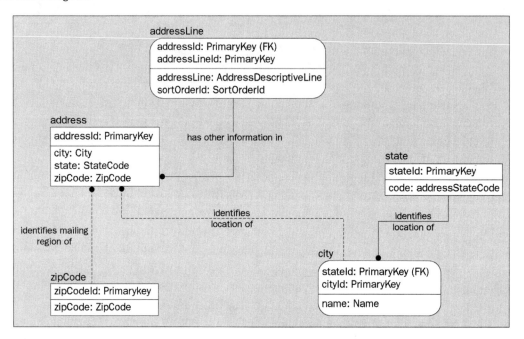

The next stage of the process is to determine the exact relationship between `city` and `zipCode`. Because one zip code may cover an entire small town, but a large city may contain many zip codes, the relationship is of a many-to-many variety. Having created city, state, and address entities, you now need to be able to combine their attributes so that you can search for addresses using full rows. To do this you create a new entity, `zipCodeCityReference`, which brings together the attributes `CityID`, `StateID`, and `zipCodeID`, and includes a new attribute `PrimaryFl`. The primary flag will allow you to set which city is the "primary" city in the `zipCode`, an attribute that the postal service will sell along with a database of zip codes and cities. In this way, your user can usually access full address details by entering only the `zipCode` attributes into an application. Building this gives you the following model.

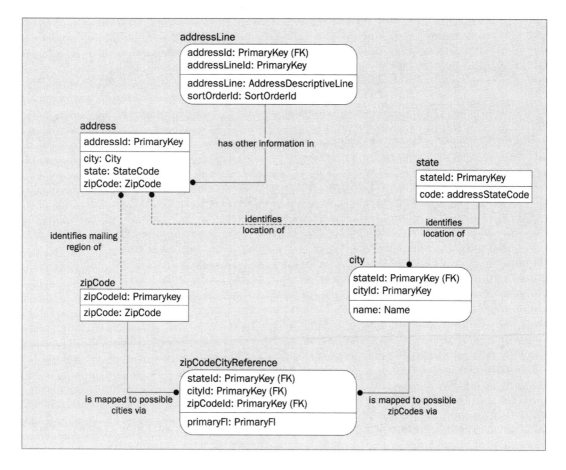

Example 3—check.UsageType

The usageType attribute was first envisioned as a way to tag a check as being used for a certain purpose. In practice however, a single check can be written for many different purposes, hence you have a violation of the Fourth Normal Form, because the user will not be able to put every usage of the check into a single value. To overcome this you create the checkUsage entity and associated-type domain, in a similar fashion to that what you saw in the previous example. This gives you the following model.

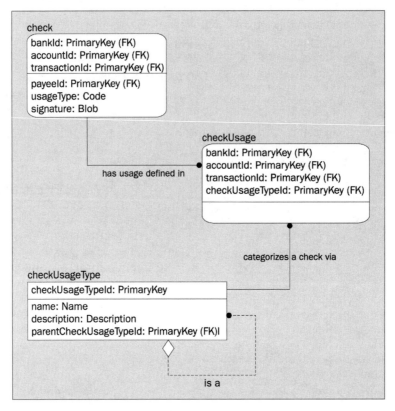

Note that the `checkUsageType` entity includes a recursive relationship that allows the user to create a tree of `usageTypes` for check categorizations, because you now allow one instance of a `checkUsageType` to be owned by another. For example, you might define the following tree as follows.

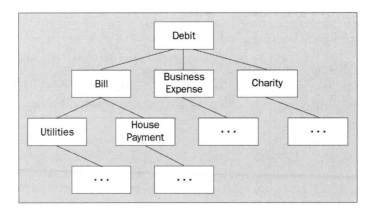

Now (using an algorithm that you'll learn about in the physical implementation part of the book in Chapter 12), you can summarize all of the bills, which in your tree include utilities and house payments, or all debits, which include business expenses and charity.

Recursive relationships may sound daunting, but aren't at all terribly difficult to deal with. The base of the algorithm is pretty simple once you understand it. First take all of the rows without parents (Debit), and go down the tree one level at a time. The first pass gives you Bill, Business Expense, and Charity, and the next pass gives you Utilities and House Payment. On each pass through the tree, you simply summarize and add to the previous levels. As mentioned previously, there's a very simple example of this in Chapter 13.

Now you need to finish the `checkUsage` entity. You've allowed the user to determine multiple usages for a check, but you haven't allowed him to allocate the amount of the check to go to each. There are two possible data solutions to the problem, either allocating check usage by percentage or by amount. In your solution, you'll choose to allocate by amount. Allocating by amount gives the user a way to discretely assign the allocation amounts to each usage type and if the amount of the check changes, the allocation will have to change. If allocating by percentage, it's too easy to forget what values were intended to be set.

Hence, you end up with the following set of entities, with the new attribute `allocationAmount`.

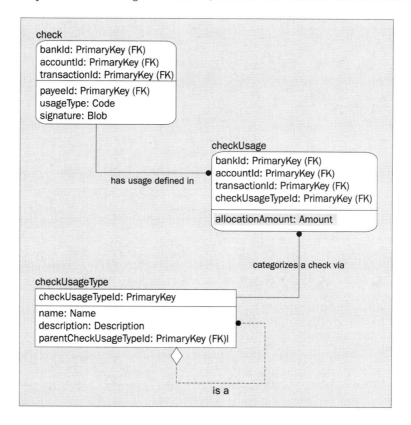

In your documentation, you'll need to record your first identified inter-entity business rule. You won't allow the sum of the `checkUsage+allocationAmount` values to be greater than the transaction amount for the check. You should also have another rule that states that `checkUsage+allocationAmount` values never come to less than the transaction amount for the check. This is impossible to implement in SQL Server 2000, but needs to be noted for middle-tier or front-end implementation because this is a type of constraint that SQL Server doesn't have (a database or end-of-transaction constraint, in which you check to make sure that everything is in balance after a transaction).

You now have most of the attributes required to actually implement your checking system. You won't enhance the attributes of the model by adding any further information in this normalization exercise. It's very important at this stage that you review the model that you've created to ensure that everything makes sense and looks complete enough. It's also time to review the data model with the client, to make certain that the model precisely models the client's business. In later chapters you'll occasionally have to make changes to your structures, because you'll do some further review and begin to consider how the users will be using the data.

The final logical data model of your system is as follows:

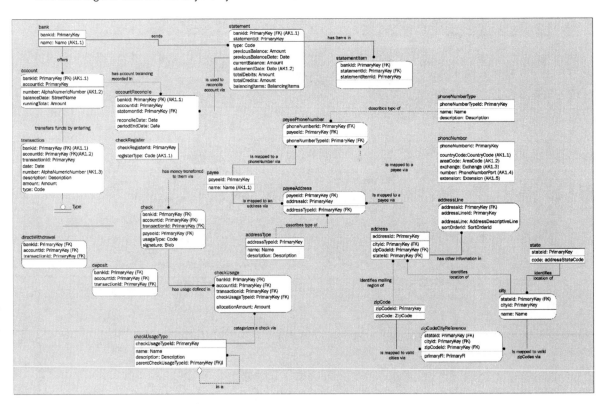

Best Practices

❑ **Follow the rules of Normalization as closely as possible**: They are summarized in the following section. These rules are optimized for use with relational database management systems, such as Microsoft SQL Server. Keep in mind that SQL Server has tools and will continue to add them to help with normalized and denormalized structures, because the goal of SQL Server is to be all things to all people. The principles of normalization are 30-plus years old, and are still valid today.

❑ **All attributes must describe the essence of what is being modeled in the entity**: Be certain to know what that essence is. For example, when modeling a person, only things that describe or identify a person should be included.

❑ **At least one key must uniquely identify and describe the essence of what is being modeled by the entity**: Uniqueness isn't a sufficient criterion for being the only key in an entity. It isn't wrong to have a uniqueness-only key, but it should not be the only key.

❑ **Choice of primary key isn't necessarily important at this point**: Possibly this is a heretical statement, but keep in mind that the primary key is changeable at any time. You have taken a stance that artificial keys are sufficient keys, even in logical modeling, but this isn't a required stance; it's just a convenience that must not supplant the choice of a proper key.

❑ **Normalize as far possible during the logical phase**: There is little to lose by designing complex structures in the logical phase of the project; it's trivial to make changes at this stage of the process. The well-normalized structures, even if they aren't implemented as such, will provide solid documentation on what the actual "story" of the data is.

Summary

In this chapter, you have been presented additional criteria for normalizing your databases beyond the forms presented in the previous chapter. At this stage it's pertinent to quickly summarize the nature of the normal forms outlined in this and the preceding chapter so far.

First Normal Form	All attributes must be atomic, one single value per attribute.
	All instances of an entity must contain the same number of values.
	All occurrences of an entity in an entity must be different.
Second Normal Form	The entity must be in the First Normal Form.
	All attributes must be a fact about the entire key and not a subset of the key.

Third Normal Form	The entity must be in the Second Normal Form. An entity is in the Third Normal Form if every non-key attribute is a fact about a key attribute. All attributes must be a fact about the key, and nothing but the key.
Boyce-Codd Normal Form	All attributes are fully dependent on a key; all attributes must be a fact about a key, and nothing but a key. An entity is in the Boyce-Codd Normal Form if every determinant is a key.
Fourth Normal Form	The entity must be in the Boyce-Codd Normal Form. There must not be more than one multivalued dependency represented in the entity.
Fifth Normal Form	The entity must be in Boyce-Codd Normal Form. Entity keys are broken down as far as possible without losing their meanings.

All of the information you've learned in these two chapters can then be boiled down into the following statement:

> **All entities must be relations and must be single themed!**

Clearly, if the entity is representing one single thing (a person, place, thing, or idea), then the attributes of that entity will necessarily only be describing that one single thing. In this way, any time you change an attribute of an entity, you're simply changing the description of that single entity, and cannot affect an incidental change in the data. The process of stepping through all of the normal forms takes you to a place where your databases require very little special coding to keep the data clean.

In the next chapter, you'll look at the issues that remain in the logical design phase of your project.

Ending the Logical Design Phase

Here's a review of what you've learned so far in this book:

- ❑ You've gathered information pertaining to the solution.

- ❑ You've covered relational theory.

- ❑ You've designed a logical model of your database using the IDEF1X modeling methodology.

- ❑ You've normalized that model.

Now you're almost ready to start your database implementation, but there are a few issues to consider before you start creating tables and generating code.

While you're still in the right frame of mind and still have reasonably free contact with the users, you should try to get answers to a few additional questions. These questions aren't exactly logical modeling, but they aren't exactly physical modeling either. One thing, however, is clear: The things you'll consider now can make the difference between a brilliant project and an adequate or even substandard one. At this point it's a good idea to make certain that there is a review with the project sponsor for a last check on whether the design covers all the requirements. Also, consider preparing a sign-off document for supporting documentation. There is nothing worse than building a "beautiful" solution to a problem, only to find out that the problem solved wasn't quite the problem that needed to be solved.

From a database standpoint, you've developed a structured data model and you're just about ready to begin implementing it in SQL Server. In this chapter, you'll take a brief look at the tasks that you must finish prior to beginning implementation, and you'll examine the final technical issues that are critical to getting the database implemented properly, such as the following:

❑ Data usage

❑ Volumetrics

❑ Project plan

❑ Test plan

❑ Final documentation review

Each of these is important to the process of implementing the database that you'll begin in the next chapter. Taking care of these important technical issues now will allow you to make changes if you missed something, which will often happen, because no one is perfect.

It's good practice to enlist the aid of other developers to validate the design. This "peer review process" will almost always save time and energy because any given applications will have similarities with other applications. By enlisting the help of others, a few things can be learned from how they approached the design. Take the ideas and suggestions offered in the reviews and evaluations to refine the model and add any additional detail that may have been omitted.

Lastly, no matter how good a job is done during the initial interviews, getting exact descriptions of all data needed from the clients is pretty much impossible. Take the time to meet with clients and ask them any questions that remain unanswered, and make sure to be clear about what is and isn't possible. Point out what assumptions have been made during the logical design and what the impacts may possibly be. This isn't so much to cover the backside as to leave the client with realistic expectations for the project. If the design doesn't match the desires of the client, it's critical to work out the details now, even if the outcome is to go back to the start of the process and discover what was misunderstood, or even cancel the project.

> *The truth will always set you free, and the time for the user to discover the gory details of how little you understand his business isn't after the database is implemented.*

Data Usage

So far, I've mapped out what data you need. You've taken copies of the client's reports, screens, and documents to try to glean the data you'll need to store, but you haven't fully considered what that data will actually be used for. In this section, you'll look at the following:

❑ Common processes

❑ Reporting

❑ Data usage and ownership

❑ Interfaces to external systems

Common Processes

Data models don't deal with how data is used (processes) or who uses the data (users). In order to completely describe the system and build full-featured systems, you need to know something about these topics. There are a few very important reasons for this:

❑ Security

❑ Ensuring that the data required to support the process exists

❑ Building stored procedures and triggers to support the processes

For example, let's say you've been developing a your data model in support of getting a book published. You have at the very least the following users:

❑ Publisher

❑ Printer

❑ Editor

❑ Writer

You would also have the following processes that need to be supported:

❑ **Suggest book**: Writers suggest topic that they want to write about.

❑ **Accept book**: The publisher decides to publish the book and create a contract.

❑ **Write book**: The least fun process, definitely can't be automated (I've tried) so likely there wouldn't turn out to be a computer-based task, but more of a wait state.

❑ **Edit book**: Take the product of the writers' delusions, and make sure everything makes sense, looks good, and is worth purchasing.

❑ **Print book**: Take the files that make up the book, and print it.

❑ **Pay for book**: Every author's favorite step, mine included.

This certainly doesn't include all of the processes required to model the book publishing process, but it's good enough for this example. Each process will typically need at least some basic data stored to explain what it means beyond a basic explanation. The following table shows a possible description for one of your processes:

Name	Write book
Description	The process of taking an idea and expanding it into several hundred pages
InvolvesUsers	Author
Pre-Conditions	Book must have been suggested and approved Outline must have been completely fleshed out and ready to write Author must be willing to forsake family and pets
Post-Conditions	A written piece of prose will be completed and ready for editing
Steps to complete	Take outline Write introduction Write all chapters Write summary

Between the model and the descriptions, you can see at a glance not only who the users are, but also what their interactions are with your system of writing a book.

There are tools out there that can be used to make this task easier, such as methodologies like UML to make the process richer in detail, as well as more useful during the implementation phase of a product. A good book on this subject is Terry Halpin's *Information Modeling and Relational Databases*.

Reporting

Reporting is one of the most important parts of any system, and this is especially the case when building a database-centric system. Almost every bit of data that you've been modeling will need to be viewed by someone in the organization in some way, either directly or perhaps as part of a calculation.

During the course of many projects, reporting gets treated as an add-on and the design and implementation of reports is an afterthought rather than something integrated into the primary project. This certainly isn't advisable, but it does happen. This is more common with corporate or internal projects, but it does happen on consulting and external projects as well.

The following Gantt chart shows a typical project timeline:

ID	Task Name	Start	End	Duration	Feb 2001				Mar 2001				Apr 2001		
					2/4	2/11	2/18	2/25	3/4	3/11	3/18	3/25	4/1	4/8	4/15
1	Implement Module1	2/1/2001	02/03/2001	22d	███████										
2	Implement Module2	28/02/2001	26/03/2001	19d				████████							
3	Implement Module 3	13/03/2001	13/04/2001	24d						███████					
4	Design Reports	13/04/2001	13/04/2001	1d											▮
5	Implement Reports	16/04/2001	18/04/2001	3d											■

Even on the rare occasion when a reasonable amount of time is scheduled for reports, the time is commonly tagged to the end of the design and development periods, because you really must finish designing and implementing the database before you can start querying and actually implementing reports from it. Then, if the project timeline slides–as they have a tendency to do for one reason or another–the time allocated for reports can be pinched even tighter.

Sometimes, when the clients begin to realize that it's getting late in the process and the reporting design still hasn't been done, they will mention it and force the issue, making sure that their reports are considered. However, even if clients don't jump up and down shouting about how important reports are to them, users *always* care tremendously about reports, because reports are what most customers use to run their business. Reports are how they get the information out and look at it, slice it, dice it, plan for it, and–most important of all–get paid for it. In some cases, reports are the only bit of a project that the user will see.

Before you end the logical design phase, it's very important to make sure that you understand what the user wants to get out of the database. Even if you cannot do a full design of the reports, at the very least you need to understand what the needs are going to be and get the general structure right.

Report Discovery Strategy

You need to be concerned with the following two different sorts of report:

❑ **Standard reports**: The reports that the user must have to get her job done. Frequently, these are very simple reports. They generally make up the core of a user's needs.

❑ **Specialized reports**: Reports that allow users to go the extra mile by giving them more than the average information that they would think of themselves.

These are two distinctly different things. Standard reports are reports that take no special skills to develop–for example, the displaying of the account balance. It's expected that the produced system will be able to produce these reports. Specialized reports are those that aren't quite so expected–they're the ones that take some specialized skill or understanding of the business process–for example, consolidating accounts on a multinational corporation. In this phase of the project it's extremely important to plan for both.

Standard Reports

Most database systems have some fixed set of required reports that are necessary for the running of the business. These may be daily, weekly, or yearly reports, all fixed to show the performance of the situation that is modeled by the database system that is being created. High profile examples that you see all of the time might include the following:

❑ **Neilsen ratings**: There is a database somewhere that tests what people watch, based on boxes they have in their houses. Daily, hourly, and weekly, it ranks the television shows based on the number of users who watch. These numbers are used to determine which shows stay and which go.

❑ **Movie ticket sales**: Every week in the papers there is always a list of the top ten grossing movies of the week. This comes from a typical database just like any other.

A less high profile example might be the following:

❑ **Utility bill**: A report of a meter reading, amount being charged, previous charges, and possibly even last year's charges.

❑ **Traffic report**: In the area where I currently live (Nashville, TN), there are cameras and detectors set up all over the highways, providing commuters with online reports of traffic flows.

Specialized Reports

Beyond the scope of the standard reports, the contacted users will have special desires for the data that will be stored in the database. It's important to meet with the clients to identify how these special reporting requirements can be met. Users frequently have great ideas in their heads waiting to get out, and they won't always be heard.

Keep in mind that the realities involved in implementing a report, or the storage for it, aren't important during the interview–though be careful not to be the one to plant unrealistic ideas in the mind of the client (all of a sudden there will exist an unwritten specification that will be a future road block if it isn't checked). The simplest strategy to employ is to ask the users to list all of the questions that they might conceivably want to ask of the data that will be stored. This serves two very important purposes. You get the following:

❑ An idea of what types of things they are thinking of for the future.

❑ Find out if you've overlooked anything in your original database design.

Using your report examples, you might ask the following types of questions:

❑ **Neilsen ratings**: The user would probably like to know about the person who was watching the TV program, whether she was watching or taping it, and if she watched the tape after she recorded it.

- **Movie ticket sales**: The age and gender of the people seeing the movie, when they saw it, how many were in the average party, and how many people walked out because they found it dull.

- **Utility bill**: How the values were affected each day by the weather, holidays, or any other situation.

- **Traffic report**: Trend analysis on how many vehicles are on the road, how the traffic flowed during the day, the effects of accidents, and so on.

There are many challenges in developing reports for the user. In fact, at first it may even seem impossible. However, by breaking down the requirements and evaluating them, you're in a better position to advise on what is possible and what isn't. Reporting requirements should be prioritized and then, taking into account time and resources (never promise more than can be delivered!), broken down into required and future needs. Note that, as the designer, it's important not to be afraid to say no if a reporting requirement is actually impossible to fulfill.

Let's look at the utility bill report mentioned previously:

- **Required needs:** Reading of meter, amount being charged, previous charges

- **Future needs**: Last year's meter reading and average temperature

- **Impossible needs**: Daily values (cannot be made due to the limitations of the analog equipment)

Document, document, document! This information will be important to someone, and even if the budget doesn't currently fit, it may later. Even if the information is for an internal customer, you should keep in mind that if the users do a better job, the information could stimulate revenue and keep the company thriving. As the data architect with a large organization, you might not be able to ask these types of questions—it will likely be someone else, just make sure to speak out whenever it's reasonable.

> **Avoid hiding "the impossible" from the members of the design team. It may not be impossible—that is why you have teams.**

Prototype Reports

Once you've defined what reports are necessary, you need to build prototypes of what the reports will need to look like and what data will be placed on them. Nearly every computer system design uses prototypes of the screens that make up an application as a blueprint of what the client wants and what you'll deliver. You must establish the same kind of thing for reports.

There are two schools of thought when it comes to what kinds of data to put on the prototype report:

❑ **Using unreal data:** Of course, it's important to make sure not to make the data bizarrely unrealistic to the client, just keep the sample data unreal enough to avoid drawn-out discussions of how the exact situation in the report has never actually happened. For example, "You've never sold products to Company X, though you've considered it." Prototype reports merely reflect possible sets of data for a given reporting situation, not exact situations. In many cases, the client's exact current data won't be fully understood until later in the development process. This sort of data allows you to cover many hypothetical situations without confusion with what has happened.

❑ **Using real data:** By making the prototype report as close as possible to the final report, you give the user a feeling of how well the data is understood. Using current and familiar data draws the user closer to the design. In addition, it provides early feedback to the designers of the report as to whether they understand the requirements, and whether their design will produce the desired result. This will not allow for freedom to cover as many possibilities, because things that have happened may not cover an adequate set of situations.

I generally fall in the first camp, but it's totally dependent on the situation, the client, and–most important–how vital reports are to the process. Either way, you'll most likely be using current data in the development of the reports, and where data conversion is included in the development process you'll want to run your developed reports using the converted data.

Determine Data Usage and Ownership

Understanding what the data will be used for and who owns it is a critical factor for the completion of the logical phase. First off, you need to check that your understanding of the following is still up-to-date by asking the following questions:

❑ Who will be using the data and what will they be doing with it?

❑ Who will be allowed to do what, to what data?

❑ From where will they access it?

❑ What applications will be used to access the data?

❑ How many users will access the data?

❑ How many of these users will need to access the data concurrently?

These will likely have been covered during the early analysis. It's incumbent on you to make certain that you totally understand the needs for the data, considering you may have discovered new data during the logical modeling phase. You'll now move on and begin to deal with complex architecture issues like security and data access architecture.

Security

Unless the client has a predefined architecture for securing his data from unwanted modifications and access, you'll find that the matter of security frequently gets pushed even further back than reporting. While it may possibly be the least important part of the project to the data architect, it's certainly important to the database administrator, so it isn't something that can be simply ignored.

When it comes to reports, security is an issue that is ultra-important. Its importance tends to depend on the information contained in the reports that the client may be using, but seldom will an organization want every user to have access to all data. A good approach is for the designer to establish a "reports classification table" and seek instructions from the project sponsor on the classification of each report and which users or user groups will have access to each report.

Including security information in the process descriptions of every actor in the system is a very useful technique. Security is implied by every process since, if the process documentation includes every possible report and every possible process, it will follow that if a process is not linked to a user, then they cannot perform some function.

For example, take your example process from earlier in this chapter.

Name	Write book
Description	The process of taking an idea and expanding it into several hundred pages
Involves	Users Author
Pre-conditions	Book must have been suggested and approved Outline must have been completely fleshed out and ready to write
Post-conditions	A written piece of prose will be completed and ready for editing
Steps to complete	Take outline Write introduction Write all chapters Write summary
Security	Author

The writer will need to have access to whatever data it takes to map the "write book" module work. No one else will have access to this data unless it's used in a different module as well.

Now consider what happens if you add a report called the "Book Report" (you could ask your 13-year-old daughter to do it). You might also define a process for it and note that it gives quite a bit of information like name, description, picture, staff comments, and sales information.

The writer may be able to view the report, but his view should be limited and should lack things like detailed sales information, for instance. In the user definition, you might include the following:

Name	Author
Description	The actor who writes the text of the book
Security notes	May only see the light version of the book report, because it contains sensitive information

Of course, you'll probably use some form of tool that should either have space for such documentation or notes columns to use instead. Either way the gist will be the same; all of the high-level tasks that are performed are documented, including who can use what and what might need to be done to secure access to it. In the "Book Report" process, you'll document the versions and security constraints for the report, along with how it's used.

Known Architecture Limitations

You'll look at determining final architecture later in the book, but I'll introduce it here, because this stage in the process is probably the last chance you'll get to ask the client questions regarding the actual demands that will be placed on the database. You need to know about the following:

❑ **Bandwidth limitations**: How will the clients actually access the data: the Web, local applications?

❑ **Likely system demand**: Minimum and maximum number of users on the system, and the required hours of operation.

❑ **Hardware limitations**: This could be political or budgetary, but imagine you figured that the user is going to purchase a million dollars worth of equipment, and the client figured on five thousand.

You need to get some handle on limitations to **performance** (how fast the database goes) and **scalability** (how performance changes as the number of users increases) before you get down to physical implementation.

Interfacing with External Systems

When I speak of "external systems," I'm referring to other databases that aren't an internal part of the system you're creating, but to which an interface will be created. Common examples include any off-the-shelf product (human resources system, payroll system, and so on) that an organization has that needs to communicate with your database.

The main problem with external systems is that some are poorly designed. Quite a few off-the-shelf systems still in use today were developed as mainframe or record manager systems and hastily ported over to a relational database system because it was the fashion at the time, and there was little understanding of relational programming.

The examples in this section are based on real-world situations so, even if they seem unreal, they do mimic real problems in real products. They're included mostly for shock value, but also to give some idea of what may be ahead of you if you wait too late in the process before taking into account the external systems that you need to interface with.

Example 1—A Problematic Enterprise Resource Planning System

A purchasing and requisitioning application I've worked with had nearly a thousand tables, but only one domain table to serve as the domain for all tables in the system. Instead of having a single table modeled, as shown in the following figure.

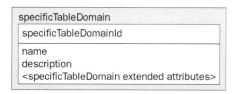

Here a single table has been modeled for each place where the client needed one—for example, payment type, resource type, purchase type, and so on. Some programmer got the bright idea to implement a single table like this, as shown in the following figure.

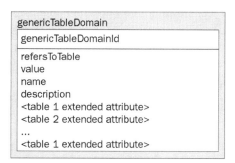

The programmer's idea was that, in getting a single table to do many things, only a single editor would be needed to manage all domain values.

Unfortunately, there are quite a few major problems with using SQL on the data in this implementation. There are the obvious implementation difficulties—like not being able to use declarative referential integrity because the specialized tables required a key value, which isn't possible in any RDBMS (relational database management system)—as well as data conversion issues. There were over 80 different distinct values in the domain table's refersToTable column. Because this method of building a domain table wasn't standard, no data conversion tool supported this type of query, and the new system you were developing certainly didn't mimic this design. Many ugly queries had to be hand-coded to extract the data.

Example 2—Another "How Not To Do It" Example

The next example arose with a third-party product I've had the "pleasure" of interfacing with, and it makes the previous situation look easy. I was implementing a system that had to interface with a business unit that the company had been using for quite a while, and it could not be replaced. The system stored its data in SQL Server, but was implemented in such a manner as to hinder interfacing with other systems. The database used structures that masked the column names in such a way that required client software to go through its interfaces just to figure out what a table had in it. For example, the following table shows the metadata that is used to define the columns in a table:

Actual Table Name	Actual Column Name	Logical Attribute Name (the name that you want to know the attribute as)	Type	Nullable
TABLE1	COLUMN1	KeyId	Varchar(30)	No
TABLE1	COLUMN2	CreatedBy	Sysname	Yes
TABLE1	COLUMN3	CreateDate	Int	No
TABLE1	COLUMN5	ModifyDate	Datetime	No
TABLE1	COLUMN6	Field1	Varchar(10)	Yes
TABLE1	COLUMN7	Field2	Varchar(10)	Yes
TABLE1	COLUMN8	Field3	Varchar(15)	Yes
...	...	...	...	...
TABLE1	COLUMNn	FieldN	Varchar(30)	Yes

The designers of the product did this in part to encapsulate the implementation away from the users. As a mechanism to prevent competitors from gaining an understanding of their structures, it works fabulously. However, building an interface to retrieve data for reports was a nightmare, requiring statements such as the following:

```
SELECT    COLUMN7 as field1,
          COLUMN8 as field2,
          COLUMN9 as field3,
          COLUMN10 as field4,
          COLUMN11 as field5,
          ...
          COLUMNn as fieldN
FROM      TABLE1
WHERE     COLUMN9 = '<field1Value>'
```

Performing data conversions, by building statements to modify the data in the tables from the new system, was a heinous and time-consuming task.

Example 3—Systems Suffering from Denormalization

One of the more frequent problems that you'll face with other systems is denormalization. Systems may be denormalized for many reasons. Maybe the database designer wasn't very proficient, or maybe it's a legacy system in which the technology doesn't support full normalization. It isn't at all uncommon to see a database with one, two, or maybe three tables where fifty are required to properly flesh out the solution. For example, you know that a table that models a person should only have attributes that specifically describe the person, but a poorly designed table may look like the following figure.

Hopefully there are very few systems as ridiculously denormalized as this one, but even the least amount of denormalization in the source system will require complex queries to load the data into your tables.

As mentioned in the normalization chapters, inadequate normalization can have the result of having data that appears to represent multiple things, when it's only meant to be a single value.

```
person
 socialSecurityNumber

 firstName
 lastName
 homeAdddressLine1
 homeAddressLine2
 homeCity
 homeState
 homeZipCode
 officeAddressLine1
 ...
 officeZipCode
 spouseName
 dateOfBirth
 homeTelephoneNumber
 officeTelephoneNumber
 computerUserName
 computerPassword
 printerPassword
 salesTotalQuarter1ofYear2000
 salesTotalQuarter2ofYear2000
 salesTotalQuarter3ofYear2000
 salesTotalQuarter4ofYear2000
 childName1
 childName2
 <and it goes on like this
 for quite a while>
```

Additional Issues when Interfacing with Third-Party Systems

One of the primary issues when interfacing with external third-party systems is coupling. The reason you've modeled the entire database without care for external interfaces is that, for the most part, it's important to keep your systems loosely coupled to the interfaces that use the data.

A technique for integrating with external systems that share similar but different data structures is to build views on the data contained in the external systems. Imagine an SKU (stockkeeping unit system) with a core SKU table that stores the data in a particular structure, and a cash register system that stores it in a slightly different format, but from which you need to access the same information. The abstraction layer created by the views allows the core system to be modified without needing to change the external cash register system.

Another good reason for identifying all external systems to which you might need to interface is that you don't want to start a data store for information that already exists and is available to you. There's no point in creating a new `employee` table if an external system has an employee table that you can use.

Volumetrics

Volumetrics is defined as "of or relating to measurement by volume," and deals with determining how large the database will grow based on the size of rows and rowcounts. This type of information will be very useful when you get to physical modeling. Typically, some idea of the size of the tables that are being designed will be acquired from conversations with the client and by looking at previous systems that are being replaced.

You can start to gather the following basic pieces of information at this point in the process:

❑ Average length of attribute data (including text and BLOB data)

❑ Percentage of data that will be filled in for every attribute

❑ How much data will likely be in the table initially

❑ Number of rows in a table and by how much this number will grow

❑ How long the life of the project is expected to be

For example, in your customer database you might have the following table of values to help estimate database sizes:

Table Name	Initial Rows	Growth in Rows per Month	Max Rows
customerType	4	0	20
customer	0	30	3000
order	0	1000	Unlimited

In this case, you're saying that you'll start out with 4 rows in the customerType table, that you don't expect much if any growth, and that you should accommodate a maximum of 20 rows. In the customer table, you'll start out with no data but you expect to add 30 rows a month, with an expected ceiling of 3000 rows. In the order table, you hope that you'll keep adding 1000 rows per month forever.

Having this kind of information at the beginning of hardware planning will be extremely useful.

Project Plan

Eventually, you'll need a project plan. Every step from here on will be relatively straightforward to plan for, especially after you've been through the process of creating databases ten or twenty times. The following bits of information should be included:

❑ What tasks need to be accomplished

❑ What tasks must be finished before others

❑ Milestones to reach for user review

❑ How long each task should take

The task of building the project plan will lie directly with the project managing team and, as such, is strictly beyond the scope of this book. Further coverage of building project plans can be found in *Professional VB6 Project Management* by Jake Sturm.

Test Plan

Another task that needs to be considered before implementation is testing, or a test plan. At this point you've designed what you're going to build; now you have to consider how do you know when you're done with the project. Obviously the test plan should include all elements of a system (UI, web pages, objects, and so on), but what you'll deal with here is simply the database portion of the project.

Initially, what is needed is a list of scenarios that you must be able to fulfill with the system. For example, say your system is horribly simple, and consists of the following single table:

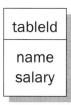

tableId
name
salary

And the only requirement is that name must be smaller than 30 characters but greater than 2. The salary value must be a nonnegative value, and must be accurate to two digits.

The test plan for this "system" would at the very least need to validate that:

❑ The name value must be between 3 and 30 characters; not less and not more.

❑ Any value put into the salary value is greater than 0.

❑ The rounding of values placed into the salary column is proper up to two digits.

A simple checklist of things to verify may be enough, though a better method is to expand each of the stated criteria into actual test data that must be run through the system to verify that the system actually works. For example, consider the table you've defined. You might define the test plan to include creating the following data:

Joe   23,400.45
Bob   34,232.59

These two rows would be your verifiable result. Then, you need to try the following:

```
Insert into table (name, salary) values ('Joe',23400.446000)
Insert into table (name, salary) values ('Bob',34232.590212)
```

205

These two rows provide the positive test and tests the rounding. On the other side, you'll try the following three statements:

```
Insert into table (name, salary) values ('J',23,000)
Insert into table (name, salary) values ('12345678901234567890123456789012345678901',20)
Insert into table (name, salary) values ('Fred',0)
```

These statements do a base-level test of the system by trying a few workable values, and some nonworking values that will cause specific errors. Obviously building statements that cover all of the possibilities will, without question, be very hard work. Most of the time these queries would not be handwritten, but would be expressed as scenarios to test with the application. A great technique for building repeatable tests is to use Profiler and capture the test statements that are being executed via the application. Then you can use the captured scripts to test and retest the data layer to show that the database does work.

> **Reality Check: Test plans are incredibly valuable when the end of the project comes along and you want to say you're finished. The user can see that the functionality that was agreed upon does in fact work. However, building full-blown test plans are often beyond the capability of smaller teams due to time and money constraints. There is no situation in which a test plan is bad outside of these boundaries.**

Final Documentation Review

Throughout the process of designing your system, you've likely amassed a great deal of documentation.

The final documentation review means exactly what it sounds like. All documentation should be read through, corrected, and synchronized. This step is frequently missed or axed from project plans when time is short—which is exactly when good documentation can make a big difference. Throughout the design process, documentation frequently gets out of synch with itself, especially when a large team is involved.

As an example, I was the data architect on a project for a moderately sized manufacturing plant. The gist of the project was to store measurements on samples of the materials that the plant was producing, for quality control purposes. I gathered information about what the company did, what it wanted, and how it would use the data. I determined its needs, mocked up screens, and designed a database for solving its problems. The problem was that, though I understood the fundamentals of the reporting needs, I didn't understand everything that was required.

❏ The reporting was so complex—due to intricate calculations (one of the queries was over 250 lines of code)—that, when I had mocked up a test query and verified the results, I failed to check exactly how the plant would use the data. It took more than 50 old measurements to calculate a new value, and what happened if someone went back and changed one of those old readings? The managers wanted graphs with the last hundred calculated values, so computing on-the-fly wasn't an option. I just failed to understand much of how these calculated values were used, or how to make them more valuable to their staff.

❏ Second, I failed to understand the organizational structure of the company. I dealt with the two people who were running the project and they seemed experienced enough, but looks were deceiving. During the design phase of this project, the primary user contact was still in training. Near the end of the six-month project, they finally understood the exact needs for the system I was developing, but it was too late in the process

❏ The third problem was the worst. I failed to properly review the documentation and make sure that everything that was agreed upon was written down. I did this because it was a time-and-materials contract. Unfortunately, I had to give them an estimate of what the costs would be like. I got the figure wrong by at least 200 percent, and the project took three times as long to complete. Consequently, I lost the follow-up work to a different consulting firm.

The important moral in this story is that all three of these problems would have disappeared if I had fully reviewed the documentation and made the clients sign off that they had agreed to what had been designed. If the entire plan had been meticulously written down, the additional time required would not only have been foreseen but likely accepted. Instead, I ran into trouble because I had other projects to move on to.

It isn't always possible to document every last detail of a system that is being built. However, it's extremely important at this stage to review the documentation, and make sure that what has been specified can actually be built in the amount of time specified, and that the requirements aren't too open-ended. Regardless of the type of project —corporate, time-and-materials, or fixed bid—it will always make sense to protect yourself by developing decent documentation.

Future Requirements

As a final step, you should document any future requirements that the client may have for the system you're creating. As the designer, you should try to discover the future plans for the system, and what requirements may arise from them. Wherever feasible, the design for the current project should take these into consideration, as long as it doesn't significantly increase costs. You'll look pretty silly (and turn out to be a lot poorer) if, six months after a project completes, the client asks for what he considers to be a trivial change, and you have to tell him it will take six months to implement because 50 tables will have to be changed—especially when you knew that this might have been a possible request from the outset.

A little advance planning might mean a two-week turnaround, a happy customer, and possible future business. Obviously, you cannot kill yourself trying to second-guess the client's every need or whim—you have to be sensible about this. Be up front with the client. "If you spend an extra two days adding X, then it will make it much easier to add Y should you need it in the future." If the client says, "Nah! You'll never need that" then fair enough—but write that down (if a signature can be acquired to validate it even better!). Be proactive. As a professional designer, it's important to be thinking beyond the simple limits set by the client. Suggesting possible future enhancements and planning for them shows an understanding of his business and rarely hurts the bank balance.

Case Study

Previously, you had built your data model for your case study, and you were ready to start building. But not quite—you still have a few more pieces of information to gather.

User and Process Identification

In your system, the interviewer identified two users, a *general account user* and the *accounting clerk* (note, the process of the interview goes outside of your scope of topic, but will uncover information that you have to have). Where an account user will want to be able to perform actions such as getting account information, withdrawing money, making deposits, and so on, the accounting clerk needs to be able to do tasks such as accessing accounting information and entering transactions. You can summarize the user and processes you've identified as being of interest to you when you start to build security and write procedures, as follows:

Name	Description
General account user	Any user who can deposit or withdraw money from the account
Accounting clerk	User who has the ability to enter and maintain accounts

Next, the following processes are defined, including the users that will need to execute the processes.

Name	Description	User
Get account information	Allows users to retrieve account information such as name of bank, balance, and so on	General account user, account clerk
Enter transaction	Allows user to record that a transaction has occurred	Account clerk
Enter check	Allows user to specifically record a check-type transaction	Account clerk
Balance	Allows user to reconcile items that have been reported by the bank	Account clerk

Name	Description	User
Download statement	Allows user to download the items from the bank that the bank has committed	Account clerk
Withdraw money	Users getting money from account to spend	General account user
Make deposit	Users putting money into account	General account user
Write check	Users writing a paper document and giving it to another person to transfer funds	General account user

In developing a real system, understanding process is a very important part of design. However, because this book is geared totally towards building the database, I won't be expanding and perfecting the list of processes.

Reports

When you ask the users what kind of reports they must have, you get the following list:

❑ **Account summary**: Simply a categorized list of transactions, based on the checkUsage attribute. This report must let the user determine the level of subcategories to show. For instance, she could simply ask for all debits vs. credits, or another level down where she could see the basic categorization—all bills, business expenses, and charitable donations made (as you saw in the checkUsageType table example in the previous chapter).

❑ **User activity**: A list of all transactions attributed to a given user, or simply grouped by user. Also needs to be able to show any transactions that haven't been attributed to the user who actually spent the money.

❑ **Account balance**: A list of all accounts and balances.

Further discussion led the users to give you the following specialized reports:

❑ **Spending trends**: A very useful report that should be fairly easy to program (but certainly isn't required) gives the trends of where the money goes in a more graphical easy-to-understand manner than the Account Summary Report.

❑ **Future balance estimator**: The client would like to take spending for previous months and extrapolate to get an estimate of what he'll probably spend in future months. This would be in lieu of a budget-type tool. This report would also come in handy when building budgets.

❑ **Automatic check writing**: Sometime in the future the client would like to have a facility to automatically pay bills, including the ability to have automatic payment with some intelligence built in, for situations in which the required amount isn't available in the account.

The client would also like to build data marts based on company data, in order to get multigrouped reports based on payee, payee location, where the money goes, how much the amount was, and so on. This is clearly above and beyond the current scope, but is very interesting to know.

Note that you've discovered at least one new data element and a new table for the database in the User Activity Report. So you add a user table, and associate a user with a check and a deposit as shown in the following figure.

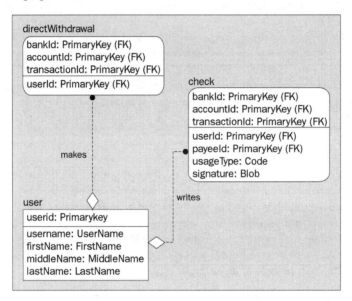

This will allow you to track the user who writes a check. This is another example of why you need to go through the entire design process, without leaving out any steps or leaving any stone unturned.

Prototype Report

You'll now produce prototype reports of those listed in the previous section. To save space in this case study, I've I chosen just one–the Account Summary Report–for illustration purposes.

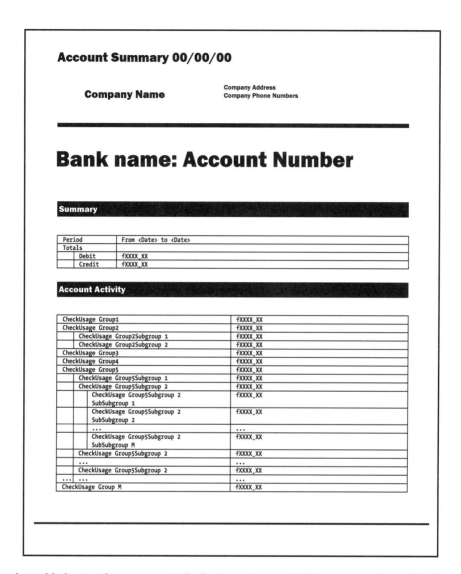

The user has added a simple summary to the basic requirements that you were given. You then have each of the check usage–type groups summarized, and the amounts listed in the second column.

You'll create prototypes for each of the three required reports. These reports should be well handled by your design structures. The specialized reports that users have requested could be tackled in the next iteration of the system.

Interfacing to External Systems

The only external system that you'll need to deal with belongs to the bank. From the original interview documents, you have the format of the bank's automatic register, repeated here.

Column	Datatype	Required
Transaction Date	Date Only	Yes
Transaction Number	String(20)	Yes
Description	String(100)	Yes
Item Amount	Money	Yes

Transaction
  Transaction Date
  Transaction Number
  Description
  Item Amount

In the paper version, you have extra summary-type values that you apparently don't get from the electronic version. You'll likely want to make your statement attributes optional, or possibly fill them in from a summary of items. You also need to add a few attributes to your data model for the statementItems, and you note that you had not even considered how an item would be considered reconciled. So you adjust your data model as shown here.

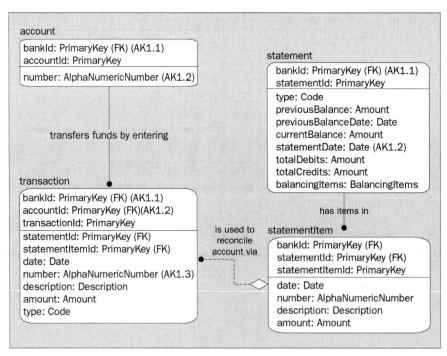

Note that you added the four attributes to the `statementItem` table for each of the columns in the bank's downloadable statement items. In order to use these items for balancing, you need to link the item used for balancing to the item in the register.

> **You discover new things about your solution as you go along. All you're doing now is making important tweaks, closing important holes that you didn't find the first time around.**
>
> **At this point you must attempt to avoid "analysis paralysis," because over-analyzing, continually questioning the client, and making more and more changes to the design prevents you from getting to the implementation phase. At some point a line must be drawn in the sand and you must start the implementation phase, even it isn't 100-percent perfect. You'll deal with additional shortfalls as they are discovered. Experience dictates exactly when you have designed enough.**

Data Conversion Plan

In your system, the client has decided to start afresh with her check register; hence you won't have to do any data conversion. You'll simply start the account out with a credit or debit for the initial balance.

This is the simplest type of data conversion plan—that is, none. Because you're replacing a paper-based system, if the clients had wanted to do data conversion, they would have needed to enter all of the data by hand. Frequently this isn't a possibility because it's too costly and problematic.

Volumetrics

For volumetrics, you build a simple table containing details of all of the other tables in your database, with the expected number of rows that the tables will initially contain. The best way to approach this is to take the system's important tables—as shown in the data model in Chapter 7—and work from there. Say you decide that a good starting point for your estimates is the `transaction` table. You then simply inquire from the user about each table or group of tables, and extrapolate out to some of the other tables—especially the ones that you've added yourself.

Note that you'll also need to gather some statistics on columns. You'll make quite a few decisions concerning how columns are implemented, and the users may be able to assist in estimating the numbers. You can also refer to the existing system as a guide.

Let's take the transaction table first. In your case, the users have decided to start fresh with no actual transactions. They expect to have around 300 transactions per month, with 245 of those being checks, 5 being deposits, and 50 being direct withdrawals.

From there you get estimates on the number of different payees they want to start with, and how many they expect to add. You basically guess the rest of the numbers based on these values. For instance, from the estimate of 245 checks per month, you guess that they have 100 payees that they can set up, and they'll likely add 30 new payees a month. Obviously, the more input you get from the clients, the better informed these estimates will be.

You end up with the following table of approximates that will need to be reviewed with the client.

Table Name	Initial Rows	Growth in Rows per Month	Max Rows
account	1	0	20
accountReconcile	0	1	36
address	50	30	600
addressLine	55	35	700
addressType	5	0	10
bank	1	0	5
check	0	245	10000
checkRegister	0	1	36
checkUsage	75	400	12000
checkUsageType	20	0	40
city	450	20	25000
deposit	0	5	4000
directWithdrawal	0	50	1000
payee	100	30	300
payeeAddress	100	30	600
payeePhoneNumber	100	30	600
phoneNumber	50	30	600
phoneNumberType	5	0	10
state	50	0	70
statement	0	1	36
statementItem	0	300	15000
transaction	0	300	15000
user	10	2	50
zipCode	1000	10	99999

Here is a description of the previous table:

❑ **Initial Rows**: How many rows do you expect to be added to the table when system goes live (zero indicates no rows yet)?

❑ **Growth in Rows per Month**: The number of rows you expect the table to grow to (zero means little to no growth).

❑ **Max Rows**: A crude estimate of the maximum number of rows ever.

Project Plan

You make some estimates concerning how long the process will take in the project plan. For example, to finish the task of building this database, you might have a Gantt chart as shown here.

ID	Task Name	Start	End	Duration	May 2004					Jun 2004				Jul 2004			
					4/20	5/3	5/13	5/20	5/27	6/3	6/10	6/17	6/24	7/1	7/6	7/15	7/22
1	Physical Modeling	5/1/2004	5/7/2004	5d	■												
2	Design Data Protection	5/8/2004	6/1/2004	19d		■■■■											
3	Implement Access Code	6/4/2004	7/5/2004	24d							■■■■						
4	Implement Reports	7/5/2004	8/15/2004	30d											■■■■		

You would need to drill down into each task, as follows:

Physical modeling:

Choose data types – 1 day
Designing optimistic locking mechanisms – 2 days

Or something like this. The amount of time things will take is really subjective, but should be based on previous experience and not on how much Dilbert you hope to read as you sit at your desk and look busy. The project plan is beyond the scope of the book and won't be discussed further.

Test Plan

You won't define a test plan here in the case study.

Final Documentation Review

Once you've finished, you stack up all of your papers, make copies, distribute them, and call a meeting a few days later. During this meeting, your goal is to have the client sign off on everything you've claimed in your documentation. This is what I like to call the point of no return. Once the client signs off on the blueprints for the system, the code-writing race can begin. You probably won't spend very much more time with the user, except for progress reporting progress.

This isn't to say that the plans are fixed in stone, because you'll likely find things that you didn't do well enough. Hopefully, though, any changes will be in the form of an additional attribute, not an entire module of tables with screens.

Best Practices

- ❑ **Understand how the user will use the system**: Your logical design process has largely been surrounding *what* data is needed, but when you start to implement it, it's important to understand what the user will be doing with the system. How many users, where will they be located, and so on. This information will feed into architecture decisions.

- ❑ **When choosing an architecture, make decisions based on need, not fad**: The type of architecture chosen can be easily be based more on what magazine is sitting on a nontechnical manager's desk rather than sound technical planning. It goes without saying that that would be a bad idea, but decide how to implement the system based only on needs, requirements, and available resources and limitations.

- ❑ **Don't underestimate the effort needed to interface to external systems**: The majority of software written will *not* be easy to build interfaces to.

- ❑ **Remember reports**: Reports are usually the most important part of the system. It isn't uncommon that executive types will **only** see printed output from the system. Make sure that they aren't an afterthought.

- ❑ **Understand the processes that the system is used for**: This can make a big difference in how the system is architected, not to mention that therein lies data that you'll likely need to support some of the processes. This process information will also serve as the basis of the security for the system.

Summary

The goal of logical design, however unreachable, is to discover everything that you need to implement a system. Once the implementation battle has begun, it can be very hard to change plans. However, I'm assuming that because you're reading this book, you at least have the common sense to not continue the *design-review-repeat* process forever until analysis paralysis sets in, but to find the best point when the design is ready to be implemented.

Throughout the entire logical design part of the book, you've been trying to design well enough to avoid having to change directions once you get rolling. You've gathered data, interviewed clients, pored over documentation, built models of your data, and finally normalized them, all so that the design should be ready for implementation.

In this chapter, you skirted very close to physical implementation in your attempts to finish off this part of the process. You've looked at planning your data needs, from security issues to reporting. You've also added your input to the project plan and made some estimates concerning the size and growth of the data you'll be storing in your tables.

Once this stage was complete, you reviewed the design—going back to make sure that you designed what you set out to design, and that any changes from the original requirements had been noted. If you're lucky, your documentation will now be in such a state that you don't need to actually go back and touch it again.

The output from the logical design phase is a blueprint, much like that which a building architect develops with a client, getting their hopes and dreams for the system, then tempering them with the reality and physics required to actually construct it. Once the client has approved the final blueprint, subcontractors are called in to add walls, lighting fixtures, plumbing, wires, and all the other various bits that go into putting together a physical structure.

Your blueprint isn't unlike a building's blueprint, with written descriptions, models, diagrams, and so on for physical implementation. The next phase of the project will now take you away from this very abstract world into the phase where you start hammering nails, erecting walls, and moving towards a database where your data can live and be safe.

Planning the Physical Architecture

In this chapter, you start the process of physical implementation by considering questions about how you should architect the solution. In order to illustrate the type of judgments you may have to make, consider the following scenarios and assess what each requires for successful implementation. Consider some of the possibilities discussed earlier in the book, such as an ODS or operational data store (used to separate reasonably current read-only structures for reporting) or simply additional hardware to improve query performance. Each is a realistic example of databases that are quite commonplace today. Let's assume in each case that the logical design is complete and appropriate in each case.

Scenario 1

The database contains 100 tables. One of the tables will have a million rows and will grow at a rate of one hundred thousand rows a day. There are 2,000 users entering data into the system, and only three people carry out reporting all day long.

Scenario 2

The database contains 20 tables. All of the tables have relations to at least one other table, and 10 of the tables grow at a rate of 100 rows per day. Three people enter all of the rows twenty-four hours a day, while reports are run by an automatic process and sent via e-mail to the senior executives in the organization.

Scenario 3

The database has two million users, fifteen thousand of whom will be accessing the database at any given time. Every minute, each of the users will create two new rows in a database.

The Solution

So what is the solution? Can you make a decision with the information you have? Unfortunately, the answer is no, because none of the scenarios contains sufficient information to allow you to make an informed decision.

In Scenario 1 for example, in order to determine whether there is a need to build a special database to support day-to-day reporting needs, you would need to know how long it takes for the two thousand users to enter the hundred thousand rows. This could take all day, or it could be rows from users who are actually machines that automatically enter data in an hour every day. Furthermore, while you could anticipate that data in this case has to be transformed, summarized, and stored in a data warehouse to do reporting against, the exact nature of any reporting needs isn't outlined in this case.

Scenario 2 may seem simpler, because you might suppose that adding one thousand rows to a database a day isn't that many, especially if a single user enters them. As an automatic process runs reports, you know that it can be scheduled to run at an opportune time. In this case, you probably will not need any kind of special database for reporting, because the system should not be busy, thus the querying of the OLTP database can take place directly. However, you should take into consideration that you're going to add several hundred thousand rows per year to the database, which, while certainly not a large number of rows, may be a problem depending on the type of data in the rows and the type of reporting required. Simple aggregations that are supported intrinsically by SQL Server will probably be no problem, while more complex statistical operations may require special handling. You'll look deeper at the topic of complex reporting needs later in this chapter.

Scenario 3 is indicative of a website. It's also arguably the simplest of the scenarios to solve. The primary reason for this is that if the user has a database with two million users and fifteen thousand active connections, there will probably be money to throw as much hardware at the situation as is needed. However, aside from the hardware investment solution, there are still important issues to resolve regarding the nature of the rows that will be generated, and what reporting requirements there will be.

This chapter was actually the hardest for me to write, because a good logical design is dictated by the problem being analyzed, without the trade-offs required during implementation in allowing for performance and usability issues. Good logical modelers will generally come to similar conclusions for the same problems. You follow the same type of design methodology, regardless of whether you're working on a small database to store a television schedule or a large database to store engineering-quality control data. After doing it well a couple of times, doing it over and over again, with consistent, expected results will be less of an arduous task.

Determining how the physical database solution should finally be laid out and implemented is a different story altogether. Here you must take a set of parameters and build the solution that represents the logical model in a manner that allows the business to meet all its expected requirements. Be certain that this isn't always easy to get right every time. In implementation, not only must the logical design model be considered, but also the work of the other IT staff (the network engineers, DBAs, database programmers, and so on) in order to make the best choices when selecting hardware, coding SQL procedures, building transformations from the OLTP database to the ODS, and so on. It isn't always possible for these people to make optimal choices and, because the database server is typically the central part of any system, it can often get the lion's share of the blame for system problems.

You'll start to look at all of the pre-implementation issues you need to deal with before creating tables. While you can't describe every situation that may be encountered in physical implementation, you can at least consider the two main factors that you have influence over, namely:

❑ **Reporting**: A key issue in all your design work is balancing the need for frequent updating of your given database with reading data in order to provide accurate reporting. Maintaining facilities to monitor the business is very important to the process of making informed decisions concerning tweaking that is required within the business to optimize its efficiency.

❑ **Performance**: Performance is a very different sort of issue. There are situations in which the well-normalized database may provide less-than-adequate performance in relation to what is required. You'll look at some of the basic things you can do to adjust performance, while still preserving your normalized database structures (in most cases as they'll provide the greatest data integrity protection).

Client-server systems are built to allow changes to be made to your *current* data, and have it applied *immediately*–not to send off a query and wait for its completion. Hence you should do whatever you can to keep the OLTP system unencumbered by users who are executing reports or simply browsing through the data. While you must consider performance (because this is what gets users all excited), you shouldn't compromise the integrity of the data that you store. It's the data architect's primary duty to store data that is needed, in a clean manner, thereby protecting it from anomalies that occur in poorly structured databases.

Reporting Issues

The goal of reporting is to arrange raw data into a meaningful format that will enable users to make timely and adequate decisions. As discussed in the previous chapter, reports are usually the most important part of the system to the end users, and in this section you'll learn about some of the ways that reports can be optimized to fit into a range of database structures. Quite a few issues arise when discussing accurate and timely reporting, not all of which are as obvious as you might think.

Size of Data

One of the most frequent problems in reporting is that the volume of data needed to answer a user's questions is too large to perform queries on in a reasonable manner. The nature of the problem is dependent upon what hardware that SQL Server is running on, be it a desktop computer with 16MB of RAM or an 8-node cluster with 4GB of RAM each. Generally however, querying techniques will need to be refined based on the volume of data involved, though determining when "small" volumes become "large" ones can become somewhat problematic, as the following examples illustrate:

> *Imagine that the United States government has a database somewhere that contains every social security number it has issued, along with every transaction that it has made for the purpose of adding money to, or distributing money from, the social security accounts. It's clear that over the past 50-plus years, there would have been millions upon millions of rows added each month.*

While this may seem like a large quantity of data, it's dwarfed by databases being created by some Internet service providers and Internet sites in their desire to log every click, purchase, and search that their users perform. In this way, e-commerce websites track as much information as they can about their visitors, in order to personalize their site to show goods that they predict the visitor will have an interest in. Such applications are likely to log immense amounts of information concerning the millions of daily visitors to such sites, all of which will be required for analysis by the site owners.

Another example of logging activities that are becoming commonplace is that of manufacturing quality-assurance databases, in which a robot takes large numbers of measurements to ensure that the items being manufactured fall within a specified tolerance. This kind of application will obviously generate a tremendous number of rows, and these rows will need to be available to reverse any bad situations that are ongoing in the manufacturing process.

In these situations, there are a few basic approaches you can take to try to solve the problem:

❑ **Optimization**: If you're faced with a situation in which you seem to have reached the limit for the amount of data that your system can handle, there are many times when a simple change in your system setup (such as adding processors, increasing bandwidth, or even separating data out into different file groups) will correct the problem. While large numbers of indexes (or indeed a lack of them), or poorly considered optimizer hints (overriding how the optimizer chooses to deal with queries), can kill performance, in many cases cries of "too much" anything may well have more to do with the less-than-optimal setup of the server or databases.

❑ **Data access**: Consider a case in which you were using a tool that implemented joins at the client level, rather than in the database server. Performing a join may well involve bringing each of the linked tables to the client before creating the join using its own query engine, which isn't a great idea when you're dealing with thousands of rows, and is probably unfeasible in the case of millions of rows. However, the query might run admirably if performed using SQL Server. In many cases, problems with large amounts of data are linked more to the actual passing of data over a wire, rather than the SQL operation itself. More on data access times will follow later in this chapter.

❑ **Powerful hardware**: Perhaps you might be able to simply put together more efficient hardware that will handle the amount of data that you have to deal with. Using a faster CPU, or as much RAM that will fit in the machine, as well as fully optimized disk arrays may not be the only solutions to the problem, but will certainly go a long way toward helping you understand the problem. Hardware will be discussed in some depth in Chapter 14.

❑ **Reporting database**: As discussed in Chapter 1, and as you'll see in Chapter 15, you can build a copy of your data that contains the answers to many of the queries that the user will want to make, in order to support your day-to-day operations. In the previous e-commerce example, you saw that building a cached copy of your data in order to answer queries on user activities is a relatively easy process. The alternative to this is to scan through all of the rows that have logged all of the actions of not only the single user, but *all* the users that have been through the site: a *real* pain to carry out!

In all likelihood, you'll end up using a mixture of these ideas, though the first two are a good place to start, because they don't require huge capital expenditures and can be a fun challenge (but don't let your pointy-haired boss hear you say that or you might have a cubiclemate before you know it!).

Complexity

The complexity of the reporting required directly depends on how you use basic SQL operations. Simple queries, using only intrinsic SQL operations, are generally no problem (though poorly designed queries can cause nasty situations, like forgetting a WHERE clause and duly locking up an entire table, thereby preventing others from modifying it), but it isn't always possible to restrict calculations to these operations alone. For example, I have implemented reports that utilize a single SQL statement containing over 300 lines of code. While the time required to execute the statement wasn't tremendous (in seconds) the operation proved costly in terms of resource utilization (disk and CPU usage), thereby limiting concurrency. What the users wanted to be able to do was see the last 100 executes of this query on a graph, with each aggregation using the previous 100 values in the table to make up the calculation. This required the execution of a 300-line query up to 200 times. Sounds nuts, but since each query required the previous 100 values, it was necessary to recalculate each of the values since the previous 100 values would be needed, and their value may have changed. It is clear that to have users running this process hundreds of times a day would have been unreasonable.

In this case, and in others involving extremely complex reporting circumstances, it may become necessary to store some precalculated data. This data will violate the Third Normal Form, but it's invaluable when additional data or business rules require the answers to the same queries over and over to do their jobs. This is an illustration of the denormalization process that was touched on in Chapter 7.

Note of course that the precalculated data could come from calculations outside of SQL Server. When using precalculated data you must ensure that if the underlying data changes, the calculated code is executed again, and the stored values change. In the previous example, a change of a single value could cost as much as 100 executes of a very complex process in order to repair the denormalized data. There isn't much that can be done about this, because modification anomalies of this sort are at the core of the normalization argument. To ensure data integrity, all references to the same data must be changed simultaneously.

Search Requirements

If a report requires a large amount of search freedom (for example when users need to perform queries on many different columns from many different tables), the complexity can increase to the point that it's unmanageable. The tables in a normalized database aren't optimized for querying, precisely because the process of normalization attempts to create single-themed tables. One of the ways to work around this type of problem is to use **indexed views**. This provides a means of precalculating a view based on its own definition, and so the precalculation could be used to build a view that presents the users with the data in an understandable interface, which they can then query in a straightforward manner. This method suffers from the same performance issues that storing your own denormalized data does, because SQL Server has to maintain the indexed view in a similar manner whenever the underlying data changes.

223

User Access Contention

For any given system, the more concurrent users there are, the more contention you're going to have between them. In OLTP operations, transactions and queries should be designed to last for an extremely minimal amount of time. Reports are another matter. Many report queries can take quite a while to execute; it isn't uncommon to have reports that take 15 minutes, an hour, or even several hours to execute.

Problems may occur when, for example, there is a particularly knowledgeable user (though one who really doesn't understand concurrency issues) who writes ad hoc queries. If the user doesn't have any understanding of exactly how SQL Server concurrency works, then they may try and execute queries that involve numerous joins between large tables of data, thereby taking many hours to complete their actions. Because of this they are liable to eventually begin blocking other users' activities. This is despite row-level locking implemented in SQL Server 7.0, which is designed to greatly decrease the likelihood of exactly this type of blocking scenario. However, the way that row-level locking was implemented allows the optimizer to choose between row-level, page-level, and table-level locks. When a user writes a particularly poorly constructed query that accesses many pages in a table, the optimizer will eventually escalate the locks to a page or even table lock. Occasionally, when users perform such queries, the eventual locks will include pages and tables still being modified by the active users, thereby causing a great deal of frustration!

Timeliness

Timeliness refers to how current the data needs to be in order to support the user's needs in making informed decisions. For example, suppose that you build an operational data store from your OLTP data, feed a data warehouse and data marts from it, and refresh the data daily. This entire setup will be useless to the user if all decisions are to be made using up-to-the-second data.

How quickly you can provide data access depends not only on the amount of time it takes for the data to travel from one location to another (**latency**) but also on your design. Your different approaches may be summarized as follows:

❑ **Current**: Current access is the most problematic because there is very little you can do about it. There are many ways to handle these needs and all of them cause you performance problems. You'll frequently just have to build stored procedures that read data directly from your tables, thereby accessing data in such a manner so that you avoid locking data (such as using the READ UNCOMMITTED isolation level). If it isn't possible to do this without an unreasonable performance "hit," then you can use indexed views or possibly even denormalized structures in your stored procedures. Sometimes the performance hit is unavoidable and actually represents an acceptable drawback in relation to your data-presentation needs. Equally you may be able to devise a compromise situation, such as randomly sampling data, rather than including every value, to improve your speed of data retrieval.

❑ **Some allowable latency**: If the user doesn't have an instantaneous read requirement for data, you can use any of the other methodologies. You can build ODS structures that are refreshed as often as the data size allows and the business rules permit. Care will need to be taken to ensure that the frequency of update is at least greater than the user's needs.

❑   **Large latency**: When time isn't a primary issue, and particularly when tremendously large amounts of historical data are involved (such as trend analysis over periods of time), the data warehouse or companion data marts are the best approach, because you can have most of the possible (and all of the frequently used) aggregations and queries set up.

Frequency

Frequency in this context refers to the number of times a report will be run. One of the systems that I've previously worked on had a report that was considered central to a client's efforts. It was run every 24 hours at midnight and would take 3 hours to run. Because it was run during the slower hours of the day, the users could live with a small degree of performance degradation.

On the other hand, many other systems have users who need to keep tabs on how things are going throughout the day, such as a bank manager who needs to make sure that the bank has enough money on hand, or a broker who needs to run up-to-the-minute trend reports on each of his clients or funds. Reporting of this type will probably require super-powered hardware and extremely optimized queries as well as some denormalized structures.

Performance Concerns

If you take the example of a database built to monitor and store consumer activity at a website, not only will you design this database logically to log every activity, but you also might store every item, and every page that is displayed on the screen as well. This is a very large database (think terabytes), and with its data stored in a normalized fashion, a single database would quite possibly not be able to withstand both users modifying the data, and web users querying its pages.

In the following section, you'll look at some of the possible computer and networking configurations (commonly referred to as **topologies**) that you'll use to combat a number of common performance issues.

Connection Speed

Of primary concern here are WANs **(wide area networks)** as well as web applications (which you could technically regard as a WAN in different clothing). Let's take, as a very simple example, the classic two-tier client server system as shown here.:

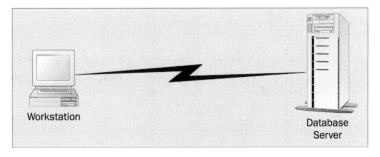

Varying the connection speed or distance between the client and the database server will considerably change the way you end up organizing your database system. In the following list, you'll look at some of the common networking speeds and how they'll affect your decision to vary from this simple topology:

- **Very fast connection, such as a 10 Mbit, 100 Mbit network or greater**: These types of connections are most commonly seen within a company's physical network. Unless you have database-size issues, you should have little problem employing a simple two-tier client-server system as shown in the previous diagram. The user could connect directly to the SQL Server and require very few special optimizations.

- **Moderate connection, such as an ISDN, DSL, cable (2 Mbit down to 128 Kbit) connection**: In general, basic client-server applications are fairly workable over such connections, but you might need to ensure that you optimize all of your calls to the database, in order to reduce the number of bytes that go back and forth over the network and the number of separate communications involved. A possible enhancement would be to optimize your client software by caching frequent calls to the database that may be repeated, and to batch multiple operations together.

- **Slow connection, such as a dial-up (56 Kbits in principle, often more like approximately 28.8 Kbits)**: Dial-up applications are still more prevalent than one might realize. Many sales or support workers have dial-up connections that they use to run their database applications every night from their hotels. While users who access their applications via a dial-up connection are generally more understanding when it comes to access speed, the applications must work adequately. In these cases, you'll certainly have to optimize the applications, or possibly even move to a replication scheme to present parts of the database to the client using some form of compression. You'll look at replication in some length later in this chapter.

No matter how fast the workstation or database server is, the speed at which users connect to the server is crucial to performance. If someone is trying to push 1000 rows back to the client where the row has 3000 bytes, and doing this over a 128 Kbit ISDN line, the client is going to be really unhappy, because it will take approximately 3 minutes (3000 * 1000 * 8 (bits per byte)) / (128 * 1000 = 187.5 seconds) to complete. This doesn't allow for networking overhead or any other users. If 10 users were trying to use the same bandwidth, then it would take 31-plus minutes for them to all receive their data!

> *It should be noted that this solution could be optimized to retrieve rows and display them as needed, instead of retrieving all 1000 rows at the same time. For instance, you might show 20 rows in one page, and as the users scroll through the results, the remaining rows would then be downloaded in chunks. However this isn't always the case when using third-party tools, such as Query Analyzer.*

The reality is that very few of the larger systems today are being built with a simple client-server architecture. Most of them have parts distributed all over the network, and even the world. The following example is a pretty wild-looking design that includes web servers, data warehouses, and even a legacy mainframe system.

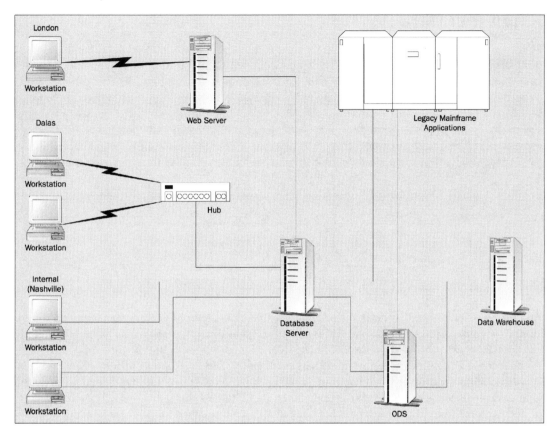

This diagram shows a very minor example of how complex the architecture may get. The complexity of your solution is bounded only by the architect's imagination (and oftentimes fate plays a large part because the most difficult foe of architecture is usually the way an organization is located in a building or multiple buildings). Some organizations have tens or even hundreds of database servers, many of which are connected together via all sorts of connections with all sort of different reliability factors. In this case, each one of the lines between items represents a network connection. At any of these connection points, you have speeds that may vary from blisteringly fast to doggedly slow, and each point should be considered as a liability (in design terms), because networks tend to be less than 100-percent reliable.

Although it's important for the database designer to at least be aware of how connection speed affects the performance of applications, the system administrator will handle some of the wider aspects of networking issues.

Amount of Data

SQL Server 2000 is a very scalable database server. It scales from Windows Pocket PC handheld devices, through a single Pentium-200 MHz laptop with 32MB of RAM running Windows 95, or a dual Pentium 4 desktop with a half gigabyte of RAM, all the way up to a 16-server cluster of 8-processor servers with 4GB of RAM each, and everything in between. The amount of data that can be supported goes from a megabyte or two on a Pocket PC to multiple terabytes on the server cluster. The size of data will affect your coding methods. You can get away with some programming conveniences (ignoring optimizations and such) with ease if your primary table in the database will have one thousand rows as opposed to one billion. As an illustration, take this simple example:

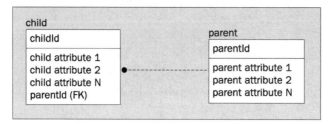

As a matter of definition, if a row in the child table exists, the migrated key from the parent table must exist. Now consider the situation in which you want to delete a row from the parent table. It then becomes apparent that the size of the child table will be extremely important. If there are ten rows in the child table, to delete a single row in the parent table SQL Server must scan through ten rows. This is no big deal, but if there are a million rows, it isn't quite so simple a task for SQL Server (even with indexes this could take an unreasonable amount of time). It follows that if you're dealing with a billion rows in the table, the row may not be able to be deleted in a fortnight (of course that would give the user time to watch Wimbledon!). In this case, you would probably implement an additional column in the parent table to indicate that the row can no longer be used, but you wouldn't actually delete the row. However, setting this flag on the parent table only will leave rows in the child table related to the flagged row, which requires careful handling. Hence in either case, you may not be able to handle the situation in what is an optimal manner.

Budget

Any solutions you devise must be based on what is appropriate for the organization, because increasing the size of the budget to pay for expensive hardware may not always be an option.

The following are three main areas of concern:

❏ **Hardware**: Not enough can be said to emphasize how inappropriate hardware will cause heinous problems. In Chapter 14, you'll look at sizing hardware for database growth, the number of users, and so on. "Never skimp on production hardware" is the simple message. In Chapter 15, you'll look in some depth at the concept of having at least three different environments, one each for development, testing, and production. In order to build, verify, and implement a proper database system, at least two separate servers will be needed.

❑ **Software**: Budget sufficiently for the operating system, database software licenses, and any tools needed for building the software. Read with care the licensing agreements on the software to avoid overpaying for it.

❑ **Staffing**: Depending on the size of the project, be prepared to have staff capable of handling each part of the database system that is being developed. Very few database architects are also great networking specialists, great database administrators, great documenters, great testers, great coders, and great...(you get the point).

Number of Users

One of the most difficult performance issues to deal with concerns the number of users (or connections) to be supported. As each connection requires approximately 12KB + (3 * (network packet size *<size varies but defaults to 4KB>*)), or 24KB, most system architects aren't exactly concerned with the number of users that a system will have. However, in this day of database-supported websites, the effective user totals that could be accessing your database could be anything from 10 to 10 million or even more! In attempting to deal with such vast numbers of users there are a number of methods that you can use including the following:

❑ **Connection pooling**: If a user connects and disconnects many times in her applications, it can be advantageous to use the connection-pooling features in ODBC 2.5 and beyond, or OLE DB. These features allow the drivers to let the user "think" that they disconnected but actually hold the connection open and wait for a further command.

As a brief word of caution, connection pooling does NOT do its own cleanup when you tell a connection to end. Most importantly, any open transactions may not be closed out and could affect later connections, even in the case of multiple users sharing a connection, so suitable caution should be exercized.

❑ **COM+ (or any variation on the n-tier applications)**: COM+ enables offloading of some of the processing that could have been done on the client end, and pool connections among many different users, so that a good bit of the overhead of creating and destroying connections is eradicated. By pooling connections, 10,000 concurrent connections can look like 1000, or even 100.

❑ **More power, more memory**: Just add more hardware doggone it! Unfortunately budget constraints may mean that this solution isn't possible. As mentioned previously, each connection to the server requires ≈ 24KB of RAM. This may not seem like too big of a deal, but if there are 10,000 connections to the server, it could equal 240,000KB, which is a good part of the 256MB that a standard SQL Server can use. If you add in the processor overhead of manipulating all that RAM over and over again, then you quickly see how problems can develop.

❑ **Clustering servers**: Microsoft SQL Server and Windows 2000 support clustering multiple database servers and treat them as a single server. Using clustering allows you to build very large, very powerful database-server systems. The idea with these systems is to distribute the load of an application across a number of servers, so that additional servers can be added as the number of requests increases in order to deal with the additional load. This process is known as **load balancing**. Because each server (ideally) is capable of handling a client's request individually then if one server breaks down, or there is a need for additional servers to be added to the cluster, there is no breakdown in performance.

❑ **Application-specific read-only copies of data**: This is a technique that works well when building websites. Most of the data that you require when building data-driven web pages is read-only. For instance, consider a hypothetical product description database, in which you have all of your products stored in a strictly normalized set of structures, so you can avoid all of the pitfalls of redundancy. Then consider the web page that the user will see that has some current price, color, sizes, shapes, specifications, and so on all listed on the same page. In this case, you might build a table that has all of the values that the web page needs in one table, instead of 50 tables, and 300 rows. You probably wouldn't want to pre-generate the entire user's page, because you certainly would want to be able to personalize it (add in discounts, and so on) and indeed change its look and feel on the fly. Additional storage will be required, but your processing needs will be greatly reduced thanks to the reduction in the number of joins performed.

SQL Server Facilities

Having considered many of the issues relating to the performance of your database systems, you should now look at the tools that SQL Server offers the designer. In this section, you take a quick look at what these tools are and how they can be used primarily for those who don't have much SQL Server experience. Regular SQL Server users can skip this section and head for the topology examples in the next section.

Replication

Replication is a wonderful facility that assists in making copies of databases and maintaining them at some interval for you. This interval can vary from immediately to days or weeks. Replication can be carried out between SQL Servers, or even from SQL Server to Microsoft Access, Oracle, or almost any database that supports the Subscriber requirements for SQL Server (see SQL Server Books Online for more information).

A couple of terms that we need to introduce here are as follows:

❑ **Publication**: The source of the data being replicated, though it may or may not be the original creator. Much like a physical printed publication (hence the name), a publication is a database that has been marked for other databases to **subscribe** to. The database is split up into tables marked for replication referred to as **articles**.

❑ **Subscription**: When a database uses a publication to get a replica of one or more articles of a publication, it's referred to as the **subscriber**. The subscription can be to a single article or all articles.

SQL Server provides several models for implementing replication:

❑ **Snapshot replication**: Makes a copy of the data of the Publication database and replaces the entire set of data in the Subscription database on a periodic basis.

❑ **Transactional replication**: Initially makes a snapshot of a Publication into the Subscription (just like snapshot replication), and then applies any transaction asynchronously to the Subscription as they occur on the Publication.

❑ **Merge replication**: Allows for the building of multiple databases (one of which is chosen as Publisher and the others are Subscribers) in which all changes from the Publisher are added to the Subscriber and vice versa. This allows editing data in either place and changes are applied to the other automatically. Merge replication is very useful for mobile clients where maintaining a connection to the primary server is unfeasible. Merge replication also has default and custom choices to allow for conflict resolution in the case where multiple users edit the exact same pieces of data.

Linked Servers

Linked servers allow you to access heterogeneous SQL Server or OLE DB data sources directly from within SQL Server. Not only can you simply access the data, but you're able to issue updates, commands, and transactions on this data. For example, to access a SQL Server named LOUSERVER, you would execute the following:

```
sp_addlinkedserver @server = N'LinkServer',
    @provider = N'SQLOLEDB',
    @datasrc = N'LOUSERVER',
    @catalog = N'Pubs'
```

Then you can execute a query to retrieve rows from this data source as follows:

```
SELECT *
FROM LinkServer.pubs.dbo.authors
```

This is a simple example, but it shows that you use common SQL code, instead of complex code, to access external data sources. With linked servers you're able to access additional SQL Servers, Oracle servers, Access databases, and Excel spreadsheets, just to name a few. And the beauty of it is that no additional syntax has to be learned to access a myriad of different types of data. The ugly side of it is that to join the given set to another set, a great deal of data *may* have to be passed from one SQL Server into temporary storage on another, before the join is performed, which can have serious performance side effects.

Data Transformation Services (DTS)

When replication will not work due to changes (transformations, hence the name) that need to be made in the data, Microsoft has provided DTS, which transforms data and transfers it between OLE DB sources. DTS also allows you to transfer indexes and store procedures between SQL Servers.

DTS lets you build packages that group together multiple transformation operations and objects that can be run either synchronously (one operation waiting for another to complete) or asynchronously using the full power of SQL Server. For example, you can build data-scrubbing (removal or cleaning of data) transformations from one table to another, with the ability to calculate new values using simple VBScript.

DTS is a fully-featured data-scrubbing tool and as such has a plethora of settings and possibilities. Further details can be found in *Professional SQL Server 2000 DTS* by Apress.

Distributed Transaction Controller (DTC)

DTC is the facility that implements a **two-phase commit** to enable transactions involving more than one server. The process is called a two-phase commit because each of the servers that are involved in the transaction is sent two special commands to start and end the process.

❏ **Prepare**: The Transaction Manager sends a command to each database server from its resource manager. The server then prepares to accept the commands that will be sent.

❏ **Commit or rollback**: Once the "user(s)" have completed whatever tasks and commands they want to execute, the commit or rollback phase begins, working much like executing a COMMIT TRANSACTION on each server.

In a strictly SQL Server coding manner, once DTC has been turned on and linked servers have been created, you can update the authors table both on the server where this code is executing, and the linked server.

```
USE pubs
GO
BEGIN DISTRIBUTED TRANSACTION

UPDATE authors
SET au_lname = 'Davidson'
WHERE au_id = '555-55-5555'

IF @@error <> 0
BEGIN
    ROLLBACK TRANSACTION
    RETURN
END

UPDATE linkserver.pubs.dbo.authors
'SET au_lname = 'Davidson'
'WHERE au_id = '555-55-5555'
```

```
IF @@error <> 0
BEGIN
    ROLLBACK TRANSACTION
    RETURN
END

COMMIT TRANSACTION
GO
```

Note that the DTC controller works with data of any type where there exists an OLE DB driver that supports the distributed transaction interfaces. It should also be recognized that if DTC hasn't been installed, the BEGIN DISTRIBUTED TRANSACTION statement will fail.

SQL Data Management Objects (SQL-DMO)

SQL-DMO is a set of COM objects that encapsulates almost every feature of SQL Server. From DMO you can carry out tasks such as creating tables and indexes, and automating object creation and administration tasks. The objects can be used from any tool that allows the instantiation of COM objects, such as Visual Basic, VBScript, VB for Applications, C++, and as you'll see in the next section, SQL Server itself. There are many good examples in the SQL Server Books Online that illustrate the power of SQL-DMO.

COM Object Instantiation

Another nifty feature that has existed since the 6.x versions of SQL Server is COM object instantiation. Using a pretty powerful (if a bit clunky) T-SQL interface, you can make a call to most COM objects and have them do almost anything you require.

In the following example, you instantiate the SQLServer DMO object and then connect to it as follows:

```
DECLARE @objectHandle int, @retVal int

--instantiate the sqlserver object
EXECUTE @retVal = sp_OACreate 'SQLDMO.SQLServer', @objectHandle OUT
IF @retVal <> 0
BEGIN
    EXECUTE sp_displayoaerrorinfo @objectHandle, @retVal
    RETURN
END

--connect to server
EXECUTE @retVal = sp_OAMethod @objectHandle, 'Connect', NULL,
'LOUSERVER','louis', '<none of your business what my password is>'
IF @retVal <> 0
BEGIN
    EXECUTE sp_displayoaerrorinfo @objectHandle, @retVal
    RETURN
END
```

While instantiating a COM object is very useful, it can also be a slow process. The object must be created (and memory allocated for it), executed, and finally destroyed, all in a manner that is specifically non-SQL-like. Make use of this functionality only when a SQL-based solution isn't possible, or in procedures that won't be called that often.

SQL Mail

SQL Mail allows SQL Server to send and receive mail using a simple Outlook or Exchange interface and either an Exchange or POP3 server. The server can be made to answer e-mails that contain queries, thus returning the answering resultset as an e-mail. It can also be added to stored procedures and triggers when required.

Examples of how useful this facility can be are tasks such as sending reminders for items on a calendar, or indeed sending warnings to tell the user that a certain condition has occurred, such as a negative balance on their bank account. In the following code snippet, you use SQL mail to send you a very happy e-mail:

```
EXEC xp_sendmail @recipients = 'yourname@domain.com',
                 @query = 'SELECT * FROM Authors',
                 @subject = 'SQL Server Report',
                 @message = 'Hello!',
                 @attach_results = 'TRUE'
```

Full Text Search

Full-text searching with SQL Server allows you to build very powerful searches that work much like any Internet search site would. Using full-text search lets you search through text columns as well as external system files. The query syntax for full-text search is simply an extension of regular SQL Server commands.

For example, consider the following query:

```
SELECT title_id, title, price
FROM pubs..titles
WHERE CONTAINS (title, '"Database" near "Design"')
```

Using the CONTAINS keyword, you're searching not only for titles that have "database" and "design" in the title, but for locations where titles are close together.

Note that while full-text capabilities ship with SQL Server 2000, they do not come installed by default. If you try to execute that statement in pubs without configuring the pubs database, yet also configure the title column in the titles table for full-text support, you'll receive an error message and the previous example will fail. The full-text indexes are stored separately from the SQL Server, and as such may be slower than intrinsic SQL Server operations. Further details regarding setting up and implementing full-text searches can be found in *Professional SQL Server 2000 Programming* by Wrox Press.

SQL Server Agent

Last in the section on SQL Server Facilities, but far from least, is the job-scheduling capability of SQL Server Agent, which is the glue that makes your systems operate. Replication uses the agent to process transactions, schedules DTS packages to run at certain times, and also schedules your own stored procedures to execute and launch operating-system programs.

Setting up the SQL Server Agent is beyond the scope of this book; the reader should consult SQL Server Books Online for further details. Suffice to say that SQL Server has a built-in facility, running in its own security context, that will execute almost anything your database will require.

Basic Topology Discussion

In this section, we'll take a look at some of the more important topologies that you might choose to employ when you're building your applications.

Thin Client vs. Thick Client

The "thickness" of a client relates directly to how much processing is done by the end user's client program. A client may be thick by doing all their own data processing, for example, in loading data into Excel, or they may be thin by processing all data on a server and having it simply delivered through a web browser. SQL Server can be used in a variety of manners, either just as an optimized file structure delivering to thick clients or as a fully featured data-centric server delivering to thin clients. You'll look at the following generic classes of client involvement "size":

❑ Thick clients

❑ Thin clients

❑ Somewhere in between thick and thin

Thick Client

The best example of a thick client would be an application written in Visual Basic that accesses text file databases using ODBC. Because a text file is certainly not an RDBMS (relational database management system) and as such cannot protect or manipulate itself, you must include every bit of data-validation code in the client. Even operations such as browsing the data must be managed by individual pieces of code that are located on every client.

However, a thick client isn't without its problems. Because you've already prevalidated the data, it seems like overkill to have SQL Server validate it. On the other hand, unless the client is the *only* method of getting data into the server, you leave your data open to errors whenever manipulation is done without the application. This may seem like a small price to pay to have a user-friendly application, but rarely can all data edits be made strictly through a single piece of software.

Another problem is that as data size increases, manipulating all the data may become problematic. This may require faster and faster resources on the client as the size of the data grows.

Thin Client

On the other end of the spectrum is the thin client. In this scenario, the client code would not validate the data that is being entered at all, and would trust that the SQL Server mechanisms will take care of any errors and report them. A pretty good example of a very thin client is the SQL Server Enterprise Manager Query window:

au_id	au_lname	au_fname	phone	address	ci
172-32-1176	White	Johnson	408 496-7223	10932 Bigge Rd.	M
213-46-8915	Green	Marjorie	415 986-7020	309 63rd St. #411	C
238-95-7766	Carson	Cheryl	415 548-7723	589 Darwin Ln.	B
267-41-2394	O'Leary	Michael	408 286-2428	22 Cleveland Av. #	S
274-80-9391	Straight	Dean	415 834-2919	5420 College Av.	C
341-22-1782	Smith	Meander	913 843-0462	10 Mississippi Dr.	L
409-56-7008	Bennet	Abraham	415 658-9932	6223 Bateman St.	B
427-17-2319	Dull	Ann	415 836-7128	3410 Blonde St.	P
472-27-2349	Gringlesby	Burt	707 938-6445	PO Box 792	C
486-29-1786	Locksley	Charlene	415 585-4620	18 Broadway Av.	S
527-72-3246	Greene	Morningstar	615 297-2723	22 Graybar House l	N
648-92-1872	Blotchet-Halls	Reginald	503 745-6402	55 Hillsdale Bl.	C
672-71-3249	Yokomoto	Akiko	415 935-4228	3 Silver Ct.	W
712-45-1867	del Castillo	Innes	615 996-8275	2286 Cram Pl. #86	A
722-51-5454	DeFrance	Michel	219 547-9982	3 Balding Pl.	G
724-08-9931	Stringer	Dirk	415 843-2991	5420 Telegraph Av	C
724-80-9391	MacFeather	Stearns	415 354-7128	44 Upland Hts.	C
756-30-7391	Karsen	Livia	415 534-9219	5720 McAuley St.	C

Data in Table 'authors' in 'pubs' on '(local)'

Pretty much whatever you enter into the fields will be taken by the entry form and passed to SQL Server (it will actually do a small amount of validation based on some of the column properties). The entry form in turn will take the data and save it unless it has been instructed not to do so based on any of the domain information for the column in the table. One of the great things about using thin SQL Server clients for all data editing is that you never have to worry about where the data comes from because, if you have coded your server properly, all data in the database will be clean. Data is also validated once and only once. This will improve the performance of your applications, especially when the instances of errors are very low.

The downside is a decrease in application usability. Because the application has no idea of what the data should look like, it cannot assist the user in avoiding errors. This is very apparent in applications that have rules that affect more than a single column. Take the following example.

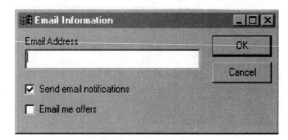

It's easy to see that you need to have a rule to prevent you from checking either of these checkboxes unless the user has an e-mail address. In the database this is simple to implement, but if you don't program any of this logic into the front end there is no way that you can avoid the situation shown in the following figure.

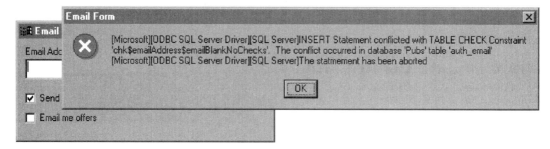

In this case, you had a rule that made certain that if the user didn't enter an e-mail address, then none of the checkboxes on the form are allowed to have values. This situation was clearly violated by your data. You could devise a fairly complex error-mapping scheme, in order to map the error in a more user-friendly format, but the underlying process will never be a very good way to handle the situation.

Somewhere In Between Thick and Thin

This brings us nicely to "somewhere in between." Almost every application built around a database server will fall into this category. The most important point to be made is that the data is the most important thing. The goal is pristine data. There are however certain types of rule that aren't suited for thick client implementation, such as the following:

❑ Inter-table rules

❑ Uniqueness of data

❑ Foreign key relationships

For these types of issues, you need to make sure that you cover them at the database-server level. The reason for this is that enforcing such rules can require lots of data to be touched to execute the validation. For example, consider foreign key relationships. To insert or delete a row with a foreign key relationship, it's essential that you consider every row in the related table. Doing this at the client level would require that the entire table be pulled down to the client.

If you go back to your previous example VB form, you would need to do something similar to the following figure.

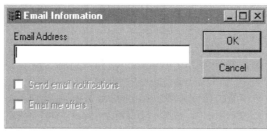

Here the two checkboxes have been disabled so that the user cannot interact with them until the e-mail address has been filled in. Just how far you go with the prevalidation of data is a cautious mix of usability with maintainability. (For example, changes to the data schema may also require changes to the VB program and, as a consequence, retesting of both the schema and VB code.) If you wanted to validate that the e-mail address typed in was valid, you might simply let the SQL Server perform the validation using a check constraint, thus mapping the check to a suitable message for the users.

Client to Data Configurations

Now you'll look at some of the basic configurations that you can use when building database-server systems. Although the group you'll cover isn't inclusive, it will certainly give you a basis for customized configurations that solve your own individual problems.

Classic Client Server

This is the old faithful configuration, and yet it's still important after all these years. Thirteen years ago this was a very new concept. Twelve years and 364 days ago you all began trying to come up with a better configuration, and while many applications are now of an *n*-tier type, client-server is still appropriate in a number of situations in which SQL Server is employed.

Basically, you have one or more workstations directly networked to a SQL Server database server. The connection needs to be a reasonably fast one, because primarily all that needs to be transmitted across the network are SQL commands sent to the server and a resultset that's returned to the client.

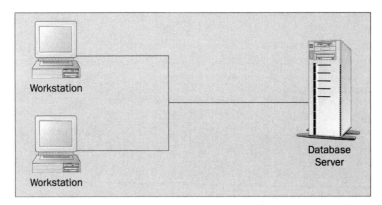

One of the primary merits of this configuration is simplicity. The client software sends commands directly to the database to retrieve or change what it needs. If these commands are well thought out and well encapsulated (a topic you'll look at in some depth in Chapter 12), and the results you receive from the server are as narrow (as few columns) and as short (as few rows) as possible, attaining required performance usually won't be too difficult. If you have a relatively small number of users who access your data, this configuration is a suitable one. However what constitutes a "small" number will depend directly upon the type of hardware the database server is run on.

When the number of users grows very large, or when you have to handle machine-driven data entry, the overhead of the client-server system configuration can become too much to bear. One of the primary reasons for this is that the most expensive operations are connecting and disconnecting to and from the server. Most applications require several connections to the server and, to reduce network overheads, are frequently written to hold on to their connections. As mentioned previously, keeping around 5,000 to 10,000 open connections to the database server can be a heavy drain on processing resources.

Three-Tier Configuration

Three-tier configurations (and more generally n-tier configurations) are pretty much the norm when it comes to medium- to large-scale projects. The goal is to separate the presentation logic from the business logic and the business logic from the data logic. As depicted in the following diagram, the user's workstation generally never connects to the database server; it simply connects to a group of objects on a middle tier.

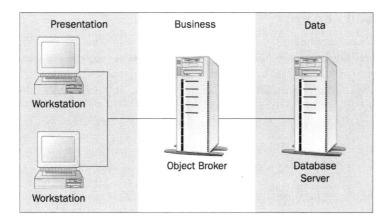

Ideally, the business objects that are in the business layer have two very important tasks.

Connection Pooling

To reduce the overhead of the client-server model, the object broker pools connections. Because clients tend to make the same requests over and over, despite needing an open connection to the database server for a much smaller time than they usually have them, the object broker maintains a pool of connections that it uses to connect to the database server. You may also have many instances of objects cached for use on the object broker as well as the ability to have multiple object brokers. Essentially, the philosophy behind this configuration is to take the job of connecting to the client out of the hands of the database server and put it on a more scalable device.

Enforcing Business Rules

You may well encounter performance problems with certain business rules that appear somewhat arbitrary, and include a large number of AND, NOT, and OR clauses that make them inefficient to code. An example of such a rule might be the following:

A user's subscription covers weekdays from Monday to Friday, but NOT Saturdays and Sundays, unless they take out the enhanced cover, which includes weekends, though not bank holidays. If an engineer is requested outside the hours of nine and five this will cost an additional fee, payable to the visiting engineer.

Rules like this generally aren't conducive to being dealt with in Transact-SQL code, because the handling will require feedback from the user after the first time they try to save the row and the rules are liable to change frequently depending on management's changing needs. If you code in a functional language able to interact with the users, business rules are easier to implement, and indeed alter. In the next two chapters, you'll see that the only rules that you should implement in SQL Server are all nonchanging rules that will be enforced on the data in the database. This may sound as if most rules are constantly changing and require feedback, but this is seldom the case. There are usually very few such rules, but they're quite often the more important rules, and most of the time they're very challenging to implement.

Heavy Use Web Servers

Another scenario that is becoming somewhat more common is that of having thousands or even millions of read-only users connected to your database. In this situation, you can make one or more read-only copies of your data (in a heavily denormalized, read-optimized form). The load-balancing switch (and a whole lot of setting up that is way beyond my core abilities) takes requests from the client, routes these requests to a web server (each web server being a copy of the same web server), then the web server calls one of the database servers (again routed by the load-balancing switch), as shown in the following figure.

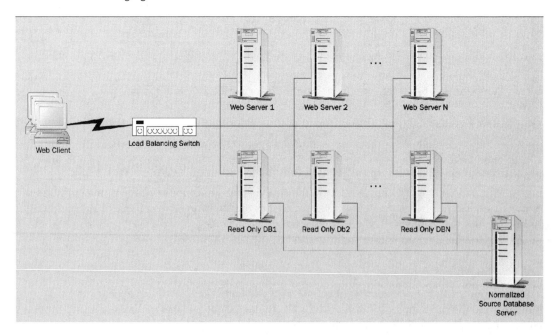

The normalized database is the source of all edits on the data, and if the user needs to modify data (such as make an order, or save some settings) then you can provide interfaces to the source database server or possibly to another server that you use only for editing data. Take for example a large media and books e-commerce site with tens of thousands of CDs, books, and so on. Users will not sit still and wait to see the list of products containing the phrase "Garfield" more than a fraction of a second, and there are far more lookers than there are purchasers. All information regarding these items will exist in a normalized database configured to ensure data integrity. For performance reasons, you could take this data from its normalized form, and transform it into prebuilt, prejoined queries in order to build the web pages that the customers of the website will view. You might also partition the data across servers. Based on factors such as frequency of use, you might put classical music on one server, rock music on another, and so on.

Wide Area Network

In the global economy, many organizations are spread over an entire country, or indeed different continents. In some cases, you can build simple client-server, or even multitier applications that will be sufficient for your data editing needs. However, there are also many cases for which it's impractical to edit and report on data over a WAN. Hence you can build a topology that is basically as shown in the following figure.

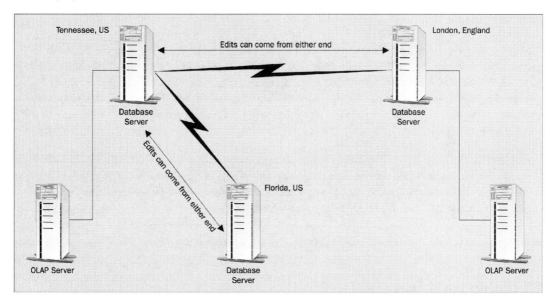

You can use merge replication to allow for editing on either end of the pipe, then merge changes back into all of the servers. In this manner, each of the offices in your diagram will feel as if they have their own database, where they could edit all rows in the database. You might partition the data to avoid having one user in Tennessee edit one row, at the same time as another in London, but you might simply let SQL Server's conflict resolution facilities handle the cases where this occurs.

Case Study

In our case study, we're going to assume the simplest topology possible while still showcasing all of the ideas that we've looked at. We'll use a simple client-server setup as well as an ODS.

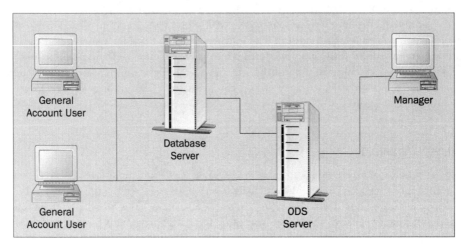

One of the main reasons to stick to a tried and true client-server topology is that our goal is to display the power of the relational database engine and demonstrate how to implement data protection using these facilities. To make this example clear we'll be implementing business rules on the database server when at all possible. I'll certainly discuss any situation where this client-server topology is a hindrance. Obviously, it isn't required that you implement your systems in exactly this way, but the goal in this book is to demonstrate the power of the SQL Server relational engine. In this chapter, I intended to make it clear that the physical implementation may take on many different forms, yet still remain adequate.

> **No matter how the solution is architected, the data still reigns as king of the database system. Invalid data of any kind can take what should be very valuable data and reduce it to a mere pile of ones and zeros.**

Best Practices

❑ **Avoid jumping to conclusions**: Take the documentation that you've gathered and understand the needs of the customers before deciding upon architecture. Often what seems to require a certain type of architecture may not, based on the time of use, frequency of use, or number of users.

❑ **Choose an architecture that meets your needs**: Fads come and go, but the most important thing is to build solid, responsive database systems that treat the data as money. The end user cares about the data, and could care less about the architecture (other than some basic morbid curiosity, that is).

❑ **Make certain to understand reporting needs**: Reports are the life of many companies. A good percentage of your time will be spent producing reports for management.

❑ **Analyze the situation completely**: Before determining architecture, be certain to understand the parameters of the client's issues. Do they have enough bandwidth to go a certain direction, will there be too much data, how many users, how much money can they spend now and later?

❑ **Use the tools that come with SQL Server to their fullest**: SQL Server provides a rich set of tools that are good enough for most users. Consider these tools when building systems. There are also fine third-party tools to supplement the SQL Server tools.

Summary

It's probably easy enough to guess from all the other chapters of this book that there are absolutely NO easy answers for dealing with the extremely wide range of possible situations, configurations, and parameters that can affect the implementation. It's very important that you not only take what you've learned in this chapter, but, depending on your role, learn everything you possibly can about how SQL Server and its additional tools work. Use other books and SQL Server Books Online.

You've looked at merely a small subsection of the different possible ways to connect a database to a client, or to architect a solution. This chapter doesn't tell you everything you could possibly need to know about the physical architecture of a database design. That would require a whole book in itself. In this chapter, I sought to give you the bulk of the information to allow you to get a feel for the subject, and solve 80 percent of problems you'll face. You'll also decide where to find further information to tackle the remaining 20 percent of problems.

The next chapter explores the process of building tables, including a full look at the basic SQL Server objects, such as indexes and datatypes, which you'll use to build your eventual databases.

10

Building the Basic Table Structures

The goal in this chapter is to turn your logical model into the physical tables that will comprise your database. This can be a laborious task, but using any of the readily available commercial database design tools will make the task far easier. During this implementation phase, you have to reorganize your objects, add implementation details, and finally turn it all into code.

In this chapter, you'll build your code without the benefit of any tools or code generators, so you get to see exactly what is going on. Instead, you'll use Query Analyzer and hand-edit the DDL (data definition language) for defining tables. You'll look at the code to generate tables and relationships, but not any extended code that defines data domains, beyond choosing appropriate datatypes. You'll examine datatypes, discuss some of the extensions to these that you may possibly want to use, and define some basic columns and datatypes that you'll probably want to reuse. The next chapter will deal with extending the definition of domains to further constrain data values beyond sizing or typing issues.

Finally, you'll define the unique constraints and indexes on your tables in order to make certain that you have proper keys defined in order to ensure that you only have unique rows in your tables.

When you finish with the topics in this chapter, you'll have a database schema comprising a group of tables with indexes and relationships. You'll have established a firm basis for the implementation of business rules that will be covered in the next chapter.

Database Generation Tools

What you're about to do should, in practice, only be done with a decent database generation tool. There are several excellent database generation tools that are equally good for database modeling. It isn't impossible to maintain a database server without them, but in many cases, the original structures will have been generated by a tool–it's recommended to use them.

Most database schema generation tools will be data modeling tools, such as those you used in the first part of the book to build the diagrams. Most data modeling tools allow you to convert a logical model into a physical model without losing the original logical model. You'll make some changes to the model during physical modeling, but it's important to keep a logical model so you can see the original specification for the database.

During this phase of the implementation, many programmers will be eager to start writing code. If you have to build all of your tables and code by hand, it will take a huge amount of time to complete. The first system that I wrote database code for included over 800 stored procedures and triggers, developed by hand over eight months. This was ten years ago, and it was a fantastic learning exercise. Today, advanced database design tools let you build databases with comparable code in a matter of weeks.

> *There are tools that do much of the "detail" work for you, but if you don't have a full understanding of what they're doing it can make it very hard for you to be successful. Doing it by hand before using these great tools is worth all of the blood, sweat, and tears it will cost.*

However, in order to show you how the physical implementation process works, you aren't going to use any of these tools for the next five chapters. You'll build by "hand" the scripts that a tool would generate automatically. This will help you to understand what the tool is building for you. This is also a good exercise for any database architect or DBA if he wishes to review the SQL Server syntax; except maybe on a database with 90 tables unless you have a few months where you're trying to look busy.

You'll deal primarily with a development database in these chapters. These are characterized as containing data that has no actual business value. Developers should be able to modify or destroy any of the sample data (not structures) when developing code to access a database. Unfortunately, many programmers will beg for real data in the database straight away.

Physically Designing the Schema

In the logical design part of the book, I discussed in quite some detail how to design your objects. In this section, you'll begin to take this blueprint and develop actual database objects from it. Just as building engineers take an architect's blueprint and examine it to see what materials are needed and make sure that everything is actually realistic, you'll take your logical model and tweak out those parts that might be unfeasible or just too difficult to implement. Certain parts of an architect's original vision may have to be changed to fit what is realistic, based on factors that were not known when the blueprint was first conceived, such as ground type, hills, and so on. You too are going to have to go through the process of translating things from raw concept to implementation. During logical design, you hardly looked at any real code examples and did your best to consider only features common to all relational database systems. The logical model you've designed could be implemented in Microsoft SQL Server, Microsoft Access, Oracle, Sybase, or any relational database management system.

From now on, I'm going to assume that you have Microsoft SQL Server 2000 installed, and that you've created a development database to work with. You'll look at many of the features that SQL Server gives you, though not all.

Throughout the chapter, your goal will be to map the logical design to the physical implementation in as faithful a representation as possible. You'll look at the following:

- ❑ Transforming the logical design into your physical design
- ❑ Creating tables
- ❑ Creating columns
- ❑ Datatypes
- ❑ Physical-only columns
- ❑ Collation
- ❑ Keys
- ❑ Creating relationships
- ❑ Sharing your metadata with the developers

Each of these steps will be covered in detail, because a proper understanding of what is available is fundamental to getting the actual design and implementation correct.

Transforming the Logical Design

In earlier versions of SQL Server, a section like this on physical design would have been much longer than just the few pages here, but hardware and software advances, coupled with data warehousing methodologies, potentially allow you to implement your database almost exactly as you logically designed it. However, care must still be taken when designing the physical database, because you should never try to implement something that is too difficult to use in practice.

Subtypes

You may have to stray from your logical design when you deal with subtypes. You'll recall that a subtype in database modeling terms indicates a specific type of one-to-one relationship, in which you have one generic table–for example, `person`–and you then have one or more subtyped tables that further extend the meanings of this table–such as `employee`, `teacher`, `customer`, and so on. They're particularly significant in logical design, but there are also good reasons to keep them in your physical design, too.

Depending on how you end up doing your logical modeling, you may have to tweak more than just subtypes. Always bear in mind that there are as many ways of designing databases as there are data architects.

I will now present examples of cases in which you *will* and *will not* want to keep the subtyped tables.

Example 1

Say you have a Movie table that lists the names of movies (as well as other information, such as genre, description, and so on). You also have a movieRentalInventory table that defines videos or DVDs for rental. You specify a number to be used as the alternate key, and an itemCount that specifies the number of videos or discs that are in the rental package. There is also a mediaFormat column that shows whether the item is a video or a DVD.

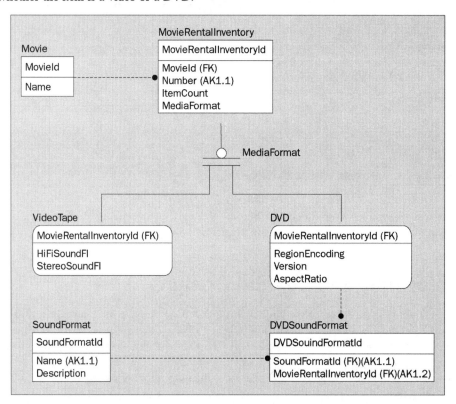

You define subtypes of the mediaFormat value for videoTape and DVD. You need to know the format because DVDs differ from videos, especially with regards to region encoding and sound format. You implement a special DVDSoundFormat for DVD as a many-to-many relationship—because DVDs support an ever-changing set of sound formats—while, for the videoTape type, you just have columns for hi-fi and stereo sound.

There are a few things about this implementation that are interesting:

❑ In order to create a new media rental, you have to create rows in at least two tables (movieRentalInventory and videoTape or DVD, and another in DVDSoundFormat for a DVD). This isn't a tremendous problem, but can require some special handling.

❑ If you want to see a list of all of the items you have for rental, including their sound properties, you'll have to write a very complex query that joins movieRentalInventory with videoTape, and merges this with another query between movieRentalInventory and DVD, which may be too slow or simply too cumbersome to deal with. (You'll learn about queries in some detail in Chapter 12.)

These are common issues with subtypes. When considering what to do with a subtype relationship, one of the most important tasks is to determine how much each of the subtyped entities have in common, and how many attributes they have in common.

A simple survey of the attributes of the subtyped tables in this example shows that they have much in common. In most cases it's simply a matter of cardinality.

Take the DVD. Region encoding is specific to this medium, but some videos have different versions, and technically every video product has an aspect ratio (the ratio of the height and width of the picture) that will be of interest to any enthusiast. While it's true that you can specify the sound properties of a videotape using two simple checkboxes, you can use the same method of specifying the sound for a DVD. You'll just have to limit the cardinality of soundFormat on a video to one, while DVD may have up to eight.

So you redraw the subtype relationship as follows:

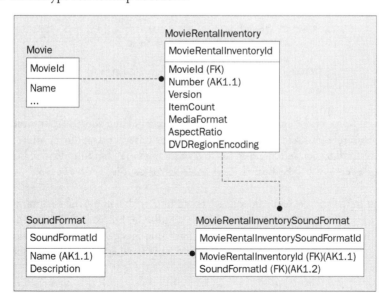

The last point is that, because you have changed your structure and are storing multiple types of information in the same entity, you now have to be careful not to allow improper data to be entered into the table. For example, when `mediaFormat` is video, the `DVDRegionEncoding` column doesn't apply and must be set to `NULL`. These business rules will have to be enforced using constraints and triggers, because the values in one table will be based on the values in another.

Rolling up (or combining) the subtype into a single table can seem to make implementation easier and more straightforward, though it actually just offloads the work somewhere else. Knowing how the values are used will certainly help you decide if rolling up the subtype is merited.

Example 2

As a second example, let's look at a case for which it doesn't make sense to roll up the subtype. You'll generally have subtypes that shouldn't be rolled up in the case for which you have two (or more) objects that share a common ancestor, but, once subtyped, the subtypes of the items have absolutely no relationship to one another, as shown in the following figure.

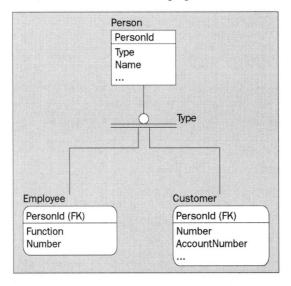

You have a `person` table with a name and other attributes, including some that are implemented as additional tables with relationships to the `person` table (such as address, contact information, contact journal, and so on). In this example, employees and customers may both be people, but the similarities end there. So, in this case, it will be best to leave the subtype as it is.

The only problem here is that, when someone wants to look at the employee's name, you have to use a join. This isn't a real problem from a programming standpoint, but you're concerned from a technical standpoint. In many cases, the primary features that make subtypes more reasonable to use revolve around creating views that make the `employee` table look as if it contains the values for `person` as well.

Determining when to roll up a table is one of those things that comes with time and experience. As a guideline it's usually best to do the following:

- ❏ Roll up when the subtyped tables are very similar in characteristics to the parent table, especially when you'll frequently want to see them in a list together.

- ❏ Leave as subtypes when the data in the subtypes share the common underpinnings, but aren't logically related to one another in additional ways.

A Reason Not to Stray from the Logical Design

The most frequent cause of straying from the logical model is denormalized structures—usually summary data to summarize a given set of rows, as shown in the following figure.

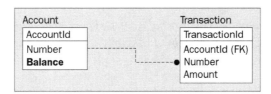

Here, the `balance` attribute will be equivalent to the summary of all of the transaction amount values for a given `accountId`. You'll learn how to implement this type of summary data using triggers, because sometimes introducing denormalized data may be required to solve a particular performance problem.

Introducing this at an early point of physical design may seem like a reasonable thing to do. However, it should be stressed that denormalization isn't something that should be done unless there are compelling reasons, because denormalization usually causes more problems than it solves. It can be hard for novice architects to understand why it's better to retrieve values through joins instead of propagating duplicate values all around a database to speed up a query or a set of queries. Joins in SQL Server are extremely efficient and very often will provide adequate performance.

The rule of thumb that we'll take in this book regarding denormalization is that it's only to be used as a last resort, when other nonstructure-changing methods for increasing performance have been taken.

Tables

Tables are the central objects you'll deal with. The basics of the table are very simple. If you look at the full syntax for the CREATE TABLE statement, you'll see that there are many different optional parameters. Throughout this chapter, and part of the next, you'll look at table creation statements and how best to choose what to do with each variation.

The first required clause is very straightforward:

```
CREATE TABLE [<database>.][<owner>.]<tablename>
```

We'll expand upon the items between the angle brackets (< and >). Note that anything in square brackets ([and]) is optional and may be omitted.

❑   <database>: You usually don't specify the database in your CREATE TABLE statements. If not specified, this will default to the current database where the statement is being executed. Specifying the database means that the script will only be executable in a single database, which precludes using the script to build alternate databases on the same server should the need arise without editing the script.

❑   <owner>: This is the name of the owner of the table. This must be a current user in the database or dbo for the database owner. If the statement is executed by a member of the sysadmin server role, or the db_dbowner or db_ddladmin fixed roles, then an object can be created for any user by specifying a name. Generally it isn't necessary to specify the owner, but it can be handy to make certain that the table is owned by dbo to specify dbo as the owner.

> *Best practice is to minimize the number of owners. Having multiple owners causes "ownership chain" issues between dependent objects. It's most common to have all objects owned solely by a single user known as dbo.*

Naming

The entry for <tablename> gives the table a name. The name must fit into the system datatype of sysname. In SQL Server, this is defined as a 128-character (or less of course) string using double-byte Unicode characters. The combination of owner and tablename must be unique in a database.

SQL Server's rules for the names of objects consist of two distinct naming methods.

The first uses delimiters (either square brackets or double quotes) around the name (though double quotes are only allowed when the SET QUOTED_IDENTIFIER option is set to on). By placing delimiters around an object's name, you can use *any* string as the name. For example, [Table Name] or [3232 fjfa*&(&^(] would both be legal (but annoying) names. Delimited names are generally a bad idea when creating new tables, and should be avoided if possible as they make coding more difficult. However, they can be necessary for interacting with data tables in other environments.

The second and preferred naming method is to use nondelimited names, but they have to follow a few basic rules:

❑   The first character must be a letter as defined by Unicode Standard 3.1 (generally speaking, Roman letters A to Z, upper- and lowercase) or the underscore character (_). The Unicode standard can be found at www.unicode.org.

❑   Subsequent characters can be Unicode letters, decimal numbers, the ampersand (@), or the dollar sign ($).

❑ The name must not be a SQL Server reserved word. There is a pretty large list of reserved words in SQL Server 2000 Books Online (look in the *Reserved Keywords* section).

❑ The name cannot have spaces.

While the rules for creating an object name are pretty straightforward, the more important question is, "What kind of names should you choose?" The answer is predictable: "Whatever you feel is best as long as others can read it." This may sound like a cop-out, but there are as many different naming standards as there are data architects out there. The standard I generally go with is the standard we'll use in this book, but it certainly isn't the only way. Basically, you'll stick with the same standard that you started with in logical naming. With space for 128 characters, there is little reason to do much abbreviating. It's most important to be clear when choosing names.

> *Because most companies have existing systems, it may be a good idea to know the shop standard for naming tables so that new developers on your project will be more likely to understand your database and come up to speed more quickly.*

As an example, let's name the object that you might use to store a television schedule item. The following list will show several different ways to build the name of this object:

❑ television_schedule_item: Using underscores to separate values. Most programmers aren't big friends of the underscore because they're cumbersome to program until you get used to them.

❑ [television schedule item] or "television schedule item": Delimited by brackets or quotes. Not favored by most programmers, because it's impossible to use this name when building variables in code, and it's easy to make mistakes with them.

❑ televisionScheduleItem: Mixed case to delimit between words. This is the style that you'll make use of in your case study, because it's the style that I like.

❑ tvSchedItem or tv_sched_item or [tv sched item]: Abbreviated forms. These are problematic because you must be careful to always abbreviate the same word in the same way in all of your databases. A dictionary of abbreviations must be maintained or you'll get multiple abbreviations for the same word, for example, description as desc, descr, descrip, and description.

Choosing names for objects is ultimately a personal choice, but should never be made arbitrarily, and should be based on existing corporate standards, existing software, and legibility.

Owner

The user who creates a database is called the database owner, or dbo. The dbo is a member of the system administrators or database creator system roles. Any user can be added to the database owners group in the database by being added to the db_owner role, which means that the user can create and delete *any* data, table, view, and stored procedure in the database.

When any non-dbo user creates an object, that object is owned by that user (and the dbo or db_owner roles). If a user called Bob tries to access a table without specifying an owner, as follows:

```
SELECT * FROM tableName
```

SQL Server first checks to see if a table named tableName and owned by Bob actually exists. If not, it then checks to see if a table with this name owned by the dbo exists. If it does, and the dbo hasn't given Bob rights to access the table, the statement will give an error. To access a specific owner's table directly in code, you need to specify the owner of the table using a two part name, as follows:

```
SELECT * FROM dbo.tableName
```

If you do specify a specific table and its owner, like you did in the previous line of code, and this table doesn't exist, then you raise an error.

The owner gets implicit rights to create, modify, and delete data from the table as well as the table itself. Any other user has to be given the rights to do so. At this point, it's simply important to understand that every table, view, and stored procedure in SQL Server has an owner.

You should also note that SQL Server uses a naming scheme with up to four parts:

[<server>.][<database>.][<owner>.]<objectName>

❑   server: Identifies the server where the object is located. For objects on the same server, the server name should be omitted. Objects on different servers can only be accessed if the system administrator has set up the server as a linked server.

❑   database: Identifies the database where the object resides. If omitted, the object is looked for in the database from which the object is being accessed.

❑   owner: Identifies the user who created or owns the object. If omitted, SQL Server uses the user who is connected as the default.

❑   objectName: Identifies the name of the table, view, or stored procedure.

This was briefly mentioned in Chapter 9 during the discussion of linked servers.

Limits

Before going any further, you need to look at a few of the limits that you'll have to work with when building tables in SQL Server. Four limits are important to you when building a table:

❑   **Number of columns:** The maximum number of columns (that is, data columns) in a table is 1024. If the database is properly normalized, this is way beyond normal requirements.

- ❑ **Number of bytes per row:** The maximum number of bytes in a row is 8060 (this is the number of usable bytes on a page, after overhead). Unlike the number of columns, the maximum number of bytes isn't quite as hard to reach. You'll see why this is when you start to look at character and binary data.

- ❑ **Number of bytes per index entry:** The limit on this is 900 bytes and for good reason. A page is roughly 8060 bytes, so if an index was much larger than 900, it would become very ineffective.

- ❑ **Number of indexes:** The limit is 1 clustered and 249 nonclustered indexes per table. You might get close to this limit in data warehousing systems, but rarely in an OLTP system. Having 250 indexes on a table in an OLTP system would reduce performance drastically because of the frequent modifications that are likely to be made to the data. You'll learn about clustered and nonclustered indexes later in this chapter.

A more conclusive list of the basic requirements will be given in Chapter 14, when you look at hardware requirements.

Columns

The **bold** lines are the lines that you'll use to define a column:

```
CREATE TABLE [<database>.][<owner>.]<tablename>
(
    <columnName> <data type> [<NULL specification>]
    — or
    <columnName> AS <computed definition>
)
```

There are two types of columns that you'll deal with: physical and computed (or virtual).

- ❑ **Physical columns:** This is an ordinary column in which physical storage is allocated and data is actually stored for the value.

- ❑ **Computed (or virtual) columns:** Columns that are made up by a calculation including any of the physical columns in the table.

You'll primarily deal with physical columns, but computed columns are pretty useful as well.

Naming

The <columnName> placeholder is where you specify the name that the column will be known by.

The naming rules for columns are the same as for tables as far as SQL Server is concerned. As for how you choose a name for a column–again, it's one of those tasks for the individual architect, based on the same sorts of criteria as before (shop standards, best usage, and so on).

The following set of guidelines will be followed in this book:

❑ Other than the primary key, my feeling is that the table name should rarely be included in the column name. For example, in an entity named `person`, you shouldn't have columns called `personName` or `personSocialSecurityNumber`. No column should be prefixed with `person` other than the primary key of `personId`. This reduces the need for role naming (modifying names of attributes to adjust meaning, especially used in cases for which you have multiple migrated foreign keys).

❑ The name should be as descriptive as possible. You'll use very few abbreviations in your names. There are three notable exceptions:

Complex names: Much like in table names, if you have a name that contains multiple parts, like "Conglomerated Television Rating Scale," you might want to implement a name like `ConTvRatScale`, even though it might take some training before your users become familiar with its meaning.

Recognized abbreviations: As an example, if you were writing a purchasing system and you needed a column for a purchase order table, you could name the object PO because this is very widely understood.

Datatype indicators: You'll sometimes add a short string (say, two characters) to the end of the column name. For example, a column that you use as a Boolean will end in the suffix "fl", short for flag, and a date column would end in "dt", obviously short for datetime. Note that you won't use these suffixes to indicate precise datatypes (for example, you might implement a Boolean with an `int`, `tinyint`, `smallint`, `bit`, or even a string containing "`Yes`" or "`No`").

> *Note that you haven't mentioned Hungarian-style notation to denote the type of the column. I've never been a big fan of this style. If you aren't familiar with Hungarian notation, it means that you prefix the names of columns and variables with an indicator of the datatype and possible usage. For example, you might have a variable called* vc100_columnName, *to indicate a* varchar(100) *datatype. Or you might have a Boolean or bit column named* bCar, *or* isCar.

In my opinion, such prefixes are overkill because it's easy to tell the type from other documentation you can get from SQL Server or other methods. Your usage indicators typically go at the end of the name and are only needed when it would be difficult to understand what the value means without the indicator.

By keeping the exact type out of the names, you avoid clouding the implementation details with the entity identity. One of the beauties of using relational databases is that there is an abstraction layer hiding the implementation details. To expose them via column naming is to set in concrete what changing requirements may make obsolete (for example, extending the size of a variable to accommodate a future business need).

Domains

In logical modeling, the concept of domains involved building templates for datatypes and columns that you use over and over again. In physical modeling, domains are the same, but with additional properties added for physical needs.

For example, in the logical modeling phase, you defined domains for such columns as name and description, which occur regularly across a database. The reason for defining domains might not have been completely obvious at the time of logical design, but it becomes very clear during physical modeling. For example, for the *name* domain, you might specify the following:

Property	Setting
Name	Name
Datatype	varchar (100)
Nullability	Not NULL
Check Constraint	LEN(RTRIM(Name)) > 0 – may not be blank

Most tables will have a name column and you'll use this same template to build every one of them. This serves at least two purposes:

❑ **Consistency:** If you define every name column in precisely the same manner, there will never be any question about how to treat the column.

❑ **Ease of implementation:** If the tool you use to model or implement databases supports the creation of domain and template columns, you can simply use the template to build columns and not have to set the values over and over. If the tool supports property inheritance, when you change a property in the definition, the values change everywhere.

Domains aren't a requirement of good database design, logical or physical, nor are they mapped precisely by SQL Server, but they enable easy and consistent design and are a great idea. Of course, consistent modeling is always a good idea regardless of whether or not you use a tool to do the work for you.

Choosing the Datatype

Choosing proper datatypes to match the domain chosen during logical modeling is a very important task. One datatype might be more efficient than another of a similar type. For example, storing integer data can be done in an integer datatype, a numeric datatype, or even a floating-point datatype, but they certainly aren't alike in implementation or performance.

It's important to choose the best possible datatype when building the column. The following list contains the intrinsic datatypes and a brief explanation of each of them:

- ❑ **Precise Numeric Data:** Stores numeric data with no possible loss of precision

  - ❑ **Bit:** Stores either 1, 0, or NULL, used for Boolean-type columns

  - ❑ **Tinyint:** Nonnegative values between 0 and 255

  - ❑ **Smallint:** Integers between –32,768 and 32,767

  - ❑ **Int:** Integers between –2,147,483,648 to 2,147,483,647 (-2^{31} to $2^{31} - 1$)

  - ❑ **Bigint:** Integers between –9,223,372,036,854,775,808 to 9,223,372,036,854,775,807 (that is, -2^{63} to $2^{63} - 1$).

  - ❑ **Decimal**: All numbers between $10^{38} - 1$ through $10^{38} - 1$

  - ❑ **Money**: Values from –922,337,203,685,477.5808 through 922,337,203,685,477.5807

  - ❑ **Smallmoney**: Values from –214,748.3648 through 214,748.3647

- ❑ **Approximate Numeric data**: Stores approximations of numbers; gives a very large range of values

  - ❑ **Float (N)**: Values in the range from –1.79E +308 through to 1.79E +308

  - ❑ **Real**: Values in the range from –3.40E +38 through to 3.40E +38. `real` is a synonym for a `float(24)` datatype

- ❑ **Date and Time**: Stores date values, including time of day

  - ❑ **Smalldatetime**: Dates from January 1, 1900, through to June 6, 2079

  - ❑ **Datetime**: Dates from January 1, 1753, to December 31, 9999

- ❑ **Binary data**: Strings of bits, for example files or images

  - ❑ **Binary**: Fixed-length binary data up to 8,000 bytes long

  - ❑ **Varbinary**: Variable-length binary data up to 8,000 bytes long

  - ❑ **Image**: Really large binary data, max length of $2^{31}-1$ (2,147,483,647) bytes or 2GB

- ❑ **Character (or string) data**

  - ❑ **Char**: Fixed-length character data up to 8,000 characters long

  - ❑ **Varchar**: Variable-length character data up to 8,000 characters long

  - ❑ **Text**: Large text values, max length of $2^{31} -1$ (2,147,483,647) bytes or 2GB

  - ❑ **Nchar, nvarchar, ntext**: Unicode equivalents of char, varchar, and text

❑ **Other datatypes**

 ❑ **Variant**: Stores any datatype

 ❑ **Timestamp (or rowversion)**: Used for optimistic locking

 ❑ **Uniqueidentifier**: Stores a GUID (globally unique identifier) value

The list given here is just a brief reference for the datatypes. For more complete coverage, in Appendix D, you'll take a deeper look at the intrinsic datatypes and see the situations and examples of where they're best used (see the Apress web site). The most important thing is that when choosing a datatype, you choose the one that most matches what you're trying to store. For example, say you want to store a person's name and salary.

You could choose to store the name in a text column, and the salary in a variant column. In all cases these choices would work just fine, but they wouldn't be *good* choices. The name should be in something like a `varchar(30)`, and the salary should be in a money column. Notice that you used a `varchar` for the name. This is because you don't know the length, because most names will not be nearly 30 bytes, this will save space in your database.

Obviously, in reality you would seldom make such poor choices, and most choices are reasonably easy. However, it's important to keep in mind that the datatype is the first level of domain enforcement in that you have a business rule that states the following:

❑ The name must be greater than or equal to 5 characters and less than or equal to 30 characters.

You can enforce this at the database level by declaring the column as a `varchar(30)`. This column will not allow a value longer than 31 characters to be entered. You cannot enforce the greater than or equal to 5 characters, but you'll learn more about how to do that in chapters 11 and 12 as we discuss more about integrity enforcement.

Optional Data

You discussed in logical modeling that values for an attribute, now being translated to a physical column, may be optional or mandatory. Whether or not a column value is mandatory or optional is translated in the physical model as nullability. Before you get to how to implement NULLs, you need to briefly discuss what "NULL" means. While it can be inferred that a column defined as NULL means that the data is optional, this is an incomplete definition. A NULL value should be read as "unknown value" in the column create phrase, as follows:

```
<columnName> <data type> [<NULL specification>]
```

Here, you simply change the `<NULL specification>` to `NULL` to allow `NULL`s or `NOT NULL` to not allow `NULL`s, as shown here:

```
CREATE TABLE NULLTest
(
    NULLColumn varchar(10) NULL,
    notNULLColumn varchar(10) NOT NULL
)
```

Nothing particularly surprising there. If you leave off the `NULL` specification altogether, the SQL Server default is used. To determine what the current default property for a database is, you execute the following statement:

```
EXECUTE sp_dboption @dbname = tempdb, @optname = ANSI NULL default
```

which gives you the following:

OptionName	CurrentSetting
ANSI NULL default	off

To set the default for the database, you can use the **sp_dboption** procedure. (I would recommend that this setting is always off so, if you forget to set it explicitly, you won't be stuck with nullable columns that will quickly fill up with `NULL` data that you'll have to clean up). To set the default for a session use the following command:

```
set ansi_NULL_dflt_on off -- or on if you want the default to be NULL
```

Here's an example:

```
--turn off default NULLs
SET ANSI_NULL_DFLT_ON OFF

--create test table
CREATE TABLE testNULL
(
    id    int
)

--check the values
EXEC sp_help testNULL
```

which returns, among other things, the following:

Column_name	[...]	Nullable
id	...	no

Alternatively, you could try the following:

```
--change the setting to default not NULL
SET ANSI_NULL_DFLT_ON ON

--get rid of the table and recreate it
DROP TABLE testNULL
GO
CREATE TABLE testNULL
(
    id    int
)

EXEC sp_help testNULL
```

which returns this:

Column_name	[...]	Nullable
id	...	yes

In Chapter 14, you'll look at some of the difficulties with null data, especially when doing comparisons. For now, you should know that NULL means that the value of the column may be filled in the future; it simply isn't known at the current time.

Identity Columns

For any of the int or decimal (with a scale of 0) datatypes, there is an option to create an automatically incrementing column whose value is guaranteed to be unique for the table it's in. The column that implements this identity column must also be defined as not NULL.

```
CREATE TABLE testIdentity
(
    identityColumn int NOT NULL IDENTITY (1, 2),
    value    varchar(10)   NOT NULL
)
```

In this CREATE TABLE statement, I've added the IDENTITY function for the identityColumn column. The additional values in parentheses are known as the seed and increment. The seed of 1 indicates that you'll start the first value at 1, and the increment says that the second value will be 3, then 5, and so on.

In the following script you insert three new rows into the testIdentity table:

```
INSERT INTO testIdentity (value)
VALUES ('one')
INSERT INTO testIdentity (value)
VALUES ('two')
INSERT INTO testIdentity (value)
VALUES ('three')

SELECT * FROM testIdentity
```

This produces the following results:

IdentityColumn	value
1	one
3	two
5	three

The identity property is fantastic for creating a primary key type pointer that is small and fast. (Another reminder–it must not be the only key on the table or you technically have no uniqueness, except for a random value!) The int datatype requires only four bytes and is very good, because most tables you create will have fewer than 2 billion rows.

One thing of note: Identity values are apt to have holes in the sequence. If an error occurs when creating a new row, the identity value that was going to be used will be lost. Also, if a row gets deleted, the deleted value will not be reused. Hence, you shouldn't use identity columns if you cannot accept this constraint on the values in your table.

> If you need to guarantee uniqueness across all tables, or even multiple databases, consider creating a column with the uniqueidentifier datatype and with a default to automatically generate a value. You'll discuss this implementation later in this section on datatypes.

User-Defined Datatypes

The primary value of user-defined types is to allow the architect to build an alias for a frequently used datatype. In the user-defined type declaration, you can specify the following:

❑ A name for the datatype

❑ The system datatype, including any length information

❑ Whether or not the datatype will allow NULLs

To create a user-defined type for your corporate serial number, you might do the following:

```
EXEC sp_addtype @typename = serialNumber,
    @phystype = 'varchar(12)',
    @NULLtype = 'not NULL',
    @owner = 'dbo'
GO
```

When the type is used, you can override the nullability by specifying it, but you cannot override the datatype. You can then use this type much like you use all of SQL Server's datatypes–as a way to keep the implementation details of all usages of a type exactly the same. You can bind a rule (to limit values that are entered into it across all usages) and defaults (to give a default value if a value isn't supplied) to the datatype.

User-defined datatypes, because they're implemented in SQL Server, have some drawbacks that make them somewhat confusing to use, such as the following:

❑   Error reporting using rules

❑   Inconsistent handling as variables

❑   Datatypes of columns defined with user-defined types will not change if the user-defined type changes

We'll look into these problems now.

Error Reporting Using Rules

It's possible to create a user-defined datatype to encapsulate rules and error reporting. Create the user-defined type, create a rule for it, and bind it to a column. Now when a table is created with a column with the new datatype, the rule is enforced, as expected. However, the error messages that are produced are worthless!

For example, let's create a very useful datatype called socialSecurityNumber, add a rule, and bind it to a column.

```
--create a type, call it SSN, varchar(11), the size of a social security
--number including the dashes
EXEC sp_addtype @typename = 'SSN',
    @phystype = 'varchar(11)',
    @NULLtype = 'not NULL'
GO

--create a rule, call it SSNRule, with this pattern
CREATE RULE SSNRule AS
    @value LIKE '[0-9][0-9][0-9]-[0-9][0-9]-[0-9][0-9][0-9][0-9]'
GO

--bind the rule to the exampleType
EXEC sp_bindrule 'SSNRule', 'SSN'
GO

--create a test table with the new data type.
CREATE TABLE testRule
(
    id int IDENTITY,
    socialSecurityNumber    SSN
)
GO
```

This creates a table with a column that should prevent an invalid social security number from being entered. So, in the following script, we'll try to insert the following data into the table:

```
--insert values into the table
INSERT INTO testRule (socialSecurityNumber)
VALUES ('438-44-3343')
INSERT INTO testRule (socialSecurityNumber)
VALUES ('43B-43-2343')    --note the B instead of the 8 to cause an error
GO
```

The result looks like the following:

Server: Msg 513, Level 16, State 1, Line 1
A column insert or update conflicts with a rule imposed by a previous CREATE RULE statement. The statement was terminated. The conflict occurred in database 'tempdb', table 'testRule', column 'socialSecurityNumber'.
The statement has been terminated.

You can see from this that the error message isn't that helpful because it doesn't even tell you what rule was violated.

> *Note that, in your testing, you have the* NOCOUNT *option turned on for all connections. This setting will avoid the messages that tell you how many rows are modified by an action. In this case, this also makes for a better example. You can do this in code by specifying* SET NOCOUNT ON *.*

Inconsistent Handling of Variables

First, let's look at the handling of NULLs. When you created the type in the code in the previous "Error Reporting Using Rules" section, you set its nullability to NOT NULL. Now run the following:

```
DECLARE @SSNVar SSN
SET @SSNVar = NULL
SELECT @SSNVar
```

This code shows one of the inconsistencies of user-defined datatypes. When executed, you would expect an error to occur because the type didn't allow NULLs. Rather, you get the following:

```
SSNVar
-------------

NULL
```

This is fairly minor, but I would expect that the user-defined datatype wouldn't allow a NULL value.

Another problem associated with user-defined datatypes occurs when a variable is created according to the type—it doesn't employ the rule that was associated with it. It's possible to assign values to a variable defined using a user-defined datatype with a rule, but these values cannot be inserted into a column defined with the same user-defined type. You can see this effect here:

```
DECLARE @SSNVar SSN
SET @SSNVar = 'Bill'
SELECT @SSNVar AS SSNVar

INSERT INTO testRule (socialSecurityNumber)
VALUES (@SSNVar)
```

This code results in this error:

```
SSNVar
----------
Bill
```

Server: Msg 513, Level 16, State 1, Line 5

A column insert or update conflicts with a rule imposed by a previous CREATE RULE statement. The statement was terminated. The conflict occurred in database 'tempdb', table 'testRule', column 'socialSecurityNumber'.
The statement has been terminated.

In the next chapter, you'll look more closely at protecting your data from bad values, but at this point, you just need to understand why you aren't employing what looks like such a useful encapsulation tool.

Note that rules aren't the standard way of providing such protections—check constraints are. However, for a user-defined type to be of value to you, it should be an object in and of itself. For anyone that reads this book who really likes user-defined types, I think it is important to point out some of the biggest problems with them. Rules are in SQL Server 2000 as a backwards compatibility feature, and as such may not be around beyond the next version, depending on customer pressures to keep certain features. You'll use check constraints, because they're bound directly to the column and not to the datatype.

UDT Cannot Be Modified When in Use

The datatypes of columns defined with user-defined types will not change if the user-defined type changes. This is the worst problem. Consider that you need to change a user-defined datatype, say from char(1) to varchar(10), for whatever reason. There is no facility to "change" the user-defined type, and you cannot drop it if it's already in use. Hence, you have to change the datatype in every spot it has been used to the base type, change the type, and change the type back. That isn't pretty.

You won't employ user-defined datatypes in your case study for these reasons.

Calculated Columns

Now that you've been introduced to the datatypes, let's take a quick look at calculated columns. These are a really cool feature that was added in SQL Server 7.0. Strangely, they weren't implemented in the Enterprise Manager, which simply destroyed them for you when you made any changes to the table, so you had to maintain them with script. In SQL Server 2000, this feature is properly supported.

```
<columnName> AS <computed definition>
```

Calculated columns can be used to take unreadable data and translate it into a readable format in the definition of the table. In SQL Server 2000, they can now be indexed–so they're even more useful.

In particular, they came in handy in a database system I created for building a grouping on the day, month, and year. In the following code, you have an example that is close to this. It groups on the second to make the example easier to test:

```
CREATE TABLE calcColumns
(
    dateColumn    datetime,
    dateSecond    AS datepart(second,dateColumn), -- calculated column
)

DECLARE @i int
SET @i = 1
WHILE (@i < 1000)
BEGIN
    INSERT INTO calcColumns (dateColumn) VALUES (getdate())
    SET @i = @i + 1
END

SELECT dateSecond, max(dateColumn) as dateColumn, count(*) AS countStar
FROM calcColumns
GROUP BY dateSecond
ORDER BY dateSecond
```

When this code is executed, it returns the following:

DateSecond	dateColumn	countStar
20	2003-11-14 11:07:20.993	8
21	2003-11-14 11:07:21.993	900
22	2003-11-14 11:07:22.083	91

An almost dangerous feature with calculated columns is that they will be ignored when you're inserting data if you omit the insert column list. SQL Server will ignore any calculated columns and match the columns up as if they don't exist. For example, you create the following table:

```
CREATE TABLE testCalc
(
value varchar(10),
valueCalc AS UPPER(value),
value2 varchar(10)
)
```

Then you create some new values without the insert list as follows:

```
INSERT INTO testCalc
-- You should have (value, value2) here
VALUES ('test', 'test2')
```

No error occurs. When you execute as follows:

```
SELECT *
FROM   testCalc
```

You get back the following results:

Value	valueCalc	value2
test	TEST	test2

Now you have this column called valueCalc that takes value and makes it uppercase.

> **Regardless of calculated columns, it's poor practice to code `INSERT` statements with no insert list.**

Calculated columns are an extremely valuable feature, and should cause excitement to anyone who has ever had to type and retype column calculations over and over.

Physical-Only Columns

Not every column that will appear in your physical model will be or should be denoted on the logical data model. In this section, you'll discuss some of the reasons why you would have columns that don't fit the mold of a logical model column, but which are required in the physical implementation.

The primary reason for a physical-only column is that the column isn't an attribute of the entity that the table is modeling. In other words, the column is required primarily for implementation purposes. Here are a few examples of situations when such columns are needed.

Concurrency Control

When you have a database with more than one user, you need to implement some form of concurrency control mechanism. You'll want to make sure that, once a user gets a row they want to change, no other user can make changes to the row, or you might lose information. There are two different methods for performing this task.

❏ **Pessimistic locking**: This is implemented by having locks on any rows that a user reads with intent to update. It's called pessimistic because it assumes that other users will likely be trying to edit the same row as the current user. This is a very high-maintenance solution and is usually unnecessary, because in most cases no two users are likely to look at the same row at the same time. You would only use a pessimistic lock when it's completely necessary to make other clients wait until you're finished with the row before letting them get access to it. The problem is that you have to lock the row in such a way that *no one* else may look at it, or any other user may step on your changes after you've released your lock.

❏ **Optimistic Locking**: This is a far more popular solution. To implement an optimistic-locking mechanism, you simply add a column to each table that changes every time a row changes in the database. For example, User 1 retrieves a row of values. Shortly afterwards, User 2 retrieves the same row. User 1 updates a row, and the value of the lock column changes. Now, if User 2 tries to modify the row, SQL Server checks the value of the lock column, sees that it has changed, and prevents User 2's update, as shown in the following figure.

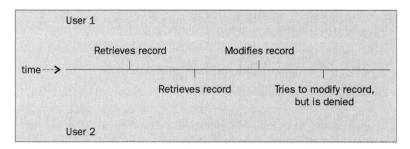

Implementing the optimistic lock is a fairly simple task, but note that every process that uses the tables must adhere to the rules of the optimistic lock. If one process ignores it, the overall process fails.

There are a few ways to implement an optimistic lock:

❏ **Using a timestamp column:** As previously discussed, the timestamp column is a special column that changes every time a row is modified. Timestamp columns are the ideal way to create an optimistic lock.

❏ **Using the last-updated date or last-updated user:** Basically this is the same method, except that you add columns to store the user that last modified a row and the time of the modification. You do this through a trigger on INSERT and UPDATE. This method is better in that it gives a human readable value for the optimistic lock, but worse in that it requires the overhead of coding triggers.

❏ **Using all columns in the WHERE clause during modifications:** This is the method provided by tools like Microsoft Access, when there is no timestamp column available. Basically, when doing a modification statement, you would include every column in the table in the WHERE clause. If the values have changed because you first retrieved the value, then someone else has likely fingered your data out from under you. Hence the optimistic lock will fail.

You'll use the timestamp column, because it's quite easy to implement and requires absolutely no code whatsoever to maintain the values in the table. You'll have to build code to do the comparisons when you're building code, however. So, you'll build the following table:

```
CREATE TABLE testOptimisticLock
(
    id int NOT NULL,
    value varchar(10) NOT NULL,
    autoTimestamp timestamp NOT NULL, --optimistic lock
    primary key (id)                  --adds a primary key on id column
)
```

Then you execute the following script. The first step is to create a new row in the table and get the optimistic lock value for the row.

```
INSERT INTO testOptimisticLock (id, value)
VALUES (1, 'Test1')

DECLARE @timestampHold timestamp
SELECT @timestampHold = autoTimestamp
FROM testOptimisticLock
WHERE value = 'Test1'

--first time will work
UPDATE testOptimisticLock
SET value = 'New Value'
WHERE id = 1
    AND    autoTimestamp = @timestampHold
IF @@rowcount = 0
BEGIN
    raiserror 50000 'Row has been changed by another user'
END
SELECT   id, value FROM testOptimisticLock

--second time will fail
UPDATE testOptimisticLock
SET value = 'Second New Value'
WHERE id = 1
    AND    autoTimestamp = @timestampHold
IF @@rowcount = 0
BEGIN
    raiserror 50000 'Row has been changed another user'
END
SELECT   id, value from testOptimisticLock
```

This will return the following:

Id	value
1	New Value

Server: Msg 50000, Level 16, State 1, Line 38
Row has been changed by another user

Id	value
1	New Value

Row Disablers

A physical-only column that is of some importance in many applications that I've created is a row disabler. For example, take a domain table that defines the type of some row; say a `contactType` as in the following example diagram.

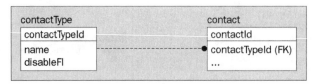

In the `contactType` table you have a `bit` column entitled `disableFl`. If this column has a value of 1, then you won't be able to use this value as a type of contact any longer. You won't have to delete or change any existing contact values to set this flag. (Note that this solution will require a trigger to enforce this rule–to check the value of `contactType.disableFl`–because this is an inter-table rule.)

Why would you want to do this? There are three very obvious problems you need to solve:

❑   If you only have ten contacts, it wouldn't be a problem to physically delete any rows in the contact table where the `contactType` instance is used. However, if you have one million contacts, all of the contacts will have to be checked. This might be too much to deal with.

❑   While the user may not foresee any further use for a particular value, there may be no reason to remove the row totally from the database.

❑   There may be existing child rows that you don't want to remove from the database.

Note that, where a list of `contactType` values is presented to the user, it would have to be filtered as follows:

```
SELECT name
FROM contactType
WHERE disableFl = 0
```

This does imply some trade-off in terms of query performance, so in some cases you may need to balance the overhead of doing the delete vs. the query costs. You might also implement both a delete and a disable flag–thereby disabling during contentious times for your database and cleaning out the rows later in the night when everything is quiet.

It should be mentioned that `disableFl` is one of those attributes that requires the Fourth Normal Form treatment, because you'll probably want to know more than whether it's disabled–like *when* it was disabled, for instance. It would be possible of course to add a `contactTypeStatus` table, in which you monitor the past and present status. In practice, this is rarely needed, but should certainly be considered on a case-to-case basis, because the first time you're asked when and why the `contactType` of "Active" was disabled and you cannot provide a simple answer, you're in trouble.

Collation (Sort Order)

The collation sequence for SQL Server determines how it will arrange character data when storing it, how data will be sorted when needed, and how data will be compared. SQL Server and Windows provide a tremendous number of collation types to choose from. To see the current collation type for the server and database, you can execute the following commands:

```
SELECT serverproperty('collation')
SELECT databasepropertyex('master', 'collation')
```

On most systems installed in English-speaking countries, the default collation type is `SQL_Latin1_General_CP1_CI_AS`, where `Latin1_General` represents the normal Latin alphabet, `CP1` refers to code page 1252 (the SQL Server default Latin 1 ANSI character set), and the last parts represent case-insensitive and accent-sensitive, respectively. Full coverage of all collation types may be found in the SQL Server 2000 documentation.

To list all of the sort orders installed in a given SQL Server instance, you can execute the following statement:

```
SELECT *
FROM ::fn_helpcollations()
```

On the computer that I perform testing on, this query returned over 700 rows, but usually you won't need to change from the default that the database administrator initially chooses. There are a few important reasons to specify a different collation.

❑ **Case sensitivity**: Depending on the application, there can be a need to have all of your code and data treated as case-sensitive. Note that this makes your code and object names case-sensitive, too.

Remember that case sensitivity causes searching difficulties. For example, when searching for all names starting with the letter "A," you have to search for all things starting with "A" or "a." You could use uppercase functions for columns or variables, but this defeats indexing and generally isn't a good idea.

❑ **Foreign character sorting**: The other reason is foreign characters. Using Unicode, you can use any character from any language in the world. However, very few languages use the same A to Z character set that English-speaking countries use. In fact, nearly all other European languages use accented letters that aren't part of the 7-bit ASCII character set. One possible use of a different collation type is in the implementation of columns for different languages. You'll see an example of this later in this section.

In previous versions of SQL Server, the entire server had a single sort order. This meant that, in every database, in every table, in every column, in every query, you were forced to use exactly the same sort order. This leads to interesting difficulties, for example when trying to implement a case-sensitive sort.

However, in SQL Server 2000, you can set the collation for your server and database as mentioned earlier, but you can also do it for a column, and even in the ORDER clause of a SELECT statement.

To set the collation sequence for a char, varchar, text, nchar, nvarchar, or ntext column when creating a table, you specify it using the collate clause of the column definition, as follows:

```
CREATE TABLE otherCollate
(
    id integer IDENTITY,
    name nvarchar(30) NOT NULL,
    frenchName nvarchar(30) COLLATE French_CI_AS_WS NULL,
    spanishName nvarchar(30) COLLATE Modern_Spanish_CI_AS_WS NULL
)
```

Now, when you sort frenchName by columns, it will be case-insensitive, but it will arrange the rows according to the order of the French character set. The same applies with Spanish regarding the spanishName column.

In the next example, we look at another cool use of the COLLATE keyword. You can use it to affect the comparisons made in an expression. You do this by changing one or both of the values on either side of the expression to a binary collation. Let's create a table, called collateTest:

```
CREATE TABLE collateTest
(
    name    VARCHAR(20) COLLATE SQL_Latin1_General_CP1_CI_AS NOT NULL
)

insert into collateTest(name)
values ('BOB')
insert into collateTest(name)
values ('bob')
```

Note that for demonstration purposes, the COLLATE statement that I've included is the default for my server. This is likely to be your collation also if you've taken the default (you should assume this collation for the rest of the book).

You can then execute the following against the database:

```
SELECT name
FROM collateTest
WHERE name = 'BOB'
```

which returns both rows:

```
name
----
bob
BOB
```

However, if you change the collation on the "BOB" literal, and execute it, as follows:

```
SELECT name
FROM collateTest
WHERE name = 'BOB' COLLATE Latin1_General_BIN
```

you only get back the single row that actually matches "BOB" character for character:

name
—————
BOB

You should have noticed that you only cast the scalar value "BOB" to a binary collation. Determining collation precedence can be a tricky matter and it's one that won't be covered here. In general, it's best to add the COLLATE function to both sides of the expression when performing such an operation.

In our case, instead of the collate on just the scalar, we would write it this way:

```
SELECT name
FROM collateTest
WHERE name COLLATE Latin1_General_BIN = 'BOB' COLLATE Latin1_General_BIN
```

We won't delve any deeper into the subject of collation. In the SQL Server documentation, there is a large amount of information about collations, including the rules for collation precedence.

Keys

As discussed in the logical modeling chapters, the definition of keys is one of the most important tasks in database design. In this section, you won't look at *why* you defined the keys you did, but rather *how* you implement them. The following different types of keys have already been discussed:

❑   **Primary**: Contains the primary pointer to a row in the table.

❑   **Alternate**: Contains alternate pointers to a row in the table, basically any unique conditions that you wish to make certain exist among one or more columns in the table.

❑   **Foreign**: Foreign keys are pointers to primary keys in other tables.

Primary and alternate keys are hybrid objects—part constraint, part index. They use unique indexes to make sure that the values are unique.   If you don't understand how SQL Server stores data and implements indexes, see Appendix B (see Apress web site).

Primary Keys

Choosing a primary key is one of the most important choices you'll make concerning an individual table. It's the primary key that will be migrated to other tables as a pointer to a particular value.

In logical modeling, you choose to use a 4-byte integer pointer for entity primary keys, which migrate to dependent child tables in this manner:

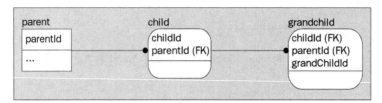

In physical modeling, this causes the number of values in the implemented keys to grow at a rapid rate. Another problem with implementing the primary keys this way is that you tend to lose sight of the fact that the key of a table must not be made up of meaningless columns. The migrated keys are fine, because they represent the values in the table that they came from, but by adding the unique value, you have essentially made this a meaningless key (because no matter what you add to a meaningless value, you'll always end up with a meaningless value). In logical modeling, this representation of the parent and child tables showed you that you could not have a grandChild without a child or a parent, and you always modeled an additional alternate key to make sure it was understood what the actual alternate key was. However, now that you're in the physical-modeling stage, you'll follow a slightly different strategy. Every table will have a *single* meaningless primary key and you'll implement alternate keys in your tables, as shown in the following diagram.

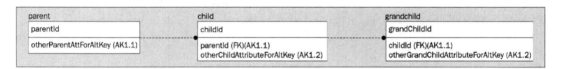

We'll choose this method for the following important reasons:

❑   You never have to worry about what to do when the primary key value changes.

❑   Every table has a single-column primary key pointer, and it's much easier to develop applications that access this pointer, because every table will have a single value as the primary key.

❑   Your primary key index will be very small, and thus operations that use it to access a row in the table will be faster. Most update and delete operations will modify the data by accessing the data based on primary keys which will use this index.

❑   Joins between tables will be cleaner to design, because all migrated keys will be a single column.

There are disadvantages to this method, such as always having to join to a table to find out what the value of the primary key actually means, not to mention other joins that will be needed to access data. Because the goals of your OLTP system are to keep keys small, speed up modifications, and ensure data consistency, this strategy isn't only acceptable, but favorable.

Implementing the primary key in this manner is very simple.

```
CREATE TABLE nameTable
(
    id integer NOT NULL IDENTITY PRIMARY KEY CLUSTERED
)
```

Note that you may not have any NULL columns in a primary key, even though you may have NULL columns in a unique index. The reason for this is actually pretty simple. The primary key is the row identifier, and a NULL provides no form of row identification.

Also you explicitly specified CLUSTERED. This is also the default for SQL Server 2000 but it's better not to leave it to chance. It's usually the best idea to let the primary key be clustered, especially when using as small a value as a integer for the primary key. This keeps the clustering key small and reduces the size of other indexes.

> *In Appendix B you'll read about some reasons why you may not desire to cluster on the primary key, because there are some other good uses for clustered indexes (see the Apress web site).*

The following will also work if you need to specify more than one column for the primary key.

```
CREATE TABLE nameTable
(
    id integer NOT NULL IDENTITY,
    pkeyColumn1 integer NOT NULL,
    pkeyColumn2 integer NOT NULL,
    PRIMARY KEY CLUSTERED (id)
)
```

As mentioned previously, if you have to provide for a key that is guaranteed to be unique across databases, or even servers, you can use the uniqueidentifier column with the ROWGUIDCOL property, as follows:

```
CREATE TABLE nameTable
(
    id uniqueidentifier NOT NULL ROWGUIDCOL DEFAULT newid(),
    PRIMARY KEY NONCLUSTERED (id)
)
```

Note that the ROWGUIDCOL doesn't enforce uniqueness, nor does it provide its own default like the identity column. Only use the uniqueidentifier when necessary, because it uses 16 bytes instead of 4 for the integer.

Alternate Keys

Alternate key enforcement is a very important task of physical modeling. When implementing alternate keys, you have two choices:

❏ Unique constraints

❏ Unique indexes

As an example, take the `nameTable` and extend it to include a first and last name. You'll then want to implement a rule that you must have unique full names in the table. You could implement an index, as follows:

```
CREATE TABLE nameTable
(
    id integer NOT NULL IDENTITY PRIMARY KEY CLUSTERED,
    firstName varchar(15) NOT NULL,
    lastName varchar(15) NOT NULL
)

CREATE UNIQUE INDEX XnameTable ON nameTable(firstName,lastName)
```

Or a unique constraint, as follows:

```
CREATE TABLE nameTable
(
    id integer NOT NULL IDENTITY PRIMARY KEY,
    firstName varchar(15) NOT NULL,
    lastName varchar(15) NOT NULL,
    UNIQUE (firstName, lastName)
)
```

Though technically they're both based on unique indexes, unique constraints are the favored method of implementing an alternate key and enforcing uniqueness. This is because constraints are semantically intended to enforce constraints on data, and indexes are intended to speed access to data. In reality, it doesn't matter how the uniqueness is implemented, but you do need to have either unique indexes or unique constraints in place.

One additional benefit of implementing them as constraints is the ability to view the constraints on the table by executing the following stored procedure:

```
sp_helpconstraint 'nameTable'
```

This returns a resultset of which the following is an abridged version:

constraint_type	constraint_name	[...]	constraint_keys
PRIMARY KEY (clustered)	PK__nameTable__1466F737	...	id
UNIQUE (non-clustered)	UQ__nameTable__155B1B70	...	firstName, lastName

This stored procedure will be used to view all constraints that you'll add to your tables in the next chapters.

Naming

Key names are relatively unimportant to the general structure of the table. However, it still pays to give the keys some recognizable name for use in error messages. SQL Server doesn't force you to give your indexes names. If you leave the name out of the constraint declaration as you have in the previous sections, SQL Server assigns a name for you. For instance, the following names were chosen when you ran the previous example code:

```
PK__nameTable__1ED998B2
UQ__nameTable__1FCDBCEB
UQ__nameTable__20C1E124
UQ__nameTable__21B6055D
```

These don't mean much to the human reader. While it isn't hard to look them up with tools like Enterprise Manager, it's probably better to make them something more intelligible. The naming standard that you'll use in this book is pretty simple:

```
<type><tableName>_<description>
```

For a primary key the type would be PK, and for an alternate key you would use AK. As for the description, you would omit that on the primary key because you can only have a single instance of a primary key. For the description of alternate keys, use either the column name for single columns or a brief description for an alternate key comprising more than one column. So, for this example, you would get the following:

```
CREATE TABLE nameTable
(
    id integer NOT NULL IDENTITY
        CONSTRAINT PKnameTable PRIMARY KEY,
    firstName varchar(15) NOT NULL CONSTRAINT AKnameTable_firstName UNIQUE,
    lastName varchar(15) NULL CONSTRAINT AKnameTable_lastName UNIQUE,
        CONSTRAINT AKnameTable_fullName UNIQUE (firstName, lastName)
)
```

This would leave you with these names, thus making it easier to work out the role of the constraints:

```
PKnameTable
AKnameTable_fullName
AKnameTable_lastName
AKnameTable_firstName
```

Other Indexes

Any indexes that you add in addition to those used to enforce uniqueness should be taken care of when dealing with performance tuning. Indexes make accessing data in a certain way faster, but they also have overhead. Every time a change affects any of the columns that are indexed, the index must be modified. For a single change, this time is negligible, but the more active the system, the more this will affect performance. In your OLTP system, only in extremely obvious cases would I advocate performance "guessing"–adding indexes before a need is shown–vs. performance "tuning" where you respond to known performance problems. Only at this time will you be able to decide how a performance "tune" will affect the rest of the database.

Relationships

You've studied relationships in some length already, so I won't say too much more about why you would use them. In this section you'll simply learn how to implement relationships. The first thing you need to do is introduce a new statement. This is the `ALTER TABLE` statement:

```
ALTER TABLE <tablename>
```

The `ALTER TABLE` statement allows you to modify and add columns, check constraints, and enable and disable triggers. In this section, you'll look at how to add constraints to tables. Note that you're also able to do this using the `CREATE TABLE` statement. However, because you frequently create all of your tables at once, it's better to use the `ALTER TABLE` command on preexisting tables rather than having to create tables in order, so that parent tables are created before dependent-child tables.

Foreign Keys

The foreign key is actually just a unique key of another table migrated to a child table where it represents the parent entity. The unique key will be the primary key of the table 99.9 percent of the time. Implementing foreign keys is a fairly simple task in SQL Server 2000. You have to work through the following issues when creating relationships:

❑ Cascading deletes (if the parent row is deleted, then delete any related children values that refer to the key of the deleted row).

❑ Relationships that span different databases.

The basic syntax of the `ALTER TABLE` statement for adding foreign key constraints is pretty simple (the `ALTER TABLE` command will be used many times throughout this chapter and the next to add constraints):

```
ALTER TABLE <tablename>
    ADD CONSTRAINT [<constraintName>]
    FOREIGN KEY REFERENCES <referenceTable> (<referenceColumns>)
```

Note that this code demonstrated the addition of a constraint. For other operations that you can carry out using ALTER TABLE, *see the SQL Server 2000 documentation.*

❑ `<tablename>` is the child table in the relationship.

❑ `<referenceTable>` is the parent table in the relationship.

❑ `<referenceColumns>` is a comma-delimited list of columns in the child table in the same order as the columns in the primary key of the parent table.

If you need to implement an optional relationship (where the migrated key is nullable) like the following figure.

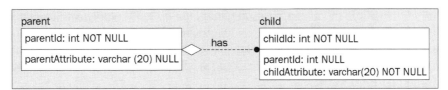

Then this is implemented almost identically to the previous situation. The ALTER TABLE statement is the same, but you'll notice that the `child.parentId` column is nullable. When the referencing key allows a NULL, SQL Server knows that you want it to be optional. You don't have to have a NULL primary key because, as discussed earlier, it's impossible to have a NULL attribute in a primary key.

It's as simple as this to protect the parent-child relationships that you've set up in your design. You'll read some examples of relationships and cascading deletes as well as a brief discussion of cross-database relationships, shortly.

Naming

When choosing names for your objects, you've usually created names that allowed the user to interact with the objects. For constraints and indexes, you need names that indicate the usage of the object. The same goes for the naming of relationships, though it's possible in certain circumstances to have chosen the same name for two relationships though you cannot implement this in SQL Server. Hence, you need to consider designing names for relationships.

Throughout the book you'll use very descriptive names for your objects that tend to be quite long. For example, the naming standard for relationships that you'll adopt for this book takes the verb phrase from the logical model and includes the parent and child table names in the object name, to create a unique name as well as making any constraints easy to identify when listed by name.

You use the following template for your name:

```
<parentTable>$<verbPhrase>$<childTable>
```

For example if you had a company table related to a product table you would define the relationship name as company$sells$product, and as with the naming of foreign keys, implement this using the following syntax:

```
ALTER TABLE product
    ADD CONSTRAINT company$sells$product FOREIGN KEY
    REFERENCES parent (companyId)
```

Note the use of the dollar sign in the name. Referring back to the identifier standards discussed earlier in the chapter, there aren't any really good values to delimit or separate between parts of a name other than the dollar sign. Other than letters and numbers, you were allowed only three special characters: the dollar sign, the ampersand, and the underscore. The underscore is frequently used within the names of objects (instead of the camel-case formatting that you're using). The ampersand is often used for variables, which these aren't. Hence, for clarity, you'll use the dollar sign between names.

This makes any system messages that pertain to the constraints easier to trace. However, in the final analysis, any naming convention will suffice as long as you name all objects and don't just leave it up to SQL Server to pick a name for you.

Cascading Deletes and Updates

In our previous example, the database prevented us from deleting the parent table if a child table existed with a reference to the parent as an attribute. This is great in most cases, but there are cases in which the data in the child table is so integrated with the data of the parent table that, when the parent table is changed or deleted, SQL Server will always seek to modify or delete the child row without any further interaction with the user.

Consider the case of a product and a table that stores descriptive specification information:

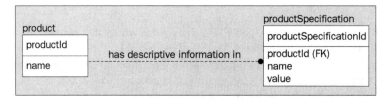

In this case, if you wanted to delete a row from the product table, it's unlikely that you'd want to keep the productSpecification table either.

The ability to affect some implicit change automatically on a child table, as a result of an explicit action on a parent table, is known as **cascading** changes.

For a delete, you could set a constraint that would automatically delete the children of a relationship as a result of some action on the parent table. For an update, if you modify the value of the primary key of the parent table, then the change would cascade down to the child table's foreign key value. There is another lesser-used cascading action that SQL Server doesn't in fact implement—a type of cascading action for which the child table isn't deleted altogether but its key reference is set to NULL.

This can only be implemented on optional relationships because, if the foreign key value doesn't allow NULLs, it will fail. A discussion of how to implement such a situation will be left to the next chapter because it has to be built with triggers.

Two of the most exciting new features of SQL Server 2000 are the ability to have cascading deletes in declarative referential integrity, and cascading updates. In previous versions of SQL Server, a cascading operation required a trigger. This was troublesome because you could no longer employ foreign key relationships and tools that would use declarative relationships.

The syntax for implementing cascading operations is simple. You simply add ON DELETE CASCADE or ON UPDATE CASCADE to your constraint declaration as follows:

```
ALTER TABLE <tablename>
    ADD CONSTRAINT <constraintName>
    FOREIGN KEY REFERENCES <referenceTable> (<referenceColumn>)
    [ON DELETE <CASCADE> | <NO ACTION>]
    [ON UPDATE <CASCADE> | <NO ACTION>]
```

Using the NO ACTION option for either of the declarations sets the relationship to the "normal" restrictive case–when a child row exists and a change to the key or a delete is affected on the parent, an error occurs.

> *No action may seem like a strange way to put it, but what is being said is that, if the delete fails, you take NO ACTION and end the operation.*

To continue your childhasparent constraint example, you just found out that, after creating the child row, you could not delete the original parent. So, you'll adapt this example to allow cascading deletes.

```
--note that there is no alter constraint command
ALTER TABLE child
    DROP CONSTRAINT child$has$parent

ALTER TABLE child
    ADD CONSTRAINT child$has$parent FOREIGN KEY (parentId)
    REFERENCES parent
    ON DELETE CASCADE

SELECT * FROM parent
SELECT * FROM child
```

It returns the following:

parentId	parentAttribute
2	parent

childId	parentId	childAttribute
2	2	child

Then you run the delete and re-execute the selects as follows:

```
DELETE FROM parent
SELECT * FROM parent
SELECT * FROM child
```

and this returns the following:

parentId	parentAttribute

childId	parentId	childAttribute

It would be trivial to implement an example of cascading an update in much the same way. Note, however, that the primary key cannot be implemented as an identity column to make use of the cascading update, because identity values cannot be updated.

Cross-Database Relationships

The primary limitation on constraint-based foreign keys is that the tables participating in the relationship cannot span different databases. When this situation occurs, you must implement your relationships via triggers.

It's generally a bad idea to design databases with cross-database relationships. A database should be considered a unit of related tables that are always kept in sync. When you design databases that extend over different databases or even servers, you spread around references to data that isn't within the scope of the database, and you cannot guarantee its existence. However, there are times when cross-database relationships are unavoidable.

Sharing the Details of Your Database with Developers

In the logical-modeling phase of design, you spent many hours entering definitions of your tables, columns, and other objects. In this section, you'll look at some of the tools that you should give to your clients who will need to understand what you've created for them. These tools will provide reports of all the database objects and their properties, both implemented and informational.

However, building these reports, keeping them up-to-date, and distributing them can be quite a task. In this book, we're only going to explore the tools that SQL Server 2000 provides for you. There are several methods that are built into SQL Server:

❑   The Information Schema and system stored procedures

❑   Descriptive properties

❑   Metadata services

You'll learn about the first two in this list in some detail, but you won't look at metadata services here. They're very valuable but impractical from a simple usage standpoint. They're primarily used for exchanging metadata between modeling tools, DTS, and OLAP, and aren't really relevant to the subject matter of this book.

Information Schema and System Stored Procedures

For simply letting your users look at the structures of your tables, SQL Server offers you the Information Schema and system stored procedures.

The Information Schema is a set of 20 views based on the ANSI SQL-92 standard definition of a mechanism to provide a standard set of metatables to foster cross-platform development. They define many of the objects in SQL Server–all those that are understood by the SQL-92 standard–and they provide a quick reference to the structures of your tables.

In these views, you tend to use a slightly different, but fairly easy-to-understand set of semantic representations for common objects:

SQL Server Name	INFORMATION_SCHEMA (SQL-92) Name
database	catalog
owner	schema
user-defined datatype	domain

The following table gives a list of metadata procedures and the corresponding INFORMATION_SCHEMA views. The explanation in the third column of the table is simply a brief note of what the different procedures and views are used for. It's advisable for any database programmer to have a good understanding of how to use these objects to query the metadata of the model. The best way to do this is to look up the complete documentation on them in SQL Server 2000 Books Online.

SQL Server offers two completely different ways of viewing the same system data. From a comparison of the two different methods, there are two things that stand out for me. The system stored procedures are very much SQL Server implementation oriented. The INFORMATION_SCHEMA tables give the impression of being developed by a committee, on which not everybody got their way. However, the definitions that they give tend to be generic but very useful. In my opinion, it's best to use the INFORMATION_SCHEMA views whenever possible, because they're based on the SQL 92 standard and would likely be improved in the future. In addition, because every SQL 92–compliant database will eventually have an identical set of views implemented, using these views should facilitate understanding of other database systems.

System Stored Procedure	Corresponding INFORMATION_SCHEMA View	Explanation
sp_server_info	N/A	Gives a listing of settings and information concerning the server. Server information isn't in the INFORMATION_SCHEMA.
sp_tables	TABLES, VIEWS	Gives listings of the tables and views in the system. sp_tables lists system tables, user tables, and views. Strangely, the TABLES view lists tables and views, while the VIEWS view only lists views. It does have extended information about views, such as updatability, definition, check option, and a few other things.
sp_columns	COLUMNS	While the sp_columns procedure requires a parameter delineating the table it's used for and the COLUMNS view doesn't, both contain useful, interesting information about columns.
sp_stored_procedures	ROUTINES	Both list stored procedures and functions, but where sp_stored_procedures has a few columns that haven't yet been implemented, the ROUTINES view has lots. Both of these methods show hints of what is to come for SQL and SQL Server.
sp_sproc_columns	PARAMETERS	Both list the parameters of stored procedures and functions.
N/A	ROUTINE_COLUMNS	Lists the columns of the tables returned by functions, when they return tables, of course.
sp_helptext	VIEWS, ROUTINES	sp_helptext is one of those procedures that should be understood by any administrator. Using this procedure, you can get the text of any procedure, default, extended stored procedure (which returns the DLL it's in), and function in the system. The VIEWS and ROUTINES views are related because they too will return the definition of the view or routine, much like Help text.
sp_column_privileges	COLUMN_PRIVILEGES	Both list the different rights available on the columns in the tables.
sp_special_columns	N/A	Returns the primary key of the table.

System Stored Procedure	Corresponding INFORMATION_SCHEMA View	Explanation
sp_statistics	N/A	sp_statistics displays information on a table's indexes. There is no information about indexes in the INFORMATION_SCHEMA.
sp_fkeys	TABLE_CONSTRAINTS, CONSTRAINT_TABLE_USAGE, REFERENTIAL_CONSTRAINTS, KEY_COLUMN_USAGE	sp_fkeys gives you a list of the foreign key constraints on a table. TABLE_CONSTRAINTS and CONSTRAINT_TABLE_USAGE list all constraints on the table, one from the table's perspective, and the other from the constraint's. REFERENTIAL_CONSTRAINTS lists all of the foreign key constraints in the database. KEY_COLUMN_USAGE lists the columns in primary and foreign key constraints.
sp_pkeys	KEY_COLUMN_USAGE, TABLE_CONSTRAINTS	p_pkeys gives a list of primary keys on a table. The TABLE_CONSTRAINTS has already been mentioned in the previous section on sp_fkeys.
sp_helpconstraint	REFERENTIAL_CONSTRAINTS, CHECK_CONSTRAINTS, TABLE_CONSTRAINTS, CONSTRAINT_COLUMN_USAGE, CONSTRAINT_TABLE_USAGE	sp_helpconstraint gives you an overview of a table's constraints. You have read about all of the other INFORMATION_SCHEMA views already.
sp_table_privileges	TABLE_PRIVILEGES	sp_table_privileges displays a list of privileges available for a given table that may be granted. The TABLE_PRIVILEGES view lists one row for each privilege that has been granted to a user. They're related, but are actually opposite. sp_table_privileges is centered on what *can be* granted, while TABLE_PRIVILEGES is centered on what *has been* granted.
sp_datatype_info	DOMAINS	sp_datatype_info lists all datatypes that are available in the system and their properties, while the DOMAINS view lists only user-defined datatypes.
N/A	DOMAIN_CONSTRAINTS, COLUMN_DOMAIN_USAGE	Two additional views are added for domains that can really come in handy. DOMAIN_CONSTRAINTS lists all of the constraints (rules) that have been added to a domain. COLUMN_DOMAIN_USAGE lists every table in which the domain has been used in a table.

There are some bits of information in this group of functions that you haven't yet begun to investigate, most notably those functions that deal with privileges. You'll look at them in Chapter 12.

As an exercise, it's up to the reader to execute the procedures, look through the tables, and study SQL Server 2000 Books Online in the "System Stored Procedure" section (particularly the catalog procedures, but it's all good) as well as the section on the "Information Schema Views." With a combination of catalog procedures, INFORMATION_SCHEMA objects, and T-SQL functions, you can get a look at almost every piece of metadata concerning the databases you've created.

Descriptive Properties

In your modeling, you've created descriptions, notes, and various pieces of data that will be extremely useful in helping the developer to understand the whys and wherefores of using the tables you've created. In previous versions of SQL Server, it was very difficult to actually make any use of this data directly in the server. In SQL Server 2000, Microsoft introduced extended properties that allow you to store specific information about objects. This is really great because it allows you to extend the metadata of your tables in ways that can be used by your applications using simple SQL statements.

By creating these properties, you can build a repository of information that the application developers can use to do the following:

❑ Understand what the data in the columns is used for

❑ Store information to use in applications, such as the following:

   ❑ Captions to show on a form when a column is displayed

   ❑ Error messages to display when a constraint is violated

   ❑ Formatting rules for displaying or entering data

Extended properties are stored as sql_variant columns, so they may hold any datatype other than text or image columns.

For the purposes of attaching extended properties, the objects in SQL Server have been classified into a three-level naming scheme. The following tree illustrates this hierarchy:

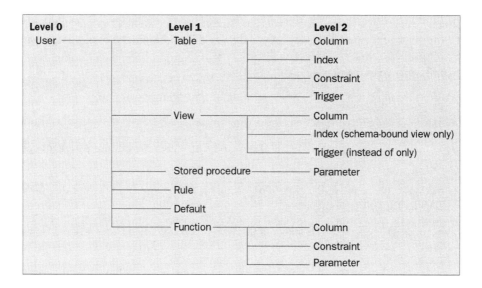

Note that in this diagram a new term has been mentioned: schema-bound. Schema binding refers to a mechanism that is new to SQL Server 2000; when you create a schema-bound view or schema-bound user-defined function, you can instruct SQL Server not to allow any changes to the base tables it uses. You'll cover this in greater detail in Chapter 12.

These are the only objects on which you can define extended properties, because SQL Server will check the names that you use for these properties. The naming scheme is fairly simple. You can add a property to a user requiring no other information, but to add a property to a table, you first must have a reference to the user who owns the table. To attach one to a column, you must know the user who owns the table, as well as the table name, column name, and so on.

To maintain extended properties, you're given the following functions and stored procedures:

❏ `sp_addextendedproperty`: Used to add a new extended property.

❏ `sp_dropextendedproperty`: Used to delete an existing extended property.

❏ `sp_updateextendedproperty`: Used to modify an existing extended property.

❏ `fn_listextendedproperty`: A system-defined function that can be used to list extended properties.

In the following example, you'll look at the specific syntax of each command as you use them, but it's important to understand the basic way the commands work. Each has the following parameters:

- ❑ @name: The name of the user-defined property.

- ❑ @value: What to set the value to when creating or modifying a property.

- ❑ @level0type: Either user or user-defined datatype.

- ❑ @level0name: The name of the object of the type that is identified in the @level0type parameter.

- ❑ @level1type: The name of the type of object that is on the level 1 branch of the tree under user, such as Table, View, and so on.

- ❑ @level1name: The name of the object of the type that is identified in the @level1type parameter.

- ❑ @level2type: The name of the type of object that is on the level 2 branch of the tree under the value in the @level1Type value. For example, if @level1type is Table, then @level2type might be Column, Index, Constraint, or Trigger.

- ❑ @level2name: The name of the object of the type that is identified in the @level2type parameter.

For example, let's say you create a table named **person** with the following script:

```
CREATE TABLE person
(
    personId int NOT NULL IDENTITY,
    firstName varchar(40) NOT NULL,
    lastName varchar(40) NOT NULL,
    socialSecurityNumber varchar(10) NOT NULL
)
```

To do this, you're going to add a property to the table and columns named MS_Description. Why MS_Description? Because this is the name that Microsoft has chosen to use in the Enterprise Manager to store descriptions.

> *Note that this is subject to change. I found the name of the property by using the SQL Profiler to trace how SQL Server saved the property, and then fabricated my own version of the script. Profiling how Enterprise Manager does things is a quick way to discover how to script out tasks that are seemingly only possible using the GUI tools.*

You execute the following script after creating the table:

```
--dbo.person table gui description
EXEC sp_addextendedproperty @name = 'MS_Description',
   @value = 'Example of extended properties on the person table',
   @level0type = 'User', @level0name = 'dbo',
   @level1type = 'table', @level1name = 'person'

--dbo.person.personId gui description
EXEC sp_addextendedproperty @name = 'MS_Description',
   @value = 'primary key pointer to a person instance',
   @level0type = 'User', @level0name = 'dbo',
   @level1type = 'table', @level1name = 'person',
   @level2type = 'column', @level2name = 'personId'


--dbo.person.firstName gui description
EXEC sp_addextendedproperty @name = 'MS_Description',
   @value = 'The persons first name',
   @level0type = 'User', @level0name = 'dbo',
   @level1type = 'table', @level1name = 'person',
   @level2type = 'column', @level2name = 'firstName'

--dbo.person.lastName gui description
EXEC sp_addextendedproperty @name = 'MS_Description',
   @value = 'The person's last name',
   @level0type = 'User', @level0name = 'dbo',
   @level1type = 'table', @level1name = 'person',
   @level2type = 'column', @level2name = 'lastName'

--dbo.person.socialSecurityNumber gui description
EXEC sp_addextendedproperty @name = 'MS_Description',
   @value = 'descrip of sociSecNbr colmn',
   @level0type = 'User', @level0name = 'dbo',
   @level1type = 'table', @level1name = 'person',
   @level2type = 'column', @level2name = 'socialSecurityNumber'
```

Now when you go into Enterprise Manager, right-click your table and select Design Table, and you'll see your description as follows:

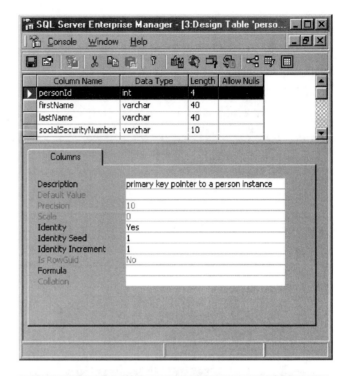

And looking at the properties of the table (click the icon to the right of Save) shows that you now have a description.

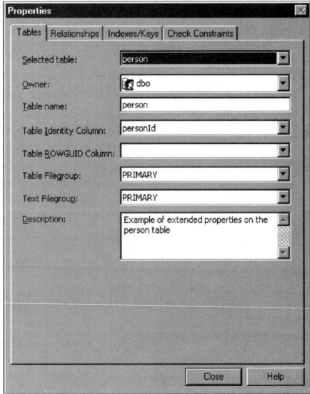

Obviously this would be quite a pain in the fingertips if you went to every table and column and hand-entered every one of the descriptions over again. However, if the tool that is being used has advanced capabilities for building scripts, you should be able to push out this data to make Enterprise Manager that much more useful as a tool for your programmers.

To change a property, you would use the following type of script:

```
--see if the property already exists
IF EXISTS ( SELECT *
    FROM ::FN_LISTEXTENDEDPROPERTY(MS_Description,
        'User', 'dbo',
        'table', 'person',
        'Column', 'socialSecurityNumber') )
BEGIN
    --if the property already exists
    EXEC sp_updateextendedproperty @name = 'MS_Description',
    @value = 'the persons government id number',
    @level0type = 'User', @level0name = 'dbo',
    @level1type = 'table', @level1name = 'person',
    @level2type = 'column', @level2name = 'socialSecurityNumber'
END
ELSE
BEGIN
    --otherwise create it.
    EXEC sp_addextendedproperty @name = MS_Description,

    @value = 'the persons government id number',
    @level0type = 'User', @level0name = 'dbo',
    @level1type = 'table', @level1name = 'person',
    @level2type = 'column', @level2name = 'socialSecurityNumber'
END
```

The fn_listExtendedProperty *object is a system-defined function that you'll explore further in Chapter 12.*

Your final extension to this example is to add an extended property to the table that the user-processes can use when executing the program. For this you'll add an input mask property to the table, so that you can build a general method of data entry for the column.

```
exec sp_addextendedproperty    @name = Input Mask,
    @value = ###-##-####,
    @level0type = 'User', @level0name = 'dbo',
    @level1type = 'table', @level1name = 'person',
    @level2type = 'column', @level2name = 'socialSecurityNumber'
```

Note that you can create *any* extended property you want. The names must fit into the sysname datatype, and may include blank, nonalphanumeric, or even binary values.

This new documentation feature has some interesting possibilities for creating applications and making the most of the metadata you have stored in various locations, even beyond the tremendously valuable documentation uses. For more information, check the SQL Server 2000 Books Online section on "Using Extended Properties on Database Objects."

Case Study

Returning to your case study, you now need to get down to building the physical structures to put the theory into practice. You'll follow your prescribed path whereby you identify situations that are going to be too difficult to implement and drop them from the implementation. You then choose your primary keys and datatypes, and then present the physical model that you'll implement. You'll then use a T-SQL script to implement your database, including adding your description information from your initial analysis.

Cleaning Up the Model

The first step is to clean up any situations that exist in the model that are too difficult to implement. In some cases, you'll have to leave out large areas of implementation that you would otherwise want, thereby ending up with a less-than-perfect solution. Depending on your situation, your tools, or even your corporate standards, you may have to change the way of implementing things, though you must still finish up with a solution that is functionally equivalent to the logical model. Each transformation you make in the model during the physical-modeling phase shouldn't change the set of data that is stored by your database, unless you discover further attributes that are required and that must be added to the logical model.

Subtypes

One of the most difficult situations to implement in SQL Server is the subtype. In your logical model (which you finished at the end of Chapter 8), you have an example of just such a case: the transaction subtype. You modeled it as a complete subtype; that is, all possible cases were represented in the diagram.

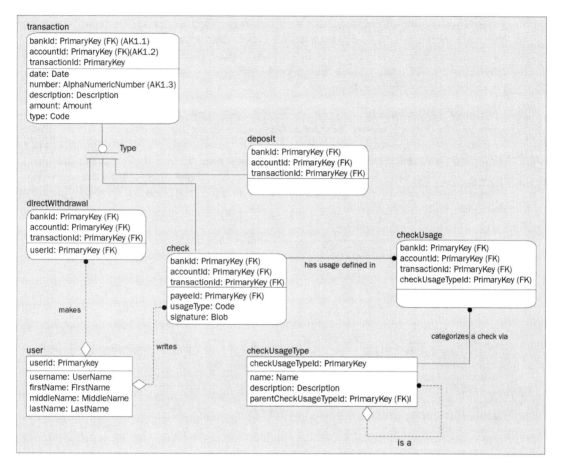

However, you didn't identify any additional attributes for a "deposit" or "direct withdrawal" to add to the model. In this case, you could simply change your subtype to an incomplete version (in which not every subtype value is actually materialized into a table) and remove the "deposit" and "direct withdrawal" entities. Depending on how large the subtype is (one or two attributes, or more, plus related tables), you may just want to assign these attributes to the parent of the relationship. This is what you'll do in this example. The primary reason for this is practicality, because each of the subtypes is very close to the same object. Later, you'll have to write some specialized code to protect the data from unreasonable data entry into the subtype tables.

In the subtype it's quite obvious which columns are valid, based on what value the discriminator is (in this case the discriminator is the type of transaction because it determines in which child table you should look for the subtype values), but once you take all of the attributes of all of the subtyped entities and reassign them to the parent, it can become less obvious. In your case, you have the following three attributes to deal with:

❑ **Payee:** Checks always have payees. Direct withdrawals might work also, but deposits never have payees. You could enhance your tables to allow the documentation of where the money for the deposit comes from, but you won't do this because you want to keep a limit on the size of the project and because such a change would breach the implementation plans that were previously approved by the client.

❑ **Signature:** Only checks have signatures. This attribute seems a little pointless, but you'll leave it this way for the purpose of the example. If you were taking this system to full fruition, this attribute would probably extend to a large domain tree and would pertain to deposits, direct withdrawals, and checks. However, you'll use the logic from the previous point and state that, because the client didn't ask for it, you don't put it in. You'll also change this value to a string because you'll only store the name of the person who signed the check, rather than a picture of the signature.

checkUsageType: This one is pretty simple; you'll change this to transactionAllocationType, where the user can set the usage and allocation for every type of transaction.

So you remodel the tables like this:

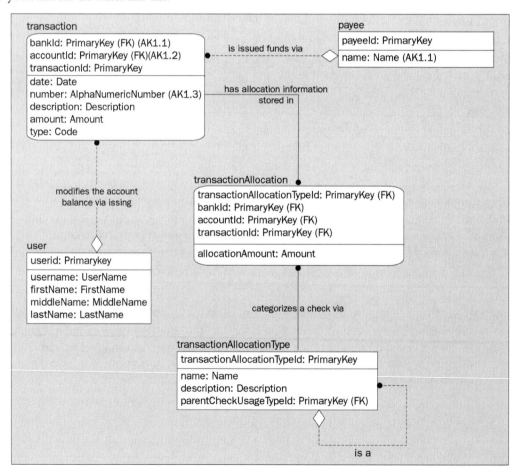

One thing should be noted. The `transaction` table cannot be so named in the physical implementation because it's a reserved word and SQL Server will not allow you to use it in code. So you have several choices of ways to handle this.

❑   Rename the table to a different name, say `xaction`.

❑   Always refer to the table with bracketed notation: `[transaction]`.

Neither of these is overly pleasant, and transaction was the best name for the table and referencing tables. For this example, you'll choose to keep the name transaction and use bracketed notation whenever using the table. This will keep the table name more recognizable to the client and give you a reason to use the bracket notation in your coding examples. You'll only refer to the table as `[transaction]` when you're using it in code.

We'll look at how to implement the specific data rules that you'll have to handle in the next chapter.

Simplification of Complex Relationships

In some cases, you'll model things during the logical design phase that are a little too complex to actually implement. In your logical model, you have one situation that you might find too difficult to implement as designed. In order to have a unique postal address, you have to look across two tables. In your model, the `address` and `addressLine` tables are like this:

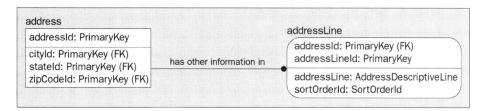

This allows for an address of unlimited size and structure, but this probably isn't necessary for the physical implementation. So you'll simply rebuild the address table as follows:

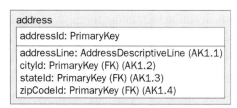

The `addressLine` column allows for all of the street, post office box, and other information, the size of which you'll decide upon when you choose datatypes.

Domain Tables

In the `transaction` table, you have a column named **type** to denote the type of transaction.

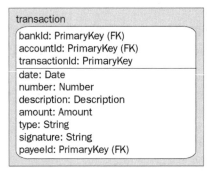

Usually, you won't want to have a freeform data entry column when you need to be able to group on the column, or, in the case of the `transaction type` column, when you'll likely need to use the domain value for special handling in your user interface.

You might even want to add implementation-specific information to your address-type table, such as icon file name locations, so that the UI could show a little check by the check type, an ATM card by the direct withdrawal, and so forth. In your `transactionType` table, you add `name` and `description` columns. This way you can include more information to explain what each value in the table means. Again, each of these attributes would have to be passed by the client and possibly added to the logical model. You see these changes, plus three other logical columns in the following diagram.

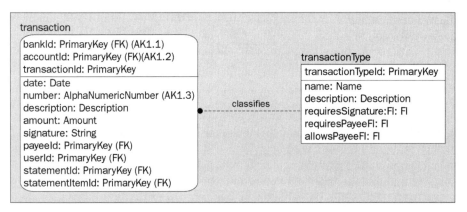

Now you can write code that forces the `signature` column to be filled in for a certain type of transaction, or you can specify that the payee is mandatory or optional. Building the UI would be easier, because you have data that will tell you when a value is required and changing the requirement will not require any extra code. Each of these flag columns would be considered as valid logical columns because they support the implementation of information already in the current design.

You'll also use this table as your transaction type for the `statementItem` table (though you won't use the flag columns). Because your transaction types will match the bank's, you won't be able to have duplicate data in the table, plus it will make matching the items during the balancing of the account much easier—but you certainly won't *require* that the transaction types match.

Trimming Down Unneeded Entities

After further review, you note that the `checkRegister` table won't really turn out to be an implemented table at all, because the check register is a concept that doesn't really match a computer table. Hence, you remove it from your physical model, though it still has value in the logical model because it's an actual entity that you may have to deal with.

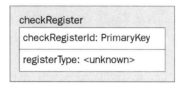

Correcting Errors in the Model

As you go through the process, you'll find errors in the model even if you use the best modeling tools and work at an unhurried pace. For instance, in the original model you had the following relationship.

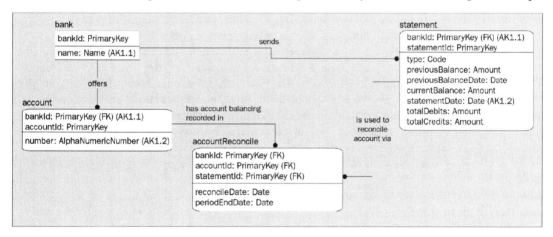

The error is the relationship between the `bank` and `statement` tables: "banks send statements." The relationship should be "banks send statements for accounts" and, to implement this, the relationship between bank and statement should be replaced by a relationship between account and statement. You move the `periodEndDate` column to the statement, because this will be a part of the statement rather than a value you store when you're marking the statement as reconciled. You'll also drop the relationship between account and `accountReconcile`, because you'll mark a statement as reconciled.

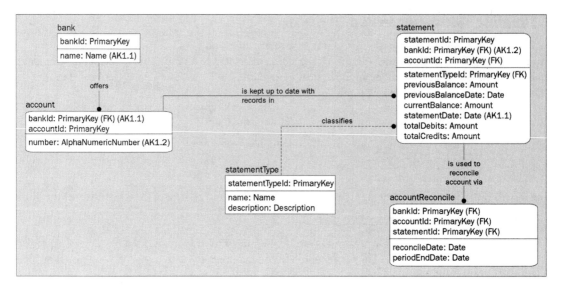

One of the interesting parts of this model is that, in order to find out when an account was last reconciled, you have to go through the `statement` table to the `accountReconcile` table. Though this may seem odd to those uninitiated to normalized database programming, this is one of the tell-tale signs of a well-designed database. In a larger system, you might have to go through 5, 10, or 20 tables to find out information like this. The principle of having one piece of data stored in one place can make your databases more interesting to traverse, but on the other hand will eliminate redundant data and modification anomalies—if an account number is stored in more than one place and it needs to be changed, it has to be changed in every place otherwise your data would be inconsistent. As you'll see in the next chapter, not having the ability to accidentally mess up your data is worth the extra initial coding pain.

You shouldn't look at finding errors like this in your model as a failure. Very often you'll miss stuff as you go through the design phase. Often your clients will make a change in their database requirements that must be dealt with. Errors cannot be entirely eliminated because every database architect is human. Often, it isn't until you've completed the first draft of a design that you're able to spot the more complex problems and consider their solutions. Sometimes one design decision may determine or modify several others. Database design should always be an iterative process.

Preparing the Model for Implementation

Once you've cleared up the logical model in the way I just outlined, you can move on to preparing your tables for generation. Here you should take steps to make the system easy to create, thereby adding columns for optimistic locking and row disabling (and anything else that suits your particular needs). You'll then add primary keys, unique keys, and finally choose datatypes.

Once you've completed these final tasks, you'll be ready to script your database objects and implement the database in SQL Server.

Physical-Only Columns

As a brief reminder, physical-only columns don't relate to any of the database objects. They're simply included in the database to make coding easier. The two examples you've already examined have been added to the following table.

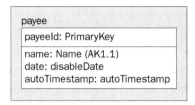

In this table you have a `disableDate` column as opposed to the `disableFl` that was previously discussed. `disableDate` sets the date and time after which the payee can no longer receive monies from transactions in your database. You could also add tables to store the reasons for and history of payee status, but you won't here in order to keep things simple. `disableDate` works the same way as `disableFl` except that, instead of a simple flag, you implement a date so you can see if you set it to some future date and time.

You've also added an `autoTimestamp` column to every table on the model, which, as previously discussed, will form the basis of an optimistic lock mechanism.

These are the only physical-only columns you'll add to your current database.

Primary Keys

Primary key columns are technically physical-only columns, because you'll never show them to the user and they exist primarily for your benefit in implementation, though you've represented them both on the logical and physical models.

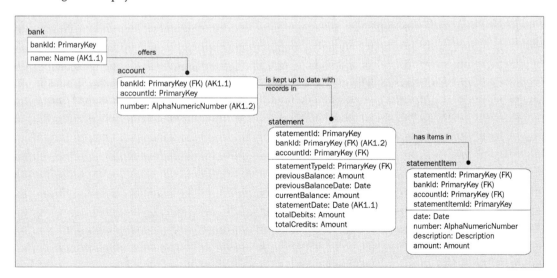

The bankId pointer migrates from the bank table all the way down to the statementItem table. This is fine for logical modeling but, for multipart keys in physical tables, this can cause more trouble than it's worth. The main reason for this is that you may need two, three, or even more columns to uniquely identify a table. If you have to join across ten tables to find related information, then you're in trouble. So, if your database was implemented as shown here and you asked the question–"For the First National Bank, in which cities did we spend the most money on textiles?"–this query would involve every table and, by the time you had included all of the multipart keys, the query would be unmanageable.

Another reason for making the primary key a physical-only column is that, if you change the composition of the *logical* primary key for the object, you wouldn't affect the *implemented* primary key of the object. This will reduce the effect that the change will have on any dependent objects. In this example, take your "bank to account to statement to statementItem" set of relationships. If you decided that the bank table was no longer needed and you deleted the table from the model, the account, statement, and statementItem tables would have their primary keys changed.

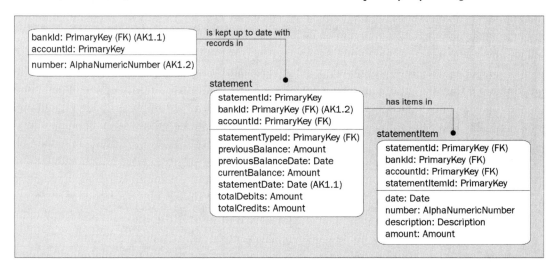

This isn't an optimal solution to your coding problem because all of the code that used these entities would now be broken. However, if each table had a single column primary key, only the account table would be forced to change. The meaning of the objects would change, because they would no longer be identified by the corresponding bank; but to the programmer, the actual values of the primary keys would still be the same. An account would still have statements and transactions.

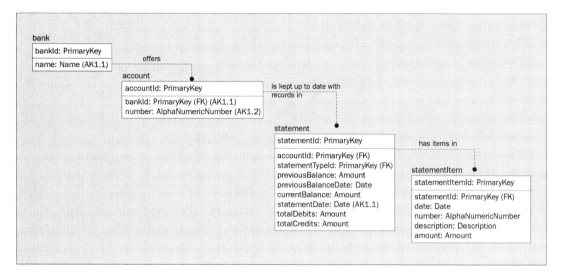

Now, note what happens when you remove the bank table from this model.

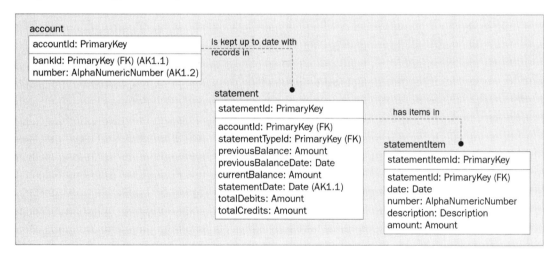

The `statement` and `statementItem` tables are unchanged. Hence, the programs that access them won't change. The `account` programs will only have to change to reflect the fact that there no longer is a `bankId` column in the table–a fairly minor change in comparison with what might have been required. Note that, once you've changed the keys, the implementation of the tables has changed, though what the tables represent hasn't.

One thing about the new tables–each of them has a unique key containing the migrated part of the previous primary key. For instance, before the changes were made the `statement` table looked like the following figure.

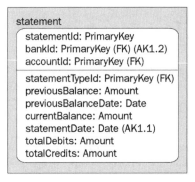

statement

statementId: PrimaryKey
bankId: PrimaryKey (FK) (AK1.2)
accountId: PrimaryKey (FK)

statementTypeId: PrimaryKey (FK)
previousBalance: Amount
previousBalanceDate: Date
currentBalance: Amount
statementDate: Date (AK1.1)
totalDebits: Amount
totalCredits: Amount

This table has no easily identifiable natural key, because you didn't previously specify any alternate keys in your design. Upon further review, there is a possible key that you can use–the `date` value (likely with time stripped off). You've defined this program to allow online account balancing, which you might do daily but no more frequently than that (check with client before making such decisions). So, you could use the `date` as part of the alternate key, as modeled in the following diagram.

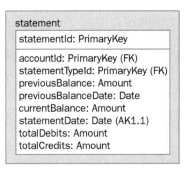

statement

statementId: PrimaryKey

accountId: PrimaryKey (FK)
statementTypeId: PrimaryKey (FK)
previousBalance: Amount
previousBalanceDate: Date
currentBalance: Amount
statementDate: Date (AK1.1)
totalDebits: Amount
totalCredits: Amount

Normally, you wouldn't use dates in your keys, even alternate ones, if you can possibly help it–especially a key that you implement as a full 8-bit `datetime` value. There are two very important reasons to avoid this practice:

❑   **Ease of accessing data:** When you need to use the key to access a given row in the table, if your key is defined with the date value, it can be very hard to type in the actual value of the date by hand. For instance, a `datetime` value contains day, month, year, hour, minute, second, and parts of a second (and `smalldatetimes` include values up to the minute). This can be cumbersome to deal with, especially for the average user.

❑   **Precision:** In most cases, the precision of the date variables is more than is required for the average key. Usually, when you want to put the date in the key it's because you simply want the day and year.

In your case, you'll use a `datetime` type, probably a `smalldatetime`, because you'll want to be able to have a statement produced at multiple times during the day and it works best here. Plus, you'll be stripping off some of the time values.

Datatypes

During the modeling, you've chosen logical domains for your attributes. Now you'll take your design and turn the attributes into real columns and assign real datatypes. To decide on datatypes, you'll create a table of the domains that you've chosen, and then assign datatypes and definitions to them—choosing the datatype, nullability options, and any additional information on a domain-by-domain basis. Once you've done this task, you'll go through each of your tables, setting the datatype to the domain values you've chosen.

> *The domains that you've been applying to your logical model throughout this exercise have the following form, in which* `primaryKey` *and* `otherDomainName` *are considered the domain for the different attributes.*

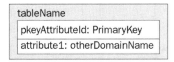

The following list contains all of the domains that you've used by name. We'll go through and make some guesses as to what the datatype seems to call for. Then, once finished, you'll use these as first passes to your datatype choices. You'll find that there is a very good hit ratio and you won't have to change many. You will, however, have to go through all of the tables to verify they're right (of course you'll only do a few tables here).

Name	Comment	Datatype	Nullability
addressDescriptiveLine	Used to store the address information.	varchar(800) adequate size; keeps the unique index under 900 bytes	NOT NULL
addressStateCode	The two character state code that is recognized by the US post office.	char(2)	NOT NULL
alphaNumericNumber	Alphanumeric "number" that is usually an alternate key value for a row in a table. An example is an account number.	varchar(20)	NOT NULL
amount	Generic domain for monetary amounts.	money	NOT NULL

Name	Comment	Datatype	Nullability
areaCode	Code that identifies a dialing region of a state.	varchar(3)	NOT NULL
autoTimestamp	Automatically incrementing optimistic locking value.	timestamp	NOT NULL
countryCode	Dialing code that identifies the country being dialed.	char(1)	NOT NULL
date	Default datetime values. Defaults to smalldatetime values because you'll seldom need the precision of the datetime datatype.	smalldatetime	NOT NULL
description	Brief, unstructured comments describing an instance of a table to further extend another user's ability to tell them apart.	varchar(100)	NOT NULL
disableDate	Used to disable a row without deleting it, such as for historical purposes.	smalldatetime	NULL
exchange	The area code that comes before the telephone number.	char(5)	NOT NULL
extension	A string that allows a set of numbers that can be dialed after the connection has been made.	varchar(20)	NULL
firstName	Used to store a person's first name.	varchar(60)	NOT NULL
Fl	Generally a logical value. Implemented as a NOT NULL bit column where 0 is false and nonzero is true.	bit	NOT NULL
lastName	Used to store a person's last name.	varchar(60)	NOT NULL
middleName	Used to store a person's middle name.	varchar(60)	NOT NULL
name	The name that an instance of a row will be uniquely known as. This isn't a person's name, rather, this is usually an alternate key value for an object.	varchar(60)	NOT NULL

Name	Comment	Datatype	Nullability
number	General value that is a number. Defaults to integer.	int	NOT NULL
phoneNumberPart	The telephone number.	char(4)	NOT NULL
primaryFl	Bit flag that is used to point to the primary row of a group.	bit	NOT NULL
primaryKey	Auto-generating identity column used as the pointer for an instance of an entity.	int	NOT NULL, IDENTITY
String	Generic string values. You used this as the default when you didn't know what the string was going to be used for. NOT NULL by default.	varchar(20)	NOT NULL
Username	Used to store the name of a user in the system.	sysname (a SQL Server user-defined datatype that they use to store usernames. You'll store SQL Server names here to map to real names, because you'll give rights to any user who has rights to enter a check to look at the transactions and accounts, based on the use cases.	NOT NULL
ZipCode	Five-digit zip code that identifies a postal region that may span different cities, states, and may also simply identify a part of a city.	char(5) (Note that you've used the zipCode to link back to the city. This is done with the five-character zipCode. You've ignored the +4 zip code again for simplicity.)	NOT NULL

It should be noted that all of my addresses and phone numbers are very US-centered. This serves one purpose—simplicity.

Once your list has been completed, you step through each of the tables and look at each datatype and NULL specification for every column to see how they work in the individual situation. If you find out that some don't match the specifications as outlined earlier, and assuming that you were going to repeat this process many times, you would likely want to create new domains for future use. You won't go along this route; rather, you'll just make the necessary changes if there are any. One additional point—you'll also want to finalize the definitions for your attributes, because you've added and changed many of them along the design path.

> *In each of the following sections, you'll take one of your entities, match the domain name with those from the list, present what the default choices were for datatypes, and then follow that with a discussion and any overrides to the datatype from the default.*

You start with the bank entity, as shown here.

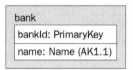

❑ **bankId**
PrimaryKey, int NOT NULL IDENTITY: Which is exactly what is needed.
Define as: "Non-human readable pointer used to identify a bank instance."

❑ **name**
Name, varchar(60): Which should be sufficient to handle any bank name.
Define as: "The name that an instance of bank will be uniquely known as."

Note that you go for very technical definitions for the attributes, because these will be used by developers who haven't been involved in the design phase and this will be the first time that they will see the database specification. In logical modeling (from Chapter 5), you defined the "Bank Name" attribute as "the name of the bank you're dealing with," which means the same thing but is in a softer format that will be understood by all users. When developing systems using database modeling tools, you'll need to be able to reconcile the definitions that you've chosen.

Finally, you end up with the following, as shown here.

```
bank
bankId: int IDENTITY
name: varchar(60) NOT NULL (AK1.1)
autoTimestamp: timestamp NOT NULL
```

> *Note that you've also added the column autoTimestamp, which is defined as the "Automatically incrementing optimistic locking value." You'll add this to all tables.*

Next you'll look at the `account` table.

```
account
  accountId: PrimaryKey
  bankId: PrimaryKey (FK) (AK1.1)
  number: AlphaNumericNumber (AK1.2)
```

❑ **accountId**
  `primaryKey`, `int NOT NULL IDENTITY`: Which is exactly what is needed.
  Define as: "Non-human readable pointer used to identify an account instance."

❑ **bankId**
  `primaryKey`, `int NOT NULL`: Which is exactly what is needed because it's a foreign key value with nulls that aren't allowed.
  Define as: "Non-human readable pointer used to identify a bank instance."

❑ **number**
  `AlphaNumericNumber`, `varchar(20) NOT NULL`: which should be sufficient to handle almost any account number. Some additional research might be needed to determine if all of the client's values will fit.
  Define as: "Account number that is provided by the bank to identify the account."
  Note that while the value is referred to as a number, it's actually an alphanumeric string because it may contain leading zeros or letters.

This results in the following:

```
account
  accountId: int IDENTITY
  bankId: int NOT NULL (FK) (AK1.1)
  number: varchar(20) NOT NULL (AK1.2)
  autoTimestamp: timestamp NOT NULL
```

For your last illustration, let's look at the `transaction` table.

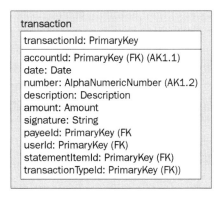

```
transaction
  transactionId: PrimaryKey
  accountId: PrimaryKey (FK) (AK1.1)
  date: Date
  number: AlphaNumericNumber (AK1.2)
  description: Description
  amount: Amount
  signature: String
  payeeId: PrimaryKey (FK
  userId: PrimaryKey (FK)
  statementItemId: PrimaryKey (FK)
  transactionTypeId: PrimaryKey (FK))
```

❑ **transactionId**
PrimaryKey, int NOT NULL IDENTITY: Which is exactly what is needed.
Define as: "Non-human readable pointer used to identify a transaction instance."

❑ **accountId**
PrimaryKey, int NOT NULL: Which is exactly what is needed because it's a foreign key with nulls that aren't allowed.
Define as: "Non-human readable pointer used to identify an account instance."

❑ **number**
AlphaNumericNumber, varchar(20) NOT NULL: Which should be sufficient to handle almost any check number, or number from the deposit or ATM (automatic teller machine) slip. Some additional research might be needed to determine if all of the client's values will fit.
Define as: "Account number provided by the bank to identify the account."

Note that while the value is referred to as a number, it's actually an alphanumeric string because it may contain leading zeros or letters.

❑ **description**
description, varchar(100) NOT NULL: In this case, you should probably give them additional space to describe the use of a check, ATM, or deposit. However, you also have a checkAllocation table in which usage is broken down. For this, you'll change the description column type to varchar(1000) in order to give the freedom to describe the transaction in greater detail if required.
Define as: "Unstructured comments, describing an instance of a transaction, to further extend another user's ability to tell them apart."

❑ **amount**
amount, money, NOT NULL: These will be sufficient to describe the amount of a transaction.
Define as: "The amount of money that is to change hands via the transaction."

❑ **signature**
String, varchar(20) NOT NULL: This is where you would possibly want to extend the string to handle an entire name. You also might want to use some form of image datatype to store an image of the signature. In your tables, you'll simply choose to change it from a varchar(20) to a varchar(100), in order to allow the user to enter the name of the person to whom the signature belongs.
Define as: "A textual representation of the signature that was entered on a transaction."

❑ **payeeId**
primaryKey, int NOT NULL: Which isn't exactly what is needed because this is an optional relationship. So you make sure that this column is set to NULL.
Define as: "Nonhuman readable pointer used to identify a payee instance, which may only be filled in based upon the allowsPayeeFl value in the related transactionType table."

❑ **userId**
primaryKey, int NOT NULL: Which isn't needed because this is an optional relationship. So you make sure that this column is set to NULL.
Define as: "Nonhuman readable pointer used to identify the user who was responsible for the transaction."

❏ **statementItemId**

primaryKey, int NOT NULL: Which isn't needed because this is an optional relationship. So you make sure that this column is set to NULL.

Define as: "Nonhuman readable pointer used to identify the statementItem that was used to reconcile this transaction item."

❏ **transactionTypeId**

primaryKey, int NOT NULL: Which is exactly what is needed because it's a required column. Define as: "Nonhuman readable pointer used to identify a transaction-type row that identifies the type of transaction you're dealing with."

The results are in the following table.

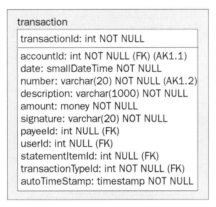

You continue through all of the tables in your model in this manner, until you've determined all of the datatypes and definitions. In the next two sections, you'll see the final physical model that you'll implement, followed by the script for the three tables you've created in this section. The entire schema script (and supporting code) will be located at http://www.apress.com.

> *Before you continue, you need to make a note about collations (the character sets and ordering settings you looked at earlier) on datatypes. Setting individual column collations is quite an advanced topic, and it's useful for a very specific set of situations. In your case study you won't make use of collations, but I mention them again here to remind you that it's possible to set the collation of a single column if desired.*

Physical Model

At this point, the model on paper should be given a "sanity check," preferably in conjunction with a coworker, so that you can ensure your model is efficient and usable, but also understandable to someone else.

So here's the final physical model for your database system. As far as you're concerned, these are the models that you'll implement and create on the database server:

Part One

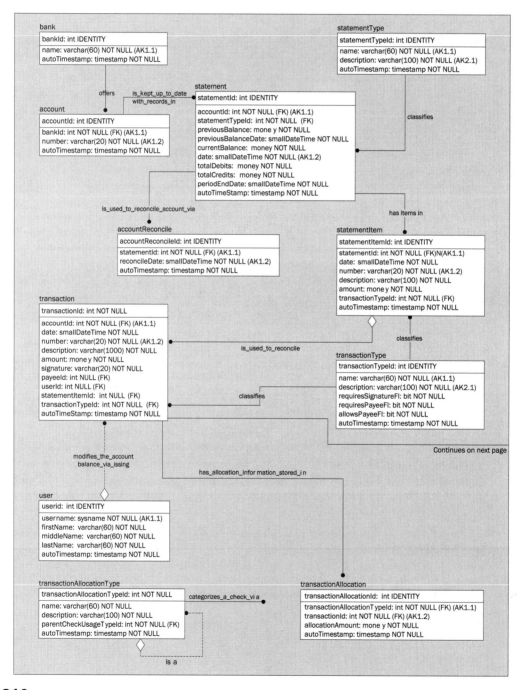

Continues on next page

Part Two

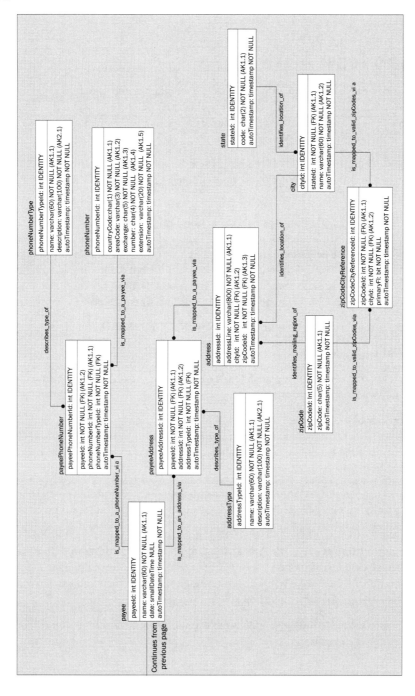

> The full version of the source code to create the database objects will be available from http://www.apress.com. The full script for even this small database is quite long, and is quite repetitive.

Best Practices

- ❑ **Make sure you've invested in proper database generation tools**: Implementing tables, columns, relationships, and so on is a very tedious and painful task when done by hand. There are many great tools that double as logical data-modeling tools and also generate these objects as well as the objects and code you'll be learning in the next three chapters.

- ❑ **Maintain normalization**: Try to maintain the normalizations you've set up in Chapter 6 and 7 as much as possible. It will help keep the data better protected, and will be more resilient to change.

- ❑ **Be careful when implementing subtypes**: Carefully consider if leaving them as multiple tables makes more sense than rolling them up into a single table. The single table solution will always *seem* to be the best idea, but it can end up causing much trouble because you end up with tables that have complex logic that determines which columns are valuable in a given situation or not. It will actually make UI coding more troublesome, because it isn't overly apparent which columns fit in which situation, whereas it's clear when the objects are subtyped.

- ❑ **Develop a real strategy for naming objects**: Keep the basics in mind.

- ❑ **No plural names for tables or columns.**

- ❑ **Give all objects reasonably user-friendly names, so that it's obvious to at least support personnel what is being done.**

- ❑ **Develop template domains**: Reuse definitions in every case for which a similar datatype is needed. This will cut down on time spent implementing, and will make users of the data happy, because every time they see a column called description, it's very likely that it will be the same datatype.

- ❑ **Carefully choose the datatype and nullability for each column**: These are the first levels of data protection that you deal with. Also, improper datatypes can cause precision difficulties with numbers and even performance issues.

- ❑ **Make certain that every table has at least one UNIQUE constraint that doesn't include an artificial value**: It's a good idea to consider using an identity column as the primary key. However, if that's the only UNIQUE constraint on the table, then you can have duplication in the *real* columns of the table, which is a very bad idea.

- ❑ **Avoid user-defined datatypes**: They aren't well implemented and are more trouble than they're worth at this point.

❏ **Include optimistic lock values in every table**: This will preferably be a timestamp column because they're guaranteed to be unique and are maintained by SQL Server. Make use of them in applications in which the client reads in a dataset (usually via a disconnected recordset), makes some changes, and pushes the changes back to the client. If the timestamps match, then the row is the same row that was cached in the disconnected recordset.

❏ **Implement all foreign keys using foreign key constraints**: They're fast, and no matter what kind of gaffes are made from a client, the relationship between tables cannot be wrong if a foreign key constraint is in place.

❏ **Use extended properties to communicate the system documentation to the user and programmers**: You can even let the value show up in the Microsoft tools, given the proper name of the property.

Summary

This has been a long chapter that covered a lot of ground. Understanding how to build tables and how they're implemented is the backbone of every database designer's knowledge. You've taken your logical model and examined each entity to determine how feasible it is to implement. You've dealt specifically with subtypes and learned that they can be problematic. You've also considered possible deviations from your strict normalization rules in extreme cases (though you've fought this as much as possible), and cleaned your database structures by dealing with the errors that exist in the model.

After you were satisfied that you had a model you could implement, you took a deep look at SQL Server tables, and walked through limits on tables and the `CREATE TABLE` and `ALTER TABLE` syntax. You learned the rules for naming objects, columns, indexes, and foreign key constraints.

The two most important sections of this chapter dealt with choosing datatypes and implementing unique keys. You completed this process by defining the primary keys and at least one alternate key per table, and a `timestamp` column for the purpose of illustrating optimistic locking. The final model and a script to implement the system is available from the Apress website.

In the next chapter, you'll finish the task of implementing the OLTP system by implementing the business rules required to keep the data in your database as clean as possible.

11

Declarative Data Protection

In this chapter, you'll finalize the predicates and domains that have been specified during the design process. When you discuss data integrity, you're looking at applying a body of rules to a given table, or set of tables, to ensure that stored values are always valid. Maintaining your database in a state where data is always within your original design specifications is at the heart of a great implementation. No matter how good or bad the tables have been designed, the way the user perceives the database will be based on how well the data is safeguarded. When developing a data integrity strategy, you need to consider several different scenarios:

❑ Users using custom front-end tools

❑ Users using generic data tools such as Microsoft Access

❑ Routines that import data from external sources

❑ Raw queries executed by data administrators to fix problems caused by user error

Each of these poses different issues for your integrity scheme, and what is more important, each of these scenarios (with the possible exception of the second) form part of every database system that you develop. To best handle each scenario, you must safeguard the data, using mechanisms that work independently of the user. This makes sure that the user/programmer does not "forget" about a rule and accidentally input incorrect data. There are four possible ways you can use code to maintain consistent data:

❑ **Datatypes and constraints** are simple, straightforward resources that form an integral part of the table definition. They are very fast mechanisms that require little coding, and their use can give you some important performance gains. Such constraints include actions such as defining data ranges in columns (for example, column must be greater than 10, or if column1 = 1 then column2 > 1).

This is the best place to protect the data because most of the work is handled by SQL Server, and the user cannot get around this by any error in an external program.

❑ **Triggers** differ from constraints in that they are pieces of code attached to a table (or tables). This code is automatically run whenever the event(s) you have specified occur in the table(s). They are extremely flexible and can access multiple columns, multiple rows, multiple tables, and even multiple databases. As a simple case, let's consider a situation in which you want to ensure that an update of a value is performed on both the tables where it occurs. You can write a trigger that disallows the update unless it occurs in both tables.

This is the second best place to protect the data. You do have to code every trigger rule in T-SQL, but the user cannot get around this by any error in an external program.

❑ **Stored procedures** are pieces of code, stored in the database, that deal with tables in a very flexible manner, so that different business rules can be applied to the same table under different circumstances. A simple example of a stored procedure is one that returns all the data held in a given table. In a more complex scenario, they can be used to grant different permissions to different users regarding manipulation of tables. This isn't all that great a solution to protect the data because you have to code the rules into any procedures that access the data. However, because it's in the central location, you can use this to implement rules that may be different based on various situations.

❑ **Client executable code** is useful to deal with situations in which business rules are optional or flexible in nature. A common example is asking the user "Are you sure you wish to delete this row?" SQL Server is a server product, and if you ask it to delete data, it deletes data. Most server products work in this manner, leaving the client programs the responsibility of implementing flexible business rules and warnings. Bear in mind that applications come and go, but the data must always be protected.

In moving down this list the solutions become less desirable, yet each one has specific benefits that are appropriate in certain situations. All of these features will be considered in turn; however let's begin by introducing a new feature in SQL Server 2000, which is essential in building constraints, triggers, and stored procedures. This feature is called UDFs (User-Defined Functions).

Example Tables

In the examples provided, the various concepts under consideration throughout this chapter are illustrated. You'll use the following tables:

```
CREATE TABLE artist
(
    artistId int NOT NULL IDENTITY,
    name varchar(60),
    --note that the primary key is clustered to make a
    --point later in the chapter
    CONSTRAINT XPKartist PRIMARY KEY CLUSTERED (artistId),
    CONSTRAINT XAKartist_name UNIQUE NONCLUSTERED (name)
)

INSERT INTO artist(name)
VALUES ('the beatles')
INSERT INTO artist(name)
```

```
VALUES ('the who')
GO

CREATE TABLE album
(
    albumId int NOT NULL IDENTITY,
    name varchar(60),
    artistId int NOT NULL,
    --note that the primary key is clustered to make a
    --point later in the chapter
    CONSTRAINT XPKalbum PRIMARY KEY CLUSTERED(albumId),
    CONSTRAINT XAKalbum_name UNIQUE NONCLUSTERED (name),
    CONSTRAINT artist$records$album FOREIGN KEY (artistId) REFERENCES artist
)

INSERT INTO album (name, artistId)
VALUES ('the white album',1)
INSERT INTO album (name, artistId)
VALUES ('revolver',1)
INSERT INTO album (name, artistId)
VALUES ('quadrophenia',2)
```

You'll use these tables to demonstrate how to protect your database using the different mechanisms you're given. This table will be used again in the next chapter as you continue to refine your solution.

Constraints

As you've seen before, constraints are SQL Server resources that are used to automatically enforce data integrity. One of the greatest things about using constraints instead of triggers is that the Query Optimizer can use them to optimize queries. For instance, if you tell SQL Server that a certain variable can only have values between 5 and 10, and then perform a query for all rows that have the value of this variable greater than 100, the optimizer will know without even looking at the data that there will be no rows that meet the criteria.

There are five different kinds of constraints that you have in SQL Server:

❑ **NULL**: Though NULL constraints aren't *technically* constraints, they behave as constraints.

❑ **Primary keys** and **unique constraints**: To make sure that your keys contain only unique combinations of values.

❑ **Foreign keys**: Used to make sure that any migrated keys have only valid values that match the keys that they reference.

❑ **Default**: Default constraints are used to set an acceptable default value for a column.

❑ **Check**: Constraints that are used to limit the values that can be entered into a single column or an entire table.

Having previously considered the first three of these in Chapter 10, we'll now focus your attention on the latter two here.

Default Constraints

I consider default values to be a very important part of safeguarding data. If a user doesn't know what value to enter into a table, the value can be omitted and the default constraint will set it to a valid predetermined value. Though you can prevent the user from entering invalid values, you cannot keep them from putting in illogical values. For example, consider that an experienced SQL Server user must enter a value into a column called `boogleFl`, which is a bit column (`boogleFl` was chosen because it has just as much meaning to you as some of the columns that make sense have for other users). Not knowing what `boogleFl` means, but forced to create a new row, the user may choose to enter a 0. Using default values gives the users an example of a likely value for the column. There is no question that setting default values for columns is very convenient for the user!

The command to add a default follows the following structure:

```
ALTER TABLE <tableName>
    ADD [ CONSTRAINT
    <DefaultName> ]
    DEFAULT <constantExpression>
    FOR <columnName>
```

You'll use a similar naming structure for your previous naming, expanding the default name to use the following pattern:

```
dflt<tableName>$<columnName>$<genericDatatype>$<description>
```

which results in the following altered syntax:

```
ALTER TABLE <tableName>
    ADD [ CONSTRAINT    <constraintName> ]
     DEFAULT <constantExpression>
     FOR <columnName>
```

The `<constantExpression>` is a scalar expression that can be either a literal value, a `NULL`, or a function. You'll look at several different scenarios for constant expressions in the following section.

There are two styles of defaults you'll look at:

❑ **Literals**: A single value that will always be the same value

❑ **Functions**: Uses functions to set a default value based on a situation

Literal Defaults

A literal is a simple single value in the same datatype that requires no translation by SQL Server. For example, the following table has sample defaults for a few datatypes:

Datatype	Possible Default Value
int	1
varchar(10)	'Value'
binary(2)	0x0000
datetime	'12/31/2000'

So in your database, let's say you want to default all albums to "the Beatles." Unless the user specifies otherwise, you might do a select from the artist table to see what the `artistId` of the Beatles entry is, as follows:

```
SELECT * FROM artist
```

artistId	name
1	the beatles
2	the who

So you specify the following default value:

```
ALTER TABLE album
    ADD CONSTRAINT dfltAlbum$artistId$integer$one
    DEFAULT (1)
    FOR artistId
```

A word of warning about literal defaults. It's better not to supply a literal default value to a column that is part of a unique index. This is because any column that has a default value set is less likely to contain unique values. Also, in any index, having large numbers of repeating values is never good for performance.

Functions

An alternative to hard coding a default value is to use a function to return the default value. A very common example is a physical-only column that tells you when the row was created. For example, let's define a simple table:

```
CREATE TABLE insertDate
(
    insertDateId  int identity,
    value         varchar(10) not null,
    createDate    datetime DEFAULT (getdate())
)
```

When you insert the following row and look at it

```
INSERT INTO insertDate (value)
VALUES ('test')

SELECT *
FROM insertDate
```

you get the following output (of course the time will change for you!):

insertDateId	value	createDate
1	test	2003-09-05 18:13:27.240

In the next chapter you'll look at how you might build a method of tracking when a row is updated, rather than when it is created.

As a slightly more complex example, let's consider your earlier literal example when you wanted to set the default artist to "the Beatles." To do this you add a column to the artist table, `defaultFl` with a default of 0. You do this because you only want to have a single value that was 1, plus you want to force the user to *choose* the default row.

```
ALTER TABLE artist
    ADD defaultFl bit NOT NULL
        CONSTRAINT dfltArtist$defaultFl$boolean$false
        DEFAULT (0)
```

You now set "the Beatles" row to 1:

```
UPDATE artist
SET defaultFl = 1
WHERE name = 'the beatles'
```

The table now includes a column where the user can choose which value is required as the default. So what do you do next? You want to have your album table default to whatever value is the default in the artist table. So, you build a user-defined function that returns the primary key value for the artist that is default (if the function doesn't make sense, please refer to Appendix C for a full explanation of how user-defined functions work; refer to the Apress web site).

```
CREATE FUNCTION artist$returnDefaultId
(
)
RETURNS int
WITH SCHEMABINDING
AS
BEGIN
    DECLARE @artistId int

    SELECT @artistId = artistId
    FROM dbo.artist
```

```
        WHERE defaultFl = 1

        RETURN @artistId
END
GO
```

Now if you execute the following statement:

```
SELECT dbo.artist$returnDefaultId( ) AS defaultValue
```

you'll get this:

defaultValue
_____

1

Because that is the primary key value for the row that you set to default. Note that this value may vary in your example if you don't do *exactly* what is done in the sample code, but it will not change a thing if your default value is 1 or 100. So for your solution, you can code this as follows:

```
ALTER TABLE album
    ADD CONSTRAINT dfltAlbum$artistId$function$useDefault
    DEFAULT dbo.artist$returnDefaultId( )
    FOR artistId
```

Now you have the exact functionality that you wanted, and in doing so you've created a function that any other process may employ. To test it out, execute the following INSERT statement, leaving out the artistId:

```
INSERT INTO album(name)
VALUES ('rubber soul')

SELECT album.name AS albumName, artist.name AS artistName
FROM album
    JOIN artist
    ON album.artistId = artist.artistId
WHERE album.name = 'rubber soul'
```

You'll see that it contains the row that you created:

albumName	artistName
rubber soul	the beatles

Default constraints in SQL Server 2000 are a tremendously powerful resource with which to supply initial values to columns. Because you can set default values in one table from within another, there are few limits to their uses.

Check Constraints

Check constraints are used to disallow improper data from being entered into a single column in a table. Check constraints are executed after default constraints (so you cannot specify a default to supply an improper value) and INSTEAD OF triggers (which you'll cover in detail in the next chapter). They cannot affect the values that you're trying to put in the table, but are used to verify the validity of the supplied values. There are two separate types of check constraint: column and table. Column constraints reference a single column, and are only used when the individual column is referenced in the modification. Table constraints are used regardless of which columns are referenced.

Fortunately, you don't have to worry about declaring a constraint as either a column constraint or table constraint. When SQL Server compiles the constraint, it verifies whether it needs to check more than one column and applies the appropriate constraint accordingly. In each of your examples of constraints, you'll learn whether it's a column or table constraint.

The basic syntax of the ALTER TABLE statement that concerns check constraints is as follows:

```
ALTER TABLE <tableName> [WITH CHECK | WITH NOCHECK]
    ADD [CONSTRAINT <constraintName>]
    CHECK <searchConditions>
```

Some of the syntax will not be familiar, so here is an explanation of the new parts. When you create a check constraint, the WITH CHECK setting (as the default setting) gives you the opportunity to decide whether or not to check the existing data in the table. WITH NOCHECK allows existing data to be invalid, but will not allow future values to violate the constraint requirements. Sometimes the WITH NOCHECK setting may be necessary, if you're adding a constraint to an existing table in which it's unrealistic to check all existing data, but you still want to check all subsequent data entries. It's always good practice to avoid using NOCHECK unless absolutely necessary.

While it's obvious what <columnName> is referring to, why is it optional? It's simply a means to incorporate the column that you're trying to protect in the constraint's name. However, when you're dealing with a constraint that works with multiple columns, you shouldn't include a column name in the name. If you declare a column name, it will only be checked when that particular column is modified.

The <searchConditions> value is analogous to the WHERE clause of a typical SELECT statement, with no subqueries allowed. It may access system and UDFs, and use the name or names of columns in the table. However, it cannot access any other table, nor can it access any row other than the current row. If multiple rows are modified, the constraint deals with each row individually. The result of the searchConditions part must be a logical expression with only two possible values, TRUE or FALSE.

A common check constraint that you'll add to almost every string (varchar, char, and so on) serves to prevent blank data from being entered. For example, in your album table, you have a name column. This column doesn't allow NULLs, so the user has to enter something, but what about a single space character?

```
INSERT INTO album ( name, artistId )
VALUES ( '', 1 )
```

If you allowed this in your database, you would certainly end up with a blank row because there would likely be one occasion for which a user would enter a row prematurely after having failed to input his name. The second time a space is entered instead of the name, an error would be returned:

Server: Msg 2627, Level 14, State 2, Line 1
Violation of UNIQUE KEY constraint 'XAKalbum_name'. Cannot insert duplicate key in object 'album'.
The statement has been terminated.

Alternatively, you may have a nonunique constraint-bound column, like a description or notes column, where you might have many blank entries. So you might add the following constraint to prevent this from ever happening again:

```
ALTER TABLE album WITH CHECK
    ADD CONSTRAINT chkAlbum$name$string$noEmptyString
    --trim the value in name, adding in stars to handle
    --values safer than just checking length of the rtrim which
    --will be NULL if name is NULL, and a single char if not.  The coalesce
    --makes certain
    CHECK (( '*' + COALESCE(rtrim(name),'') + '*') <> '**' )
```

The final CHECK function here utilizes the COALESCE operation to ensure that if there are no characters other than space then a zero-length string is returned, and if a NULL is entered then it's returned. Of course, you know that you already entered a value that will clash with your constraint, so you get the following error message:

Server: Msg 547, Level 16, State 1, Line 1
ALTER TABLE statement conflicted with COLUMN CHECK constraint 'chkAlbum$name$string$noEmptyString'. The conflict occurred in database 'master', table 'album', column 'name'.

If you specify the constraint using WITH NOCHECK:

```
ALTER TABLE album WITH NOCHECK
    ADD CONSTRAINT chkAlbum$name$string$noEmptyString
    --trim the value in name, adding in stars to handle
    --values safer than just checking length of the rtrim
    CHECK (('*' + COALESCE(rtrim(name),'') + '*') <> '**' )
```

The statement will be added to the table definition, though the NOCHECK means that the bad value is retained in the table. However, any time a modification statement references the column, the check constraint will be fired. The next time you try to set the value of the table to the same bad value, an error will occur.

```
UPDATE album
SET name = name
WHERE name = ''
```

323

This gives you the following error message:

```
Server: Msg 547, Level 16, State 1, Line 1
UPDATE statement conflicted with COLUMN CHECK constraint
'chkAlbum$name$string$noEmptyString'. The conflict occurred in database 'master', table 'album',
column 'name'.
The statement has been terminated.
```

In the next example, you'll look at ways of coding UDFs in order to perform both simple and complex checks. In the case of the function that checks for empty strings you can build your own UDF as follows:

```
CREATE FUNCTION string$checkForEmptyString
(
    @stringValue varchar(8000)
)
RETURNS bit
AS
BEGIN
    DECLARE @logicalValue bit
    IF ( '*' + COALESCE(RTRIM(@stringValue),'') + '*') = '**'
        SET @logicalValue = 1
    ELSE
        SET @logicalValue = 0

    RETURN @logicalValue
END
```

and then build constraints such as the following:

```
ALTER TABLE album WITH NOCHECK
    ADD CONSTRAINT chkAlbum$name$string$noEmptyString
    --trim the value in name, adding in stars to handle
    --values safer than just checking length of the rtrim
    CHECK (dbo.string$checkForEmptyString(name) = 0)
```

Now if the method for determining if a value is empty ever changes, it will be encapsulated within a function, and will only change in a single place.

Most check constraints will consist of the simple task of checking the format of a single column, but the check need not be so simple. The user-defined function can be complex, and may touch tables in the server. In the next two examples, you'll employ UDFs to provide generic range-checking functionality and powerful rule checking, which can implement complex rules that would prove difficult to code using just straight SQL.

In the first example, let's add a catalog number column to the album table, and stipulate that the catalog numbers are alphanumeric values with the following format:

```
<number><number><number>-
<number><number><alphaOrNumber><alphaOrNumber><alphaOrNumber>-<number><number>
```

An example of such a catalog number might be '433-43ASD-33', with all characters in the string being required.

So you define a UDF called `album$catalogNumberValidate,` which will encapsulate the validation of `catalogNumbers`. This function will have two purposes, namely validating the column in a check constraint, and validating any bulk row inserting and data cleaning. Your function will return a bit value of 1, 0, or NULL for a NULL value that you can use to deal with the checking of the data.

The first step is to add your new column to the database.

```
ALTER TABLE album
    ADD catalogNumber char(12) NOT NULL
    --temporary default so you can make the column
    --not NULL in initial creation
    CONSTRAINT tempDefaultAlbumCatalogNumber DEFAULT ('111-11111-11')

 --drop it because this is not a proper default
ALTER TABLE album
    DROP tempDefaultAlbumCatalogNumber
```

Then you create your function that is used to check the values of the `album.catalogNumber` column, as follows:

```
CREATE FUNCTION album$catalogNumberValidate
(
    @catalogNumber char(12)
)
RETURNS bit
AS
BEGIN
    DECLARE @logicalValue bit
    --check to see if the value like the mask you have set up
    IF @catalogNumber LIKE
            '[0-9][0-9][0-9]-[0-9][0-9][0-9a-z][0-9a-z][0-9a-z]-[0-9][0-9]'
        SET @logicalValue = 1 —yes it is
    ELSE
        SET @logicalValue = 0 —no it is not
    --note that we cannot just simply say RETURN 1, or RETURN 0 as the
    --function must have only one exit point
    RETURN @logicalValue
END
```

You'll check to see if the constraint works, as follows:

```
IF dbo.album$catalogNumberValidate('433-11qww-33') = 1
    SELECT 'Yes' AS result
ELSE
    SELECT 'No' AS result
```

which returns the following:

```
result
------
Yes
```

All that is left is to build a function based check constraint, as follows:

```
ALTER TABLE album
    ADD CONSTRAINT
    chkAlbum$catalogNumber$function$artist$catalogNumberValidate
    --keep it simple here, encapsulating all you need to in the
    --function
    CHECK (dbo.album$catalogNumbervalidate(catalogNumber) = 1)
```

By testing the new constraint, you see that the following incorrect catalog number makes the system generate an error as follows:

```
UPDATE album
SET catalogNumber = '1'
WHERE name = 'the white album'
```

It returns the following:

Server: Msg 547, Level 16, State 1, Line 1
UPDATE statement conflicted with COLUMN CHECK constraint
'chkAlbum$catalogNumber$function$artist$catalogNumberValidate'. The conflict occurred in
database 'master', table 'album', column 'catalogNumber'.
The statement has been terminated.

Executing it with proper values will work just fine, as shown here:

```
UPDATE album
SET catalogNumber = '433-43ASD-33'
WHERE name = 'the white album'
```

As a second example, let's add a column to the `artist` table that will hold the LIKE mask. Note that it needs to be considerably larger than the actual column, because some of the possible masks use multiple characters to indicate a single character. You should also note that it's a `varchar`, because using `char` variables as LIKE masks can be problematic due to the padding spaces.

```
ALTER TABLE artist
    ADD catalogNumberMask varchar(100) NOT NULL
    -- it's acceptable to have a mask of percent in this case
    CONSTRAINT dfltArtist$catalogNumberMask$string$percent
    DEFAULT (' per cent')
```

Then you build the function, and it will access this column to check that your value matches the mask, as shown:

```
ALTER FUNCTION album$catalogNumberValidate
(
    @catalogNumber char(12),
    @artistId int —now based on the artist id
)
RETURNS bit
AS
BEGIN
    DECLARE @logicalValue bit, @catalogNumberMask varchar(100)

    SELECT @catalogNumberMask = catalogNumberMask
    FROM artist
    WHERE artistId = @artistId

    IF @catalogNumber LIKE @catalogNumberMask
        SET @logicalValue = 1
    ELSE
        SET @logicalValue = 0

    RETURN @logicalValue
END
GO
```

Now you give the artist columns the correct masks, as follows:

```
UPDATE artist
SET catalogNumberMask =
            '[0-9][0-9][0-9]-[0-9][0-9][0-9a-z][0-9a-z][0-9a-z]-[0-9][0-9]'
WHERE artistId = 1 --the beatles

UPDATE artist
SET catalogNumberMask =
            '[a-z][a-z][0-9][0-9][0-9][0-9][0-9][0-9][0-9][0-9][0-9]'
WHERE artistId = 2 --the who
```

and you test that the function works like this:

```
IF dbo.album$catalogNumberValidate('433-43ASD-33',1) = 1
    SELECT 'Yes' AS result
ELSE
    SELECT 'No' AS result

IF dbo.album$catalogNumberValidate('aa1111111111',2) = 1
    SELECT 'Yes' AS result
ELSE
    SELECT 'No' AS result
GO
```

Now you can add the constraint to the table, as shown here:

```
ALTER TABLE album
    ADD CONSTRAINT
    chkAlbum$catalogNumber$function$artist$catalogNumberValidate
    CHECK (dbo.album$catalogNumbervalidate(catalogNumber,artistId) = 1)
```

327

However, your data doesn't match, as shown here:

Server: Msg 547, Level 16, State 1, Line 1
ALTER TABLE statement conflicted with TABLE CHECK constraint
'chkAlbum$catalogNumber$function$artist$catalogNumberValidate'. The conflict occurred in
database 'master', table 'album'.

You could use the NOCHECK option because this will mean that any existing data will be improper
when you save the constraint, although any new data will automatically be validated. There is an issue
in this example however, in that the constraint will not prevent the user changing the mask. If this is a
problem, you might need to implement a time-based table, where you can state that the catalog
number mask will take a certain value for a publishing date in the period '1/1/1970'–'12/31/1995' and
a different value for the period '1/1/1996' until the present.

This query will find the problems in the table:

```
--to find where your data is not ready for the constraint,
--you run the following query
SELECT dbo.album$catalogNumbervalidate(catalogNumber,artistId)
    AS validCatalogNumber,
    artistId, name, catalogNumber
FROM album
WHERE dbo.album$catalogNumbervalidate(catalogNumber,artistId) <> 1
```

This gives you a list of rows with invalid data. Using similar code to your previous examples, you can
correct the error and then add the constraint. When you attempt to add an incorrect value, as follows:

```
UPDATE album
SET catalogNumber = '1'
WHERE name = 'the white album'
```

it results in the following error:

Server: Msg 547, Level 16, State 1, Line 1
UPDATE statement conflicted with COLUMN CHECK constraint
'chkAlbum$catalogNumber$function$artist$catalogNumberValidate'. The conflict occurred in
database 'master', table 'album', column 'catalogNumber'.
The statement has been terminated.

Now you'll try a correct one, as shown here:

```
UPDATE album
SET catalogNumber = '433-43ASD-33'
WHERE name = 'the white album' --the artist is the beatles
```

Using these approaches, you can build any single row validation code for your tables.

However, there is a drawback to this coding method. As described previously, each UDF will fire once for each row and each column that was modified in the update, and making checks over and over again may lead to a degradation in performance. The alternative method–it will be presented later on–would be to use a trigger to validate all table predicates in a single query.

Despite the drawback, this way of solving row validation issues is very clean, easy to understand and easy to maintain. However, if your check constraints are complex and require access to many tables, performance may be affected and using a trigger is more appropriate. If the validation needs to be done one row at a time, then it's certainly better to use a check constraint vs. using a cursor in a trigger.

Handling Errors Caused by Constraints

Handling errors is one of the most important parts of writing any data-modifying statement in SQL Server. Whenever a statement fails a constraint requirement, you've seen that an error message is generated. SQL Server provides you with very rudimentary error-handling tools to determine what happened in a previous statement, and you'll consider them here. Throughout this chapter, you've been executing statements to prove that constraints execute. When the constraints fail, you get error messages like this:

```
Server: Msg 547, Level 16, State 1, Line 1
UPDATE statement conflicted with COLUMN CHECK constraint
'chkAlbum$catalogNumber$function$artist$catalogNumberValidate'. The conflict occurred in
database 'master', table 'album', column 'catalogNumber'.
The statement has been terminated.
```

This is the error message that the Query Analyzer tool sees as well as the error message that user applications will see. The error message is made up of a few basic parts:

❑   **Error number**, Msg 547: The error number that's passed back to the calling program. In some cases this error number is significant; however in most cases it's simply enough to say that the error number is nonzero.

❑   **Level**, Level 16: A severity level for the message. 0–18 are generally considered to be user messages, with 16 being the default. Levels 19–25 are really severe errors that cause the connection to be severed (with a message written to the log) and typically involve data corruption issues.

❑   **State**, State 1: A value from 1–127 that represents the state of the process when the error was raised.

❑   **Line**, Line 1: The line in the batch or object where the error is occurring. Very useful for debugging purposes.

❑   **Error text:** A text explanation of the error that has occurred.

However, in your SQL Statements you only have access to the error number. You do this simply using the @@error global variable.

```
SET @<errorVariableName> = @@error
```

This will capture the value of the error number of any message that has occurred as a response to the previous statement. This value will have one of the following values:

0	No error.
1–49999	System errors, either from constraints, or from real system errors that aren't under your control. Examples of such system errors include syntax errors, disk corruptions, invalid SQL operation, and so on.
50000	Ad hoc error messages with no number specified, or any general message that no user process will need to differentiate from any other message.
50001 and higher	User-defined. If the client system can make use of the error number, then it isn't a bad idea to develop a corporate or personal standard for error numbers. You'll look at error-handling schemes in Chapter 12.

The maximum error number is the maximum value for the bigint datatype.

When you execute an INSERT, UPDATE, or DELETE statement anywhere in your script, trigger, or stored procedure code, you must always check the error status of the command. Note that this value is changed for every command in your database, so any statement following *every* modification statement should get the value stored in @@error. (Also, you could get the value of @@rowcount after a SET statement because this statement doesn't affect the @@rowcount value.)

What you do with the error value depends on the situation you face. It's generally better to execute every statement that modifies data inside its own transaction, unless you're executing a single statement. In the following example code, you'll try to update an album with an invalid catalog number. This will raise an error that you'll handle by issuing a RAISERROR which will inform the user what is happening. Each time you execute the UPDATE command again, you'll check whether @@error variable is zero, and if not you'll make sure that the command isn't executed:

```
BEGIN TRANSACTION

    DECLARE @errorHold int

    UPDATE album
    SET catalogNumber = '1'
    WHERE name = 'the white album'

    SET @errorHold = @@error --store the value because the value of @@error will
                             --no longer be valid after another statement is run
    IF @errorHold <> 0
    BEGIN
```

```
            RAISERROR 50000 'Error modifying the first catalogNumber for album'
            ROLLBACK TRANSACTION
      END

      IF @errorHold = 0 --you could have coded as an ELSE but in real code you might
                        --not have immediately went into the next statement.
      BEGIN
          UPDATE album
          SET catalogNumber = '1'
          WHERE name = 'the white album'

          SET @errorHold = @@error
          IF @errorHold <> 0
          BEGIN
              RAISERROR 50000 'Error modifying the second catalogNumber'
              ROLLBACK TRANSACTION
          END
      END

   IF @errorHold = 0
      COMMIT TRANSACTION
   ELSE
      RAISERROR 50000 'Update batch did not succeed'
```

By executing that batch you get back the following three errors:

Server: Msg 547, Level 16, State 1, Line 1
UPDATE statement conflicted with TABLE CHECK constraint
'chkAlbum$catalogNumber$function$artist$catalogNumberValidate'. The conflict occurred in
database 'master', table 'album'.
The statement has been terminated.

Server: Msg 50000, Level 16, State 1, Line 12
Error modifying the first catalogNumber for album

Server: Msg 50000, Level 16, State 1, Line 33
Update batch did not succeed

Note that we included several RAISERROR statements after the error was discovered. By coding the extra error messages, you can build error-reporting chains that tell you precisely where an error occurs in a batch, allowing for easy debugging.

Case Study

In your case study, you'll take the basic implementation that you produced in the previous chapter, implement the business rules that have been previously identified during the logical design phase, and add whatever data protection measures are necessary to meet the business rules. You'll follow the same path that you did during the chapter, building your constraints first, followed by triggers, then any optional rules that you've identified. You've already assigned datatypes, and built NULL and foreign key constraints when you created your tables.

Default Constraints

You need to add several sets of default constraints to your columns.

zipCode and city

Note that you've built a `zipCode` to `city` reference table. It might seem a good idea to allow the user to simply choose the zip code or city and apply a default for the other one. However, it's impossible to do such a default because you have to enter the `city` and `zipCode` at the same time, and defaults cannot access any other columns during the insert or update. You'll use this table as a basis for a trigger validation later in the case study.

Bit Columns in transactionType

In the `transactionType` table, you have three columns in which you can supply default constraints. You'll set them to the most lenient settings, as follows:

❑   `requiresSignatureFl`: Set to 0 to state that a signature isn't required

❑   `requiresPayeeFl`: Set to 0 to state that a payee isn't required

❑   `allowPayeeFl`: Set to 1 to state that they can put it in a payee

which you'll script as follows:

```
ALTER TABLE transactionType
ADD CONSTRAINT dfltTransactionType$requiresSignatureFl$bit$false
DEFAULT 0 FOR requiresSignatureFl

ALTER TABLE transactionType
ADD CONSTRAINT dfltTransactionType$requiresPayeeFl$bit$false
DEFAULT 0 FOR requiresPayeeFl

ALTER TABLE transactionType
ADD CONSTRAINT dfltTransactionType$allowPayeeFl$bit$true
DEFAULT 1 FOR allowPayeeFl
```

Phone Number Columns

Another use for defaults is to set columns that users typically leave blank. Two fairly good examples are the country code and area code for a phone number. You would set the country code to '1', because this is the default for all United States phone numbers, and, say, '615' for the area code, or whatever the code is for the area where the users of the system are located.

```
ALTER TABLE phoneNumber
ADD CONSTRAINT dfltPhoneNumber$countryCode$string$charNumberOne
DEFAULT '1' FOR countryCode

ALTER TABLE phoneNumber
ADD CONSTRAINT dfltPhoneNumber$areaCode$string$localAreaCode
DEFAULT '615' FOR areaCode
```

Check Constraints

In almost any database you design, you'll require far more check constraints than triggers or optional rules. Your database will be no different. As examples, you'll be adding four different sets of check constraints in order to disallow empty strings, prevent future financial transactions, force specification of the range of a financial transaction, and ensure that addresses may only have certain columns filled in a given condition. Of course, you'll be building UDFs to support many of these constraints as needed.

Disallowing Empty Strings

In many string columns, you'll want to prevent your users from entering an empty string. As discussed earlier in this chapter, you can prevent the entry of empty strings using the following code:

```
CHECK (( '*' + COALESCE(RTRIM(<column>),'') + '*') <> '**' )
```

but in practice, you'll want to encapsulate such algorithms into a function wherever possible. In this case, you'll build the following function:

```
CREATE FUNCTION string$checkEntered
(
    @value varchar(8000)     --longest varchar value
)
RETURNS bit
AS
--used to check to see if a varchar value passed in is empty
--note: additional function required for unicode if desired
BEGIN
    DECLARE @returnVal bit --just returns yes or no

    --do an RTRIM, COALESCED to a '' if it's NULL, surround by *, and compare

    IF ( '*' + COALESCE(RTRIM(@value),'') + '*') <> '**'
        SET @returnVal = 1 --not empty
    ELSE
        SET @returnVal = 0 --empty

    RETURN @returnVal
END
GO
```

Now you must test the code. When problems arise, it's always nice to be able to check the code quickly, so you test your constraint code by forcing it to fail and succeed as illustrated here:

```
-- empty condition
IF dbo.string$checkEntered('') = 0
   SELECT 'Empty'
ELSE
   SELECT 'Not Empty'

-- not empty condition
IF dbo.string$checkEntered('Any text will do') = 0
   SELECT 'Empty'
ELSE
   SELECT 'Not Empty'
```

As expected, the first code returns Empty and the second, Not Empty.

Next you'll want to create your check constraints. You could look at every column in the database you've designed and identify columns, but a better place to start is your domain list. In the following table you have all of the varchar and char domains you previously identified, and you determine which of them need to be validated with a check constraint.

Again keep in mind that your examples don't consider non-US address or phone numbers for the simplicity of the example.

Name	Datatype	Nullability	Check Nonempty
addressDescriptiveLine	varchar(2000)	NOT NULL	Yes
addressStateCode	char(2)	NOT NULL	Yes
alphaNumericNumber	varchar(20)	NOT NULL	Yes
areaCode	varchar(3)	NOT NULL	Yes
countryCode	char(1)	NOT NULL	Yes
description	varchar(100)	NOT NULL	Yes
exchange	char(5)	NOT NULL	Yes
extension	varchar(20)	NULL	No, in this case if it's known that there is no extension, a blank would indicate that; if unknown, NULL fits.
firstName	varchar(60)	NOT NULL	Yes
lastName	varchar(60)	NOT NULL	Yes
middleName	varchar(60)	NOT NULL	No, if the user didn't give a middle name, a blank would signify.
name	varchar(60)	NOT NULL	Yes
phoneNumberPart	char(4)	NOT NULL	Yes

Name	Datatype	Nullability	Check Nonempty
string	varchar(20)	NOT NULL	No because this is the generic case, and these cases would need to be evaluated on a case-by-case basis.
username	sysname (A SQL Server user-defined datatype that they use to store usernames. You'll store SQL Server names here to map to real names because any user who has rights to create a check row should be given rights to look at that transaction and accounts, based on the security we will define.)	NOT NULL	Yes
zipCode	char(5) (Note that you've used the zipCode to link back to the city. This is done with the five character zipCode. You've ignored the +4 zip code again for simplicity.)	NOT NULL	Yes

To illustrate the way in which you format your constraints let's consider the example of the bank table. To build a constraint for its name column, you use the following:

```
ALTER TABLE bank
ADD CONSTRAINT chkBank$name$string$notEmpty
CHECK (dbo.string$checkForEmptyString (name) = 1)
```

The same would be true for the account table's number column:

```
ALTER TABLE account
ADD CONSTRAINT chkAccount$number$string$notEmpty
CHECK (dbo.string$checkForEmptyString (number) = 1)
```

Preventing Post-Dated Financial Transactions

Your specifications state that you shall prevent transactions that appear to occur in the future from being entered, so you'll apply a constraint to prevent exactly this. In order to determine whether a transaction has yet occurred, you need to carry out some preliminary operations on your date-time data. For instance, you won't store the time in your transactions, so you need to strip the time element from your date-time variables in your check constraint. You'll implement time-stripping in your column in the trigger section in the next chapter, but you'll simply trust here that it has taken place.

335

The ability to check whether a date is in the future or the past is quite a useful facility, and you can build a UDF to do this for you, as follows:

```
CREATE FUNCTION date$rangeCheck
(
    @dateValue datetime,              -- first date value
    @dateToCompareAgainst datetime    -- pass in date to compare to
)
RETURNS int
AS
BEGIN
    DECLARE @returnVal int
    IF @dateValue > @dateToCompareAgainst
    BEGIN
        SET @returnVal = 1                 -- date is in the future
    END
    ELSE IF @dateValue < @dateToCompareAgainst
    BEGIN
        SET @returnVal = -1                -- date in is the past
    END

    ELSE
        SET @returnVal = 0                 -- dates are the same
    RETURN @returnVal
END
GO
```

Again you need to check out your function to make sure that it works, as shown:

```
--empty condition
SELECT dbo.date$rangeCheck('1/1/1989',getdate()) as [should be -1]
SELECT dbo.date$rangeCheck(getdate(),getdate()) as [should be 0]
SELECT dbo.date$rangeCheck('1/1/2020',getdate()) as [should be 1]
```

You then create a function to strip off the time part of the date-time value, as follows:

```
CREATE FUNCTION date$removeTime
(
    @date datetime
)
RETURNS datetime AS
BEGIN
    SET @date = CAST(datePart(month,@date) as varchar(2)) + '/' +
                CAST(datePart(day,@date) as varchar(2)) + '/' +
                CAST(datePart(year,@date) as varchar(4))
    RETURN @date
END
GO
```

This function could be coded using the CONVERT *function with a format of 110. Either way will work just fine.*

Now you can go to your transaction table and build a constraint against the date column as follows:

```
ALTER TABLE [transaction]
ADD CONSTRAINT chkTransaction$date$date$notFuture
--0 is equal, -1 means in the past, 1 means in the future
CHECK (dbo.date$rangeCheck(date,dbo.date$removeTime(getdate())) > 0)
```

Specifying the Range of a Financial Transaction

Now you can go back to your `transaction` and `transactionType` tables, as shown in the following figure.

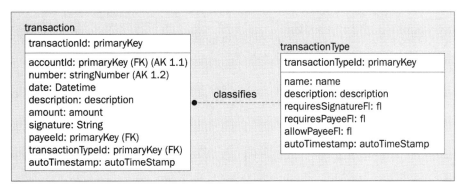

You need to ensure that all deposits are positive values, and that all checks and electronic withdrawals are negative values. Instead of building a check constraint based on the value of a foreign key, you could add a new column to the `transactionType` table called `positiveAmountFl`, but this isn't flexible enough for your needs. Some items may allow negative values, zero or only positive numbers. You might also decide that a particular type of transaction has a maximum value imposed on it, such as an automatic "cash machine" withdrawal of 500 dollars. So a straightforward way to implement this would be to allow the user to create a range by adding the `minimumAmount` and `maximumAmount` attributes to your `transactionType` table, as shown here:

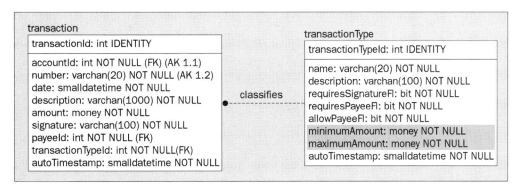

Here you add a simple constraint to ensure that the minimumAmount isn't greater than the maximumAmount value you've entered:

```
ALTER TABLE transactionType
ADD minimumAmount money NULL
--Here you need to load values for the column
ALTER COLUMN minimumAmount money NOT NULL

ALTER TABLE transactionType
ADD maximumAmount money NULL
--Here you need to load values data for the column
ALTER COLUMN maximumAmount money NOT NULL

--simple check constraint to make certain that min is less than max
ALTER TABLE transactionType
ADD CONSTRAINT chkTransactionType$minAndMaxRangeCheck
CHECK (minimumAmount <= maximumAmount)
```

Now you can create a UDF that will confirm that a value for a transaction of a given transactionType is within the range defined by the minimumAmount and maximumAmount columns, as follows:

```
CREATE FUNCTION transactionType$validateAmountInRange
(
    @transactionTypeId int,
    @amount money
)
RETURNS bit
AS
BEGIN
    --1 means within range, 0 out of range
    DECLARE @returnValue bit
    IF EXISTS ( select *
        FROM transactionType
        WHERE @amount NOT BETWEEN minimumAmount AND maximumAmount
            AND transactionTypeId = @transactionTypeId)
        BEGIN           SET @returnValue = 0
        END
    ELSE
        SET @returnValue = 1
        RETURN @returnValue
END
```

Finally, you alter the transaction table and add a check constraint to validate the data as it's being entered into the table, as shown here:

```
ALTER TABLE [transaction]
ADD CONSTRAINT chkTransaction$amountProperForTransactionType
CHECK
    (dbo.transactionType$validateAmountInRange(transactionTypeId, amount) = 1 )
```

Note that the signature required constraint; payee required or payee allowed constraints based on the flags in the transactionType table would be built in much the same manner, so you won't include them here.

Best Practices

❏   Use the five different kinds of constraints as much as possible:

    ❏   **NULL**: Set during column declaration. Defines if column can store the NULL or unknown value.

    ❏   **Primary keys** and **unique constraints**: Used to make certain that no two rows will be alike, a very important goal for every table.

    ❏   **Foreign keys**: Used to make sure that any migrated keys have only valid values that match the keys that they reference.

    ❏   **Default**: Default constraints are used to set an acceptable default value for a column. Define defaults in every case where they make sense. Try to use these default values in applications whenever possible so that users know what they will be defaulted to.

    ❏   **Check**: Constraints that are used to limit the values that can be entered into a single column or an entire table.

❏   **Make use of user-defined functions**: Use them in constraints when you need complex check and default constraints.

❏   **Develop an error-handing strategy**: Constraints return horrible error messages, so it's very important to map the messages to what is actually happening.

Summary

You've made a solid start on the task of developing the data protection layer for your databases. In this chapter you used the declarative mechanisms in SQL Server to safeguard your data using defaults and constraints.

You've covered DEFAULT constraints, which are used to set values for columns when the user doesn't enter a value herself. While it might not seem like defaults can be considered data protection resources, they can be used to automatically set columns where the purpose of the column might not be apparent to the user (and the database adds a suitable value for the column).

Next you learned about CHECK constraints, which you'll use to protect a single row of a table from invalid data. They can be table-level or column-level constraints. The primary difference is that a column constraint is fired when the column is modified, and the table-level constraints fire no matter which columns are modified. You don't have to make this decision; rather SQL Server determines which columns are referenced for you.

Once you've built and implemented a set of appropriate data-safeguarding constraints, you will then move on to deal with more complex business rules that cannot be expressed in constraints or default constraints. You use UDFs for this.

In the next chapter, you'll look at more advanced techniques for building data-protection mechanisms with which it isn't possible to use declarative constraints.

12

Programmatic Data Protection

In this chapter, you'll examine the predicates and domains that could not be implemented using simple check or default constraints. To implement these types of checks you have three different mechanisms at your disposal.

❑ **Triggers**: These differ from constraints in that they are pieces of code that you attach to a table (or tables). This code is automatically run whenever the event(s) specified occur in the table(s). They are extremely flexible and can access multiple columns, multiple rows, multiple tables, and even multiple databases. As a simple case, let's consider a situation in which you want to ensure that an update of a value is performed on both the tables where it occurs. You can write a trigger that will disallow the update unless it occurs in both tables.

This is the second best place to protect the data. You do have to code every trigger rule in T-SQL, but the user cannot get around this by any error in an external program.

❑ **Stored procedures**: Stored procedures are pieces of precompiled T-SQL stored in the database, dealing with tables in a very flexible manner, so that different business rules can be applied to the same table under different circumstances. A simple example of a stored procedure is one that returns all the data held in a given table. In a more complex scenario, they can be used to grant different permissions to different users regarding manipulation of tables. This isn't all that great a solution to protect the data because you have to code the rules into any procedures that access the data. However, because it's in the central location, you can use this to implement rules that may be different based on various situations.

❑ **Client executable code**: Useful in dealing with situations in which business rules are optional or are flexible in nature. A common example is asking the user "Are you sure you wish to delete this row?" SQL Server is a server product, and if you ask it to delete data, it deletes data. Most server products work in this manner, leaving the client programs the responsibility of implementing flexible business rules and warnings. Bear in mind that applications come and go, but the data must always be protected.

In moving down this list the solutions become less desirable, yet each one has specific benefits that are appropriate in certain situations.

Your test tables are the same tables as the ones you used in the previous chapter, and all of the modifications you had previously made are intact.

Triggers

Triggers are a type of stored procedure attached to a table or view and are executed only when the contents of a table are changed. They can be used to enforce almost any business rule, and are especially important for dealing with situations that are too complex for a check constraint to handle.

Triggers need to be used when one of the following needs to be done:

❑   Perform cross-database referential integrity

❑   Check inter-row rules, where just looking at the current row isn't enough for the constraints

❑   Check inter-table constraints, when rules require access to data in a different table

❑   Introduce desired side effects to your data modification queries

The main advantage that triggers have over constraints is the ability to directly access other tables, and to execute multiple rows at once. In a trigger you can run almost every T-SQL command, except for the following:

ALTER DATABASE	CREATE DATABASE	DROP DATABASE
RESTORE LOG	RECONFIGURE	RESTORE DATABASE

There are two different models of triggers that you'll look at using the following:

❑   **AFTER**: Meaning the trigger fires after the command has affected the table, though not on views. AFTER triggers are used for building enhanced business rule handlers and you would generally put any kind of logging mechanisms into them. You may have an unlimited number of AFTER triggers that fire on INSERT, UPDATE, and DELETE or any combination of them. Even if you have an INSTEAD-OF trigger, you may still have as many AFTER triggers as wanted, because they can all be combined into a single trigger.

❑   **INSTEAD OF**: Meaning that the trigger operates instead of the command (INSERT, UPDATE, or DELETE) affecting the table or view. In this way, you can do whatever you want with the data, either modifying it as sent, or putting it into another place. You can have only a single INSERT, UPDATE, and DELETE trigger of this type per table. You can however combine all three into one and have a single trigger that fires for all three operations.

The following section will describe some common techniques for employing triggers in your data protection code. For a deeper explanation on how to code triggers, see Appendix E.

Using AFTER Triggers to Solve Common Problems

In this section you'll look at how you use triggers to solve typical problems, such as the following:

- ❑ Cascading inserts
- ❑ Range checks
- ❑ Cascading deletes setting the values of child tables to NULLs

It's important to consider that whatever you're doing with AFTER triggers depends on preexisting data in your table passing all constraint requirements. For instance, it wouldn't be proper to insert rows in a child table (thereby causing its entire trigger/constraint chain to fire) when the parent's data hasn't been validated. Equally you wouldn't want to check the status of all the rows in your table until you've completed all of your changes to them; the same could be said for cascading delete operations. The three examples that follow are but a small subset of all the possible uses for triggers; they are just a sample to get things rolling. Each of the snippets we'll present in the next three subsections will fit into a trigger (of any type) which will be of the following basic format:

```
CREATE TRIGGER <triggerName>
ON <tableName>
FOR <action> AS
-------------------------------------------------------------------------------
-- Purpose : Trigger on the <action> that fires for any <action> DML
-------------------------------------------------------------------------------
BEGIN
   DECLARE @rowsAffected int,      --stores the number of rows affected
   @errNumber int,                 --used to hold the error number after DML
   @msg varchar(255),              --used to hold the error message
   @errSeverity varchar(20),
   @triggerName sysname,

   SET @rowsAffected = @@rowcount
   SET @triggerName = object_name(@@procid)       --used for messages

   --no need to continue on if no rows affected
   IF @rowsAffected = 0 return

<insert snippets here >

END
```

You'll generally write your triggers so that when an error occurs, you'll raise an error, and roll back the transaction to halt any further commands. The <insert snippets here> section will be replaced by chunks of code that do some check or some action as outlined in the following sections covering some uses of AFTER triggers.

Cascading Inserts

By cascading inserts, you refer to the following situation: After a row is inserted into a table, one or more other new rows are automatically inserted into other tables. This is especially important when you're creating mandatory one-to-one or one-to-many relationships. For example, say you have the following set of tables:

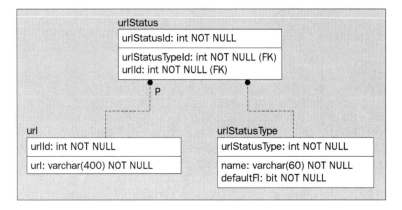

In this case the url table defines a set of URLs for your system, despite the fact that the relationship between url and urlStatus is a one-to-many. You begin by building a trigger that inserts a row into the urlStatus table on an insert that creates a new row with the urlId and the default urlStatusType based on defaultFl having the value of 1. (We'll assume for now that there is a maximum of one row with a defaultFl equal to 1, and will implement a check to make sure this is so.)

```
--add a row to the urlStatus table to tell it that the new row
--should start out as the default status
INSERT INTO urlType (urlId, urlTypeId)
SELECT INSERTED.urlId, urlType.urlTypeId
FROM INSERTED
    CROSS JOIN urlType       --use cross join with a where clause
                             --as this isn't technically a join between
                             --INSERTED and urlType
WHERE urlType.defaultFl = 1

SET @errorNumber = @@error
IF @errorNumber <> 0
BEGIN
    SET @msg = 'Error: ' + CAST(@errorNumber as varchar(10)) +
                            ' occurred during the creation of urlStatus'
    RAISERROR 50000 @msg
    ROLLBACK TRANSACTION
    RETURN
END
```

A trigger might also be needed to disallow the deleting of the default urlType, because you would always want to have a default urlStatus value. However, creation of this trigger will leave a situation where you want to do the following:

❑ Delete a url, but you cannot because of urlTypes that exist

❑ Delete the urlTypes, but you cannot because it's the last one for a url

This is a difficult situation to handle using conventional triggers and constraints, and may well be easier to solve by adding a column to the table informing the triggers (or constraints) that the row is available for deletion. This is a general problem in the case of tables in which you want to implement a two-way relationship, but also want to enforce a one-way relationship under certain circumstances.

Range Checks

A range check means simply ensuring that a given range of data conforms to the data validation rules. Some examples are as follows:

❑ Balancing accounts to make sure that there isn't a negative balance left by the transaction

❑ Ensuring that a proper number of rows exist for a relationship (cardinality), such as a "one-to-between-five-and-seven" relationship

❑ Making sure that in a table (or group of rows in the table) there exists only a single row that is the primary or default row

For our example, we make sure that there is no more than a single default flag set to true or 1 in the table; the others must be 0 or false. You'll also throw in, for good measure, code that will take any new value where the defaultFl column is 1 and set all of the others to 0. If the user manually sets more than one defaultFl column to 1, then a check is made afterwards to cause the operation to fail.

We'll use as our example table the urlStatusType table you built earlier, as shown here:

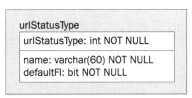

and you'll implement out range checking criteria as follows:

```
--if the defaultFl column was modified
IF UPDATE(defaultFl)
BEGIN
    --update any other rows in the status type table to not default if
    --a row was inserted that was set to default
    UPDATE urlStatusType
    SET defaultFl = 0
    FROM urlStatusType
            --only rows that were already default
    WHERE urlStatusType.defaultFl = 1
            --and not in the inserted rows
      AND urlStatusTypeId NOT IN
      ( SELECT urlStatusTypeId
      FROM inserted
      WHERE defaultFl = 1
      )

    SET @errorNumber = @@error
    IF @errorNumber <> 0
    BEGIN
        SET @msg = 'Error: ' + CAST(@errorNumber as varchar(10)) +
                    ' occurred during the modification of defaultFl'
        RAISERROR 50000 @msg
        ROLLBACK TRANSACTION
        RETURN
    END

    --see if there is more than 1 row set to default
    --like if the user updated more than one in a single operation
    IF ( SELECT count(*)
          FROM urlStatusType
          WHERE urlStatusType.defaultFl = 1 ) > 1
    BEGIN
        SET @msg = 'Too many rows with default flag = 1'
        RAISERROR 50000 @msg
        ROLLBACK TRANSACTION
        RETURN
    END
END
```

Cascading Deletes Setting the Values of Child Tables to NULL

When you have tables with optional alternate keys, instead of cascading on a parent delete, you may sometimes wish to remove the link and set any foreign key references to NULL. To do this in a DELETE trigger, you simply update every row in the child table that refers to the value in the row(s) you're deleting. Take the following relationship for example:

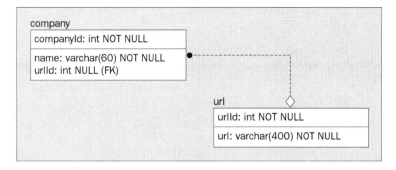

The url table contains all of the Internet addresses for your system, and the company uses one of the values for a company URL. If you want to delete one or more of the url table's rows, you don't want to delete all the companies that use the URL. So you might implement this by setting the child rows to NULL instead of deleting the rows themselves. Because SQL Server only implements a cascading delete where the child row is deleted, you'll have to use a trigger. The trigger code that does this is as follows:

```
UPDATE company
SET urlId = NULL
FROM DELETED
    JOIN company
    ON DELETED.urlId = company.urlId

SET @errorNumber = @@error
IF @errorNumber <> 0
BEGIN
    SET @msg = 'Error: ' + CAST(@errorNumber as varchar(10)) +
                        ' occurred during delete cascade set NULL'
    RAISERROR 50000 @msg
    ROLLBACK TRANSACTION
    RETURN
END
```

Uses of INSTEAD OF Triggers

INSTEAD OF triggers can be used to automatically set or modify values in your statements. INSTEAD OF triggers fire prior to both constraints and AFTER triggers, so you should know that they can be used to modify data en route to the table. You'll consider three examples of how they can be used.

Automatically Maintaining Columns

As an example, you're going to build two triggers, an INSTEAD OF INSERT trigger and an INSTEAD OF UPDATE trigger, which will automatically set the first letter of the names of your artists to uppercase, instead of the current all lowercase format. You'll make use of a function called string$properCase. This function is created in Appendix C during the exercise on creating scalar functions (see the Apress web site). It's also located in the code downloads. You don't need the exact implementation here. It's simply a function that takes a name and cleans up the format as you'll see in the following example:

347

```
CREATE TRIGGER artist$insteadOfInsert ON artist
INSTEAD OF INSERT
AS
INSERT INTO artist(name, defaultFl, catalogNumberMask)
SELECT dbo.string$properCase(name), defaultfl, catalogNumberMask
FROM INSERTED
GO


CREATE TRIGGER artist$insteadOfUpdate on artist
INSTEAD OF UPDATE
AS
UPDATE artist
SET name = string$properCase(INSERTED.name),
         defaultFl = INSERTED.defaultFl,
         catalogNumberMask = INSERTED.catalogNumberMask
FROM artist
JOIN INSERTED ON artist.artistId = INSERTED.artistId
GO
```

To test your INSERT trigger, you execute the following:

```
-- insert fairly obviously improperly formatted name
INSERT INTO artist (name, defaultFl, catalogNumberMask)
VALUES ('eLvIs CoStElLo',0,'77_____') -- then retrieve the last inserted
value into this table
SELECT artistId, name
FROM artist
WHERE artistId = ident_current('artist')
```

which returns the required response, as shown here:

artistId	name
19	Elvis Costello

Next you'll test the UPDATE trigger. First, you check all of the values in the table as they stand right now:

```
SELECT artistId, name
FROM artist
```

This returns a list of untidily formatted rows:

artistId	name
19	Elvis Costello
1	THE BEATLES
15	The Monkees
2	THE WHO

Then you run the following query, which looks as if it will set the names to all uppercase:

```
UPDATE artist
SET name = UPPER(name)
```

However, you see that all of the rows are not in uppercase, though they are now formatted in a tidier manner.

artistId	name
19	Elvis Costello
1	The Beatles
15	The Monkees
2	The Who

INSTEAD OF triggers are the best place to do this sort of data manipulation, because it saves you from inserting bad data, then having to take an additional step in an AFTER trigger to update it. Any time you need to extend the way that an INSERT, UPDATE, or DELETE operation is implemented in a generic way, INSTEAD OF triggers are great.

Conditional Insert

During our demonstration of error handling, a batch insert was created that added albums to a table based on the catalogNumber, though it didn't match the mask we had set up for an artist. Here, you'll build a more streamlined example, where the table (or tables) in such a system will accept any data from the user, while placing any invalid data in an exception-handling table so that someone can later fix any problems. First you'll have to drop the original constraint that you added in the previous chapter:

```
ALTER TABLE album
DROP CONSTRAINT chkAlbum$catalogNumber$function$artist$catalogNumberValidate
```

At this point you're unprotected from any invalid values inserted into the catalogNumber column. However, you'll build an INSTEAD OF trigger that will take all valid rows and insert (or update) them in the album table. If they are invalid, you'll insert them in a new table that you'll create called albumException, which will have the same structure as the album table, with a different primary key value and a new column called operation (for insert or update).

```
CREATE TABLE albumException
(
    albumExceptionId int NOT NULL IDENTITY,
    name varchar(60) NOT NULL,
    artistId int NOT NULL,
    catalogNumber char(12) NOT NULL,
    exceptionAction char(1),
    exceptionDate datetime
)
```

Now you create a simple INSTEAD OF trigger to intercept the user's data and attempt to validate the catalog number. If the data is valid, you update the table, otherwise it will be added to the exception table.

```
CREATE TRIGGER album$insteadOfUpdate
ON album
INSTEAD OF UPDATE
AS

DECLARE @errorValue int -- this is the variable for capturing error status

UPDATE album
SET name = INSERTED.name, artistId = INSERTED.artistId,
            catalogNumber = INSERTED.catalogNumber
FROM inserted
JOIN album
    ON INSERTED.albumId = album.albumId
    -- only update rows where the criteria is met
    WHERE dbo.album$catalogNumbervalidate(INSERTED.catalogNumber,
          INSERTED.artistId) = 1

-- check to make certain that an error did not occur in this statement
SET @errorValue = @@error
IF @errorValue <> 0
BEGIN
    RAISERROR 50000 'Error inserting valid album rows'
    ROLLBACK TRANSACTION
    RETURN
END

-- get all of the rows where the criteria isn't met
INSERT INTO albumException (name, artistId, catalogNumber, exceptionAction,
                            exceptionDate)
SELECT name, artistId, catalogNumber, 'U',getdate()
FROM INSERTED
WHERE NOT(       -- generally the easiest way to do this is to copy
                 -- the criteria and do a not(where ...)
          dbo.album$catalogNumbervalidate(INSERTED.catalogNumber,
          INSERTED.artistId) = 1 )

SET @errorValue = @@error
IF @errorValue <> 0
BEGIN
    RAISERROR 50000 'Error logging exception album rows'
    ROLLBACK TRANSACTION
    RETURN
END
GO
```

Now, updating a row to a proper value can simply happen with the following statements:

```
-- update the album table with a known good match to the catalog number
UPDATE album
SET catalogNumber = '222-22222-22'
WHERE name = 'the white album'

-- then list the artistId and catalogNumber of the album in the "real" table
SELECT artistId, catalogNumber
FROM album
WHERE name = 'the white album'

-- as well as the exception table
SELECT artistId, catalogNumber, exceptionAction, exceptionDate
FROM albumException
WHERE name = 'the white album'
```

The catalog number matches what you've updated it to and there are no exceptions in the albumException table:

ArtistId	catalogNumber
1	222-22222-22

artistId	catalogNumber exceptionAction exceptionDate

Then you do an obviously invalid update:

```
UPDATE album
SET catalogNumber = '1'
WHERE name = 'the white album'

-- then list the artistId and catalogNumber of the album in the "real" table
SELECT artistId, catalogNumber
FROM album
WHERE name = 'the white album'

-- as well as the exception table
SELECT artistId, catalogNumber, exceptionAction, exceptionDate
FROM albumException
WHERE name = 'the white album'
```

You see that you haven't updated the row–no error was returned, but you've now added a row to your exception table, thereby alerting you to the error:

artistId	catalogNumber
1	222-22222-22

artistId	catalogNumber	exceptionAction	exceptionDate
1	1	U	2001-01-07 01:02:59.363

It's left to the reader to create the INSTEAD OF INSERT trigger to accompany the UPDATE case. You would also probably want to extend the exception table to include some sort of reason for the failure if you had more than one possibility.

Modifying the Data Represented in a View

In general, doing inserts, updates, and deletes on views has always had its drawbacks, because the following criteria must be met to execute a modification statement against a view:

❑ UPDATE and INSERT statements may only modify a view if they only reference the columns of one table at a time.

❑ DELETE statements can only be used if the view only references a single table.

However, by using INSTEAD OF triggers, you can implement the INSERT, UPDATE, and DELETE mechanisms on views. In this example, you'll create an extremely simple view and an insert trigger to allow inserts:

```
-- create view, excluding the defaultFl column, which you don't want to let
-- users see in this view, and you want to view the names in upper case.
CREATE VIEW vArtistExcludeDefault
AS
SELECT artistId, UPPER(name) AS name, catalogNumberMask
FROM artist
GO


-- then you create a very simple INSTEAD OF insert trigger

CREATE TRIGGER vArtistExcludeDefault$insteadOfInsert
ON vArtistExcludeDefault
INSTEAD OF INSERT
AS
BEGIN
    --note that you don't use the artistId from the INSERTED table
    INSERT INTO artist (name, catalogNumberMask, defaultFl)
    SELECT NAME, catalogNumberMask, 0 --only can set defaultFl to 0
                                      --using the view
    FROM INSERTED
END
GO
```

Then you simply insert using the view just as you would the table (excluding the identity column, which you cannot set a value for), as shown here:

```
INSERT INTO vArtistExcludeDefault (name, catalogNumberMask)
VALUES ('The Monkees','44_____')
```

However, the view has other ideas, as follows:

Server: Msg 233, Level 16, State 2, Line 1
The column 'artistId' in table 'vArtistExcludeDefault' cannot be NULL.

This isn't what you expected or wanted. So you have to reformulate your insert to include the `artistId` and an invalid value. Now the insert works just fine, as shown:

```
INSERT INTO vArtistExcludeDefault (artistId, name, catalogNumberMask)
VALUES (-1, 'The Monkees','44_____')

SELECT * FROM vArtistExcludeDefault
WHERE artistId = ident_current('vArtistExcludeDefault')
```

which gives you back the value that you hoped it would:

artistId	name	defaultFl	catalogNumberMask
15	THE MONKEES	0	44_____

It should be noted that if you had two or more tables in the view, and you execute an insert on the view, you could insert data into *all* of the tables that make up the view. This neatly sidesteps the requirement that INSERT and UPDATE statements on views can touch only single tables at a time, which is very cumbersome. (Further details on views can be found in the next chapter.)

Client Code and Stored Procedures

For quite a while, there has been a programmatic drive to move much of the business rule implementation and data protection code out of SQL Server and into a middle-tier set of interface objects. In this way the database, client and business rules exist in three units that can be implemented independently. Thus business rules that you may well have thought about implementing via constraints and triggers get moved out of this "data" layer and into client-based code, such as a COM object and stored procedures.

Such a multitier design also attempts to make the life of the user easier, because users edit data using custom front-end tools, although the middle-tier services maintain and protect data that passes through them, thereby insulating the users from all the required SQL code. Not only that, but these services can also directly handle any errors that occur and present the user with meaningful error messages. Because application users primarily edit rows one at a time, rather than a large number of rows, this actually works really great.

The other point is that, in most enterprise applications (for instance situations with hundreds of thousands of users on a website), the database is usually considered as the "system bottleneck." Though it's possible to distribute the load on a single server, in many cases it can be much easier to spread the load across many application servers as you learned in Chapter 9.

However, almost any data protection mechanism that is enforced without the use of constraints or triggers may prove problematic. Let's consider your list of possible users that you introduced at the very beginning of the chapter, namely the following:

❑   Users using custom front-end tools: When users all use the custom front-end tools that are developed for the interface, there is no problem with employing the middle tier. In fact, it can have some great benefits, because as discussed, the object methods used to enforce the rules can be tuned for maximum performance.

❑   Users using generic data tools such as Microsoft Access: Let's consider a case in which a user needs to modify a set of "live" data, but only needs it for a week, or a weekend, and there is no time to write a full-blown application. You won't be able to let them directly access the data because it's in a raw unprotected state. Hence, you'll either have to code a relevant business rule into the Access database, or deny the user and make them wait until an application is created. This type of thing is relatively rare, and you can usually stop this kind of activity with strict policies against such access.

❑   Data import routines that acquire data from external sources: Almost every system of any magnitude will include some import facilities to take data in a raw format from external systems, maybe from another part of your company or another company altogether, and place this data in a table on the database server. This can be in as simple a form as a user application to import a spreadsheet, or as complex as an interface between all of the schools in a state and the respective state department of education. The tools will range from user applications, DTS, or even BCP (bulk copy program that comes with SQL Server). When the middle tier owns all of the business rules and data-integrity checks, you'll either have to go in through the middle tier (frequently one at a time) or extract all of the business rules and code them into your import routines.

❑   Raw queries executed by data administrators to fix problems caused by user error: Almost anybody with administration experience has had to remove a few rows from a database that users have erroneously created but cannot remove, and in so doing may have mistakenly deleted the wrong rows, for example, active account rows rather than inactive ones. In this situation, if you had business rules built into a trigger that allowed the deletion of inactive accounts only, an error message would have been returned to the user warning that active accounts could not be deleted. Obviously you cannot protect against a really bad action, such as systematically deleting every row in a table, but when a fully featured database is implemented and the data protected using constraints and triggers, it's next to impossible to make even small mistakes in data integrity.

As the data architect, I very much desire the possibilities offered by multitier development. However, the load of business rule and data-integrity rule implementation should be "shared" between the middle tier and database server as appropriate. Two very specific types of such rules that are far better implemented in the database are as follows:

❑   Any rule that can be placed in a NULL, foreign key, or check constraint: This is due to the fact that, when building additional external interfaces, this kind of check will generally make up quite a bit of the coding effort. Furthermore, base data integrity should be guaranteed at the lowest level possible, which will allow as many programs as possible to code to the database. As a final point, these constraints will be used by the optimizer to make queries run faster.

❑   Rules that require inter-table validations: Whenever you save a value, you must check to see if a value exists in a different table. The additional table will have to be accessed automatically to make certain that the state that was expected still exists. In some cases the middle tier will try to cache the data on the database to use in validation, but there is no way to spread this cached data to multiple servers in a manner that ensures that the value you're entering has proper data integrity.

Having considered some of the possible drawbacks to middle-tier coding, let's now look at cases where a stored procedure or user code is the optimal place to locate the business rules.

Mutable Rules

For a given set of criteria, on one occasion when they are met, the rule evaluates to true and an action is carried out, whereas on another occasion, the rule evaluates to false and a different action is carried out. The best litmus test for such a rule is to see whether the user is able to bypass it. For instance, in the chapter example, you could attempt to implement the following rule: "The user should enter a valid artist for the album."

As a reminder, you have the album table that contains a NOT NULL foreign-key relationship to the artist table. Hence, you're forced to put in a valid artistId when you modify the table. From here you have two courses of action.

❑   Make the artistId in the album table nullable and hence optional, thereby allowing the user to select an album without supplying an artistId. To follow the rule "should," the front end would then likely open a dialog box asking the user, "Are you sure you don't want to assign an artist to this album?"

❑   Alternatively, you could rephrase the business rule as "the user could enter an invalid artist." This would mean that the database could allow any value from the artistId and indeed let the client application handle the validation by checking the value to see if it's correct and then send a dialog box stating the following: "Are you sure you don't want to assign an artist to this album?" or worse still: "You have entered an invalid artistId, you should enter a valid one." You would then have to drop the database validations in case the user says, "Nah, let me enter the invalid value."

The point I'm trying to make here is that SQL Server cannot converse with the user in an interactive manner. The hard and fast trigger and constraint validations still depend largely on the process of submitting a request and waiting to see if it completes successfully, and you need a more interactive method of communication in which you can influence events after the request has been submitted, and before the result comes back.

In the following examples, you'll look at situations concerning rules that cannot be realistically implemented via triggers and constraints.

> *Admittedly where there's a will there's a way. It's possible, using temporary tables as messaging mechanisms, to "pass" values to a trigger or constraint. In this manner, you can optionally override functionality. However, triggers and constraints aren't generally considered suitable places to implement mutable business rules.*

Optionally Cascading Deletes

Cascading deletes are a great resource, but you should use them with care. As discussed, they automatically remove child rows that are dependent on the content of the deleted parent row, and you would rarely want to warn the user of the existence of these child rows before they are deleted. However this wouldn't be ideal in the case of a bank account. Let's say that you have the following tables:

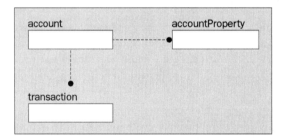

In this case, it will make sense to automatically cascade deletes of an `accountProperty` row if you want to delete a row from the `account` table. However, if an account has entries in the `transaction` table, you need to ensure that the user is aware of these, and thus warn them if a cascading delete is requested. This will of course increase complexity, because you won't be able to delete an account as well as its properties and transactions in a single statement.

Instead of a single statement, you'll have to execute the following steps:

❑ Run a `SELECT` statement for each child table that you'll want to optionally cascade delete to, in order to show the user what exists.

❑ If the user accepts, execute a `DELETE` statement for each child table that had rows related to your primary table, and in the same atomic operation, delete the row you're interested in.

This code could be built into a single stored procedure that checks for the children, and if they exist, returns a resultset of rows for the user to see what needs to be deleted. It will also include a parameter to allow the user to ignore the existence of rows and go ahead and delete them. The following shows you an example of how you might handle this situation (note that for clarity I've removed transactions and error handling, which will be covered in greater depth in the next chapter):

```
CREATE PROCEDURE account$delete
(
    @accountId int,
    @removeChildTransactionsFl bit = 0
) as

-- if they asked to delete them, just delete them
IF @removeChildTransactionsFl = 1
    DELETE [transaction] --table named with keyword
    WHERE   accountId = @accountId
ELSE --check for existence
  BEGIN
        IF EXISTS (SELECT *
                    FROM   [transaction]
                    WHERE  accountId = @accountId)
         BEGIN
                RAISERROR 50000 'Child transactions exist'
                RETURN -100
         END
  END

DELETE account
WHERE   accountID = @accountId
```

Now the user could try to execute the stored procedure with the flag equal to 0, and if any children existed, the user would get notification. If not, the account would be deleted, and presumably the properties would be removed as well via a cascading relationship.

Rules That Are Based Upon How a Person Feels

Sadly for the system architect, this is a reality that must be faced. In a typical system, you'll have many hard and fast business rules that cannot be broken. However a large number of mutable rules appear as hard and fast rules. As an example, consider the following statement:

> *It's the company's policy that you don't ship the product out to a customer until you have payment.*

This doesn't seem at all problematic until you get a request for a shipment to take place as a goodwill gesture.

As a further example consider the following rule:

Products will be shipped out in the same sequence as the orders were received.

Consider the case of a quality-control system that deals with product Y. Let's say that a constraint is applied such that a given customer specification must be met, otherwise the product cannot be shipped to the customer. So the user calls up and requests a large shipment, and the clerk who handles these orders calls up the user interface to choose some of product Y to ship. However there aren't enough products to fulfill the order. When the clerk contacts the customer to inform him of this problem, the customer requests a closely related product rather than waiting for more product Y to become available. What the clerk now discovers is that because the business rules stand, she is unable to process this request, and so has to send it to the ordering manager to fulfill.

A stored procedure approach to this problem might allow users of a different security group to override the given settings where appropriate. In this way the clerk can get a list of product Y to ship, choose materials, add them to an order, and press a button that starts shipping the product, thereby calling a stored procedure `productOrder$ship`. This procedure will check that the product is within the customer specifications, and then set the order to be shipped. If the values are out of specification, it would deny the user. However, the ordering manager will be able to execute a different stored procedure, say `productOrder$shipOutOfSpec`, that would allow the user to ship an out-of-specification product.

The following are two things of note in this scenario:

❑   The front-end would be responsible for knowing that the product was out of specification and wouldn't allow the user to execute the `productOrder$shipOutOfSpec` procedure, even though knowing this might be based on querying the rights on each stored procedure (using the `PERMISSIONS` function).

❑   `productOrder$ship` and `productOrder$shipOutOfSpec` would probably end up calling a different stored procedure that would be used to encapsulate the actual time to start shipping the order. However, by presenting actual object and method names that are different, you can limit any situational coding in your procedures (if this type of user, do this, else do this) and present a secure interface based just on the stored procedures that are used for the enforcement.

The reality for a data architect is that there will always be those who work "outside the rules" for both proper and improper reasons, and you must take this into account whenever you build a truly user-friendly system.

Case Study

Continuing with the data protection code, you'll now build a few of the necessary triggers, and you'll finally learn a few optional rules that you'll need to implement your system.

Remove the Time from Transaction Dates Trigger

The first trigger you'll create is an INSTEAD OF trigger to format the transaction date. There is no reason to store the time for the transaction date, and so you start out with your template trigger code, and add code to remove the time element from the dates using the date$removeTime function used previously for a check constraint, as shown here:

```
CREATE TRIGGER transaction$insteadOfInsert
ON [transaction]
INSTEAD OF INSERT
AS
-------------------------------------------------------------------------
-- Purpose : Trigger on the insert that fires for any insert DML
--  : * formats the date column without time
-------------------------------------------------------------------------
BEGIN
    DECLARE @rowsAffected int,     -- stores the number of rows affected
        @errorNumber int,          -- used to hold the error number after
DML
    @msg varchar(255),             -- used to hold the error message
    @errSeverity varchar(20),
    @triggerName sysname

    SET @rowsAffected = @@rowcount
    SET @triggerName = object_name(@@procid) --used for messages

    --no need to continue on if no rows affected
    IF @rowsAffected = 0 RETURN

    --perform the insert that you're building the trigger instead of
    INSERT INTO [transaction] (accountId, number, date, description,
                                amount, signature, payeeId,
                                transactionTypeId)
    SELECT accountId, number, dbo.date$removeTime(date) AS date,
           description, amount, signature, payeeId, transactionTypeId
    FROM INSERTED

    SET @errorNumber = @@error
    IF @errorNumber <> 0
    begin
        SET @msg = 'Error: ' + CAST(@errorNumber AS varchar(10)) +
                    ' occurred during the insert of the rows into ' +
                    ' the transaction table.'
        RAISERROR 50000 @msg
        ROLLBACK TRANSACTION
        RETURN
    END
END
```

Ninety-five percent of the update trigger is the same code, so this is left to the reader.

Validate City and Zip Codes Match Trigger

In your address table, you have the cityId and zipCodeId columns, which are foreign keys to the zipCode and city tables, respectively. You have also included a zipCodeCityReference table that is used to help the user select city and state from the zip code. You would fill this table from a commercially available zip code database (like from the US Postal Service). A final purpose of this table is to validate the city and zipCodeId values. As a reminder, here was the physical data model for these tables:

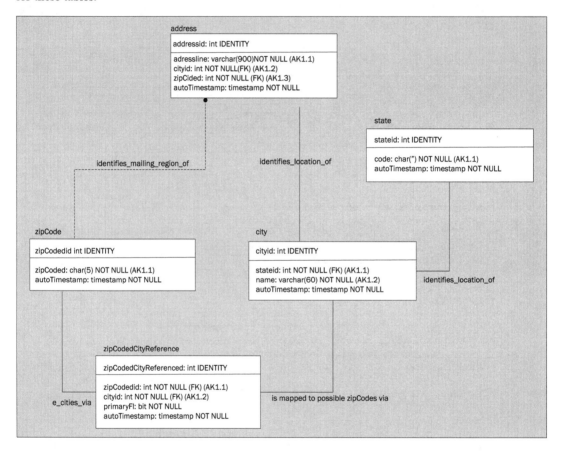

You can do this by making sure that the cityId and zipCodeId pair that has been entered is found in the reference table, as follows:

```
CREATE TRIGGER address$afterInsert
ON address
AFTER UPDATE
AS
--------------------------------------------------------------------------
-- Purpose : Trigger on the <action> that fires for any <action> DML
--------------------------------------------------------------------------
BEGIN
    DECLARE @rowsAffected int, -- stores the number of rows affected
    @errNumber int, -- used to hold the error number after DML
    @msg varchar(255), -- used to hold the error message
    @errSeverity varchar(20),
    @triggerName sysname

    SET @rowsAffected = @@rowcount
    SET @triggerName = object_name(@@procid) --used for messages

    --no need to continue on if no rows affected
    IF @rowsAffected = 0 RETURN

    DECLARE @numberOfRows int
    SELECT @numberOfRows = (SELECT count(*)
                            FROM INSERTED
                                JOIN zipCodeCityReference AS zcr
                                    ON zcr.cityId = INSERTED.cityId
and
                                        zcr.zipCodeId =
INSERTED.zipCodeId)
    IF @numberOfRows <> @rowsAffected
    BEGIN
        SET @msg = CASE WHEN @rowsAffected = 1
                        THEN 'The row you inserted has ' +
                            'an invalid cityId and zipCodeId pair.'
                        ELSE 'One of the rows you were trying to insert ' +
                            'has an invalid cityId and zipCodeId pair.'
                    END
    END
    RAISERROR 50000 @msg
    ROLLBACK TRANSACTION
    RETURN
END
```

Ninety-nine percent of the insert trigger is the same code, so this is left to the reader.

Transaction Allocations Cannot Exceed the Amount Stored Trigger

In this example, you consider the transaction allocation amounts for transactions. The column you're concerned with is the allocationAmount on the transactionAllocation table:

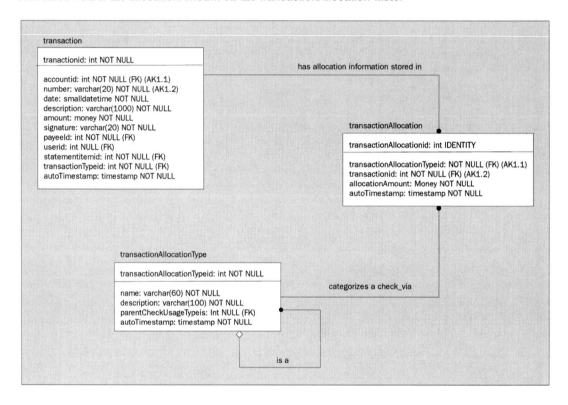

Whenever a user modifies an existing allocation, you check to make sure that he hasn't allocated more money to the transaction than what actually exists. So you write the following trigger:

```
CREATE TRIGGER transactionAllocation$afterInsert
ON transactionAllocation
AFTER INSERT AS
---------------------------------------------------------------------------
-- Purpose : Trigger on the insert that fires for any insert DML
-- : * protects against allocations that are greater than 100%
---------------------------------------------------------------------------
BEGIN
    DECLARE @rowsAffected int,      -- stores the number of rows affected
    @errNumber int,                 -- used to hold the error number after DML
    @msg varchar(255),              -- used to hold the error message
    @errSeverity varchar(20),
    @triggerName sysname

    SET @rowsAffected = @@rowcount
    SET @triggerName = object_name(@@procid) --used for messages
```

```
-- no need to continue on if no rows affected
IF @rowsAffected = 0 RETURN

-- get the total of all transactionAllocations that are affected by your
-- insert and get all transactions affected

IF EXISTS (
    SELECT * FROM (
        SELECT transactionId, sum(amount) AS amountTotal
        FROM transactionAllocation
                                --note this transactionId expands your
                                --query to look at all allocations that
                                --are for any transaction who's
                                --allocation you have touched
        WHERE transactionId IN (SELECT transactionId FROM INSERTED)
        GROUP BY transactionId ) AS allocAmounts

    -- join to the transaction to get the amount of
    -- the transaction
    JOIN [transaction]
        ON allocAmounts.transactionId = [transaction].transactionId

    -- check to make sure that the transaction amount isn't greater
    -- than the allocation amount
    WHERE [transaction].amount > allocAmounts.amountTotal )
    BEGIN
        SET @msg = CASE WHEN @rowsAffected = 1
                        THEN 'The row you inserted has' +
                             'made the transaction exceed its transaction.

                        ELSE 'One of the rows you were trying to insert '

                             'has made the transaction exceed its ' +
                             'transaction.'
                    END
    END
    RAISERROR 50000 @msg
    ROLLBACK TRANSACTION
    RETURN
END
```

Note that you solved a fairly complex problem using a complex query, and you've used neither cursors nor temporary tables. It's important to formulate your queries in triggers using as few operators as possible, so that you can minimize the possibility of introducing logic errors into very hard-to-find places when building complex queries. There will always be trade-offs in usability vs. readability or understandability. In almost any system, slow triggers will be a problem, especially if you have to insert a large number of rows at a time.

Again, 95 percent of the update trigger for this and the transaction table is the same code, so it isn't included here.

Optional Rules

In your system, you have a few optional business rules that need implementing. The following were identified in your original analysis:

❑ **User should get a warning if they attempt to withdraw too much money**: You would likely create a stored procedure that checks the balance of the user account prior to saving a transaction amount. The client-side code would compare the balance with the amount of the transaction that was attempting to complete.

❑ **Account must be balanced weekly**: When starting up, the application would need to call a stored procedure that finds out when the account was last balanced, compares it to the current date, and issues a reminder or warning: a reminder might be sent to a manager to advise if the balancing was severely overdue.

In Chapter 14 you'll look at the best practices for building stored procedures.

Best Practices

❑ **Use triggers to perform data validations that check constraints cannot handle**: The work of some trigger functionality may be moved off into middle-tier objects, though triggers do have performance benefits. Use triggers when the following types of validations need to be made:

  ❑ *Cross-database referential integrity:* Just basic RI, but SQL Server doesn't manage declarative constraints across database boundaries.

  ❑ *Intra-table inter-row constraints:* For example, when you need to see that the sum of a column value over multiple rows is less than some value (possibly in another table).

  ❑ *Inter-table constraints:* For example, if a value in one table relies on the value in another. This might also be written as a functions-based check constraint.

  ❑ *Introducing desired side effects to your queries:* For example, cascading inserts, maintaining denormalized data, and so on.

❑ **Make sure that triggers are able to handle multi-row operations**: Although most modifications are in terms of a single row, if a user enters more than one row there is a possibility of invalid data being entered.

❑ **Use client code as a last resort**: When constraints and triggers will not solve the problem, then you cannot implicitly trust that the data in the table will meet the requirements. This is because triggers and constraints cannot be gotten around unless a conscious effort is made by dropping or disabling them.

  ❑ *Note: This best practice pertains only if you use SQL Server as more than a data storage device, which is a role that SQL Server plays very well. Many systems will use it with only base table structures and unique constraints (if that). However, the best practice for using SQL Server is to apply the protection code as close to the table as possible so no mistakes can be made by having code to protect the data in multiple locations.*

Summary

You've now finished the task of developing the data storage for your databases. In the last two chapters you've built the physical storage for the data by creating the tables. In this chapter you took the next step and completed your scheme to safeguard it. During this process, you looked at the following resources that SQL Server gives you to protect your data from having invalid values:

❑ **Defaults**: Though you might not think defaults can be considered data-protection resources, you should know that they can be used to automatically set columns where the purpose of the column might not be apparent to the user (and the database adds a suitable value for the column).

❑ **Check constraints**: These are very important in ensuring that your data is within specifications. You can use almost any scalar functions (user-defined or system) as long as you end up with a single logical expression.

❑ **Triggers**: Triggers are very important resources that allow you to build pieces of code that fire automatically on any INSERT, UPDATE, and DELETE operation that is executed against a single table.

❑ **Stored procedures/front-end code**: I've simply made mention of these mechanisms of data protection because you'll want to ensure that they are used prudently in handling business rules.

Throughout this process you've made use of user-defined functions, which are a new resource that SQL Server 2000 offers you. With them you can encapsulate many of the algorithms that you employ to enhance and extend your defaults, check constraints, triggers, and as you'll find in the next chapter, stored procedures.

Once you've built and implemented a set of appropriate data-safeguarding resources, you can then trust that the data in your database has been validated. You should never need to revalidate your data once it's stored in your database, but it's a good idea to do random sampling so you know that there are no integrity gaps that have slipped by you. Every relationship, every check constraint, every trigger that you devise will help to make sure this is true.

In the next chapter, you'll look at some more advanced data access and modification methods, in particular the use of views and stored procedures.

13

Advanced Data Access and Modification

In previous chapters, you've designed your databases, built your storage, and made protection schemes for your data. Throughout this book, I've assumed that you're relatively proficient in Transact-SQL, and that you have some experience in writing stored procedures and views, all of which are skills that you'll further develop in the course of this chapter.

Now you'll meet more advanced concepts for accessing data in your OLTP database. You'll learn major query considerations, such as how transactions, temp tables, cursors, and NULLs make your coding both easier and more *interesting*. You'll take an in-depth look at the issues surrounding using views and stored procedures, and look at a full discussion of the pros and cons of building applications using stored procedure access, ad hoc query access, and a mixture of both.

After reading about querying matters, you'll learn how you can use SQL Server security to limit access to the data in your systems. Finally, you'll briefly examine how building applications that access data across different servers affects your architecture and coding.

One thing to note. For the data architect in some organizations, performing a few of the tasks described in this chapter will be beyond the call of duty. Perhaps creating stored procedures and views will come close to stepping on the DBA (database administrator) or database programmer's toes. Alternatively, it may well be that data architect is just one of many hats that must be worn. Whatever the case, I feel that it's important for every data architect to endeavor not to lose those SQL coding skills. A thorough understanding of these issues is very beneficial to the design role. If you aren't skilled in SQL then you run the risk of designing a database that will be indefensible when others begin to complain that it's too hard to work with. It would be a lie if I didn't tell you that it will initially be easier to deal with a well-normalized database. In this chapter, you won't be looking at easier ways to access the data but rather, how you can build a database more "correctly."

Query Considerations

In this section, you'll look at some of the important issues that need to be understood to implement efficient database access and modification features. Transactions, locking, NULLs, cursors, temporary tables, stored procedures, and views are all essential to the architecture of a database system.

In this chapter, you'll look at how these issues affect your coding of applications, rather than how they affect your creation of objects.

Transactions

Transactions play a very important role in accessing your data. A transaction is a sequence of operations performed as a single logical unit of work. They're very important to coding strategy because they allow you to take multiple statements and allow those statements to execute as one single unit of work.

Transaction usage can make or break a system. Often underusing transactions is quite often more of an issue than overuse.

For example, consider that you have a system that takes orders and in the process takes payment information. When trying to insert the data into the table, you use the following two pseudostatements:

```
INSERT INTO into order (…) VALUES (…)
INSERT INTO into payment (…) VALUES (…)
```

What happens if the order row is created, but the payment isn't? The user gets her product and doesn't have to pay. Or the opposite occurs and she pays but doesn't get her stuff. Not good. So you use transactions to recode this as follows (still in pseudocode):

```
BEGIN TRANSACTION
INSERT INTO into order (…) VALUES (…)

IF @@Error <> 0
   BEGIN
         ROLLBACK TRANSACTION
         RETURN
   END

INSERT INTO into payment (…) VALUES (…)
IF @@Error <> 0
   BEGIN
         ROLLBACK TRANSACTION
         RETURN
   END
COMMIT TRANSACTION
```

Now you're safe. Either all will succeed, or all will fail.

In the following sections, you'll look at the following tips for using transactions:

- ❑ Use transactions as much as needed
- ❑ Avoid long-running transactions
- ❑ Transaction shouldn't span batch boundaries

Use Transactions As Much As Necessary

Most issues with transactions occur because of a lack of a transaction, rather than overuse. The data is what's important and performance comes second. If you have subsecond response times from every one of your queries, but the data cannot be trusted, then you really don't have much.

In every case where there are multiple statements when two statements are executed and BOTH need to complete, or neither of them do, you should use a transaction. Obviously, users waiting for the first resource will have to wait for the whole transaction to be complete, but this is preferable to corrupting your data.

Avoid Long-Running Transactions

You've seen this suggestion several times already. However, *how long* is a long transaction? A long running transaction may take half of a second, one minute, one hour, or even a day. What matters most is that you minimize the transactions that are affecting your users and their access to data.

Rather than loading values from an outside source directly into your users' table, it may be better to load the rows into a new intermediate table and then insert the rows into the users' table during off-peak hours. The overhead of doing this will be far less than bulk copying directly into a table.

In very exceptional circumstances when a transaction cannot be kept down to a short time, you'll either have to redesign the procedure or live with it. When it comes to transactions lasting a couple of seconds or less, there isn't much that can be done programmatically to reduce this stress. If this duration isn't within acceptable levels, this is where performance tuning comes into play.

Transactions Shouldn't Span Batch Boundaries

When sending multiple batches of commands to the server, it's best not to start a transaction in one batch and finish it in another.

By following this *critical* recommendation, you can greatly reduce some of the more performance-hindering situations that will occur.

Consider the following example. In the following diagram you have two commands that update `tableA` and then `tableB`. It has been determined that you need to make these commands into a transaction, and you've built a tidy little set of methods for dealing with this situation. You call a `begin_transaction()` method that connects to the server and begins the transaction. Next, it sends a command to update `tableA`, followed by a command to update `tableB`, but somewhere during the last call, the LAN breaks down:

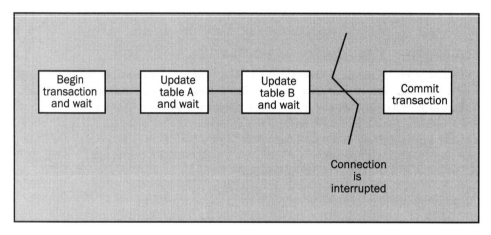

SQL Server may not see that the connection has been severed, so it keeps the connection open waiting to commit or roll the connection back. However, the transaction is only part of the way through, and neither a commit nor a rollback will occur until SQL Server realizes that the connection has been broken due to inactivity. Your data will be just fine as the transaction created update locks to protect it. The only problem is that, depending on the actual WHERE clause, the row, rows, or possibly the whole `tableA` table will be locked up tight. Hence, when another user comes by to simply look at a row in `tableA`, he is forced to wait or click the Stop button on the browser.

The answer to this problem is to roll these commands up into a single batch, which executes all at once, for instance:

```
BEGIN TRANSACTION

UPDATE tableA SET …
SELECT * FROM tableB
UPDATE tableB SET …

COMMIT TRANSACTION
GO
```

In this manner, if SQL Server gets the commands and begins to execute them, either *all* the operations will occur or none will. You won't end up with any locked resources just waiting for a user to send another batch.

So why would you consider sending transactions in multiple batches? A couple of reasons:

❑ Apparent speed–once each statement is finished, it's possible to update a progress bar and tell the user that tableA has indeed been updated, now I'm moving on to tableB, and so on.

❑ It's easy to do without knowing it–especially using tools such as ADO. Consider the following ADO code sample, culled from SQL Server 2000 Books Online in the "Performing Transactions in ADO" section:

```
Dim cn As New ADODB.Connection
Dim rs As New ADODB.Recordset
. . .
' Open connection.
cn.Open


' Open titles table.
rs.Open "SELECT * FROM titles", Cn, adOpenDynamic, adLockPessimistic
. . .
' Begin the transaction.
rs.MoveFirst
cn.BeginTrans

' User loops through the recordset making changes.
. . .
' Ask if the user wants to commit all the changes made.
If MsgBox("Save all changes?", vbYesNo) = vbYes Then
    cn.CommitTrans
Else
    cn.RollbackTrans
End If
```

This code will do exactly what I was discussing earlier, but in a much nicer-looking wrapper. By executing the BeginTrans method on the connection, a BEGIN TRANSACTION command is sent in one batch to the server. For each touch of a row in the loop (not coded, just mentioned), a data modification statement will be sent to the server. Finally, if all goes well in the code, the CommitTrans or RollbackTrans method will be called, sending a COMMIT TRANSACTION command. If there is any mistake inside here, or even a connection burp, then the users of the titles table will be waiting for quite a while. Note also that an adLockPessimistic lock is called for, which will likely implement an isolation level of read committed or possibly even serializable–so no other user can touch the rows while this user has them in this loop. This is a simple example of code for teaching how a few methods of the connection objects work, but it isn't a good example to follow when building multiuser programs.

However, if you stored each statement in this situation, instead of actually sending them to SQL Server one at a time, you could execute the batch of statements once the user has finished. The user may have to wait a bit longer for the operation to finish than when each step was performed separately. Actually, less time will be taken overall but the user gets the impression that nothing is going on, and the time will *seem* longer. In this case, however, if the connection is interrupted after the server receives the batch of work, you can be sure that the user's changes will be applied and all locks used to maintain consistency will be immediately released.

By following the very simple rule of keeping transactions within the same batch, you won't leave transactions hanging because SQL Server will make sure that everything that is required for a transaction is ready before a single command is executed. If you get disconnected, it's guaranteed that either all or none of your command will be executed, and you won't affect any other user's performance any longer than necessary.

One thing should be mentioned however. When the executed code returns data, you may still get into a situation that is similar to this. Take the previous code and add a SELECT statement as follows:

```
BEGIN TRANSACTION

UPDATE tableA SET …
SELECT * FROM tableB
UPDATE tableB SET …

COMMIT TRANSACTION
GO
```

If the client doesn't fetch and exhaust the resultset from the SELECT statement, you'll have the same issues as if it were in two batches. The commit transaction will never be gotten to. This is because, depending on the cursor type, the resultset may be editable, so the UPDATE statement is dependent on results of the SELECT.

Major Coding Issues

Any discussion of data access and modification techniques using queries wouldn't be complete without covering three features that most affect SQL Server's performance:

❑ Temporary tables

❑ Cursors

❑ NULLs

You'll look at these topics in some depth, to make sure that you can deal with them effectively and avoid potential performance issues that can result from their misuse.

Temporary Tables

Temporary tables (usually called temp tables) were briefly mentioned earlier in the book when you were discussing table creation. They're like permanent tables, but are removed from the system when they go out of scope. There are three different kinds:

❑ **Variable-based temp tables**: These are scoped to the batch of code being executed.

❑ **Local temp tables** (whose names are prefixed with #): These are scoped to the connection to SQL Server. Use only when a variable-based temp table will not work, for example when an EXECUTE statement is required or the amount of data is so great that an index is required.

❑ **Global temp tables** (names prefixed with ##): These can be viewed by any connection and any user in the system. They don't fully go out of scope until the connection that creates them is destroyed *and* any other connections that are using the tables stop accessing them. You seldom need to use global temp tables for any reason, unless you have to share temp data across connections.

Temp tables allow you to create your own temporary storage and add some data into it, using most of the same INSERT, UPDATE, and DELETE statements as you do with permanent tables. Global and local temporary tables can also be indexed if necessary. In fact, a temp table is just an ordinary table that has a very short life span. Note too that any user can create and use them as they see fit. Variable-based temporary tables will also not work by taking the results of an EXECUTE statement, for example:

```
INSERT INTO @TEMP
EXECUTE ('<statement>')
```

> In earlier versions of SQL Server, temp tables were frequently used as workarounds to overcome certain limitations. With SQL Server 2000, they should be far less frequently employed. Using a temp table in a query will always be slower than one executed in straight SQL.

For example, imagine you want to try to determine the number of stored procedures and functions that have either two or three parameters. Using a temp table for this might seem the ideal solution:

```
--create the table to hold the names of the objects
CREATE TABLE #counting
(
    specific_name sysname
)

--insert all of the rows that have between 2 and 3 parameters
INSERT INTO #counting (specific_name)
SELECT specific_name
FROM information_schema.parameters as parameters
GROUP BY specific_name
HAVING COUNT(*) between 2 and 3

--count the number of values in the table
SELECT COUNT(*)
FROM #counting

DROP TABLE #counting
```

This code will return the right value (which of course will vary from SQL Server to SQL Server):

355

With a bit more thought, you can avoid using the temp table altogether and execute the query in SQL only—thereby boosting the query speed, as shown here:

```
SELECT count(*)
FROM (SELECT specific_name
    FROM information_schema.parameters AS parameters
    GROUP BY specific_name
    HAVING count(*) between 2 and 3 ) AS TwoParms
```

You'll explore this example of parameter counts again in the next section on cursors.

Temp tables could be avoided more easily if you made better use of the following under-used T-SQL features:

❑ **Derived tables**: One of the most important additions to the T-SQL language has been the ability to include subqueries in joins. This is an extremely useful technique, and it allows you to do most of the things that you would previously have done with temp tables in your queries, as shown here (and in the previous example):

```
SELECT tableName.subqueryTableName,
        alias.subqueryTableNameId AS aliasKey
FROM tableName
JOIN ( select subqueryTableNameId, tableNameId
        from subqueryTableName ) AS alias
    ON tableName.tableNameId = alias.tableNameId
```

The bold code acts exactly like a single-use view in the query and because it allows you to use GROUP BY and HAVING clauses, a temp table isn't required to perform the query, which will be much faster because of this. Note that you can nest derived tables within other derived tables, if needed.

❑ **UNION [ALL]**: Frequently, a temp table will be built to take two sets and put them together. In many cases, a UNION ALL could be used to put the sets together instead. There have been times when I've gained a 40-percent speed improvement by using a UNION ALL where I might have used a temp table in the past. Also, if some final WHERE clause is applied to the entire set, you can put the unioned set in a derived table!

❑ **Large numbers of tables in one query**: In some cases, it may seem prudent to divide long queries into smaller, more palatable chunks of code by breaking them up into calls to temporary tables. However, SQL Server 2000 will allow up to 256 permanent tables to be accessed in a single query, and it will often do a better job of choosing how to execute the query than you can.

This all sounds like there are no good uses of temp tables. This is definitely not the case. They can be useful when you need to manipulate the data in some manner that needs more than a single pass. I use temp tables quite frequently when implementing a recursive tree for display on the screen—adding the values for each level of the tree to the next level. A temp table is ideal in this specific situation because you have to iterate through the set to touch each level of the tree, and you need somewhere to store the intermediate values.

In this example, you'll take a recursive tree table called **type**. Each of the types may have an unlimited number of subtypes. You need to order and display them as a tree, with subitems directly following other subtypes. The tree of data has the following nodes that you'll deal with:

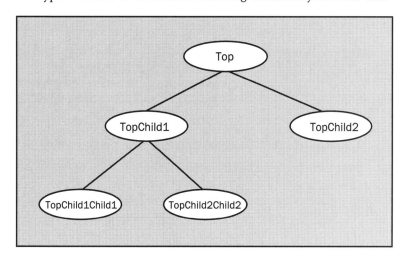

First, let's set up the scenario:

```
--first you create the type table
CREATE TABLE type
(
    typeId int,                  --not identity because you need to reference
                                 --it in this test script
    parentTypeId int NULL,
    name varchar(60) NOT NULL,
)

--then you have to populate the type table
INSERT INTO type (typeId, parentTypeId, name)
VALUES (1, NULL, 'Top')
INSERT INTO type (typeId, parentTypeId, name)
VALUES (2,1, 'TopChild1')
INSERT INTO type (typeId, parentTypeId, name)
VALUES (3,1, 'TopChild2')
INSERT INTO type (typeId, parentTypeId, name)
VALUES (4,2, 'TopChild1Child1')
INSERT INTO type (typeId, parentTypeId, name)
VALUES (5,2, 'TopChild1Child2')
```

Now you build the query using a temp table that will display the tree. Note that you use the temp table here as an array to hold some values while you make extra passes–a **SELECT** statement won't suffice:

```
CREATE TABLE #holdItems
(
    typeId int NOT NULL,         --pkey of type table
    parentTypeID int NULL,       --recursive attribute
    name varchar(100),           --name of the type
    indentLevel int,             --level of the tree for indenting display
    sortOrder varchar(1000)      --sort order for final display
)
```

You now add the top of the tree items into the temp table as follows:

```
--get the toplevel items
INSERT INTO #holdItems

-- First pass will start at indentLevel 1. You put the parent primary key into
-- the sortOrder, padded with zeroes to the right, then you'll append each
-- level of child to each sublevel
SELECT typeId, parentTypeID, name, 1 AS indentLevel,
        LTRIM(replicate('0',10 - LEN(CAST(typeId AS char(10)))) +
        CAST(typeId AS char(10))) AS sortOrder
FROM dbo.type
WHERE parentTypeID IS NULL            --parent is NULL means top node
```

Then you have to code a loop to work down the table levels, one at a time, ordering the rows for output:

```
DECLARE @currLevel int
SET @currLevel = 2

WHILE 1=1                         -- because there is no repeat until in T-SQL
    BEGIN

        INSERT INTO #holdItems

        -- add the sort order of this item to current sort order
        -- of the parent's sort order
        SELECT type.TypeId, type.parentTypeID, type.name,
               @currLevel AS indentLevel,
               RTRIM(#holdItems.sortOrder) +
               LTRIM(replicate('0',10 - LEN(CAST(type.typeId AS char(10)))) +
               CAST(type.typeId as char(10)))
        FROM dbo.type AS type

        -- this join gets you the child rows of the items in the
        -- #holdItemsTable
        JOIN #holdItems
            ON Type.parentTypeId = #holdItems.typeId

            -- currlevel tells you the level you're adding, so you need the parent
            -- in the @join
            WHERE #holdItems.indentLevel = @currLevel - 1

        -- if there are no children on the new level, you break
        IF @@rowcount = 0
            BREAK

        -- otherwise you simply increment the counter and move on.
        SET @currLevel = @currLevel + 1
    END
```

Now you have all of the data setup that you need to display the tree, as shown here:

```
SELECT typeId, parentTypeId, CAST(name AS varchar(15)) AS name, indentLevel
FROM #holdItems
ORDER BY sortorder, parentTypeID

-- drop table isn't explicitly required if in a stored procedure or if
-- you disconnect between executions
DROP TABLE #holdItems
```

This all yields the following set of rows:

typeId	parentTypeId	name	indentLevel
1	NULL	Top	1
2	1	TopChild1	2
4	2	TopChild1Child1	3
5	2	TopChild1Child2	3
3	1	TopChild2	2

This forms the basis of a routine that deals with binary (recursive) trees coded in SQL tables. By extending this algorithm, you can do almost anything you need to do with binary trees, with remarkably good performance.

Don't forget though—if you could do this without the temp tables, it would be faster still. Basically, before using a temp table, make sure that it isn't possible to code the solution without it.

Cursors

In SQL, the typical way to deal with data is a set at a time. You've seen this over and over again in your examples. However, it isn't always possible to deal with data in a set-based manner. **Cursors** are a mechanism in T-SQL that allow you to get to an individual row and perform an action on it, rather than operating on a preselected group of rows.
There are two different types of cursors that are frequently used:

❑   **External, database API cursors**: These are specific cursors that are used to provide external interfaces to SQL Server. Common examples are ODBC, OLE DB, and ADO. By using cursors associated with these technologies, programmers can build streams of data for their applications.

API cursors are primarily used by application programmers and because of this, they're beyond the scope of this book.

❑   **Transact-SQL cursors**: These cursors are used in T-SQL code and you'll look at them in detail in this section. You'll use them to loop through SQL-based steps to perform an action one row at a time.

People tend to have very opposite opinions of cursors in T-SQL code. The two main schools of thought are as follows:

❑   Cursors are evil

❑   Cursors are very useful tools that you must have available

The reasons why cursors have been described as "evil" are twofold:

❑ First, they tend to lead to poor implementations of solutions to problems that are better resolved using set-based SQL. In these cases, the performance of a query using cursors will frequently be an order of magnitude slower than when using set-based operations.

❑ Unless you use the proper cursor types, you'll end up placing locks around your database for each row that you access. When using T-SQL cursors, this may be less of a problem because your T-SQL code will never have to wait for user interaction, but the problem certainly still exists.

The second school of thought on the use of cursors also rings true because there are occasions where you do have to use them. With the advent of user-defined functions, however, there is really only one situation in which the cursor provides the only possibility for implementation–when you need to perform some command on each row in a set. For instance, a cursor allows you to perform a custom-stored procedure, containing business logic, on every row in a table.

Uses of Cursors

Although I would warn against getting into the habit of using cursors, they can be very useful in certain situations. Here are the circumstances under which I consider cursors to be very helpful:

❑ Executing system commands, such as DBCC, or system stored procedures

❑ Executing stored procedures for each row in a set

❑ Where you must access each row individually, rather than a set it at a time

The first two of these should be fairly self-explanatory. A common example of a system stored procedure that you may need to execute using cursors is **sp_adduser**. If you're provisioning users, such as from a spreadsheet, you would likely import the data into a temp table in SQL Server, iterate through the values using a cursor, and add the new users to the database.

The second is different from the first, but not by much. When the need arises to execute a stored procedure once for each row in a set, a cursor will usually have to be employed. This is a relatively common activity (such as implementing business rules from a stored procedure) though it isn't the optimal way to handle the situation. For instance, if you don't own the system tables but you have to add data to them, you'll probably accept that calling a stored procedure in a loop is the only way to carry out this task. If you were the owner of these tables, you could carry out this task using triggers instead.

The third situation is where you can get yourself into trouble. There are an extremely limited number of reasons why you might have to go through each row in your set one after the other. The only common situation where I would use a cursor, and where I wasn't calling to some type of function, is demonstrated in the following example. Here you're going to implement an artificial sort order on a set. You'll load the set with random values, then finally renumber the set in a uniform manner using a cursor. Consider that you have the following table:

```
-- table to demonstrate cursors
CREATE TABLE item
(
    itemId int IDENTITY
    CONSTRAINT XPKItem PRIMARY KEY,
    sortOrderId int
    CONSTRAINT xAKItem_sortOrder UNIQUE
)
```

The first step is to load the table by filling the sort order with random numbers:

```
DECLARE @holdSortOrderId int, @counter int
SET @counter = 1                              --initialize counter

WHILE @counter <= 5
    BEGIN
        --use random numbers between 0 and 1000
        SET @holdSortOrderId = CAST(RAND() * 1000 AS int)

        --make sure the random number doesn't already exist as
        --a sort order
        IF NOT EXISTS (SELECT *
                         FROM dbo.item
                         WHERE sortOrderId = @holdSortOrderId)
        BEGIN
            --insert it
            INSERT INTO dbo.item (sortOrderId)
            VALUES (@holdSortOrderId)

            --increment the counter
            SET @counter = @counter + 1
        END
    END
```

Once you've loaded your table, you should take a look at the results as shown here:

```
SELECT *
FROM dbo.item
ORDER BY sortOrderId
```

This gives you a fairly random set of numbers, which you'll want to reorganize in the next step, as follows:

itemId	sortOrderId
4	29
2	35
1	71
3	72
5	81

Now you'll build a cursor to move through all of the items in your table, ordered by the sort order, and you'll update each row separately:

```
DECLARE @cursor CURSOR,                    --cursor variable
        @c_itemId int, @c_sortOrderId int, --cursor item variables
        @currentSortOrderId int            --used to increment the sort order
SET @currentSortOrderId = 1                --initialize the counter

--use static cursor so you don't see changed values
SET @cursor = CURSOR FORWARD_ONLY STATIC FOR SELECT itemId, sortOrderId
        FROM dbo.item
        ORDER BY sortOrderId
OPEN @cursor                                      --activate the cursor

--get the first row
FETCH NEXT FROM @cursor INTO @c_itemId, @c_sortOrderId

--fetch_status = 0 says that the fetch went fine
WHILE @@fetch_status = 0      --this means that the row was fetched cleanly
    BEGIN
        --update the table to the new value of the sort order
        UPDATE dbo.item
        SET sortOrderId = @currentSortOrderId
        WHERE itemId = @c_itemId

        --increment the sort order counter to add 100 items of space
        SET @currentSortOrderId = @currentSortOrderId + 100

        --get the next row
        FETCH NEXT FROM @cursor INTO @c_itemId, @c_sortOrderId
    END
```

Because you added the line to output the keys of every row, you get the following output:

c_itemId c_sort	OrderId current	SortOrderId
4	29	1
2	35	101
1	71	201
3	72	301
5	81	401

Next you look at the values in the table:

```
SELECT *
FROM dbo.item
ORDER BY sortOrderId
```

If everything went well, the rows are output in the same order as shown here:

```
itemId sort    OrderId
------------------------------
4              1
2              101
1              201
3              301
5              401
```

As an example of why to be careful with your cursor types, what if you change to a DYNAMIC cursor type, like the FAST_FORWARD cursor? If you change the FORWARD_ONLY STATIC part of the cursor declaration to FAST_FORWARD, you'll get results like the following:

```
c_itemId c_sort    OrderId current     SortOrderId
--------------------------------------------------------------
4                  29                  1
2                  35                  101
1                  71                  201
3                  72                  301
5                  81                  401
2                  101                 501
1                  201                 601
3                  301                 701
5                  401                 801
2                  501                 901
```

The reason for this is that the values in the cursor *change*, and end up reordered by the sort order. Because the sort order is changed to more than the next value of sort order, you'll never get to the end.

> **Always specify the type of cursor desired because unpredictable results may occur otherwise.**

NULL Handling

In Chapter 10, I discussed implementing optional values by setting columns to allow storing null values. In this section, we need to shed light on programming with NULLs and, especially, how NULL comparisons are handled in SQL Server and what this means to coding.

NULLs can be tricky to work with, and it's hard to avoid having them in the database. This may seem a bold statement. Could you not set every column in the database to NOT NULL? Yes, but any time you use an outer join in a statement, the values that aren't returned will all be filled with NULLs.

Now you'll examine a slightly different way of looking at what "NULL" refers to when used in a logical expression (I'm indebted to Dr. David Rozenshtein for introducing me to this concept). You'll see some of the more interesting and most overlooked problems that arise when dealing with NULL data.

What does NULL mean? According to SQL Server 2000 Books Online, "[a] value of NULL indicates the value is unknown. A value of NULL is different from an empty or zero value. No two NULL values are equal. Comparisons between two NULL values, or between a NULL and any other value, return unknown because the value of each NULL is unknown."

So it's fairly clear that NULL means unknown. And this meaning serves you well in the case of a column being left NULL, and even in the case of a join, where the match of one set to another is unknown. However, when programming using three-value logic (true, false, and NULL) you have to be a bit craftier than that.

The problem is a fairly simple one to demonstrate. Consider the following statement:

```
SELECT CASE WHEN NOT(1=NULL) THEN 'True' ELSE 'False' END
```

It's obvious that (1=1) gives True and (1=0) gives False. What about (1=NULL)? I believe that False is the logical answer. And, obviously, NOT(False)=True. Yet executing this query returns a different value, as follows:

```
--------
False
```

Well, OK then: if NOT(1=NULL) is False, then NOT(NOT(1=NULL)) must be True, right? So you execute the following:

```
SELECT CASE WHEN NOT(NOT(1=NULL)) THEN 'True' ELSE 'False' END
```

This returns False again!

This fundamental property of three-valued logic is one of the least understood principles in SQL Server programming.

The problem lies with the definition of NULL as unknown. Logically speaking, what is the opposite of unknown? Known. So, consider that you replace (1=NULL) with Unknown because, logically, if NULL is Unknown then it's still Unknown if it's equivalent to 1. Therefore, NOT(1=NULL) must be NOT(Unknown). And this equals Known, right? Perhaps in an English lesson, but not in three-valued logic.

Maybe

What if you use Maybe instead of Unknown? So, (1=NULL) is Maybe. And the opposite of Maybe? Maybe.

Consider the following truth tables (it just wouldn't be a computer book without at least one truth table, but no worries, there are more than one!):

AND	True	False	OR	True	False
True	True	False	True	True	True
False	False	False	False	True	False

Taking a look at a few examples from this table, you see that True AND True=True and True AND False=False.

Next, you look at the standard truth tables including NULL. These tables come from SQL Server 2000 Books Online, but have Unknown replaced with my Maybe:

AND	True	False	Null	OR	True	False	Null
True	True	False	Maybe	True	True	True	True
False	False	False	Maybe	False	True	False	Maybe
Null	Maybe	Maybe	Maybe	Null	True	Maybe	Maybe

So you see that, while True AND NULL=Maybe, True OR NULL=True.

The other interesting comparison is (NULL=NULL). It sure looks like True, but how can two unknown values be equal? They aren't—the result is Maybe.

Here are the NOT AND and NOT OR truth tables:

NOT AND	True	False	Null	NOT OR	True	False	Null
True	False	True	Maybe	True	False	False	False
False	True	True	Maybe	False	False	True	Maybe
Null	Maybe	Maybe	Maybe	Null	False	Maybe	Maybe

It's important to test these last two tables using (1=1) is True, (1=0) is False, and (1=NULL) is Maybe, for example:

```
SELECT CASE WHEN (NOT((1=1) OR (1=NULL)) AND (1=1))
            THEN 'True'
            ELSE 'False'
       END
```

You take each logical expression and evaluate it as follows:

```
(NOT(True OR Maybe) AND True) = NOT(True AND True) = NOT(True) = False
```

which you see by executing the following statement:

```
---------
False
```

An underlying issue in understanding some ugly logic errors in SQL Server programming is getting to grips with the fact that SQL Server evaluates the statement using the proper three-valued logic but, in the final analysis, treats the NULL value as False. However, because a great number of the most important queries you'll write will include many search criteria, it's important to understand that the NULL value is kept as a NULL until the very end.

Consider that you're looking at a WHERE clause for a given row, trying to figure out why it isn't returning a value when you expect one:

```
WHERE NOT ((column1=@column1) OR (column2=@column2))
```

In the following line, I've replaced all of the column and variable values in the code with the data that is being compared:

```
WHERE NOT ((1=1) OR (NULL=NULL))
```

So you end up with NOT(True OR Maybe)=NOT(True)=False. This seems fairly reasonable. However, let's change the values just slightly:

```
WHERE NOT ((2=1) OR (NULL=NULL))
```

Now you have NOT(False OR Maybe)=NOT(Maybe)=Maybe.

> Note that when SQL Server ends a comparison with the Maybe value, it treats it as a False at that point.

Presumably it's safer to work in this pessimistic way, because a Maybe could well be false.

> *While the ANSI standard for the comparison is that* (NULL=NULL) *evaluates to* NULL, *SQL Server 6.5 and earlier versions assumed that* (NULL=NULL)=True. *There is a setting in SQL Server 2000* (SET ANSI_NULLS) *that allows this to be toggled so that you can make* (NULL=NULL)=True. *However, using this setting isn't recommended unless you have backward-compatibility issues. It tends to cause more trouble than it solves and the setting will likely not exist much longer.*

Problems with comparing data that includes NULLs are very common, and can only be combated by being extremely careful with NULL usage. You must be sure to understand the following:

❑   (NULL = 3) has a value of Maybe

❑   (NULL > 3) also has a value of Maybe

And the example of where it will bite you: NOT(column1=3), where column1 is NULL, will evaluate to NOT(Maybe)=Maybe. SQL Server finally evaluates this to False.

IS NULL

The only comparison that works all of the time with NULLs is the IS NULL operator. You can discover which values are NULL by using the following:

```
WHERE column1 IS NULL
```

This will return True if the column is NULL, or False if it's not. There is also an IS NOT NULL operator that does the logical opposite of the IS NULL operator. Using these two operators, you can formulate proper comparisons with two values that are NULL. For example, if you want to determine whether two nullable values are "equal," that is, they have the same value or both are NULL, you would need the following three-part comparison:

```
WHERE column1 = @column1
  OR (column1 IS NULL
  AND column2 IS NULL)
```

This may seem pretty obvious but, of all the logical coding bugs I find and contribute to, by far the most pervasive are those involving transformations with a column that requires NULLs.

Suppose that I have a view from which I'm building the transformation, and a child row of one of the tables–giving a person's address–isn't available. However, not all people have an office address, so you have to use an outer join.

```
CREATE VIEW v_person
AS
SELECT person.personId, person.lastName
       address.streetName
FROM dbo.person AS person
LEFT OUTER JOIN dbo.personAddress AS personAddress
   JOIN dbo.address as address
      ON address.addressId = personAddress.addressId
      AND personAddress.type = 1                        --office address
   ON person.personId = personAddress.personId
```

385

Now a transformation query is built to insert any rows where the `personId` doesn't exist in the table. This is pretty easy to deal with. Next you code the following UPDATE statement to change the values for a person if any have altered:

```
UPDATE person
SET person.lastName = v_person.lastName,
    person.streetName = v_person.streetName,
    person.streetName = v_person.streetName
FROM ODS..person AS person
JOIN dbo.v_person AS v_person
    ON person.personId = v_person.personId
WHERE person.lastName <> v_person.lastName
        OR person.firstName <> v_person.firstName
        OR person.streetName <> v_person.streetName
```

This looks pretty much correct, yet there is a gaping hole in there. Even assuming that all columns in your base tables don't allow NULLs, a left outer join exists in your view. `streetName` can be NULL. If the `personAddress` row doesn't exist, circumstances could arise where `v_person.streetName` is NULL but, if `person.streetName` isn't NULL, this still evaluates to a `False` condition. Substituting real data into the following:

```
WHERE person.lastName <> v_person.lastName
        OR person.streetName <> v_person.streetName
```

you would get the following:

```
WHERE 'Davidson' <> 'Davidson'
        OR 'Worthdale' <> NULL
```

Looking back at the truth tables, this evaluates to (`False or Maybe`)=`Maybe`. And in the final analysis, SQL Server evaluates this to `False`! It's very easy to do this, so the query will need to be written as follows:

```
WHERE person.lastName <> v_person.lastName
        OR  person.firstName <> v_person.firstName
        OR (person.streetName <> v_person.streetName
        OR (person.streetName IS NULL AND person.streetName IS NOT NULL )
        OR (person.streetName IS NOT NULL AND person.streetName IS NULL ) )
```

This code is painful to write, but it's the only way you can effectively deal with comparisons to NULL.

NULLs In Other Operations

The last point to be made about NULLs concerns their use in other operations. When dealing with a NULL in a situation other than a logical comparison, it's best to consider it as Unknown. NULL doesn't mean, nor should it ever mean, "Nothing" (Where Nothing=Nothing, Null <> NULL). NULL is something, so it must be treated as such, though its identity is unknown. Consider the following issues:

❑ **Numerical calculations:** NULL + 10 evaluates to Unknown because, if you don't know how many you start with, then no matter what you add to it you still don't know what you have (Unfortunately, 0 * NULL = NULL)

❏ **String concatenations:** `'*' + NULL + '*'` also evaluates to Unknown, because there is no way of knowing what the string should actually be

❏ **NULL + NULL:** Obvious really, two Unknowns cannot possibly produce anything other than Unknown

Hence, when dealing with an operation where one or more factors could well be NULL, you'll frequently need to use one of several mechanisms that SQL Server provides–the keyword CASE, and the functions ISNULL and COALESCE.

For example, to perform the following concatenation:

```
SELECT '*' + @column + '*'
```

where @column may be NULL, and you wish to receive a non-NULL result if the @column is NULL, you can take the following three paths:

```
SELECT CASE @column
    WHEN NULL THEN ''
    ELSE @column
END
```

or

```
SELECT ISNULL(@column,'')
```

or

```
SELECT COALESCE(@column,'')
```

Each of these has different merits:

❏ **CASE:** The use of CASE here is pretty self-explanatory. It's a very powerful tool that goes far beyond simple NULL validations.

❏ **ISNULL:** Has two parameters. It checks to see if the first is NULL and then returns the second (in the case above, an empty string) if it is. If the second parameter is NULL, NULL is still returned.

❏ **COALESCE:** Allows you to supply multiple parameters and it chooses the first non-NULL value. For example, `COALESCE(@column, @variable, @variable2 + '*', '')` would first check @column, then @variable, and so on. This is the equivalent to a CASE statement that does the following:

```
SELECT CASE WHEN @column IS NOT NULL THEN @column
            WHEN @variable IS NOT NULL THEN @variable
            WHEN @variable2 + '*' IS NOT NULL THEN @variable2 + '*'
            ELSE ''
END
```

Hopefully, this section has highlighted some of the problems you'll need to keep in mind when programming with NULLs. They can be troublesome to implement, but there is no way to avoid having to deal with them.

Views

As discussed in Chapter 3, views can be thought of as virtual tables and have most of the characteristics of a normal database table. As far as your SQL statements are concerned, they *are* tables, and while they do support modification statements in very specific circumstances (only one table at a time, or by using an instead-of trigger). Usually you wouldn't really want to use views for modification purposes because they're meant to simplify your viewing of data.

> *Views aren't precompiled objects like stored procedures, but are simply implemented as text that can be inserted into a query where needed, just as you insert a derived query into a statement.*

There are a few general cases in which views will be employed in your database:

❑   **To encapsulate implementation details:** They can be used to hide a large number of joins from the user.

❑   **As a real-time reporting tool:** They can be used to implement reports that touch your live data and don't affect performance, by specifying a set of known queries that users frequently employ.

❑   **As security mechanisms:** By giving access to a view and not the base table, you can implement row-based or column-based security.

You'll look at these situations now.

Views as an Encapsulation Device

Views are excellent encapsulation devices. You can take your highly normalized tables, join them back to the other tables in your database, and give your users data presented as they expect it to be, hiding from them the underlying database and the complexities of the actual mechanism by which the data was accessed. Views can also screen out all the unwanted data, enabling the user to focus on what is really important.

Suppose that you have the following two tables in a sales database. The item table represents items that are for sale, and a sale table indicates the number of items sold:

```
--items that you sell
CREATE TABLE item
(
    itemId int NOT NULL IDENTITY,
    name varchar(60) NOT NULL,
    price money
)

--records sales
CREATE TABLE sale
(
    saleId int NOT NULL IDENTITY,
    itemId int NOT NULL,          --foreign key to the item table
    date datetime NOT NULL,
    itemCount int NOT NULL        --number of items sold
)
```

You might wish to build a view to encapsulate the item and the sales information into a single table for the user to view.

```
CREATE VIEW v_sale
AS
SELECT sale.saleId, sale.itemId, sale.date, sale.itemCount,
       item.name, item.price
FROM dbo.sale AS sale
JOIN dbo.item AS item
    ON sale.itemId = item.itemId
```

Now, whenever the user needs to look at a sale, the view will save them from having to manually join in the item table. This is a pretty simple example, but when ten or more tables are included in a view, the time savings in coding can be pretty great. Plus, if the tables' columns change–or you do further normalization and, instead of storing the price in the item table, you store a reference to a separate price table where the value is stored–the user of the view never has to know about it.

Views in Real-Time Reporting

Real-time reporting is a term that indicates that a report can have no latency, that is, its data is continually updated. If you want immediate, up-to-the-second reports, one way to implement this is with a view. A view offers you a couple of benefits over writing a query directly against the tables, as with typical report-writing code:

❑   **Views prevent ad hoc report queries of base tables**: Ad hoc querying against live tables can produce big performance hits. By building a view or views, you can attempt to channel any real-time querying needs into using a set of queries that have been optimized, tested, and have a smaller chance of affecting overall system performance.

389

❑ **Views can be used to avoid locking**: You can usually build reports in such a way that they will ignore locks in the database and, more importantly, don't *leave* locks in the database either. This is achieved by using the `readuncommitted` (or `nolock`) optimizer hint. This hint should only be used when estimated data is acceptable because some of the rows it reads may be in a transaction that could be rolled back. This way, no matter what the user tries to do with the view, it will not lock any resources.

Going back to your tables, let's say the user needs to see up-to-the-minute sales figures on an hourly basis. You discover from the user that you can ignore those instances where a sale is recorded but might be removed later. So, you might create the following view for the user to build queries with:

```
CREATE VIEW v_saleHourlyReport
AS
SELECT item.itemId, dbo.date$removeTime(sale.date) AS saleDate,
       datePart(hour,sale.date) AS saleHour,
       sum(sale.itemCount) AS totalSold,
       sum(sale.itemCount * item.price) AS soldValue
FROM dbo.item as item (readuncommitted)
JOIN dbo.sale as sale(readuncommitted)
   ON sale.itemId = item.itemId
--group by item ID information, then the day and the hour of the day, to
--give what was asked
GROUP BY item.itemId, item.name, dbo.date$removeTime(sale.date),
         datePart(hour,sale.date)
```

Note that here you're using the `datePart` system function for extracting the hour from the date, and a function you created in Chapter 11 to remove the time from the date.

Now this query can be executed repeatedly with less effect on ongoing processes, because you've removed the chances of the data holding read locks as it's used (with the `readuncommitted` statements).

Of course, these measures are only as good as the tools that are built to use them. Even without locking, it's possible to use vast system resources if a view is joined to other views in an unfavorable manner.

Views as Security Mechanisms

There are two properties of views that you'll make use of to build a more secure database. The first is assigning privileges to a user so that she can use a view, though not the underlying tables. For example, consider that you have a `person` table as follows:

```
CREATE TABLE person
(
    personId int IDENTITY,
    firstName varchar(20) ,
    lastName varchar(40)
)
```

You could construct a view on this:

```
CREATE VIEW vPerson
AS
SELECT personId, firstName, lastName
FROM dbo.person
```

Selecting data from either of these returns the exact same data. However, they're two separate structures that you can separately assign access privileges to.

The second property of views that is useful as a security mechanism is the ability to partition a table structure, by limiting the rows or columns visible to the user. Suppose you have the following table structure:

	Column1	Column2	...	ColumnN
Row1	Secretary1's salary	Secretary1's SSN		Secretary1's address
Row2	Manager1's salary	Manager1's SSN		Manager1's address
...				
RowN	CEO's salary	CEO's SSN		CEO's address

Views let you cut the table in sections that include all columns, but not all the rows, based on some criteria. This is **row-level security**, or **horizontally partitioning** your data. In this example, you might only allow Secretary1 to see Row1, while the rest of the rows don't even appear to exist:

	Column1	Column2	...	ColumnN
Row1	Secretary1's salary	Secretary1's SSN		Secretary1's address

Hence, by giving the view access to this row only, any user who has privileges for the view will only have rights to see this particular row.

Returning to your code example, you'll take the previous view you created and use it as the basis for a very specific view—one that would only be of interest to the manager of the product with an itemId of 1. This will allow the manager to monitor the level of sales for this product over the course of a day:

```
CREATE VIEW v_saleHourlyReport_socksOnly
AS
SELECT itemId, saleDate, saleHour, totalSold, soldValue
FROM dbo.v_saleHourlyReport
WHERE itemId = 1
```

You would typically implement a far more comprehensive security plan than hard-coding an itemId in a view, but this is to give a quick example of row-level security. You'll look at such a plan later in the chapter.

Alternatively, you could use **column-level security**. Unsurprisingly, this is also known as **vertically partitioning** the data because you'll be dividing the view's columns. In the `item` table you have three columns, `itemId`, `name`, and `price`. It wouldn't be abnormal to allow every user of the database to see all of the items with their names, but price might be a different story altogether. Hence, you might put together a view like this:

```
CREATE VIEW v_itemNoPrice
AS
SELECT itemId, name
FROM dbo.item
```

Of course, there is no reason why you cannot horizontally and vertically partition your tables at the same time, giving the user as small an amount of data as need be:

	Column1
Row1	

Once you've built the necessary views, you wouldn't allow access to the base table, but would give users who need to see the data access to the views instead. A more advanced discussion on security is included in the latter part of this chapter.

Powerful View Features

There are two very powerful extensions to views in SQL Server 2000 that bear looking at. These features are as follows:

❑   View indexing

❑   Partitioning views

Both of these features will be examined in some detail next.

Indexed Views

By indexing a view, you now have the ability to build triggerless summary data, which is automatically maintained by SQL Server in a way that makes a usually tricky operation as simple as writing a query. Instead of the view definition being used as in ordinary views, the Query Optimizer can choose to use the index, which has the current values for the index prematerialized.

So, instead of building triggers that summarize your data in other tables, you could create a view. For example, going back to your `item` and `sale` tables, you could create the following view. Note that only schema-bound views may be indexed. This makes certain that the tables and structures that the index is created upon will not change underneath the view.

```
CREATE VIEW v_itemSale
WITH SCHEMABINDING
AS
SELECT item.itemId, item.name, sum(sale.itemCount) AS soldCount PRIMARY KEY,
sum(sale.itemCount * item.price) AS soldValue
FROM dbo.item
JOIN dbo.sale
ON item.itemId = sale.itemId
GROUP BY item.itemId, item.name
```

This would do the calculations at execution time. If this weren't fast enough, or if it used too many resources to execute, you might add an index on the view like this:

```
CREATE INDEX XV_itemSale_materialize
ON v_itemSale (itemId, name, soldCount, soldValue)
```

SQL Server would then build the view and store it. Now your queries to the view will be *very* fast. However, though you've avoided all of the coding issues involved with storing summary data, you have to keep your data up-to-date. Every time data changes in the underlying tables, the index on the view will change its data, so there is a performance hit due to maintaining the index for the view. Hence, indexing views means that performance is great for reading but not necessarily for updating.

There are some other caveats too. The restrictions on what can be used in a view, prior to it being indexed, are fairly tight. The most important things that cannot be done are as follows:

❑ Use the SELECT * syntax—columns must be explicitly stated

❑ Use UNION in the view

❑ Use any subqueries

❑ Use any outer joins or recursively join back to the same table

❑ Specify the TOP keyword

❑ Use DISTINCT

❑ Include a Sum( ) function, if it references more than one column

❑ Use almost any aggregate function against a nullable expression

❑ Reference any other views

❑ Reference any nondeterministic functions

And this isn't all! There are several pages of requirements that must be met, documented in SQL Server Books Online in the "Creating an Indexed View" section, but these are the most significant ones that you'll need to consider before using indexed views.

While this may all seem pretty restrictive, there are good reasons for all of these rules. For you to maintain the indexed view is analogous to you writing your own denormalized data-maintenance functions. The more complex the query is to build the denormalized data, the greater the complexity in maintaining it. I'm speculating, but it's likely that these rules will become more lenient in later versions of SQL Server.

Distributed Partitioned Views

A distributed partitioned view is basically like any other view, in that it represents data spread across several tables. However, these tables may exist on completely different SQL Servers. This process is known as **federation**. Here, you're referring to a group of servers that are independently administered, but that share the processing load of a system. This can bring incredible performance improvements by boosting the parallel I/O from the system.

Because we're primarily interested in the design aspects of such a view, we'll look at the steps for building the schema:

❑ Take a table and create several replicas of it

❑ Partition the data along some value (month, type, and so on) into these tables, and apply a check constraint to enforce the partition

❑ Finally, define a view that uses UNION ALL (with no duplicate removal and no sort criterion) to combine the replica tables into a single resultset

For example, take your sale table. Say you have just two items—ItemA with itemId = 1, and ItemB with itemId = 2. You might then define the following tables:

```
CREATE TABLE sale_itemA
(
    saleId int NOT NULL,
    itemId int NOT NULL
    CONSTRAINT chk$sale_itemA$itemId$One CHECK (itemId = 1)
    itemCount int NOT NULL,
)
CREATE TABLE sale_itemB
(
    saleId int NOT NULL,
    itemId int NOT NULL
    CONSTRAINT chk$sale_itemA$itemId$One CHECK (itemId = 2)
    itemCount int NOT NULL
)
```

Next, you create a view that references these two new tables:

```
CREATE VIEW v_sale
AS
SELECT saleId, itemId, itemCount
FROM dbo.sale_itemA

UNION ALL -- no sort or duplicate removal

SELECT saleId, itemId, itemCount
FROM dbo.sale_itemB
```

SQL Server is smart enough to automatically assign two processors, if available, to deal with queries of this view.

There is some performance cost associated with going outside a server to process a query, but, depending on how large the data set is, using federated partitioned views can create incredible performance gains. Obviously, you wouldn't use it to store a simple contact list, but when storing session information for half a million active Internet users at any time, it may very well pay to partition data across multiple servers.

Batches of SQL Code

A batch of SQL code is one or more SQL statements executed by the server as a group. We'll look at two different types of batches and the differences in how you must handle them. We'll consider the following:

❑   **Single-statement batches**: These contain only a single statement to the server

❑   **Multistatement batches**: Used to perform multiple operations in a way that a single statement, or even a single stored procedure, cannot easily do

Note that the concept of single- or multistatement batches has no meaning to SQL Server. It executes the whole batch, regardless of how many statements it contains, and returns whatever. You make the distinction because you must code differently for the two different cases.

> *One small point; in this section, you aren't dealing with database creation scripts, which are one-time operations. In contrast, you're discussing building an application to touch and modify data.*

Single-Statement Batches

A single-statement batch is a single SQL statement–usually an INSERT, UPDATE, DELETE, or SELECT statement, but it can be a stored procedure or a system function like a DBCC.

The only time you do *not* have to consider adding extra code to execute a batch is when you execute a single statement. Note, however, that you're very limited as to what you can do with these statements. You can send a SQL statement of any type, but it isn't possible to make more than one modification to the data. Hence, no prevalidation or manipulation of data is allowed, and error handling within the statement is effectively prohibited. For example, if you execute the following:

```
UPDATE customer
SET firstName = 'Andy'
WHERE customerId = 100
```

you cannot assume that this operation succeeded because there may have been an error. It's incumbent on the actual calling program to check the error status and handle the errors themselves. There is another concern, however. Does this row even exist? If not, the command will not update any rows. Many times I've seen statements (executed from VBScript in an ASP page) like this:

```
UPDATE customer
SET firstName = 'Andy'
WHERE customerId = 0
```

which weren't executed because a user had misspelled a variable name, or had forgotten to turn on Option Explicit, but *had* specified On Error Resume Next. What's more, if the database requires a manually maintained optimistic locking mechanism, unless it's remembered to pass in the timestamp, or whatever optimistic locking value has been chosen, *every time a row is modified*, the optimistic lock is valueless.

It's my suggestion that, if you're going to use batches of uncompiled code to do data modifications, then you should build a generic object to handle the modifications. Make sure as well that you get this object right, because experience has taught me that there are many ways to make a goofy mistake that is very hard to locate in your code.

Multistatement Batches

When discussing multistatement batches, you'll basically follow the same structure that you did in stored procedures. However, you must consider two topics that need a different treatment in this context:

❑   Transactions

❑   Handling errors

Transactions

As noted in the "Transactions" section at the beginning of the chapter, it's very important that, when you converse with SQL Server, you make certain that you never start a transaction from your client software without closing it in the same batch of statements.

Handling Errors

When you batch together multiple statements, you have to consider what to do in the case of failure. You have the RETURN statement when coding stored procedures, but RETURN doesn't work in a batch. When you decide that you're through with the batch and wish to quit, the way to deal with the situation is to set a variable and use it to conditionally execute blocks of code.

Suppose that you have statements that you want to execute, and you need to make sure that each of them runs prior to finishing. You put them in a transaction, but what if one fails?

```
begin transaction
<Statement1>
<Statement2>
<Statement3>
commit transaction
```

You can code around it as follows:

```
DECLARE @errornbr int,    -- holds error numbers after any statement
        @returnvalue int, -- holds return values from stored procedures
        @errorout bit     -- flag to tell later statements to execute or not
SET     @errorOut = 1
BEGIN TRANSACTION

<Statement1>
SET @errorNbr = @@error
IF @error <> 0 or @returnValue < 0
    BEGIN
        RAISERROR 50000 'Error executing <statement1>'
        SET @errorOut = 0
    END

IF @errorOut = 1
    BEGIN
        <Statement2>
        SET @errorNbr = @@error
        IF @error <> 0 or @returnValue < 0
        BEGIN
            RAISERROR 50000 'Error executing <statement2>'
            SET @errorOut = 0
        END
    END

IF @errorOut = 1
    BEGIN
        <StatementN>
        SET @errorNbr = @@error
        IF @error <> 0 OR @returnValue < 0
            BEGIN
                RAISERROR 50000 'Error executing <statement2>'
                SET @errorOut = 0
            END
    END
```

```
IF @errorOut <> 0
   BEGIN
      RAISERROR 50000 'Error executing batch'
      ROLLBACK TRANSACTION
   END
ELSE
   COMMIT TRANSACTION
```

> *Once again don't forget that if an error occurs in a trigger, the batch will come screeching to a halt and all of your exterior error handling will never be called. Coding all access in this manner is a good idea anyway because any constraint errors will not kill the batch.*

Whenever you want to send multiple statements from the client and need to have them all execute or fail, a scheme like this needs to be used. Note that I've included lots of seemingly redundant error messages for debugging purposes. Obviously, a message about the first error that causes the batch to go wrong is the most important to get to the user, translated into a readable form for them.

Note the different shading of sections of this batch. If you're simply batching together a set of statements, probably with no resultsets, it shouldn't be a problem to build a batching mechanism to add a set of statements to a queue and then build a script out of it. You might also add a bit of descriptive text to the error message, so that something like "Error executing <statement1>" becomes more along the lines of "Error deleting customer with customerId = 1234". When you go to execute this batch, the shaded parts are added to the ends, and you would add the error handlers after each statement.

Of course, this isn't the only way to build an error handler. I frequently use another technique. Instead of using this as follows:

```
IF @errorOut = 1
```

to build up scripts, I code a GOTO in the error handler:

```
<statement2>
SET @errorNbr = @@error
IF @error <> 0 OR @returnValue < 0
BEGIN
   RAISERROR 50000 'Error executing <statement2>'
   GOTO errorOut
END
```

and end the batch like this:

```
COMMIT TRANSACTION
GOTO endOfBatch
errorOut:
   RAISERROR 50000 'Error executing batch'
   ROLLBACK TRANSACTION

endOfBatch:
```

This is an acceptable solution, even though it makes use of the seemingly dreaded GOTO statement. The primary value of this method is the ability to simply append the error code to the end of each statement, but basically this was a bit of laziness on my part. The most important thing is that you keep your batches safe and you make sure that the transaction is closed. If it doesn't close, two really freaky things will occur:

❑ Whatever data is modified will be locked up tight, possibly causing other users to get blocked behind this transaction.

❑ Because the application doesn't know that it's hanging a transaction, any other commands you send will also be running under this same transaction.

Make certain to complete any batches sent to the server, or completely cancel them. If an error occurs in the middle of the batch, the batch waits for someone to handle the error before moving on. We'll discuss this further in "Error Handling" in the "Stored Procedures" section

Stored Procedures

Stored procedures are basically multistatement batches that are stored in the database. The major difference between stored procedures and batches lies in performance, with stored procedures being precompiled.

In this section, you won't look specifically at the syntax of stored procedures; rather, you'll look at some of the features of stored procedures that are of interest when implementing a database system and how to use them properly.

Stored procedures are very similar to user-defined functions, with a few important differences:

❑ Stored procedures return resultsets in a very loose manner, in that you don't have to declare what you'll be returning to the client, and you can return any number of resultsets

❑ Stored procedures may have multiple output parameters, whereas scalar functions may only have a single return value of any type and may not have output parameters

❑ Scalar functions can be used in scalar expressions, while stored procedures cannot

❑ Stored procedures allow you to alter the database (in the form of updates, changing settings, and so on), whereas functions may not change anything during execution

Each of these distinctions will dictate when you use stored procedures as opposed to functions, especially the last two. In the rest of this section, you'll look at the following:

❑ Returning values from stored procedures

❑ Error handling

❑ Using stored procedures for an encapsulation layer between your applications

❑   Using stored procedures as security mechanisms

❑   Using stored procedures to solve common problems

Regardless of the overall architecture, stored procedures are database features that every SQL programmer should use and use well. Writing efficient stored procedures takes a lot of skill and experience, so it's a good idea to experiment on dummy data and try out different construction methods.

Returning Values from Stored Procedures

There are three ways that stored procedures can communicate with the outside world:

❑   **Return values:** Used to return a status value

❑   **Output parameters:** Used to return single values through a parameter

❑   **Resultsets:** Used to return tables of information

Each of these has a very specific purpose that you'll explore in the following sections.

Return Values

Unlike with user-defined functions, the RETURN statement of a stored procedure can only return an integer value, which is usually used to indicate status. The following is a common suggestion for a return value protocol, with the meanings for each value:

Value	Meaning
> 0	Procedure succeeded, with some meaning that can be inferred from the procedure definition.
0	Procedure succeeded, but no extended information can be learned.
−1 to −99	Procedure failed with a system error. The meaning cannot be inferred, other than the fact that a system failure has occurred.
−100	General user-defined error has occurred that cannot be handled in Transact-SQL.
< −100	Specific user-defined error message, based on whatever is built into the stored procedure.

The reason for this protocol is fairly simple. If any error occurs in the stored procedure and needs to signal its caller, then a simple check for a negative return value shows there is a problem, and a nonnegative return value indicates success.

For example, let's build a simple procedure that returns an integer value passed to it, as follows:

```
CREATE PROCEDURE returnValue$test
(
      @returnThis int = 0
)
AS
RETURN @returnThis
```

The next stored procedure is set up to use the value from the first:

```
CREATE PROCEDURE caller$testreturnvalue
(
      @testValue int
)
AS

DECLARE @returnValue int
EXEC @returnValue = returnValue$test @testValue
SELECT @returnValue AS returnValue

IF @returnValue < 0 --negative is bad
    BEGIN
        SELECT 'An error has occurred: ' + CAST(@returnValue AS varchar(10))
AS status
    END
ELSE                  -- positive or zero is good
    BEGIN
        SELECT 'Call succeeded: ' + CAST(@returnValue AS varchar(10))
                       AS status
    END
GO
```

Executing this with a negative value:

```
EXEC caller$testreturnvalue -100
```

tells you that an error has occurred as shown here:

```
returnValue
----------------
-100

status
------------------------------------
An error has occurred: -100
```

Obviously, if you change the parameter to a nonnegative number, you get the message that no error occurred.

401

Output Parameters

Output parameters allow you to return a scalar value of any type to a calling procedure, and will allow the passing of the cursor datatype if needed.

The output parameter is the best way to return a scalar from one procedure to another, because it's considered bad practice to use the return value for this purpose, even if the value you're returning happens to be an integer. You can have as many output parameters as necessary. Use the following syntax:

```
DECLARE @variable int
EXEC storedProcedure @variable = @variable OUTPUT
```

Using output parameters can increase performance in T-SQL code when returning a single row, thereby avoiding the overhead of a resultset.

Resultsets

Returning resultsets to the client is as simple as including a SELECT statement in code:

```
CREATE PROCEDURE test$statement
AS

SELECT 'Hi' AS hiThere
SELECT 'Bye' AS byeThere
GO
```

Executing this stored procedure:

```
EXEC test$statement
```

will return the following two resultsets:

```
hiThere
-------------
Hi

byeThere
-------------
Bye
```

What's interesting (because this is a pretty simple example) is that there are several communications back and forth with SQL Server in this batch: one to send the statement, two to get rows, a couple more to tell the server you're finished with the resultset, and so on.

This seems very simple but bear in mind that, because stored procedures are precompiled batches of code, they must be self-contained. They shouldn't contain code that requires interaction with the client, whether human or another program. Stored procedures aren't transactions by themselves and, if a connection cuts midway through a stored procedure (like while you're fetching data from a resultset), the rest of the procedure will not complete or roll back. This is why output parameters and return values aren't available to the caller until *after* all resultsets have been retrieved or canceled, and the stored procedure is finished.

Error Handling

Error handling in SQL Server code is one of its weakest points. There is no error trapping in SQL Server. However, you can always determine if a statement has caused an error, and take appropriate action.

Consider, for example, this call to a nonexistent stored procedure:

```
EXEC dbo.doesntExist
```

This returns the following standard error message:

```
Server: Msg 2812, Level 16, State 62, Line 1
Could not find stored procedure 'dbo.doesntExist'.
```

If you look in the `master.dbo.sysmessages` table for error number 2812, you'll see the following:

```
SELECT error, description
FROM master.dbo.sysmessages
WHERE error = 2812
```

complete with all the static text needed to build the error message and a tag for holding the parameter values:

```
error    description
-------------------------------------------------------------
2812     Could not find stored procedure ' %.*ls'.
```

You can also create an error in code using the RAISERROR statement, which you've used before to send an error message to the client. RAISERROR is a very powerful and robust tool and you can do a lot more with it.

You can use the RAISERROR command to create your own messages and have them saved in the sysmessages table. It's important to mention how flexible RAISERROR is. It has built-in language support so, if you need to internationalize the database code, you can create versions of your messages in other languages. The appropriate message will be displayed according to the language setting of the user.

RAISERROR will do the following for you:

❑ Return an ad hoc message

❑ Return a message that you store in the master.dbo.sysmessages table with special formatting

❑ Return an error number (between 50000 and the maximum bigint value)

❑ Return a severity that tells you how bad the message is, from "informational" to "hardware corruption"

❑ Return a state value that indicates the source from which the error was issued

The simplest syntax for the RAISERROR command is as follows:

```
RAISERROR <error number> <message>
```

This allows you to specify an error number and some text describing the error. The message value can be a varchar value or the contents of a varchar variable, for example:

```
RAISERROR 911911911 'This is a test message'
```

will return the following:

```
Server: Msg 911911911, Level 16, State 1, Line 1
This is a test message
```

So, in your stored procedures, you can build a statement that tests whether the output parameter value is less than zero and, if so, raises an error:

```
CREATE PROCEDURE test$validateParm
(
    @parmValue int
) AS

IF @parmValue < 0
    BEGIN
        DECLARE @msg varchar(100)
        SET @msg = 'Invalid @parmValue: ' + CAST(@parmValue AS varchar(10)) +
                    '. Value must be non-negative.'
        RAISERROR 50000 @msg
        RETURN -100
    END
SELECT 'Test successful.'
RETURN 0
GO
```

Then, when you pass in a 0 to test it as follows:

```
dbo.test$validateParm 0
```

you get the following:

```
----------------------
```
Test successful.

If you pass in a negative number, you get this error:

Server: Msg 50000, Level 16, State 1, Procedure test$validateParm, Line 11
Invalid @parmValue: -1. Value must be non-negative.

The other place where it's helpful to include an error message is after an INSERT, UPDATE, or DELETE statement. The reason is the same. If an error occurs, you can pinpoint exactly which statement caused the failure. Say you have the following table:

```
CREATE TABLE test
(
    testId int IDENTITY,
    name varchar(60) NOT NULL
    CONSTRAINT AKtest_name UNIQUE
)
```

you build the following stored procedure to create new values:

```
CREATE PROCEDURE test$ins
(
    @name varchar(60)
) AS

INSERT INTO dbo.test(name)
VALUES(@name)
IF @@error <> 0
    BEGIN
        -- raise an error that tells the user what has just occurred.
        RAISERROR 50000 'Error inserting into test table'
    END
GO
```

and then you execute a statement:

```
EXEC dbo.test$ins @name = NULL
```

The result is as follows:

Server: Msg 515, Level 16, State 2, Procedure test$ins, Line 6
Cannot insert the value NULL into column 'name', table 'master.dbo.test'; column doesn't allow NULLs. INSERT fails.

Server: Msg 50000, Level 16, State 1, Procedure test$ins, Line 10
Error inserting into test table
The statement has been terminated.

405

This may seem to make the code messier because you have error handlers everywhere, but it's crucial to check the return code and error status after every modification statement or stored procedure call. If you do this, you can see what error occurred and you know exactly where. This is very helpful because there will be occasions when, instead of inserting one row into a single table once, you might be inserting many rows into the table from your client application, or you might be calling this stored procedure from another server. This sort of error handling will save debugging time.

There are two things that you can do to improve SQL Server's error reporting:

❏ Build an error message mapping database so you can map constraint messages to more meaningful custom messages

❏ Create an error message tag format to return extended messages to the client

Constraint Mapping

In this section, you'll look at a technique to map the errors raised by your constraints to more comprehensible messages, which can be a largely automated process. The standard SQL Server constraint messages aren't meant for end-user consumption. Consider the case in which you have tried to enter a NULL value into a column–in this case a name column in the test table.

Server: Msg 515, Level 16, State 2, Procedure test$ins, Line 6
Cannot insert the value NULL into column 'name', table 'database.dbo.test'; column doesn't allow NULLs. INSERT fails.

By parsing some of the basic information from this message (the error number–which tells you that it's a NULL violation–and the column and table from the message) as follows:

Server: **Msg 515**, Level 16, State 2, Procedure test$ins, Line 6
Cannot insert the value NULL into **column 'name', table 'database.dbo.test'**; column doesn't allow NULLs. INSERT fails.

you can produce the following error message, which is much better for the user:

You must enter a value for the name column in the test table.

Violations of non-NULL constraints are fairly simple to identify and report, but what about others? Consider check constraints. Imagine you add a check constraint to the test table to prevent Bob from accessing it as follows:

```
ALTER TABLE dbo.test
ADD CONSTRAINT chkTest$name$string$notEqualToBob
CHECK (name <> 'Bob')
```

If a user now tries to enter Bob's name

```
INSERT INTO dbo.test (name)
VALUES ('Bob')
```

the result is this standard SQL Server error message:

Server: Msg 547, Level 16, State 1, Line 1
INSERT statement conflicted with COLUMN CHECK constraint
'chkTest$name$string$notEqualToBob'. The conflict occurred in database 'master', table 'test',
column 'name'.
The statement has been terminated.

In this case, you should prefer a custom message to be returned, if a user called Bob attempts to access the table. The standard error message is sketchy because you only get back the error definition, but you can use this as the basis of a custom message. To do this, you make use of the new extended properties that you discussed in Chapter 10.

In this case, you'll create a property for the constraint that declares the message that you want violating users to see:

```
EXEC sp_addextendedproperty @name = 'ErrorMessage',
       @value = 'You may not access the test table',
       @level0type = 'User', @level0name = 'dbo',
       @level1type = 'table', @level1name = 'test',
       @level2type = 'constraint', @level2name =
              'chkTest$name$string$notEqualToBob'
```

Once the extended property has been put into the database, SQL Server outputs the message as normal when the error arises. The client machine intercepts it, pulls out the constraint name, and queries the extended property to get the custom message, which is then sent to the client.

```
SELECT value AS message
FROM ::FN_LISTEXTENDEDPROPERTY('ErrorMessage', 'User', 'dbo', 'table', 'test',
              'constraint', 'chkTest$name$string$notEqualToBob')
```

So the user will see this new message:

message

You may not access the test table

This model can be extended to make it much more flexible by automatically setting each of the possible constraints up with messages. Then you can map each message to a real message for the client. There's one thing you should know: I generally prefer to have a method on the client to see the standard SQL Server error message, so that I can see what really happened (for example, an additional information button on the message dialog box).

This method does cost another round-trip to the server. A front-end object could be coded so that when you're developing your applications you go to the server to process the error messages, but when you come to the release version of the software, you can roll up the error messages into a DLL that is distributed for faster access.

Tagging Error Messages

Once you've mapped the messages that SQL Server sends to you, it's important to make sure that the messages that you send back to the client are as useful as possible.

When building ad hoc messages, you're very limited as to what you can return in a message. I add an encoded tag to the end of the message:

```
'message text' +
                '<tagName1=tagValue1;tagName2=tagValue2;...;
    tagNameN=tagValueN>'
```

Here, each tag indicates a value that may be important to the client software:

obj	The object that raised the error (P=procedure, TR=trigger, and so on).
type	The type of object that raised the error.
call	Previous call or action that caused the error.
col	Column values that required the error to be raised.
key	The key values of the row with the problem. This could be used if an entire batch of stored procedure calls were sent to SQL Server and you need to differentiate between them.
action	Specific action that the caller should take to repair the problem.
severity	Severity, like "warning," "severe," and so on.
occurrence	Number of times that an execution of the same type might have taken place.

In your examples, you'll be using the obj, type, *and* action *tags for simplicity.*

For example, in the block in each stored procedure where you declare your variables (such as variables to hold row counts, messages, and so on), you have the following:

```
--used to hold the first part of the message header
DECLARE @msgTag varchar(255)
--preset the message tag with the name of the object and its type
SET @msgTag = '<obj=' + object_name(@@procid) + ';type=P;'
```

Then, whenever you need to raise an error, you make a call like the following:

```
SET @msg = 'Ad hoc message' + @msgTag + ';action=(insert test)>'
RAISERROR 50000 @msg
```

and this returns a message like this:

Server: Msg 50000, Level 16, State 1, Line 5
Ad hoc message<obj=test$ins;type=P;action=(insert test)>

This message makes it easier to find out exactly what was going on and where it occurred in the test$ins stored procedure. Stripping off the text between the < and > delimiters and parsing out each tag's value, to give a more readable message to the user, is simple as well. Now you can tell the client if your message is just a warning, or if it's more serious. This method has the advantage of not requiring any extra code.

Consider the following stored procedure. It simulates an error by setting the @error variable (that you typically would use to trap the @@error value) to a nonzero value:

```
CREATE PROCEDURE test$errorMessage
(
    @key_testId int
) AS

--declare variable used for error handling in blocks
DECLARE @error int,                --used to hold error value
        @msg varchar(255),         --used to preformat error messages
        @msgtag varchar(255)       --used to hold the tags for the error message

--set up the error message tag
SET @msgTag = '<' + object_name(@@procid) + ';type=P'
                  + ';keyvalue=' + '@key_routineId:'
                  + CONVERT(varchar(10),@key_testId)

--call to some stored procedure or modification statement on some table

--get the rowcount and error level for the error handling code
SELECT  @error = 100              --simulated error

IF @error != 0                    --an error occurred outside this procedure
    BEGIN
        SELECT @msg = 'A problem occurred calling the nonExistentProcedure. ' +
                    @msgTag + ';call=(procedure nonExistentProcedure)>'
        RAISERROR 50000 @msg
        RETURN -100
    END
```

This procedure is fairly long, yet all it does is raise an error! Unfortunately though, nearly all of this code (except the error tagging code) is generally required when you're calling other stored procedures or making changes to other tables. You need to check the return value and the value of @@error every step of the way. Executing this procedure as follows:

```
test$errorMessage @key_testId = 10
```

returns the following message:

```
Server: Msg 50000, Level 16, State 1, Procedure test$errorMessage, Line 23
A problem occurred calling the nonExistentProcedure.
<test$errorMessage;type=P;keyvalue=@key_routineId:10;call=(procedure nonExistentProcedure)>
```

This tells the support person a few things. First of all, there would probably have been an error raised before this message that told you what the real problem was. Second, the nonExistentProcedure was the source of the problem, it came from the test$errorMessage procedure, and the value of the @key_routineId parameter was 10.

Encapsulation

The encapsulation of SQL code from the user is one of the most important reasons for using stored procedures, which allow you to execute many commands with a single call to a stored procedure. This is fantastic for two reasons:

❏ **How an action takes place can change, as long as the action itself doesn't**: In other words, as long as the code you've written works, the actual implementation doesn't matter. In this way, you can performance-tune the inner workings of the stored procedure without having to change the interface that the external users see. You might even change all of the underlying table names and structures, yet the stored procedure will still have the same effect.

❏ **An interface can be built entirely by encapsulating SQL calls into stored procedures**: In this manner, the client programs would never embed any tricky calls in SQL to the database server; they would simply be able to use the stored procedures. This clarifies which operations can be performed because you can see the list of possible procedures.

I will try to demonstrate the first point with a quick example. Suppose you're asked to write a procedure that pulls the names of clients from the person table, and the following specifications have been provided:

❏ Name: person$get

❏ Parameters: @personId (int)

❏ Resultsets: a single resultset, containing a row from the person table comprising personId, firstName, and lastName, with personId filtered by the @personId parameter.

The following code might be produced as follows:

```
CREATE PROCEDURE person$get
(
    @personId int
) AS

SELECT personId, firstName, lastName
FROM person
WHERE personId = @personId
```

When just starting out in the SQL programming world, you might have produced the following, however (and don't think this is stretching it: I've seen this sort of thing from programmers tutored a different paradigm like Clipper or Foxpro where this type of operation was not only natural, but often faster than using SQL).

```
CREATE PROCEDURE person$get
(
    @personId int
) AS

CREATE TABLE #person
(
    personId int,
    firstName varchar(30),
    lastName varchar(30)
)

DECLARE @cursor cursor, @c_personId integer, @c_firstname varchar(30),
        @c_lastname varchar(30)

SET @cursor = cursor fast_forward for select personId, firstName, lastName
    FROM person

OPEN @cursor
FETCH NEXT FROM @cursor INTO @c_personId, @c_firstName, @c_lastName

WHILE @@fetch_status = 0
    BEGIN
        IF @personId = @c_personId
            BEGIN
                INSERT INTO #person
                VALUES (@c_personId, @c_firstName, @c_lastName)
            END
        FETCH NEXT FROM @cursor INTO @c_personId, @c_firstName, @c_lastName
    END
SELECT * FROM #person
```

While this code is riddled with bad SQL, it does exactly what is advertised; it looks for a person row with a matching personId and returns a single row. It will return the proper values and, if the amounts of data are small, its performance will be unnoticeable in a small set of data and will probably be used on the development server. However, because you encapsulated the call, it's easy to rewrite this code in the proper fashion shown initially. What's more, the client software using this stored procedure need not even notice that a change has been made.

The last point I want to make is that, when using stored procedures, you don't even need an actual table structure to start building applications. By using some form of code generation, you should be able to produce a set of methods (stored procedures) for your database that do nothing, but appear to the programmer as if they do enough to get started. Commonly called **dummy procedures**, they're often used to test the user interface before it's fully implemented.

In the previous example, you could have built the following dummy procedure to get the programmer started:

```
CREATE PROCEDURE person$get
(
    @personId int
) AS
SELECT 1 AS personId, 'Joe' AS firstName, 'Jones' AS lastName
```

While this procedure doesn't do anything, and though it just ignores the parameter, it will return a row that an application programmer can use to see if a screen works while proper code is written. What is important is that the public interface isn't violated.

Security

As with views, security in stored procedures is handled at the object level. Just because a user can use a stored procedure doesn't necessarily mean that he has to have rights to every object that the stored procedure refers to.

You can use stored procedures as your primary security mechanism by requiring that all access to the server be done through them. By building procedures that encapsulate all functionality, you can then apply permissions to the stored procedures to restrict what the user can do.

This allows you to have **situational control** on access to a table. This means that you might have two different procedures that functionally do exactly the same operation, but giving a user rights to one procedure doesn't imply that she has rights to the other. So, if a screen is built using one procedure, the user may be able to use it, but not when the screen uses the other procedure.

Having two procedures that do exactly the same operation may seem unrealistic, but it illustrates the fact that you can build objects that access the same tables, in different ways, and you can grant access independently of the underlying objects. You may have a summary procedure that gives a count of people whose names start with each letter of the alphabet, which a user may use, and a procedure that lists the very same names that he cannot use. A similar situation can be implemented with views, but with procedures, you can create, modify, and delete data as well as look at it. You'll look in more detail at using SQL Security to lock down access to your objects later in the chapter.

Transaction Count

The transaction count (denoted by @@trancount) tells you how many active transactions are currently open. When you employ transactions in your batches of code, you must be very careful to open and close them before the end of the batch, so you don't leave any locks that might affect other users.

In stored procedures, you have to be cognizant of the transaction count. Whatever the transaction count is when the procedure is started, it must be the same value when the procedure ends. This concept makes perfect sense, because any procedure that calls the procedure would have to make certain that a transaction had not been rolled back after every call to a stored procedure. It does however make coding transactions interesting in stored procedures. Take the following two procedures:

```
CREATE PROCEDURE tranTest$inner
AS
BEGIN TRANSACTION

--code finds an error, decides to rollback
ROLLBACK TRANSACTION
RETURN -100
GO
```

```
CREATE PROCEDURE tranTest$outer
AS
DECLARE @retValue int
BEGIN TRANSACTION

EXEC @retValue = tranTest$inner
IF @retValue < 0
    BEGIN
        ROLLBACK TRANSACTION
        RETURN @retValue
    END
COMMIT TRANSACTION
GO
```

To see what is happening, you'll consider the following call and slowly work through the execution. This can be a painful process, but in many cases it's the only way to completely understand the code.

```
EXEC tranTest$outer
```

413

Step	Procedure	Operation	Comment	Result
1	tranTest$outer	DECLARE @retValue INT	Sets up the variable to hold the return value from the procedure	@retvalue = NULL
2	tranTest$outer	BEGIN TRANSACTION	Starts a new transaction	@@trancount = 1
3	tranTest$outer	EXEC @retValue = tranTest$inner	Calls the tranTest$inner procedure	
4	tranTest$inner	BEGIN TRANSACTION	Starts a second transaction	@@trancount = 2
5	tranTest$inner	ROLLBACK TRANSACTION	Rolls back all transactions	@@trancount = 0
6	tranTest$inner	RETURN −100	Returns a negative value to the calling procedure to tell it something happened	ERROR: Transaction count has changed
7	testTran$outer		Upon returning, the value of @retValue is populated	@retValue = −100
8	testTran$outer	IF @retValue < 0	Conditional to determine if an error has occurred	
9	testTran$outer	ROLLBACK TRANSACTION	Rolls back all transactions	ERROR: @@trancount already zero

Because the transaction count changed between step 3 when you started the procedure and step 6 when you ended it, you would have received the following error message:

Server: Msg 266, Level 16, State 2, Procedure tranTest$inner, Line 6
Transaction count after EXECUTE indicates that a COMMIT or ROLLBACK TRANSACTION statement is missing. Previous count = 1, current count = 0.

Instead of using straight transactions, you'll begin a new transaction when you start the stored procedure, and then set a transaction save point. Note that you set a variable for the save point that is the procedure name plus the nest level, so it will be unique no matter how deeply you nest your procedure and trigger calls:

```
DECLARE @tranPoint sysname              --the datatype of identifiers
SET @tranPoint = object_name(@@procId) + CAST(@@nestlevel AS varchar(10))

BEGIN TRANSACTION
SAVE TRANSACTION @tranPoint
```

So you recode your procedures in the following manner:

```
CREATE PROCEDURE tranTest$inner
AS
DECLARE @tranPoint sysname                    --the datatype of identifiers
SET @tranPoint = object_name(@@procId) + CAST(@@nestlevel AS varchar(10))

BEGIN TRANSACTION
SAVE TRANSACTION @tranPoint

--again doesn't do anything for simplicity
ROLLBACK TRANSACTION @tranPoint
COMMIT TRANSACTION
RETURN -100
GO
```

```
CREATE PROCEDURE tranTest$outer
AS
DECLARE @retValue int
DECLARE @tranPoint sysname                    --the datatype of identifiers
SET @tranPoint = object_name(@@procId) + CAST(@@nestlevel AS varchar(10))

BEGIN TRANSACTION
SAVE TRANSACTION @tranPoint

EXEC @retValue = tranTest$inner
IF @retValue < 0
    BEGIN
        ROLLBACK TRANSACTION @tranPoint
        COMMIT TRANSACTION
        RETURN @retvalue
    END
COMMIT TRANSACTION
GO
```

Now you rerun your previous exercise, and step through the process again as follows:

```
EXEC tranTest$outer
```

Step	Procedure	Operation	Comment	Result
1	tranTest$outer	DECLARE @retValue int	Sets up the variable to hold the return value from the procedure	@retvalue = NULL
2	tranTest$outer	DECLARE @tranPoint sysname SET @tranPoint = object_name(@@procId) + CAST(@@nestlevel AS varchar(10))	Sets up a name for the transaction save point	@tranPoint = 'tranTest$outer1'

Table continues overleaf

415

Step	Procedure	Operation	Comment	Result
3	tranTest$outer	BEGIN TRANSACTION	Starts a new transaction	@@trancount = 1
4	tranTest$outer	SAVE TRANSACTION 'tranTest$outer1'	Saves the transaction, but doesn't change @@trancount	@@trancount = 1
5	tranTest$outer	EXEC @retValue = tranTest$inner	Calls the tranTest$inner procedure	
6	tranTest$inner	DECLARE @tranPoint sysname SET @tranPoint = object_name(@@procId) + CAST(@@nestlevel AS varchar(10))	Sets up a name for the transaction save point	@tranPoint = 'tranTest$inner2'
7	tranTest$inner	BEGIN TRANSACTION	Starts a second transaction	@@trancount = 2
8	tranTest$inner	SAVE TRANSACTION 'tranTest$inner2'	Saves the transaction, but doesn't change @@trancount	@@trancount = 2
9	tranTest$inner	ROLLBACK TRANSACTION 'tranTest$inner2'	Rolls back to the tranTest$inner2 save point	@@trancount = 2
10	tranTest$inner	COMMIT TRANSACTION	Commits the transaction and returns @@trancount back to the value when you started the procedure in step 5	@@trancount = 1
11	tranTest$inner	RETURN −100	Returns a negative value to the calling procedure to tell it something happened	
12	testTran$outer		Upon returning, the value of @retValue is populated	@retValue = −100
13	testTran$outer	IF @retValue < 0	Conditional to determine if an error has occurred	

Step	Procedure	Operation	Comment	Result
14	testTran$outer	ROLLBACK TRANSACTION 'tranTest$outer1'	Returns you back to your save point, no change to @@trancount	@@trancount = 1
15	testTran$outer	COMMIT TRANSACTION	Commits the final transaction	@@trancount = 0
16	testTran$outer	RETURN @retValue	Returns the return value of the inner call back to the caller	

This code helps prevent you from ever being out of the transaction protection–and, as a result, prevents you from possibly having invalid data saved after the transaction is rolled back–because, as you saw, the code in the second stored procedure didn't necessarily stop executing because of the transaction count error.

The code changes you've made really only apply to the inner stored procedure, in that the failure of the inner transaction must not bring down the outer transaction. Failure of the outer transaction isn't a problem because @@trancount would go to zero, which is where it started.

A positive side effect of all this is that you had the possibility to let the outer transaction occur. There are some cases in which you might want to allow part of a transaction to complete when part of it failed, and this gives you that flexibility.

Common Practices with Stored Procedures

The real purpose of this section is to give the basic building blocks of common stored procedures. You'll explore these procedures and discuss some of the pros and cons of each solution. Stored procedures are wonderful tools, though, because you'll see, on occasion you're forced to hammer a square peg into a round hole.

You'll build your objects to access the following table:

```
CREATE TABLE routine
(
    routineId int NOT NULL IDENTITY CONSTRAINT PKroutine PRIMARY KEY,
    name varchar(384) NOT NULL CONSTRAINT akroutine_name UNIQUE,
    description varchar(100) NOT NULL,
    ts_timestamp timestamp
)
```

To load some basic data into the table, you execute this script:

```
INSERT INTO routine (name, description)
SELECT specific_catalog + '.' + specific_schema + '.' + specific_name,
    routine_type + ' in the ' + specific_catalog + ' database created on ' +
    CAST(created AS varchar(20))
FROM <database>.information_schema.routines

SELECT count(*) FROM routine
```

Here you'll replace <database> with your database names. In this example you'll use Northwind, Master, and Pubs for a total of around 1000 rows. I'm executing these examples on a Pentium II 400 laptop with 256MB of RAM—a pretty out-of-date computer. This will give you a baseline for some basic testing of stored procedure performance because you look at possible ways to build stored procedures for your applications.

Retrieve

This code fills a list control in an application, and is a very common procedure in my applications. Each of the parameters is a filter to the list, so that the user can see the list in their own way. Here's the stored procedure:

```
CREATE PROCEDURE routine$list
(
    @routineId int = NULL,          --primary key to retrieve single row
    @name varchar(60) = ' %',        --like match on routine.name
    @description varchar(100) = ' %' --like match on routine.description
)

-- Description : gets routine rows for displaying in a list
--            :
-- Return Val : nonnegative:  success
--            : -1 to -99:  system generated return value on error
--            : -100:  generic procedure failure

AS

-- as the count messages have been known to be a problem for clients
SET NOCOUNT ON

-- default the @name parm to ' %' if the passed value is NULL
IF @name IS NULL SELECT @name = ' %'

-- default the @description parm to ' %' if the passed value is NULL
IF @description IS NULL SELECT @description = ' %'

--s elect all of the columns (less the timestamp) from the table for viewing.
SELECT routine.routineId AS routineId, routine.name AS name,
        routine.description AS description
FROM dbo.routine AS routine
WHERE (routine.routineId = @routineId
        OR @routineId IS NULL)
        AND (routine.name LIKE @name)
        AND (routine.description LIKE @description)
ORDER BY routine.name
RETURN
```

Though the stored procedure itself is pretty rudimentary, we need to discuss the WHERE clause. I'm checking all of the parameters against the set, regardless of which parameter the user is sending. SQL Server builds its plan based on the fact that some value is being passed in. So how does it perform? For average-sized tables, extremely fast. It isn't, however, the optimal solution to the problem.

To show this, you'll pull out the actual query from the stored procedure and execute it, wrapped with GETDATE() statements and turning SET STATISTICS IO on. This will allow you to check the performance of the code in a very straightforward way.

Note that this is just one of the performance tests to run on your code. Looking at the query plan in Query Analyzer is also a very good way to get an understanding of what is going on. I feel it makes it easier to follow an argument by looking at the amount of time, and how much I/O it takes to execute a statement.

Apart from timing the code, you'll measure the following:

❑ **Scan count**: The number of scans through the table that were required

❑ **Logical reads**: The number of pages read from the data cache

❑ **Physical reads**: The number of pages that were read from the physical disk

❑ **Read-ahead reads**: The number of pages placed into the cache

Taking the logical reads and the physical reads together is a good indicator of how the query is performing. For larger queries and busier systems, logical reads will become physical reads as cache contention increases.

```
SET STATISTICS IO ON
DBCC freeproccache     --clear cache to allow it to choose best plan

SELECT GETDATE() AS before

--run the procedure version
EXEC routine$list @routineId = 848

SELECT GETDATE() AS middle

--then run it again as an ad-hoc query
SELECT routine.routineId AS routineId, routine.name AS name,
       routine.description AS description
FROM dbo.routine AS routine
WHERE (routine.routineId = 848 OR 848 IS NULL)
      AND (routine.name LIKE ' %')
      AND (routine.description LIKE ' %')
ORDER BY routine.name

SELECT GETDATE() AS after
```

This code gives you the following results (I haven't shown the actual results from the query to save space):

```
before
------------------------------------------------
2001-01-17 20:41:16.300
```

Table 'routine'. Scan count 1, logical reads 12, physical reads 0, read-ahead reads 0.

```
middle
------------------------------------------------
2001-01-17 20:41:16.330
```

Table 'routine'. Scan count 1, logical reads 2, physical reads 0, read-ahead reads 0.

```
after
------------------------------------------------
2001-01-17 20:41:16.330
```

This tells you that executing the statement and retrieving the data took 0.03 seconds for the stored procedure, and less than 0.03 seconds for the ad hoc version (the datetime datatype's granularity is 0.03 seconds). Not an appreciable difference at all. Will this always be the case? No—as you'll see when you execute this same test, filtering on the description column (which isn't indexed):

```
SET STATISTICS IO ON
DBCC freeproccache        --clear cache to allow it to choose best plan

SELECT GETDATE() AS before

EXEC routine$list @description = 'procedure in the master named sp_helpsql %'

SELECT GETDATE() AS middle

SELECT routine.routineId AS routineId, routine.name AS name,
       routine.description AS description
FROM dbo.routine AS routine
WHERE (routine.routineId = NULL OR NULL IS NULL)
   AND (routine.name LIKE ' %')
   AND (routine.description LIKE 'procedure in the master named sp_helpsql %')
ORDER BY routine.name

SELECT GETDATE() AS after
```

After removing the actual rows returned from the results, this gives you the following:

```
before
------------------------------------------------
2001-01-17 21:13:49.550
```

Table 'routine'. Scan count 1, logical reads 2022, physical reads 0, read-ahead reads 0.

middle

2001-01-17 21:13:49.620

Table 'routine'. Scan count 1, logical reads 19, physical reads 0, read-ahead reads 0.

after

2001-01-17 21:13:49.640

Here you see that there isn't much difference between the times taken to execute the tests, 0.07 against 0.02 seconds. But this time the stored procedure attempt requires ten times the number of logical reads. Because logical reads come directly from memory, this makes almost no difference even on my slow machine. Depending on the number of users, the memory, the processor speed, and so on, these reads may not be logical reads; they may turn into physical reads, or at least partially physical reads.

There are a couple of stored procedure alternatives. You could do the following:

❏   Use the WITH RECOMPILE option in the stored procedure. This causes a new plan to be generated every time the query is executed. Building a plan takes time but because a poor plan will lead to real performance problems, this isn't a bad idea at all. Unless the procedure is called very frequently, the cost of compilation is usually quite small compared to the gain due to the better plan. Of course the actual amount of time to recompile any given procedure may or may not be an issue, depending on many of the same factors that were discussed when I discussed logical reads earlier, in addition to the complexity of SQL in the procedure.

❏   Build an IF THEN nest, with every possible parameter combination that the user may send in, and custom-build a query for each possibility. The main problem with this is that there are many (n! + 1) possible combinations of parameters.

❏   Pick out individual cases and build additional stored procedures to handle the slow ones. In your case with description, if this performance wasn't acceptable, a second stored procedure could be created that was faster. Then, before the SELECT statement, you break out into another stored procedure for the given case.

❏   Continue to implement using a stored procedure, but use a dynamic query. This solution will perform best, but when you execute code in a stored procedure, you lose the security benefits of stored procedures because the user then needs rights to run the dynamic query.

Let's demonstrate the dynamic query alternative. Here, you'll build up the text into varchar variables and then run the query using EXEC:

```
CREATE PROCEDURE routine$list
(
    @routineId int = NULL,          -- primary key to retrieve single row
    @name varchar(60) = '%',        -- like match on routine.name
    @description varchar(100) = '%' -- like match on routine.description
) AS

--as the count messages have been known to be a problem for clients
SET NOCOUNT ON

-- create a variable to hold the main query
DECLARE @query varchar(8000)
-- select all of the columns from the table for viewing
SET @query = 'SELECT routine.routineId AS routineId, routine.name AS name,
                    routine.description AS description
              FROM dbo.routine AS routine'

-- create a variable to hold the where clause, which you'll conditionally
-- build
DECLARE @where varchar(8000) SET @where = '' --because NULL + 'anything' =
-- NULL

-- add the name search to the where clause
IF @name <> ' %' AND @name IS NOT NULL
    SELECT @where = @where + CASE WHEN LEN(RTRIM(@where)) > 0
    THEN ' AND ' ELSE '' END + ' name LIKE ''' + @name + ''''

-- add the name search to the where clause
IF @description <> ' %' AND @description IS NOT NULL
    SELECT @where = @where + CASE WHEN LEN(RTRIM(@where)) > 0
    THEN ' AND ' ELSE '' END + ' name LIKE ''' + @description + ''''

-- select all of the columns from the table for viewing
IF @routineId IS NOT NULL
    SELECT @where = @where + CASE WHEN LEN(RTRIM(@where)) > 0
    THEN ' AND ' ELSE '' END +
    ' routineId = ' + CAST(@routineId AS varchar(10))

-- create a variable for the where clause
DECLARE @orderBy varchar(8000)
-- set the order by to return rows by name
SET    @orderBy = ' ORDER BY routine.name'

EXEC (@query + @where + @orderBy)
GO
```

This procedure will run optimally for any set of parameters that are passed in, but for such a simple query this is a lot of really hard-to-maintain code. Consider the fact that some basic stored procedures to retrieve a set of rows may have 20 lines or more of SQL, with quite a few different joins. Then you'll begin to understand why dynamically building the query in a stored procedure (or even from the client) is such a hard thing to do.

In my experience, a procedure is optimized if it runs within specifications and doesn't interfere with other processes. I tend to generate database code that is as generic as the example list procedure, and optimize when needed. Seldom will I need to optimize this particular query, but in those cases where it runs too slowly or is causing other processes to wait, one of the listed alternatives will always fix the problem.

In the next three sections, you'll look at stored procedures that create, modify, and destroy data. Though retrieving data gave you difficulties, these types of data modification are pretty much plain sailing.

Although users will frequently demand to look at a thousand rows of data, rarely will they want to update a thousand rows at a time. It does happen, and you can code these statements when necessary, but data modification is generally done by primary key. Nearly every OLTP form I've been connected with over the years has followed this pattern:

❑ Find a row from a list

❑ View the details of the row

❑ Modify the row, delete the row, or add a new row

❑ View the row after performing the action

❑ See the row in the list

In this section, you'll look at building basic stored procedures that create, modify, and destroy single rows. From there, it should be easy to extend the examples to modify multiple rows, simply by repeating parts of the code.

Create

The CREATE stored procedure:

```
CREATE PROCEDURE routine$ins
(
    @name varchar(384),
    @description varchar(500),
    @new_routineId int = NULL OUTPUT
) AS

-- declare variable used for error handling in blocks
DECLARE @rowcount int,        -- holds the rowcount returned from dml calls
    @error int,               -- used to hold the error code after a dml
    @msg varchar(255),        -- used to preformat error messages
    @retval int,              -- general purpose variable for retrieving
                              -- return values from stored procedure calls
    @tranName sysname,        -- used to hold the name of the transaction
    @msgTag varchar(255)      -- used to hold the tags for the error message
```

```
-- set up the error message tag
SET @msgTag = '<' + object_name(@@procid) + ';type=P'

-- default error handling code used for most procedures
-- generic tran name generation guarantees unique transaction name,
-- even if the procedure is called twice in a chain, because if one is active
-- and another gets called it cannot be at the same nest level
SET @tranName = object_name(@@procid) + CAST(@@nestlevel AS varchar(2))


- note that including this transaction isn't actually necessary because you only
-- have a single statement. I like to include this just as a precaution for
-- when the need arises to change the code.

BEGIN TRANSACTION           -- start a transaction
SAVE TRANSACTION @tranName -- save tran so you can roll back your action without
                           -- killing entire transaction

-- perform the insert
INSERT INTO routine(name,description)
VALUES (@name,@description)

-- check for an error
IF (@@ERROR!=0)
   BEGIN
   -- raise an additional error to help you see where the error occurred
   SELECT @msg = 'There was a problem inserting a new row into the ' +
      'routine table.'  + @msgTag + ';call=(insert routine)>'
   RAISERROR 50000 @msg
   ROLLBACK TRAN @tranName
   COMMIT TRAN
   RETURN -100
END

-- then retrieve the identity value from the row you created error
SET @new_routineId = scope_identity()

COMMIT TRANSACTION
GO
```

Now you test the code:

```
BEGIN TRANSACTION -- wrap test code in a transaction so you don't affect db
DECLARE @new_routineId int
EXEC routine$ins @name = 'Test',
   @description = 'Test', @new_routineId = @new_routineId OUTPUT
-- see what errors occur
SELECT NAME, DESCRIPTION FROM routine WHERE routineId = @new_routineId

--to cause duplication error

EXEC routine$ins @name = 'Test',
   @description = 'Test', @new_routineId = @new_routineId OUTPUT

ROLLBACK TRANSACTION -- no changes to db
```

This returns two things. First, a resultset that has the new row in it:

```
name                description
----------------------------------------------
Test                Test
```

Then a set of three distinct messages:

Server: Msg 2627, Level 14, State 2, Procedure routine$ins, Line 29
Violation of UNIQUE KEY constraint 'akroutine_name'. Cannot insert duplicate key in object 'routine'.

Server: Msg 50000, Level 16, State 1, Procedure routine$ins, Line 37
There was a problem inserting a new row into the routine table.<routine$ins;type=P;call=(insert routine)>

The statement has been terminated.

Your clients will need to translate the first message into something that the user can read. The second tells you what procedure was called and what it was trying to do, so you can debug.

However, note that where the selecting procedure had trouble in building a decent WHERE clause for the Query Optimizer, you're going to have to specify a fixed number of columns for the insert. This has a fairly annoying side effect of not allowing you to use the default values you've defined on your columns. This isn't usually a problem because, when user interaction is required, any defaults that the user might choose will be shown on the UI, and any that they cannot change will not have to be a part of the INSERT statement.

Modify

Modifying or updating data in the table is again a fairly simple task:

```
CREATE PROCEDURE routine$upd
(
    @key_routineId int, -- key column that you'll use as the key to the
                        -- update. Note that you cannot update the primary key
    @name varchar(384) ,
    @description varchar(500),
    @ts_timeStamp timestamp  --optimistic lock
)
AS

-- declare variable used for error handling in blocks
DECLARE @rowcount int,      -- holds the rowcount returned from dml calls
        @error int,         -- used to hold the error code after a dml
        @msg varchar(255),  -- used to preformat error messages
        @retval int,        -- general purpose variable for retrieving
                            -- return values from stored procedure calls
        @tranname sysname,  -- used to hold the name of the transaction
```

```
          @msgTag varchar(255) -- used to hold the tags for the error message

-- set up the error message tag

SET @msgTag = '<' + object_name(@@procid) + ';type=P'
                    + ';keyvalue=' + '@key_routineId:'
                    + CONVERT(varchar(10),@key_routineId)

SET @tranName = object_name(@@procid) + CAST(@@nestlevel AS varchar(2))

-- make sure that the user has passed in a timestamp value because it will
-- be very wasteful if they have not
IF @ts_timeStamp IS NULL
   BEGIN
   SET @msg = 'The timestamp value must not be NULL' + @msgTag + '>'
   RAISERROR 50000 @msg
   RETURN -100
END

BEGIN TRANSACTION
SAVE TRANSACTION @tranName

UPDATE routine
SET NAME = @name, description = @description
WHERE routineId = @key_routineId AND ts_timestamp = @ts_timeStamp

-- get the rowcount and error level for the error handling code
SELECT @rowcount = @@rowcount, @error = @@error

IF @error != 0   --an error occurred outside of this procedure
   BEGIN
      SELECT @msg = 'A problem occurred modifying the routine row.'   +
         @msgTag + ';call=(UPDATE routine)>'
      RAISERROR 50001 @msg
      ROLLBACK TRAN @tranName
      COMMIT TRAN
      RETURN -100
   END
ELSE IF @rowcount <> 1  -- this must not be the primary key
                        -- anymore or the row doesn't exist
   BEGIN
      IF (@rowcount = 0)
         BEGIN
            -- if the row exists without the timestamp,
            -- it has been modified by another user
            IF EXISTS ( SELECT *
               FROM routine
                  WHERE routineId = @key_routineId)
                  BEGIN
                     SELECT @msg = 'The routine row has been modified' +
                                   ' by another user.'
                  END
            ELSE
               BEGIN
                  SELECT @msg = 'The routine row doesn''t exist.'
               END
```

```
                    END
            ELSE
                BEGIN
                    SELECT @msg = 'Too many rows were modified.'
                END

                SELECT  @msg = @msg + @msgTag + ';CALL=(UPDATE routine)>'
                RAISERROR 50000 @msg
                ROLLBACK TRAN @tranName
                COMMIT TRAN
                RETURN -100

        END

    COMMIT TRAN
    RETURN 0
```

I will not demonstrate this code; you'll have to run it from the sample code. Note the use of the timestamp column as the optimistic lock. This is how you deal with it:

❏   Do the update, using the primary key *and* the timestamp.

❏   Then, if there are no errors, you test to see how many rows are modified as follows:

> ❏   If one row is modified, everything is great.
>
> ❏   If more than one row is modified, then too many rows are changed. It might be overkill to check for this, but it's a small cost to prevent a messy event from occurring. It's important to make sure that exactly what is expected to occur actually occurs. In this case, only one row should be updated, so you check to make sure that this happened.
>
> ❏   If no rows were updated, you check to see if the row with the primary key value exists in the table. If it does, then the row exists but it has been modified. Otherwise, it never existed in the first place.

You check each of these cases because it keeps stupid errors from occurring. Many times I've seen queries written to modify rows, and instead of passing in null values for missing foreign key values, they pass in zeroes. Five minutes using Profiler (the most important tool of the database code tester!) and the problems are found. Adding complete error handling to the procedure keeps every situation that may occur from biting you, with very little cost.

Note that, again, you have to update all of the columns at once. It would be deeply inefficient to write an update stored procedure that updated the columns based on which column was passed in.

One thing that can be done, however, is to take into consideration any columns that have extremely costly validations (or, in some cases, denormalization routines). You can take the following two paths:

❏   Break the statement into two updates. One to update the costly column(s) and another to update the others. This would only be proper if there are several columns and the costly columns are seldom updated.

❑   A more reasonable path (if there are only one or two columns to deal with) is to check to see if the values have changed, and then decide whether or not to update them. Build two (or more) possible update statements that update the columns in question.

Let's look at a part of the second path. You'll consider the case where changing the `description` column of your table causes all sorts of costly validations (and possibly even the dreaded denormalizations), taking well over a second to occur–but the value in the `description` column only changes 10 percent of the time. You could replace the following:

```
UPDATE routine
SET name = @name, description = @description
WHERE routineId = @key_routineId AND ts_timestamp = @ts_timeStamp

-- get the rowcount and error level for the error handling code
SELECT @rowcount = @@rowcount, @error = @@error
```

with this:

```
-- leave the timestamp out of this statement because you don't want
-- to update the description column because the timestamp has changed
IF EXISTS (SELECT * FROM routine WHERE routineId = @key_routineId
               AND description = @description)
   BEGIN
      UPDATE routine
      SET name = @name WHERE routineId = @key_routineId
         AND ts_timestamp = @ts_timeStamp

      -- get the rowcount and error level for the error handling code
      SELECT @rowcount = @@rowcount, @error = @@error
   END
ELSE
   BEGIN
      UPDATE routine
      SET name = @name, description = @description WHERE routineId =
               @key_routineId
      AND ts_timestamp = @ts_timeStamp

      -- get the rowcount and error level for the error handling code
      SELECT @rowcount = @@rowcount, @error = @@error
   END
```

Notice that you don't change the meaning and you still check the same things out in the error-handling code. It appears that the procedure will be slower to execute now because there is more code to deal with, and it will be slower when the description value is changed. However, overall, the total time executed for all calls will be significantly lower, because the `description` column will be checked far less and you won't incur those costs when it doesn't change.

Destroy

The destroy or DELETE stored procedure that I'll demonstrate here is very similar to the update procedure, other than the fact that the row will no longer exist, of course.

```
CREATE PROCEDURE routine$del
(
    @key_routineId int,
    @ts_timeStamp timestamp = NULL   --optimistic lock
)
AS

-- declare variable used for error handling in blocks
DECLARE @rowcount int,          -- holds the rowcount returned from dml calls
        @error int,             -- used to hold the error code after a dml
        @msg varchar(255),      -- used to preformat error messages
        @retval int,            -- general purpose variable for retrieving
                                -- return values from stored procedure
calls
        @tranname sysname,      -- used to hold the name of the transaction
        @msgTag varchar(255)    -- used to hold the tags for the error mes-
sage

-- set up the error message tag
SET @msgTag = '<' + object_name(@@procid) + ';type=P'
                + ';keyvalue=' + '@key_routineId:'
                + CONVERT(varchar(10),@key_routineId)

SET @tranName = object_name(@@procid) + CAST(@@nestlevel AS varchar(2))

BEGIN TRANSACTION
SAVE TRANSACTION @tranName

DELETE routine WHERE routineId = @key_routineId AND @ts_timeStamp = ts_time-
stamp

-- get the rowcount and error level for the error handling code
SELECT @rowcount = @@rowcount, @error = @@error

IF @error != 0  -- an error occurred outside of this procedure
    BEGIN
        SELECT @msg = 'A problem occurred removing the routine row.'   +
        @msgTag + 'call=(delete routine)>'
        RAISERROR 50000 @msg
        ROLLBACK TRAN @tranName
        COMMIT tran
        RETURN -100
    END
ELSE IF @rowcount > 1  -- this must not be the primary key anymore or the
                       -- row doesn't exist
    BEGIN
        SELECT   @msg = 'Too many routine rows were deleted. ' +
        @msgTag + '; call=(DELETE routine)>'
```

```
            RAISERROR 50000 @msg
            ROLLBACK TRAN @tranName
            COMMIT tran
            RETURN -100

    END
ELSE IF @rowcount = 0
    BEGIN
        IF EXISTS (SELECT * FROM routine WHERE routineId = @key_routineId )
            BEGIN
                SELECT @msg = 'The routine row has been modified' +
                        ' by another user.' + ';call=(delete routine)>'
                RAISERROR 50000 @msg
                ROLLBACK TRAN @tranName
                COMMIT TRAN
                RETURN -100
            END
        ELSE
            BEGIN
                SELECT @msg = 'The routine row you tried to delete' +
                        ' does not exist.' + @msgTag + ';call=(delete rou-
tine)>'
                        raiserror 50000 @msg
                -- the needs of the system should decide whether or
                -- not to actually implement this error, or even if
                -- if you should quit here and return a negative value.
                -- If you were trying to remove something
                -- and it doesn't exist, is that bad?
            END
    END

COMMIT TRAN
RETURN 0
```

The performance of the DELETE procedure is extremely good. You want to destroy one row by primary key, so you give it the primary key and the row is deleted. There is no chance of deleting only parts of the row, or of not passing in the correct number of values.

These are four central stored procedures. You have now effectively built a set of access methods that will present a fairly easy-to-use interface for building an application. They will also provide hooks into the security system for your application, because you can clearly choose the operations that a user can perform at a finer-grained level than INSERT, UPDATE, DELETE, or SELECT.

Obviously, you'll need more than these four stored procedures to build an application, but they cover 80 percent of the requirements and allow the building of editing applications in a very generic manner. When the database interface always follows a very similar design, the code to access it can also follow a very generic path.

Compiled SQL vs. Ad Hoc SQL for Building Apps

When building OLTP applications, you have to make a very big choice. Do you or do you not use stored procedures? And if you do, should you require that *all* database access go through them? In this section, we'll examine the different arguments and give a recommendation for the best way to build applications.

Ad Hoc SQL

Ad hoc SQL is sometimes referred to as **straight SQL** because it's code that has nothing added to it. The "normal" way that most tools tend to want to converse with SQL Server is by using ad hoc batches of SQL code. As you've seen, it's useful when T-SQL statements are batched together and, sometimes, this is the only way you can build scripts to do one-time changes to data. But what about when you're building a permanent interface to your OLTP system data?

Using uncompiled, ad hoc SQL has some advantages over building compiled stored procedures:

❏ More flexibility

❏ Better performance in some situations

More Flexibility

Because you build it at the very last minute, ad hoc SQL doesn't suffer from some of the stern requirements of stored procedures. For example, say you want to build a user interface to a list of customers. You have ten columns that can be added to the SELECT clause, based on the tables that are listed in the FROM clause. It's very simple to build into the user interface a list of columns that the user will be able to use to customize her own list. Then the program can issue the list request with only the columns in the SELECT list that are requested by the user. Because some columns might be very large and contain quite a bit of data, it's better to only send back a few columns instead of all ten.

For instance, consider that you have the view v_customer, with columns customerId, name, number, officeAddress (with each line of the address separated by slashes), phoneNumber, lastSaleDate, and yearToDateSales. You certainly don't want to show users the customerId, though you'll always need it. If a user is in sales, he might set up a profile to return name, number, lastSaleDate, lastContactDate, and yearToDateSales. The user interface would send the following query to the server to get the requested rows:

```
SELECT    customerId, name, number, lastSaleDate, yearToDateSales
FROM      v_customer
```

Another user may simply want to see name and number, so you would execute the following:

```
SELECT    customerId, name, number
FROM      v_customer
```

This will save you bandwidth when transmitting the query back to the user. But you've still calculated yearToDateSales, lastContactDate, and lastSaleDate. As you've seen, in a well-designed database these values are likely to be calculated rather than stored, which will cause this query to incur a lot of unnecessary overhead.

In this case, you can split the query into two possibilities. If the user asks for a sales column, then the client will send the whole query:

```
SELECT customer.customerId, customer.name, customer.number,
       sales.yearToDateSales, sales.lastSaleDate
FROM   customer
         LEFT OUTER JOIN
           (SELECT customerId,
            SUM(itemCount * pricePaid) AS yearToDateSales,
               MAX(date) AS lastSaleDate
         FROM   sales
         GROUP  by customerId) AS sales
         ON customer.customerId = sales.customerId
```

If the user doesn't ask for a sales column, the client will send the following:

```
SELECT customer.customerId, customer.name, customer.number
-- note the commas on the front of the row. This allows you to easily comment
-- out a row of columns easily, or programatically remove them in a real app
--          ,sales.yearToDateSales, sales.lastSaleDate
FROM   customer
--         LEFT OUTER JOIN
--             (SELECT   customerId,
--                  SUM(itemCount * pricePaid) AS yearToDateSales,
--                     MAX(date) as lastSaleDate
--              FROM    sales
--              GROUP   BY customerId) AS sales
         ON customer.customerId = sales.customerId
```

In this way you have the flexibility to only execute what is actually needed.

The same can be said for INSERT and UPDATE statements. One of the issues that we found when we built these two types of stored procedures was that it was very hard to vary the columns in the INSERT and UPDATE lists. It will be trivial (from a SQL standpoint) to build your applications to only include the columns that have changed in the column lists. For example, take the customer columns from above: customerId, name, and number. In your stored procedure, the UPDATE always had to send all the columns:

```
UPDATE customer
SET name = @name,
    number = @number
WHERE customerId = @customerId
```

But what if only the `name` column changed? And what if the `number` column is part of an index, and it has data validations that take three seconds to execute? Using straight SQL, you simply execute the following:

```
UPDATE customer
SET name = @name
--      ,number = @number
WHERE customerId = @customerId
```

Better Performance

Performance gains from using straight SQL calls are basically centered around the topics that you looked at in the previous section on flexibility. Because you can omit parts of queries that don't make sense in some cases, you don't end up in the situation where you're executing unnecessary code. SQL Server 7.0 and 2000 cache the plans of ad hoc calls, but bear in mind that the statements that are sent must be identical, except possibly for the scalar values in search arguments. Identical means identical; add a comment or even a space character and the plan is blown. SQL Server can build query plans that have parameters–which allow plan reuse by subsequent calls; but, overall, stored procedures are better when it comes to using cached plans for performance.

Compiled SQL

Compiled SQL is split into two types of objects. One type is stored procedures (and the functions compiled within them). The other type is triggers; we won't concern ourselves with triggers here because I think it's clear that if validations are needed that require a trigger, we'll build a trigger rather than sending ad hoc SQL to do the validations with the ad hoc modification query. In this section, you'll look at the four particular properties of stored procedures that make them outstanding tools for building applications:

❑ Limited access path to data

❑ Performance

❑ Encapsulation

❑ Security

Limited Access Path to Data

Though a stored procedure can perform multiple operations, it appears to the user like a single call. You can build almost object-oriented methods for your database objects, so that the user never has to execute ad hoc query calls. This gives you a very large organizational gain. If you force users to only use stored procedures, you know the finite set of paths that users may take to access the data. Hence, if you have a performance problem, you can optimize the stored procedure in a rather simple manner (much as you did in the "Encapsulation" section earlier) instead of having to comb through lines and lines of code to find the problem.

Performance

Stored procedures can improve performance by storing the optimized query plan the first time the procedure is executed. Subsequent calls use the exact same plan as the first. With all of the join types, possible tables, indexes, view text expansions, and so on, optimizing a query is a nontrivial task that may take quite a few milliseconds. Now, admittedly, when building a single-user application, you might say, "Who cares?" but because user counts go up, this really begins to add up.

As discussed in the "Ad Hoc SQL" section a moment ago, SQL Server can cache plans of SQL calls, and even though there are a few stringent rules governing how this occurs, it can really make a difference.

However, when accessing stored procedures, the rules are far less stringent. Every time you call with any set of parameters, it uses the same plan (unless you force it not to using WITH RECOMPILE). This saves milliseconds, which are important if there are lots of users accessing the system. While SQL Server does a pretty good job of caching ad hoc SQL calls, it's excellent when it comes to caching stored procedure calls.

One thing to understand is that stored procedures are optimized based on the initial parameters that are passed in. This very occasionally causes a problem if the exact same procedure is executed with two very different parameters. For example, you might have a table with a nonclustered index on a column, where 60 percent of the items in the table have the exact same value while all other values in the table are unique. If the search argument is in the nonunique values, the index wouldn't be the best way to retrieve the rows (because the overhead of fetching through the index to the data pages would likely be greater than just touching all of the data rows directly). If the search argument is against the unique values, using the index would be best. Whichever value is passed in first becomes the plan that is used by all subsequent queries.

There are two ways to deal with this, if it's a problem:

❑ Add the WITH RECOMPILE option to the stored procedure declaration, causing the plan to be dropped every time.

❑ Build a procedure that calls two other procedures, one for the unique cases and another for the nonunique. This is pretty cumbersome, but for a frequently accessed stored procedure, this would be the best way.

Encapsulation

One really great benefit of using stored procedures as an encapsulation layer between the user and the tables is that it simplifies calls to access data. Even a simple SELECT statement that accesses a single table can be difficult to formulate and send from the client, much less a multitable query or even a multistatement query. For example, consider this single table statement:

```
SELECT personId, firstName, lastName
FROM person
WHERE personId = 1
```

In pseudocode, you might have to do the following:

```
query = "SELECT personId, firstName, lastName FROM person WHERE personId = 1"
```

You could then execute this using ADO or some other set of objects that allow clients to consume data from SQL Server. If you were executing a stored procedure, you might simply do the following:

```
DIM query AS STRING
query = "EXECUTE person$get @personId = 1"
```

You can build this on the server as follows:

```
CREATE PROCEDURE person$get
(
    @personId  int
) AS

SELECT personId, firstName, lastName FROM person WHERE personId = @personId
```

The first thing you'll probably notice is that the stored procedure took more effort to build. However, this is a very simple example. Considering that most SELECT statements in this code are at least 5 or 6 lines, and sometimes closer to 15 or 20, it's far easier for clients to use the code in a single line of text.

Consider also that, though your examples have been single statement queries, you looked earlier at multistatement queries. When you need to execute more than one statement in a procedure, such as when filling a temporary table or possibly even updating multiple tables, you have to use the far more complex batching syntax you looked at in the "Batches of SQL Code" section. Trying to build up the script programmatically and then executing it this way is pretty messy.

An encapsulation layer of stored procedures between the user and the tables also gives optimization benefits. As discussed in the "Stored Procedures" section, because the details are encapsulated and therefore hidden from the user of the data, and because you have a finite set of queries to optimize, when a user says that a given procedure is slow, you can fix it easily. Although stored procedures make perfect optimization more difficult to attain, they lend themselves to code reuse and far easier troubleshooting, because all SQL in a procedure is fixed.

Security

You can restrict users' access to specific stored procedures, and consequently, specific base tables by using stored procedures to encapsulate SQL calls The result is that, by employing stored procedures, it's easy to build a proper set of rights that limit the user to seeing only what you want them to see.

Tips to Consider

Each of the two choices has pros and cons. On the one hand you have ad hoc SQL. This is very flexible–leading to faster development times but some associated performance hits (mild when the load is small, but greater as the load on the server gets greater). All that flexibility can also create chaos when trying to performance-tune the application. On the other hand, by using stored procedures for access you save some compilation time on multiple uses, and gain encapsulation of the database structure from the actual user of the data–in essence putting a protective database-access tier between the user and the data itself.

All things considered, the best choice for most OLTP databases is to build them using stored-procedure access. You might guess that the primary reason for this is performance. Using stored procedures does enhance performance, especially when the database is used very actively. Once Microsoft added query plan caching for ad hoc SQL calls to SQL Server 2000, a great deal of this performance value was eliminated.

Consequently, the greatest reward from stored-procedure use is encapsulation. Maintaining a layer between applications and data structures is an invaluable tool for building solid applications and reducing maintenance costs.

The key to this is simple. Once users have worked with the application for a while, changes are inevitable. With stored procedures, you can encapsulate these changes to tables and never have to change your applications. Stored procedures also make your applications cleaner by taking much of the error handling of DML operations out of the presentation code. When you send batches of code to SQL Server, you're basically sending a stored-procedure definition anyway, so why not build the SQL once and use it generically?

Security Considerations

Security is another database administrator job that you need to understand at a fairly high level, so that you can architect suitable applications that protect, not so much against improper data, but against improper data usage.

How data access applications will use the security is something that you'll routinely have to specify. You'll shy away from any really technical security discussions–such as whether or not to use trusted connections (Windows Authentication) or standard SQL Server Security–largely because, from a design standpoint, you don't really care. Inside the database the security will be set up exactly the same.

Using SQL Server Security, you'll want to build a security plan that will prevent any unwanted usage of your objects by any user, whether he's part of your organization or a hacker. As data architects, it's extremely important to carefully design your security needs in terms of who can do what with what (as you started to do with your processes back in Chapter 5). Your goal is to allow the user to perform whatever tasks she needs to, but prohibit any other tasks without letting her see any data that she shouldn't. Creating roles and associating users to them is a fairly easy task using the Enterprise Manager, and one that you won't be looking at.

In SQL Server, you can control rights to almost every object type. The following table shows the kinds of operations that you'll be interested in dealing with for each object type, with regard to security in your databases:

Object	Rights
Table	SELECT, INSERT, UPDATE, DELETE
View	SELECT, INSERT, UPDATE, DELETE
Column (view and table)	SELECT, INSERT, UPDATE, DELETE
Function	EXECUTE
Stored procedure	EXECUTE

There also exists a References *right on tables that give tables owned by a user the rights to include tables owned by another users. It isn't pertinent to this discussion because, in practice, when you build a system to use only tables owned by the dbo, you'll always have References rights between tables.*

You can then grant or deny usage of these objects to your users. You certainly don't want to have to grant access to each user individually because you may have a multitude of users in your databases. So SQL Server provides you with the concept of a **role** (previously known as groups in SQL Server 6.x and earlier) that you can grant rights to and then associate with users.

Every user in a database is a member of at least the public role, but may be a member of multiple roles. In fact, roles may be members of other roles. Take, for example, any typical human-resources system that has employee information like name, address, position, manager, pay grade, and so on. You'll likely need several roles, such as the following:

❑ **HRManagers:** Can do any task in the system.

❑ **HRWorkers:** Can maintain any attribute in the system, but approval rows are required to modify salary information.

❑ **Managers:** All managers in the company would be in this role, but they can only see the information for their own workers.

❑ **Employees:** Can only see their own information, and can only modify their own personal address information.

Each of the roles would then be granted access to all of the resources that they need. A member of the Managers role would probably also be a member of the Employees role. Then, as stated, they could see the information for their employees as well as themselves.

There are three different commands that SQL Server uses to give or take away rights from each of your roles:

❑ **GRANT:** Gives the privilege to use an object

❑ **DENY:** Denies access to an object, regardless of whether the user has been granted the privilege from any other role

❑ **REVOKE:** Removes any GRANT or DENY permissions statements that have been executed; behaves like a delete of a permission.

Typically, you'll simply give permissions to a role to perform tasks that are very specific to the role. The DENY command should only be used as more of a punishment-type command because, no matter how many other times the user has been granted privileges to an object, she will not have access to it while there is one DENY. As an example, take the HR system I just mentioned. You wouldn't deny access to the Employees role, because managers are employees also and would need to have rights to it.

Once you have built all of your objects–including tables, stored procedures, views, and so on–you can grant rights to them. I've already mentioned in the object specific sections that–with stored procedures, functions, and views–you don't have to grant rights to the underlying objects that are used in these objects. This is true as long as the user that builds the object is also the user that owns the object. Because you'll build your objects as the database owner, this isn't usually a problem.

One additional issue is that each database has a special set of built-in roles as follows:

❑ db_accessadmin: Users associated with this role can add or remove users from the database

❑ db_backupoperator: Users associated with this role are allowed to back up the database

❑ db_datareader: Users associated with this role are allowed to read any data in any table

❑ db_datawriter: Users associated with this role are allowed to write any data in any table

❑ db_ddladmin: Users associated with this role are allowed to add, modify, or drop any objects in the database (in other words, execute any DDL statements)

❑ db_denydatareader: Users associated with this role are denied the ability to see any data in the database, though they may still see the data through stored procedures

❑ db_denydatawriter: Much like the db_denydatareader role, users associated with this role are denied the ability to modify any data in the database, though they still may modify data through stored procedures

❑ db_owner: Users associated with this role can perform any activity in the database

❑ db_securityadmin: Users associated with this role can modify and change permissions and roles in the database

Deciding whether to make users members of any of these roles is totally up to the situation. I like to build a user administrator role–a user who can add users to the database and associate them with roles. Building an application that displays these values is a fairly easy task with SQLDMO (SQL Distributed Management Objects). Then, once a user has been created by the DBA, the user in the administrator role can associate them to their database roles.

Programmatically, you can determine some basic information about a user's security information in the database as follows:

❑   `is_member(<role>)`: Tells you if the current user is the member of a given role

❑   `user`: Tells you the current user's name

❑   `permissions(object_id('<objectName>'))`: Lets you see if a user has rights to perform some action

For example, you could build a query to determine all of the routine stored procedures that the user can execute as follows:

```
SELECT specific_name,
       CASE WHEN permissions(object_id(specific_name)) & 32 = 32
           THEN 1
           ELSE 0
       END
AS canExecute
FROM information_schema.routines
WHERE specific_name LIKE 'routine$%'
```

When you execute it, you get the following list:

```
specific_name         canExecute
-----------------------------------------------
routine$del           1
routine$ins           1
routine$list          1
routine$upd           1
```

If you've only given limited access to the base tables, you've already built every bit of security into the system that the user or programmer will ever need to deal with. For example, take the four procedures listed earlier. By restricting access to the `routine$list` procedure, the user interface can look in this access list and determine if it should even try to execute the list. The same is true for the INSERT, UPDATE, and DELETE procedures. If the UI cannot use the `routine$del` procedure, it won't even show Delete in its menus.

PERMISSIONS() is a very versatile function that can be used to determine if a user can do most operations in SQL Server (consult SQL Server Books Online for more information). When building applications, you'll try your best to use the facilities of SQL Server for your security needs–this will help you to avoid building tables of users and their rights ever again.

In the rest of this section, you extend this concept of using SQL Server Security to deal with a few methods that you'll occasionally have to employ. You'll look at the following:

❑ Row-level security

❑ Column-level security

Row-Level Security

This generally refers to the situation where you want to give a user the rights to use a table, and use all of the columns of the table, but you don't want them to be able to see all of the rows, based on some criteria.

Row-level security was very difficult to implement in previous versions of SQL Server. In SQL Server 2000, you can build a fairly simple solution to this problem with user-defined functions.

For your first example, let's use the `artist` and `album` tables from the previous chapter. You're going to deal with only letting the users see Beatles albums if they're a member of the `BeatlesFan` role. Assuming you've created the role, you'll create the following user-defined function:

```
CREATE VIEW v_album
AS
    SELECT albumId, name, artistId FROM dbo.album
    WHERE artistId <> 1 --Beatles
        OR is_member('BeatlesFan') = 1
GO
```

Then you select from it as follows:

```
SELECT *
FROM dbo.v_album
```

This returns the following:

albumId	name	artistId
3	quadrophenia	2
9	tommy	2

because I'm not a member of the `BeatlesFan` role. This certainly isn't very robust. What if you want to deny users from seeing other artists' work? You need to extend the example. You could build a table with group to `artist` relationships, here named `rlsAlbum` (`rls` meaning row-level security).

```
CREATE TABLE rlsAlbum
(
    rlsAlbumId int NOT NULL identity, artistId int, memberOfGroupName sysname
)
```

You then build a view that correlates the security to the artist table:

```
--you build a view that includes your row-level security table.
ALTER VIEW v_album
AS
SELECT album.albumId, album.name, album.artistId
FROM   dbo.album AS album
          JOIN (SELECT   DISTINCT artistId
                  FROM rlsAlbum
                     WHERE is_member(memberOfGroupName) = 1) AS security
                        ON album.artistId = security.artistId
GO
```

Then you select from the view before adding any groups

```
--executed as member of no group
SELECT * FROM v_album
```

and you get no rows:

```
albumId   name                   artistId
-------------------------------------------------------------
```

Next, you can add some groups to the rlsAlbum table to let the db_owners and other logical roles see the values in the table:

```
--db_owner, probably added in insert trigger on albumTable
INSERT INTO rlsAlbum(artistId, memberOfGroupName)
VALUES (1, 'db_owner')
INSERT INTO rlsAlbum(artistId, memberOfGroupName)
VALUES (2, 'db_owner')

INSERT INTO rlsAlbum(artistId, memberOfGroupName)
VALUES (1, 'BeatlesFan')
INSERT INTO rlsAlbum(artistId, memberOfGroupName)
VALUES (2, 'WhoFan')
GO
```

Now a user will not be able to see any rows, unless you've specifically given rights to view to the role of which they're a member. It can be fairly tedious to set up, but when row-level security is required, this is a pretty easy scheme to implement.

Column-Level Security

SQL Server Security does have facilities to grant and revoke rights to a particular column, but they're painful to use. They also will not work when you use views and stored procedures to access your data because objects use the security of their *owner*. If you want to use stored procedures to access all of your data (which is my preference), you need to look at different possibilities.

441

In this section, you'll give a possible alternative to building multiple views or procedures to vertically partition your data. A possible way to implement this is to use a technique very much like the row-level example so you can blot out a column that the user doesn't have rights to see. Using SQL Server permissions, you can extend your previous view to only return values for columns that the users have access to:

```
ALTER VIEW v_album
AS
SELECT album.albumId, --assume the user can see the pk pointer
CASE WHEN PERMISSIONS(OBJECT_ID('album'),'name') & 1 = 1
THEN NAME
ELSE NULL
END AS NAME,
CASE WHEN PERMISSIONS(object_id('album'),'artistId') & 1 = 1
THEN album.artistId
ELSE NULL
END AS artistId
FROM dbo.album AS album
JOIN (SELECT DISTINCT artistId
FROM rlsAlbum
WHERE is_member(memberOfGroupName) = 1) AS security
ON album.artistId = security.artistId
```

Note that you return NULL as the indicator here, because the column is a not-NULL value. In some cases, like when NULL is actually an allowable value for a column, you might need to add an additional column—perhaps something like canSeeNameFl (bit)—which tells the application if the user is allowed to see the column or not.

This may cause a bit of overhead, but then, almost any solution for column- and row-level security will. The important aspect of this solution is that you can now use this view in a stored procedure and, regardless of who owns the stored procedure, you're able to restrict column usage in a very generic manner that only uses SQL Server Security.

Cross-Database Considerations

So far, all of the code and issues discussed have been concerned with a single database. In general, there is little difference in accessing data beyond the confines of the local database. This generally makes working with the data harder, especially because foreign key constraints cannot be used to handle referential integrity needs. Additionally, because the other database must be backed up differently, you lose some of the protection you have in a single database world, because when a database restore is made, you cannot be certain that the data in the two databases are in sync, which is a task that's far easier in a single database.

Though accessing data in outside databases causes difficulties, sometimes it's unavoidable. A typical example might be trying to tie an off-the-shelf system into a homegrown system. In this section, you'll identify some of the issues that arise when working with other databases. You'll break things into two sections:

❑ Same server

❑ Different server

Same Server

Accessing data in a different database but on the same server is pretty similar to the normal (same database, same server) situation. There are a few issues, however—regarding naming, security, and data modification—that you should examine.

Same Server Naming

This is pretty simple. To access data beyond your database, you simply include the database in the name of the object you're accessing. You use the following convention:

```
<databaseName>.<owner>.<objectName>
```

This is true for tables, stored procedures, functions, and so on.

Same Server Security

Prior to service pack 3 (SP3), if you had two databases on the server, there was no way to correlate the two owners and allow them to transfer rights to objects via a stored procedure. For example, consider this procedure:

```
USE Northwind
GO
CREATE PROCEDURE dbo.procedure$testCrossDatabase
AS
SELECT au_id
FROM pubs.dbo.authors
GO
```

The user wouldn't only have needed access privileges to the procedure$testCrossDatabase procedure, but in the pubs database you would have had to grant them explicit access to the database *and* the object.

In SP3, a significant modification was made to allow for cross-database security chaining. The commands for the server (all commands in the master database) are as follows:

```
EXEC sp_configure 'Cross DB Ownership Chaining', '0'; RECONFIGURE
--'1' turns it on, '0' turns if off
```

To modify the setting for a database, use the following:

```
EXEC sp_dboption 'Northwind', 'db chaining', 'ON'
EXEC sp_dboption 'Pubs', 'db chaining', 'ON'.
```

443

What this changes is that instead of looking at the owner of the object in terms of database user, it's regarded in terms of the login user. So, in the example, because the Northwind database and the pubs database are both owned by the same login user, if an owner-owned object in one Pubs accesses an owner-owned object in Northwind it will have access and will not require rights given directly to the user to the object in the different database.

A word of caution. It's common practice for the same user (the DBA) to own every database on many SQL Server installations. If this setting is enabled for the entire server, and there are databases which are owned by different people, but *technically* owned by different *people*, a significant security hole will be opened, where a user can create a procedure as dbo in one database that accesses objects in a different database and have full access, even if they're not allowed user access in the other database.

Same Server Data Modification

In the first part of this chapter, you looked at how SQL Server uses transactions and locks to make certain that your operations either finish totally or not at all, and, more importantly, finish without interruption from other processes. There is no difference in coding when you access data in a different database. You simply use the same syntax and touch the data in both databases. The same transaction mechanisms work seamlessly in either case.

For example, say you have an old in-house requisitioning system, and a new purchasing system that was created by a different company. When you built the former, you included a table that was a queue of items that the purchasing people needed to purchase, and that showed where the items were to be delivered to. Now that you have the new third-party purchasing system, you want to utilize its purchase-order functionality. You would like to automatically create a purchase order whenever a requisition is accepted by the person with authority. So, in the requisition$finalize stored procedure, the call to INSERT INTO the aforementioned queue will be changed to INSERT INTO the purchase order table:

```
CREATE PROCEDURE requistion$finalize

...misc code removed for clarity...

BEGIN TRANSACTION
INSERT INTO dbo.requisitionStatus (requisitionNumber, statusId)
VALUES (@requisitionNumber, @statusId)
--error handling

INSERT INTO purchasing.dbo.purchaseOrder(number, date)
VALUES (@purchaseOrderNumber,getdate())
--error handling

--also insert items
COMMIT TRANSACTION
```

Because the two databases are on the same server, the operation appears seamless to the user. However, because there are now multiple transaction logs in the mix, SQL Server cannot do a simple transaction. It must use a very important concept called a **two-phase commit**.

Two-Phase Commit

The two-phase commit is basically a protocol that allows a server to communicate with a database that it wants to perform tasks in two different logical areas as a single unit of work. The same protocol is used when COM+ is using COM objects to perform nondatabase tasks within a transaction. Using COM+, you can mix transactions of database objects with file system objects, using the two-phase commit to pretty much ensure transactional integrity (there is some possibility of failing to finish a transaction on one source and not another, simply because of latency, but the possibility is very small).

Keep in mind that the controller starts transactions just as it normally does. A transaction is started on each individual database or resource exactly as it would if it was the only transaction. Then, when you send the final commit to return the transaction count to zero, the two-phase commit begins, as follows:

❑ **Prepare phase:** Sends a prepare message to each of the resources and tells it to finish the transaction. The resource then takes care of all logs and does everything necessary to make the transaction action permanent. When it finishes, it messages the transaction initiator, and tells it whether or not it was successful.

❑ **Commit phase:** Once it receives successful messages from the resources, a final message of commit is sent to each resource. If either of the resources claims failure, then all transactions are rolled back.

During the commit phase, if a command is received by one of the resources but not by another and the controller should fail, work may be lost. There is no way around this. However, this is *extremely* improbable because these commands go really fast, and during the commit phase, there should be no possibility of blocking occurring–you already have the items locked and all that's left is to send out the final commit command.

Different Server (Distributed Queries)

I just want to briefly mention distributed queries and introduce the functions that can be used to establish a relationship between two SQL Servers, or a SQL Server and an OLE DB or ODBC data source. There are two methods that can be used:

❑ **Linked servers**: You can build a connection between two servers by registering a "server" name that you then access via a four-part name (`<server>.<database>.<owner>.<table>`), or through the openquery interface

❑ **Ad hoc connections**: Using the openrowset or opendatasource functions, you can return a table of data from any OLE DB source

Just as your transactions could span multiple databases, you can also have transactions that span different servers using T-SQL. If needed, you can update data in your distributed data source by using the DTC (Distributed Transaction Controller) service that is a part of SQL Server and COM+. You use the following command:

```
BEGIN DISTRIBUTED TRANSACTION

UPDATE externalServer.database.owner.table
...

COMMIT TRANSACTION
```

You can write your code almost exactly as if it were on the same server. Note that if you had written BEGIN TRANSACTION instead of BEGIN DISTRIBUTED TRANSACTION, the transaction would have been local to this server, and the action that touched the other server wouldn't be part of the transaction.

I won't be going into the details of these commands because they can be quite complex and have many different settings for many different situations. I've seldom used them in building OLTP systems and prefer, when possible, to import or replicate all data into the same SQL Server—mostly for performance purposes. Linked servers are used frequently when establishing replication relationships. For more information on distributed queries and replication, see SQL Server 2000 Books Online.

Case Study

You're now ready to begin building the access to the database structures that you created in the past two chapters. For this part of the case study, you have three specific tasks to deal with. These tasks will allow the other programmers who are working on your database to begin writing actual code to use the structures:

❑   Create the base modification stored procedures (insert, update, delete)—which are sometimes referred to as the CRUD procedures (create, read, update, delete)—as well as a list procedure and a domain fill for your domain tables

❑   Build custom stored procedures that support the important tasks of your system, as noted in the process table

❑   Specify a set of security groups, and outline what objects they will probably have use of at a very high level

Base Stored Procedures

Referring back to your diagram in Chapter 10, you'll build the following four stored procedures, for four different tables:

❑   transaction$ins

❑   bank$upd

❑   payee$del

❑   account$list

You'll also build a `transactionType$domainFill` procedure. Note again that this code can be downloaded from http://www.apress.com.

Transaction Insert Procedure

This is essentially the insert stored procedure that you developed earlier in this chapter, with a few more comments. In this procedure, you insert every column in the table, and include error handling to get back extra information if an error occurs. As usual, you must bracket the `transaction` table name, because it's a reserved word.

```
CREATE PROCEDURE transaction$ins
(
    @accountId int,
    @number varchar(20),
    @date smalldatetime,
    @description varchar(1000),
    @amount money,
    @signature  varchar(100),
    @payeeId int,
    @transactionTypeId int,
    @new_transactionId int = NULL OUTPUT   --contains the new key
                                           --value for the identity
                                           --primary key
) AS
  BEGIN

    --error handling parameters
    DECLARE   @msg AS varchar(255),      -- used to preformat error messages
              @msgTag AS varchar(255),   -- used to hold the first part
                                         -- of the message header
              @tranName AS sysname       -- to hold the name of the savepoint

    -- set up the error message tag and transaction tag
    -- (nestlevel keeps it unique amongst calls to the procedure if nested)
    SET   @msgTag = '<' + object_name(@@procid) + ';TYPE=P'
    SET   @tranName = object_name(@@procid) + CAST(@@nestlevel AS VARCHAR(2))

    BEGIN TRANSACTION
    SAVE TRANSACTION @tranName

    INSERT INTO [transaction](accountId, number, date, description, amount,
                         signature, payeeId, transactionTypeId  )
       VALUES(@accountId, @number, @date, @description, @amount, @signature,
                @payeeId, @transactionTypeId )

       -- check for an error
       IF (@@error!=0)
          BEGIN
             -- finish transaction first to minimize chance of transaction
-- being hung waiting on a message to complete
             ROLLBACK TRAN @tranName
             COMMIT TRAN
             SELECT @msg = 'There was a problem inserting a new row into ' +
                         ' the transaction table.' + @msgTag +
```

447

```
                                    ';CALL=(INSERT transaction)>'
            RAISERROR 50000 @msg
            RETURN -100
        END

    -- scope_identity keeps you from getting any triggered identity values
    SET @new_transactionId=scope_identity()

    COMMIT TRAN

    END
```

Bank Update Procedure

In the update procedure, you'll simply update the name of the bank to the value passed in. Note the timestamp parameter and how you use it to implement an optimistic lock for the users of this procedure.

```
CREATE PROCEDURE bank$upd
(
    @key_bankId int, -- key column that you'll use as the key to the
                     -- update. Note that you cannot update the primary key
    @name varchar(384),
    @ts_timestamp timestamp -- optimistic lock
)
AS
-- declare variable used for error handling in blocks
DECLARE @rowcount AS int,      -- holds the rowcount returned from dml calls
        @error AS int,          -- used to hold the error code after a dml
        @msg AS varchar(255), -- used to preformat error messages
        @retval AS int,         -- general purpose variable for retrieving
                                -- return values from stored procedure calls
        @tranname AS sysname,   -- used to hold the name of the transaction
        @msgTag AS varchar(255) -- to hold the tags for the error message

    -- set up the error message tag
    SET @msgTag = '<' + object_name(@@procid) + ';TYPE=P'
                    + ';keyvalue=' + '@key_bankId:'
                    + CONVERT(varchar(10),@key_bankId)

    SET @tranName = object_name(@@procid) + CAST(@@nestlevel AS VARCHAR(2))

    -- make sure that the user has passed in a timestamp value because it will
    -- be very wasteful if they have not
    IF @ts_timeStamp IS NULL
        BEGIN
            SET @msg = 'The timestamp value must not be NULL' +
                @msgTag + '>'
                RAISERROR 50000 @msg
                RETURN -100
        END

    BEGIN TRANSACTION
    SAVE TRANSACTION @tranName
```

```
UPDATE bank
SET name = @name
WHERE bankId = @key_bankId
    AND autoTimestamp = @ts_timeStamp

-- get the rowcount and error level for the error handling code
SELECT @rowcount = @@rowcount, @error = @@error

IF @error != 0   -- an error occurred outside of this procedure
    BEGIN
        ROLLBACK TRAN @tranName
        COMMIT TRAN
        SELECT @msg = 'A problem occurred modifying the bank row.' +
            @msgTag + ';CALL=(UPDATE bank)>'
        RAISERROR 50001 @msg
        RETURN -100
    END
ELSE IF @rowcount <> 1   -- this must not be the primary key
                         -- anymore or the row doesn't exist
    BEGIN
        IF (@rowcount = 0)
            BEGIN
                -- if the row exists without the timestamp, it has been modified
                -- by another user
                IF EXISTS (SELECT * FROM bank WHERE bankId = @key_bankId)
                    BEGIN
                        SELECT @msg = 'The bank row has been modified' +
                                ' by another user.'
                    END
                ELSE    -- the primary key value did not exist
                    BEGIN
                        SELECT @msg = 'The bank row doesn't exist.'
                    END
            END
        ELSE            -- rowcount > 0, so too many rows were modified
            BEGIN
                SELECT @msg = 'Too many rows were modified.'
            END

    ROLLBACK TRAN @tranName
    COMMIT TRAN
    SELECT @msg = @msg + @msgTag + ';CALL=(update bank)>'
    RAISERROR 50000 @msg
    RETURN -100

    END

COMMIT TRAN
RETURN 0
```

Payee Delete Procedure

In terms of its code, the payee delete is very much like the update. This procedure allows the user to delete a payee row from the table.

```
CREATE PROCEDURE payee$del
(
    @key_payeeId int,
    @ts_timeStamp timestamp = NULL   --optimistic lock
)
AS
--declare variable used for error handling in blocks
DECLARE @rowcount AS int,           -- holds the rowcount returned from dml
calls
        @error AS int,              -- used to hold the error code after a dml
        @msg AS varchar(255),      -- used to preformat error messages
        @retval AS int,            -- general purpose variable for retrieving
                                   -- return values from stored procedure calls
        @tranName AS sysname,       -- used to hold the name of the transaction
        @msgTag AS varchar(255) -- used to hold the tags for the error mes-
sage

-- set up the error message tag
SET     @msgTag = '<' + object_name(@@procid) + ';TYPE=P'
                + ';keyvalue=' + '@key_payeeId:'
                + convert(VARCHAR(10),@key_payeeId)

SET     @tranName = object_name(@@procid) + CAST(@@nestlevel as varchar(2))

BEGIN TRANSACTION
SAVE TRANSACTION @tranName

DELETE payee
WHERE   payeeId = @key_payeeId
   AND @ts_timeStamp = autoTimestamp

-- get the rowcount and error level for the error handling code
SELECT @rowcount = @@rowcount, @error = @@error

IF @error != 0  -- an error occurred outside of this procedure
    BEGIN
        SELECT @msg = 'A problem occurred removing the payee row.' +
               @msgTag + 'call=(delete payee)>'
        ROLLBACK TRAN @tranName
        COMMIT TRAN
        RAISERROR 50000 @msg
        RETURN -100
    END
ELSE IF @rowcount > 1  -- this must not be the primary key anymore or the
                       -- row doesn't exist
    BEGIN
        SELECT @msg = 'Too many payee rows were deleted. ' +
               @msgTag + ';call=(delete payee)>'

        ROLLBACK TRAN @tranName
        COMMIT TRAN
```

```
                RAISERROR 50000 @msg
              RETURN -100


     END
ELSE IF @rowcount = 0
     BEGIN
         IF EXISTS (SELECT * FROM payee WHERE payeeId = @key_payeeId)
             BEGIN
                 SELECT @msg = 'The payee row has been modified' +
                               ' by another user.' + ';call=(delete payee)>'

                 ROLLBACK TRAN @tranName
                 COMMIT tran
                 RAISERROR 50000 @msg
                 RETURN -100

             END
         ELSE
             BEGIN
                 SELECT @msg = 'The payee row you tried to delete' +
                               ' does not exist.' + @msgTag +
                               ';call=(delete payee)>'
                     RAISERROR 50000 @msg
                         -- it depends on the needs of the system whether or not
you
                         -- should actually implement this error or even if
                         -- if you should quit here, and return a negative value.
                         -- If you were trying to remove something
                         -- and it doesn't exist, is that bad?
             END
     END

COMMIT TRAN
return 0
GO
```

Account List Procedure

To build this procedure you need to include the account information and a few possible filters–in this case, number, bankId, and bankName. When you see a list of accounts, you'll want to see the bank information too, so you'll join this in.

```
CREATE PROCEDURE account$list
(
 @accountId int = NULL,          -- primary key to retrieve single row
 @number   varchar(20) = '%', -- like match on account.name
 @bankId   int = NULL,
 @bankName  varchar(20) = '%'
)
AS
-- as the count messages have been known to be a problem for clients
SET NOCOUNT ON

-- default the @number parm to '%' if the passed value is NULL
```

```
        IF @number IS NULL SELECT @number = '%'

        -- select all of the columns (less the timestamp) from the table for viewing.
        SELECT account.accountId, account.bankId, account.number,
                bank.name AS bankName
        FROM dbo.account AS account
        JOIN dbo.bank AS bank
            ON account.bankId = bank.bankId
        WHERE (account.accountId = @accountId OR @accountId IS NULL)
            AND (account.number Like @number)
            AND (account.bankId = @bankId OR @bankId IS NULL)
            AND (bank.NAME LIKE @bankName)
        ORDER BY account.number

        RETURN 0
        GO
```

Transaction Type Domain Fill Procedure

The domain fill procedure is used to fill a combo box of transaction types, like on a transaction form. Note that you turn the site name into a description column, even though there is a description column in the table. This is because, even when there is no name or a description in the table, you would still return a description to make user coding simpler.

```
        CREATE PROCEDURE transactionType$domainFill

        AS

            BEGIN

                -- all domain fill procedures return the same column names, so that the
                -- user can code them the same way using a generic object
                SELECT transactionTypeId AS ID, transactionType.NAME AS description
                FROM transactionType
                ORDER BY transactionType.NAME

            END
```

Custom Stored Procedures

You'll focus on two of the processes and consider how you might build stored procedures to support them. You'll look at the following:

❑   Balance account

❑   Get account information

Balance Account Process

Referring back to the use process table in Chapter 4, you'll recall that I identified a process entitled `Balance` and described it as follows: "Allows user to reconcile items that have been reported by the bank." You won't be writing any actual SQL code for this process, but you'll consider this fairly complex situation and how you'll solve it in your database.

To perform the balancing operation, you'll probably need to have the following stored procedures coded:

❑ `Statement$insert`, `statmentItem$insert`, and possibly `statement$insertItems`. Because you'll possibly be downloading the `statementItem` rows from an Internet site, you might use the last procedure to load the values into a temporary table and insert the lot at once. You could add an `INSTEAD OF` trigger to put all of the invalid rows into an exception handling table when they're retrieved from the download file.

❑ `transaction$listPossibleMatchesToStatementItems`: This procedure would do a join of unreconciled transactions to `statementItems` and give all of the exact matches, based on `transaction.number` to `statementItem.number` for checks, and `transactionType` if available. You would need to make certain that the join produces a one-to-one relationship for `transaction` to `statementItems`.

❑ `Transaction$reconcile`: This will allow you to associate a `transaction` with a `statementItem` for reconciliation.

❑ A batch of stored procedure calls would need to be coordinated from the screen that uses the `transaction$listPossibleMatchesToStatementItems` to execute the query.

❑ You would need a procedure much like your generic `transaction$list` filtered by account, to only show unreconciled items.

❑ `statementItem$list`: This would give you a list of items that haven't been associated with a given `transaction`. This procedure and the previous one would give you the ability to have a side-by-side form (UI again) that you could use to associate items.

❑ `Statement$finalizeReconciliation`: This would place a row in the `accountReconciliation` table to tell the statement that it's finished. You would want to add a trigger to the statement table that checks to make sure that the total credits and total debits (positive and negative transactions) in the `transaction` table matched the totals in the statement. An enhancement to the requirements of the system might be to allow an offset transaction to be automatically added to the table in order to balance the statement when a small error could not be tracked down.

Keep in mind that I've added to the requirements for the system in the last bullet. This functionality should be considered an enhancement and discussed with the project manager and the user. This may not be a feature that the client wanted or it may have slipped the client's mind. Throughout the process of implementing the system, you'll think of new and cool features to add to the project. The architecture that you're creating should be clean enough to support new features, but you should never add new features that aren't in the specifications to a product without getting client agreement (and an increase in your fee).

As you can see, this is quite a list of procedures to write. Depending on the coding staff, the next step could be to have stub versions of these procedures written so that UI coders can continue with their work. You've also discovered a few additional triggers that need to be written to cover the statement and accountReconcile tables. Discovering additional triggers and requirements will not be uncommon—no design process is perfect.

Get Account Information Process

You should be able to support this process with a fairly simple stored procedure, and you'll write it here. You should consider that the UI has been specified to give a list of accounts, with a way to drill down and see current information, including the following:

❑ Current balance (total debits, total credits)

❑ Total unreconciled amounts

❑ Total number of transactions

❑ Last statement date

❑ Last reconcile date

So you write the following procedure:

```
CREATE PROCEDURE account$getAccountInformation
(
    @accountId int
) AS

--  Note that because you built your transaction table using a reserved word,
--  you have to use bracketed names in your query.

SELECT account.accountNumber,
       statement.DATE,          --  if this value is NULL then no statements
                              --  ever received
       accountReconcile.DATE, --  if this value is NULL, then the account
                              --  has never been reconciled
    SUM([transaction].AMOUNT) AS accountBalance,
    SUM(CASE WHEN [transaction].AMOUNT > 0
```

```
            THEN [transaction].AMOUNT
            ELSE 0
        END) AS totalCredits,
        SUM(CASE WHEN [transaction].AMOUNT < 0
        THEN [transaction].AMOUNT
        ELSE 0
        END) AS totalDebits,
        SUM(CASE
        WHEN transactionReconcile.transactionReconcileId IS NOT NULL
            THEN transactionAmount
            ELSE 0 END) AS unreconciledTotal
    FROM   dbo.account AS account
    --   accounts may have no transactions yet
        LEFT OUTER JOIN dbo.[transaction] AS [transaction]
            --   transaction may not have been reconciled yet
            LEFT OUTER JOIN dbo.transactionReconcile AS transactionReconcile
                ON [transaction].transactionId =
                                            transactionReconcile.transactionid
            ON account.accountId = [transaction].accountId
            --   account may never have received a statement
        LEFT OUTER JOIN dbo.statement AS statement
            LEFT OUTER JOIN dbo.accountReconcile AS accountReconcile
                ON statement.statementId = accountReconcile.statementId
            ON account.accountId = [transaction].accountId
    WHERE accountId = @accountId
    GROUP BY account.accountnumber, statement.DATE, accountReconcile.DATE
```

Security for the Processes

Finally, you need to specify your security. Your example does have two security roles specified, and you'll probably want to add another role for administration purposes:

❏   AccountUser: Based on the processes you specified, this role will simply be able to view account information. The custom stored procedure account$getAccountInformation would certainly be required as well as any supporting stored procedures to build the form.

❏   AccountingClerk: As specified, this role will have rights to every defined procedure in the system.

❏   UserAdministrator: This role would be a member of the db_securityadmin and db_accessadmin fixed database roles.

There is some ambiguity in the specifications, but you've chosen to implement a user that can view all account information–AccountUser. You certainly need to ask the project manager and the client whether certain accounts should be off-limits to certain users. If so, then you might want to add a row-level security system to implement this.

Best Practices

❑ **Transactions**: Use liberally as needed because the data is the most important thing. Obviously it's best to limit their scope to only relevant statements, because they do hinder performance and concurrency. However, it's better to over-protect than to under-protect. Clients will accept a bit of slowness, but they will not accept poor data quality.

❑ **Batches**: Avoid spreading transactions across batches. This will help to avoid long-running transactions if the connection is broken.

❑ **Temporary tables**: Avoid if at all possible by using different SQL structures like derived tables and UNION. Use variable-based tables where it makes sense or local temporary tables. Global temporary tables are limited in use, but can be good tools if you need to share temporary data between connections.

❑ **Cursors**: Avoid these like a visit to the dentist. When the SQL language will not work to solve a problem, they're necessary (like when you have a toothache you have to go see the dentist!) but if possible, code around cursors.

❑ **When using cursors, always choose the type of cursor**: Otherwise the type chosen by SQL Server might not be what you want.

❑ **Stored procedures**: Execute code from stored procedures as often as reasonable. These provide many advantages over executing "plain" SQL, such as performance due to precompilation; security; and encapsulation of implementation details from users.

❑ **Views**: Views are excellent for partitioning tables for security or performance.

❑ **Nulls**: Be careful with null columns, especially when the column will be used in comparisons. Null comparisons are problematic and can cause some strange results.

❑ **When executing batches of multiple SQL statements be careful with error handling and transactions**: It can seem unnatural to apply the necessary code from front-end or middle-tier objects, but it's essential to the protection of the data, and it's necessary so that the desired results will always be the ones obtained.

❑ **Security**: Define security in terms of roles, so that it's clear what a user will get if added to a role.

❑ **Cross-database security chaining**: Use this whenever you have two databases owned by the same user. Also use it when you need stored procedures, triggers, functions, and views to use objects between databases. It will keep the security benefits of stored procedures intact, regardless of whether you're using objects outside of the database. However, it can mask security issues when two databases are technically owned by the dbo, but are actually owned by two different people.

Summary

In this chapter, you've looked at many of the most important issues that you should be aware of when implementing data access and modification in your applications.

You've examined the pros and cons of using stored procedures, ad hoc SQL, and views. You learned what can be done to tackle errors–error handling being one of SQL Server's weak points–and you looked at implementing security through stored procedures and user roles.

You've looked in detail at transactions and locking, temporary tables, NULLs, and cursors. Finally, you drew up some of the core stored procedures required to implement your case-study database.

Hopefully, this chapter has answered many of the questions regarding data access and modification, and has raised your awareness of important issues. It should be interesting to see how these ideas affect your own designs.

In the next chapter, you'll look at one of the most difficult tasks for the database designer–translating system requirements into actual hardware requirements.

14

Determining Hardware Requirements

This chapter consists of tasks that don't play a large role in database design, and therefore aren't normally considered part of the data architect's remit. However, now that you've physically implemented your design, you have some idea of the volume of data the hardware will be required to handle. In considering these requirements, the rest of this chapter is a primer rather than a complete reference for such matters, because you won't always have the luxury of database administration staff to handle them.

The hardware configuration that SQL Server runs on top of can make or break your applications. How do you know how much hardware is really needed by your applications? How do you know if your applications have grown to the point where they're now overloading your system? This chapter gives you the information you need when choosing the hardware on which your database will be hosted. More specifically, you'll see how much space your database will need (a topic known as **volumetric analysis**) and look at the performance of your server.

Volumetric analysis is a process in which you examine the types of data stored and their expected rate of growth. An analysis of the types of databases you'll encounter is necessary. Following this, we'll engage in formulaic analysis of tables and attempt to simplify this analysis for the vast majority of cases. Archiving of old, unused data is an important and often overlooked area of performance improvement.

Server performance involves analyzing the various properties of a server and the database system.

Types of Databases

Obviously there are innumerable applications with a plethora of databases that support them. Although it's always difficult to draw clear, distinct lines, databases are generally separated along two lines: online transactional processing (OLTP) and online analytical processing (OLAP). In this section, we'll take a look at each of these in turn.

OLTP Databases

OLTP databases generally have highly normalized tables that experience growth through numerous short transactions. Point-of-sales or bank account automated teller machine (ATM) databases are good representations of OLTP databases. Due to the normalized nature of the tables, row sizes and index usage are usually minimized. The main tables in these databases will generally grow at a constant rate of X (a calculable number of) rows per time period. This time period could be hours or days, or indeed, months or years. As you seek to gather the data storage requirements for an OLTP database, you'll need to gauge this growth rate, forecasting it as accurately as possible.

Some OLTP databases may support more than one application, a good example being accounting applications in which you might have a separate database for each of the general ledger, accounts payable, and accounts receivable modules. On the other hand, due to the nature of SQL Server security and system table infrastructure, you'll often see such applications written with a single database for all these modules. Thus, such an accounting database may have subsets of tables that support individual general ledger, accounts receivable, and accounts payable modules. Essentially, from a volumetric growth perspective, these subsets can be considered as individual applications of tables and analyzed separately.

OLAP Databases

OLAP databases are used for summarizing and reporting on the data generated from OLTP applications and nonrelational sources. Take, for example, an insurance company that collects claims data in one of its OLTP databases. The company might have separate OLAP databases that summarize this data for the purposes of regulatory requirements and business-decision analysis reports. Some will call these databases "operational data stores" and reserve the OLAP acronym for the specialized star-schema databases that are a further refinement of the operational data store. For our purposes, we'll use the common acronym OLAP when talking about reporting databases running on top of the SQL Server engine.

Data is generally loaded into these databases through discrete batch loads during less busy periods. Usage is primarily limited to read-only selects, and tables are often denormalized and will frequently have large row sizes, in an effort to reduce the number of joins used in queries. To speed the execution of queries, each table in an OLAP database usually possesses many indexes. These databases grow based on the anticipated growth of their source feeds. However, the indexes must always be accounted for as well. Also, as new reporting requirements occur, new tables and/or new indexes will be added.

Just as in life, everything is not black and white. Although most databases generally will either be of the OLTP or OLAP type, a few will support applications that have both OLTP and OLAP components. A payroll database, for example, will provide the routine OLTP transactional entries related to ongoing pay cycles. At the same time, quarterly and annual report tables of an OLAP nature will often be generated from this data to supply governmental tax requirements. Again, in this instance, the OLTP and OLAP portions of the databases should be analyzed separately.

Growth of OLTP Tables

Not all of the tables in an OLTP database can be expected to grow at the same rate. Some of them will capture everyday data (for example, a publishing house may expect to receive new orders daily), whereas others will expect less rapid growth (we would hope to get new customers, but not at the same rate as we receive orders). In this section, we'll look at these scenarios in more detail.

Rapid Growth

Usually, most OLTP applications will have two to five tables that contain the vast majority of the data for the application. The size of the tables will usually be a factor of volume increasing constantly over time. A purchasing application, for example, will usually have a `PurchaseOrder` table and a `POLineItem` table. For each purchase order, you'll have one or more line items in the `POLineItem` table. In many applications, you might have a variety of subapplications.

For example, an HR payroll application would have a set of tables that primarily support the HR side of the application and a set of tables for the payroll side of the application. In the former, tables covering the history of the employees' human resource attributes of training, assignments, personal data, and company data would capture much of the data. In the latter, history tables covering payments to the entire sundry list of salary payments, taxes, and deductions from salary would contribute to most of the growth of the database.

Slow Growth

In addition to the tables mentioned previously, there are secondary tables that increase in size over time, albeit less rapidly. In the purchasing application, this would include the domain table that covers the list of vendors, purchasers, and allowable products. In the HR payroll application, this would cover the employee personal and corporate assignment tables. Often these tables are relatively small compared to the main tables and, if accounted for with a large estimate, can be assumed to be constant over the life of the application.

No Growth

Obviously, there are certain domain tables that will usually be populated initially and have very little change over the life of the application. For the purchasing application, this would cover attributes of the purchase order such as unit-of-issue. For the HR payroll application, this would include such domain tables as job codes and their descriptions. These tables can generally be assumed to be constant over time after their initial load. Thus, while you're calculating table growth, you don't have to factor the time element into the size of these tables. In fact, if your time period for analysis is long enough, you can often totally ignore these tables for size calculation purposes, which dramatically simplifies your task.

To summarize, a single OLTP application will often have 20 to 40 tables. Two to five main tables will grow at a continuous rate and will take up the vast amount of the space requirements. Some supporting domain tables will grow at a slower rate. Other domain tables will receive an initial load and their growth (and often size itself) is negligible over time.

Growth of OLAP Tables

OLAP tables are also expected to grow. There may be many reasons for this: the amount of data from the OLTP database will have an effect, or the number of precalculated queries may change. We'll now go on to look at these types of growth.

Batch Growth

As opposed to OLTP databases, OLAP databases, due to their often denormalized nature, will have fewer domain tables and more summary tables that experience routine batch growth. Typically, OLAP databases will take one of two forms. A large operational data store will have a number of large summary tables with some supporting domain tables. Where a specialized OLAP engine isn't used, some OLAP databases will have a **star schema**, a single large summary table with rays emanating to a number of domain tables.

The volumetric growth of an OLAP database has a number of factors, such as the underlying data and its growth, the amount of denormalization necessary to speed queries, and the frequency with which data is introduced into the database from the source or sources. Almost all growth can be defined as discrete events. The most obvious growth of the database is due to the routine batch loads from one or more sources. Each source needs to be analyzed based on the periodicity of the batch feeds and the amount of growth this translates to in the summary tables of the OLAP database.

Not to be confused with this routine entry of data from various sources is the denormalization and summarization that often occurs in OLAP databases. Although the data might be loaded in and this causes growth, data will also be summarized in "time batches." For example, tables with different levels of detail might be loaded for periods covering quarter-to-date, year-to-date, prior year, and older-than-prior-year time periods. Care must be taken to estimate the potential geometric growth factor this can have on OLAP database growth.

OLAP databases are well known for combining heterogeneous data sources to provide analysis. Along with these disparate sources, you'll have to account for their disparate batch-load frequencies. Batches may range from daily to quarterly depending on the source and allowable latency in your reporting requirements.

Growth Through Company Growth

Less obvious in the growth of an OLAP database is the growth of a company. Because OLAP databases are often used for executive reportage, the database needs to be sized to accommodate not only the growth of its original sources, but also the growth due to mergers and acquisitions of the parent company. For example, a medical insurance company might build an OLAP database providing profit and loss reportage on claims from a specific geographic area. When it acquires another insurance company covering a separate geographic area, suddenly the original database must now accommodate the data from this acquisition in order to give an accurate profit and loss statement for the new, expanded company.

Coincident with our thoughts about growth here due to mergers and acquisitions, you might do well to consider designing your OLAP table structures very generically with variable size columns. SQL Server 2000 introduces the SQL_variant datatype, and this is a place where you may want to take advantage of it. Implicit with the use of variable size columns and SQL_variant columns is that they take more space than a simple integer or a big integer column for the same representation. Furthermore, certain functions (AVG, SUM, etc.) can't be used on SQL_variant columns.

"We Need More Reports!"

Remember also that OLAP databases play a vital role in getting timely and valuable analyses of information to the key decision-makers in the organization. As the data begins flowing in and business decisions are made, as often as not a need for new reports and information is realized. Accommodating this need often means new summarization of the data or a new column or index on an existing table.

Don't Forget the Indexes

In OLAP databases, the volumetric impact of indexes can't be overlooked. A single table with tens of gigabytes of data may have an equal amount of data necessary for indexes. Thus, as the calculation of table volume is discussed, the equally important calculation of index sizes will also be discussed.

Calculating Complete Table Size

As you would expect, table size is roughly the product of the number of rows and the row size. However, a number of factors increase the complexity of the calculation. These include the number and type of indexes, the index key columns, the number and percent usage of variable length columns, and the size of text and image blobs.

463

You can follow these steps to estimate the amount of space required to store the data on a table:

1. Compute the space used by the data in the table

2. If one exists, compute the space used by a clustered index

3. If any exists, compute the space used by each nonclustered index

4. Add these values together

SQL Server Books Online does a nice job of explaining how tables and indexes are sized based on these parameters. What isn't included there, however, is a programmatic method for performing the tedious job of gathering information on column size, column characteristics, and index key columns and then completing the calculations. We've included a set of three stored procedures with this book for just this job, and you'll be working through them shortly.

The three procedures (explained in detail later) that you need to create in the master database are as follows:

❑   sp__table$calcDataSpace

❑   sp__index$getKeyData

❑   sp__table$indexSpace

To use the procedures, you first need to actually create the empty tables and indexes in the master database. Additionally, you need to have thought through the expected row size and the percentage that variable length columns will be filled. These procedures were designed for SQL Server 7.0 and SQL Server 2000 and won't be valid for SQL Server 6.5.

Data Size Calculation

First you need to compute the space used by the data in the table. For this exercise's purposes, assume that you've already created a table with its appropriate columns and indexes. Alternatively, you can work through the case study at the end of the chapter. If you have variable-length columns such as varchar, nvarchar, and varbinary, then you'll need to make an estimation of the percentage that these columns will be filled. For the sp__table$calcDataSpace procedure outlined in this section, this is a single value for all columns. This is a single number for the whole table you'll store as @variFillPercent.

> With the introduction of user-defined extended properties (discussed in Chapter 10) in SQL Server 2000, you can now create a percentFillExpectation property for each of your variable-length columns that are programmatically accessible. This is just one of the many ideas that developers and DBAs are going to come to terms with for using these user-defined extended properties.

The size of a table is based on the number of columns, the length of those columns, and the number of rows. First you need some basic information. This section will walk you through the buildup of the procedure sp__table$calcDataSpace. (The variable declarations are assumed.) The default page size for SQL Server 2000 is 8192 bytes. You can get this programmatically using the following query:

```
SELECT @pagesize = low FROM master.dbo.spt_values WHERE number = 1 AND type = 'E'
```

For planning purposes, you'll need to estimate the number of rows that you expect in the table. If you want to default to the number already in the table, you can get this programmatically through the following query:

```
SELECT @rowcount = rows FROM sysindexes WHERE object_name(id)= @tablename
                                         AND indid IN (0,1)
```

You then need the number of variable-length columns, the size of those variable-length columns (which is a function of their maximum size times the percent that you expect them to be filled, @variFillPercent), the total column count, and the size of fixed columns. The following two queries return these results, the key difference in the queries coming in the variable column value from the systypes table:

```
SELECT @varicolcount=count(c.name), @maxvaricolsize=ROUND((@variFillPercent *
ISNULL(sum(c.length),0)),0) FROM syscolumns c JOIN systypes t
    ON c.xusertype = t.xusertype
join sysobjects o on c.id = o.id WHERE t.variable = 1 AND o.name = @tablename
    GROUP BY o.name

SELECT @columncount=count(c.name)+@varicolcount,
    @fixcolsize=ISNULL(sum(case WHEN c.length IS NULL THEN t.length ELSE
c.length
    end),0)
FROM syscolumns c JOIN systypes t ON c.xusertype = t.xusertype
JOIN sysobjects o ON c.id = o.id WHERE t.variable = 0 AND o.name = @tablename
```

A portion of each row is reserved for calculating the nullability of each column. This is a bitmapping for each column plus some overhead. The section of the row is called the **null bitmap**. You need only the integer portion of the calculation, and the query to calculate is as follows:

```
SELECT @nullBitmap=2+FLOOR((@columncount+7)/8)
```

If there are any variable-length columns, you'll adjust the maximum variable length column size for a row by adding 2 bytes for the table and 2 bytes for each variable-length column:

```
SELECT @maxvaricolsize=@maxvaricolsize+2+@varicolcount*2
```

The full row size is the sum of the fixed column size, the null bitmap size, the max variable column size, and the data row header of 4 bytes:

```
SELECT @maxrowsize = @fixcolsize+@nullbitmap+@maxvaricolsize + 4
```

Next, you have to be concerned with whether the table is a heap of rows or it's ordered by a clustered index. If the latter is true, then you need to calculate the amount of free space between rows due to a fill factor of less than 100. Each table always has a row in **sysindexes** with either an index ID of 0 for a heap table without a clustered index or an index ID of 1 for a table physically sorted along the clustered index key. Obviously, if the table is a heap table with no fill factor, you don't need to find the fill factor and calculate free space. You extract the fill factor with the following query:

```
IF ((SELECT indid FROM sysindexes WHERE object_name(id) = @tablename
    AND indid IN (0,1)) = 1)
SELECT @fillfactor=OrigFillFactor FROM sysindexes
    WHERE object_name(id)=@tablename AND indid = 1
```

> **The default for fill factor is 0; legal values range from 0 through 100. A fill factor value of 0 doesn't mean that pages are 0 percent full. It's treated similarly to a fill factor value of 100, in that SQL Server creates clustered indexes with full data pages and nonclustered indexes with full leaf pages. It's different from 100 in that SQL Server leaves some space within the upper level of the index tree. For the purposes of table data space calculation here, a fill factor of 0 will be identical to a fill factor of 100.**

If you have a heap table, you'll continue the formula for calculating the number of free rows per page by setting the fill factor to 100. Once you have the fill factor for a table ordered by a clustered index, you calculate the amount of free space inserted in each page:

```
SELECT @freeRowsPerPage = (@pagesize*(100-@fillFactor)/100/(@maxrowsize+2))
```

Notice that if the fill factor is 100, the preceding query will always have a 0 value for free rows per page. This is true whether the table is a heap table or it's ordered by a clustered index with a fill factor of 0 or 100.

Before you look at the next query for calculating the total data space in a table, a little explanation is necessary. Embedded in this query is a formula for the number of rows in a page. This is represented programmatically by FLOOR((@pagesize-96)/(@maxrowsize+2)). It's the space on the page not used by row points and page headers (@pagesize-96), divided by the rowsize plus 2 bytes between each row (@maxrowsize+2). You then use the FLOOR function to round the quotient down to the nearest integer, because rows can't span pages and a complete row must fit on each page. From this result you subtract the number of free rows per page. The resulting number of useful rows per page is then divided into the estimated or actual rowcount set forth earlier to yield the total number of pages your data would need. Round up using the CEILING function to get complete pages. You could stop at this point if you're interested only in the number of pages you need. Multiplying by the actual page size yields the number of bytes that the data would need.

```
SELECT @data_space_used = @pagesize *
    CEILING(@rowcount/((FLOOR((@pagesize-96)/(@maxrowsize+2)))-@freeRowsPerPage))
```

Reviewing Index B-Tree Structures

Before you begin calculating index space, it's helpful to review how indexes are put together. Indexes are essentially shortcut pointers to rows in a database. All indexes contain at least one level, the **root node** level. This is a single page where queries of the index begin. Unless the table is so small that the root node page is also the bottom level leaf node page on a nonclustered index, the root node will point to the next level in the index. This may be a page from an index node level or it may be a page from the one and only leaf node level. Each index node level points to a lower index node level until the leaf node level is reached. As you can see from the following diagram, this example index has three levels: the root node level, a single index node level, and the leaf node level.

The leaf node level will take one of three forms. If the index is a clustered index, the leaf node level is the actual data sorted along the clustered index key. The remaining two forms of leaf nodes are for nonclustered indexes and depend on whether the table has a clustered index or not. If the index is a nonclustered index on a table with a clustered index, each row of the leaf node level will contain pointers to the corresponding clustered index key for that row. Thus, the size of each row in the leaf row level in this instance is essentially the size of the clustered index key.

We should briefly mention here that this is the principal reason for keeping clustered index keys very short. When a query gets through traversing a nonclustered index in this form, it must then traverse the clustered index to find the actual row. Remember, the shorter your index key, the fewer levels your index will have.

The third form of leaf node is for a nonclustered index on a table without a clustered index (aka a heap table). Each row in the leaf row level is an 8-byte row pointer to the actual row in the table (4 bytes for the page pointer and 4 bytes for the row offset on the page).

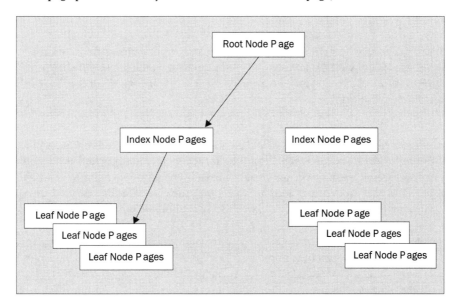

To summarize this section:

- ❏ For clustered indexes, leaf node pages are the data pages.

- ❏ For nonclustered indexes on a table with a clustered index, leaf node pages contain pointers to a clustered index key.

- ❏ For nonclustered indexes on a table without a clustered index, leaf node pages contain pointers to the actual rows on the table.

When an index has fewer node levels, it's said to be "flatter." You can see that flatter indexes mean fewer page reads for a query because each node level is a page read. Fewer page reads mean less of that expensive disk activity and fewer CPU cycles. Overall, flatter indexes are better when you need to go all the way to the table data to obtain your information.

Index Size Calculation

The space taken up by the data in a table is only half of the equation for the total space used by a table. The other half is the space taken up by indexes. With OLAP databases, it isn't unusual to see total index space equal or exceed that used by the actual data.

We'll look at two more stored procedures, sp__table$indexSpace and sp__index$getKeyData. The first, sp__table$indexSpace, is the main procedure, and the second, sp__index$getKeyData, is an auxiliary procedure called from the first. As we outlined previously for table size calculations, we make a simplification by estimating the percentage that variable-length columns will be filled. As before, variable declarations are assumed.

> When you run the sp__table$indexSpace procedure, in addition to the overall size of the table, you'll get information on the size of the data alone in the table, the size of each index, and how many B-tree node levels are necessary for a given record count in the table.

You'll begin your analysis of sp__table$indexSpace by getting some housework out of the way. You need the page size for the server, the number of rows for the table if not supplied as an input parameter, and the overall space consumed by just the data. The page size and row count queries were outlined in the "Data Size Calculation" section. To get the space used for the actual data, you'll call the stored procedure sp__table$calcDataSpace, whose analysis we outlined previously.

Next, you create a temporary table, #keyColumns, with columns for index ID, column name, column length, whether the column is variable or not, and the fill factor from the index of the index ID. You pass this table name off to the stored procedure sp__index$getKeyData, whose sole task is to populate the #keyColumns table.

In sp__index$getKeyData, a cursor is set up on the index ID for each index, whether clustered or nonclustered, on the table. If there are no indexes, the @@fetchstatus for the cursor will be less than 0 and you return to the main procedure; otherwise, you cursor through the index IDs.

Every index will always have at least one column in it. To get the data for this column to put in #keyColumns (the name of which was passed into the procedure as the variable @tempTableName), you'll generate a character string dynamically and execute it. Dynamic character string execution is a great skill to master, so it's worth going through the following query in detail.

Loaded into the variable @exct_stmt is a USE statement for the database name. Then you generate an INSERT for the temporary table #keyColumns (passed as @tempTableName) and its columns, indid, colname, variable, collength, and fill_factor. The data loaded into these columns is the index ID from the cursor, @indid, the column name generated by the INDEX_COL function, the variable value for the column datatype from systypes, the length of the column from syscolumns, and the fill factor value, which is also part of the cursor key. After you load the string into the @exct_stmt variable, you simply execute it inside a set of parentheses.

```
SELECT @exct_stmt = 'use ' + quotename(@dbName, '[')+ ' INSERT ' +
                            quotename(@tempTableName,']') +
                    ' (indid,colname,variable,collength,fill_factor)
SELECT '+convert(varchar(10),@indid) + ',
        INDEX_COL('+quotename(@tablename,'''')+','' +
        convert(varchar(10),@indid) + ',1),
        t.variable,
        c.length,' +
        convert(varchar(3),@fill_factor)+
        ' FROM '+@dbname+'.dbo.syscolumns c
JOIN '+ @dbname+'.dbo.systypes t
    ON c.xusertype = t.xusertype
    WHERE c.id = '+convert(varchar(16),@objid)+'
    AND c.name=INDEX_COL('+quotename(@tablename,'''')+'
        ','+ convert(varchar(10),@indid)+',1)'
EXEC (@exct_stmt)
```

If you don't understand how to execute character strings, it will be helpful to consider this procedure in more detail. Open the code for the procedure in SQL Server 2000 Query Analyzer. The color-coding in Query Analyzer will help you understand what you're doing. Notice that because you use the INDEX_COL function, you don't have to make a call on the SYSINDEXES table. Trust us, you don't want to have to call SYSINDEXES to get out column names. The INDEX_COL function is more than sufficient.

After you get the first column name, use the increment key ID field for the INDEX_COL to get the next column name. If the column name is NULL, you know that you've exhausted the columns for a particular index and you go to the next index in the cursor if there is one. Although the column name from the INDEX_COL function isn't NULL, you loop through a WHILE loop, executing a character string similar to that previously to insert the next row into #keyColumns.

When you've exhausted the last column for the last index, return control to the sp__table$indexSpace procedure with a now populated #keyColumns table.

First you test #keyColumns to see if the table has a clustered index. If so, you set a flag variable in your procedure to indicate that there's a clustered index. This is important for two reasons. First, remember that from the index structure review, the leaf node level for a clustered index is the data. You already have this information from the sp__table$calcDataSpace procedure. Second, if you have a clustered index, each row in the leaf level of any nonclustered indexes will be the size of the clustered index key rather than an 8-byte row pointer. This is how you test for the existence of a clustered index, whose index ID is always 1:

```
IF EXISTS (select 1 from #keyColumns where indid = 1) select @clus_flag = 1
```

You then branch conditionally into calculating the non-leaf-level sizes of the clustered index or immediately continue by calculating the size of any nonclustered indexes. Because you can have up to 253 nonclustered indexes, you set up a cursor to work through each nonclustered index based on its index ID from the data in #keyColumns. With the exception of the leaf level, the calculation of the sizes of the other levels for all indexes is similar.

You begin by calculating the key size for the index. In an index page, the key length is the row size. This is very similar to calculating the row size in sp__table$calcDataSpace, and we won't go through the specific details, except to say that the data in this case comes from the #keyColumns table that you generated rather than the actual system tables, as in sp__table$calcDataSpace. Here are the three summations from the sp__table$indexSpace procedure for the respective cases of a clustered index row size, a nonclustered index row size on a table with a clustered index, and a nonclustered index row size on a heap table:

```
@CIndex_Row_Size =
@Fixed_CKey_Size + @Variable_CKey_Size + @CIndex_Null_Bitmap + 1 + 8

@Index_Row_Size=
@Fixed_Key_Size+@Variable_Key_Size+@Index_Null_Bitmap+1+@CIndex_Row_Size

@Index_Row_Size=
@Fixed_Key_Size+@Variable_Key_Size+@Index_Null_Bitmap+1+8
```

Notice that, in the latter two instances for nonclustered index row size, the difference in the sums is the difference between the clustered index row size, @CIndex_Row_Size, and the set value for a heap table row pointer of 8 bytes. Furthermore, in the first instance note that the clustered index row size, @CIndex_Row_Size, will always be at least 10 bytes and, more likely, at least 13 bytes in size. Thirteen bytes is the case in which your clustered index is a single 4-byte integer column. Some would think that we're making the point that it might be better to not have a clustered index. Not at all! When intelligently done, a clustered index can give significant performance gains. The point we're making is to keep your clustered index key size and row size as small as is practical due to the feedback effect on nonclustered index row size.

> **Think of it this way. Reducing your clustered index key length by 1 byte will cause a reduction in 1 byte for every single row of every single page of every single level of every single index on your table outside the clustered index leaf node level. It adds up. It means flatter indexes and faster queries.**

After you have the key length for the index, you have to calculate the leaf level size first (or in the case of the clustered index, the index level immediately above the leaf level). If this level has only one page, you don't have to go any further. If it's more than one page in size, you have to calculate the next level up progressively until you get to the point where a level is only one page in size. This level is, by definition, the root node level. Here's the WHILE loop code for looping through index-level page calculations while checking whether that particular level is only one page in size:

```
SELECT @this_Num_Pages_Level =
CEILING((@Num_Rows / @Index_Rows_Per_Page — @Free_Index_Rows_Per_Page))
SELECT @Num_Index_Pages = @this_Num_Pages_Level
WHILE @this_Num_Pages_Level > 1
  BEGIN
    SELECT @level_cnt = @level_cnt + 1
    SELECT @this_Num_Pages_Level =
CEILING(@this_Num_Pages_Level/@NL_Index_Rows_Per_Page)
    SELECT @Num_Index_Pages = @Num_Index_Pages + @this_Num_Pages_Level
END
```

First you calculate the number of pages for the current level, @this_Num_Pages_Level. You've already initialized the @level_cnt variable with a value of 1. You add @this_Num_Pages_Level to the overall count you're keeping for the number of pages in the index, @Num_Index_Pages. Although @this_Num_Pages_Level is greater than 1, you loop through and calculate the number of pages for each successively higher index level until you get to the root level consisting of a single page. The calculations for the clustered index are similar.

At this point, you've calculated the pages necessary for each index and the number of B-tree levels for each index. You report this information out and add it to the overall page count you're keeping for the entire table. When you've finished with the indexes, you add the index page count to the data page count to get the overall table size.

Obviously, over time, data increases in tables and indexes. Is there any way to intelligently reduce the number of records in a table and the number of levels in your indexes? We discuss this in the "Archive Data When It Makes Sense" section later in this chapter.

Transaction Log Size

Once you've calculated estimates for all your table sizes, you also need to account for transaction log sizes. Generally, transaction logs are initially set as a percentage of database size. This percentage is based primarily on the expected transaction level and the rate that transaction logs are dumped to either disk or tape.

For OLTP databases in which transactions are the bread and butter of the database, it isn't unusual to see transaction log sizes exceeding 50 percent of the database size. OLAP databases, on the other hand, routinely operate with 10 percent or less dedicated to a transaction log.

This brings up the issue of recovering transaction logs, as the ability to recover them will affect their size. For large batch loads, in SQL Server 7.0 a procedure was often developed in which the transaction log was placed in `truncate log on checkpoint` mode while a batch load was taking place. The developers of SQL Server 2000 recognized this routine process and added a Bulk-Logged option to the transaction logging process:

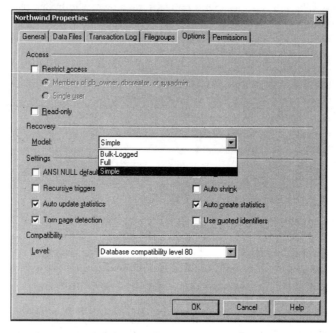

A Full recovery model is one in which the individual transaction, including bulk inserts and SELECT INTOs, can be recovered transaction by transaction. It makes for large transaction logs, particularly for OLAP databases that have large batch transactions.

The Bulk-Logged model is a compromise that's normally reserved for OLAP databases. Here, for bulk insert, SELECT INTO, and BCP, batches of inserts are recorded instead of individual transactions. It can mean that in the event of a failure, whole batch transactions may need to be manually repeated, but at the gain of smaller transaction logs.

The Simple recovery model is synonymous with setting a database to `truncate log on checkpoint` in SQL Server 6.5 and 7.0. Essentially, a database is recoverable to the last full backup and no further in this model. It's usually recommended for nonproduction environments.

So how much transaction log is enough? Generally start small and turn on and monitor auto growth for the transaction log files. We recommend starting with 20 percent of expected data size for an OLTP database and 5 percent for an OLAP database in Bulk-Logged recovery mode.

Archive Data When It Makes Sense

Given all these sources of data, you can quickly see that even in a moderately sized company, the volume of data can become huge. This is particularly relevant in the denormalized OLAP world. Very early in a volumetric sizing analysis, a decision needs to be made about when data will be archived to a long term "offline" storage container (tape; Write-Once, Read Many [WORM] drive; CD-ROM; DVD; and so forth). Although data may no longer be needed for reportage or transactional processing, there may be a legal or regulatory reason that the data must be maintained. You need to remember that although these regulations very often specify a time requirement for maintaining the data, they seldom specify the media (paper hard-copy, read-only storage, rotating disk, clay or stone tablet, and so forth) that the data is stored on. It can get very expensive to keep massive amounts of data spinning around for years and years when it may more appropriately be "shelved" on read-only media.

Even if the data volume is not huge and it can still stay in a SQL Server database, it may make sense to archive it away from your main tables. As we pointed out earlier in the book, the single greatest expense that we always seek to minimize in database usage is reads from disk. The more data we need to read from disk, the slower an application will appear to an end user. If reads from disk are considered to be slow, reads from archived, offline storage can be an order of magnitude (or more) slower. A general rule of thumb is that no data should be archived from disk where there is a routine operational need to access that data.

On the other hand, once data is no longer routinely operationally necessary, it should aggressively be archived either to another table, another database, another server, or a totally different medium. The gains from querying smaller indexes and, less desirably, tables can become enormous. What does "routine operational need" mean? The emphasis here should be on the word "routine." When data is accessed monthly, quarterly, or even yearly, it might be best to keep it spinning on a hard disk.

The nonroutine events category could include IRS audits, legal suits, and company acquisitions. Such events happen rarely. When they do, the time expense of loading the data into either hard disk or RAM from an offline storage device and the customized querying that may be needed are usually acceptable expenses to the database operating system and the DBA.

The Cost of Archiving

Like all performance improvements, every optimization needs to be analyzed from a cost-benefit standpoint. Although the benefits include increased performance, the costs of archiving are primarily threefold. The first is the cost of the archive subsystem and its physical implementation. There might be the upfront cost of a dedicated WORM drive, for instance. Additionally, the server engineers have to develop and maintain skills for its implementation and maintenance.

We shouldn't gloss over the word "maintain" too quickly in the previous sentence. We all know that the rapid pace of change in software is matched by the pace of improvements in hardware. If you are an old hand, you can remember that little more than a decade ago we were running around with TRS-80 processors and 5.25-inch (or worse still, 8-inch) floppies. Think of what it would take to load and read an 8-inch floppy today. This doesn't even get into the software formatting of the disk implicit to the operating system it was saved under. Imagine that you have a requirement to save data for 25 years. You need to account for the "costs" of being able either to read data from an *ancient* format or to periodically reformat that data from old media onto more modern media.

Once the physical archive storage device exists, additional and significant costs can be generated in intelligently removing the data from the active online databases. As often as not, some detailed analysis is necessary. Heaven forbid that you archive business data that is operationally necessary. The cost and time for this analysis needs to be factored into your design.

> **Archiving data doesn't mean you're throwing it away; you still have to be able to use it.**

Finally, there's the cost of designing the code necessary to access the data once it's archived. There may be a nonroutine, exceptional need for the data. It's incumbent on the archive designer to account and prepare for this exceptional need.

Archiving Details

Now that you're totally convinced of the need for archiving, you need to know the details. Obviously, every database will have differing criteria depending on the parameters previously set forth. But you should generally start thinking about archiving by looking at the following areas:

- Archiving by time period
- Archiving by fact table date-partitioning
- Archiving by fact table characteristics
- Accessing archived data

Archiving by Time Period

Briefly, we need to begin by discussing the concept of **fact tables**. Fact tables are generally the largest tables in the database because they contain detailed data about the underlying transactions.

The most obvious method of archiving is to pull historic data from fact tables and populate a parallel table structure with the archived data. Although usually straightforward, as in "we will archive all data that is 3 years old," some things may not be obvious. Sometimes fact tables may have several dates associated with them. For example, a purchase order detail record may have the date the purchase order was initiated, multiple dates it was approved at various levels of approval authority, the date the purchase order was submitted to the vendor, the date the vendor acknowledged receiving the purchase order, the date or dates that the order was fulfilled, and the date that the purchase transaction was finally completed. It isn't unusual to see 6 months or a year go by before some purchase orders are finally fulfilled, particularly on manufacturing contracts. Do you want to archive based on the date the purchase order number was assigned or based on the date that the purchase order was finally fulfilled? This is the work of a skilled data analyst who gets paid well. And it could be you.

What about domain tables that support fact tables? Take the vendor table that provides a `vendor_id` column to the purchase order detail record. Generally, you'll have a foreign key on the purchase order record referencing the primary key on the vendor column. Take the scenario in which a vendor goes out of business. Now it's 3 years later and you have archived all rows that this vendor record key supported from your purchase order rows. All of the sudden, you no longer have programmatic enforcement of the primary key's persistence by a row with the foreign key. You need to think of such things as you prepare to archive. As we all know, good programmers make it work; great programmers make it break correctly.

Archiving by Fact Table Date-Partitioning

Much of the data that you insert into your databases is easily partitioned along date lines. For example, ATM transactions have a very definite date on which they were conducted. Further, once the transactions have been recorded, the data is essentially read-only. Rather than going back and undoing a disputed transaction, another correcting transaction is entered at a later date. Thus, it's easy to see how all the transactions for a particular month could be inserted throughout the month in a particular table. For example, table `ATM_200104` (or actually a subset of dated tables with referential integrity that would really cover all the ATM transactions) could be all the ATM transactions for the month of April in the year 2001. Once April is over, no more transactions will go in this table. Once the bills for April 2001 are issued and summary tables for OLAP analysis have been generated, this table is a great candidate for archival onto read-only media. Such huge fact tables are routinely offloaded onto tape, CD-ROM, or DVD for infrequent reference. Now that you know this, you can understand why the bank charges you a hefty fee for a copy of a previous monthly statement. In some instances, companies will simply refuse to generate duplicate detail records from these fact tables (short of court action).

Archiving by Fact Table Characteristics

Similar to archiving by date-partitioned fact tables, you can also archive an individual row from an online table according to a particular set of circumstances for the row. In this case, you aren't taking the whole table offline. Rather, you're culling individual rows and groups of rows from tables based on specified criteria. A good example might be a transaction completed more than 2 years ago. Obviously, while the transaction is open and has detail records inserted against it, you wouldn't want to archive it. Even after it's recently closed, you wouldn't want to archive it because it's still used for year-to-date and last-full-year reporting and analysis. Depending on your business rules, though, a transaction more than 2 years old might be a prime target for archiving.

Another example of a row that might be archived based on specified criteria would be a row representing a potential customer who never materialized. You might have a customer table listing all your current, previous, and prospective customers. You use this table not only to record customer activity, but also as a sales-generation tool for mailings and leads. Routinely, potential customers are put into the tables in lists that your company buys from a list broker. Many of these potential customers will be turned into customers. Some will not. Periodically you would want to prune this list to make your queries easier. You specify criteria for archiving off potential customer "deadwood." Such criteria might be "never was an active customer" and "we've carried this customer on the list for 3 years with no activity generated." Remember, though, you paid good money for this list. You don't just delete these potential customers. They go in the ever-expanding deadwood archive table or tables on read-only media. Who knows? You may be able to bring this wood back to life and move the row back to an active customer.

> **When you're designing a database, the moment you start thinking about putting large amounts of data into a table is the moment you should start thinking about archiving data out of the table.**

It's important to note that archiving shouldn't be an afterthought to designing a database and an application. Archiving can represent a significant area for performance gains. If, however, your table structure isn't designed to support archiving, or applications weren't designed to access archived data, you may be out of luck. It will be very hard to sell the customer the idea of removing data from their database, paying the cost of redesigning the application or database, and giving you more money to do this once the original application is online. Worse still, when your application starts choking on data that should otherwise be archived, the customer will blame you.

Accessing Archived Data

Once you've removed data, two questions come to mind: "How do you get back to this data when you need it?" and "If you offloaded data onto alternative media, what is their shelf life?"

Regarding the first question, an application will often be made archive-aware by inserting a small row in the active table keyed to the archived row. When a user requests this archive row, a process is set in place to deal with the request. This process may involve a simple query to another table, a jukebox loading a CD-ROM, a message sent to a computer room attendant to mount a tape, or a message sent back to the original user asking him if he really, really needs this data.

Much of this process depends on how the data is archived. If the archived data is still in the database, but just moved to an alternate location (so that queries of the main fact table are faster and indexes are flatter), then getting to the data will be almost transparent to the users. At the other extreme, when the archived data is stored on reel-to-reel tapes that have to be mounted manually, the end user may decide that she doesn't really need the data.

The second question to keep in mind when archiving data is the issue of media and its shelf life. More and more when data is archived, it's stored on either CD-ROM or DVD-ROM. What about the situation in which it's placed on magnetic tape? We recently came across a story about the US National Aeronautics and Space Administration (NASA). NASA satellites routinely download information onto tape for later study and analysis by scientists in NASA-funded laboratories. The amount of data is staggering. It turns out that this tape has a shelf life of 10 years. It also turns out that if NASA took all the tape drives that are serviceable today to begin recopying this data onto more reliable and longer lasting media, it would take significantly longer than 10 years. In short, be careful where you store your archived data if you have a requirement to use it later.

Server Performance

We could present an intricate analysis of the memory breakdown of exactly what aspects of RAM are inhabited by each portion of SQL Server, but this subject has been exhausted in other books. We'll limit our analysis to a quick overview, emphasizing where you can obtain the greatest performance gains.

Although all versions of Windows Server are built from the same kernel, they're certainly not the same in terms of performance. Each successive version of the kernel, from Windows NT 4.0 to Windows 2000 Server to Windows Server 2003, has seen improvements in areas that directly impact database performance. These areas include memory management, process management, I/O management, and networking.

If you're buying a new server today, definitely get the latest (at the time of this writing) server operating system, Windows Server 2003. Windows Server 2003's network stack, for example, is 25-percent faster than Windows 2000 Server's network stack when it comes to TCP/IP send performance (i.e., returning the results of a query to the client). This and many more improvements to the core kernel make Windows Server 2003 the optimum platform for SQL Server 2000.

It should be noted that there's one limitation on running SQL Server 2000 on top of Windows Server 2003. You must be running Service Pack 3 of SQL Server 2000. If your database application isn't supported under Service Pack 3, this could be a problem. Increasingly, though, application vendors are releasing upgrades that work on top of SQL Server 2000 Service Pack 3.

Windows Server 2003 Editions

Databases love RAM, and Microsoft didn't disappoint them with the release of the various editions of Windows Server 2003. You should definitely be running Windows Server 2003 as the base operating system for SQL Server 2000 if you have a choice. However, you need to understand the features and limitations of the various editions in order to make an intelligent choice.

We'll start by describing the cheapest and most limited edition: the Web Edition. It supports only two symmetric multiprocessors and a maximum of 2GB of RAM. Even more limiting is that it supports only ten inbound Server Message Block (SMB) connections. SMB connections are the connections you need to make to managing files on the server or for using a named pipes SQL connection. The most limiting feature, though, is that it supports only the Microsoft SQL Server Database Engine (MSDE) with a maximum of 25 concurrent connections. Essentially, the Web Edition was designed with a price point and feature set to compete with Linux/Apache/MySQL installations. If you're going to use this for a small-to-(maybe)medium website, it will make a good platform for the MSDE version of SQL and you can be happy. For anything else, we recommend using the Windows Server 2003 Standard Edition.

The Standard Edition is a fully capable server. The vast majority of SQL Server instances will be homed on this 32-bit operating system, which supports up to four CPUs and 4GB of RAM. Out of the box, it comes with an MSDE instance supporting five concurrent connections. You will, of course, want to avoid this instance in favor of the fully featured and non-governor-limited SQL Server Standard Edition. Together, Windows Server 2003 Standard and SQL Server 2000 Standard editions make the best price/performance point for most applications.

The Enterprise Edition of Windows Server 2003 is designed for medium-to-large-sized businesses. It comes in both a 32-bit edition and a 64-bit edition. It supports up to eight processors and up to 32GB of RAM for the 32-bit edition and 64GB of RAM for the 64-bit edition. It has some features that the Standard Edition of the operating system lacks. One of the slam-dunk features is that it will run an application called Windows System Resource Manager (WSRM). This allows you to allocate those eight CPUs and 32/64GB of RAM on a per-application basis. If you're running multiple instances of SQL Server, this could be a real cost-saver for you. If you plan to run SQL Server 2000 Enterprise Edition, you generally want to run it on this platform.

The Datacenter Edition of Windows Server 2003 is only available through an OEM load of a very high-end server hardware package. You'll find it marketed by companies such as Hewlett-Packard (HP) and Unisys. It's enough to say that the 32-bit edition supports 32 CPUs, and the 64-bit edition supports 64 CPUs. If that weren't enough, a 128-CPU, 64-bit edition should be available by this book's publication that is really just two 64-CPU partitions. Although the 32-bit edition supports 64GB of RAM, the 64-bit edition is constantly expanding the amount of RAM it will support and is really only limited by the hardware vendors. As of this writing, a 512GB installation was being tested. As you can imagine, putting half a terabyte of RAM in one place will make for a pretty nice DBMS.

Memory Subsystems

In short, if there's any money left over in the budget for your hardware, the first rule of SQL Server performance tuning is to use this money for RAM. SQL Server thrives on RAM. Although we'll go into depth on disk subsystem performance gains, the performance gain you get from RAM is, dollar for dollar, greater than that of disk subsystems.

Within reason, you should seriously consider getting the maximum amount of RAM that your motherboard can hold. If you don't do so, make sure you buy RAM chips that maximize each RAM slot on the motherboard, by getting the largest possible memory module size possible for the slot, as this will make any future memory upgrades easier.

As an example, say you're buying a server that has eight RAM slots with a capacity of 512MB in each slot, for a total maximum of 4GB. You've checked your budget and can justify only 2GB in your boss's mind. There are two different ways that your server vendor can fill this requirement. The cheaper way is with eight RAM chips of 256MB each. The better way and the price that you want to present to your boss is four RAM chips of 512MB each, leaving four empty slots. The slight premium you pay for this configuration will more than pay for itself when your data requirements expand and you need to buy that extra 2GB.

Memory Subsystems on Windows NT Server

Speaking of 4GB of RAM, there are some limitations for the operating systems on which SQL Server runs. Though SQL Server will run on Windows 9*x*/ME systems, we're only going to look at SQL Server on the Windows NT/2000/2003 product line. An important point to note about the Windows 9*x* operating system family is that because they have a different virtual memory design from Windows NT and Windows 2000, the algorithms used for SQL Server optimization are different.

Windows NT Server comes in two different editions: the Standard Edition and the Enterprise Edition. Although both of the Windows NT versions support a maximum of 4GB of RAM, they divide this 4GB differently. The Standard Edition will support only a maximum of 2GB of memory dedicated to any one process. This dedicated memory includes both RAM and virtual memory, where a portion of the hard disk is set aside to act like RAM, albeit very, very slowly. Thus, even though you might have 4GB of RAM in your server, the service process that starts at operating system boot-up and in which SQL Server runs would be able to use only 2GB of this memory. The other 2GB would be set aside for the operating system. The Enterprise Edition raises this level to 3GB, allowing essentially a 50-percent boost in performance. This is done through a BOOT.INI switch.

Memory Subsystems on Windows 2000 Server

Windows 2000 memory architecture is a little more complex. To begin with, there are now three editions of the operating system: Standard, Advanced, and Datacenter. The Standard Edition is much like the standard version of Windows NT. It will support 4GB of RAM, with a maximum of 2GB for any single process.

Windows 2000 Advanced Server scales up to 8GB of RAM. It does this in two different ways. The first is called **application memory tuning** or **4-gigabyte-tuning** (4GT). 4GT is very similar to the way the NT Enterprise version handles memory. It is for applications that run on servers with between 2GB and 4GB of RAM and has a maximum process limit of 3GB.

479

To make full use of the 8GB of RAM on Windows 2000 Advanced Server, you need to implement Physical Address Extension (PAE) X86. The hardware requirements for PAE X86 are more stringent than those for 4GT. To determine if your hardware is supported, please consult the Windows 2000 Hardware Compatibility List (http://www.microsoft.com/windows2000/server/howtobuy/upgrading /compat/default.asp/) and search for the keywords **Large Memory**.

Technology	Hardware Requirements
Physical Address Extension (PAE) X86	❏ Pentium Pro processor or later
	❏ 4GB or more of RAM
	❏ 450 NX or compatible chipset and support or later
Application memory tuning, also known as 4-gigabyte tuning (4GT)	❏ Intel-based processor ❏ 2GB or more of RAM

With PAE X86 implemented, both SQL Server 7.0 and SQL Server 2000 Enterprise editions use Microsoft Windows 2000 Address Windowing Extensions (AWE) to address approximately 8GB of memory. In SQL Server 2000, this is on a per-instance basis because it supports more than one instance of SQL Server. Each instance using this extended memory, however, must have its memory allocated manually instead of letting SQL Server manage it automatically using its dynamic memory management routines.

Windows 2000 Datacenter is the most ambitious operating system Microsoft has ever marketed. In addition to supporting up to 32 processors, using PAE X86 it will support 64GB of RAM. Only SQL Server 2000 Enterprise Edition is set up to run in this environment. Additionally, the Windows 2000 Datacenter Server operating system will load only on an approved hardware configuration. Approved hardware configurations are available under the Windows Datacenter Program and are available from major vendors such as Compaq, Dell, Unisys, IBM, and HP. Unisys, for example, markets the ES7000 with 32 CPUs and up to 64GB of RAM. Its disk I/O subsystem supports up to 96 channels.

Memory Subsystems on Windows Server 2003

Windows Server 2003 memory architecture is still a little more complex than Windows 2000 Server, primarily because Windows Server 2003 introduces the 64-bit platform. Going forward, this platform will distinguish SQL Server in the marketplace. There are now four editions of the operating system: Web, Standard, Enterprise, and Datacenter. However, because there are 64-bit editions of the Enterprise and Datacenter products, we'll treat these as separate editions, for a total of six editions. Generally, you'll want to determine what the application needs to perform, and then you'll pick the operating system to match those needs. Obviously, you still get what you pay for, with the Web Edition being the cheapest and least capable of the editions.

The Web Edition is really a boutique server build designed to compete with Linux/Apache on both performance and price levels. As such, it won't be a good player for a SQL Server under most applications. That said, if you have a relatively lightweight database behind your website, the 25-concurrent-connection MSDE that ships "out of the box" with Web Edition is for you. The next step up is a "per CPU" license for SQL Server 2000 Standard Edition, and this starts to get expensive.

The Standard Edition still supports 4GB of RAM like the 2000 version. As with Windows 2000, you're still limited to a 2GB address space for SQL Server.

As previously noted, the Enterprise Edition is really two different editions: the 32-bit edition and the 64-bit edition. An easy way to remember the RAM capabilities here is that the 32-bit edition has a maximum of 32GB of RAM, and the 64-bit edition has a maximum of 64GB of RAM. In the 32-bit edition, however, you still have to use AWE to make use of the full amount. In the 64-bit edition, a flat memory map is used, and it's much cleaner. For this reason, in a comparison of two servers with roughly the same processor totals and speed, a 64-bit server Itanium 2 server will often outperform a 32-bit Pentium server by a factor of 2 or 3 or more.

The Datacenter Editions also come in 32-bit and 64-bit editions. The maximum RAM for the AWE-utilized, 32-bit edition is 64GB. The 64-bit Datacenter server is Microsoft's scalability platform for beating Oracle. Microsoft is constantly expanding its capabilities based on what the big hardware vendors are showing up with at the door. At the time of this writing, the maximum supported amount of RAM for the 64-bit version of Datacenter Server was a whopping 512GB of RAM.

Memory Performance Monitoring

Now that you know the memory limitations in SQL Server imposed by the operating system, what can you do to optimize that memory and determine if you need more? This is where we get into what is popularly called "the art of performance monitoring."

We'll generally focus our efforts on tuning SQL Server 7.0 and SQL Server 2000 engines. These engines made dramatic improvements over SQL Server 6.5 in their memory management algorithms. Unlike SQL Server 6.5, they dynamically acquire and free memory as needed. It's typically not necessary for an administrator to specify how much memory should be allocated to a SQL Server 7.0 or SQL Server 2000 server, although the option still exists and is required in some environments.

Due to the dynamic nature of the memory in SQL Server 7.0 and SQL Server 2000, Microsoft removed support for one of the most useful tools available in SQL Server 6.5: DBCC MEMUSAGE. Now, to get this information, you have to monitor a variety of performance counters in the Buffer Manager object and the Cache Manager object because the information is no longer statically mapped in a table like sysconfigures. Although this handy tool is listed as "Unsupported" now and no longer returns the breakdown of memory usage, try running it. You'll see that this unsupported snapshot continues to return the top 20 list of buffered tables and indexes. This can be a very handy list. When you're analyzing performance of an individual application in a test environment, it can be invaluable.

The Art of Performance Monitoring

Performance monitoring is an art, in that it's a combination of talent, experience, knowledge, and sometimes just plain luck. How do you know if you can do it? You have to try, try, and try again. Keep at it and read up on it. Keep a performance monitor continually open against your production server. Here are some guidelines to get you started:

1. Make sure that you're running your typical processes (SQL Server) and workloads (queries and stored procedures) during your monitoring.

2. Don't just do real-time monitoring of your servers. Capture long-running logs. In Windows NT, install the Datalog/Monitor service from the NT Resource Kit; this functionality is available out of the box in Windows 2000 Server and Windows Server 2003.

3. Always have disk counters turned on by running from a command prompt the command DISKPERF –Y and then rebooting. Even in a production environment, the overhead is minimal. The last thing you want to do in the middle of a crisis in which logical and physical disk counters are necessary is have to reboot.

4. For routine, daily, desktop monitoring, set up the chart window with an interval of 18 seconds. In both the Windows NT PerfMon and the Windows 2000/2003 MMC SysMon, this will give your chart a window of 30 minutes. For us, this has proven to be the ideal interval for both seeing the past and minimizing the impact on the server.

5. Use SQL Profiler for individual queries and processes in coordination with PerfMon or SysMon to get a good picture of the impact of individual queries.

6. Know the terminology of performance monitoring. **Objects** are lists of individual statistics available. An example is the Processor object. A **counter** is a single statistic that falls under the heading of an object. An example is the % Processor Time counter under the Processor object. An **instance** is a further breakdown of a counter statistic into duplicate components. Not all counters will have separate instances. The % Processor Time counter has instances for each processor and a _Total instance as a summary of all processor activity.

7. Know your tools. Although you may know how to set up a chart in PerfMon, learn how to set up a log with Datalog or Performance Log. Other tools to be familiar with are DBCC MEMUSAGE, Task Manager, and SQL Enterprise Manager Current Activity.

8. Don't be afraid to experiment. The BackOffice Resource Kit contains tools for creating test data (DataSim), creating test databases (DBGen), and simulating loading from multiple clients (SqlLS) .

SQL Performance Monitoring and Bottlenecks

Bottlenecks occur when the hardware resources can't keep up with the demands of the software. For example, when a software process or combination of processes wants more I/O from a disk than the disk can physically deliver, a bottleneck occurs at the disk. When the CPU subsystem becomes too saturated and processes are waiting, a bottleneck has occurred. Bottlenecks are usually fixed in one of two ways. The first is to identify the limiting hardware and increase its capabilities. In other words, get a faster hard drive or increase the speed of the CPU. The second way is to make the software processes use the hardware more efficiently. This could be done by putting an index on a table so that either the disk I/O necessary to service a query is reduced or the CPU units necessary to process a join are lessened.

The following are five key areas to monitor when tracking server performance and identifying bottlenecks. Each bottleneck candidate will have varied performance monitoring objects and counters to consider.

- ❏ Memory usage: This relates to SQL Server requirements, relative to itself and to the operating system memory. If SQL Server has enough memory but the operating system is starved of memory such that it has to frequently swap through the page file to disk, overall performance will suffer dramatically.

- ❏ CPU processor use: High CPU usage rates indicate the CPU subsystem is underpowered. Solutions could be upgrading the CPU or increasing the number of processors.

- ❏ Disk I/O performance: Failure of the disk or disk controller to satisfy read or write requirements in a timely manner impacts performance.

- ❏ User connections: Improperly setting the number of user connections could rob memory otherwise available to SQL Server.

- ❏ Blocking locks: One process keeps another process from accessing or updating data. This is particularly noticeable to users and is the cause of some of the most severe performance problems from a user perspective.

Memory Tuning: The Operating System and SQL Server

Start your intensive analysis of memory by looking at two counters:

- ❏ Memory: Available Bytes

- ❏ Memory: Pages Faults/sec

The Available Bytes counter indicates how much memory is available for use by processes. The Pages Faults/sec counter indicates the number of hard page faults, pages that had to be retrieved from the hard disk because they weren't in working memory. It also includes the number of pages written to the hard disk to free space in the working set to support a hard page fault.

A low number for `Available Bytes` indicates that there may not be enough memory available, or processes, including SQL Server, may not be releasing memory. A high number of `Page Faults/sec` indicates excessive paging. You should further examine individual instances of `Process:Page Faults/sec` to see if the SQL Server process, for example, has excessive paging. A low rate of `Page Faults/sec` (commonly 5 to 10 per second) is normal, as the operating system will continue to do some housekeeping on the working set.

As previously noted, starting with SQL Server 7.0, memory is autotuning by default. In general, though, you want to give SQL Server as much dedicated memory as possible. This is mostly dependent on what other applications may be running on the server. By using the `sp_configure` stored procedure, you can set the values for `MIN SERVER MEMORY` and `MAX SERVER MEMORY` to dedicated values.

If SQL Server is the only application on the server, set `MIN SERVER MEMORY` and `MAX SERVER MEMORY` to the same value. If SQL Server coexists with one or more applications, lower the `MIN SERVER MEMORY` setting to account for the memory demands of the other application(s). If the other application fails to start in a timely manner, it may be because SQL Server has been operating at or near the `MAX SERVER MEMORY` setting and is slow in releasing memory to the new, and now starved, application. In this instance, lower the value of `MAX SERVER MEMORY`. Obviously, `MAX SERVER MEMORY` always needs to be greater than or equal to `MIN SERVER MEMORY`.

> **If you've installed and are running the full-text search support (Microsoft Search service, also known as MSSearch), then you must set the `MAX SERVER MEMORY` option manually to leave enough memory for the MSSearch service to run. Microsoft supplies a handy formula here: Total Virtual Memory – (SQL Server MAX + Virtual Memory for Other Processes) = 1.5 * Server Physical Memory.**

Once you've tuned the SQL Server memory settings, it's a good idea to decide if you want SQL Server 7.0/2000 to tune the process memory automatically or have values set for the configuration. For better performance, you can lock the amount of working set memory that SQL Server reserves. The trade-off here is that you may receive "out of memory" messages from other applications on the same server. If you do decide to fix the amount of working set memory, two configuration settings are necessary. First, equalize the `MIN SERVER MEMORY` and `MAX SERVER MEMORY` settings. Then turn on the `SET WORKING SET SIZE` configuration flag using `sp_configure`. `MAX SERVER MEMORY` should generally not exceed the RAM available for the server.

SQL Server 2000 Dynamic Memory Tuning

Just how does dynamic tuning work? The screen shot that follows shows the memory property settings for an instance of SQL Server 2000. This instance is called CD1\MS8D1. This means that it's on server CD1 and is a second or later instance, as the default first instance would simply have the name of the server. Deep down under the covers, the instance is running with a process identified by MSSQL$InstanceName–in this case, MSSQL$MS8D1. The default instance, as in SQL Server 6.5 and SQL Server 7.0, has a process name of MSSQLServer. Instance CD1\MS8D1 has a minimum setting of 60 and a maximum of 512, which is the total RAM installed on this particular server. With these settings, you would think that when you start up instance CD1\MS8D1, it would immediately take 60MB of RAM and could potentially take all 512MB. This isn't the way dynamic memory works.

When you first start an instance of SQL Server 2000, it initially takes 8 to 12MB of RAM. It will only acquire more RAM for its process as users connect and workload increases. In the case of CD1\MS8D1, it will gradually increase its memory space allocated to the MSSQL$MS8D1 process. Once it reaches the threshold of the configure value of 60MB, it won't go below this setting. At the same time, as workload increases, the instance will gradually acquire memory. It will, however, not reach 512MB, the value of installed RAM on the server. Instead, Microsoft designed a series of algorithms that kick into place. These algorithms have two specific goals:

❏   Maintain the operating system's free memory within 4MB and 10MB

❏   Distribute memory between instances of SQL Server based on their relative workloads

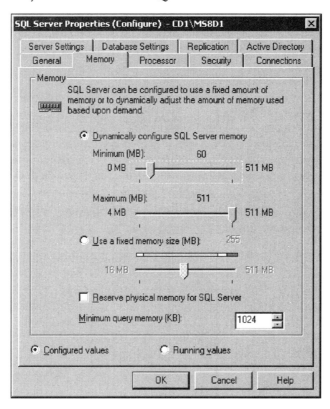

Free Memory Target

As previously noted, the maximum setting for instance CD1\MS8D1 in the preceding screen shot was 512MB, the value of installed RAM on the server. Experiments by Microsoft have shown that maintaining 4 to 10MB of memory on a Windows server will minimize page-file swapping. The specific value that the SQL Server seeks to maintain in this 4 to 10MB window is called the **free memory target**. The algorithms were designed such that, as SQL Server consumes more and more memory for its data cache, the amount of free memory for the operating system decreases. When the 4 to 10MB threshold is reached, SQL Server will stop acquiring memory. The free memory target is at 10MB for a lightly loaded SQL Server system, and it gradually goes down to 4MB for a heavily loaded SQL Server. This free memory target is a reflection of the page life expectancy in the SQL Server buffer pool. When a server is heavily loaded, pages are more frequently loaded into the buffer cache and old pages are removed, decreasing page life expectancy. As page life expectancy goes down, SQL Server will maintain operating system free memory at the low end (4MB) of the target 4 to 10MB range. When it's less busy and page life expectancy goes up, it maintains a free memory target closer to 10MB.

Thus, going back to the instance of CD1\MS8D1, the maximum memory will never approach 512MB of RAM. Rather, it would probably be somewhere around 460 to 470MB, because a relatively clean operating system takes 30 to 40MB of RAM and the free memory target of 4 to 10MB of RAM is always maintained free for the operating system, in order to avoid paging.

So what happens when you're running SQL Server and it's maintaining a free memory target of 4 to 10MB of RAM available for the operating system, and you suddenly start a large process that consumes 20 to 25MB of RAM? It turns out that SQL Server will dynamically reduce its memory in data cache to maintain the 4 to 10MB of free operating system memory. It can do this very quickly, on the order of several megabytes per second.

Multiple Instance Memory Tuning

When SQL Server has to share the operating system with another process (for example, with the MSSearch service), SQL Server's maximum memory has to be manually configured. As you probably know by now, SQL Server 2000 allows multiple instances of SQL Server on the same operating system. This is true whether the operating system is Window NT or Windows 2000. What about the situation in which two or more instances of SQL Server are installed on the same server?

In this case, SQL Server is smart enough to balance the loads between the two instances. Remember from the previous section the instance CD1\MS8D1. Obviously, the default instance is called CD1. We'll look at these two instances, but the theory would be the same for three or more.

> How many instances can you run on a single server? Microsoft recommends one, the default instance, for a production server. We've heard of separate tests running 10 and 16 successfully. We certainly don't recommend more than 10. Generally, you would want to run multiple instances on a single server to support, for example, a development environment in one or more instances, and a quality assurance or testing environment in another instance. All of this, of course, is contingent on the overall capabilities of the hardware underneath the instances.

On system start-up, each of the instances, CD1 and CD1\MS8D1, will immediately acquire 8 to 12MB of RAM. They'll remain at this level until user connections and workloads start increasing on one or both. They'll then acquire RAM independently of one another only until the operating system has 4 to 10MB of free RAM available as outlined in the previous section. At this point, they start competing with one another for memory based on their free memory target values.

As an example, if the default instance has heavy workload, its free memory target will be around 4MB. The CD1\MS8D1 instance is more lightly loaded and has a free memory target of 10MB. Assume that only 7MB of free memory is available for the operating system. As you would expect, the heavily loaded CD1 instance with a target of 4MB will keep on acquiring memory. Because the lightly loaded CD1\MS8D1 doesn't see 10MB free, it will release memory to the operating system to try and reach its target of 10MB free. Don't think about how much memory is allocated to each process. Rather, think about the page life expectancy and the value of its corresponding free memory target for that instance.

A negative feedback loop is thus set up to balance the amount of memory each instance acquires relative to its workload. As the CD1, the heavily loaded instance, gets more memory, it can keep pages in memory longer, increasing its page life expectancy. As page life expectancy goes up, the free target memory value, which had been 4MB, goes up. On the lightly loaded instance, CD1\MS8D1, memory is released so that SQL Server attempts to raise the operating system's free memory to the 10MB target. As memory is released, pages are kept in memory for a shorter period, decreasing their page life expectancy. As page life expectancy goes down, the free target memory value goes down from 10MB. At some point, the lightly loaded instance will have released enough memory (at least down to its minimum value) such that the free memory target of the two instances is the same.

What is the final result? The free memory target (and corresponding page life expectancy) of the two instances is the same. The heavily loaded instance is still heavily loaded. Except, now given the approximately 460MB of RAM available to all SQL Server instances, the heavily loaded instance has, as an example, 430MB of RAM allocated to it. The lightly loaded instance has around 100MB of RAM. The equilibrium lasts only as long as the relative workloads of the instances remain steady. As soon as the workload on one or the other instance increases or decreases, the page life expectancy and corresponding free memory target will respond and drive the instances to a new equilibrium.

SQL Server Process Memory Tuning

Once you've gotten the overall operating system and SQL server memory tuned, look further at the SQL Server memory usage. Four counters are desirable here:

❑   Process: Working Set:sqlservr

❑   SQL Server: Buffer Manager: Buffer Cache Hit Ratio

❑   SQL Server: Buffer Manager: Free Buffers

❑   SQL Server: Memory Manager: Total Server Memory (KB)

The Working Set:sqlservr instance shows the amount of memory that SQL Server is using. If the number is consistently lower than the amount SQL Server is configured to use by the MIN SERVER MEMORY and MAX SERVER MEMORY options, then SQL Server is configured for too much memory. Otherwise, you may need to increase RAM and MAX SERVER MEMORY.

Buffer Cache Hit Ratio should be consistently greater than 90. This indicates that the data cache supplied 90 percent of the requests for data. If this value is consistently low, it's a very good indicator that more memory is needed by SQL Server. If Available Bytes is low, this means that you need to add more RAM.

When Free Buffers is low, this means that there isn't enough RAM to maintain a consistent amount of data cache. It too is indicative of a need for more memory.

If Total Server Memory for SQL Server is consistently higher than the overall server memory, it indicates that there isn't enough RAM.

Adjusting Server Performance

If this server is dedicated to SQL Server or if SQL Server is considered to be the most important application on the machine, there's a configuration change that you can supposedly make to increase performance. You can control the relative amounts of processor time that will be given to foreground applications compared to background applications. The default value for Windows NT is to give foreground applications the highest priority and, therefore, the best response time.

To configure this setting, open Control Panel from the Settings folder menu of the Start menu. Open the System applet in Control Panel and select the Performance tab, as shown in the following screen shot. Use the slider control on this tab to adjust the foreground and background priorities. In Windows NT Workstation, the operating system scheduler will always give background threads two clock ticks. Clock ticks can be 7 to 15 ms depending on the hardware abstraction layer (HAL). Depending on the position of the slider, the foreground applications will get either two, four, or six clock ticks for each thread, corresponding to None to Maximum.

A little-known fact is that in Windows NT Server, this has absolutely no impact. The slide on the GUI works, but nothing changes underneath. All threads get 12 clock ticks. Period.

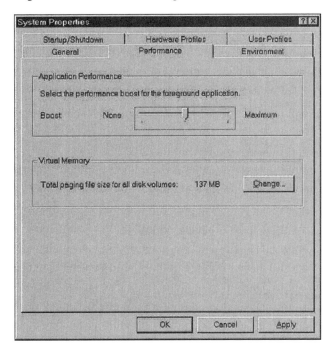

Unlike Windows NT Server, in Windows 2000 Server this actually works. But it's a little simpler. In both the server product and the workstation product, called Windows 2000 Professional, you access the following dialog box by clicking the Performance Options button in the Advanced tab of the Control Panel | System applet.

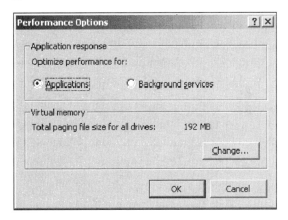

When you optimize performance for Applications in Windows 2000, you get the background thread to foreground thread ratio of two clock ticks to six clock ticks that Windows NT Workstation uses when it's optimized for foreground applications. When you select the Background services choice for Windows 2000, you get the performance of Windows NT Server: 12 clock ticks for all threads.

489

It's recommended that you keep this at the **Background services** selection on all Windows 2000 servers running SQL Server to provide equal processor time to both foreground and background applications. This will give Microsoft SQL Server a greater percentage of the processing power, as it's almost always run as a background service.

Windows Server 2003 uses a slightly different scheme to manage these performance options. Begin in Control Panel. As in Windows 2000 Server, click the **System** applet. Go to the **Advanced** tab and under the **Performance** section, click the **Settings** button. The **Performance Options** dialog window opens. Click the **Advanced** tab in this dialog box, which will expose the ability to change **Processor scheduling, Memory usage,** and **Virtual memory.**

Processor scheduling refers to how the processor resources are distributed between running programs. Selecting **Programs** will assign more resources to the foreground programs that are responding to user input. In doing so, you'll allocate short variable time slices, or quanta, of the processor control to these foreground programs. Not good. Generally on a SQL Server, you want to select **Background services.** When you do this, Windows Server 2003 will assign an equal number of resources to all programs and use long, fixed quanta. This is good.

Memory usage refers to how Windows Server 2003 allocates memory resources between running programs. For a SQL Server, you should select **System cache.** If you were using the server as a workstation (not a recommended practice), you would select **Programs.**

CPU Subsystems

The CPU subsystem is the heart and soul of your server. As such, it's a primary candidate for performance tuning. In recent years, symmetric multiprocessor (SMP) configurations have abounded. Windows NT Server supports four processors out of the box with no special vendor HAL. Windows 2000 Server maintained support at four processors; Windows 2000 Advanced Server raises the bar to eight processors. The Windows 2000 Datacenter Server further raises this up to 32 processors. Windows Server 2003 expands this even further. Although the Web and Standard Editions are limited to two and four processors, respectively, the Enterprise Edition supports eight processors in both the 32- and 64-bit editions. Like Windows 2000 Datacenter, the 32-bit Windows Server 2003 **Datacenter** supports 32 processors. The 64-bit edition of Windows Server 2003 Datacenter supports 64 processors. Microsoft is marketing a 128-processor SKU on the 64-bit Datacenter frame, but at the time of this writing, it isn't supported yet. We're talking some significant computation at this level.

Should you use Windows 2003, Windows 2000, or Windows NT? Definitely Windows 2003. For a four-processor server, Windows 2003 Server shows up to a 140-percent performance improvement over a similarly equipped Windows NT Server. Windows NT doesn't support anything over four processors, short of specialized OEM builds. Windows 2003 also supports processor affinity. This is where a process such as the SQL Server process is assigned to one or more processors. This effectively replaces the SMP concurrency that was written out of SQL Server as a configuration option after SQL Server 6.5. Please note that just as in SQL Server 6.5 with SMP concurrency, you should exercise caution when using processor affinity because it will often have the impact of keeping a process such as SQL Server from being able to use a less-used processor.

Although most people won't run a 64-processor server, many will run 2- and 4-processor servers. The newer servers have a technology called **hyperthreading**. Hyperthreading allows a processor to time-share within itself such that to the rest of the hardware it appears as two processors. Though you obviously aren't going to get the performance of two processors, you usually get the performance of 1.4 to 1.6 processors. Windows Server 2003 fully supports hyper threading, making it another slam-dunk choice for you to run if given the option.

Currently there appears to be a price-performance "sweet spot" at the four-processor level. So how should you configure SQL Server to maximize CPU usage? For SQL Server 7.0 and SQL Server 2000, one thought is necessary: hands off! Although some arguments may have been made for tuning a CPU subsystem in SQL Server 6.5, SQL Server 7.0 and SQL Server 2000 are highly tuned to take maximum advantage of any CPU setup that you throw at them.

CPU Performance Monitoring

In CPU performance monitoring, you'll use several counters:

❑   Processor: % Processor Time

❑   Processor: % Privileged Time

❑   Processor: % User Time

Generally, CPU performance monitoring is straightforward. You need to start by monitoring Processor: % Processor Time. If you have more than one processor, you should monitor each instance of this counter and also monitor System to determine the average for all processors.

Usage rates consistently above 80 or 90 percent may indicate a poorly tuned or designed application. On the other hand, if you've put all the other recommendations of this book into use, they may indicate a need for a more powerful CPU subsystem. In general, we recommend spending a little bit of time analyzing the applications before immediately going out and buying three more processors. Spending this time experimenting to discover CPU performance problems and correcting them through software improvements will often keep you from just spending money on a more powerful CPU that only "covers up" poorly written software for a short time.

If you do see high CPU usage, you then want to monitor Processor: % Privileged Time. This is the time spent performing kernel-level operations, such as disk I/O. If this counter is consistently above 80 or 90 percent and corresponds to high disk performance counters, you may have a disk bottleneck rather than a CPU bottleneck.

What about SQL Server? Processor: % User Time measures the amount of processor time consumed by non-kernel-level applications. SQL Server is such an application. If this is high and you have multiple processes running on a server, you may want to delve further by looking at specific process instances through the instances of the counter Process: % User Time. This can be very useful, for example, when your operating system engineers install new antivirus software on all your servers. It may temporarily bring the servers to their knees until you're able to determine the culprit through analyzing Process: % User Time for the antivirus software instance.

491

Textile Management

In the parlance of CPU usage, **threads** are a single process run by a CPU. Threads are managed by the operating system in kernel mode. SQL Server can maintain up to 255 open threads, with each thread used for batch processing. With the introduction of SQL Server 7.0, a new term, **fibers**, was introduced. Although threads are handled by the operating system in kernel mode, fibers are handled in user mode by the application itself.

In a high-capacity OLTP environment, the number of batches, and thus threads, thrown at a CPU subsystem may be very high, typically approaching the configured default of 255 threads. Each time a thread context is switched for a CPU, the CPU has to come out of user mode, go through a context switch to kernel mode, take up the new thread, and then context-switch back into user mode. For a CPU, a context switch is relatively expensive.

With fibers, SQL Server will spawn a few threads and then have multiple fibers in each thread. The management of fibers is relegated to the SQL Server application-level code rather than the operating system kernel. Because fibers run in user mode, when the CPU switches between one fiber and another in the same thread, there are no context switches for the CPU. The difference in CPU cycles between a CPU taking up a new thread that has to go through a context switch down into kernel mode and back out, and a CPU taking up a new fiber that doesn't undergo this process, is an order of magnitude.

Fibers aren't for every situation. Fibers are confined to a single thread, which is always assigned to a single CPU. Thus, whereas a process thread could be serviced by one CPU and then another, a process fiber would be confined to a single CPU. OLTP applications are emphasized because they typically have very short, defined transactions running in a process, be it contained in thread or fiber. Use the following checklist to determine if fibers may be for you:

1. Your server should be entirely dedicated to SQL Server usage and generally use it for an OLTP environment.

2. You are experiencing a very high CPU usage rate (> 90 percent).

3. You see an abnormally high rate of context switches using the counter `System:Context Switches/sec`.

If these parameters fit your system, you may want to experiment with fiber usage by switching the "lightweight pooling" configuration setting from 0 to 1.

Disk Subsystems

The second most important system characteristic for good performance of your SQL Server application is the disk subsystem. Remember, performance is mostly determined by maximizing the number of data reads from high-speed memory. Getting this data in and out of high-speed memory and storing it is the responsibility of the disk subsystem.

The Basic Disk Subsystem

The basic disk subsystem involves a hard disk and a hard disk controller interfacing with the motherboard. Hard disks have various performance characteristics. You can look at them from the standpoint of reading and writing, the standpoint of reading data off the disk sequentially or randomly, and the standpoint of how fast the disk is turning.

The reading characteristics are naturally different from the writing characteristics of a disk. As you would expect, writing is relatively slow compared to reading. Thus, you want to minimize the waiting time for disk writes. SQL Server naturally optimizes this by using a combination of individual worker threads and the lazy writer system. These two systems combine to scan through the buffer cache in active memory and decrement a counter indicating the relative busyness of a page in the buffer cache. Accessing the page causes an increment in its counter. In this way, frequently accessed pages are maintained in the buffer cache. If a buffer cache page's counter reaches zero and the page's dirty page indicator is set, either an individual worker thread or, less frequently, the lazy writer will schedule a flush to disk of the page. The key is that this is done asynchronously with the thread's read efforts, so that waiting time for writing is minimized.

Reading data from the disk is where most performance gains are concentrated. It's much more efficient to read data sequentially (rather than randomly) off a disk. Thus, the use of clustered indexes for loading large amounts of data into the data cache for analysis is always optimal.

Finally, if you're given a choice between a disk that turns at 7200 rpm and one that turns at 15,000 rpm, naturally choose the latter. Disks that turn faster get the data under the read head faster and into the data cache faster. Of course, they're more expensive.

You may have the fastest hard disk in the world, though, and have a poorly performing system if you don't have a good controller interface between the hard disk and the motherboard. The controller's performance is measured in bit path throughput. Obviously, 64 bits is better than 32.

What's also important about controllers is their caching capability. Today's controllers have both read-ahead and write-ahead or write-back caching capability. When a controller reads ahead, it uses sophisticated algorithms to anticipate data needs and place this data in fast cache before the CPU is ready for it. Write-ahead or write-back caching involves the controller posting data to high-speed cache and returning a completion status to the operating system. The data is then actually written to the disk by the controller, independent of the operating system. Significantly, caching capability is marked by the amount of high-speed RAM dedicated to caching this information. Again, more is better, but it's also more expensive.

Write Caching and SQL Server

Many controllers have a feature called **write caching**. This is where the controller will receive the data from the operating system and essentially tell the operating system that the data is written to disk, when in fact it has been stored in high-speed RAM for eventual writing to disk.

493

This can be highly problematic. SQL Server's whole scheme of ensuring data integrity in the event of a server failure is dependent on transaction logs being written to disk before the underlying tables are actually changed on disk. With a write-caching controller, SQL Server can be mistakenly told that a transaction log is sitting firmly on a hard disk, when in fact it's still residing in the high-speed RAM of the caching controller. If during that moment the server fails, the integrity of SQL in recovering committed transactions and rolling back dirty transactions is potentially defeated.

Most medium- to high-end servers today have write-caching controllers with on-card battery backups just for the controllers and their array of disks. In the instance of this battery backup, you should be safe in turning on write-caching controllers. However, what happens if the battery goes bad? The server engineers will tell you not to worry. They get alarms/paged. However, it's our personal experience that even with a very competent set of server engineers and a high-end server from one of the leading and best-known server manufacturers, we only found out that the first of two redundant power supplies for a server had failed when the second one also failed and brought down the whole server. Even though paging was turned on, for some reason it didn't work.

In short, with very, very few exceptions, Microsoft almost always recommends that write caching be turned off on controllers through which SQL Server writes to disk. Based on our experience, we heartily agree. Except for a very few OLTP applications, this small performance hit is well offset by the extra hours of sleep your DBA will get. Just think of it this way: Remember the first (and hopefully only time) you typed a ten-page term paper into a word processor without frequently saving and the lights blinked? If you're going to turn write caching on, you really need to have a very compelling performance reason and very high confidence in the hardware, engineers, and systems maintaining and monitoring it.

The RAID Subsystem

Disks and controllers can be joined together in Redundant Array of Inexpensive Disks (RAID) combinations. The primary purpose of such combinations is to provide fault tolerance (in other words, redundancy), such that the failure of any one component won't bring down the whole system. RAID combinations can be either software based, in which the Windows NT or Windows 2000 operating system maintains the array, or hardware based, in which a specialized controller maintains the RAID configuration.

Generally there are three plus one ways of looking at a RAID configuration. The three ways are called RAID 0, RAID 1, and RAID 5. The extra one is called either RAID 10 or RAID 0+1. RAID 0, RAID 1, and RAID 5 are found in both software and hardware solutions. RAID 10 is only found in hardware solutions.

RAID 0

In RAID 0, data is striped across disks in blocks, usually about 64KB each. A single controller or the operating system would write a 64KB block to one disk and then proceed to write a block to the next disk. Writing to and reading from such arrays can be extremely fast. Reads and writes are rapid, as you have multiple drive heads, which can read the blocks of data concurrently.

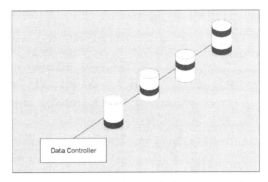

Many people will tell you that RAID 0 is not really RAID because it isn't redundant. We personally agree. If any one of the disks fails, then your system comes to a screeching halt and you may have (gasp!) lost data. There's an advantage in RAID 0 in terms of speed. Because no parity information is maintained on any other disks, data is written rapidly in stripes or blocks of data across each disk. Similarly, for reads (in particular, sequential reads) the performance can be extraordinarily good. In addition to speed, though, another advantage of the RAID 0 configuration is that it can support very large arrays. Even though it isn't really a "redundant" array, it's important to detail it, because its performance means that it's one of two RAID configurations that will come into play later when we discuss RAID 10, the other being RAID 1.

RAID 1

RAID 1 is called **mirroring** when one controller mirrors two disks, or **duplexing** when two controllers each control a separate disk to maintain mirrored copies of data. Often, the term mirroring is used when duplexing would be more technically correct. It's usually enough to know that identical subsystems are being referenced. Essentially, two identical disk volumes, A and B, are set up. When data is written to A, it's simultaneously written to B. The volumes are kept in perpetual synchronization. When either A or B fails, the disk subsystem doesn't miss a beat. It just raises (hopefully) all sorts of alarms to tell you that it's no longer redundant. To recover, you have to "break the mirror," snap in a new drive, and resynchronize the mirror. Most subsystems that support mirroring will let you do this without ever taking down the server. What suffers? Remember the *I* in RAID? It stands for inexpensive. With RAID 1, you have to buy 2 bytes of storage for every 1 byte of data. In addition to costs, a disadvantage of the RAID 1 configuration is that it can only be as large as a single hard disk size.

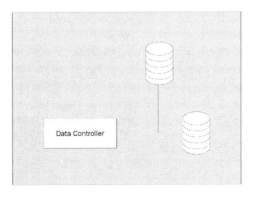

RAID 5

RAID 5 is the most common RAID configuration, and like RAID 0, data is written across a set of disks in blocks. However, whereas RAID 0 only requires two disks, RAID 5 requires at least three or more disks. Each stripe, though, will now have a parity block written to alternating disks. For example, if you have four disks in a RAID 5 array, every stripe will write three blocks of data and one block of parity information. The parity information will be rotated from disk to disk such that no one disk has all the parity information.

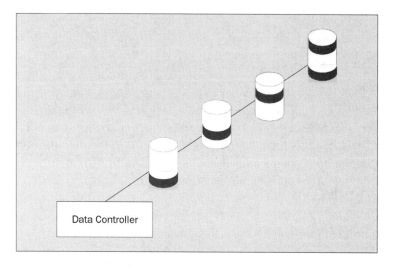

Data Controller

When a single disk fails in a RAID 5 array, the other disks will pick up the load. When the read should have come from the failed disk, the controller or operating system will read the parity information and compare it to the data from all the other intact disks, computing the data that would otherwise be present on the failed disk.

> **RAID 3 is very similar to RAID 5, except that rather than spreading the parity across all disks in the array, a single disk is used for the parity storage and all other disks are used for data storage.**

Obviously, a disk failure in a RAID 5 configuration means that data reads become significantly slower than a failure of a RAID 1 system, in which data reads aren't really affected. Just as obviously, the overhead to maintain redundancy is only 1/N of your storage space, where N is the number of disks participating in the array. Another advantage of RAID 5 arrays is that the array can be sized very large. I've seen RAID 5 arrays with hundreds of gigabytes. For the vast majority of midrange servers and applications, hardware-based RAID 5 is the disk subsystem of choice.

We should mention here that some hardware vendors are implementing a modified RAID 5 array scheme in which a second redundant disk is added to the array, allowing for failure of two disks while still maintaining the integrity and uptime of the data.

RAID 10: Where 0+1 Does Not Equal 1

As you can see, RAID 0 has the best throughput and extensibility of all arrays, but no redundancy. RAID 1 has the best redundancy, but it's very limited in its extensibility. Thus, the best RAID arrays on the market today are those that are characterized as RAID 0+1 or RAID 10. To build a RAID 10 array, you first make two separate but identical RAID 0 arrays in which data is striped in blocks across two or more disks. These two identical RAID 0 arrays are then mirrored to each other. This solution is only implemented by high-end RAID controllers.

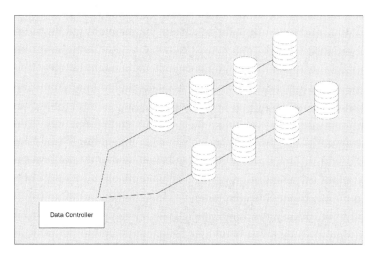

Data Controller

Although RAID 10 is often considered one of the best RAID solutions, it should be pointed out that RAID 5 and RAID 1 are often used because of their lower cost and equal redundancy.

Multiple Controller/Channel Solutions

Up to now, we've addressed only a single channel of data. Many controllers can have dual channels, and certainly you can install extra controllers on a server. Remember, SQL Server is essentially a multilevel system. When a single record is written to disk, it's preceded by the transaction log write and, as often as not, accompanied by one or more index writes. Alongside the SQL writes, the operating system is continually pruning the operating system memory and paging inactive memory to disk. If these writes can be written by different controllers to different disk array subsystems, then the transaction throughput will be multiplied.

Data reads from disk to data cache can also greatly benefit from multiple channels. A well-optimized database will have complementary tables that are most frequently joined. By putting the data from one table on controller A, the indexes from that table on controller B, the data from another table on controller C, the indexes from that table on controller D, and TempDB on controller E, the data reads can be happening simultaneously and very quickly.

Overall, although RAID 0+1 would probably be the fastest single disk subsystem, given the same amount of budget, a better buying decision for most applications would be to buy three or four RAID 5 subsystems. Then the transaction logs would be dedicated to one subsystem, the data from some tables and indexes from others to another subsystem, and the remaining tables and indexes from the first tables on the third. The page file and other operating system components may be on the fourth, if it's available.

Another viable solution that's frequently used is to put the write-intensive transaction log on a RAID 1 mirrored configuration. RAID 1 writes are faster because mirrored drives are doing simultaneous writes and don't have the overhead of calculating and writing the parity bit for a stripe. Because the data requires more extensibility, one or more RAID 5 subsystems are incorporated for the data and indexes.

Disk Tuning and Performance Monitoring

An earlier section titled "The Art of Performance Monitoring" made mention of setting up disk performance counters. The overhead of the disk performance counters on processor CPU utilization is very small. In the early days of Windows NT, it was said that the overhead of disk performance counters was, at worst, one-half of 1 percent of processor usage on a single CPU 486DX66 server. With Pentium 3s running at 10+ times that clock speed today in symmetric multiprocessor environments, the concern about disk performance counter overhead is negligible.

The greatest risk of bottleneck, after memory, is equally shared between the disk subsystem and the processor(s). A table scan on a large table can literally bring a server to its knees. Worse still, an ill-advised Cartesian join of two large tables is a death sentence for disk performance. You'll want to monitor disk performance when such events creep into your systems (and they will at the worst possible times). Imagine the head of the human resources department trying to run a summary query during payroll processing. It happens.

Begin disk performance monitoring by looking at the following counters:

❑   PhysicalDisk: % Disk Time

❑   PhysicalDisk: Current Disk Queue Length

❑   PhysicalDisk: Avg. Disk Queue Length

Applications and systems that are I/O-bound may keep the disk constantly active. This is called **disk thrashing**.

> You should always know how many channels you have, what types of arrays you have, how many disks are in each array, and which array/channel your data and transaction logs are located on before you start thinking about disk-performance tuning.

The `PhysicalDisk: % Disk Time` counter monitors the percentage of time that the disk is conducting read or write activity. If the `PhysicalDisk: % Disk Time` counter is high (more than 90 percent), check the `Physical Disk: Current Disk Queue Length` counter to see the number of requests that are queued up waiting for disk access.

It's important at this point to be familiar with your disk subsystem. If the number of waiting I/O requests is a sustained value more than 1.5 to 2 times the number of spindles making up the physical disk, you have a disk bottleneck. For example, a RAID 5 configuration with seven spindles/disks would be a candidate for disk-performance tuning should the `Current Disk Queue Length` continually rest above 12 to 14.

To improve performance in this situation, consider adding faster disk drives, moving some processes to an additional controller-disk subsystem, or adding additional disks to a RAID 5 array.

Most disks have one spindle, although RAID devices usually have more. A hardware RAID 5 device appears as one physical disk in Windows NT PerfMon or Windows 2000 SysMon. RAID devices created through software appear as multiple instances.

> *WARNING: The* `% Disk Time` *counter can indicate a value greater than 100 percent if you're using a hardware-based RAID configuration. If it does, use the* `PhysicalDisk: Avg. Disk Queue Length` *counter to determine the average number of system requests waiting for disk access. Again, this is indicative of a performance problem if a sustained value of 1.5 to 2 times the number of spindles in the array is observed.*

User Connections

In SQL Server 6.5, user connections were an important tuning option. SQL Server 7.0 and SQL Server 2000 have reduced this importance. User connections in these versions are a dynamic, self-configuring option. In most cases you shouldn't adjust the user connections settings because if 100 connections are necessary, 100 connections are allocated. Running the following commands will give the current settings of user connections and the maximum allowed number of user connections:

```
EXEC sp_configure "user connections"
SELECT @@MAX_CONNECTIONS
```

You may use `sp_configure` to tune the number of user connections, but we highly recommend avoiding doing this in SQL Server 7.0 and SQL Server 2000. Each user connection consumes about 40KB of memory. When you start specifying the maximum number of user connections instead of letting SQL Server maintain the number, the allocation of memory is no longer dynamic. Instead, 40KB of memory times the number of maximum users set will be consumed immediately. Generally, you only want to configure the number of user connections in an environment in which spurious users could spawn a large number of user connections.

Many administrators and managers confuse user connections and client access licenses (CALs) . They are apples and oranges. In SQL Server 2000, a CAL is a license for either a single user (a named person) or a single device (usually a computer, but it could be your cell phone) to connect to SQL Server. The people who manage your licenses should explicitly assign the license to a user or to a device. Once that user or device is licensed with a single CAL, he or she/it can connect and open as many user connections as the server will allow. It isn't unusual to see a single computer with a single device CAL open 20+ user connections to one server and five to another server. In short, there is no correlation between user connections and CALs. Please don't think that this short explanation solves all your legal issues (which is what a CAL essentially is). Microsoft's licensing structure is more complex than this short explanation about the difference between user connections and CALs. Furthermore, the licensing structure is known to change routinely, and this explanation could be out of date by the time this book goes to print. The professional thing to do is *read your licenses.*

It's important to monitor user connections in your performance tuning. The counter is SQL Server:General:User Connections. In a troubleshooting or testing environment, you may want to monitor SQL Server:Databases:Active Transactions:database.

The number of user connections is based on the requirements of your application and users. OLE DB applications need a connection for each open connection object. ODBC connections are spawned for each active connection handled in an application. DB-Library uses a connection for each occurrence of the dbopen function. N-tier applications that make use of connection pooling would tend to minimize the number of open connections.

Because SQL Server is a transaction logging system, you may want to be aware of the presence of long-running transactions. It's commonplace to dump the transaction logs every hour or two. The transaction log is maintained open back to the longest open transaction. If a transaction remains open for an extended period of time, the transaction log will grow and grow, with each dump getting larger and larger. In a default situation, SQL Server will automatically grow the transaction log. It can get really huge, and we've seen it reach the capacity of a disk. We've traced third-party applications that begin a session with a DB-Library dbopen function call, immediately followed by a BEGIN TRAN statement. Monitor the sizes of your transaction log dumps. If they get progressively larger throughout the day for a particular database, you may have this condition. You can see long-running open transactions by issuing the following T-SQL command:

```
DBCC OPENTRAN <database>
```

You may even consider writing a T-SQL job that alerts you to the presence of long-running open transactions.

Locking and Blocking

Locks in and of themselves are a very good thing. They guarantee that the data you read is the data actually in the database. Locks held too long are a problem. They lead to what we call **blocking**.

Blocking Demonstration

Start Query Analyzer. Open two connections to the same server, and then tile the windows vertically by using the menu option Windows | Tile Vertically.

In the first window, type and execute the following code:

```
USE pubs
GO
SELECT au_fname FROM AUTHORS -- (NOLOCK)
   WHERE au_lname = 'Green'
```

You should return a value of Marjorie.

In the second window, type and execute the following code:

```
USE pubs
GO
BEGIN TRAN
   UPDATE authors SET au_fname = 'Harry'
   WHERE au_lname = 'Green'
- ROLLBACK TRAN
```

Ensure that there are two dashes in front of the ROLLBACK TRAN statement. You should get a message back.

(1 row(s) affected)

Now re-execute the first query. Open a third window (by typing *CTRL+N*) and run the following command:

```
sp_who2
```

Scroll through the list and notice the blkby column. This shows that your select transaction is blocked by your update transaction. Close the third window. If necessary, realign your windows using the Windows | Tile Vertically menu option again. In your update transaction window, highlight the phrase ROLLBACK TRAN and execute it. Notice what happens to the select query.

Try the experiment again, only this time uncomment the (NOLOCK) clause by removing the two dashes from in front of it. Because you're now using NOLOCK, you'll not see your select statement blocked in SP_WHO2 this time. This is a good example of a dirty read.

Monitoring Blocking

Sometimes things just don't get better. In SQL Server 6.5, there was a very handy performance counter, SQLServer-Locks:Users Blocked, that we always used to show active blocking on our servers. This was such an important counter that we would magnify the scale of the counter by 10 and increase the width of the counter line to a very thick line. Thus, when even a single lock popped up on our servers, a large thick line popped up in our performance monitor charts.

Unfortunately, this counter went away in SQL Server 7.0 and stayed away in SQL Server 2000. What to do?

Use the user-defined performance counters. Most people never use these counters and don't know how they work. In SQL Server 6.5, when a counter was called, it automatically updated itself. In SQL Server 7.0 and SQL Server 2000, it doesn't. Each user-defined counter has to be explicitly updated with an integer value by running the stored procedure sp_user_counterX Y, where X is the user-defined counter number and Y is the integer value assigned to the counter.

In SQL Server Enterprise Manager, drill down in the management tree to Management | SQL Server Agent | Jobs. Right-click Jobs and choose New Job. Then enter a name and description for User Defined Performance Counter 1.

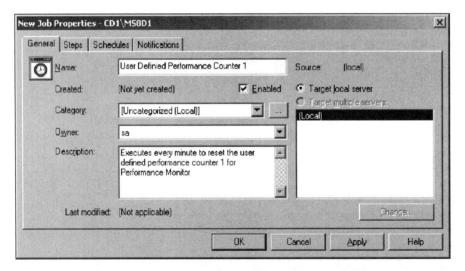

Click the Steps tab and then the New button to add a step. In the New Job Step dialog window, create a single step called Reset Counter in this job with the following T-SQL script executing in the master database:

```
SET NOCOUNT ON
DECLARE @blocks int
SELECT @blocks = count(blocked) FROM
          master.dbo.sysprocesses (nolock)
   WHERE blocked > 0
EXEC sp_user_counter1 @blocks
GO
```

The window should look like this:

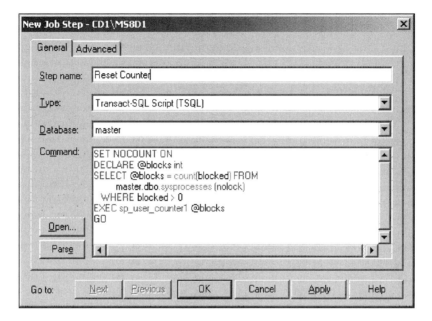

Click OK to close the New Job Step dialog box.

In the Schedules tab, click the New Schedule button. Select the Start whenever the CPU(s) become idle option because you want this job to happen in the background and not interfere with more important ones.

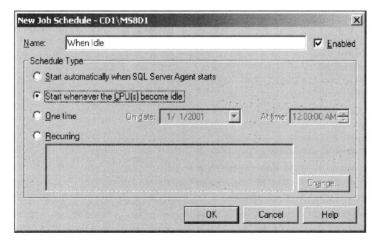

Click OK to save this schedule, and then click OK in the New Job Properties dialog box to save the job.

Now in either Windows NT PerfMon or Windows 2000 SysMon, add the instance SQLServer:User Settable:Query:User counter 1. Run the blocking tests outlined in the "Blocking Demonstration" section to verify your work.

If you decide you want to add other user-defined performance counters later, you can just add them to the T-SQL script in the Reset Counter step you defined previously and invoke the counter in Windows NT PerfMon or Windows 2000/2003 SysMon.

Case Study

In this segment of the case study, we'll look at taking the volumetric values we gathered in Chapter 8 and finally turn them into real numbers. We've taken the following table from the end of Chapter 8 and will now extrapolate what the new values will be, as we now have some new tables. Most notable of these are the following three rows:

Table Name	Initial Rows	Growth in Rows per Month	Max Rows
Deposit	0	5	4000
Check	0	245	10000
directWithdrawal	0	50	1000

In our tables, we took the subtyped tables of transaction and turned them into the table `transaction`. We'll add them all together into a single row:

transaction	0	300	15000

We do the same for each of the tables and arrive at the following table of the conditions of initial row size, row growth, and maximum expected rows:

Table Name	Initial Rows	Growth in Rows per Month	Max Rows
account	1	0	20
accountReconcile	0	1	36
address	50	30	600
addressType	5	0	10
bank	1	0	5
city	450	20	25000
payee	100	30	300
payeeAddress	100	30	600
payeePhoneNumber	100	30	600
phoneNumber	50	30	600
phoneNumberType	5	0	10
state	50	0	70

Table Name	Initial Rows	Growth in Rows per Month	Max Rows
statement	0	1	36
statementItem	0	300	15000
statementType	3	0	5
transactionAllocation	75	400	12000
transaction	0	300	15000
transactionAllocationType	20	0	40
transactionType	3	0	5
user	10	2	50
zipCode	1000	10	99999
zipCodeCityReference	1100	10	99999

Next, we need to calculate the sizes of the tables. Using the sp_table$indexSpace procedure, we'll calculate values for initial rows, growth in rows per month, and maximum rows conditions. For each table, an assumption needs to be made regarding the percentage to which variable length columns are filled. For the purposes of this case study, we'll assume 50 percent. A sample query for maximum row condition in the transaction table is as follows. There are three variable length columns in the transaction table: number, which is VARCHAR(20); signature, which is VARCHAR(20); and description, which is VARCHAR(1000). The 50-percent assumption would need to be evaluated with these in mind.

```
EXEC SP_Table$IndexSpace
    @tablename = 'transaction',
    @variFillPercent = 50,
    @num_rows = 16000
```

The results for all tables and all conditions we've considered are presented in the following table. As you look at the results for each table, notice that the growth per month doesn't seem to be cumulative. This is because we were using the rows per month as the input parameter for rows for the stored procedure sp_table$indexSpace. Whether there is one row or several, the output of the procedure will always be in discrete 8KB multiples. Thus, the size is particularly relevant for the initial row size and maximum row conditions. Also, remember, that as an index grows, the node levels gradually fill up. At a certain point, they'll need to "grow" an additional leaf node level. Thus, index growth in general will be nonlinear, particularly for larger tables.

The clustered index size is relatively flat (a single root node page of 8KB) for virtually all conditions. This is because the clustered index that we're talking about here is the single root node page that points to the page of the actual data. All of our clustered indexes are single column keys of a 4-btye integer datatype, and 455 of these page pointers will fit on the root node page. This will almost always yield the flattest realistic clustered index you can have. Once the data pages exceed the 455-page count, the clustered index will increase in levels and include an additional index node level. This is only seen in the transaction table for the max row condition. Due to the relatively large row size of the transaction table (remember that the description column is VARCHAR(1000) and we assume it's 50-percent filled), the number of pages exceeds the 455-page threshold.

Because all of our tables have clustered indexes, it might be more accurate to say the clustered index size is the sum of the "CInd Size" column and the "Data Size in KB" column, which is actually the leaf node of the clustered index. We break these out in the stored procedure and in the following table for analysis purposes.

Table	Condition	Rows	Data Size in KB	CInd Size	CIndex Lvls	NCInd Size	NCInd Lvls
account	Initial Row Size	1	8	8	1	8	1
account	Growth Per Month	0	0	0	0	0	0
account	Max Rows	20	8	8	1	8	1
accountReconcile	Initial Row Size	0	0	0	0	0	0
accountReconcile	Growth Per Month	1	8	8	1	8	1
accountReconcile	Max Rows	36	16	8	1	24	2
address	Initial Row Size	50	24	8	1	32	2
address	Growth Per Month	30	16	8	1	24	2
address	Max Rows	600	272	8	1	296	3
addressType	Initial Row Size	5	8	8	1	8	1
addressType	Growth Per Month	0	0	0	0	0	0
addressType	Max Rows	10	8	8	1	8	1
bank	Initial Row Size	1	8	8	1	8	1
bank	Growth Per Month	0	0	0	0	0	0
bank	Max Rows	5	8	8	1	8	1
city	Initial Row Size	450	32	8	1	40	2
city	Growth Per Month	20	8	8	1	8	1
city	Max Rows	25000	1456	8	1	1496	3

Table	Condition	Rows	Data Size in KB	CInd Size	CIndex Lvls	NCInd Size	NCInd Lvls
payee	Initial Row Size	100	8	8	1	8	1
payee	Growth Per Month	30	8	8	1	8	1
payee	Max Rows	300	24	8	1	32	2
payeeAddress	Initial Row Size	100	8	8	1	8	1
payeeAddress	Growth Per Month	30	8	8	1	8	1
payeeAddress	Max Rows	600	24	8	1	32	2
payeePhoneNumber	Initial Row Size	100	8	8	1	8	1
payeePhoneNumber	Growth Per Month	30	8	8	1	8	1
payeePhoneNumber	Max Rows	600	24	8	1	32	2
phoneNumber	Initial Row Size	50	8	8	1	8	1
phoneNumber	Growth Per Month	30	8	8	1	8	1
phoneNumber	Max Rows	600	32	8	1	40	2
phoneNumberType	Initial Row Size	5	8	8	1	8	1
phoneNumberType	Growth Per Month	0	0	0	0	0	0
phoneNumberType	Max Rows	10	8	8	1	8	1
state	Initial Row Size	50	8	8	1	8	1
state	Growth Per Month	0	0	0	0	0	0
state	Max Rows	70	8	8	1	8	1
statement	Initial Row Size	0	0	0	0	0	0
statement	Growth Per Month	1	8	8	1	8	1
statement	Max Rows	36	8	8	1	8	1
statementItem	Initial Row Size	0	0	0	0	0	0
statementItem	Growth Per Month	300	32	8	1	24	2
statementItem	Max Rows	15000	1584	8	1	600	2
statementType	Initial Row Size	75	8	8	1	8	1
statementType	Growth Per Month	400	48	8	1	32	2

Table continued overleaf

Table	Condition	Rows	Data Size in KB	CInd Size	CIndex Lvls	NCInd Size	NCInd Lvls
statementType	Max Rows	12000	1264	8	1	672	2
transaction	Initial Row Size	0	0	0	0	0	0
transaction	Growth Per Month	295	176	8	1	24	2
transaction	Max Rows	15000	9144	32	2	640	2
transactionAllocation	Initial Row Size	1	8	8	1	8	1
transactionAllocation	Growth Per Month	0	0	0	0	0	0
transactionAllocation	Max Rows	20	8	8	1	8	1
transactionType	Initial Row Size	3	8	8	1	8	1
transactionType	Growth Per Month	0	0	0	0	0	0
transactionType	Max Rows	5	8	8	1	8	1
user	Initial Row Size	10	8	8	1	8	1
user	Growth Per Month	2	8	8	1	8	1
user	Max Rows	50	16	8	1	8	1
zipCode	Initial Row Size	1000	32	8	1	40	2
zipCode	Growth Per Month	10	8	8	1	8	1
zipCode	Max Rows	99999	2544	8	1	2656	2
zipCodeCityReference	Initial Row Size	1000	32	8	1	40	2
zipCodeCityReference	Growth Per Month	10	8	8	1	8	1
zipCodeCityReference	Max Rows	99999	2936	8	1	2944	2

The total space for the table would thus be the data size plus the size of the clustered and nonclustered indexes. Our tables have only one nonclustered index on each of them for the alternative key. Obviously, as you add more nonclustered indexes for performance reasons, you would then need to review the results from sp_table$indexSpace for each additional nonclustered index that you add and the row total conditions listed previously.

Summary

In this chapter we took a look at how you can estimate what requirements your database will have, not just at the time of deployment, but also in a year or so down the line. Data sizing, index sizing, and row estimations are intricately tied to future performance. Archiving is one of the most overlooked methods for obtaining significant performance improvements in a mature database. We looked at the most important hardware requirements: those of storage space, processing power, and online memory. Consistent with this is a requirement on your part that you spend time familiarizing yourself with the performance analysis tools so that, when push comes to shove, you'll have the skills to isolate causes of performance problems. More specifically, we covered what hard drive configurations are available and what they offer in terms of performance and data redundancy. Obviously, the higher the processor speed and the more memory you acquire, the better. But you also learned how important it is to configure SQL Server to take advantage of the processor and memory, especially where it might be fighting for resources with other applications. You're now in a position to finish the design project, which you'll go on to do in the next chapter.

15

Completing the Project

Ah, the crowd sighs a collective sigh of relief. It's over, done. Throughout the past 14 chapters you've taken your database system from conception to a working database. You've gathered data on what the user wanted, built models of this data, created tables, considered various safeguarding mechanisms, and finally added code to act as a kind of tier between the user and the data. So your development work is at an end then? Well, though the OLTP part of the system is now complete, you still have a few (not insignificant) things to tidy up.

❑ **Performance tuning**: Though you've learned about performance tuning in previous chapters, you've mostly been concerned with how transactions can affect the system. Now you need to make sure that the choices you've made for hardware and data structures will work.

❑ **Reports**: Now that your OLTP database has solidified and you're able to work with it, you can optimize it for the reporting needs that you determined in the logical design phase. For larger mission-critical projects (especially those involving vast amounts of data, or even mechanical clients tearing away at the data 24 hours a day) you may need to take the additional step of building a read-only copy (or partial copy) of the data for reporting. This will decrease the contention for data in your primary databases. You'll look at designing a read-only database to meet such needs. You'll also learn about a few other uses of read-only extracts other than simple reporting, such as building an ODS (operational data store).

❑ **Enterprise modeling**: As a corporate data architect, you must build a model that not only encompasses the work you've done on one project, but all projects that came before it, and even out-of-the-box packages that were built by different vendors. The goal of enterprise modeling is to keep a record of all of the data in your organization in order to enhance overall normalization on a corporate level.

❑ **Three-phase implementation**: This refers to the setting up of a design and implementation cycle involving the development, QA (quality assurance) and production phases. You'll discuss how to construct such an environment.

You'll look at a few guidelines for protecting against system problems in the production phase such as power outages and general hardware failures. Though the production phase system setup isn't strictly the responsibility of the data architect, in my experience, the data architect *is* often involved and can end up taking the blame if the proper backup and disaster recovery plan wasn't specified in the architecture for the system.

Performance Tuning

The performance-tuning process is complex, and is completely separate from database design. You should also bear in mind that it's a never-ending process. Developers may need performance enhancements, and testers (especially those performing stress testing) will hopefully find almost every additional place to tune performance. Once the real system is up and running, you'll again tune performance (of course by then it's a trial by fire, because real users using a real system tend to get annoyed and start firing off e-mails all over the place when a system is running too slow).

Performance tuning is the responsibility of the DBA, not the data architect. Nevertheless, when designing the database you must be aware of critical matters that will affect the DBA's task, and you should investigate them regularly. The following list represents reasons why I've skirted away from a deep discussion of performance tuning during your design:

Performance tuning shouldn't be a matter of guessing: Performance must be considered over the entire system, and basing performance considerations on previous experiences isn't always optimal. SQL Server provides some extremely powerful tools for tracking down problem areas in your systems. By using the SQL Server Profiler, you can determine which queries take a long time to run, and look at how long processes take before and after a change. This, coupled with good stress testing, can determine if indexes, hardware improvements, or even denormalization is the best thing for the overall system package. It should be noted in passing that performance testing doesn't mean distorting the database model through denormalizing, and indeed, denormalization for the sake of it may well lead to degraded performance when attempting to manipulate the database tables. Though denormalization may be desirable in some cases, it will begin to reintroduce the kinds of modification anomalies that you strove to remove in the normalization process. You either have to live with these anomalies or you have to write additional code to deal with them. An effective database administrator who can tune a database without having to carry out denormalization is worth his weight in gold.

Performance-tuning changes in SQL Server versions: Though earlier versions required the designer to perform a large amount of manual optimization, recent versions (7.0 and 2000) have added a rich layer of functionality to performance tuning. Generally I've now found that it's often best to give back control of optimization to SQL Server.

Superfluous indexes are very costly: In a system that is write-intensive, such as an OLTP database, too many indexes can cause performance problems. This is due to the fact that when changes are made to the underlying structure, you greatly increase the cost of doing inserts, updates, or deletes because both the table structures and indexes have to be manipulated. When you run into a slow-running read query, the use of indexes can be an appealing solution, but the overall performance of the system can be affected, especially if the data is continually being added to. The problems will probably not become apparent until the system is under a heavy load of a very real nature. On the other hand, appropriate use of indexes will usually be a real boost to performance.

When performance problems arise you can use the SQL Server Profiler to see the exact calls that your clients are making. The Query Analyzer then allows you to consider the following:

❑ **Query plan**: By looking at how SQL Server is planning on performing the query, you can see if it's making any illogical assumptions that you need to improve upon, either by rewriting your queries (like removing data from the query that you never make use of), using the Query Optimizer hints to tweak the query, or possibly adding indexes with suitable caution.

❑ **Statistics time and statistics IO**: You can set the Query Analyzer to return information about how long the query took, or how much and what types of disk activity the query required.

❑ **Index Tuning wizard**: Using this tool will determine if optimal indexes are being used in a database for a given set of SQL commands.

❑ **DBCC commands**: DBCC stands for database consistency checker, and there are quite a few very useful DBCC commands that can be used for performance tuning. These include `SHOW_STATISTICS`, which shows statistics pages for indexes to help determine why they're used or unused, and `SHOWCONTIG`, which shows how fragmented a table or an index is.

These tools only scratch the surface. There are many other methods that you can use to tune your queries, databases, and servers in order to obtain maximum performance. Creating indexes is always a valid thing to do to boost performance, but too many can cause real problems. Limited denormalization may be undertaken, such as dropping back a level in particular tables where there is a problem (usually associated with dropping back from the Fourth Normal Form or higher), but only after some level of testing has been performed.

Read-Only Support Databases

If your reporting needs aren't real-time, you can allow some latency between the current data and the data that users are dealing with, and then you can build a read-only database that mirrors your active databases. Users who need to run expensive queries against the data could then utilize this read-only database. Depending on how the database is utilized (and after you've loaded the data into the database), it's possible to set the database as read-only by using the following:

```
EXEC sp_dboption '<databaseName>', 'read only', 'true'
```

You can then flip the switch back to write mode whenever you need to load more data into the database (because it isn't possible to refresh the database when it's set to read-only, for pretty obvious reasons). Setting the database to read-only has the very great benefit of telling SQL Server that it doesn't actually have to use locks on database resources, because no one can make changes to the data or structures of the database. Basically, you try to do all writes to the read-only database when no users want to read the data.

The question to answer before you go any further is "Why build a read-only database?

The answers to this question are one or all of the following:

1. To maximize concurrency in your user database systems

2. To maximize performance on a set of queries

3. To consolidate data from multiple sources

The bottom line is that, though all of your data ought to have had its original home in a proper normalized OLTP database, there are situations where this will definitely not be the case, such as the following:

❑ **Legacy databases**: Mainframes are classically referred to as legacy systems, but as the years begin to pass because the mini and even PC platform began developing server platforms, you can get legacy databases based on any platform.

❑ **User databases**: Unfortunately, not all databases are built on a database server. Many exist as Access, Foxpro, or other database platforms.

❑ **Other**: Categorized as "other" because there are too many to mention. Spreadsheets, text files, and many other ways of storing data may be in use in a particular organization, and required for entry into the read-only systems.

Once you've transformed the data from your databases into the read-only system, you get the following benefits:

❑ **Limited contention**: Because all users of the database will be unable to modify the data, there is very little chance of concurrent users locking the same piece of data from one another. Whenever you can guarantee that no process will write to the database, you can set the database to read-only and no locks will be able to run. If you have a continuously updating system, you could run reports in the repeatable read-isolation level, which will mean you need never worry about an outside process changing the results of your reports as you run them. Note, of course, that you cannot eliminate contention within your hardware subsystem, or indeed loading methods, because whatever portion of the data is being copied from your OLTP system will be blocked to users though the transfer is taking place.

❑ **Fast performance**: Depending on the situation, specific queries in your user database can be optimized, or if desired, you can move all querying out of the user databases. Bear in mind that greater performance benefits will be attained when the read-only databases don't reside on the same server as the user databases.

In the following section, you'll look at a few possibilities for structuring your read-only database, and I'll discuss the effect on performance, give you a few tips on implementing the solution, and finally, show you a few examples of how to employ such databases in the real world. It should be noted that I won't be going to the level of data warehouse or data mart (implemented in OLAP) in these discussions. Instead, you're looking at more generic solutions to immediate problems such as heavy use clients, ad hoc reporting of current data, and ODS. (See Chapter 9 for more solutions.)

Read activity is a very important part of allowing your OLTP system to stay as normalized as possible. Read activity takes a load off your servers by reducing contention between readers and writers.

Modeling the Transformation

In this section, you'll use the following set of four simple tables for illustrative purposes:

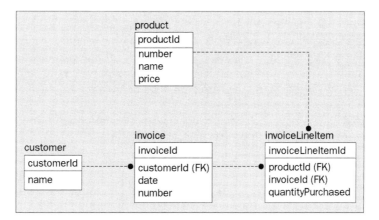

It should be obvious that this is a simplified model of an invoice system, and that I've ignored the fact that the price value will change over time. However, this set of tables will serve as an illustration of a common system from which reports need to be generated. In reality, you may have a much more complex situation like this:

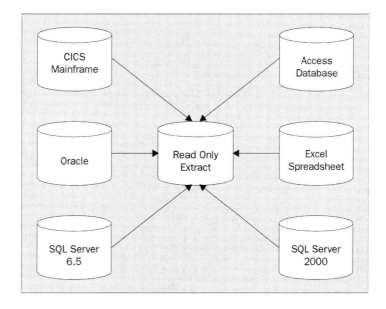

Which means that the data store could pull data from more that just one database. Note that I included an Excel spreadsheet on the diagram: it isn't uncommon for a spreadsheet to become the "home" of a piece of data especially where there isn't the technical expertise to create and administer a database. Note of course that you aren't advocating the use of spreadsheets as permanent data stores, but simply admitting that using them does happen frequently. Fortunately, you can import data from almost anywhere either by using DTS (Data Transformation Services), building ADO clients, or by utilizing some of the functions in SQL Server that I've discussed.

Modeling a read-only system is the same as the task of modeling the OLTP database, except that you can largely ignore normalization rules beyond the first one. Having functional dependencies in your data isn't a bad thing as long as none of the data can be edited and gotten out of sync. There are two methods that I've found useful for performing this task. One is very pragmatic and the other is an open-ended solution that allows a more free-form perusal of the data:

❑   **Table oriented**: A very open method of building a reporting database, in which every important table that doesn't simply contain domain data is represented.

❑   **Solution oriented**: If you have a very specific problem to solve, there is generally no need to take as drastic an approach as the previous method. I'll discuss why you might want to just include what is necessary to meet a particular need.

Bear in mind that, because always, I'm not stating that these are the only methods for doing this sort of operation. The methods listed here are intended to be as much food for thought as they are precise solutions to a particular problem. Because you're looking at read-only databases, you must make sure that the data in the database matches the source data in value at some recognized point in time. Beyond that, structure is of lesser concern, precisely because the data isn't modified, except by system processes that are isolated from the user.

Table Oriented

What you'll try to do is to take a copy of your OLTP database and expand each entity so that it includes as much data from parent tables as possible. In the example scenario, the invoice table has the customer table as a parent, and the invoiceLineItem table has invoice and customer on one path, and product on another. In this case, the essence and definition of the invoiceLineItem table includes both the definition of what was purchased and the invoice, customer, and product.

There are benefits to this approach, because any time a user wants to see an invoiceLineItem, she will usually want to know which customer purchased it. Hence you include a reference to the customer in the invoiceLineItem table. One concept in this scenario doesn't change, in that every attribute of an object must describe the object, even if only indirectly. Because you'll include customer information in the invoice line item, you're clearly breaking normalization rules, though the values in the table do actually describe something about the invoice line item, namely the customer who purchased it.

You can also include additional columns for summary data that pertains to the object. If you want to store the sum total of all invoice items, then you store it in the `invoice` table, and not the `invoiceLineItem` table. The goal isn't to totally eliminate joins, but to have as few as possible in order to maintain a reasonably logical structure though maximizing your overall performance.

> *One additional concern must be mentioned: disk space. Your disk space requirements for such a database, fully expanded into the final format, will be much larger than the original database and in some cases may actually be prohibitive depending on the size of the source data. Obviously the entire system wouldn't have to be done this way if only small parts were required for queries.*

The first step is to walk down your relationship trees and move attributes down. From the example diagram, you work from top to bottom, starting with `invoice`, adding the parent columns like so:

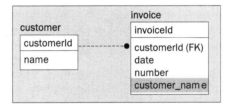

The column `customer_name` is now a part of the `invoice` table, because the invoice is for a customer. The `customerId` column already exists in the `invoice` table, so no need to do anything there. The next step is to look at the `invoiceLineItemTable`. You include the attributes of the invoice and product tables and come to the following:

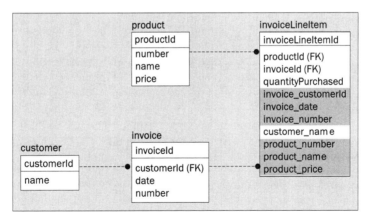

The next step is to take any values on which you might need to perform calculations or string concatenation operations, and add a column to contain the result. In the `invoiceLineItem` table, you have a `quantityPurchased` column as well as a `product_price` column, and you would want to multiply together the values of these columns to find the value of the line item, so you add a column to hold this value as shown:

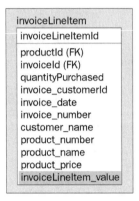

The last step is to go back up the chain and summarize all children. In this case, you can take the `invoice` to `invoiceLineItem` relationship and summarize all products on an invoice, as follows:

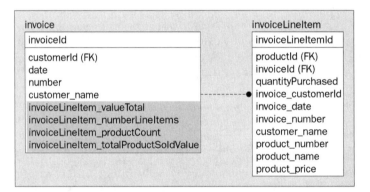

Take for example the *invoiceLineItem_valueTotal* column. This will be filled with the summation of all *invoiceLineItem_value* (*quantityPurchased* * *productPrice*) columns for a given invoice. The *invoiceLineItem_numberLineItems* would be the total count of line items.

You do the same for `product`, and then `customer`, to arrive at the following diagram:

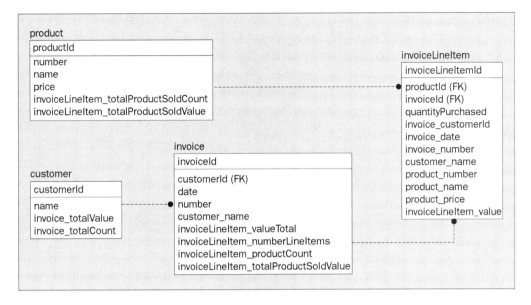

There are a few benefits of this approach:

❑ **Ease of use**: Because all related data is in the same table, having a user or programmer build a report using a tool such as Seagate Crystal Reports is much easier, because you've removed all joins from the data.

❑ **Recognizable data**: Users will know the names of the tables, and the columns within the tables, because you've gone to great lengths to make sure that you've named your objects in a way that is meaningful to them.

❑ **Useful summary data**: The goal is to simply try to push data down the tree to eliminate joins. What this does is to place all of the data that you'll need at one level in the relational hierarchy of the database.

❑ **Relatively easy to implement**: In most cases you perform simple queries that include one or more children and one or more parents. This isn't to oversimplify of course, because everything will depend heavily on how complex the database structures are.

For example, to load the product table, you could run the following code:

```
INSERT orderReport.dbo.product (productId, number, name, price,
                                invoiceLineItem_totalProductSoldCount,
                                invoiceLineItem_totalProductSoldValue)
SELECT product.productId, product.number, product.name, product.price,
       SUM(invoiceLineItem.quantityPurchased)
          AS invoiceLineItem_totalProductSoldCount,
       SUM(product.price * invoiceLineItem.quantityPurchased)
          AS invoiceLineItem_totalProductSoldValue
```

```
FROM [order]..product AS product
JOIN [order]..invoiceLineItem AS invoiceLineItem
    ON product.productId = invoiceLineItem.productId
GROUP BY product.productId, product.number, product.name, product.price
```

Not every answer will be readily available, but you're basically trying to allow ad hoc reporting by making the data output easier for the user to understand. This is possible because you've removed all hierarchy from the data model and put the data right where the user needs it. For example, if you want to know the total value of product number 'XYY43233', which was invoiced in January 2001 to customerId 10, you might simply code a SELECT from a single table:

```
SELECT sum(invoiceLineItem_value)
FROM invoiceLineItem
WHERE invoice_customerId = 10
    AND invoice_date < 'Feb 1 2001'
    AND invoice_date >= 'Jan 1 2001'
    AND product_number = 'XYY43233'
```

Alternatively, you could transform the data, pre-aggregating difficult values, and (once you've moved the data to the read-only database) consider using views to perform any reasonably simple calculations. This will certainly lower the coding needed to set up this read-only database system as well as reduce the data space requirements. Using views in this way may prove more efficient than coding, though it will also allow more flexibility if the reporting requirements change at some future date.

Solution Oriented

The solution-oriented method of creating a read-only database is easier to explain than the table-oriented method. In some cases you simply need a way to get certain data faster than you can retrieve it from your OLTP database, and you can build a solution-oriented extract of your data to do so.

Instead of building the entire database model as you did previously, you could decide to provide answers to a very specific set of questions. Take, for example, a report of customers and the products purchased by them in the past week, month, and year. Using the same database illustration from the previous example, you could build a query using nothing but the invoiceLineItem table, and if you do decide to build a full, table-based database as before, you could create an additional table to handle this situation.

However, consider a situation in which a query takes 40 minutes to execute from the original OLTP database, and the sales staff need this data at their fingertips quickly and efficiently. In this case you may simply want to build a table like this:

customerProduct
customerId
productId
customer_name
product_name
product_price
product_number
week_quantityPurchased
week_valuePurchased
month_quanityPurchased
month_valuePurchased
year_quanityPurchased
year_valuePurchased
build_date

At the most basic level, the table will contain the answer to the sales staff's query. Here, you've intersected the customer and product tables, and provided data for the product sales for the past week, month, and year. This model is extendable in that if a requirement was made so that a user wanted to summarize on types of products, you could add a column for type, but unless you're dealing with tens of thousands of products, it's probably fine to allow summation by grouping on the type of product.

You include the ID columns as the primary key, in order that this table can be linked to the original OLTP. In addition to this summary table, the user might need more detailed customer information, in which case you can add a child table to supply this information.

The place that I use this kind of summary data the most often has nothing to do with sales but rather web content, for example, when serving up a set of personalized pages to a type of user. The normalized internals of a web-content database may be extremely ugly, yet you must maintain a very high level of concurrency when presenting pages and let the user do whatever she wants with the OLTP data she requires. Once the content is prepared, say for a corporate front page of a site, a read-only version of the data might be built to support the web site.

What you end up with here is a very denormalized database, possibly containing one single table. Though it's similar to the table-based solution, in this case you have fewer tables (and so a smaller subset of data) and each of these tables is oriented around a specific query rather than around an identifiable object.

Performance

As with the OLTP system, you again have to consider performance when creating your read-only database, but this time you do want to make a preemptive strike, in that you not only performance guess, but take it to the extreme and cover any and all scenarios for database use. Because the consistency of the read-only data is handled by the transformation subsystems, all you need to care about is making the reporting run fast. In this section, you'll look at two of the most important issues for the read-only system, hardware and indexes.

Hardware

Because this topic was covered in the previous chapter, I'll just remind you of the importance of not skimping on hardware when building the read-only system. It may even be advantageous to have a separate server to house the data, depending on the size of the operation. If you physically locate the read-only data on the same server as the one running the OLTP database, though you'll reduce contention within the database, you can still end up with hardware contention. Even if you've built the best disk subsystem possible, you may still have to purchase an extra server due to processor limitations in simultaneously handling users who are running long reports and other users who are trying to update the OLTP master database.

Indexes

In building a read-only database, indexes are intrinsically part of the design, especially because you allow true ad hoc querying of the data. Because the read-only database will be updated infrequently, putting in too many indexes is unlikely to be a major problem. This of course depends on the actual size of the database, because if there is a terabyte of data in the read-only system, it may not be feasible to do what I'm suggesting here.

In the ad hoc environment, one strategy that will give great benefits is to index every column individually in every table. Consider your example of the `invoiceLineItem` table you built for your table-oriented extract:

invoiceLineItem
invoiceLineItemId
productId (FK)
invoiceId (FK)
quantityPurchased
invoice_customerId
invoice_date
invoice_number
customer_name
product_number
product_name
product_price
invoiceLineItem_value

On this table you would build indexes on all of the columns individually. This will allow the Query Optimizer to choose to use any or several of the indexes on the table to perform the query, possibly using a covered query if you don't ask for too many columns of the table.

> *A covered query is one where SQL Server doesn't have to look into the actual tables to get the data it needs. Because the nodes of the index contain the data that is needed to build the index, if you only reference columns in an index or indexes, SQL Server will never have to read from the actual data.*

Note that you can even include indexes on columns that it might otherwise seem silly to index. Take the case of a column that contains gender ("M", "F"). This is generally considered a horrible index for finding a row. However, it isn't too bad if you're dealing with only a column or two. If you want to see how many male or female values are in a table, you can perform a covered query on the gender index, and thereby only access the gender column. This will save large amounts of IO because it will be a very thin index, and is certainly more efficient than touching all data pages, especially in the read-only expansions of your tables.

Take for example, a query to access the `invoiceLineItem` table:

```
SELECT sum(invoiceLineItem_value)
FROM invoiceLineItem
WHERE invoice_customerId = 10
    AND invoice_date < 'Feb 1 2001'
    AND invoice_date >= 'Jan 1 2001'
    AND product_number = 'XYY43233'
```

From the `invoiceLineItem` table you've only accessed the `invoiceLineItem_value`, the `invoice_customerId`, the `invoice_date,` and the `product_number` columns. By having an index on each column you've given SQL Server the chance to decide what the best first step is, by using the index statistics to ask a few simple questions:

❑ How many rows will I get back from `invoice_customerId = 10`?

❑ How many rows will I get back from `invoice_date < 'Feb 1 2001'` and `invoice_date >= 'Jan 1 2001'`?

❑ How many rows will I get back from `product_number = 'XYY43233'`?

❑ How expensive will it be to go get the `invoiceLineItem_value` value from the table rather than from the index?

The Query Optimizer will not only choose the best plan, but also determine whether you have one invoice or a million between the specified dates. In addition, it determines the likelihood of a row even existing with the specified `product_number`. You don't do this in your OLTP database due to the large overhead in maintaining the indexes, but you should presume that in most cases you'll do your writes to the read-only database when no users want to read the data.

Latency

Latency in this case refers to the amount of time it takes for a piece of data to be created before it's available in your database. In this section you'll look at the factors surrounding the latency of your read-only database.

Determining Build Frequency

Determining how often to update the read-only database depends on several factors, which are explained in the following list. You should make it clear that because financial and network resources are limited, in practice you'll seldom be able to reach the ideal of instant updates.

❑ **How often the user needs it**: If the data is needed immediately, then you may have to pull out all the stops to get it there as rapidly as possible.

❑ **How busy the OLTP server actually is**: If the server is used to store measurements from manufacturing robots, or to handle online orders, it may not be feasible to analyze the data immediately due to the load on the database servers.

❑ **Connection properties**: Depending on the connection speed, competing demands on your bandwidth, and the relative proximity of the OLTP system to the read-only version, it may not be reasonable to move massive amounts of data across the network during business hours.

❑ **Connection status**: When it comes to some clients who receive the extracts, they may not even be able to connect to the server except on demand. This might include a Pocket PC or laptop user who gets a copy of the data from the server.

❑ **Data size**: The quantity of important data in a system varies from a few rows to terabytes of data. If you consider an OLTP system with 200GB of data, you might not be able to extract the whole database, but it will certainly be possible to extract and aggregate a certain amount of data for faster use. Data size brings up the unfortunate truth that the more you need to take the additional steps to build a read-only database, the harder it actually becomes to implement. In some cases you may be able to carry out incremental updates, because there is rarely a need to ship the entire database every time.

❑ **Availability of resources**: If a good base-level server can be afforded, it may actually hurt more to spend the time transforming the OLTP data into a read-only database, rather than carrying out some denormalization of the OLTP data in the same database and building stored procedures or views as necessary.

I would like to build a matrix of the factors surrounding latency, but I can't. There is no single function or set of functions that you can use to decide what to do and when. The interplay between these factors is complex and each project must be treated individually in determining update frequency, though the individual user's needs come first wherever possible.

Implementation

Implementation of read-only databases is much easier to deal with than OLTP databases. You have three facilities readily available to you for transforming the data from the OLTP database.

❑ **DTS**: A powerful tool for transforming data from one form to another. It allows for graphical transformation of the data, as well as the use of scripting languages (VBScript, JavaScript) in the transformations.

❑ **Stored procedures**: You can write queries that take data in one form and insert it as rows into the new database. For many jobs this is the cleanest and fastest way to build the transformations, especially when they operate between databases on the same server.

❑ **Replication**: Used as a tool to replicate data from database to database, a really neat manner of implementing the transformation is by using **stored procedure replication**. In this manner you can publish one database to another, overriding the typical SQL inserts, updates, and deletes for replication and using stored procedures instead. In the read-only database, you can build stored procedures to handle each situation where a row or table is modified and have the data in the summary tables change accordingly. A drawback to this plan is that you must still implement the initialization stored procedures which can be really tricky, because instead of doing clean transformations, you have to add to or subtract from summaries.

As an example, let's say that you have a running total on the customer table of all purchases that have been made. You would need to code an INSERT stored procedure that increments the value of the running total. For a DELETE, you would decrement the value, and for a modifying UPDATE command, you would have to subtract the previous value and add the new value.

You can also use replication as your distribution agent to re-distribute the entire extracted database to all users.

With each of these tools, extracts can be created to suit a variety of needs. Let's consider a situation where you have an order processing establishment in Nashville, and a headquarters in New York. Though orders are both taken and invoiced in Nashville, the corporate headquarters, to which reports summarizing sales are sent, is located in New York. Because the headquarters in New York doesn't have enough space to house any of the primary corporate computers, the following design is devised:

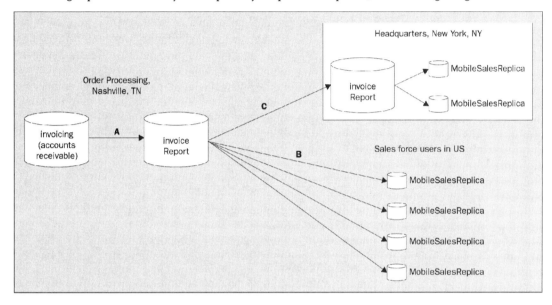

You have three separate problems to deal with in turn:

❑   **Transforming the data (A)**: You have to take the normalized data and turn it into the report.

❑   **Loading the data onto lightweight clients (B)**: This is unlikely to entail loading all the data onto the client, but rather a very small, very specific data set that enables the user to do his job better.

❑   **Loading the data from one physical plant to another (C)**: With your business becoming more and more globalized, you need to be able to transport your data across a network.

You'll now go on to look at each of these concerns individually.

Transforming the Data

To transform the data from the original normalized format, there are two possible courses of action:

❑   **Rebuild every time**: Anytime you build a read-only database, you always have to create a method of initially loading the database. If transformations are required, you'll have to synchronize the database with the OLTP database's current state. If the size of the data is reasonably small and there is a period of time when usage of the database is low, you can simply delete the data and start over. This is the easiest method to use when creating a daily extract.

❏ **Transactionally using replication procedures**: If you must keep the data updated frequently, or the data is too large to handle by wiping and synchronizing, you can write replication procedures to maintain the data in the database.

As an example, let's code a procedure from the four-table example, and look at what you'll have to do when a new `invoiceLineItem` row is inserted. You won't only have to insert a new `invoiceLineItem`, but also update the `product` table as well as the other tables up the relationship chains:

```
CREATE PROCEDURE invoiceLineItem$replInsert
(
    @invoiceLineItemId int,
    @productId int,
    @invoiceId int,
    @quantityPurchased int
) AS


-transaction and error handling not present for clarity

INSERT INTO invoiceLineItem (invoiceLineItemId, productId, invoiceId,
    quantityPurchased, Invoice_customerId,
    invoice_date, invoice_number,
    customer_name, product_number, product_name,
    product_price, invoiceLineItem_value)
SELECT @invoiceLineItemId, @productId, @invoiceId,
    @quantityPurchased, Invoice.customerId,
    invoice.date, invoice_number,
    customer.name, product.number, product.name,
    product.price, invoice.quantityPurchased * @quantityPurchased
FROM invoice
    JOIN customer


    ON customer.customerId = invoice.customerId
            -cross join is used because in a normal query you would join
            -these two sets to the invoiceLineItem table, which is represented
            -by the variable values, guaranteeing a Cartesian product of two
            -single rows, which return a single row.
    CROSS JOIN product
WHERE product.productId = @productId
    AND @invoiceId = invoice.invoiceId

UPDATE product
    -add the quantity purchased to the products sold count
SET invoiceLineItem_totalProductSoldCount =
    invoiceLineItem_totalProductSoldCount + @quantityPurchased,
    -add the quantity purchased * price to the products sold value
    invoiceLineItem_totalProductSoldValue =
    invoiceLineItem_totalProductSoldValue +
    price * @quantityPurchased
WHERE productId = @productId

-same type of thing for invoice and product

GO
```

Note that you won't do any summarizing, because you only insert a row at a time. However, you have to offset the amounts that are inserted. In general, this should run pretty fast. Unfortunately, this may actually be more costly than deleting all the data and summarizing it again for data sets that are subject to constant change (these are generally smaller in nature). It may be best to simply truncate the data and add it back to start with, because this requires much less effort on your behalf.

Loading the Data onto Lightweight Clients

Lightweight clients are those working with either laptops or PDAs. The best method for implementing an "on demand" client when working with disconnected clients is to implement **pull replication subscription** (because you don't have control over when and where clients will connect from). This allows the client to connect from wherever he wants, and in much the same way as a mail program calls to the server to get your e-mail, SQL Server calls the main server and requests any changes. This type of replication can also be used in cases when you need to update rows in other tables.

Loading the Data from One Physical Plant to Another

In this case **transactional replication** (where every transaction that is applied to one database will be used for replication) would be the way to go, with as much latency as the client can allow, or at the very least, tuned to happen primarily when loads are lowest on the servers.

> *Note that any type of replication uses the transaction log to do the synchronization, so if you've made many changes to any of the databases and want to replicate them, the transaction log will continue to grow until the distribution or merge agent has been able to apply all of the log entries to the target database.*

Uses

We'll take the opportunity here to briefly list a few possible uses of read-only databases:

❑ **Simple reporting needs**: *Simple* here refers to single database-type report extracts.

❑ **Operational data store**: The database where you consolidate data from all your external sources.

❑ **Websites**: Because most of the content from a website is read-only, any of the content that users need can be transformed from normalized structures into a format that's tailored to any particular site.

❑ **Laptop computers**: You might wish to factor in users of portable computers (who may be carrying around copies of sales figures or even actuarial tables), so that they have instant access to the latest figures.

Obviously the sky is the limit in this case. By separating the heavy readers of the data from the heavy writers, you give both sets of users a tremendous boost in performance. Now you'll take a deeper look at a couple of read-only database uses.

Simple Reporting Needs

Note that when I say simple, I'm referring neither to the queries that you can support, nor the complexity of reports, but rather to the work involved in setting up the reporting. In general, you'll create your reporting databases from a single database. This is a fairly common use of read-only databases, because with only a small amount of work, you can give the user what she needs in order to answer questions, without fearing that she'll accidentally modify something in the primary system.

Generally, you can go down two paths in this case. You can support particular reports that the user needs, much like you did in the `customerProduct` table earlier:

```
customerProduct
  customerId
  productId
  customer_name
  product_name
  product_price
  product_number
  week_quantityPurchased
  week_valuePurchased
  month_quanityPurchased
  month_valuePurchased
  year_quanityPurchased
  year_valuePurchased
  build_date
```

You do this by removing all joins and giving them a report that they can customize the parameters on. Because most reports are based on a single resultset of information, this works really well for less knowledgeable clients with very specific needs.

If you have more knowledgeable clients, however, then you could implement something closer to the table-based solution that was developed previously.

English Query

A tool for ad hoc reporting that I wanted to make sure to mention is **English Query**. It's a product that ships with SQL Server (since version 6.5) and is used to put a very natural language interface on a SQL database, by translating a question such as the following:

What was the total value of EPROMs that was invoiced to Bob's Electronics last year?

into a native SQL call to your extract table:

```
SELECT sum(invoiceLineItem_value)
FROM invoiceLineItem
WHERE product_name = 'EPROM'
    AND customer_name = 'Bob''s electronics'
    AND invoice_date >= 'jan 1, 2000'
    AND invoice_date < 'jan 1, 2001'
```

Of course it would also work against OLTP databases as well, and could create the following query:

```
SELECT sum(invoice.quantityPurchased * @quantityPurchased)
FROM invoiceLineItem
    JOIN invoice
    JOIN customer
    ON customer.customerId = invoice.customerId
    ON invoiceLineItem.invoiceId = invoice.invoiceId
    JOIN product
    ON product.productId = invoiceLineItem.productId
WHERE product.name = 'EPROM'
    AND customer.name = 'Bob''s electronics'
    AND invoice.date >= 'jan 1, 2000'
    AND invoice.date < 'jan 1, 2001'
```

If this sounds like magic, it isn't. There is a very detailed Semantic Modeling Format (which is an XML-based language) that you must use to store a "model" of the database with descriptors for every table, attribute, and relationships, so that *total value* and *were invoiced* in your question can be turned into both of the previous queries, in different databases. You would, of course, have to model the entire database that you wanted English Query to recognize in order for it to be able to perform these queries.

Operational Data Store

This is a database where you take all of the data from any (and possibly all) of your databases, as illustrated in the following diagram:

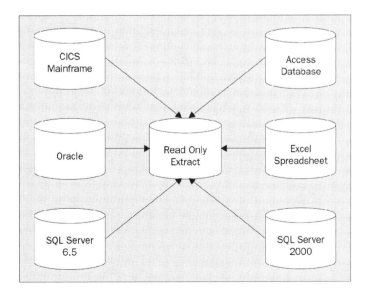

529

It's the database where you consolidate data from all of your external data sources. In the ODS, you'll employ many of the normalization (and for reporting, some denormalization) techniques that you've used to build your OLTP database, in order to create a reasonably up-to-date set of data. This will allow you to make decisions that will enable the overall business organization to run more efficiently.

The ODS will contain a model that is pretty much like your OLTP database, with some degree of denormalization. The goal isn't to build one ODS per OLTP database; rather it's to merge organizational data from ALL corporate sources into a common storage, fully cleaned and with common data matched to common data. For example, say you have two databases, one out-of-box and one developed in-house, with each database employed by different business units. Not surprisingly, each database has a vendor table filled with vendors that each unit does business with.

The first step to take is to model each of the source databases using common terms. For example, you may have two databases each of which models the vendor tremendously differently:

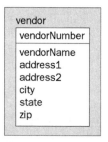

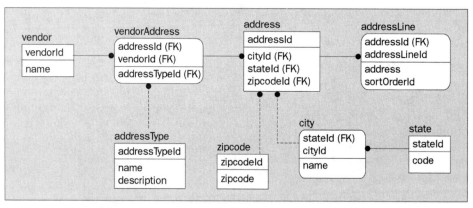

In the case of these tables, you should build your ODS model using the normalized structures and transform the data from the first structure into the second. The distressingly difficult part of building the ODS is merging existing databases. Thinking back to the first chapter, you had this diagram:

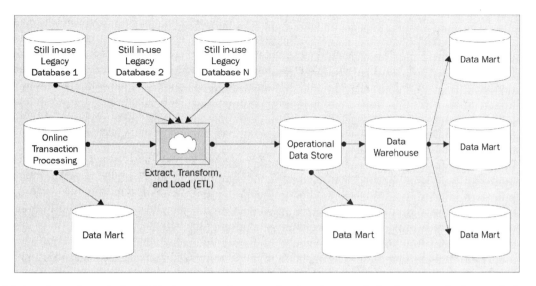

All data flows through this ETL cleaning cycle to get the data from each database matched up with the corresponding data from the other databases. In the final ODS, you'll want to store the data in exactly the same manner for every instance of it, so if you have ten vendor tables in ten different databases (or spreadsheets, or whatever data storage is in use) and you have five different spellings of the name 'Joe's Fish Market' ('Joe''s Fish Market', 'joes phish markt', 'joe fish', and 'joe market'), which all represent the same fish market, you consolidate the contents from all these rows into the same row in your ODS.

Enterprise Data Models

The concept of an **enterprise data model** is relatively straightforward: it's a model that shows every table and every relationship in every database that you deal with. In this way, the architect gains a complete overview of all the data that the corporation uses. Sounds like a good idea? Unfortunately achieving a perfect enterprise data model is extremely difficult.

In your case study system that you've been building throughout the book, you've created nearly 20 tables in order to perform a very small function. Now consider a corporation of almost any size and how much more complex its banking system would be if it contained, say, 200 tables. Then note that most corporations have more than one database, and several more management systems that they have purchased from vendors. In many cases these systems require interfaces from other systems. This can lead you to a system such as the one shown schematically in the next diagram:

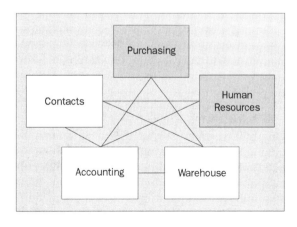

The darkened rectangles denote systems that have been purchased, and the lines represent where an interface is built. Each of these systems will require hundreds of tables in their own right, and you've probably built several tables to support each communication between them. The goal of an enterprise model is to fuse all of the models into one "grand model," whereby you can see all of the interactions and get a clear picture of what you have and how they interact. This is no simple task, whatsoever, for several reasons:

❑ **Sheer volume of the data**: Suppose that your previous example contains 1000 tables.

❑ **Proprietary nature of third-party systems**: Even some of the best third-party tool developers feel the need to hide the implementation details of their systems from prying eyes. The business case for such schemes aside, it makes understanding and using the data next to impossible.

❑ **Multiple database server types**: SQL Server 4.2, 6.5, 7.0, 2000; Oracle 6, 7, 8; Informix, and so on, leave you confused as to exactly what is going on in the server.

❑ **Fluctuations in the model**: Keeping a data model synchronized with a single database is a pretty steep task without very strict rules governing who can change it.

❑ **Cost**: Considering the rest of the bulleted points, this operation can be quite expensive.

You can remove some of these issues by deciding to simply implement a logical enterprise model, by quite possibly removing proprietary systems from your view, and by including only the interface tables (either ones you create will interface with processes, or actual system tables that you care about). This leads you to a totally different problem, namely, that of ensuring that the logical model for one database squares with its physical model. A further complication is that some of the systems that you'll create may include multiple "modules" of a given system, such as an accounting system:

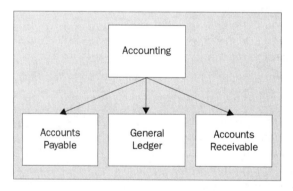

The goal of any section in this book is to outline a situation, a description of the problem, and then suggest what to do about it. In this case, the answer isn't easy. The only way to keep a logical model in sync with the physical model and more importantly, the physical implementation, is by being disciplined. The only way to take the smaller models and build an enterprise model is again through discipline. Fixed processes must be in place to take code from the on-paper stage to the built stage.

Changes to the database schema need to follow some process such as the following:

❑ Create or modify the logical model to contain all of the data that it currently needs to store.

❑ Update the physical model to reflect these changes in the manner decided.

❑ Make changes to physical structures.

❑ Update the enterprise model to reflect the current status of the system every time anything changes.

How to actually turn the goal of an enterprise model into reality will depend heavily on what tools are used to model the data and enterprise. It's critical to find the right modeling tool and repositories that will allow you to build the model and maintain it over time as situations change.

Moving from a Test Environment

When developing software, you have to be realistic. Your design will never be perfect, and neither will the coding. If it were, you could just develop new software, hand it over to users, and move to the next project. The second reality is that once the users have had an opportunity to use the software, there will be changes required. Typically, there is an iterative process in developing databases, involving three key stages:

❑ Development

❑ Quality assurance

❑ Production

Each environment plays a fundamental part in the process of getting code created, tested, and utilized by users. The goal is to have a process for which your code moves through a series of phases that appear as shown in the following figure.

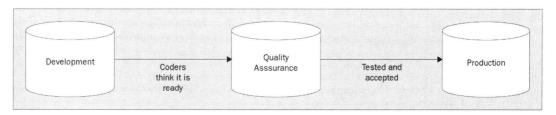

Code starts in the development database, then moves into QA, and finally into production. Though this is the goal, it certainly isn't reality. It's almost impossible to develop a system of any complexity and not find any errors. Usually, at a minimum, the process is more like the following figure.

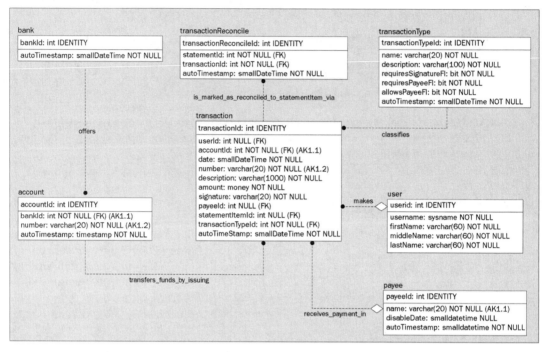

And realistically, you could draw lines from every database to every other database. However, when bugs are located in production, in most cases you still have to go through this same cycle of developing code, testing the code for quality, and finally putting it into production.

In addition to this three-phase model, it's common to have a preproduction phase between QA and production, depending on the importance of the system. You may also have two or more QA databases for different types of testing (load testing, user-acceptance testing, validity testing, and so on) in order to determine that all algorithms are proper, based on the system and requirements. Some organizations will need to have multiple development areas to maintain different versions of the code to support the production system that the users are currently using, and another area for new versions of the code.

However, you won't learn much about this, because no matter how many actual systems have to be dealt with, the same areas must be addressed.

Development

This is the environment in which you'll build your databases at the beginning. In this area, you shouldn't have any users or testers, but rather you'll have the architects, DBAs, user-interface programmers, and database coders testing out and creating new code.

Development Hardware

The hardware for development should be minimal, but reasonable. If the test server is as powerful as the production database servers, the developers will tend to try to use every bit of juice to solve a problem, and it will be very hard to discover any kind of tuning issues that may occur once the data moves to production. The same kind of thing is true when it comes to networking bandwidth. If you're building a WAN application with a 2Mbit connection between client and server, and the development is happening on a 100Mbit network, it can be difficult to develop the proper solution.

Bear in mind, however, that the server shouldn't be so slow as to impede process. Finding the proper balance for a development environment is a difficult task, and it's probably better to err on the side of too much hardware. This decision must also be tempered with the knowledge that most test servers aren't simply used for one database system and end up chock full of databases, web servers, file shares, and so on. These things start finding their home on the server over time in order to save money on hardware costs (even though you ask nicely for them to not put more stuff on the database server). For example a new vendor product is acquired and it just "has to be tested somewhere and your server isn't that busy, and it's only for a few days." ("A few days" being a manager phrase that loosely translates to: "As long as I want it to be there.")

Quality Assurance

Once software (or parts of the software) has been developed to a level where it's supposed to be ready to be given to users, it must be tested. The QA environment is used as a proving ground in several ways:

- ❏ **Quality testing**: Ensuring that the software (database and code that accesses the database, like the UI) performs as the programmers advertise. It also checks that the system meets the users' needs. This will include testing the validity of the system (that all algorithms are correct), security audits, and basically that every thing works.

- ❏ **Load testing**: Used to put the software through a realistic (and in many cases beyond realistic) load to see if it can handle the loads it will be exposed to in production.

- ❏ **Acceptance testing**: Before the user can begin to utilize the new database, or certain changes are made to it, the users will typically have to approve of the software that has been written in order to agree that it does everything that was on the initial specification.

QA Hardware

The key to the right level of QA hardware is scale. Not every organization will be able to completely duplicate the hardware of their production servers, because the server(s) may end up costing a large percentage of the entire budget for the system being developed. However, consider it this way. If the entire QA system has 10 percent of the power of the production one, you should be able to handle ten times as much activity on the production system. Note of course, that rarely will you be able to scale every part of your system to exactly the same levels, but a great DBA should be able to approximate the process and get a reasonable scale factor for testing.

Minimal hardware is required for the other task of QA, which is to make sure that whatever has been developed meets the agreed specifications. During such testing the stress-testing hardware will more than suffice for running test scripts that identify inputs to processes and procedures and corresponding proper values as well as application testing.

Production

The production environment is where the user actually uses the database. Once you've promoted code from development, through the QA process, in theory, it should be bugfree (of course, in practice it generally takes a few cycles through the development-to-QA path to get it close to bugfree). Though setting up the production database isn't the data architect's job, in my experience, the data architect *is* often involved with specifying how this system is used and maintained (especially in smaller organizations) and can take a good amount of blame if the proper database and hardware isn't specified.

In Chapter 14, I gave a basic introduction to some of the hardware issues that you'll face as well as some formulas and stored procedures that you can use to assist with the database-sizing issues. You also calculated the sizes (and projections of future sizes) of the data that will be stored in your database. In most cases, this will be entirely the job of the DBA, but it's critical to understand the basics, because not all DBAs understand hardware fully, and in many cases there may not even be a dedicated DBA, and you may have to participate in a request for hardware for a database system.

Maintenance and Disaster Recovery Plans

Though you won't be looking at how to back up databases, you do need to examine a few of the important factors to consider when the system moves towards production. Generally, this kind of information will be specified when the data architect has nearly finished the job. There are two areas of concern here: maintenance and disaster recovery, and there is a difference between the two.

For a maintenance plan and a disaster recovery plan, we're out to save ourselves from simple hardware and software problems like UPS failures and hard-disk crashes. These are relatively straightforward problems to deal with as long as the DBA understands a few particulars:

❑ **Size of data**: Using the formulas discussed in the previous chapter, you can give projections of the size of the data based on its expected growth, as estimated at the end of the logical-design phase.

❑ **Acceptable loss of data**: This one is easy! None. Of course, this isn't a valid answer, because you have to accept that you'll always have some window of time when there is a loss of data due to a massive system failure. However, because the acceptable risk time gets smaller, the cost of meeting this goal goes up exponentially. If you can lose a day's data, you simply have to back up every night onto some storage that isn't located on the same machine. If an hour is acceptable loss, you can do the same thing with transaction logs though users are using the data, and you can eliminate almost any loss of data using clustering techniques (there is always some minimal latency that cannot be avoided). Of course clustering is far more expensive than a tape drive and with clustering you still need the tape drive. Cost, of course, is more of a matter for the client and the project manager to duke it out over.

❑ **Acceptable level of service**: This would generally be some indication of the expected load at different times during the day. It would also detail the expected and contracted uptimes that the database must be active. Of course, this sounds quite like the "Acceptable Loss of Data" bullet mentioned earlier, because the expected level of service is full barrel, anytime the client wants it; but this isn't a realistic expectation, and will not be contracted as such. To completely cover this requirement, you must also have an understanding of how long it will take to bring the servers back online.

For a disaster recovery plan, you have to plan for "real" problems, such as hurricanes, fires, tornadoes, and even a blown transformer from a neighboring construction site (I learned about this when a worker tossed a metal gutter across a power line in a building I was working in. Transformers give off really cool colors when they're exploding!). A full plan would simply be an extension of the maintenance plan, but will escalate from hardware failures to include the following:

❑ **Power failures**: Power failures are a very important concern. How many times have you heard stories about the online retailer that was down for a few hours? Not a great way to get recognition. Having a generator that will kick in well before the UPS gives way is the best way to make certain that that there will be no interruptions in service, regardless of the power supply.

❑ **Weather disasters**: What if all of the power is out due to a hurricane? Or a tornado? Or even a flood? In a global economy, if servers are down for a week, you'll likely be in the nightly news (or worse the financial news), and you may have sunk your company. You'll probably need to have this covered with out-of-town servers.

❑ **Other disasters**: Disasters come in all shapes and sizes, and you cannot even begin to make an exhaustive list. Building wiring faults, poorly set-up systems, mice, insects, a volcano eruption, or (unfortunately) even the poorly planned software upgrade can all cause the system to be down for an unacceptable amount of time.

The last, and certainly most important, issue surrounding maintenance and disaster recovery plans is testing them. The best laid plans of mice and DBAs or something like that. The most impressive disaster recovery plan may be designed including the most impressive generator and UPSs, but if you only stock enough fuel to run the generators for a day, and subsequently an ice storm hits, taking the power out for two days, and there is no fuel to be purchased (apparently everyone needs fuel in these types of disasters!), then the plan will be somewhat ineffectual. In the same manner, if you pull the plug on the main UPS only to discover that the generator cannot be up and running in time before the UPS runs out of juice, then it's possible that the time spent roasting marshmallows might be spent repairing operating systems, databases, and file shares.

Case Study

In this final case study, you have one final task to perform–that of building a reporting database. If you really were building this system, you probably wouldn't actually build a reporting database, because your system is small with low concurrency requirements. However, for completeness you'll build a table to support a specific report that you discovered in the "Case Study" section of Chapter 8. It was described as follows:

> **User activity: A list of all transactions attributed to a given user, or simply grouped by user. Also needs to be able to show any transactions that haven't been attributed to the user who actually spent the money.**

Hence you need to get the tables related to the transaction, which are as follows:

❑   **transaction**: The transaction itself

❑   **account**: The account that the check came from

❑   **bank**: The bank where the account is held

❑   **payee**: For checks, and possibly others based on the `transactionType` table

❑   **user**: A list of users who are known to the system that write checks

❑   **transactionType**: Classifies the type of transaction

❑   **transactionReconcile**: If a row exists in this table for the transaction, it has been reconciled.

The relation between these is summarized in the following figure.

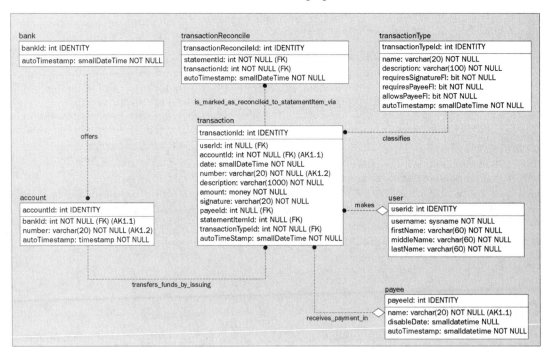

You'll roll up many of the columns in these tables into a single table as follows:

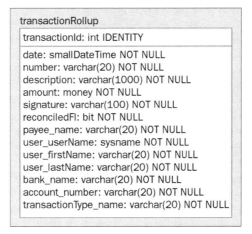

Because your system isn't a high-access system, you'll simply build a stored procedure to truncate the data in the `transactionRollup` table, and replace it with the proper values. Instead of moving this table to a different database, you'll choose to place it in the same database and never give users access to modify it. For smaller systems, this allows giving users a read-only extract without needing to build an additional database.

In the following code, you build the transform procedure. Though it's pretty long, it's also pretty straightforward. It simply resolves all of the joins to the parent tables of the `transaction` table as follows:

```
CREATE PROCEDURE transactionRollup$transform
AS

--declare variable used for error handling in blocks
DECLARE @rowcount int, --holds the rowcount returned from dml calls
    @error int, —used to hold the error code after a dml
    @msg varchar(255), --used to preformat error messages
    @retval int, --general purpose variable for retrieving
    --return values from stored procedure calls
    @tranName sysname, --used to hold the name of the transaction
    @msgTag varchar(255), --used to hold the tags for the error message
    @key_bankId int   --used in @msgTag
--set up the error message tag
SET @msgTag = '<' + object_name(@@procid) + ';type=P'
    + ';keyvalue=' + '@key_bankId:'
    + convert(varchar(10),@key_bankId)

SET @tranName = object_name(@@procid) + cast(@@nestlevel as varchar(2))

BEGIN TRANSACTION
SAVE TRANSACTION @tranName

TRUNCATE TABLE transactionRollup
IF @error != 0 —an error occurred outside of this procedure
```

```
    BEGIN
    SELECT @msg = 'A problem occurred truncating the transactionRollup table'
    + @msgTag + 'call=(truncat transactionRollup)>'
    rollback TRAN @tranName
    COMMIT TRAN
    RAISERROR 50000 @msg
    RETURN -100
    END


INSERT INTO transactionRollup (transactionId, date, number, description,
    amount, signature, reconciledFl,
    payee_name, user_userName, user_firstName,
    user_middleName, user_lastName, bank_name,
    account_number, transactionType_name)
SELECT xaction.transactionId, xaction.date, xaction.number,
    xaction.description, xaction.amount, xaction.signature,

    --if the outer join to the transactionReconcile table leaves the
    --not nullable COLUMN null in the join. Hence if you check for null
    --in this COLUMN, you can tell if the ROW has been reconciled
    CASE WHEN transactionReconcile.transactionReconcileId IS NULL
    THEN 1
    ELSE 0
    END AS reconciledFl,
    payee.name, [user].userName, [user].firstName, [user].middleName,
    [user].lastName, bank.name, account.number, transactionType.name

FROM dbo.xaction AS xaction

    --get the account and bank
    JOIN dbo.account AS account
    JOIN dbo.bank AS bank
    ON bank.bankId = account.bankId


    ON xaction.accountId = account.accountId

    --get the type of the transaction
    JOIN dbo.transactionType AS transactionType
    ON transactionType.transactionTypeId =
    xaction.transactionTypeId
    --not all transactions will have a payee
    LEFT OUTER JOIN dbo.payee AS payee
    ON payee.payeeId = xaction.payeeId

    --not all transactions have to be associated to user
    LEFT OUTER JOIN dbo.[user] AS [user]
    ON [user].userId = xaction.userId

    --left outer join in case the value has not been reconciled yet
    LEFT OUTER JOIN dbo.transactionReconcile AS transactionReconcile
    ON transactionReconcile.transactionId = xaction.transactionId

IF @error != 0 --an error occurred outside of this procedure
    BEGIN
    SELECT @msg = 'A problem occurred truncating the transactionRollup table'
```

```
        + @msgTag + 'call=(truncat transactionRollup)>'
        ROLLBACK TRAN @tranName
        COMMIT TRAN
        RAISERROR 50000 @msg
        RETURN -100
        END

    COMMIT TRANSACTION
```

Of course you've read about other tasks, such as setting up production environments, performance tuning, and so on. However, these tasks are beyond the scope of this case study and were covered more to note their existence for times when you get called in to help specify hardware, such as when the DBA staff all land new jobs. Having an understanding of how everything works, even if you never have to turn SQL Server's knobs and dials, is very important.

Best Practices

❏ **Put off performance tuning until as late in the process as possible**: Now that the project is finished, you can make tweaks to the database as needed. If you've encapsulated what the user (object, programs, front-ends, and so on) needs well enough, you can tune without changing anything other than some database or middle-tier code.

❏ **Do what is required to avoid ad hoc usage of the OLTP system**: The better known the SQL that will be executed in the database the better. Build read-only databases to allow the user to query the data with no contention to the active users. Even if this is simply replicating a copy of the database transactionally, it will keep the users and reporters happy because no one will be blocking anyone from doing actual revenue-generating activity just to look at some data.

❏ **Develop an enterprise model**: Every time some user wants data stored or retrieved, it's essential to know what data is currently stored, and where. Without this tool you may have no idea what you have and run a high risk of storing duplicated data in multiple databases, systems, or file types, and so on.

❏ **Maintain multiple environments for the system**

   ❏ *Development:* For building new additions to the programs and database

   ❏ *Quality Assurance:* For making sure that what has been developed is up to the challenge

   ❏ *Production:* Where actual money making goes on

Summary

In this chapter, you've considered some of the issues that you may well face at the end of your design projects, just as you're thinking about packing up and moving on to the next job.

I began by discussing the need for performance tuning, and recommended building queries and performance tuning after design. SQL Server is a great performer, so the practice of proactively tuning SQL Server queries, even before they have been executed once, can do more harm than good.

I then discussed all of the basics of building read-only extracts of your databases. The easy part of this task is to model what you want the data to look like, but the other tasks, such as setting up replication, using DTS, and so on, are a lot more complex and involve other individuals such as the DBA. Included in this discussion was the idea of maintaining an enterprise model that outlines all of your database resources. The most important reason to do this is to ensure that you store any one piece of data only once in a database.

Finally, you had a high-level look at how to organize your development environment, utilizing a three-phase iterative process involving development, quality assurance, and production. Such a cycle requires consideration of issues such as hardware, size of data, and the nature of testing that you need to perform. You also looked at the need for devising both maintenance and disaster recovery plans.

Having looked at all these issues you should now be able to send the database away to the users and let them begin using your creation, while you mosey off into the sunset to face the next great database challenge.

Index

Numbers and Symbols

4GT (4 Gigabyte Tuning), 479
\# prefix, local temporary tables, 373
\#\# prefix, global temporary tables, 373
$ (dollar sign) delimiter, 280
@@error variable
  accessing error numbers from SQL, 330
@@rowcount variable
  interrogating after SET statements, 330
@@trancount variable
  stored procedures must leave unchanged, 413
@name
  and other extended property sproc parameters, 288
[] (square brackets)
  enclosing SQL Server object names, 252
  enclosing table named as reserved word, 295
" " (double quotes)
  enclosing SQL Server object names, 252
<searchConditions> value
  check constraints, 322

A

abbreviations
  exceptions to the rule of avoiding in names, 256
  naming of attributes should avoid, 101, 128
abstract entities, 59
acceptance testing, 535
access contention. *See also* concurrency, conflict resolution
  ad hoc user queries, 224
access privileges

allocating to security roles, 438
  partitioned data, 391
  restricting to views instead of tables, 391
accessing archived data, 476
ActiveX Data Objects. *See* ADO (ActiveX Data Objects)
actors, use case models
  checking register case study, 208
  including security information, 199
ad hoc queries
  table-oriented read-only databases, 520
ad hoc SQL, 431, 433
Address Windowing Extensions. *See* AWE (Address Windowing Extensions)
addresses
  checking register case study, 157, 159, 160, 183, 295
  examples of First Normal Form violations, 134, 135
  examples of locator attributes, 65
ADO (ActiveX Data Objects)
  API cursors, 377
  may send transactions in multiple batches, 371
AFTER triggers
  enforcing mandatory relationships with, 344
  matching zip codes with cities, 360
  range checking, 345
  transaction allocation check, 362
age of data
  archiving by time period, 474
aliases
  allowed by user-defined data types, 262
alphabetization. *See* collation types
ALTER TABLE statement
  adding constraints with, 278
  introduced, 278

alternate keys
  implementing to enforce uniqueness, 276
  introduced, 37
  representation in IDEF1X standard, 97
  role in maintaining uniqueness, 36
ANSI_NULLS option, 384
API cursors, 377
Application Memory Tuning, 479
application types
  determine number of user connections, 500
architecture limitations
  demands placed on the database and, 200
archiving policy, 473, 474
  accessing archived data, 476
  costs of archiving data, 473
  fact table date partitioning, 475
  flagging archived data, 476
  hardware and software obsolescence, 474
  should not be an afterthought, 476
arrays
  using temp tables as, 375
atomicity
  access to external tables, 355
  attributes, requirement of First Normal
  Form, 133
  checking register case study, 155
  OLTP transactions and, 5
  optionally cascading deletes, 356
  updating telephone area codes and, 137
attribute definitions
  checking register case study, 127
attribute history
  Fourth Normal Form violations and, 176
attributes
  adding descriptive information, 120
  attributes of attributes, 32
  building standard, using IDEF1X domains,
  100
  checking register case study, 78
  columns identified with, 31
  deriving from sample documents, 79, 81
  difference from columns, 65, 96
  domains and, discovering in data from
  customers, 56
  Enterprise Manager diagramming tool, 117
  finalizing definitions, 307
  identifying additional data, 75
  moving, when building read-only databases,
  517
  multi-valued, Fourth Normal Form and, 166,
  173

must be atomic in First Normal Form, 133
must fully depend on a key in BCNF, 151
naming conventions, 100
order is not inherent in, 31
representation in IDEF1X standard, 96
Second Normal Form, must describe the
  entire key, 141
tabulated examples, with entities and
  domains, 66
audit requirements, 22
audit trails
  defer to physical design stage, 60
auto dealership example
  use of summary data, 150
Available Bytes counter, 483
AWE (Address Windowing Extensions), 480

B

Back Office Resource Kit
  source of performance tuning tools, 482
balance account use case
  custom stored procedure, 453
bandwidth
  reducing, using a thick client, 235
bank account example. *See* checking register
case study
bank register
  deriving attributes from electronic format, 82
bank statement
  sample, as source of attribute information, 81
batching
  batch growth of OLAP databases, 462, 472
  database calls over moderate connections,
  226
  SQL statements executed as a group, 395
  transactions should not span boundaries, 369
BCNF. *See* Boyce-Codd Normal Form (BCNF)
BEGIN DISTRIBUTED TRANSACTION,
446
binary collation example, 272
Binary Large Objects. *See* BLOB (Binary Large
Objects)
binary relationships, 48
binary trees. *See* recursive tree example
blanks. *See* empty strings
BLOB (Binary Large Objects)
  table of domains, case study, 126
blocked access, 501

key cause of bottlenecks, 483
lock escalation by query optimizer, 224
testing with user definable counters, 503
book publishing example
    illustrating Second Normal Form violation, 141
    illustrating Third Normal Form violation, 146
    use case models, 199
Books Online, 253
    Creating an Indexed View, 393
    definition of null values, 382
    distributed queries and replication, 446
    Performing Transactions in ADO, 371
    permissions function, 439
    replication from other databases, 230
    sizing tables and indexes, 464
    SQL-DMO, 233
    System Stored Procedures, 286
    Using Extended Properties, 291
bottlenecks, 483
    disk and CPU, 491
    disk performance and, 498
bought-in systems
    inaccessiblity of implementation details, 532
Boyce-Codd Normal Form (BCNF)
    checking register case study, 157, 162
    clues to violations as for 2NF and 3NF, 154
    replacement for Second and Third Normal Forms, 151
bracketed notation, 252, 295
B-trees
    using to calculate index space, 467
budget
    effect on performance optimization options, 228
Buffer Manager
    counters, 488
    bugs. *See also* debugging
    associated with use of NULLs, 385
bulk copying
    intermediate tables to cut overheads, 369
bulk logged transactions, 472
Business Analyst role, 14
business decisions. *See also* decision support
    day-to-day, based on ODS, 6
business layer
    connection pooling by object broker in, 239
    enforcing business rules, 240
business rules
    care required in formulating, 72

coding in functional language, not in SQL, 240
defined, 71
defining in data structures, 178
discovering in customer interview notes, 86
discovering in data from customers, 56, 71
enforcing with triggers, 342
implementation by middle-tier services, 353
importance of complete discovery, 71
optional rules in case study, 364
sharing between middle tier and database, 355
table of new processes in banking example, 87
usage and relation to predicates explained, 35

C

caching
    by disk controllers, 493
    database calls over moderate connections, 226
    pages to speed data accesss, 493
    query plans, 433, 434
    validation data can compromise data integrity, 355
    write caching, 493
CAL (Client Access Licenses)
    distinction from user connections, 500
calculated columns, 266. *See also* computed columns
    building read-only databases, 518
camel notation, 95
candidate keys
    avoiding duplicate information, 35
    Boyce-Codd Normal Form, 160
capitalizing words in strings
    INSTEAD OF trigger to capitalize names, 347
cardinalities
    enforcing, as use for after triggers, 345
    of relationships, discussed, 48
    table showing six possible, 106
    use of for rowcounts, 38
cascading deletes
    optionally cascading, 356
    using an after DELETE trigger, 346

cascading inserts
 using AFTER triggers, 344
cascading modifications
 cascading updates and deletes, 280
 foreign keys and cascading deletes, 278
 setting child key references to NULL, 281
CASE keyword
 use of to allow for possible null values, 387
case sensitivity
 changing collation to introduce, 271
case studies. *See* checking register case study
casting
 datetime data to a string, 336
 scalars to a binary collation, 272
categorization relationships, 110
 complete and incomplete categories, 111
CEILING function, 466
character strings
 dynamic execution techniques, 469
check constraints, 322
 checking register case study, 333
 deriving from domain lists, 334
 function-based, 326
 inter-column dependencies solved by, 41
 introduced, 34
 one of five constraint types, 317, 339
 rules should be enforced at database level,
 355
 triggers may perform better in validation,
 329
 validating ranges using, 338
 violations, custom error messages, 407
CHECK option
 check constraint, 322
CHECK_CONSTRAINTS listing
 Information Schema, 285
checking register case study
 applying business rules, 331
 Boyce-Codd Normal Form, 157
 building a reporting database, 537
 building the database access structures, 446
 building the physical implementation, 292
 check constraints and UDFs, 333
 combo boxes, 452
 data model after Boyce-Codd normalization,
 162
 data model after full normalization, 188
 data types, 303
 default constraints, 332
 delete stored procedure, 450
 entity discovery, 77

external systems, 212
First Normal Form violations, 155
Fourth Normal Form violations, 181
information gathering stage, 22
insert stored procedure, 447
introduced, 10
listing stored procedure, 451
marking document attributes, 79
optional business rules, 364
physical model, 310
physical-only columns, 299
range checking, 337
reporting, 209
security issues, 455
simple client-server topology, 242
table of domains, 126
table of entities, attributes and domains, 82
transaction subtype, 292
update stored procedure, 448
use case modelling, 208
volumetric analysis, 504
volumetrics, 213
checks
 sample, as source of attribute information, 79
Chen ERD methodology, 116
child tables
 problems from deleting parent records, 228
 setting foreign key references to NULL, 346
Client Access Licenses. *See* CAL (Client Access
Licenses)
client executable code
 securing data integrity with, 316, 341
clients
 thick and thin, 235
client-server systems
 checking register case study, 242
 connection speed effects, 226
 large systems depart form simple
 architecture, 226
 simplest configuration for SQL Server use,
 238
clustered indexes
 calculating testing for presence of, 470
 checking register case study, 506
 free space from fill factor, 466
 reasons to keep index keys short, 467, 470
 reasons to keep row size short, 470
clustered servers, 230, 536
COALESCE function
 check constraints, 323
 use to allow for possible null values, 387

Codd, Edgar F.
    database laws, 38, 39
    normalization pioneer, 132
    relational database pioneer, 1
    relational operators formulated by, 42
coding
    applications, distinct from object creation, 368
    logical errors due to NULLs, 385
    round normalization problems, 145
COLLATE clause, 272
collation types, 271
    checking register case study, 310
column constraints
    type of check constraint, 322
COLUMN_DOMAIN_USAGE listing
    Information Schema, 285
COLUMN_PRIVILEGES listing
    Information Schema, 284
column-level security, 392, 441
columns
    attributes of, 32
    difference from attributes, 65, 96
    indexing all in read-only support databases, 522
    limiting visibility with views, 391
    maximum permitted number, 254
    physical and computed, 255
    SQL Server definition, 30
    using CREATE TABLE to define, 255
    which are costly to update, 427
COLUMNS listing
    Information Schema, 284
COM (Component Object Model)
    COM object instantiation, 233
    COM+ use of two-phase commit, 445
compiled SQL, 433, 435. *See also* triggers, stored procedures
Component Object Model. *See* COM (Component Object Model)
composite keys
    non-foreign keys suggest 2NF violation, 145
    Second Normal Form applies to, 140
compound keys, 123
computed columns
    introduced, 255
concurrency
    maximizing by building read-only databases, 514
concurrency control, 267

conditional inserts
    using INSTEAD OF triggers, 349
conference planning example
    resolving ternary relationships, 166
conflict resolution
    widely distibuted systems, 241
connection loss
    minimizing effects by batching transactions, 370
Connection Objects, ADO
    possible locking problems, 371
connection pooling
    performed in business layer of n-tier system, 239
    technique for multi-user systems, 229
connection speed
    WANs and web applications, 226
consistent data. *See* data integrity
constant expressions
    default constraints, 318
constraint errors
    mapping to user-friendly messages, 406
CONSTRAINT_COLUMN_USAGE listing
    Information Schema, 285
CONSTRAINT_TABLE_USAGE listing
    Information Schema, 285
constraints, 317
    adding with ALTER TABLE, 278
    advantages of triggers over, 342
    end-of-transaction, not available in SQL Server 2000, 188
    five types introduced, 317
    introduced and classified, 34
    securing data integrity with, 315
contact design model
    multi-valued attribute example, 174
contention. *See also* concurrency.
    read-only support database, 514, 521
context-switching
    use of fibers to avoid, 492
contracts and work orders
    as source of data rules, 21
copy databases. *See also* read-only databases
    read-only, to protect the primary database, 513
corporate data structure
    four functional modules, 3
covered queries, 522
CPU subsystem
    performance monitoring counters, 491
    performance tuning, 490

tuning not to be attempted, 491
CREATE TABLE statement, 251
    using to define columns, 255
CREATE VIEW statement, 385, 389, 390, 391
cross joins
    example of the product operator, 44
cross-database data access, 442
    databases on different servers XE, 445
    databases on the same server, 443
cross-database relationships, 282
crow's foot symbols
    use of by Information Engineering, 115
cursor types
    effect on sort order example, 381
    importance of specifying, 381
cursors, 377
    circumstances in which to use, 378
    use of by volume-estimating stored
    procedure, 469
custom error messages, 406
    check constraint violations, 407
    tagging values to include in, 408
custom stored procedures
    for calculating complete table size, 464
    for calculating index size, 468
customer consultation
    establishing reporting requirements, 196
    identifying further sources from, 23
    marking up interview notes, 77, 78, 86
    must precede data modeling, 13
    reviewing first draft document, 76
    suggested questions for interviews, 18

D

data access. *See also* security issues
    from a different database, 442
    protecting against unauthorized, 436
    using stored procedures to limit paths, 433
data access times
    performance of systems with high data
    volumes, 222
Data Architect role, 14
data cubes
    as data mart querying technology, 11
    introduced, 7
data domains
    attributes and, discovering in data from
    customers, 56

discovered at the same time as attributes, 62
    introduced, 64
    tabulated examples, with entities and
    attributes, 66
data duplication
    minimizing, 131
data integrity
    four methods of securing, compared, 315
    middle tier and database involvemnt, 355
    OLTP primary goal, 4
    problems from importing data, 354
    problems with pre-aggregated data, 223
    securing with constraints, 315
    write caching could compromise, 494
data loss
    acceptable levels for maintenance plans, 536
Data Management Objects. *See* DMO (Data
Management Objects)
data marts
    accessible via tools not involving coding, 8
    data warehouse segments, 7
    distinguished from OLAP and cubes, 11
data modeling
    as alternative to unwieldy lists, 86
    checking register case study, 162
    identifying processes relevant to, 74
data models
    invoice system for transforming to read-only,
    515
    logical and physical distinguished, 92
data modification, 367
    allowed with stored procedures but not
    UDFs, 399
    anomalies caused by 3NF violations, 146
    cross-database data access, 444
    INSTEAD OF triggers suit generic
    extensions, 349
    INSTEAD OF triggers, examples of use, 347
    problems caused by 2NF violations, 142
    problems caused by ternary relationships,
    168
data ownership, 198
data scrubbing, 232
data size calculation
    using a stored procedure, 464
data sources
    consolidating into read-only databases, 514
data transformation
    example corporate solution, 525

Data Transformation Services. *See* DTS (Data Transformation Services)

data types
  chosing to match logical domains, 259
  cursor, passing using output parameters, 402
  example of a SQL Server domain, 33
  general classes for logical design, 33
  inheritance of in IDEF1X, 98
  securing data integrity with, 315
  transformation of logical domains into, 303

data usage, 192, 198

data validation
  involving inter-table comparisons, 355
  range checks using AFTER triggers, 345
  rules, 21
  using thick and thin clients, 235

data volumes. *See also* volumetrics
  consequences of deleting parent table records, 228
  estimating, for hardware needs, 459
  estimating, for variable length columns, 464
  factors in calculating for tables, 464
  source of reporting problems, 221

data warehousing
  as decision support tool, 6
  contrasted with OLTP, 3
  diagram of a typical architecture, 9
  read-only support database alternative, 514
  storage optimized for reporting, 3, 6

database access, 367

Database Administrator. *See* DBA role

database design
  adherence to standards and normalization, 129
  compared to building construction, 217
  delayed by technological constraints, 145
  diagram of typical for large system, 9
  history, 1
  importance of approaching in stages, 56
  logical and physical design distinguished, 10
  process stages enumerated, 10
  separate roles distinguished, 14
  should incorporate archiving plans, 476
  technology slowed development of, 2
  tools provided by SQL Server, 230

database development
  an iterative process, 533

database generation tools
  introduced, 246

database objects
  heirarchy used by extended properties, 286
  SQL Server 2000 reporting tools for, 282

database owner role, 252, 253
  db_owner and other built-in roles, 438

database reorganization
  technique for coping with high data volumes, 222

database structure
  divorcing yourself from final, at discovery stage, 56

database tables
  naming conventions, 252
  terminology illustrated by sample, 29
  types of relationships between, 68

databases. *See also* read-only databases
  defined, 28
  growth of, 463
  merging into an ODS, 530
  OLTP and OLAP, 460

databases other than SQL Server
  access as linked servers, 231
  replication from, 230

Datalog/Monitor, 482

date information
  archiving by time period, 474
  checking whether a date is in the future, 335

datepart system function, 390

dates
  use of in keys not recommended, 302

datetime data type
  removing time from, 359
  stripping off the time with a UDF, 336, 390
  technically violates First Normal Form, 139

db_owner
  and other built-in roles, 438

DBA (Database Administrator) role
  distinct from database design, 14
  hardware specification, 459, 536
  performance tuning part of, 512

DBCC (Database Consistency Checker), 378, 513

DBCC MEMUSAGE, 481, 482

DBCC OPENTRAN
  detecting long running transactions, 500

DDL (Data Definition Language)
  needed by relational language to build DML objects, 47

debugging. *See* error handling; invalid data
decision support
  OLAP reporting demands and, 463
  primary use of data warehouses for, 6
default constraints, 318
  checking register case study, 332
defaults
  ensuring singularity of, 345
degrees of relations, 31
DELETE statements
  as stored procedure alternative, 429
delimiters. *See also* bracketed notation
  clue that existing data is not in 1NF, 139
  naming constraints, 280
  SQL Server naming convention, 252
denormalization, 180
  complex reporting situations may justify, 223
  introduction of summary data, 251
  last resort of performance tuning, 512, 513
  problems from denormalized external
  systems, 203
  read-only copies of data, 241
  some required in an ODS, 530
  update stored procedure, 427
denormalized data
  coding round no longer justified, 145
deny command, 438
dependent entities, 93
  foreign keys present in primary key, 94
derived tables, T-SQL
  alternative to temporary tables, 374
descriptive information
  adding to graphical data models, 119
descriptive properties
  communicating with developers, 286
design validation, 192
desktop databases
  possible location of pre-existing data, 20
destroy stored procedure, 429
determinants
  in Boyce-Codd Normal Form, 152
developers
  communicating with, 282
development databases
  contain data with no business value, 246
development phase
  hardware requirements, 535
dial-up access
  importance of for remote staff, 226
difference operator
  NOT IN SQL operator and, 46

dimension tables
  fact tables and, 7
dirty reads, 501
disaster recovery, 537
discovery and logical design
  discovery process introduced, 56
  report discovery strategy, 195
discriminators
  categorization relationships, 110
  checking register case study, 293
disk reads
  for determining perceived performance, 473
disk striping. *See* RAID, RAID 0; RAID, RAID
10
disk subsystem. *See also* RAID
  disk performance counters, 498
  importance of familiarity with, 499
  multiple disk controllers, 497
  performance tuning, 492
disk thrashing, 498
DISKPERF -Y command, 482
distibuted computing
  widely distributed systems, 241
DISTINCT keyword
  project operator example, 43
distributed computing
  clustered servers and, 230
distributed partitioned views, 394
distributed queries, 445
Distributed Transaction Controller. *See* DTC
(Distributed Transaction Controller)
divide operator, 47
DML (Data Manipulation Language)
  commands derived from basic relational
  operators, 47
DMO (Data Management Objects)
  code to instantiate and connect to, 233
  displaying database security roles, 439
documentation
  checking register case study, 23
  completing the data documentation tasks, 75
  crucial importance in database project, 15,
  197
  data modeling as alternative to unwieldy
  lists, 86
  final review, 206, 216
  identifying information elements in, 56
  need for constant updating, 56
documents
  as entities in a database, 59
domain entities, 104

domain lists
    deriving check constraints from, 334
domain names
    table, with equivalent data types, 303
domain predicates, 128
domain tables, 104
    changes to, supporting fact tables, 475
    characterised by slow or no growth, 461
    extenal system interface problem caused by,
    201
DOMAIN_CONSTRAINTS listing
    Information Schema, 285
domains, 32. *See also* logical domains; data
domains
    building does not imply implementation, 100
    checking register case study, 125, 126
    inheritance depends on modeling tools, 99
    representation in IDEF1X standard, 98
    usage explained with examples, 34
    using as a column template, 257
double quote (" ") delimiters, 252
DTC (Distributed Transaction Controller), 232
    code example *also* using linked servers, 232
    transactions spanning different servers, 445
DTS (Data Transformation Services), 232
    read-only databases and, 524
dummy procedures, 412
duplexing (RAID 1), 495
dynamic memory allocation
    upset by specifying user connections, 499
dynamic memory tuning
    SQL Server 2000, 485
dynamic queries
    stored procedures and, 421

E

email
    SQL Mail facility, 234
email addresses
    examples of First Normal Form violations,
    133
empty strings
    using UDFs to check for, 324, 333
encapsulation
    code within stored procedures, 410, 434
    code within UDFs, 324
    joins etc, to hide them from users, 388
    user-defined data types as a tool for, 263

end-user databases
    source of denormalized data, 514
English Query, 528
Enterprise Data Models, 531
    logical enterprise model, 532
Enterprise Manager
    creating security roles using, 436
    query window as example of a thin client,
    236
    setting user definable counters, 502
Enterprise Manager diagramming tool
    introduced with SQL Server 7.0, 117
    SQL Server specificity limits usefulness, 118
entities
    adding descriptive information, 120
    attributes as identifiers for, 62
    attributes must all describe, in 2NF and 3NF,
    152
    checking register case study, 77, 121
    child and parent, defined, 101
    conceptual versions of tables, 30
    database tables should each represent single,
    132
    Enterprise Manager diagramming tool, 117
    expanding for reporting databases, 516
    First Normal Form rows must have same
    number of values, 135
    identifying from customer documentation, 57
    must be relations and single-themed, 190
    naming, 95
    removing unnecessary, before
    implementation, 297
    representation in IDEF1X standard, 93, 96
    tabulated examples with attributes and
    domains, 66, 82
    tabulated for office supplier example, 61, 70,
    82
entities and relationships, 101
    discovering in data from customers, 56
error handling (debugging). *See also* invalid data
    multi-statement batches, 397, 398
    statements that violate constraints, 329
    stored procedure for testing messages, 409
    stored procedure to examine output
    parameters, 404
    stored procedure to examine return values,
    401
    stored procedures, 403
error messages
    including after modification statements, 405
    stored procedure return values and, 400

using a mapping table to customize, 406
error messages
    analyzing, 329
error numbers, 329
error reporting
    user-defined data types using rules, 263
ERwin modeling tool
    representation of alternate keys, 97
ETL (Extract, Transform, and Load) operation,
11, 531
events
    as entities in a database, 60
exception-handling tables, 349
extended properties
    defining and adding programmatically, 287
    parameters, 2884
external systems
    checking register case study, 212
    interfacing needs, 200

F

fact tables
    archiving by row characteristics, 475
    archiving by time period and, 474
    dimension tables and, 7
facts
    modifying records with variable numbers of,
    138
fault tolerance
    provided by RAID combinations, 494
federated partitioned views. *See* distributed
partitioned views
fibers
    non-kernel applications use of instead of
    threads, 492
field format
    generic checks with UDFs, 324
field values
    supplying initial with default constraints, 321
fieldnames with shared prefixes
    checking register case study, 158
    clue that existing data is not in 3NF, 149
Fifth Normal Form, 179
fill factors, 466
First Normal Form, 133
    checking register case study, 155
    clues that existing data is not in 1NF, 139
    datetime data type technically violates, 139

examples of violations, 133
requirement for record type occurrences to
be different, 136
same number of values in all entity
instances, 135
flagging
    records it is impracticable to delete, 228
flagging archived data, 476
flat indexes, 468, 470
FLOOR function, 466
fn_listextendedproperty system function, 287, 291
foreign characters. *See* languages other than
English
foreign key constraints
    one of five constraint types, 317, 339
    rules using should be enforced at database
    level, 355
foreign key relationships, 48
foreign keys
    absent from primary keys of independent
    entities, 94
    cascading deletes and multi-database
    relationships, 278
    error-proneness in unnormalized databases,
    131
    introduced, 39
    present in primary key of dependent entities,
    94
    representation in IDEF1X standard, 98, 102
    role names for attributes used as, 107
    setting to NULL in child tables, 346
forms
    scattered data sources, 22
Fourth Normal Form, 166
    checking register case study, 181
Free Memory Target, 487
    dynamic memory tuning, 486
Full Text Search, 234
functional dependencies
    higher normalization forms and, 142
    non-key attributes in Third Normal Form,
    146
    Second Normal Form, 141
functions
    using in default constraints, 320
fundamental processes, 73
future dates
    checking for with a UDF, 335
future requirements
    documenting, 207

G

generic entities
    categorization relationships, 110
get account information use case
    custom stored procedure, 454
global temporary tables
    viewable by any connection or user, 373
Globally Unique Identifiers. *See* GUID
(Globally Unique Identifiers)
GOTO statements, 399
grant command, 438
GUID (Globally Unique Identifiers)
    example of domain specification in IDEF1X, 99

H

hardware. *See also* CPU subsystem; disk
subsystem; memory
    determining requirements, 459
    development phase requirements, 535
    memory needed by server connections, 229
    need for adequate provision, 228
    performance of read-only databases and, 521
    quality assurance phase requirements, 536
    systems with high data volumes, 222
"has a" relationships
    example of one-to-X relationship, 68
heaps
    tables without clustered indexes, 466
heavy use webservers, 240
heterogeneous data sources, 231
hierarchical relationships. *See* recursive
relationships
historical information
    data warehouse storage of, 6
horizontally partitioning data, 391

I

IDEF1X (Integration Definition for
Information Modeling), 93
    domains and inheritance of data types, 98
    introduced, 93
    naming relationships, 113
    representation of entities in, 93
    treatment of relationships, 101

identifier-dependent entities. *See* dependent
entities
identifiers
    attributes suggested as suitable, 62
identifying relationships, 103
    diagrammatic representation, 102
    Information Engineering, 115
    Second Normal Form violations and, 142
identity columns
    CREATE TABLE statement, 261
    incrementing, 261
implementation
    differences from logical design, 220
    tasks to be finished before starting, 192
importing data
    data integrity problems, 354
independent entities, 93
    foreign keys absent from primary key, 94
indexed views, 392
    restrictions on prior content, 393
    use to allow complex searches, 223
indexes
    calculating data volumes for tables, 464
    calculating size using custom stored
    procedures, 468
    DBCC commands, 513
    flattening and query performance, 468
    growth tends to be non-linear, 505
    Index Tuning Wizard, 513
    leaving to performance tuning stage, 278
    maximum number of bytes per entry, 255
    maximum number of clustered and non-
    clustered, 255
    naming is optional, 277
    part of OLAP database volumes, 460, 463
    performance problems caused by too many,
    512
    read-only support database, 522
    software approach to treating bottlenecks,
    483
Information Engineering
    non-required relationships, 115
Information Engineering methodology
    representation of relationships, 115
Information Schema
    preferred to system stored procedures, 283
    reporting on table structures, 283

informative error messages. *See* custom error messages
inheritance
    data types, using IDEF1X domains, 98
    using domains depends on modeling tools, 99
INSERT statements
    should never be coded without insert lists, 267
    stored procedure alternative, 423
INSTEAD OF triggers
    creating an exception handling table, 349
    introduced, 342
    removing time from datetime values, 359
    using to modify views, 352
integrated database design
    four functional modules, 4
Integration Definition for Information Modeling. *See* IDEF1X (Integration Definition for Information Modeling)
Integrity Independence Law, 38, 39
intelligent keys, 123
interfaces
    flexibility of, using ad hoc SQL, 431
interfacing, external systems, 200
intermittent connections. *See also* on-demand connection
    read-only database update frequency and, 523
internationalization
    storage of telephone numbers and addresses complicated by, 134
intersecting tables
    solution oriented models, 521
inter-table and inter-row constraints
    enforcing with triggers, 342, 364
inter-table validations
    rules using should be enforced at database level, 355
interview technique, 17
intrinsic data types, 259
invalid data
    exception-handling tables, 349
    finding with check constraints, 328
invoice system
    model of, for transforming to read-only, 515
IP (Internet Protocol) addresses
    First Normal Form and unsigned integers, 135

"is a" relationships
    example of one-to-n relationship, 69
IS NULL operator, 385
is_member function, 439
ISNULL function
    using to allow for possible null values, 387

J

job scheduler
    SQL Server Agent as, 235
joins
    chaining together, 44
    using views for encapsulation of, 388, 389
    including subqueries in, 374
    minimizing in read-only databases, 517
    multiple data channels can speed data reads, 497

K

KEY_COLUMN_USAGE listing
    Information Schema, 285
keys
    determinants as, in Boyce-Codd normal form, 152
    implementing, 273
    naming convention for primary and alternate, 277
    nothing but the key, 147
    use of dates in is inadvisable, 302

L

LAN (Local Area Network) breakdowns
    minimizing effects by batching transactions, 370
languages other than English
    changing collation to alphabetize correctly, 271
    supported in RAISERROR, 403
laptop users
    read-only databases, 527
latency. *See also* real-time reporting
    decision support systems, 224
    factors affecting, with read-only support database, 523

unavoidable with read-only support
database, 513
lazy writer system, 493
leaf nodes
clustered and non-clustered indexes, 467
legacy data
data warehouse incorporating, 7
source of denormalized data, 514
legacy systems
possible location of pre-existing data, 19
problems interfacing with denormalized, 203
legal values
methods of restricting listed, 32
Level of Service Agreements, 21
levels of service, 537
licenses, importance of reading, 500
lightweight clients
implementing read-only databases, 527
LIKE mask
function-based check constraint, 326
limits
for dimensions of a database table, 254
linked servers, 231, 445
code example *also* using DTC, 232
list controls
filling, example stored procedures, 418
listing relationships, 70
literal defaults, 318-319
live data
excluding from development databases, 246
reporting from, using views, 388
load balancing
offered by server clustering, 230
switch, for heavy use web servers, 240
load testing, 535
local temporary tables
scoped to SQL Server connections, 373
locator addresses
as examples of attributes, 65
locking
using views to avoid, 390
blocked access caused by lock escalation,
224
optimistic and pessimistic locks, 268
risk of, from use of T-SQL cursors, 378
logging
deferring providing to physical design stage,
60
logic
three-value logic involving NULLS, 382
logical data independence

using views to provide, 40
logical design
final stages of, 191
general datatype classes suffice for, 33
reasons to stray from during implementation,
247, 251
logical domains
transformation into data types, 303
logical enterprise model, 532
logical models
checking register case study, 188
correcting errors, 297
denormalization inappropriate to this stage,
181
implementation independence, 92
should be living documents, 95
logical reads
performance measures, 419
long transactions
minimizing effects of, 369
lossy decompositions, 169

M

maintenance plans, 536
problems of archiving systems, 474
mandatory non-identifying relationships, 105
mandatory relationships
enforcing with AFTER triggers, 344
many-to-many relationships, 50, 112
diagrammatic representation, 102
resolution entities, 112
masks
use of for data validation, 326
Maybe (NULL comparisons)
as logical equivalent of Unknown, 383
MDX (Multidimensional Expressions)
data mart access need not depend on, 8
media
archiving policy and storage of, 474, 477
memory
dynamic memory tuning, 485
importance of maximizing RAM, 478
management by SQL Server 7 and 2000,
481
management of under AWE, 480
operating system free memory, 485
process memory tuning, 488
requirements of other applications, 484

requirements of server connections, 229
tuning counters available, 483
tuning multiple server instances, 486
Windows 2000 Server optimization, 479
Windows NT Server optimization, 479
merge replication, 231
widely distibuted systems, 241
metadata procedures
Information Schema views and system
sprocs, 283
Microsoft Crporation
See individual Microsoft product names
Microsoft Visio
modeling methodology, 93, 117
middle-tier services
business rule implementation moved to, 353
migrated attributes, migrated keys
See foreign keys
migration
primary key naming to facilitate, 101
primary keys, identifying and nonidentifying relationships, 103
mirroring (RAID 1), 495
mirroring (RAID 10), 497
mobile clients
merge replication suited for, 231
modeling methodologies
key to Enterprise Data Modeling, 533
representation of relationships, 115
modifying data
drawbacks to modifying views, 352
flexibility of, using ad hoc SQL, 432
including error messages, 405
modifying views with INSTEAD OF-triggers,
352
single rows, with stored procedures, 423
typical pattern of operation, 423
modifying lists
problems caused by First Normal Form
violations, 136
movie rental example
See video library example
MS_Description table, 288
multi-database relationships
foreign keys, 278
Multidimensional Expressions. *See* MDX
(Multidimensional Expressions)
multi-part fields
modifying, 137
multiple data channels, 497
multiple disk controllers, 497

multiple joins, 44
multiple keys
that Boyce-Codd Normal Form recognizes,
151
multi-statement batches
introduced, 395
row update errors, 396
multi-tier design. *See also* n-tier configurations
problems affecting data protection, 354
multi-valued attributes
lurking, 173, 182
multi-valued dependencies, 52
allowed by Fourth Normal Form, 166
contact design model, 175
mutable rules
candidates for stored procedure
enforcement, 355
examples that appear fixed, 357
MVD. *See* multi-valued dependencies

N

naming conventions
alternative table naming styles illustrated,
253
attributes, 100
cross-database data access, 443
database objects, 252
default constraints, 318
entities, 95
extended properties, 287
importance for database objects, 95
keys and indexes, 277
problems from uninformative column
names, 202
relationships, 113, 128, 279
SQL Server four-part scheme, 254
table columns, 255
table-oriented read-only databases, 519
natural keys
checking register case study, 123
should be unique identifiers, 63
natural language interface
English Query, 528
network topologies, 235
client to data configurations, 238
connection speed for client server access,
226

designed to minimize performance problems, 225
NO ACTION option
  cascading deletes, 281
NOCHECK option
  check constraint, 322, 323
NOCOUNT option, 264
non-alphabetic characters
  clue that existing data is not in 1NF, 139
non-binary relationships, 50
non-clustered indexes
  checking register case study, 508
non-identifying relationships, 103
  diagrammatic representation, 102
  mandatory and optional, 105
  Third Normal Form violations and, 147
non-key attributes
  interdependency violates Third Normal Form, 145
non-required relationships
  Information Engineering, 115
non-specific relationships. *See* many-to-many relationships
normal forms. *See* normalization; First Normal Form; Boyce-Codd Normal Form
normalization, 129. *See also* denormalization
  adjusting performance while preserving, 221
  advanced, 165
  checking register case study model after, 188
  ignoring rules with read-only databases, 516
  reasons for normalizing data structures, 130
  seven types of normal form accepted, 132
  table summarizing normal form requirements, 189
Northwind example database
  Enterprise Manager diagramming tool, 118
NOT IN operator
  difference operator and, 46
n-tier configurations
  connection pooling, 229, 239
null bitmaps, 465
null constraints
  introduced, 34
  not technically constraints, 317
  rules for using should be enforced at database level, 355
null values, 381
  Books Online definition, 382
  comparisons, 382
  inconsistent handling of by user-defined data types, 264

need for and desirability of, 38
normalizing reduces, 130
NULL specifications for logical domains, 303

O

object listing
  checking register case study, 82
object orientation
  analogy with table rows and columns, 30
  "is a" relationships parallel subclasses, 69
objects
  as entities in a database, 59
  controlling access rights, 437
  instantiating COM, 233
ODBC (Open Database Connectivity)
  API cursors, 377
  data sources and distributed queries, 445
ODS (Operational Data Store), 529
  merging data involves finding common terms, 530
  OLAP definition and, 460
  suitability for peripatetic staff, 6
ODS (Operational Data Stores)
  consolidated data for day-to-day reporting, 5
  format, key to data warehousing transformations, 9
OLAP (Online Analytical Programming)
  as data mart querying technology, 11
  characteristics of databases, 460
  data volumes should include indexes, 460, 463
  growth rates of tables, 462
  table growth through company growth, 463
  time batching may accelerate database growth, 462
old code. *See* pre-existing systems
OLE DB
  API cursors, 377
  data sources and distributed queries, 445
  DTS and DTC require compliant sources, 232
OLTP (Online Transaction Processing)
  banking illustration, 4
  characteristics of databases, 460
  contrasted with data warehousing, 3
  growth rates of tables, 461
  normalized structure of, 4

optimized for transaction speed, not reading, 3, 4
problems with addressed by ODS, 5
on-demand connection, 527
one-to-many relationships, 49, 103
Enterprise Manager diagramming tool, 117
one-to-n relationships, 48
one-to-one or one-to-many, 68
one-to-one or more relationships, 106
one-to-one relationships, 49
one-to-X relationships
table showing possible cardinalities, 106
Online Analytical Programming. *See* OLAP (Online Analytical Programming)
Online Transmission Processing. *See* OLTP (Online Transaction Processing)
Open Database Connectivity. *See* ODBC (Open Database Connectivity)
operating system free memory, 485
Operational Data Stores. *See* ODS (Operational Data Store)
operators
Codd's eight relational, 42
elements of relational algebra, 42
modification and retrieval types, 47
optimistic locking, 268
checking register case study, 299
use of by update stored procedure, 427
optimizer hints
avoiding locking using views, 390
optional business rules
checking register case study, 364
optional relationships, 105
diagrammatic representation, 102
Information Engineering, 115
must be non-identifying, 106
optional values. *See* null values
optionally cascading deletes, 356
organization chart
example of recursive relationships, 109
outer joins
as source of null values, 382, 386
output parameters
for stored procedures, 402
ownership. *See* database owner role

P

PAE (Physical Address Extension) X86, 480
page life expectancy, 486, 487
page size
accessing programmatically, 465
Pages Faults/sec counter, 483
paper files
as possible location of pre-existing data, 20
PARAMETERS listing
Information Schema, 284
parent deletes
setting foreign key child references to NULL, 346
parity information (RAID 5), 496
peer review process, 192
PerfMon (Windows NT), 482
testing blocking with user definable counters, 503
performance issues
ad hoc queries, discouraging by providing views, 389
ad hoc SQL queries, 433
add indexes at tuning stage, 278
adjusting without sacrificing normalization, 221
architecture limitations and, 200
deletions and record disablers, 270
disk reads and off-line storage, 473
distributed partitioned views, 394
flattening indexes, 468
indexed views, 393
major coding issues, 372
maximizing on queries with read-only databases, 514
numbers of users as a factor, 229
read-only databases, 521
reporting, 221
servers, 477
triggers and check constraints, 329
performance monitoring, 481
as an art, guidelines to, 482
performance problems
avoiding by using views, 388
denormalization and, 180
networking configurations to combat, 225
unnormalized systems, due to extra programming, 131
use of summary data, 150
performance testing
stored procedures, 418, 419

performance tuning, 512
  CPU subsystem, 490
  disk subsystem, 492
  disk subsystem counters, 498
  five key areas which can cause bottlenecks, 483
  Windows 2000 Performance Options, 489
permissions function, 439
person entity
  Boyce-Codd Normal Form example, 151
personal names
  examples of First Normal Form violations, 134
pessimistic locking, 268
Physical Address Extension. *See* PAE (Physical Address Extension) X86
physical implementation
  illustrative scenarios, 219
physical model
  checking register case study, 310
physical reads
  performance measures, 419
PhysicalDisk
  counters, 498
physical-only columns, 267
  checking register case study, 299
places
  as entities in a database, 58
pointers, page and row, 467
power supply failures, 536, 537
pre-aggregated data
  data integrity problems with, 223
predicates, 34
  data input rules for tables, 40
pre-existing data, 19
  merging into an ODS, 530
  must meet constraints before triggers are applied, 343
pre-existing systems. *See also* legacy systems
  dangers of emulating, 22
  inferring business rules from old code, 72
  problems arising from need to interface with, 200
preliminary documentation
  checking register case study, 24
  identifying entities by analyzing, 57
  supplementary questions after analyzing, 61
primary key constraints
  one of five constraint types, 317
primary keys
  checking register case study, 124

choice of in logical modeling, 152
entity name repeated in attribute name, 101
implementing tables with meaningless keys, 274
logical changes effect on implemented keys, 300
may not have optional attributes, 106
migrating pointer unsuitable for implementation, 274
migration distinguishes identifying and non-identifying relationships, 103
needed for IDEF1X entities, 96
physical-only columns, 299
role in maintaining uniqueness, 36
use by update stored procedure, 427
process memory tuning
  counters available, 488
process models
  custom stored procedures from, 454
processes
  discovering in customer inteview notes, 86
  identifying from customer documentation, 74
  table of new processes in banking example, 88
processor affinity, 490
processor time
  adjusting allocation to foreground and background applications, 488
Processor % counters
  CPU performance monitoring, 491
product operator
  cross joins as example of, 44
programming
  load of in unnormalized systems, 131
programming problems
  avoided by Third Normal Form, 147
  caused by Boyce-Codd Normal Form violations, 154
  caused by First Normal Form violations, 136
  rectified by Second Normal Form, 142
project operator
  DISTINCT keyword as example of, 43
project planning
  checking register case study, 215
project plans, 205
project scope
  importance of documenting, 15
proprietray systems
  inaccessiblity of implementation details, 532

prototype reports
    checking register case study, 210
    choice of data to present in, 197
prototyping a database
    risk of distorting customer expectations, 16
publications
    replication definition of, 230
pull replication subscription, 527

Q

quality assurance. *See also* performance testing
    second phase in database development, 533,
    541
    types of testing, 534, 535
queries
    customizing client queries, 432
    factors contributing to efficiency of, 368
    flattening indexes and performance, 468
    maximizing performance with a read-only
    database, 514
    performing covered, 522
    writing to allow for null values, 386
Query Analyzer
    dynamic character strings execution, 469
    error messages seen by, 329
    role in performance tuning, 513
query optimizer
    read-only database with all columns indexed,
    523
    row-level lock escalation, 224
    stored procedures easier to optimize, 435
    use of constraints by, 317
query plans
    reuse of, 433, 434, 436
    role in performance tuning, 513
    stored procedures reuse, 434
questions
    suggested for initial customer interviews, 18
QUOTED_IDENTIFIER option, 252

R

RAID (Redundant Array of Inexpensive
Disks), 494
    advantages of a multiple RAID 5 system,
    498
    RAID 0, 494

RAID 1, 495
RAID 5, 496
RAID10, 497
RAISERROR statements
    interrogating after SET statements, 330
    stored procedures, 403
RAM (Random Access Memory). *See* memory
range checking
    checking register case study, 337, 338
    generic field format checks with UDFs, 324
    using AFTER triggers, 345
read-only copies of data, 230, 513
    heavy use web server configuration, 240
read-only databases, 513
    choice of model depends on users, 528
    example corporate solution, 525
    implementation, 524
    justifications for, 513
    possible uses tabulated, 527
    update frequency, 523
    web applications using solution oriented
    methods, 521
real data type, 258
real-time reporting, 389
record disablers, 270
recording artists example database, 316
    column-level security, 441
    row-level security, 440
records of activities
    as entities in a database, 60
recursive relationships, 50, 108
    diagrammatic representation, 102
recursive tree example, 375
Redundant Array of Inexpensive Disks. *See*
RAID (Redundant Array of Inexpensive Disks)
redundant data. *See also* data duplication
    normalization helps minimize, 131
referential integrity (RI)
    cross-database with triggers, 342, 364
    OLTP transactions and, 5
REFERENTIAL_CONSTRAINTS listing
    Information Schema, 285
relational databases. *See also* databases
    programming parallels with object
    orientation, 31
    the relational model, 27
relational operators
    retrieval operators formulated since Codd's,
    47

relations
    all entities must be relations and single-themed, 190
    origins of relational database, 28
relationship trees
    building read-only databases, 517
relationship types
    between database tables, 68
    less common types described, 108
relationships
    adding descriptive information, 119
    binary and non-binary, 48
    checking register case study, 78, 122
    Chen ERD methodology, 117
    enforcing mandatory with AFTER triggers, 344
    Enterprise Manager diagramming tool, 117–118
    identifying and non-identifying, 103, 104
    implementing, 278
    naming, 279
    representation by methodologies other than IDEF1X, 115
    table of symbols used in Information Engineering, 115
    table of types in IDEF1X, 102
    table showing possible cardinalities, 106
    tabulated for office supplier example, 70
    treatment by data modeling methodologies, 101
    triggers needed by cross-database, 282
    verb phrases make into readable sentences, 113
repeatable read isolation level, 514
repeating groups of data
    clue to 3NF violations, 149
    clues to 2NF violations, 144
replication, 230
    distributed partitioned views, 394
    implementing read-only databases, 524, 526
    possibly needed for dial-up access, 226
reporting, 194, 221
    checking register case study, 209
    complexity of reports and performance, 223
    data required should be identified early, 19
    data volumes and performance, 221
    data warehouses optimized for, 3
    day-to-day based on ODS data, 5
    demand for decision support, 463
    frequency, 225
    key issue in physical design, 221
    performance of read-only databases, 521
    problems from complex searches, 223
    real-time using views, 388, 389
    simple needs, read-only databases for, 528
    standard and specialized reports, 195
    timeliness of data required, 224
    using a copy database to boost performance, 222
reporting databases. *See also* read-only databases
    checking register case study, 538
reporting tools
    database objects, 282
    table oriented approach for ease of use, 519
Request For Proposal. *See* RFP (Request For Proposal)
Request For Quote. *See* RFQ (Request For Quote)
reserved keywords, 253, 295
resolution entities, 112
restaurant database example, 29
restrict operator
    WHERE clause as example of, 43
result sets
    classed as unnamed relations (tables), 42
    returned by stored procedure SELECT statements, 402
retrieving records
    from lists, example stored procedures, 418
return values
    suggested protocol for stored procedures, 400
review
    design stage, frequently neglected, 10
    first draft document, 76
revoke command, 438
RFP (Request For Proposal)
    source of data rules, 21
RFQ (Request For Quote)
    source of data rules, 21
rights. *See* access privileges
role names
    attributes used as foreign keys, 107
roles (security), 437
rolling up subtypes, 250
root node level
    detecting in index size calculation, 471
ROUTINE_COLUMNS listing
    Information Schema, 284
ROUTINES listing
    Information Schema, 284

row identifiers
  avoiding duplicate rows, 35
row update errors, 396
row-based operations
  archiving selected fact table rows, 475
  using cursors, 377, 378
rowcount
  @@rowcount variable after SET statements,
  330
  use of term cardinality is ambiguous, 38
rowguidcol property, 275
row-level security, 391, 440
rows
  accessing individual with a cursor, 378
  creating single, 423
  limiting visibility with views, 391
  maximum permitted number of bytes, 255
  SQL Server definition, 30
rules
  user-defined data types using, 263

S

safeguarding data. *See* data integrity
savepoints
  set by stored procedures, 414
scalability. *See also* user numbers
  needs to be known before implementation,
  200
scalar expressions
  use of UDFs but not stored procedures by,
  399
scalars
  output parameters to return, 402
scenarios
  illustrating physical implementation, 219
schema binding
  introduced, 287
  views, for them to be indexed, 392
scope creep
  role of documentation in avoiding, 16
scripting
  SQL Profiler as aid to, 288
search requirements
  reporting problems from complex searches,
  223
searching
  case sensitive data can cause problems, 271

Second Normal Form
  applies to composite keys, 140
  clues that existing data is not in 2NF, 143
  identifying relationships and violations of,
  142
security
  column level, 392, 441
  situational control, 412
  stored procedures, handled at object level,
  412
security issues
  checking register case study, 455
  cross-database data access, 443
  preventing unwanted access or modification,
  199
  using sprocs to hide base table details, 435
  using views to hide base table details, 388,
  390
security roles
  creating with Enterprise Manager, 436
seed, identity columns, 261
SELECT statements
  stored procedure alternative, 418
self-referencing relationships. *See* recursive
relationships
Semantic Modeling Format
  English Query, 529
sensitive information
  disguising on sample documents, 24
servers
  adjusting server performance, 488
  clustering, load balancing and breakdowns,
  230
  distributed partitioned views over several,
  395
  multiple server instances, memory tuning,
  486
  performance issues, 477
  reorganizing to cope with high data volumes,
  222
  two or more needed for development, 228
  web applications, with read-only database
  copies, 240
set-based operations
  alternartives to cursors, 377, 378
severity levels, error messages, 329
sign offs
  advisability of regular, 77
  final documentation review, 216
  problems that can be avoided with, 207
single-statement batches, 395

size limits
  components of database tables, 254
size of data. *See* data volumes
smalldatetime data type, 258
smart keys, 63, 123
SMP (Symmetric Multi-Processor)
confgurations, 490
snapshot replication, 231
snowflake schemas, 7
software licenses, 229
solution oriented models
  reporting databases, 516
sort order. *See also* collation types
  cursor use to implement artificial sort order, 378
sp__index$getKeyData stored procedure
  auxillary role, 468
  introduced, 464
sp__table$calcDataSpace stored procedure, 464, 465
sp__table$indexSpace stored procedure, 468
  checking register case study, 505
  introduced, 464
sp_addextendedproperty stored procedure, 287
sp_adduser stored procedure, 378
sp_column_privileges stored procedure, 284
sp_columns stored procedure, 284
sp_configure stored procedure
  adjusting server memory allocation, 484
  numbers of user connections, 499
sp_datatypes_info stored procedure, 285
sp_dboption stored procedure, 260
  setting database as read-only, 513
sp_dropextendedproperty stored procedure, 287
sp_fkeys stored procedure, 285
sp_helpconstraint stored procedure, 276, 285
sp_helptext stored procedure, 284
sp_pkeys stored procedure, 285
sp_server_info stored procedure, 284
sp_special_columns stored procedure, 285
sp_sproc_columns stored procedure, 284
sp_statistics stored procedure, 285
sp_stored_procedures stored procedure, 284
sp_table_privileges stored procedure, 285
sp_tables stored procedure, 284
sp_updateextendedproperty stored procedure, 287
sp_usercounterX Y stored procedure, 502
specialized reports, 196
specific entities

categorization relationships, 110
spreadsheets
  commonly used as data stores, 516
  data integrity problems from using, 20
SQL (Structured Query Language)
  compiled vs. ad hoc, 431
  entire interfaces can be built of sprocs, 410
  operators as relational algebra of, 42
  requires atomic fields, 136
SQL Mail, 234
SQL Profiler. *See also* SQL Server Profiler
  as aid to scripting, 288
SQL Server
  database diagramming tool from version 7.0, 117
  evaluation of NULLs, 384
  relational database models and, 28
SQL Server 2000
  dynamic memory tuning, 485
  information on features of, 247
SQL Server 2000 new features
  bulk logged transactions, 472
  calculated columns fully supported, 266
  cascading updates and deletes with declarative RI, 281
  collation setting is flexible, 272
  extended descriptive object properties, 286
  indexed and partitioned views, 392
  indexed views, 223
  schema binding, 287
  user defined functions, 316
SQL Server Agent
  scheduling jobs using, 235
SQL Server Profiler, 482
  role in performance tuning, 513
  use to check applications being redesigned, 149
SQL Server Security, 436
  row-level and column-level security, 440
sql_variant data type
  storage of extended descriptive information, 286
SQL-DMO. *See* DMO
SSN (Social Security Number)
  user-defined data type example, 263
staff expertise
  required in large projects, 229
standard attributes
  building using IDEF1X domains, 100
standard reports, 196
star schemas, 7, 460, 462

state diagrams
  Fourth Normal Form violations and, 177
STATISTICS IO
  performance testing using, 419
Statistics Time and Statistics IO, 513
status information
  Fourth Normal Form violations and, 176
storage media
  archiving policy and, 477
stored procedure replication
  implementing read-only databases, 524
stored procedures, 399. *See also* compiled SQL
  batches compared to, 399
  calculating complete table size, 464
  calculating index size, 468
  can be rewritten yet still work, 410
  checking register case study, 446
  common uses, 417
  creating single rows, 423
  custom, for bank balancing operation, 453
  custom, for getting account information, 454
  data modifications allowed with, 399
  deleting single rows, 429
  encapsulation as the greatest benefit from,
  436
  enforcing business rules, 355
  error handling, 403
  executing for each row in a set, 378
  implementing read-only databases, 524
  limiting access paths to data, 433
  modifying data, 423
  optionally cascading deletes, 357
  overriding business rules, 358
  performance measures, 419
  query plans reused by, 434
  result sets returned by SELECT, 402
  returning values from, 400
  securing data integrity with, 316, 341
  security handled at object level, 412
  should avoid client interaction, 403
  transaction count must not be changed by,
  413
  truncating rolled up tables, 539
  UDFs compared to, 399
  updating single rows, 425
  views compared to, 388
strings. *See also* character strings
  capitalizing words in, 347
Structured Query Language. *See* SQL
(Structured Query Language)
sub type relationships, 110

checking register case study, 121
  diagrammatic representation, 102
subqueries
  including in joins, 374
subscriptions
  replication definition of, 231
subtypes
  checking register case study, 292
  reasons to stray from logical design, 247
summary data
  building with indexed views, 392
  checking register case study, 158
  clue to 3NF violations, 150
  incorporating into read-only databases, 517,
  518, 521
  reasons to stray from logical design, 251
support databases. *See also* read-only databases
  returning to writeable mode, 513
Symmetric Multi-Processor. *See* SMP
(Symmetric Multi-Processor)
sysmessages table, 404
SysMon (Windows 2000), 482
  testing blocking with user definable counters,
  503
sysname data type, 291
System Architect role, 14
system architecture
  demands placed on the database and, 200
  often complex, with varying connection
  speeds, 226
system stored procedures. *See also* stored
procedures; *listings under sp_*
  appropriate to use cursors when executing,
  378
  Information Schema alternative, 283

T

table constraints
  as type of check constraint, 322
table oriented models
  benefits of, 519
  reporting databases, 516
TABLE_CONSTRAINTS listing
  Information Schema, 285
TABLE_PRIVILEGES listing
  Information Schema, 285
tables. *See also* database tables
  combining with various operator types, 43

conceptual versions are entities, 30
CREATE TABLE statement, 251
exception handling, 349
factors in calculating table volumes, 463
growth of case study tables, 504
growth of OLAP tables, 462
growth of OLTP tables, 461, 463
mathematically described as relations, 28
number accessible by queries, 374
partitioning by time, archiving and, 475
partitioning structure with views, 391
relational database theory and, 28
TABLES listing
Information Schema, 284
tag format
extending error messages, 406, 408
telephone numbers
checking register case study, 159, 332
examples of First Normal Form violations, 134
problems posed by varying formats, 68
updating area codes, atomicity and, 137
templates
using domains as, for columns, 257
temporary tables
derived tables as alternative, 374
local and global distinguished by prefixes, 372
need for under SQL Server 2000, 373
recursive tree displays using, 374
UNION [ALL] operator alternative to, 374
terminology. *See also* naming conventions
for database tables and relational theory, 29
Performance Monitoring, 482
table converting SQL Server and relational theory, 53
ternary relationships, 51, 166
Fifth Normal Form, 179
resolving, 168
testing. *See* performance testing, quality assurance
textile management, 492
thick clients, 235
thin clients, 236
thin tables, 132
Third Normal Form, 145
need for normalization beyond, 165
threads
non-kernel applications use of fibers, 492

three-phase model
database development, quality assurance and production, 533
three-value logic, 382
timeliness
decision support systems, 224
timestamp columns
use by update stored procedure, 427
use for optimistic locking, 268
tools. *See also* database generation tools
provided by SQL Server, 230
topologies. *See* network topologies
Transact-SQL. *See* T-SQL (Transact-SQL)
transaction logs
sizes of in OLTP and OLAP databases, 471
transaction support
for more than one server, 232
OLTP data integrity and, 4
transactional replication, 231
appropriate to remote databases, 527
transactions, 368
best kept short and in a single batch, 369
completing partially, 417
consequences of failing to close in batches, 399
detecting long running, 500
end-of-transaction constraints not available in SS2K, 188
introduced, 5
modifying statements should be inside, 330
stored procedure transaction count errors, 413
using two-phase commit, 445
transform procedure
checking register case study, 539
transformation queries
example illustrating problems caused by NULLs, 385
triggers, 342
basic format, 343
for solving inter-row dependencies, 41
for solving inter-table dependencies, 41
cascading modifications that need, 281
checking zipcodes match with cities, 360
cross-database relationships and, 282
discovering need for late in the design process, 454
indexed views as alternatives to, 392
looping stored procedures as alternative, 378
pre-existing data must pass constraints, 343
relationships implemented in, 118

removing time from datetime values, 359
securing data integrity with, 316, 341
use for optimistic locking, 268
value in ensuring data integrity, 354
vs. constraints, 317, 329
truncate log on checkpoint, 472
truth tables
comparisons involving NULLS, 383
T-SQL (Transact-SQL). *See also* SQL
cursor solutions often slower than set-based, 378
derived tables, 374
introduced, 2
list of commands excluded from triggers, 342
T-SQL cursors, 377
vs. set-based solutions, 378
tuples
table rows as, 31
two-phase commit, 232
cross-database data modification, 445

U

UDF (User Defined Functions)
accessing variable length column data, 464
checking for empty strings, 324
range checking example, 338
stored procedures compared to, 399
Unicode character set
allowed in non-delimited names, 252
changing collation to sort, 271
UNION [ALL] operator
alternative to using temp tables, 374
distributed partitioned views, 394
union operator, 45
unique constraints
one of five constraint types, 317
use with alternate keys, 276
unique identifiers
keys as, in Boyce-Codd Normal Form, 151
unique indexes
use of with alternate keys, 276
uniqueidentifier data type, 275
Unknown
Maybe as logical equivalent, 383
unnamed relations, 42
update frequency
read-only support databases, 523
UPDATE statement

stored procedure alternative, 425
update stored procedure
columns costly to update, 427
updating single rows, 425
updating support databases, 513
usability
reduced with thin clients, 236
use case models
checking register case study, 208
custom stored procedures from, 453
descriptive tables for use cases, 193
including security information, 199
user connections
monitoring important, 500
self-configuring in SQL Server 7 and 2000, 499
user defined counters, 502
user defined error numbers, 330
user defined functions. *See also* UDF (User Defined Functions)
checking register case study, 333
user function, 439
user interfaces
unaffected by stored procedure changes, 412
user numbers
performance optimization and, 229
problem with classic client-server configurations, 239
user privileges. *See* access privileges
user-defined data types
cannot apply changes once set, 265
inconsistent handling of variables by, 264
users
controlling access to data with stored procedures, 433
effects of multi-tier design on different types, 354
importance of early identification, 18
numbers and concurrency, 198, 200
representation in use case models, 193

V

validation
record catalog numbers example, 324
single row validation code, 328
value of data
establishing for database projects, 20
variable length data

accessing fill factors with UDFs, 464
variables
  inconsistent handling of user-defined data types by, 264
verb phrases
  can be read in either direction, 114
  naming relationships, 113, 128
vertical partitioning of data
  column-level security alternative, 442
vertically partitioning data, 392
video library example
  categorization relationships, 111
  mandatory relationships, 105
  treatment of subtypes, 248
views, 388
  drawbacks to modification statements on, 352
  Information Schema as set of, 283
  introduced and their uses discussed, 39
  modifying using INSTEAD OF-triggers, 352
  partitioning table data, 391
  providing abstraction layers using, 203
  restricting access to, rather than tables, 391
  table-oriented read-only databases, 520
  use as an encapsulation device, 388
  use of INSTEAD OF-triggers to overcome single-table restrictions, 353
  vs. stored procedures, 388
VIEWS listing
  Information Schema, 284
virtual columns. See computed columns
volumetric analysis
  archiving policy should be decided early, 473
  checking register case study, 504
  introduced, 459
volumetrics
  checking register case study, 213
  planning for, 204

W

WAN (Wide Area Networks)
  connection speed and data access over, 226
  practicability of edits and reports over, 241
web applications
  connection speed and data access over, 226
  read-only copies of data, 230, 241
  read-only databases, 527

solution oriented read-only databases, 521
WHERE clauses
  including all columns in for optimistic locking, 268
  restrict operator example, 43
Wide Area Networks. See WAN (Wide Area Networks)
Windows 2000 Data Center OS, 480
Windows 2000 Server
  CPU performance improvement over NT, 490
  memory optimization, 479
Windows Authentication, 436
Windows NT Server
  CPU performance less than 2000, 490
  memory optimization, 479
wipe and start again
  implementing read-only databases, 525
WITH RECOMPILE option
  stored procedures, 421, 434
Working Set:sqlserver, 488
write caching, 493
  possible compromise of data integrity, 494
writing to disk
  optimized by lazy writer system, 493

XYZ

Zip codes, 184
  validating match with cities, 360